THE DOCTRINE OF FIRST THINGS

"...do the first works..."
Revelation 2:5

A Comprehensive Study Of The First Things We Need To Know As New Believers

Samuel Greene, *Ph.D.*

THE DOCTRINE OF FIRST THINGS

"...do the first works..."
Revelation 2:5

**A Comprehensive Study Of The First Things
We Need To Know As New Believers**

Samuel Greene, *Ph.D*

Glory Publishing, Inc.

Glory Publishing, Inc
1301-16 Monument Road
Jacksonville, FL 32225

Printed in the United States of America
ISBN 978-1-937199-12-8

Foreword

What I have to share with you today is not only important, but vital to your walk with God. As a pastor now since 1977 and a Bible teacher who has taught all over the world, I think I have somewhat to say about this. As I have traveled the world the past couple of years and have looked particularly at the state of America, I find that I agree with what the Scriptures say: most believers do not have a foundation in God. When I say this, what do I mean? I mean a strong biblical foundation in God. We have failed as a generation of leaders to teach God's people the simplistic teachings of Christ. Even the very basic teachings can be some of the heaviest and most revelatory teachings. But we have failed to teach them, instruct them, and father them. So it is time for a new priesthood to arise. It is time for you, my brother my sister, to arise. You are the one God is calling. You make sure you have a foundation in Scripture.

Psalms 11:3 declares, "*If the foundations be destroyed, what can the righteous do?*" Well first of all, we need to understand what a foundation is. All of us know that when you build a building, the first thing you put down is the foundation because the foundation upholds the building. The bigger the desired building, the bigger and stronger the foundation must be laid to handle the weight of the building. And if you and I want to "*go on unto perfection*" (Hebrews 6:1) and "*groweth unto an holy temple in the Lord*" (Ephesians 2:21) then we must have a mighty foundation in the Lord for that temple to be built. And I don't see this happening today. Today, I see mostly Christians running from conference to conference, from experience to experience, and as far as real dedicated and diligent bible study, it has escaped them. We have Christians that have been believers for 40 years that don't know the Word of God. Now you can either be angry with me for saying this or if the shoe fits, put it on. I'm saying this out of total love for God's people who want to fulfill the will of God in their generation. God is still giving us time. We still have time to change thanks to our great Husbandman who "*waiteth for the precious fruit of the earth, and hath long patience for it...*" (James 5:7).

In the Hebrew, the word for "foundation" means "a basis for support". It comes from a root word that means "to place, apply, or to lay something upon". It also means "purpose". You see without a foundation in God, you don't know what your purpose is in God. You don't know who you are in God as well as you will never get to know who God really is. This is why when I wrote the book "The God Manual" which defines about 160 different characteristics of God, I was shocked when God told me, "My people don't know Me. They know what everybody else says about Me, but they don't know what the Scriptures say about Me". Moreover the Lord pleaded with me to let Him use the Word of God to define Himself. My goodness, can't we allow God to define Himself and lay a foundation in our lives to be the basis for all that we do. In the Greek, the word "foundation" means "something put down or the bottom structure of a building".

In Ezra 6:3 Cyrus the king made a decree and told Ezra to go ahead on and rebuild the temple and he said, "*and let the foundations thereof be strongly laid*". If you are going to have a foundation, it needs to be strongly laid. Well, how do we do this? We do this by teaching people out of Hebrews 6:1-3, "*1Therefore leaving the principles of the doctrine of Christ, let us go on unto perfection; not laying again the foundation of repentance from dead works, and of faith toward God, 2Of the doctrine of baptisms, and of laying on of hands, and of resurrection of the dead, and of eternal judgment...*" First of all, there is no going on unto perfection without a foundation. Secondly, these six major doctrines are what's called the foundation of God or the principles of the doctrine of Christ. In laying these doctrines in your life, I'm not talking about reading a little booklet on one of these principles. I'm talking about studying these doctrines "*line upon line*" (Isaiah 28:9-10). There is so much to a foundation in God that we must know.

Remember what it said of Abraham that "*he looked for a city which hath foundations, whose builder and maker is God*" (Hebrews 11:10). When we go to the book of Revelation, in the end however we find a city there that does have a foundation (Revelation 21:14). It is the bride of Christ! The bride of Christ will have a foundation. She will have a strongly laid foundation. She will have a foundation that God Himself has laid and as Zechariah 4:9 says, "*The hands of Zerubbabel* (a type of the Lord Jesus) *have laid the foundation of this house; his hands shall also finish it...*" Isaiah 44:28 says, "*Thy foundation shall be laid*".

Isaiah 28:16 says, "*Therefore thus saith the Lord GOD, Behold, I lay in Zion for a foundation a stone, a tried stone, a precious corner stone, a sure foundation...*" This is the Lord Jesus. God Himself is going to lay your foundation. As He says in Isaiah 54:11, "*O thou afflicted, tossed with tempest, and not comforted, behold, I will lay thy stones with fair colours, and lay thy foundations with sapphires*". This is the problem with those that do not have a foundation. They are constantly afflicted by the pressures of the world. They don't have the deeply rooted Scriptures in them to keep them. How many people do you know that are always going through something, are not comforted, and never at peace? Nevertheless, if you will allow Him, Isaiah here assures us that the Lord will lay our foundations! God wants to lay a mighty foundation in your life.

Listen to what Jesus says in Luke 6:47-48, "*[47]Whosoever cometh to me, and heareth my sayings, and doeth them, I will shew you to whom he is like: [48]He is like a man which built an house, and digged deep, and laid the foundation on a rock: and when the flood arose, the stream beat vehemently upon that house, and could not shake it: for it was founded upon a rock.*" Contrariwise, Jesus continues in verse 49, "*But he that heareth, and doeth not, is like <u>a man that without a foundation</u> built an house upon the earth; against which the stream did beat vehemently, and immediately it fell; and the ruin of that house was great.*" We see here and know that the storms of life come to us all. Trials, testings, temptations, etc come to all of us and they will assail the house that God is building and whether you will stand or be overcome will depend upon your foundation. When storms come, students of the Word who have a foundation in God don't fall. They stand when affliction comes. When fire and water comes, they pass on through because of the Word of God that is in them cannot be destroyed (Zechariah 13:8-9)!

I Corinthians 3:11-12 says, "*For other foundation can no man lay than that is laid, which is Jesus Christ. [12]Now if any man build upon this foundation gold, silver, precious stones, wood, hay, stubble;*" It is our choice what we allow God to build in our lives. Are you building gold, which is a type of God's character, in your life? How about silver, which speaks of God's redemption? Precious stones are all the differing characteristics, fruits, and gifts in God. These things won't perish in the fire. Wood, hay, and stubble, which all speaks of the works of the flesh will all perish when it is tried by fire.

God is desperately seeking a people whom He can lay a foundation in, one so deep and strong in His Word that He can ultimately build His house and lay His government upon their shoulders.

Isaiah 58:12 says, "*And they that shall be of thee shall build the old waste places: thou shalt raise up the foundations of many generations; and thou shalt be called, The repairer of the breach, The restorer of paths to dwell in.*" That's your calling and mine. As we lay a foundation in our lives, we can be the repairers of the breach and the restorers of paths to dwell in! But we must first take care of our own situation. Do you have a foundation? II Timothy 2:19 says, "*Nevertheless the foundation of God standeth sure, having this seal, The Lord knoweth them that are his...*" God knows who has a foundation. If you don't, admit it and get started today. This book called "*The Doctrine Of First Things*" is your starting point to having a tremendous biblical foundation in God. Allow God to lay a strong and mighty foundation in your life!

Let God get glory for what He does in you. You owe it to God and to yourself to get this mighty and awesome foundation so the Lord can build the mighty structure He seeks in your life. So let's begin today. Don't wait for a "man to carry you to the pool" (John 5:7). Start where you are and go for it! In the end, you'll be a part of the great company called "the bride of Christ"! This is Jesus' goal for all of His people. So let's run the race set before us with patience. Let's begin to read, speak, and sit under the Word of God with the express purpose in mind of getting a strong, true, and Biblical foundation in our life. So when the trials of life come (and they come to us all), we will not fall but we will stand because we have a mighty foundation to uphold us. God bless you as you begin to do it.

Love, *Brother Sam*

THE DOCTRINE OF FIRST THINGS
Table Of Contents

Lesson 1
SALVATION

I.   Understanding Our Great Salvation

A.   Defining our great salvation Scripturally

1.   Hebrews 2:3 – *"...so great salvation..."*
2.   Hebrews 7:25 – *"...save them to the uttermost..."*
3.   Jude 3 – *"...the common salvation..."*
4.   Titus 2:11 – *"...salvation hath appeared to all men."*
5.   II Corinthians 6:2 – *"...now is the day of salvation."*

6.   Romans 1:16 – *"...salvation to every one that believeth..."*

a.   Luke 3:6 – *"...all flesh shall see the salvation of God."*
b.   Isaiah 52:10 – *"...all the ends of the earth shall see the salvation of our God."*

7.   Isaiah 51:6 – *"...but my salvation shall be for ever..."*

a.   Ecclesiastes 3:14 – *"...whatsoever God doeth, it shall be for ever..."*
b.   Isaiah 32:17
c.   Hebrews 10:14 – *"For by one offering he hath perfected for ever..."*
d.   Isaiah 54:10

B.   Salvation is a person and his name is Jesus (I Corinthians 1:30)

1.   Acts 4:12 – *"...for there is none other name under heaven given among men, whereby we must be saved."*
2.   Exodus 15:2 – *"The LORD is my strength and song, and he is become my salvation..."*
3.   Psalms 27:1 – *"The LORD is my light and my salvation..."*
4.   Isaiah 12:2 – *"...God is my salvation..."*
5.   Zechariah 9:9
6.   Psalms 25:5
7.   Psalms 51:14
8.   Psalms 18:2, 24
9.   Psalms 62:2 – *"He only is my rock and my salvation..."*
10. Psalms 68:19-20
11. Psalms 118:14
12. II Samuel 22:3, 47

C.   It belongs to and comes from God

1.   Jonah 2:9 – *"...Salvation is of the LORD."*
2.   Psalms 3:8 – *"Salvation belongeth unto the LORD..."*
3.   I Samuel 2:1 – *"...because I rejoice in thy salvation."*
4.   Psalms 20:5 – *"We will rejoice in thy salvation..."*
5.   Psalms 51:12 – *"Restore unto me the joy of thy salvation..."*
6.   Psalms 98:2 – *"The LORD hath made known his salvation..."*
7.   I Samuel 11:13 – *"...the LORD hath wrought salvation in Israel."*

D.   Hebrew and Greek words for *salvation:*

1. Hebrew

    a. *Shuwah* – deliverance, aid, victory, prosperity, health, help
    b. *Vesha* – liberty, deliverance, safety, prosperity
    c. *Tshuah* – rescue, same as above

2. Greek, *soteria* – rescue, safety, deliverance, health

E. Hebrew and Greek words for *saved*:

    1. Hebrew, *yasha* – to be open, wide, free, to be safe, to deliver, to help
    2. Greek, *sozo* – safe, to save, to deliver or protect, to heal or make whole, to preserve

II. Why Does Man Need Salvation?

A. The first man disobeyed God's command

    1, Genesis 2:16-17 – "[16]*And the LORD God commanded the man, saying, Of every tree of the garden thou mayest freely eat:* [17]*But of the tree of the knowledge of good and evil, thou shalt not eat of it: for in the day that thou eatest thereof thou shalt surely die.*"
    2. Genesis 3:6 – "*And when the woman saw that the tree was good for food, and that it was pleasant to the eyes, and a tree to be desired to make one wise, she took of the fruit thereof, and did eat, and gave also unto her husband with her; and he did eat.*"

B. The result of this sin came upon the human race

    1. Romans 5:12-21 – Anyone of us in Adam's place would have done the same thing. God obviously knew man would fall because He made provision for it.
    2. Revelation 13:8

C. All men have sinned

    1. Romans 3:23 – "*For all have sinned, and come short of the glory of God.*"
    2. Galatians 3:22 – "*But the scripture hath concluded all under sin...*"
    3. Isaiah 53:6 – "*All we like sheep have gone astray...*"
    4. Psalms 14:1-3
    5. Psalms 51:5

D. The result of sin

    1. Eternal death

        a. Romans 6:23 – "*For the wages of sin is death...*"
        b. Genesis 2:17
        c. Romans 5:12 – "*...and death by sin...*"

    2. Separation from God

        a. Genesis 3:24
        b. Isaiah 59:2 – "*But your iniquities have separated between you and your God, and your sins have hid his face from you...*"
        c. II Thessalonians 1:7-9

    3.   Hell will be their eternal home

        a.   Psalms 9:17 – *"The wicked shall be turned into hell..."*
        b.   Matthew 13:40-50
        c.   Revelation 20:1-15
        d.   Revelation 21:8

We see the results of sin and disobedience to God which include eternal death, separation from God's presence and hell as an eternal home. Salvation is needed to give mankind eternal life, heaven as an eternal home, and the ability to come into God's presence again.

III.   Where Does Salvation Come From? God, knowing man would fall and that he couldn't redeem himself, made provision within Himself.

    A.   Salvation is in Jesus Christ the Son of God.

        1.   He is the author of eternal salvation

            a.   Hebrews 5:9 – *"And being made perfect, he became the author of eternal salvation unto all them that obey him;"*
            b.   Hebrews 2:10 – *"For it became him, for whom are all things, and by whom are all things, in bringing many sons unto glory, to make the captain of their salvation perfect through sufferings."*
            c.   Zechariah 9:9 – *"Rejoice greatly, O daughter of Zion; shout, O daughter of Jerusalem: behold, thy King cometh unto thee: he is just, and having salvation; lowly, and riding upon an ass, and upon a colt the foal of an ass."*
            d.   Isaiah 12:2 – *"Behold, God is my salvation; I will trust, and not be afraid: for the LORD JEHOVAH is my strength and my song; he also is become my salvation."*
            f.   John 1:29 – *"...behold the Lamb of God, which taketh away the sin of the world."*

        2.   Jesus' shed blood paid our debt

            a.   Revelation 1:5 – *"...washed us from our sins in his own blood..."*
            b.   Hebrews 9:14-28
            c.   Revelation 5:9 – *"...hast redeemed us to God by thy blood..."*
            d.   I John 1:7 – *"...the blood of Jesus Christ his Son cleanseth us from sin..."*
            e.   I Peter 1:19 – *"...but with the precious blood of Christ..."*
            f.   Colossians 1:14
            g.   Romans 5:9 – *"...much more then, being now justified by his blood..."*

IV.   How Do We Receive This Salvation?

    A.   By believing Jesus is the Son of God

        1.   Acts 16:30-31 – *"...what must I do to be saved? And they said, Believe on the Lord Jesus Christ, and thou shalt be saved..."*
        2.   Romans 10:9-13 – *"That if thou shalt confess with thy mouth the Lord Jesus, and shalt believe in thine heart that God hath raised him from the dead, thou shalt be saved...."*
        3.   John 3:36 – *"He that believeth on the Son hath everlasting life..."*

    B.   By repenting of our sin

1. Matthew 4:17 – *"...Jesus began to preach, and to say, Repent: for the kingdom of heaven is at hand."*
2. Luke 13:3 – *"...except ye repent, ye shall all likewise perish."*
3. Acts 2:38
4. Acts 3:19 – *"Repent ye therefore, and be converted, that your sins may be blotted out..."*
5. Acts 17:30 – *"...but now commandeth all men every where to repent."*

C. Confession our sins to Him

1. Proverbs 28:13 – *"He that covereth his sins shall not prosper: but whoso confesseth and forsaketh them shall have mercy."*
2. I John 1:9 – *"If we confess our sins, he is faithful and just to forgive us our sins, and to cleanse us from all unrighteousness."*
3. Psalms 32:5 – *"I acknowledged my sin unto thee...and thou forgavest the iniquity of my sin."*

D. By receiving Him into our heart

1. John 1:12-13 – *"...as many as received him, to them gave he power to become the sons of God, even to them that believe on his name..."*
2. Revelation 3:20
3. John 13:20

V. There Is Salvation In No Other

A. He is the only Savior

1. Acts 4:12 – *"...Neither is there salvation in any other: for there is none other name under heaven given among men, whereby we must be saved."*
2. Jeremiah 3:23
3. John 14:6 – *"Jesus saith unto him, I am the way, the truth, and the life..."*
4. Psalms 62:6-7
5. Psalms 27:1
6. Psalms 3:8 – *"Salvation belongeth unto the LORD..."*
7. John 10:9 – *"I am the door: by me if any man enter in, he shall be saved..."*
8. I Timothy 2:5 – *"For there is one God, and one mediator between God and men, the man Christ Jesus."*

VI. Our Salvation Is Threefold – II Corinthians 1:10 – Isaiah 53:5

A. Our triune (threefold) God created a three fold man in His image. For His threefold man He created a threefold salvation and baptism. Our salvation is a complete salvation, for our whole being.

1. God is threefold: Father, Son, Holy Ghost

   a. I John 5:7 – *"For there are three that bear record in heaven, the Father, the Word, and the Holy Ghost: and these three are one."*
   b. Matthew 28:19 – *"...baptizing them in the name of the Father, and of the Son, and of the Holy Ghost."*
   c. II Corinthians 13:14 – *"...grace of the Lord Jesus Christ, and the love of God, and the communion of the Holy Ghost..."*
   d. John 14:16 – *"And I will pray the Father, and he shall give you another Comforter..."*

2. Man is threefold: Spirit, soul, body

    a.   I Thessalonians 5:23 – *"...I pray God your whole spirit and soul and body be preserved blameless..."*

    b.   Hebrews 4:12 – *"For the word of God is quick, and powerful, and sharper than any twoedged sword, piercing even to the dividing asunder of soul and spirit, and of the joints and marrow, and is a discerner of the thoughts and intents of the heart."*

    c.   Genesis 2:7 – *"...God formed man of the dust of the ground, and breathed into his nostrils the breath of life; and man became a living soul."*

    d.   Isaiah 53:5 – *"But he was wounded for our transgressions, he was bruised for our iniquities: the chastisement of our peace was upon him; and with his stripes we are healed."*

3. Salvation is threefold: Justification, Sanctification, and Glorification

    a.   Hebrews 7:25 – *"Wherefore he is able also to save them to the uttermost that come unto God by him, seeing he ever liveth to make intercession for them."*

    b.   Hebrews 2:3 – *"How shall we escape, if we neglect so great salvation; which at the first began to be spoken by the Lord, and was confirmed unto us by them that heard him;"*

    c.   II. Corinthians 1:10 – *"Who delivered us from so great a death, and doth deliver: in whom we trust that he will yet deliver us."*

    d.   Isaiah 53:5 – *"But he was wounded for our transgressions, he was bruised for our iniquities: the chastisement of our peace was upon him; and with his stripes we are healed."*

4. Threefold Baptism

    a.   Hebrews 6:2 – "Baptisms" plural

    b.   Baptism in the Body of Christ – Spirit

    c.   Baptism in Water – Body

    d.   Baptism in the Holy Ghost – Soul

B.   Understand our Threefold Salvation – When most of us think of salvation, we think of receiving Jesus as Saviour, which of course is a one-time experience. Within that salvation, however, is a three-fold outworking, each one applying to a different part of man.

1. Justification – This part of our salvation is received immediately upon conversion. This is when the blood of Jesus washes our human spirit clean. The Holy Spirit then inhabits our spirit. Our sins are forgiven and we can communicate with the Father. We've passed from death unto life. Our human spirit from this point on is incapable of sinning. (I John 5:18, Hebrews 12:23). This does not mean we will never sin again. Our souls and bodies will sin, but God inhabits our spirits. Note these scriptures: I John 1:8-10, I John 2:1-2, Romans 7:14-25. If we did not sin, there would be no need for daily repentance.

2. Sanctification – This is the work of cleansing that the Holy Spirit and the Word of God do for us in **this life**. Sanctification is a life long thing. It is not complete until all the chambers of our soul have been individually cleansed and redeemed. This is the salvation of our soulish man.

3. Glorification – This is the final aspect to our threefold salvation. It is the redemption of our physical bodies. They are fashioned like unto His glorious body (Matthew 17:1-4)

Lesson 2
SALVATION: THE BEGINNING
KNOWING HIM: THE END

I. Salvation Is The Entrance Into The Things Of God.

A. Salvation is the beginning.

1. John 3:3, 5 – – "³*Jesus answered and said unto him, Verily, verily, I say unto thee, Except a man be born again, he cannot see the kingdom of God. ⁵Jesus answered, Verily, verily, I say unto thee, Except a man be born of water and of the Spirit, he cannot enter into the kingdom of God.*" Without salvation you can't even see the kingdom, but when you are born again you enter in. This is not the end however – this <u>starts</u> us on our journey. Salvation is the doorway into everything that is of and in God through His Son Jesus.

2. I Timothy 2:4 – "*Who will have all men to be saved, and to come unto the knowledge of the truth.*" He would have all men to be saved.

    a. II Peter 3:9 – He wants all to come to repentance.
    b. II Corinthians 5:19 – Ministry of reconciliation
    c. Romans 3:22-62
    d. Romans 5:8-19

God has already paid the price for all men's sins. He wants everyone saved, and none to perish. But He also wants us to come *into the knowledge* of the truth. Salvation delivers us from Hell, eternal punishment, sickness, and poverty and brings us into a relationship with God. Salvation secures for us a heavenly home. God wants more than this though. He wants to fulfill His original plan: that man would be in His image, walking in dominion, and having a relationship with his God that is like unto a man and a wife. He wants man to *really know* Him.

3. This is a profound mystery.

    a. Colossians 1:26-27 – "²⁶*Even the mystery which hath been hid from ages and from generations, but now is made manifest to his saints: ²⁷To whom God would make known what is the riches of the glory of this mystery among the Gentiles; which is Christ in you, the hope of glory:*"
    b. Ephesians 1:9-12
    c. Ephesians 3:3-5-11
    d. Revelation 10:7 – "*But in the days of the voice of the seventh angel, when he shall begin to sound, the mystery of God should be finished, as he hath declared to his servants the prophets.*"

For this to happen, man must not just sit back after salvation, but grow up into Him.

B. When we are saved, we enter a race.

1. Hebrews 12:1 – "*...let us run with patience the race that is set before us.*"
2. I Corinthians 9:24 – "*Know ye not that they which run in a race run all, but one receiveth the prize? So run, that ye may obtain.*"
3. Philippians 3:10-14 – Amplified says, "*...I strain to reach the end of the race...*" – This is an endurance race. One in which we are striving to win a prize. The prize is the high calling of God.

4. Ecclesiastes 9:11 – "*...that the race is not to the swift, nor the battle to the strong...*"

5. Hebrew and Greek words for "race"

   a. Hebrew – foot race
   b. Greek – struggle; fight; an athletic contest

What is this high calling? It's to know Him intimately—to be *His Bride*.

C. This is a race to know Him.

1. Philippians 3:10 – "*That I may know him...*"
2. Exodus 33:13 – "*...shew me now thy way, that I may know thee...*"
3. Psalms 27:4 – "*One thing have I desired of the LORD, that will I seek after...*"
4. Hosea 6:3 – "*...if we follow on to know the LORD...*"
5. I Chronicles 28:9 – "*...Know thou the God of thy father and...if thou seek him, he will be found....*"
   To run this race, desire will not be enough – there must be a genuine seeking.

This "knowing Him" simply means an intimate knowing such as when "*...Adam knew Eve his wife...*" (Genesis 4:1). It's the consummation of a relationship of total love and devotion: an interacting and an exchanging of that love, just like a man and his wife. We are to be His bride; He is to be our Husband.

II. Understanding What It Means To Know Him

A. God's ultimate call on our lives is to know Him intimately.

1. John 17:3 – "*This is life eternal, that they might know thee...*"
2. I John 5:20 – "*...that we might know Him that is true...*"
3. Jeremiah 9:23-24 – "*...understand and knoweth me...*"
4. Hosea 6:6 – "*I desired...the knowledge of God...*"
5. Jeremiah 24:7 – "*I will give them an heart to know Me...*"

In all of the above passages there is one main theme: TO KNOW HIM is the call upon our lives.

B. What it means to know Him

1. As stated earlier, it is to know Him intimately as a husband knows his wife

   a. Genesis 4:1 – "*And Adam knew Eve his wife; and she conceived...*"
   b. Hosea 2:18-20 – "*...And I will betroth thee unto me for ever...and thou shalt know the LORD.*"
   c. Isaiah 54:5 – "*For thy Maker is thine husband...*"
   d. Ephesians 5:22-32
   e. Isaiah 62:5 – "*...as the bridegroom rejoiceth over the bride, so shall thy God rejoice over thee.*"

2. To know him means to know his ways

   a. Psalms 103:7 – "*He made known his ways unto Moses, his acts unto the children of Israel.*"
   b. Exodus 33:13-16
   c. Hebrews 3:10 – "*...they have not known my ways...*"

Those who know Him are not just acquainted with what He does (His acts), but with *who He is*. They know what moves Him, they know what pleases Him.

3. Knowing him speaks of maturity

    a. I John 2:13-14 – "*[13]I write unto you, fathers, because ye have known him that is from the beginning. I write unto you, young men, because ye have overcome the wicked one. I write unto you, little children, because ye have known the Father. [14]I have written unto you, fathers, because ye have known him that is from the beginning. I have written unto you, young men, because ye are strong, and the word of God abideth in you, and ye have overcome the wicked one.*"

"Fathers" here indicates those who are mature in the Lord, those who have grown up into a full grown son. There is an initial knowing Him as a babe in Christ, but then we start the process of growing up, to where we really know him in a mature sense.

    1) Galatians 4:19
    2) Ephesians 4:11-15

C. Knowing Him brings tremendous advantages.

    1. Daniel 11:32 – "*...The people that do know their God shall be strong and do exploits...*"
    2. II Timothy 1:12 – "*He is able to keep that which I have committed...*"
    3. Philippians 3:10-11 – "*...power of his resurrection and the fellowship of his sufferings...*"

Knowing God is the true desire of God's heart for His people, and it is the true desire of the heart of God's people. There must be a longing in all of us to truly love and know Him intimately.

III. Most People Don't Have This Revelation

A. They don't know Him (nor want to)

    1. Isaiah 1:2-3 – "*My people don't know...they don't consider...*"
    2. Jeremiah 2:32 – "*...My people have forgotten Me days without number...*"

        a. Jeremiah 2:13
        b. Hosea 8:14

    3. Jeremiah 9:3, 6 – "*...they know not Me...*", "*...they refuse to know me...*"
    4. Jeremiah 4:22 – "*My people are foolish, they have not known me; they are sottish (stupid) children...*"
    5. Luke 17: 11-19

B. Most people (when they see God for what and who He really is) don't want Him.

    1. Exodus 20:18-21
    2. John 1:11 – "*He came unto His own, and His own received Him not*"
    3. John 6:53-66 – many of his disciples turned back
    4. Luke 19:37-40, 41-44
    5. Matthew 21:12-17 – the chief priests were sore displeased

C. How many times has God tried to visit us?

1. I Samuel 3:2-9

IV. There Will Be A People Who *Do* Desire To Know Him.

   A. God is looking for those who will seek Him and come to know Him.

      1. Isaiah 55:6-7
      2. Jeremiah 29:13
      3. Matthew 7:7

   B. There will be a people who know Him.

      1. Revelation 14:1-5
      2. Revelation 2:26-28 (Genesis 15:1)
      3. Hosea 2:14-23

   C. Let's draw nigh to Him.

      1. James 4:8
      2. Psalm 63:1-2, 8
      3. Psalm 42:1-2

Lesson 3
BENEFITS OF OUR SALVATION

I.   Psalms 103:1-5 – "*...Bless the LORD, O my soul, and forget not all his benefits: Who forgiveth all thine iniquities; who healeth all thy diseases; Who redeemeth thy life from destruction; who crowneth thee with lovingkindness and tender mercies; Who satisfieth thy mouth with good things; so that thy youth is renewed like the eagle's.*"

    A.   We have benefits because we are saved. The word benefit means a gift or favor of God given to man

        1.   Psalms 68:19 – "*...who daily loadeth us with benefits, even the God of our salvation.*"
        2.   Psalms 116:12 – "*What shall I render unto the LORD for all his benefits toward me?*"
        3.   I Timothy 6:2 – "*And they that have believing masters, let them not despise them, because they are brethren; but rather do them service, because they are faithful and beloved, partakers of the benefit. These things teach and exhort.*"

    B.   Some of the benefits of our salvation

        1.   Total forgiveness of all our sins (past, present, future, Psalm 103:3)

            a.   The whole of Psalms 130
            b.   Micah 7:18-19 – "*Who is a God like unto thee, that pardoneth iniquity...*
            c.   Job 33:27-30 – "*[27]He looketh upon men, and if any say, I have sinned, and perverted that which was right, and it profited me not; [28]He will deliver his soul from going into the pit, and his life shall see the light. [29]Lo, all these things worketh God oftentimes with man, [30]To bring back his soul from the pit, to be enlightened with the light of the living.*"
            d.   Isaiah 1:18 – "*Come now, and let us reason together, saith the LORD: though your sins be as scarlet, they shall be as white as snow; though they be red like crimson, they shall be as wool.*"
            e.   Hebrews 9:14 – "*How much more shall the blood of Christ, who through the eternal Spirit offered himself without spot to God, purge your conscience from dead works to serve the living God?*"
            f.   Ezekiel 16:6-9 – "*[6]And when I passed by thee, and saw thee polluted in thine own blood, I said unto thee when thou wast in thy blood, Live; yea, I said unto thee when thou wast in thy blood, Live. [7]I have caused thee to multiply as the bud of the field, and thou hast increased and waxen great, and thou art come to excellent ornaments: thy breasts are fashioned, and thine hair is grown, whereas thou wast naked and bare. [8]Now when I passed by thee, and looked upon thee, behold, thy time was the time of love; and I spread my skirt over thee, and covered thy nakedness: yea, I sware unto thee, and entered into a covenant with thee, saith the Lord GOD, and thou becamest mine. [9]Then washed I thee with water; yea, I throughly washed away thy blood from thee, and I anointed thee with oil.*"
            g.   Ephesians 1:7 – "*In whom we have redemption through his blood, the forgiveness of sins, according to the riches of his grace;*"
            h.   Psalms 65:3 – "*Iniquities prevail against me: as for our transgressions, thou shalt purge them away.*"
            i.   I John 1:9 – "*If we confess our sins, he is faithful and just to forgive us our sins, and to cleanse us from all unrighteousness.*"

        2.   Healing for all our diseases – Psalm 103:3

            a.   It is God's will we be healed. We have a covenant with Him concerning healing.

1) Exodus 15:26 – *"And said, If thou wilt diligently hearken to the voice of the LORD thy God, and wilt do that which is right in his sight, and wilt give ear to his commandments, and keep all his statutes, I will put none of these diseases upon thee, which I have brought upon the Egyptians: for I am the LORD that healeth thee."*

2) Exodus 23:25-26 – *"And ye shall serve the LORD your God, and he shall bless thy bread, and thy water; and I will take sickness away from the midst of thee. There shall nothing cast their young, nor be barren, in thy land: the number of thy days I will fulfil."*

3) Deuteronomy 7:15 – *"And the LORD will take away from thee all sickness, and will put none of the evil diseases of Egypt, which thou knowest, upon thee; but will lay them upon all them that hate thee."*

4) Malachi 4:2 – *"But unto you that fear my name shall the Sun of righteousness arise with healing in his wings; and ye shall go forth, and grow up as calves of the stall."*

5) Matthew 8:1-17

6) Acts 10:38 – *"How God anointed Jesus of Nazareth with the Holy Ghost and with power: who went about doing good, and healing all that were oppressed of the devil; for God was with him."*

7) Isaiah 53:5 – *"But he was wounded for our transgressions, he was bruised for our iniquities: the chastisement of our peace was upon him; and with his stripes we are healed."*

    b.   Examples of God's will concerning healing

1) Matthew 8:1-3, 17
2) III John 2
3) Jeremiah 30:17
4) James 5:14-15
5) Luke 13:10-17
6) Acts 10:38
7) Isaiah 53:5
8) Matthew 6:10

3. Total redemption from our past – Psalm 103:4

We have been redeemed from the destruction we were headed into before we were saved. Not only that destruction which was passed but that which we were destined to encounter.

    a.   Galatians 3:13 - Past
    b.   Isaiah 43:1-4 – Present and Future

4. We experience His great love and mercy. He crowns us with these.

    a.   O, how great is His love. It isn't because of our greatness

1) Deuteronomy 7:7-8
2) Romans 5:8

    b.   His love is unconditional

1) Romans 8:35-39
2) Ezekiel 16:8
3) John 15:13
4) Ephesians 3:18-19

          5)   I John 4:7-11

    c.   O, how great is His mercy

        1)   Psalm 119:156
        2)   Lamentations 3:22-23
        3)   Isaiah 54:7-10
        4)   Hosea 2:19-20
        5)   Psalm 103:8

5.   He has given us prosperity – Psalm 103:5

    a.   He takes delight in us prospering.

        1)   Psalm 35:27
        2)   Zechariah 8:12
        3)   III John 2
        4)   Ecclesiastes 5:18-20
        5)   Genesis 39:2,3 20-23
        6)   Nehemiah 2:20
        7)   II Corinthians 8:9
        8)   Proverbs 10:22
        9)   Philippians 4:19
        10) Job 36:11

    b.   Hebrew and Greek words for prosperity

        1)   Greek – *Euodoo* – To help on one's way, to succeed
        2)   Hebrew – *Shalom* – Safety, peace, well, happy, health
        3)   Hebrew – *Tsaleach* – To push forward, to break out, to mightily go over

C.   Role of the Church in Salvation's benefits – The church has a responsibility to take an active role in pursuing these "benefits of salvation" for each member.

    1.   Examples of this church involvement

        a.   Provision – James 2:14-18
        b.   Healing – James 5:14-16
        c.   Fortification – Ecclesiastes 4:11
        d.   Manifestation of Vision – Nehemiah 2:12
        e.   Deliverance – Acts 12:5, 11
        f.   Comfort – I Thessalonians 4:18
        g.   Restoration – Galatians 6:1

Lesson 4
THE PRINCIPLE OF FIRST THINGS

I.   Hebrews 5:12 and Hebrews 6:1

   A.   Hebrews 5:12 – "*For when the time ye ought to be teachers, ye have need that one teach you again which be the 'first principles' of the oracles (truths) of God: and are become such as have need of milk and not of strong meat.*"

   1. Greek for "first" – chief; a beginning; to be first; that which is of worth.
   2. Greek for "principles" – something orderly in arrangement; a series of fundamental, initial things
   3. Greek for "oracles" – an utterance of God; a divine response or utterance.

By looking at the actual Greek words and then piecing them together, we come up with a basic translation: We need to be taught "the chief things...the beginnings...the things that are of worth...the first (principles)...the series of fundamental, initial things...the utterances and divine responses of God...in an orderly arrangement of the oracles."

   B.   Hebrews 6:1 – "*Therefore leaving the 'principles' of the 'doctrine of Christ'...*" → *Apostolic Doctrine*

   1. Greek for "doctrine", *logos* – an expression of thought; the divine expression; something said; the thought; from the root, *lego* – to lay forth; relate in words, discourse.

      a. Logos is the written word of God. God's doctrine is the divine expression of thought, the things He has said, laid down in a discourse of words.
      b. The First Principles then, are the initial words and thoughts of God laid down in an orderly fashion in the hearts of God's people.

   2.   The Doctrine of Christ

      a.   John 7:14-18
      b.   Matthew 7:28-29
      c.   Matthew 22:29, 33-34
      d.   Mark 1:22-28
      e.   Mark 4:1-2
      f.   Mark 11:15-18
      g.   Mark 12:38-41
      h.   John 7:14-16, 17-31
      i.   John 18:19-23
      j.   Acts 13:4-12
      k.   Acts 17:16-31 (emphasis on verse 19)   *2 Tim. 3:10*
      l.   I Timothy 6:1-3, 4-11
      m.   Titus 2:6-7, 8-10, 11-15   *Is. 41:4*   *Rev. 1:5-8*
      n.   II John 9-11   *Is. 44:6*

As we look at all of the above passages, we discover what the Doctrine of Christ entails. It is also important to note we will cover the subject of doctrine in general later in this manual, for truly, there is much written about it in Scripture. But for now, let us realize that the Doctrine of God (Deuteronomy 32:2, Proverbs 4:2), the Doctrine of the Apostles (Acts 2:42), and the Doctrine of Christ are the same thing. It is the faith, the utterances of God, the teachings of worth, the initial beginning thoughts of God that was once delivered to the saints (Jude 3).

The New Testament epistles were written primarily by the Apostles. They laid the foundation of revelation that every believer must learn to walk in and have as revelational knowledge in their hearts. Without it, there will be no going on to perfection, no true intimacy with God, no real understanding of His purpose and plan for us personally and corporately. There are seven major principles or doctrines that make up what the Word says are our foundation in God. Every believer must know and apply them to their lives. Simply put, they are the foundation for the building God wants to build in us personally and corporately.

Comprised within these seven doctrines are all of the truths God has revealed to man. They cannot be taught or understood in a several week seminar or so called, introductory foundational class. Provided in these seven doctrines is the whole of God's Word, and the whole of His revelation to His people. A thorough study of them is the only appropriate way to respond to them. This means every teaching ministry, every Pastor, and every local church is responsible to teach them. We should not need to send our sheep to Bible College or Christian Universities. The local church is, and should be our place of schooling.

These seven doctrines make up the "milk for babes," "bread for children," "meat for men," strong meat for the aged," and "hidden manna for the over comers."

3. These seven all encompassing doctrines are:

a. Repentance from dead works
b. Faith towards God
c. Doctrines of baptisms (plural)
d. Laying on of hands
e. Resurrection of the dead
f. Eternal judgment
g. Doctrine of perfection

We will teach two subjects before this foundation. One will be an intensive study of all the basic, elementary, subjects found in Scripture that we feel are vital. The second will give us the premise of "studying the Scriptures, devoting ourselves to the preeminence the Word places on itself, teaching the need to study, the why, the how, and the principles of searching the Scriptures and how and where we got the Bible. We will call those two prior teachings doctrines as well. The names of these will be, First Principles and Searching the Scriptures. We will have at the finish nine doctrines we will have studied thoroughly. I believe that when we finish, every student will have received his or her permission from God to go on to perfection. Listed below are the nine doctrines we will examine. Remember, nine is the number in Scripture for *finality*.

4. The nine doctrines we will examine:

a. The First Principles
b. Searching the Scriptures
c. Repentance from Dead Works
d. Faith Toward God
e. Doctrine of Baptisms (plural)
f. Laying on of Hands
g. Resurrection of the Dead
h. Eternal judgment
i. Doctrine of Perfection

In this first lesson of the "First Principles" study we want to see what the bible considers as first things to know, remember and walk in.

II.   What the Scriptures Say About First Things

    A.   Jesus is God's first and last word. He is the preeminent utterance, thought and revelation of God to mankind.

        1.   Jesus the first in Scripture

            a.   Revelation 1:11 (verse 8)
            b.   Revelation 22:13
            c.   Isaiah 41:4
            d.   Isaiah 44:6-8
            e.   Isaiah 48:12-13
            f.   Colossians 1:15-18
            g.   Revelation 3:14

        2.   Jesus – God's preeminent purpose and voice

            a.   Colossians 1:12-19
            b.   Colossians 2:6-10
            c.   Colossians 3:17
            d.   Ephesians 1:17-23
            e.   Hebrews 1:1-4
            f.   Acts 17:27-28

    B.   What the Scriptures call the important first things

        1.   I John 4:19 – *"We love him, because he **first** loved us."*
        2.   I Timothy 2:1-3 – *"I exhort...that, **first** of all, supplications, prayers, intercessions, and giving of thanks, be made for all men; For kings and for all that are in authority..."*
        3.   II Corinthians 8:5 – *"...**first** gave their own selves to the Lord, and unto us..."*
        4.   Romans 1:16 – *"For I am not ashamed of the gospel of Christ: for it is the power of God unto salvation...to the Jew **first,** and also to the Greek"*
        5.   Hebrews 2:3 – *"...if we neglect so great salvation; which at the first began to be spoken by the Lord, and was confirmed unto us by them..."*
        6.   II Peter 1:20 – *"Knowing this **first**, that no prophesy of the scripture is of any private interpretation."*
        7.   Revelation 2:4 – *"...because thou has left they **first** love..."*
        8.   I Corinthians 15:46 – *"Howbeit that was not **first** which is spiritual, but that which is natural..."*
        9.   Ephesians 6:2 – *"Honour thy father and mother; (which is the **first** commandment..."*
        10. I Thessalonians 4:16 – *"...the dead in Christ shall rise **first**..."*
        11. I Corinthians 16:2 – *"Now concerning the collection...upon the **first** day of the week, let everyone of you lay by him in store, as God hath prospered him..."*

            a.   II Corinthians 8:12 – *"...if there **first** be a willing mind..."*

        12. II Peter 3:3 – *"Knowing this **first**, that there shall come in the last days scoffers."*
        13. Micah 4:8 – *"And thou, O tower of the flock, stronghold of the daughter of Zion, unto thee it shall come, even the **first** dominion, the Kingdom shall come to the daughter..."*

14. Matthew 5:24 – "*Leave there thy gift before the altar, and go thy way;* **first** *be reconciled to thy brother...*"
15. Matthew 6:33 – "*But seek ye* **first** *the kingdom of God, and his righteousness...*"
16. Matthew 12:29 – "*...except he* **first** *bind the strongman...*"
17. Matthew 19:30 – "*...many that are* **first** *shall be last, and the last shall be* **first**."
18. Matthew 22:36-40 – "*...This is the* **first** *and great commandment...*"
19. Matthew 23:26 – "*...cleanse* **first** *that which is within the cup and the platter...*"
20. Matthew 7:5 – "*Thou hypocrite,* **first** *cast out the beam out of thine own eye...*"

Lesson 5
THE PRINCIPLE OF ONE THING

I. The Principle Of One Things As Found In Scripture

A. The "one things" we need to understand

1. John 9:25 – "*He answered and said, Whether he be a sinner or no, I know not: <u>one thing I know</u>, that, whereas I was blind, now I see.*" – We are a new creation and we are no longer in the dark

2. Luke 10:42 – "*But <u>one thing is needful</u>: and Mary hath chosen that good part, which shall not be taken away from her.*" – We need to sit and study the Word of God

3. Philippians 3:13-14 – "*Brethren, I count not myself to have apprehended: but <u>this one thing I do</u>, forgetting those things which are behind, and reaching forth unto those things which are before, I press toward the mark for the prize of the high calling of God in Christ Jesus.*" – We need to forget the past and run after Jesus.

4. II Peter 3:8-9 – "*But, beloved, <u>be not ignorant of this one thing</u>, that one day is with the Lord as a thousand years, and a thousand years as one day. The Lord is not slack concerning his promise...*" – We should not be ignorant that God takes His time, but His promise will come to pass.

5. Luke 18:22 – "*Now when Jesus heard these things, he said unto him, <u>Yet lackest thou one thing</u>: sell all that thou hast, and distribute unto the poor, and thou shalt have treasure in heaven: and come, follow me.*" – Give up everything important to us and follow Him. Earthly riches cannot compare to the real treasure of heaven.

6. Psalms 27:4 – "*<u>One thing have I desired of the LORD</u>, that will I seek after; that I may dwell his temple.*" – Abide in His house, behold His glory, and seek His face

7. Ecclesiastes 3:19 – "*For that which befalleth the sons of men befalleth beasts; <u>even one thing befalleth them</u>: as the one dieth, so dieth the other...*" – We will all die, so make your life count for something.

8. Psalms 56:9 – "*When I cry unto thee, then shall mine enemies turn back: <u>this I know</u>; for God is for me.*" – When we need Him most, He will be there because He is for us.

Lesson 6
THE BAPTISM OF THE HOLY GHOST & SPEAKING IN TONGUES

I. Important Words Related To The Baptism Of The Holy Ghost – All of the words we are about to look at are really definitive as to what happens to us when we are baptized in the Holy Ghost. As well as, what this baptism is all about.

   A. **Baptize** – The Greek word means to dip, to plunge, to immerse. By definition and usage the word means to put into or under, so as to immerse or submerge. This then means we are to be immersed, put into, submerge in the presence of God, which is God himself. This is something very radical. It is not a drop, a little, or a sprinkling. This means immersion in His presence. That is the baptism of the Holy Ghost. We are to be immersed in the Holy Ghost

   B. **Holy Ghost** – We are literally baptized in the third part of the Godhead. This is the only baptism where we are actually baptized in a part of the Godhead. We actually have a mighty portion of God dwelling with us. His purpose is to bring us into a greater fellowship with him, to enable us to do great works.

   C. **Fire** – Acts 2:3, *"And there appeared unto them cloven tongues like as of fire, and it sat upon each of them."* – This is an aspect of the baptism of the Holy Ghost many overlook. This aspect is not the blessing of power and of the presence, but this one is the part of his presence that comes to purge us (Luke 3:17). God's fire is sent to purge and burn away from us all that is in our lives that is not of God.

   D. **Power** – Acts 1:8, *"But ye shall receive power, after that the Holy Ghost is come upon you..."* This is the Greek word *"dunamis"* meaning force, miraculous power, and ability. It is where we get the word "dynamite". In other words, when we are baptized in the Holy Ghost we receive as we are immersed in God's supernatural miracle force. We now have God's power which makes us able to do his miraculous works.

   E. **Witness** – Acts 1:8 – *"...after that the Holy Ghost is come upon you: and ye shall be witnesses..."* Being baptized in the Holy Ghost transfers you into a bold witness for Jesus. Consider the apostles hiding for fear (John 20:10) as well as, denying the Lord (John 16:32; Matthew 26:31-35) and look at them after receiving the baptism of the Holy Ghost in Acts 2-5.

II. The Baptism Of The Holy Ghost is *"the promise of the Father"*

   1. Acts 1:4-5 – *"⁴And, being assembled together with them, commanded them that they should not depart from Jerusalem, but wait for <u>the promise of the Father</u>, which, saith he, ye have heard of me. ⁵For John truly baptized with water; but ye shall be <u>baptized with the Holy Ghost</u> not many days hence."*

      a. Luke 24:49 – *"And, behold, I send <u>the promise of my Father</u> upon you: but tarry ye in the city of Jerusalem, until ye be endued with power from on high."*
      b. Acts 2:4-5 – *"And they were <u>all filled with the Holy Ghost</u>, and began to speak with other tongues, as the Spirit gave them utterance. ⁵And there were dwelling at Jerusalem Jews, devout men, out of every nation under heaven."*
      c. Acts 2:32-39 – *"³²This Jesus hath God raised up, whereof we all are witnesses. ³³Therefore being by the right hand of God exalted, and having <u>received of the Father the promise of the Holy Ghost</u>, he hath shed forth this, which ye now see and hear. ³⁴For David is not ascended into the heavens: but he saith himself, The LORD said unto my Lord, Sit thou on my right hand, ³⁵Until I make thy foes thy footstool. ³⁶Therefore let all the house of Israel know assuredly, that God hath made that same Jesus, whom ye have crucified, both Lord and Christ. ³⁷Now when they heard this, they were pricked in their heart, and said unto Peter and to the rest of the apostles, Men and brethren, what shall we do? ³⁸Then Peter said unto them, Repent, and be baptized every one of you in the name of Jesus Christ for the remission of sins, and ye shall receive the gift of*

the Holy Ghost. [39]For <u>the promise is unto you</u>, and to your children, and to all that are afar off, even as many as the Lord our God shall call."

2. Galatians 3:13-14 – *"[13]Christ hath redeemed us from the curse of the law, being made a curse for us: for it is written, Cursed is every one that hangeth on a tree: [14]<u>That</u> the blessing of Abraham might come on the Gentiles through Jesus Christ; <u>that</u> we might receive the <u>promise of the Spirit</u> through faith."* Here it is called the *"promise of the Spirit"*. Jesus died on the cross, not only for us to be justified by faith (the blessing of Abraham), but in order that we might receive the promise of the Spirit! Jesus died on the cross so that all of His people can receive this baptism.

3. John 7:37-39 – *"[37]In the last day, that great day of the feast, Jesus stood and cried, saying, If any man thirst, let him come unto me, and drink. [38]He that believeth on me, as the scripture hath said, out of his belly shall flow rivers of living water. [39](But this spake he of the Spirit, which they that believe on him should receive: for the Holy Ghost was not yet given; because that Jesus was not yet glorified.)"*

4. Ephesians 1:13-14 – *"[13]In whom ye also trusted, after that ye heard the word of truth, the gospel of your salvation: in whom also after that ye believed, ye were sealed with that holy Spirit of promise, [14]Which is the earnest of our inheritance until the redemption of the purchased possession, unto the praise of his glory."*

5. Joel 2:28-29 – *"[28]And it shall come to pass afterward, that I will pour out my spirit upon all flesh; and your sons and your daughters shall prophesy, your old men shall dream dreams, your young men shall see visions: [29]And also upon the servants and upon the handmaids in those days will I pour out my spirit."*

III. A Few Important Questions And Facts About The Baptism Of The Holy Ghost

A. It is a second experience after salvation.

1. Acts 8:5-17 – Notice, they were born again and water baptized, then the apostles sent Peter and John to pray for them to receive the Holy Ghost.

2. Acts 19: 2-7 – *"...since you believed."* A definitive passage outlining that the baptism is a separate experience to salvation.

3. Ephesians 1:13 – *"In whom ye also trusted, after that ye heard the word of truth, the gospel of your salvation: in whom also after that ye believed, ye were sealed with that holy Spirit of promise,"*

4. John 7:38-39 – *"He that believeth on me, as the scripture hath said, out of his belly shall flow rivers of living water. [vs. 39] (But this spake he of the Spirit, which they that believe on him should receive: for the Holy Ghost was not yet given; because that Jesus was not yet glorified.)"*

    a. I Corinthians 12:13 – *"For by one Spirit are we all baptized into one body, whether we be Jews or Gentiles, whether we be bond or free; and have been all made to drink into one Spirit."*

5. Luke 10:20 – *"Notwithstanding in this rejoice not, that the spirits are subject unto you; but rather rejoice, because your names are written in heaven."* – The disciples were already saved on the day of Pentecost, so the baptism then would be a second experience. It happens after we are saved. It can happen immediately or at length after being born again. It is up to the individual

6. Mark 16:17 – *"And these signs shall follow them that believe; In my name shall they cast out devils; they shall speak with new tongues;"* – They that believe these signs follow.

B. Is It For Today Or Has It Passed Away? There is not one passage of scripture that even remotely indicates that it is not for today. Like all of God's promises, it is for today.

1. Acts 2:39 – *"For the promise is unto you, and to your children, and to all that are afar off, even as many as the Lord our God shall call."*
2. I Corinthians 1:4-8 – The gifts are operable until the coming of the Lord. The baptism enables one to move in the gifts.
3. I Corinthians 13:8-10 – What is this which the Bible calls perfect? That which is perfect is not the Bible, as some Baptists would have us believe, all though it is the inspired Word of God. I believe Paul is talking about Jesus. He is that which is perfect. If you are going to say tongues have passed away you might as well say knowledge has passed away, but, of course, Paul is not saying this. In I Corinthians 1:4-8 he already has said the gifts will be here in operation until the coming of the Lord. That is when all these things will pass away.
4. It is the will of God that every believer receives it – John 7:38-39, Galatians 3:13-14
5. Acts 10:34 – *"Then Peter opened his mouth, and said, Of a truth I perceive that God is no respecter of persons:"* – What he has done for one he will do for all.
6. II Corinthians 1:20 – *"For all the promises of God in him are yea, and in him Amen, unto the glory of God by us."* (I Kings 8:56)
7. Hebrews 13:8 – *"Jesus Christ the same yesterday, and to day, and for ever."*
8. Malachi 3:6 – *"For I am the LORD, I change not; therefore ye sons of Jacob are not consumed."* – God does not change his mind about what he gives to his people.
9. History records people believing and receiving this baptism ever since the early church.
10. I, myself, have received it. So, no matter what someone's theory may be I have personally disproved it.

C. Tongues Are the Evidence of the Baptism of The Holy Ghost

1. I Corinthians 12:7 – *"But the manifestation of the Spirit is given to every man to profit withal."* – Every man baptized in the Holy Ghost is given the manifestation of the Spirit. I believe in particular this is speaking about tongues. Evidence in all three baptisms

   a. Baptism of Blood – a clean heart, a changed life
   b. Baptism in Water – a soaking, drenched body
   c. Baptism in Holy Ghost – speaking in tongues

2. Accounts of the baptism of the Holy Ghost and the manifestation of tongues.

   a. Acts 2: 1-5
   b. Acts 10: 43-48
   c. Acts 19: 1-7
   d. Acts 9:17 – *"And Ananias went his way, and entered into the house; and putting his hands on him said, Brother Saul, the Lord, even Jesus, that appeared unto thee in the way as thou camest, hath sent me, that thou mightest receive thy sight, and be filled with the Holy Ghost"*. (I Corinthians 14:18) – In Paul's account there is no mention of him speaking in tongues, but that does not mean it did not happen. We find later in I Corinthians 14 that he does speak in tongues. This would confirm to me that he did.
   e. Acts 8:14, 18 – In this account, we notice that Simeon "saw" that through laying on of hands the Holy Ghost was given. What did he see? Let's compare this with Acts 2:33. I believe he saw and heard them speak with tongues. Even if the last two accounts (Acts 9:17 and Acts 8:14, 18) could not be proven, we have three witnesses, which according to the Word, establishers this as principle.

IV. Two Types of Speaking in Tongues – This is where most people get confused!

A. Manifestation of the Spirit (prayer language of tongues)

1. I Corinthians 12:7 – *"But the manifestation of the Spirit is given to every man to profit withal"*.
2. I Corinthians 14:2, 28 – *"²For he that speaketh in an unknown tongue speaketh not unto men, but unto God: for no man understandeth him; howbeit in the spirit he speaketh mysteries...²⁸But if there be no interpreter, let him keep silence in the church; and let him speak to himself, and to God."*
3. I Corinthians 14:14-15 – *"¹⁴For if I pray in an unknown tongue, my spirit prayeth, but my understanding is unfruitful. ¹⁵What is it then? I will pray with the spirit, and I will pray with the understanding also: I will sing with the spirit, and I will sing with the understanding also."*
4. I Corinthians 14:4 – *"He that speaketh in an unknown tongue edifieth himself; but he that prophesieth edifieth the church"*.

This is the prayer language of the Spirit, which every believer is to use to be edified, built up, pray and worship with. These tongues are simply spoken unto God.

B. The gift of Tongues

1. I Corinthians 12:10, 30 – *"...¹⁰To another the working of miracles; to another prophecy; to another discerning of spirits; to another divers kinds of tongues; to another the interpretation of tongues...³⁰Have all the gifts of healing? do all speak with tongues? do all interpret?"* – This is the supernatural gift of speaking in tongues. It is used to speak to men for God. It, along with the interpretation of tongues, is the same as the gift of prophecy.
2. I Corinthians 14: 21-27 – These are the tongues that must be interpreted. These tongues are meant not to edify the individual, but to edify and build up the church.

C. How Can We Understand This?

1. I Corinthians 12:29–30 – *"Are all apostles? are all prophets? are all teachers? are all workers of miracle"s? Have all the gifts of healing? do all speak with tongues? do all interpret?"* – These verses here bring more confusion than any others. We must rightly divide the Scriptures here.

   a. *"Are all apostles?"*
   b. *"Are all prophets?"*

This is referring to the gifts; both ministry offices and supernatural gifts. Not everyone is called to, or given the ministry offices of an apostle, nor is everyone given the supernatural gift of tongues (which is speaking for God to men, not for private worship and edification). But everyone is called to prophecy, everyone is called to preach, all are to speak with tongues (prayer language) I Corinthians 14:5, 30; I Corinthians 12:7.

V. Scriptural Reasons Why We Should Speak In Tongues

A. Tongues are a sign

1. I Corinthians 14:22 – *"Wherefore tongues are for a sign, not to them that believe, but to them that believe not: but prophesying serveth not for them that believe not, but for them which believe."*
2. Mark 16:17 – *"And these signs shall follow them that believe; In my name shall they cast out devils; they shall speak with new tongues;"*
3. Isaiah 28:11-12 – *"¹¹For with stammering lips and another tongue will he speak to this people. ¹²To whom he said, This is the rest wherewith ye may cause the weary to rest; and this is the refreshing: yet they would not hear."*

4. Acts 2:33 – *"Therefore being by the right hand of God exalted, and having received of the Father the promise of the Holy Ghost, he hath shed forth this, which ye now see and hear."*

Tongues are a sign to the unbeliever. They are a <u>supernatural</u> sign! To believers tongues are not a sign because everyone <u>should</u> be speaking in tongues. Tongues were commonplace in Paul's day and should be now.

B. It is the will of God

1. I Corinthians 14:37-39 – *"... forbid not to speak with tongues."*
2. I Corinthians 14:5, 15, 26 – *"...I will pray with the spirit, and I will pray with the understanding also: I will sing with the spirit, and I will sing with the understanding also..."* (I Corinthians 14:14 – *"For if I pray in an unknown tongue, my spirit prayeth..."*)
3. John 4:23-24 – *"23But the hour cometh, and now is, when the true worshippers shall worship the Father in spirit and in truth: for the Father seeketh such to worship him. 24God is a Spirit: and they that worship him must worship him in spirit and in truth."*
4. Ephesians 5:17-19 – *"17Wherefore be ye not unwise, but understanding what the will of the Lord is. 18And be not drunk with wine, wherein is excess; but be filled with the Spirit; 19Speaking to yourselves in psalms and hymns and spiritual songs, singing and making melody in your heart to the Lord;"*

C. It is profitable

1. I Corinthians 12:7 – *"But the manifestation of the Spirit is given to every man to profit withal."* – Tongues are profitable because they edify, build and stimulate our faith
2. I Corinthians 14:4 – *"He that speaketh in an unknown tongue edifieth himself..."*
3. Jude 20 – *"But ye, beloved, building up yourselves on your most holy faith, praying in the Holy Ghost,"* The word *"edifieth"* in I Corinthians 14:4 and *"building up"* in Jude 20 are the same Greek root word which means to build upon, housebuilder, and to construct. Speaking in tongues enhances our worship. You might ask "What good does it do to speak in tongues?" The answer is, "How good is it to praise and magnify God?"

   a. Acts 2:11 – *"Cretes and Arabians, we do hear them speak in our tongues the wonderful works of God."*
   b. Acts 10:46 – *"For they heard them speak with tongues, and magnify God. Then answered Peter,"*
   c. I Corinthians 14:17 – *"For thou verily givest thanks well..."*

D. Speaking in tongues brings rest and refreshing.

1. Isaiah 28:11-12 – *"11For with stammering lips and another tongue will he speak to this people. 12To whom he said, This is the rest wherewith ye may cause the weary to rest; and this is the refreshing: yet they would not hear."*
2. Job 32:18-21 – *"18For I am full of matter, the spirit within me constraineth me. 19Behold, my belly is as wine which hath no vent; it is ready to burst like new bottles. 20I will speak, that I may be refreshed: I will open my lips and answer. 21Let me not, I pray you, accept any man's person, neither let me give flattering titles unto man."*
3. Isaiah 41:18 – *"I will open rivers in high places, and fountains in the midst of the valleys: I will make the wilderness a pool of water, and the dry land springs of water."*
4. John 7:37-39 – *"37In the last day, that great day of the feast, Jesus stood and cried, saying, If any man thirst, let him come unto me, and drink. 38He that believeth on me, as the scripture hath said, out of his belly shall flow rivers of living water. 39(But this spake he of the Spirit, which*

they that believe on him should receive: for the Holy Ghost was not yet given; because that Jesus was not yet glorified.)"

E.   Speaking in tongues will help us say right things.   When you are speaking in tongues, you are doing one of four things.

1.   Praying according to the will of God (Romans 8:26-27)
2.   Edifying or building yourself up (Jude 20)
3.   Giving thanks or worshipping (I Corinthians 14:17)
4.   Speaking the mysteries of God (I Corinthians 14:2)

The Greek word of "*mysteries*" is "*musterion*" meaning a secret, a mystery. Among the ancient Greeks the mysteries were religious rites and ceremonies practiced by secret societies into which anyone who so desire might be received. Those who were initiated into these mysteries became possessors of certain knowledge, which was not imparted to the uninitiated. Here is a quote from Vine's dictionary: "We, then, by speaking in tongues are released into God's divine secrets and can and will possess knowledge those who do not speak in tongues will not have."

F.   Prayer

1.   Romans 8:26-27 – "*26Likewise the Spirit also helpeth our infirmities: for we know not what we should pray for as we ought: but the Spirit itself maketh intercession for us with groanings which cannot be uttered. 27And he that searcheth the hearts knoweth what is the mind of the Spirit, because he maketh intercession for the saints according to the will of God.*"

a.   We do not always know what to pray, but He does
b.   He helps our weaknesses
c.   Always prays according to the will of God

2.   Ephesians 6:18 – "*Praying always with all prayer and supplication in the Spirit, and watching thereunto with all perseverance and supplication for all saints;*" – A part of our spiritual armor.
3.   Jude 20 – "*But ye, beloved, building up yourselves on your most holy faith, praying in the Holy Ghost,*"
4.   I Corinthians 14:14-15 – "*14For if I pray in an unknown tongue, my spirit prayeth, but my understanding is unfruitful. 15What is it then? I will pray with the spirit, and I will pray with the understanding also: I will sing with the spirit, and I will sing with the understanding also.*" – When we pray in the Spirit we are not limited to our own understanding
5.   I Thessalonians 5:17 – "*Pray without ceasing.*" – The only way to pray without ceasing is in tongues.

VI.   Questions Concerning Tongues

A.   Are They The Least Of The Gifts? The answer to that is simply No. Fundamentalists have tried to make light of speaking in tongues, and have tried to de-emphasis their importance by saying that because they are the last gift mentioned in *I Corinthians 12:10* they are the least.

1.   I Corinthians 12:1-30 – These are not listed in order of importance. All of the gifts are operated by the Spirit and none are of greater importance than the other.
2.   What are the best gifts? I Corinthians 12:31 – "*But covet earnestly the best gifts: and yet shew I unto you a more excellent way.*" – These would be whatever the love of God demanded for the moment. If healing is needed, then that would be the best gift, if deliverance, faith, miracles, discernment, etc, then whatever the gift needed at the moment would be the best.
3.   If we are going to say tongues are the least simply because it is listed last then what about:

      a.   I Corinthians 13:13 – *"And now abideth faith, hope, charity, these three; but the greatest of these is charity."*

      b.   Luke 16:10 – *"He that is faithful in that which is least is faithful also in much: and he that is unjust in the least is unjust also in much."* – No matter what, God expects faithfulness even in the least gift.

      c.   Matthew 19:30 – *"But many that are first shall be last; and the last shall be first."*

      d.   Matthew 20:16 – *"So the last shall be first, and the first last: for many be called, but few chosen."*

      e.   Also, why did God seem to ignore the firstborns and choose the younger brothers?

B.   Is Love More Important?

    1.   I Corinthians 12:31 – *"But covet earnestly the best gifts: and yet shew I unto you a more excellent way."* The reason Paul says this is that love is to be the <u>motivation</u> for the gifts, not an ambitious desire to be seen of men or any other reason. He purposely put *I Corinthians 13* between chapters 12 and 14 to show us love is why we are to move in the gifts. This says to me if we refuse to move in the gifts, we are not walking in God's love.

      a.   Contents of *I Corinthians 12-14*

         1)   *I Corinthians 12* – lists the gifts
         2)   *I Corinthians 13* – love, our motivation
         3)   *I Corinthians 14* – how to operate gifts in a meeting

    2.   We can have both; I Corinthians 14:1 – *"Follow after charity, and desire spiritual gifts, but rather that ye may prophesy."*

C.   Is Tongues Of The Devil? This is one that religious people or any person who does not want to receive truth says. If it is just too hard for them, or it will cost too much, or their pride resists, or they are simply ignorant of the Scripture, or unwilling to obey God's Word because it is not something they like, or it is not of their tradition, they make it easy on themselves and use this excuse.

    1.   I Corinthians 12:3 – *"Wherefore I give you to understand, that no man speaking by the Spirit of God calleth Jesus accursed: and that no man can say that Jesus is the Lord, but by the Holy Ghost."* – There is no way anyone speaking by the Spirit (in tongues) can be of the devil.

    2.   Matthew 11:15-19 – *"15He that hath ears to hear, let him hear. 16But whereunto shall I liken this generation? It is like unto children sitting in the markets, and calling unto their fellows, 17And saying, We have piped unto you, and ye have not danced; we have mourned unto you, and ye have not lamented. 18For John came neither eating nor drinking, and they say, He hath a devil. 19The Son of man came eating and drinking, and they say, Behold a man gluttonous, and a winebibber, a friend of publicans and sinners. But wisdom is justified of her children."* – Some people will never choose or receive truth no matter what. They will always try to find a way out.

    3.   This is blasphemy of the Holy Ghost (attributing the works of God to the devil, Matthew 12:22-34).

    4.   If tongues are really a manifestation of the devil, then why don't demon possessed speak in tongues? Why don't we see people are bars speaking in tongues?

D.   Has Tongues Passed Away? The answer is NO. That is simply a theological outlook that does not hold light in the Scriptures.

1. Acts 2:39 – *"For the promise is unto you, and to your children, and <u>to all that are afar off</u>, even as many as the Lord our God shall call."*

2. I Corinthians 1:4-8 – *"⁴I thank my God always on your behalf, for the grace of God which is given you by Jesus Christ; ⁵That in every thing ye are enriched by him, in all utterance, and in all knowledge; ⁶Even as the testimony of Christ was confirmed in you: ⁷So that <u>ye come behind in no gift</u>; <u>waiting for the coming of our Lord Jesus Christ</u>: ⁸Who shall also confirm you unto the end, that ye may be blameless in the day of our Lord Jesus Christ."*

3. I Corinthians 13:8-10 – *"⁸Charity never faileth: but whether there be prophecies, they shall fail; whether there be tongues, they shall cease; whether there be knowledge, it shall vanish away. ⁹For we know in part, and we prophesy in part. ¹⁰But when that which is <u>perfect</u> is come, then that which is in part shall be done away."* – This speaks of Jesus and His manifested sons.

4. I Corinthians 14:39 – *"Wherefore, brethren, covet to prophesy, and <u>forbid not to speak with tongues</u>."*

5. Why then do so very many godly people speak in tongues?

6. I Corinthians 14:18 – *"I thank my God, I speak with tongues more than ye all"* – Paul spoke with tongues.

Lesson 7
BEING DISCIPLED IN THE HOUSE OF THE LORD

I.   Genesis 14:12-20

"¹²And they took Lot, Abram's brother's son, who dwelt in Sodom, and his goods, and departed. ¹³And there came one that had escaped, and told Abram the Hebrew; for he dwelt in the plain of Mamre the Amorite, brother of Eschol, and brother of Aner: and these were confederate with Abram. ¹⁴And when Abram heard that his brother was taken captive, he armed his trained servants, born in his own house, three hundred and eighteen, and pursued them unto Dan. ¹⁵And he divided himself against them, he and his servants, by night, and smote them, and pursued them unto Hobah, which is on the left hand of Damascus. ¹⁶And he brought back all the goods, and also brought again his brother Lot, and his goods, and the women also, and the people. ¹⁷And the king of Sodom went out to meet him after his return from the slaughter of Chedorlaomer, and of the kings that were with him, at the valley of Shaveh, which is the king's dale. ¹⁸And Melchizedek king of Salem brought forth bread and wine: and he was the priest of the most high God. ¹⁹And he blessed him, and said, Blessed be Abram of the most high God, possessor of heaven and earth: ²⁰And blessed be the most high God, which hath delivered thine enemies into thy hand. And he gave him tithes of all."

A.   Verse 12

   1.   Lot's name means – Wrapped up, hidden, covered, myrrh

This speaks of Lot's character. He had hidden, covered up sin in his life. He was a man in bondage. He was also wrapped up and all tangled up in Sodom's life. Myrrh speaks of his suffering because of it.

     a.   II Peter 2:7-8 – *"And delivered just Lot, vexed with the filthy conversation of the wicked: (For that righteous man dwelling among them, in seeing and hearing, vexed his righteous soul from day to day with their unlawful deeds;)"*
     b.   Genesis 13:11-13 – *"Then Lot chose him all the plain of Jordan; and Lot journeyed east: and they separated themselves the one from the other. Abram dwelled in the land of Canaan, and Lot dwelled in the cities of the plain, and pitched his tent toward Sodom. But the men of Sodom were wicked and sinners before the LORD exceedingly."* – parted because of strife and lust.

   2.   Sodom means – Their secret, their cement – Sodom's secret was their wickedness. Plus they were cemented in this unlawfulness
   3.   Lot made the choice to live and stay there with his family because of strife and ambition, and it would ultimately cost him dearly.
   4.   The result of allowing sin in our lives to linger

     a.   I Corinthians 5:6 – *"...a little leaven leaveneth the whole lump?"*
     b.   Song of Solomon 2:15 – *"Take us the foxes, the little foxes, that spoil the vines..."*
     c.   Proverbs 24:33-34 – *"Yet a little sleep, a little slumber, a little folding of the hands to sleep: So shall thy poverty come as one that travelleth; and thy want as an armed man."*
     d.   Ephesians 4:26-27 – *"Be ye angry, and sin not: let not the sun go down upon your wrath: Neither give place to the devil."*
     e.   Proverbs 7:9 – *"In the twilight, in the evening, in the black and dark night:"*

B.   Verse 13 – One who escapes the battle comes and tells Abram

C.   Verse 14 – *"And when Abram heard that his brother was taken captive, he armed his trained servants, born in his own house, three hundred and eighteen, and pursued them unto Dan."*

1. I believe this passage is a picture of the last day remnant who will deliver their brethren taken captive. Other translations:

   "...he led forth his trained men"
   "...he took a band of his trained men, 318 of them, we appointed

2. Word meanings

   a. Trained – Initiated, practiced; it comes from a root word meaning – to initiate or disciple.
   b. Remember that the Greek word for mystery is "musterion" which means – That which is known only by the initiated.
   c. This means that these men knew God intimately and had proved themselves well.
   d. Abram was a man who would "teach his children"
   e. These men were disciples

3. Born in his own house

   a. This symbolizes the local church
   b. We are the house of the Lord
   c. It is the responsibility of shepherds of local flocks to train disciples to get them to the place where they are initiated.

4. The number 318 - This remnant of sons will redeem their brothers from bondage in the last days.

   a. 300 – Number of a faithful remnant
   b. 18 – Number for bondage

5. Other Scriptures

   a. Judges 7:2-7 – Gideon's 300
   b. I Samuel 30:10-19 – David's 400 at Ziklag
   c. II Samuel 23 – David's mighty men

6. Dan in Hebrew means judgment
7. Abram means high, exalted father

This remnant, led by a true father ministry, trained and discipled by him, is ready to bring God's judgment of the oppressors of God's people. This speaks of the last great move of God that will be foreshadowed by true discipleship. These will be the "manifestation of the sons of God".

8. There must be discipleship and training by a true father ministry

   a. Hebrews 12:8 – *"But if ye be without chastisement, whereof all are partakers, then are ye bastards, and not sons."* Chastisement in Greek – Education or training, tutorage, disciplinary correction; it comes from a root meaning – to train up a child, educate, teach.

   b. Disciple

      1) Hebrew word – Instructed, learned, accustomed to; it comes from a root meaning – to goad, to teach, to instruct using the rod as an incentive, expert, skillful.

      2)   Greek word – A disciplined one, a learner, student of the Word.

9.   Acts 19:9-10 – *"But when divers were hardened, and believed not, but spake evil of that way before the multitude, he departed from them, and separated the disciples, disputing daily in the school of one Tyrannus. And this continued by the space of two years; so that all they which dwelt in Asia heard the word of the Lord Jesus, both Jews and Greeks."*

10.   Matthew 28:19 – *"Go ye therefore, and teach (make disciples) all nations, baptizing them in the name of the Father, and of the Son, and of the Holy Ghost:"* Greek word for teach – To become a pupil, disciple, enroll as a scholar.

11.   Isaiah 28:9-10 – *"Whom shall he teach knowledge? and whom shall he make to understand doctrine? them that are weaned from the milk, and drawn from the breasts. For precept must be upon precept, precept upon precept; line upon line, line upon line; here a little, and there a little:"*

12.   Ezekiel 44:23 – *"And they shall teach my people the difference between the holy and profane, and cause them to discern between the unclean and the clean."*

13.   Proverbs 29:21 – *"He that delicately bringeth up his servant from a child shall have him become his son at the length."*

D.   Verse 15 – *"And he divided himself against them, he and his servants, by night, and smote them, and pursued them unto Hobah, which is on the left hand of Damascus."*

    1.   Word meanings

        a.   Hobah – Hiding place
        b.   Damascus – Moist with blood, activity

Abram found their hiding place, and made the ground moist with the enemy's blood.

E.   Verse 16 – *"And he brought back all the goods, and also brought again his brother Lot, and his goods, and the women also, and the people."*

    1.   God wants us to deliver His captive people

        a.   Jesus did it

            1)   Psalms 68:18 – *"Thou hast ascended on high, <u>thou hast led captivity captive</u>: thou hast received gifts for men; yea, for the rebellious also, that the LORD God might dwell among them."*
            2)   Luke 4:18 – *"The Spirit of the Lord is upon me, because he hath anointed me to preach the gospel to the poor; he hath sent me to heal the brokenhearted, <u>to preach deliverance to the captives</u>, and recovering of sight to the blind, to set at liberty them that are bruised,"*

        b.   He requires us to do it as well

            1)   Isaiah 49:24-25 – *"Shall the prey be taken from the mighty, or the lawful captive delivered? But thus saith the LORD, Even the captives of the mighty shall be taken away, and the prey of the terrible shall be delivered..."*
            2)   Joel 2:32 – *"And it shall come to pass, that whosoever shall call on the name of the LORD shall be delivered: for in mount Zion and in Jerusalem shall be deliverance, as the LORD hath said, and in the remnant whom the LORD shall call."*
            3)   Obadiah 21 – *"And saviours shall come up on mount Zion to judge the mount of Esau; and the kingdom shall be the LORD's."*

4) Romans 8:19-22 - *"For the earnest expectation of the creature waiteth for the manifestation of the sons of God. For the creature was made subject to vanity, not willingly, but by reason of him who hath subjected the same in hope, Because the creature itself also shall be delivered from the bondage of corruption into the glorious liberty of the children of God. For we know that the whole creation groaneth and travaileth in pain together until now."*

5) Isaiah 32:2 – *"And a man shall be as an hiding place from the wind, and a covert from the tempest; as rivers of water in a dry place, as the shadow of a great rock in a weary land."*

6) Isaiah 66:19-20 - *"And I will set a sign among them, and I will send those that escape of them unto the nations, to Tarshish, Pul, and Lud, that draw the bow, to Tubal, and Javan, to the isles afar off, that have not heard my fame, neither have seen my glory; and they shall declare my glory among the Gentiles. And they shall bring all your brethren for an offering unto the LORD out of all nations upon horses, and in chariots, and in litters, and upon mules, and upon swift beasts, to my holy mountain Jerusalem, saith the LORD, as the children of Israel bring an offering in a clean vessel into the house of the LORD."*

E. Verse 18-20

"And Melchizedek king of Salem brought forth bread and wine: and he was the priest of the most high God. And he blessed him, and said, Blessed be Abram of the most high God, possessor of heaven and earth: And blessed be the most high God, which hath delivered thine enemies into thy hand. And he gave him tithes of all."

Lesson 8
BECOMING AN EXAMPLE OF TRUE DISCIPLESHIP

In this study we want to look into the Scriptures concerning us becoming true examples of what it means to be a believer. A number of Greek words are translated example and it can mean a pattern or model to be copied. It can also mean the mark left by a blow or as an impression made on wax by a seal. It also means a footprint. There was no greater example in the Word of God other than the Lord Jesus. He alone sets a standard for all of us to try and strive to live up to, by His grace. There must come a time in all of our lives when we seek to be a true disciple, to be just like Jesus, and by doing so, we prepare ourselves for His coming, and leave an impression on other believers' lives on how to live the Christian faith. It should be our hearts desire to exhort, encourage, and challenge others by our conduct to live godly and holy Christian lives.

I.   Word Definitions for "Example"

A.   Greek words

1.   *Hupodeigma* – an exhibit for imitation, a pattern; from a root, *hupodeiknumi* – to exhibit under the eyes, to exemplify, to show.
2.   *Hupogrammos* – a copy for imitation
3.   *Tupos* – a die as struck, a stamp or scar, a model or resemblance, a pattern or print; this word is also translated – *ensample, figure, print, pattern, and form*
4.   *Deigma* – a specimen, to show literally or figuratively

II.   We are Called to be Examples

A.   The call and responsibility of leadership to be examples

1.   I Peter 5:1-3 – "*The elders which are among you I exhort, who am also an elder, and a witness of the sufferings of Christ, and also a partaker of the glory that shall be revealed: Feed the flock of God which is among you, taking the oversight thereof, not by constraint, but willingly; not for filthy lucre, but of a ready mind; Neither as being lords over God's heritage, but being ensamples to the flock.*"

a.   Feed the flock of God
b.   Taking the oversight willingly
c.   Not for filthy lucre
d.   Having a ready mind
e.   Not being a lord over God's people
f.   Lead by being an example

2.   Philippians 3:17-20 – "*Brethren, be followers together of me, and mark them which walk so as ye have us for an ensample. (For many walk, of whom I have told you often, and now tell you even weeping, that they are the enemies of the cross of Christ: Whose end is destruction, whose God is their belly, and whose glory is in their shame, who mind earthly things.) For our conversation is in heaven; from whence also we look for the Saviour, the Lord Jesus Christ:*"
3.   II Thessalonians 3:7-9 – "*For yourselves know how ye ought to follow us: for we behaved not ourselves disorderly among you; Neither did we eat any man's bread for nought; but wrought with labour and travail night and day, that we might not be chargeable to any of you: Not because we have not power, but to make ourselves an ensample unto you to follow us.*"
4.   Hebrews 13:7-8 – "*Remember them which have the rule over you, who have spoken unto you the word of God: whose faith follow, considering the end of their conversation. Jesus Christ the same yesterday, and to day, and for ever.*"

5. I Timothy 1:16 – *"Howbeit for this cause I obtained mercy, that in me first Jesus Christ might shew forth all longsuffering, for a pattern to them which should hereafter believe on him to life everlasting"*

B. We are encouraged to be examples

1. I Timothy 4:12 – *"Let no man despise thy youth; but be thou an example of the believers, in word, in conversation, in charity, in spirit, in faith, in purity."*

    a. In word
    b. In lifestyle
    c. In love
    d. In spirit (or attitude)
    e. In faith
    f. In purity

2. I Thessalonians 1:5-9 - *"⁵For our gospel came not unto you in word only, but also in power, and in the Holy Ghost, and in much assurance; as ye know what manner of men we were among you for your sake. ⁶And ye became followers of us, and of the Lord, having received the word in much affliction, with joy of the Holy Ghost: ⁷So that ye were ensamples to all that believe in Macedonia and Achaia. ⁸For from you sounded out the word of the Lord not only in Macedonia and Achaia, but also in every place your faith to God-ward is spread abroad; so that we need not to speak any thing. ⁹For they themselves shew of us what manner of entering in we had unto you, and how ye turned to God from idols to serve the living and true God;"*

3. Titus 2:1-8 - *"¹But speak thou the things which become sound doctrine: ²That the aged men be sober, grave, temperate, sound in faith, in charity, in patience. ³The aged women likewise, that they be in behaviour as becometh holiness, not false accusers, not given to much wine, teachers of good things; ⁴That they may teach the young women to be sober, to love their husbands, to love their children, ⁵To be discreet, chaste, keepers at home, good, obedient to their own husbands, that the word of God be not blasphemed. ⁶Young men likewise exhort to be sober minded. ⁷In all things shewing thyself a pattern of good works: in doctrine shewing uncorruptness, gravity, sincerity, ⁸Sound speech, that cannot be condemned; that he that is of the contrary part may be ashamed, having no evil thing to say of you."*

    a. Sober minded
    b. Pattern of good works
    c. Uncorruptness in Doctrine
    d. Gravity (honesty)
    e. Sincerity
    f. Sound speech

C. Others in Scripture

1. James 5:10-11 – *"Take, my brethren, the prophets, who have spoken in the name of the Lord, for an example of suffering affliction, and of patience. Behold, we count them happy which endure. Ye have heard of the patience of Job, and have seen the end of the Lord; that the Lord is very pitiful, and of tender mercy."*

    a. Suffering affliction
    b. Patience
    c. Endurance

2. Philippians 2:20 – *"For I have no man likeminded, who will naturally care for your state."*

3. I Peter 3:1-4 – "*Likewise, ye wives, be in subjection to your own husbands; that, if any obey not the word, they also may without the word be won by the conversation of the wives; While they behold your chaste conversation coupled with fear. Whose adorning let it not be that outward adorning of plaiting the hair, and of wearing of gold, or of putting on of apparel; But let it be the hidden man of the heart, in that which is not corruptible, even the ornament of a meek and quiet spirit, which is in the sight of God of great price.*"

D. The Lord Jesus, Our Chief Example

1. I Peter 2:20-23 – "*...For even hereunto were ye called: because Christ also suffered for us, leaving us an example, that ye should follow his steps: Who did no sin, neither was guile found in his mouth: Who, when he was reviled, reviled not again; when he suffered, he threatened not; but committed himself to him that judgeth righteously:*"
2. John 13:12-17 - "*So after he had washed their feet, and had taken his garments, and was set down again, he said unto them, Know ye what I have done to you? ¹³Ye call me Master and Lord: and ye say well; for so I am. ¹⁴If I then, your Lord and Master, have washed your feet; ye also ought to wash one another's feet. ¹⁵For I have given you an example, that ye should do as I have done to you. ¹⁶Verily, verily, I say unto you, The servant is not greater than his lord; neither he that is sent greater than he that sent him. ¹⁷If ye know these things, happy are ye if ye do them.*"

E. What we should be doing

1. Hebrews 10:23-24 – "*Let us hold fast the profession of our faith without wavering; (for he is faithful that promised;) And let us consider one another to provoke unto love and to good works:*" With our example, we should be provoking one another to love and good works

2. Philippians 1:27 – "*Only let your conversation be as it becometh the gospel of Christ: that whether I come and see you, or else be absent, I may hear of your affairs, that ye stand fast in one spirit, with one mind striving together for the faith of the gospel;*"

   a. Lifestyle be becoming of the Gospel
   b. Stand fast in one spirit and one mind
   c. Striving together for the faith

3. Hebrews 13:5 – "*Let your conversation be without covetousness; and be content with such things as ye have: for he hath said, I will never leave thee, nor forsake thee.*"

   a. Lifestyle without covetousness
   b. Content with such things as you have
   c. For He will never leave or forsake you

4. James 3:13 – "*Who is a wise man and endued with knowledge among you? let him shew out of a good conversation his works with meekness of wisdom.*"

   a. A good lifestyle
   b. Your works with meekness of wisdom

5. I Peter 2:12 – "*Having your <u>conversation honest</u> among the Gentiles: that, whereas they speak against you as evildoers, they may by your good works, which they shall behold, glorify God in the day of visitation.*"
6. I Peter 3:16 – "*Having a good conscience; that, whereas they speak evil of you, as of evildoers, they may be ashamed that falsely accuse your good conversation in Christ.*"

Lesson 9
ABIDING IN HIM

I. God Has Chosen Zion

   A. Psalms 132:13 – *"For the LORD hath chosen Zion; he hath desired it for his habitation."*
   B. Revelation 3:20 – *"Behold, I stand at the door, and knock: if any man hear my voice, and open the door, I will come in to him, and will sup with him, and he with me."*
   C. Matthew 23:37 – *"O Jerusalem, Jerusalem, thou that killest the prophets, and stonest them which are sent unto thee, how often would I have gathered thy children together, even as a hen gathereth her chickens under her wings, and ye would not!"*
   D. Revelation 21:3 – *"...the tabernacle of God is with men, and he will dwell with them, and they shall be his people, and God himself shall be with them, and be their God."*

II. Commands to Abide, Greek – *Meno* – To Stay In

   A. Given place or relation

      1. John 15:4-10
      2. I John 2:28 – *"And now, little children, abide in him; that, when he shall appear, we may have confidence, and not be ashamed before him at his coming."*

III. Blessings of Abiding

   A. I John 3:6 – *"Whosoever abideth in him sinneth not..."*
   B. Psalms 91:1, 9-16 – Hebrew for evil – adversity, affliction, calamity – *"¹He that dwelleth in the secret place of the most High shall abide under the shadow of the Almighty. ⁹Because thou hast made the LORD, which is my refuge, even the most High, thy habitation; ¹⁰There shall no <u>evil</u> befall thee, neither shall any plague come nigh thy dwelling. ¹¹For he shall give his angels charge over thee, to keep thee in all thy ways. ¹²They shall bear thee up in their hands, lest thou dash thy foot against a stone. ¹³Thou shalt tread upon the lion and adder: the young lion and the dragon shalt thou trample under feet. ¹⁴Because he hath set his love upon me, therefore will I deliver him: I will set him on high, because he hath known my name. ¹⁵He shall call upon me, and I will answer him: I will be with him in trouble; I will deliver him, and honour him. ¹⁶With long life will I satisfy him, and shew him my salvation."*

IV. How Can We Abide?

   A. Exodus 15:2 – *"The LORD is my strength and song, and he is become my salvation: he is my God, and I will prepare him an habitation; my father's God, and I will exalt him."*
   B. I John 2:6, 10 – *"He that saith he abideth in him ought himself also so to walk, even as he walked. ¹⁰He that loveth his brother abideth in the light, and there is none occasion of stumbling in him."*
   C. I John 4:16 – *"And we have known and believed the love that God hath to us. God is love; and he that dwelleth in love dwelleth in God, and God in him."*
   D. Psalms 15 – *"LORD, who shall abide in thy tabernacle? who shall dwell in thy holy hill? ²He that walketh uprightly, and worketh righteousness, and speaketh the truth in his heart. ³He that backbiteth not with his tongue, nor doeth evil to his neighbour, nor taketh up a reproach against his neighbour. ⁴In whose eyes a vile person is contemned; but he honoureth them that fear the LORD. He that sweareth to his own hurt, and changeth not. ⁵He that putteth not out his money to usury, nor taketh reward against the innocent. He that doeth these things shall never be moved."*

Lesson 10
CHRIST OUR PASSOVER

I.   Jesus Christ Is Our Passover

The keynote of the New Testament message is Messianic fulfillment. Jesus is the One of whom Moses and the prophets have written (John 1:45, Luke 24:25-27, Deuteronomy 18:15, 18, John 5:39, Jeremiah 23:5-6, Hebrews 10:7). The Messiah by His life, work, death, and resurrection has accomplished, "eternal salvation" (Hebrews 5:9). This is what the law was unable to do for the law made nothing perfect (Hebrews 7:19). It only served as a schoolmaster until Jesus Christ came (Galatians 3:24). The salvation of God as demonstrated in the story of the Passover and the Exodus is thus only a foreshadowing of what was to come. All God's acts in the Old Testament point to an ultimate future, found in the Messiah, Jesus. Passover is the beginning of the journey that the Messiah completes (I Corinthians 10:1-5), whereas the historic Passover and Exodus was limited to the experience of one people (Israel). For New Testament Christians, Passover and Exodus is open to everyone, to all the nations of the world. Jesus' Messianic activity reaches a climax in the events of His last Passover. The last supper was a paschal meal without the lamb, because Jesus was to be the lamb (John 1:29, 36). There is no mention of a lamb there (I Corinthians 11:23-26). The crucifixion took place on the first day of Passover (John 18:28).

A.   Scriptures confirming Christ our Passover

   1.   Revelation 5:6 – *"...in the midst of the elders, stood a Lamb as it had been slain..."*
   2.   Revelation 13:8 – *"...the Lamb slain from the foundation of the world."*
   3.   I Peter 1:18-19 – *"...But with the precious blood of Christ, as of a lamb..."*
   4.   Hebrews 9:7-28
   5.   I Corinthians 5:7 – *"...Christ our passover is sacrificed for us."*

"Christ our Passover is sacrificed for us." Jesus is and has always been, even from the foundation of the world, the Passover Lamb.

II.   The Passover in General

A.   Hebrew and Greek words

   1.   Hebrew word for Passover – *Pecach* – exemption, from a root – to hop over, to skip, and to spare. When used as a noun (Isaiah 31:5) it means to defend or to protect.
   2.   Greek word for Passover – *Pascha* – to pass over, to spare, it signifies the Passover feast. It means the meal, the day, the feast or the special sacrifices connected with it.
   3.   Tradition – It was called a night of the preserved one from malignant spirits.

B.   Passover in general in the Old Testament

   1.   Exodus 12:13 – *"And the blood shall be to you for a token upon the houses where ye are: and when I see the blood, I will pass over you, and the plague shall not be upon you to destroy you, when I smite the land of Egypt."*
   2.   Exodus 13:3-4 – *"And Moses said unto the people, Remember this day, in which ye came out from Egypt, out of the house of bondage; for by strength of hand the LORD brought you out from this place: there shall no leavened bread be eaten. This day came ye out in the month Abib."*
   3.   Deuteronomy 16:1-8
   4.   Exodus 12:1-51
   5.   Exodus 13:3-10
   6.   Exodus 23:14-19

7. Exodus 34:18-26
8. Leviticus 23:4-14
9. Numbers 9:1-14
10. Numbers 28:16-25

III. Verse by Verse Analysis of Exodus 12 (And the corresponding revelation of how it applies to us as believers)

A. Verse 1 – God spoke to Moses in Egypt (the land of bondage) this also speaks to us in our bondage.

B. Verse 2 –

1. Abib (Deuteronomy 16:1) this is the first Jewish month. It means – an ear of corn, a green ear. The revelation here is before we embrace the Lamb of God, we are young and immature in the ways and dealings of God and man. After the Babylonian exile it was commonly called *Nison* (Esther 3:7) it means – their flight. We begin our flight in Jesus at salvation, as we believe and receive the offering of God, the Lamb Jesus.
2. This was to represent a new beginning
3. It would become the basis or foundation for Israel.

C. Verse 3

1. All the congregation, this was for all God's people
2. Tenth day – ten is the number in Scripture that means law, government, and completed cycle. This was to be a law. It would also begin the cycle for the first year for Israel. This speaks to us that this is the law or command of God, to accept his sacrifice. Also it is the beginning of us walking in the government of God, the rules and laws of the Kingdom.
3. Every man a lamb – this represents to us that Jesus died for every man (John 1:35-36). Also, it represents that man is responsible to take, accept, and receive, the Lamb of God. We must choose to take Him. He is our Passover Lamb – I Corinthians 5:7-8.

   a. John 1:29 – *"The next day John seeth Jesus coming unto him, and saith, Behold the Lamb of God, which taketh away the sin of the world."*
   b. Revelation 13:8 – *"And all that dwell upon the earth shall worship him, whose names are not written in the book of life of the Lamb slain from the foundation of the world."*
   c. Acts 8:26-35

      1) Isaiah 53:7-8
      2) Luke 24:13-21, 26-27

   d. Revelation 5:6-13
   e. Revelation 7:9-10, 14, 17
   f. Revelation 14:1 (should be translated <u>the</u> *lamb* instead of *a lamb*.)
   g. Revelation 19:7-9
   h. Revelation 21:22-23
   i. Genesis 22:1-7,8,14 – Isaac is a type of Jesus. God wanted to see if any man was willing to do what He would do.

Lesson 11
CHURCH ATTENDANCE AND THE BODY OF CHRIST

I. Hebrews 10:23-27- *"Let us hold fast the profession of our faith without wavering; (for he is faithful that promised;) 24And let us consider one another to provoke unto love and to good works: 25Not forsaking the assembling of ourselves together, as the manner of some is; but exhorting one another: and so much the more, as ye see the day approaching. 26For if we sin wilfully after that we have received the knowledge of the truth, there remaineth no more sacrifice for sins, 27But a certain fearful looking for of judgment and fiery indignation, which shall devour the adversaries."*

A. The assembling of the saints should not to be neglected, especially as the end time approaches.

B   Where should we assemble?

   1. Deuteronomy 12:5 – Where the Lord chooses – *"But unto the place which the LORD your God shall choose out of all your tribes to put his name there, even unto his habitation shall ye seek, and thither thou shalt come:"*
   2. 1 Corinthians 12:18- Where the Lord sets us – *"But now hath God set the members every one of them in the body, as it hath pleased him."*

C. When should we gather together?

   1. Acts 20:7 – First day of the week – *"And upon the first day of the week, when the disciples came together to break bread, Paul preached unto them, ready to depart on the morrow; and continued his speech until midnight."*

D. Why should we assemble together?

   1. Assemble for the Lord's Supper and ministry of the Word – I Corinthians 11:18-34
   2. Bring tithes and offerings – I Corinthians 16:1-2 – *"Now concerning the collection for the saints, as I have given order to the churches of Galatia, even so do ye. 2Upon the first day of the week let every one of you lay by him in store, as God hath prospered him, that there be no gatherings when I come."*
   3. To edify and teach each other and minister in the Holy Spirit to one another – I Corinthians 14:23-40
   4. Because we need one another – I Corinthians 12:12-27

E. Christ is the Head of the Church

   1. Ephesians 1:22 – *"And hath put all things under his feet, and gave him to be the head over all things to the church,"*
   2. Ephesians 5:23 – *"For the husband is the head of the wife, even as Christ is the head of the church: and he is the saviour of the body."*
   3. Colossians 1:18 – *"And he is the head of the body, the church: who is the beginning, the firstborn from the dead; that in all things he might have the preeminence."*

F. The meaning of the word "Church"

   1. The New Testament Greek word for church "ecclesia" (ekklesia) is used some one hundred and nini times, and over ninety times this word refers to the local church. Many local churches are named in the Scriptures, such as the seven churches of Asia, the church at the

house of Priscilla and Aquila, the church at Rome, the church at Corinth, etc. Thus the local church patterns and teaching occupy most of the New Testament references to the church.

   2. The Greek meaning for *ekklesia* – a calling out, a popular meeting, especially a religious congregation (Jewish synagogue, or Christian community of members on earth or saints in heaven or both); assembly, church. From a root word that means – to "call" (properly, aloud, but used in a variety of applications, directly or otherwise); bid, call (forth).

Ecumenicalism may bring all denominations together. When Babylon is thus solidified, it will be clear to every believer the unscriptural basis of anything except the local church of the New Testament.

G. The Church is the Body of Jesus Christ

   1. Colossians 1:18 – *"And he is the head of the body, the church: who is the beginning, the firstborn from the dead; that in all things he might have the preeminence."*
   2. Colossians 1:24 – *"Who now rejoice in my sufferings for you, and fill up that which is behind of the afflictions of Christ in my flesh for his body's sake, which is the church:"*
   3. 1 Corinthians 12:12 – *"For as the body is one, and hath many members, and all the members of that one body, being many, are one body: so also is Christ."*
   4. Ephesians 1:21-23 – *"Far above all principality, and power, and might, and dominion, and every name that is named, not only in this world, but also in that which is to come: 22And hath put all things under his feet, and gave him to be the head over all things to the church, 23Which is his body, the fulness of him that filleth all in all."*

      a. From all the above references, we see that church membership in the New Testament church is a spiritual status and a spiritual relationship. Membership today has usually degenerated to a matter of human volition, like joining a club, rather than a matter of God "setting us in the Body" or "adding to the church."

      b. Also from the above scriptures, we see that the early churches recognized what God had done in the new believers in setting them into the Body of Christ. They recognized a "fellowship" and a "bond" which the Holy Spirit had already created.

      c. We see the new believers or members recognized and acknowledged that:

         1) Jesus Christ was their Savior and Lord
         2) That He had set them in a local church body and given them a function (or ministry) there
         3) That they were to be submissive to the authority of that local church
         4) That they were to love, to give, to witness, to fellowship, to maintain unity, and to function in the Body of Christ

H. Suggested procedure for receiving members into the fellowship of the local New Testament Church

   1. From time to time in the services, the question will be asked, "Who would like to be received into the fellowship as a member of the Body?" Then the applicants will be asked to meet with one or more of the elders, who will counsel with them and examine their spiritual status.

   2. Questions for the applicant

      a. Have you accepted Jesus Christ as your Savior and Lord?
      b. Do you believe that God has set you in this local church?
      c. Do you know what this church teaches?

d. Will you abide under the authority and discipline over this local church?
e. Will you commit your life, finances, time, talents, etc. to the place God has planted you?

At the time the new members are recognized in the Body, the spiritual status and spiritual relationship of the new member to the rest of the Body of Christ should be recognized. The new members should see their dedication and submission to Christ, to the rest of the members, and to the ministers and elders over them in the Lord. The members should see their responsibility and care for the new members.

The Good Shepherd knows His sheep (John 10:14) and calls them by name (v 3). If this is true, then any Pastor, or elder, must have a way of knowing everyone who is a member of his flock. How can a church function properly (oversight of the elders, the discipline and fellowship of believers, etc.) without an up-to-date list of the members? For example, church discipline can never work (I Corinthians 5) if there is no way of knowing if the offender is one of the church or not. The procedure is simple and clear – Acts 2:38-41. They believed, were baptized, and were added to the church.

God keeps a record of His own (Luke 10:20, Philippians 4:3, Revelation 20:15). We must not object to simple and scriptural records being kept of the members of the local church.

Lesson 12
Consecration

Consecration means total separation unto the Lord. Most of the time in the Scriptures, the Hebrew meaning is "to fill or being filled or full of God." Exodus 21:1-7

Exodus 21:1-7 – "*¹Now these are the judgments which thou shalt set before them. ²If thou buy an Hebrew servant, six years he shall serve: and in the seventh he shall go out free for nothing. ³If he came in by himself, he shall go out by himself: if he were married, then his wife shall go out with him. ⁴If his master have given him a wife, and she have born him sons or daughters; the wife and her children shall be her master's, and he shall go out by himself. ⁵And if the servant shall plainly say, I love my master, my wife, and my children; I will not go out free: ⁶Then his master shall bring him unto the judges; he shall also bring him to the door, or unto the door post; and his master shall bore his ear through with an aul; and he shall serve him for ever. ⁷And if a man sell his daughter to be a maidservant, she shall not go out as the menservants do.*"

I. Verse 5 – "*...I love my master...*" – Master Was First. Do We Really Put Our Master First?

    A. Matthew 6:33 – "*But seek ye first the kingdom of God...*"
    B. Psalms 73:25-27 – "*²⁵Whom have I in heaven but thee? and there is none upon earth that I desire beside thee. ²⁶My flesh and my heart faileth: but God is the strength of my heart, and my portion for ever. ²⁷For, lo, they that are far from thee shall perish: thou hast destroyed all them that go a whoring from thee.*"
    C. Philemon 14 – "*...that thy benefit should not be as it were of necessity, but willingly.*"
    D. Acts 17:28 – "*For in him we live, and move, and have our being...*"

The first aspect of consecration is putting Him first.

II. Verse 5 – "*...my wife, and my children...*"

    A. Sometimes there is a danger in the blessings of God.

        1. Matthew 10:34-39 – Jesus said this because He knew the potential danger of being too caught up with the blessings of God.
        2. Revelation 3:14-20
        3. Hosea 4:7 – "*As they were increased, so they sinned against me: therefore will I change their glory into shame.*"
        4. Deuteronomy 8:7-20

The second aspect of consecration is remembering where you came from and WHO got you out of there!

III. Verse 5 – "*...I will not go out free.*"

    A. The third aspect of consecration is refusing to go back into the world or into any of its temptations – separation unto the Lord, your life full of God!

        1. Philemon 1 – "*Paul, a prisoner of Jesus Christ, and Timothy our brother, unto Philemon our dearly beloved, and fellowlabourer,*"
        2. I John 2:15-18
        3. II Corinthians 6:14-18

    B. God separates us to cleanse us so that we can be consecrated.

1. Saint – means separated one
2. Church – Ecclessia – "called out ones"

C. We are not just separated FROM something, but we are separated UNTO Jesus.

    1. Exodus 28:40-41
    2. II Timothy 2:4 – *"No man that warreth entangleth himself with the affairs of this life; that he may please him who hath chosen him to be a soldier."*

IV. Verse 2 – *"...six years he shall serve..."* – In Those Six Years, He Made His Decision.

A. The fourth aspect of consecration is: Consecration involves timing.

    1. Luke 1:80 – *"And the child grew, and waxed strong in spirit, and was in the deserts till the day of his shewing unto Israel."*
    2. I Timothy 1:12 – *"And I thank Christ Jesus our Lord, who hath enabled me, for that he counted me faithful, putting me into the ministry;"*
    3. Exodus 19:8-11

V. Verse 2 – During Six Years, I'm Sure He Was Given Plenty of Reasons to Leave.

A. The fifth aspect of consecration is: The devil will be out to stop, hinder, and oppose you. One day there will be a group of people who serve God no matter what.

    1. Daniel 7:25 – Wear out.
    2. Ezra 4:1-5 – Frustrate their purpose.
    3. Job 1:1-2, 3:1

VI. Verse 6 – Can It Really Be Done?

A. Genesis 5:24 – Enoch walked with God.
B. Genesis 6:5-8 – Noah found grace.

These did it even in dark times. The sixth aspect of consecration is that not only can it be done, it is the will of God.

    1. I Thessalonians 4:3 – *"For this is the will of God, even your sanctification..."*

VII. Verse 6 – *"...his master shall bore his ear through with an aul; and he shall serve him for ever."*

A. The seventh aspect of consecration is: He will put his mark upon us, and we will be with him in an eternal relationship forever.

    1. Hosea 2:19 – *"And I will betroth thee unto me for ever; yea, I will betroth thee unto me in righteousness, and in judgment, and in lovingkindness, and in mercies."*

ESSENTIALS FOR MINISTRY

I.   Separated to the Lord

    A.   Hebrew words defined

        1.   P*arad* – to break through, to spread or separate oneself, to divide, disperse, part, scatter, part, or stretch.

        2.   *Nazar* – to hold aloof, to abstain from (food, drink, perversion), to set apart

        3.   Palah – to distinguish, put a difference, show marvellous, separate, set apart, sever, make wonderfully.

        4.   *Badad* – separate, separately, alone, desolate, only, solitary.

        5.   *Badal* – to divide (in variation senses literally or figuratively, separate, distinguish, differ, select, etc.); this Hebrew word is also translated elsewhere: difference, divide (asunder), (make) separate (self, -ation), sever (out).

        6.   *Naziyr* - separate, consecrated (as prince, a Nazarite); hence an unpruned vine (like an unshorn Nazirite):

    B.   Greek words defined, *Aphorizo* – to set off by boundary, to limit, to exclude, to appoint, divide, or sever

II.   The Call to Separation

    A.   Scriptural Examples

        1.   II Corinthians 6:17 – *"Wherefore come out from among them, and be ye separate, saith the Lord, and touch not the unclean thing; and I will receive you,"*

        2.   Acts 19:9 – *"But when divers were hardened, and believed not, but spake evil of that way before the multitude, he departed from them, and separated the disciples, disputing daily in the school of one Tyrannus."*

        3.   Proverbs 18:1 – *"Through desire a man, having separated himself, seeketh and intermeddleth with all wisdom."*

    B.   His Presence Separates Us

        1.   Exodus 33:16 – *"For wherein shall it be known here that I and thy people have found grace in thy sight? is it not in that thou goest with us? so shall we be separated, I and thy people, from all the people that are upon the face of the earth."*

        2.   Jeremiah 15:17 – *"I sat not in the assembly of the mockers, nor rejoiced; I sat alone because of thy hand: for thou hast filled me with indignation."*

        3.   Genesis 49:26 – *"The blessings of thy father have prevailed above the blessings of my progenitors unto the utmost bound of the everlasting hills: they shall be on the head of Joseph, and on the crown of the head of him that was separate from his brethren."*

        4.   Deuteronomy 10:8-9 – *"At that time the LORD separated the tribe of Levi, to bear the ark of the covenant of the LORD, to stand before the LORD to minister unto him, and to bless in his name, unto this day. [9]Wherefore Levi hath no part nor inheritance with his brethren; the LORD is his inheritance, according as the LORD thy God promised him."*

    C.   To Ministry

        1.   Acts 13:2 – *"As they ministered to the Lord, and fasted, the Holy Ghost said, Separate me Barnabas and Saul for the work whereunto I have called them."*

2. Romans 1:1 – "*Paul, a servant of Jesus Christ, called to be an apostle, separated unto the gospel of God,*"

3. Leviticus 22:1-3 – "*And the LORD spake unto Moses, saying, ²Speak unto Aaron and to his sons, that they separate themselves from the holy things of the children of Israel, and that they profane not my holy name in those things which they hallow unto me: I am the LORD. ³Say unto them, Whosoever he be of all your seed among your generations, that goeth unto the holy things, which the children of Israel hallow unto the LORD, having his uncleanness upon him, that soul shall be cut off from my presence: I am the LORD.*"

4. Numbers 6:1-8

5. Numbers 8:1-14

III. Don't Complain Once You're Separated

A. Scriptural Examples

1. Isaiah 56:3-8

2. Luke 6:22-23 – "*Blessed are ye, when men shall hate you, and when they shall separate you from their company, and shall reproach you, and cast out your name as evil, for the Son of man's sake. ²³Rejoice ye in that day, and leap for joy: for, behold, your reward is great in heaven: for in the like manner did their fathers unto the prophets.*"

IV. The Need to be Discipled

A. Scriptural References Concerning Discipleship

1. 1 Chronicles 25:2-3, 6 – "*Of the sons of Asaph; Zaccur, and Joseph, and Nethaniah, and Asarelah, the sons of Asaph <u>under the hands</u> of Asaph, which prophesied according to the order of the king. ³Of Jeduthun: the sons of Jeduthun; Gedaliah, and Zeri, and Jeshaiah, Hashabiah, and Mattithiah, six, under the hands of their father Jeduthun, who prophesied with a harp, to give thanks and to praise the LORD. ⁶All these were under the hands of their father for song in the house of the LORD, with cymbals, psalteries, and harps, for the service of the house of God, according to the king's order to Asaph, Jeduthun, and Heman.*" Other Translations of "under the hands" – "*under the direction of*"

2. Luke 16:12 – "*And if ye have not been faithful in that which is another man's, who shall give you that which is your own?*" – There is a season in our lives when we are called to be faithful to and in another man's ministry before God gives us our own.

3. Matthew 28:19 – "*Go ye therefore, and <u>teach</u> all nations, baptizing them in the name of the Father, and of the Son, and of the Holy Ghost:*" – Greek for teach – disciple, to become a pupil, or to enroll as a scholar

4. Acts 19:9-10 – "*But when divers were hardened, and believed not, but spake evil of that way before the multitude, he departed from them, and separated the disciples, disputing daily in the school of one Tyrannus. ¹⁰And this continued by the space of two years; so that all they which dwelt in Asia heard the word of the Lord Jesus, both Jews and Greeks.*" – The disciples separated and taught for two years daily.

5. Mark 6:35-44 - There is a need for disciples to minister to ranks and companies.

6. I Corinthians 4:14-21 – Paul was their father. He encouraged them to be "imitators" (Greek – followers) of him (II Thessalonians 3:6-13)

7. II Timothy 2:1-3, 7 – This is the premier example of discipleship.

8. Acts 18:24-28 – Apollos receives discipleship

9. Ephesians 4:11-13

10. 2 Corinthians 15:3-8

11. Ecclesiastes 12:11

12. Philippians 2:19-24

13. I Thessalonians 2:1-12
14. I Thessalonians 5:12-14
15. Isaiah 28:9-13

V.   Discovering Truths as we Look at Several Discipleship Teams

A.   Examples of Relationships

1.   Moses and Joshua

a.   Joshua 1:1 – *"Now after the death of Moses the servant of the LORD it came to pass, that the LORD spake unto Joshua the son of Nun, <u>Moses' minister</u>," ⁵There shall not any man be able to stand before thee all the days of thy life: as I was with Moses, so I will be with thee: I will not fail thee, nor forsake thee. ⁶Be strong and of a good courage: for unto this people shalt thou divide for an inheritance the land, which I sware unto their fathers to give them. ⁷Only be thou strong and very courageous, that thou mayest observe to do according to all the law, which Moses my servant commanded thee: turn not from it to the right hand or to the left, that thou mayest prosper whithersoever thou goest."*

b.   Joshua was known as "Moses' minister, Moses' servant.

c.   A look back at Joshua's call

1)   Numbers 27:18-23 – *"And the LORD said unto Moses, Take thee Joshua the son of Nun, a man in whom is the spirit, and lay thine hand upon him; ¹⁹And set him before Eleazar the priest, and before all the congregation; and give him a charge in their sight. ²⁰And thou shalt put some of thine honour upon him, that all the congregation of the children of Israel may be obedient. ²¹And he shall stand before Eleazar the priest, who shall ask counsel for him after the judgment of Urim before the LORD: at his word shall they go out, and at his word they shall come in, both he, and all the children of Israel with him, even all the congregation. ²²And Moses did as the LORD commanded him: and he took Joshua, and set him before Eleazar the priest, and before all the congregation: ²³And he laid his hands upon him, and gave him a charge, as the LORD commanded by the hand of Moses."*

2)   Deuteronomy 3:28 – *"But charge Joshua, and encourage him, and strengthen him: for he shall go over before this people, and he shall cause them to inherit the land which thou shalt see."*

3)   Deuteronomy 31:3-8

2.   Elijah and Elisha

a.   II Kings 2:9-18

b.   A look back at his calling

1)   II Kings 3:11 – He was known as the man who poured water on the hands of Elijah

2)   I Kings 19:16, 19-21 –

3)   II Kings 2:1-10 – *"And it came to pass, when they were gone over, that Elijah said unto Elisha, Ask what I shall do for thee, before I be taken away from thee. And Elisha said, I pray thee, let a double portion of thy spirit be upon me. ¹⁰And he said, Thou hast asked a hard thing: nevertheless, <u>if thou see me</u> when I am taken from thee, it shall be so unto thee; but if not, it shall not be so."*

4)   See in Hebrew – to observe, perceive, get acquainted with, gain understanding, to examine.

5)   Can you see the man of God, who he really is, how God uses him, how is he motivated, what is his burden, do you have his heart?

6) Now that he will be taken from you, will you still see him?
7) God separated them by fire
8) Elisha recognized Elijah as the "vehicle of Israel" and the one who had the authority, "the chariot of Israel and the horseman thereof".
9) Elisha takes up the mantle
10) He had to immediately deal with rebellion
11) God didn't want Elijah's body found because Israel would have worshipped it. They weren't ready to let Elijah go.
12) Elisha had to deal with the 42 children out of Bethel.

(1) Children – a principle, a stage of growth
(2) Bethel – house of God

13) 42 is the number of the antichrist. This speaks of an antichrist spirit in these children who come out of God's house.
14) They mocked and cursed him

3. Paul – Timothy, Titus, Silvus, Barnabas, John Mark, Priscilla and Aquilla
4. Mark 3:13-15 – Jesus and the Twelve
5. Numbers 11:16-17, 24-25 – Moses and the Seventy Elders

VI. The Making of a Disciple – What God Wants for All His People

A. To Grow in Him

1. I Peter 3:18 – "*For Christ also hath once suffered for sins, the just for the unjust, that he might bring us to God, being put to death in the flesh, but quickened by the Spirit:*"

   a. 1 Peter 2:2 – "*As newborn babes, desire the sincere milk of the word, that ye may grow thereby:*"

2. Ephesians 4:12-15 – "*For the perfecting of the saints, for the work of the ministry, for the edifying of the body of Christ: [13]Till we all come in the unity of the faith, and of the knowledge of the Son of God, unto a perfect man, unto the measure of the stature of the fulness of Christ: [14]That we henceforth be no more children, tossed to and fro, and carried about with every wind of doctrine, by the sleight of men, and cunning craftiness, whereby they lie in wait to deceive; [15]But speaking the truth in love, may grow up into him in all things, which is the head, even Christ:*"

3. Isaiah 37:31 – "*And the remnant that is escaped of the house of Judah shall again take root downward, and bear fruit upward:*"

4. Isaiah 54:13 – "*And all thy children shall be taught of the LORD; and great shall be the peace of thy children.*"

5. Hebrews 5:11-14 – "*Of whom we have many things to say, and hard to be uttered, seeing ye are dull of hearing. [12]For when for the time ye ought to be teachers, ye have need that one teach you again which be the first principles of the oracles of God; and are become such as have need of milk, and not of strong meat. [13]For every one that useth milk is unskilful in the word of righteousness: for he is a babe. [14]But strong meat belongeth to them that are of full age, even those who by reason of use have their senses exercised to discern both good and evil.*"

6. II Chronicles 15:3 – "*Now for a long season Israel hath been without the true God, and without a teaching priest, and without law.*"

7. II Timothy 3:14-17 – "*But continue thou in the things which thou hast learned and hast been assured of, knowing of whom thou hast learned them; [15]And that from a child thou hast known the holy scriptures, which are able to make thee wise unto salvation through faith which is in*

Christ Jesus. [16]*All scripture is given by inspiration of God, and is profitable for doctrine, for reproof, for correction, for instruction in righteousness:* [17]*That the man of God may be perfect, throughly furnished unto all good works."*

VII. He is Looking for Disciples

A. Matthew 28:19 – *"Go ye therefore, and teach all nations, baptizing them in the name of the Father, and of the Son, and of the Holy Ghost:"*

1. Other Translations: *"...make all peoples your disciples"*
"...make disciples of all nations"

The word "teach" here is the same word translated disciple throughout the New Testament. I think we have confused this passage with the idea it is talking of making converts or believers of all the nations, but that is not what this verse means. Yes it is true God wants converts, believers, etc., but if we read this passage carefully and rightly divide it we see it really means we are to make disciples of all nations. This then should change our entire idea of evangelism. Yes, let's get as many people saved as possible, but also God doesn't want a bunch of babies; He wants full grown sons (I John 3:1-3) fashioned to His image.(Romans 8:29, Ephesians 2:13-15, 18-22, Ephesians 3:16-20, Ephesians 4:12-16, Ephesians 5:25-28)

VIII. How Discipleship Works

A. God gives every believer a Father, a discipler. This is an eternal and spiritual thing. He gives us Pastors with His heart.

1. He Gives Us Pastors

a. Ephesians 4:11-15
b. Jeremiah 3:15 – *"And I will give you pastors according to mine heart, which shall feed you with knowledge and understanding."*
c. 1 Samuel 2:35 – *"And I will raise me up a faithful priest, that shall do according to that which is in mine heart and in my mind: and I will build him a sure house; and he shall walk before mine anointed for ever."*
d. Acts 20:20-21 – *"And how I kept back nothing that was profitable unto you, but have shewed you, and have taught you publickly, and from house to house,* [21]*Testifying both to the Jews, and also to the Greeks, repentance toward God, and faith toward our Lord Jesus Christ."*
e. Ezekiel 34:23-31
f. Numbers 27:15-23
g. Mark 6:34-45
h. John 10:2-5
i. I Corinthians 4:15 – *"For though ye have ten thousand instructors in Christ, yet have ye not many fathers: for in Christ Jesus I have begotten you through the gospel."*
j. Galatians 4:1-2 – *"Now I say, That the heir, as long as he is a child, differeth nothing from a servant, though he be lord of all;* [2]*But is under tutors and governors until the time appointed of the father."*
k. Malachi 4:6 – *"And he shall turn the heart of the fathers to the children, and the heart of the children to their fathers, lest I come and smite the earth with a curse. THE END OF THE PROPHETS."*

1) Luke 1:17 – *"And he shall go before him in the spirit and power of Elias, to turn the hearts of the fathers to the children, and the disobedient to the wisdom of the just; to make ready a people prepared for the Lord."*

l. Philippians 2:19-30
m. Revelation 10:1-3, 7-11
n. I Peter 5:1-6
o. Hebrews 13:17
p. Titus 1:3-11
q. Numbers 11:9-17
r. II Corinthians 10:8, 12-15

B. Examples in the Scriptures

1. I Samuel 3:1 – Samuel and Eli – *"And the child Samuel ministered unto the LORD before Eli. And the word of the LORD was precious in those days; there was no open vision."*

2. Joshua 1:1 – Moses and Joshua – *"Now after the death of Moses the servant of the LORD it came to pass, that the LORD spake unto Joshua the son of Nun, Moses' minister, saying,"*

a. Exodus 24:13 – *"And Moses rose up, and his minister Joshua: and Moses went up into the mount of God."* – The Hebrew word for minister here means to attend to (as in doing menial tasks), to serve, to contribute, a servant.

3. Philippians 2:19-24 – Paul and Timothy (I Corinthians 4:17)
4. Mark 3:13-15 – Jesus and the Twelve – *"And he goeth up into a mountain, and calleth unto him whom he would: and they came unto him. ¹⁴And he ordained twelve, that they should be with him, and that he might send them forth to preach, ¹⁵And to have power to heal sicknesses, and to cast out devils:"*

IX. Incorrect Discipleship

A. What Saith the Scriptures?

1. How those in authority should disciple

a. II Samuel 23:3 – *"The God of Israel said, the Rock of Israel spake to me, He that ruleth over men must be just, ruling in the fear of God."*
b. I Peter 5:1-6

1) Feed
2) Do it willingly
3) Not for money
4) Never trying to lord it over someone
5) Being an example
6) Future rewards

c. II Corinthians 10:8 – *"For though I should boast somewhat more of our authority, which the Lord hath given us for edification, and not for your destruction, I should not be ashamed:"*

1) Always to edify
2) Never to use your authority for destruction

3) Greek for Destruction – to lower in violence, to destroy, to demolish.

    d.   II Corinthians 13:10 – *"Therefore I write these things being absent, lest being present I should use sharpness, according to the power which the Lord hath given me to edification, and not to destruction."*

    e.   Titus 1:5-9 – *"For this cause left I thee in Crete, that thou shouldest set in order the things that are wanting, and ordain elders in every city, as I had appointed thee: ⁶If any be blameless, the husband of one wife, having faithful children not accused of riot or unruly. ⁷For a bishop must be blameless, as the steward of God; not selfwilled, not soon angry, not given to wine, no striker, not given to filthy lucre; ⁸But a lover of hospitality, a lover of good men, sober, just, holy, temperate; ⁹Holding fast the faithful word as he hath been taught, that he may be able by sound doctrine both to exhort and to convince the gainsayers."*

    f.   Titus 2:1-9, 15

    g.   II Timothy 2:1-2 - *Thou therefore, my son, be strong in the grace that is in Christ Jesus. ²And the things that thou hast heard of me among many witnesses, the same commit thou to faithful men, who shall be able to teach others also."*

    h.   II Timothy 4:1-5 – *"I charge thee therefore before God, and the Lord Jesus Christ, instant in season, out of season; reprove, rebuke, exhort with all longsuffering and doctrine. ³For the time will come when they will not endure sound doctrine; but after their own lusts shall they heap to themselves teachers, having itching ears; ⁴And they shall turn away their ears from the truth, and shall be turned unto fables. ⁵But watch thou in all things, endure afflictions, do the work of an evangelist, make full proof of thy ministry."*

    i.   I Timothy 3:1-13

    j.   II Thessalonians 3:6-13

    k.   I Thessalonians 2:3-12

    l.   Proverbs 29:21 – *"He that delicately bringeth up his servant from a child shall have him become his son at the length."*

B.   What the Scriptures say about what not to do

1.   Jeremiah 5:31 – *"The prophets prophesy falsely, and the priests bear rule by their means; and my people love to have it so: and what will ye do in the end thereof?"*

2.   Ezekiel 34:1-10

3.   Ecclesiastes 8:9 – *"All this have I seen, and applied my heart unto every work that is done under the sun: there is a time wherein one man ruleth over another to his own hurt."*

Lesson 14
FACE TO FACE COMMUNION

I. Psalms 42:2 – *"My soul thirsteth for God, for the living God: when shall I come and appear before God?"*
John 12:21 – *"The same came therefore to Philip, which was of Bethsaida of Galilee, and desired him, saying, Sir, we would see Jesus."*

A. Man originally had face to face communion and lost it

1. Genesis 3:8 – *"And they heard the voice of the LORD God walking in the garden in the cool of the day: and Adam and his wife hid themselves from the presence of the LORD God amongst the trees of the garden."* Man lost face to face communion with God due to sin. It is important to note that the Hebrew word translated "presence" is also translated "face" elsewhere over 300 times.

2. Exodus 3:6 – *"Moreover he said, I am the God of thy father, the God of Abraham, the God of Isaac, and the God of Jacob. And Moses hid his face; for he was afraid to look upon God."* Moses was too afraid to look upon God, but later knew God face to face.

    a. Deuteronomy 34:10 – *"And there arose not a prophet since in Israel like unto Moses, whom the LORD knew face to face,"*
    b. Exodus 33:11 – *"And the LORD spake unto Moses face to face, as a man speaketh unto his friend. And he turned again into the camp: but his servant Joshua, the son of Nun, a young man, departed not out of the tabernacle."*

3. Exodus 20:18-21 – *"18And all the people saw the thunderings, and the lightnings, and the noise of the trumpet, and the mountain smoking: and when the people saw it, they removed, and stood afar off. 19And they said unto Moses, Speak thou with us, and we will hear: but let not God speak with us, lest we die. 20And Moses said unto the people, Fear not: for God is come to prove you, and that his fear may be before your faces, that ye sin not. 21And the people stood afar off, and Moses drew near unto the thick darkness where God was."* – Most don't want Him once they really see Him.

4. Exodus 33:20, 23 – *"20And he said, <u>Thou canst not see my face</u>: for there shall no man see me, and live...23And I will take away mine hand, and thou shalt see my back parts: but my face shall not be seen."*

B. A future promise of seeing His face

1. Revelation 22:3-4 – *"And there shall be no more curse: but the throne of God and of the Lamb shall be in it; and his servants shall serve him: And <u>they shall see his face</u>; and his name shall be in their foreheads."*
2. I Corinthians 13:12 – *"For now we see through a glass, darkly; <u>but then face to face</u>: now I know in part; but then shall I know even as also I am known."*
3. Revelation 1:7 – *"Behold, he cometh with clouds; and <u>every eye shall see him</u>, and they also which pierced him: and all kindreds of the earth shall wail because of him. Even so, Amen."*
4. Job 19:25-27 – *"25For I know that my redeemer liveth, and that he shall stand at the latter day upon the earth: 26And though after my skin worms destroy this body, yet in my flesh shall I see God: 27Whom I shall see for myself, and mine eyes shall behold, and not another; though my reins be consumed within me."*
5. I John 3:2 – *"Beloved, now are we the sons of God, and it doth not yet appear what we shall be: but we know that, when he shall appear, we shall be like him; for <u>we shall see him as he is</u>."*
6. Jeremiah 50:4-5 – *"In those days, and in that time, saith the LORD, the children of Israel shall come, they and the children of Judah together, going and weeping: they shall go, and seek the*

THE DOCTRINE OF FIRST THINGS

LORD their God. They shall ask the way to Zion with their faces thitherward, saying, Come, and let us join ourselves to the LORD in a perpetual covenant that shall not be forgotten." – Israel on the way to Zion with their faces toward the Lord.

C. Between what we've lost and what we will have is a lifetime of God's dealings. Below are Scriptures showing what we must become and what we must go through.

1. Matthew 5:8 – *"Blessed are the <u>pure in heart</u>: for they shall see God."*
2. Isaiah 66:2 – *"For all those things hath mine hand made, and those things have been, saith the LORD: but to this man will I look, even to him that is <u>poor and of a contrite spirit</u>, and trembleth at my word."*
3. Hebrews 12:14 – *"Follow peace with all men, <u>and holiness</u>, without which no man shall see the Lord:"*
4. Isaiah 6:1 – *"<u>In the year that king Uzziah died</u> I saw also the Lord sitting upon a throne, high and lifted up, and his train filled the temple."* – Let others go who hinder us
5. John 14:23 – *"Jesus answered and said unto him, <u>If a man love me</u>, he will <u>keep my words</u>: and my Father will love him, and we will come unto him, and make our abode with him."* – other translation, *"...If anyone really loves me, he will observe my teaching and my Father will love Him and both of us will come in face to face fellowship with him."*
6. Psalms 17:15 – *"As for me, I will behold thy face <u>in righteousness</u>: I shall be satisfied, when I awake, with thy likeness."*
7. Revelation 3:18 – *"I counsel thee to buy of me gold tried in the fire, that thou mayest be rich; and white raiment, that thou mayest be clothed, and that the shame of thy nakedness do not appear; and <u>anoint thine eyes with eyesalve</u>, that thou mayest see."*

D. In the meantime, what happens to us when we see Him.

1. II Corinthians 3:18 – *"But we all, with open face beholding as in a glass the glory of the Lord, <u>are changed</u> into the same image from glory to glory, even as by the Spirit of the Lord."*
2. Revelation 1:17 – *"And when I saw him, I fell at his feet as dead. And he laid his right hand upon me, saying unto me, Fear not; I am the first and the last:"* – death to the carnal man
3. Acts 9:3-9 – blindness to our past life and to our own selfish motives.
4. Genesis 32:24-30 – a revelation of who we are
5. Isaiah 6:1, 5 – a revelation of what we aren't

E. Our response

1. Psalms 27:8 – *"When thou saidst, Seek ye my face; my heart said unto thee, Thy face, LORD, will I seek."*
2. Lamentations 5:21 – *"Turn thou us unto thee, O LORD, and we shall be turned; renew our days as of old"*
3. I John 3:2-3 – *"2Beloved, now are we the sons of God, and it doth not yet appear what we shall be: but we know that, when he shall appear, we shall be like him; for we shall see him as he is. 3And every man that hath this hope in him purifieth himself, even as he is pure."*

F. Our prayer of blessing for one another

1. Numbers 6:24-26 – *"24The LORD bless thee, and keep thee: 25The LORD make his face shine upon thee, and be gracious unto thee: 26The LORD lift up his countenance upon thee, and give thee peace."*

Lesson 15
FAITHFULNESS

I.   Revelation 2:10 – *"Fear none of those things which thou shalt suffer: behold, the devil shall cast some of you into prison, that ye may be tried; and ye shall have tribulation ten days: be thou faithful unto death, and I will give thee a crown of life."*

      A.   Proverbs 20:6 – *"Most men will proclaim every one his own goodness: but a faithful man who can find?"* – Other translations:

"Many a person is called kind, but a trustworthy man is a rare find."
"Many a man protests his loyalty, but where will you find one to keep faith."
"A multitude of men proclaim each his kindness, and a man of steadfastness who doth find."
"Many a man claims to have unfailing love..."
"Many will say they are loyal friends, but who can find one who is truly reliable."
"Lots of people announce that they show kindness, but who can find someone faithful to do it."
"Most people will tell you what loyal friends they are, but are they telling the truth."
"Everyone talks about how loyal and faithful he is, but just try to find someone who really is"

Our precious Saviour never asks us to do something He hasn't already done. God is faithful! What this means is that He is absolutely trustworthy. He is also extremely loyal and reliable. He is the God that never fails, never leaves us or forsakes us. His Word is true. Because of this revelation we can always depend on Him to do whatever He has said. Because He also cannot lie we can rest assured if He has said something it will come to pass. His faithfulness to us means He gives perfect loyalty and consistency in being true to His name, His character, and His Word! This faithfulness is one of God's greatest moral attributes.

So when the Scriptures admonish us to be "faithful unto death," it means He desires the same kind of faithfulness out of His true, devoted, loving disciples. Should we obey this Godly request, He promises to give us a "crown of life." This "crown of life" is won by dying to self, ambition, desires, the things of this world, the lust of the flesh, the pride of life, and the deceitfulness of riches. This crown is won by being faithful to Him, His Word, His will, His purpose, His kingdom, and His people.

      1.   John 12:20-33 – *"20And there were certain Greeks among them that came up to worship at the feast: 21The same came therefore to Philip, which was of Bethsaida of Galilee, and desired him, saying, Sir, <u>we would see Jesus</u>. 22Philip cometh and telleth Andrew: and again Andrew and Philip tell Jesus. 23And <u>Jesus answered them</u>, saying, The hour is come, that the Son of man should be glorified. 24Verily, verily, I say unto you, <u>Except a corn of wheat fall into the ground and die</u>, it abideth alone: <u>but if it die</u>, it <u>bringeth forth much fruit</u>. 25He that loveth his life shall lose it; and he that <u>hateth his life</u> in this world shall keep it unto life eternal. 26If any man serve me, let him follow me; and where I am, there shall also my servant be: if any man serve me, him will my Father honour. 27Now is my soul troubled; and what shall I say? Father, save me from this hour: but for this cause came I unto this hour. 28Father, glorify thy name. Then came there a voice from heaven, saying, I have both glorified it, and will glorify it again. 29The people therefore, that stood by, and heard it, said that it thundered: others said, An angel spake to him. 30Jesus answered and said, This voice came not because of me, but for your sakes. 31Now is the judgment of this world: now shall the prince of this world be cast out. 32And I, if I be lifted up from the earth, will draw all men unto me. 33This he said, signifying what death he should die."*

In this story, certain Greeks wanted to see the real Jesus. Jesus answers them by talking about death. The revelation for us is, if we as Christians want to show the world the real Jesus through our lives, the only way to do that is if we die to ourselves so the life of God can live through us. Paul says in Galatians 2:20, *"I am crucified with Christ: nevertheless I live; yet not I, but Christ liveth in me..."* <u>Except</u> you and I die to everything in our lives (self, ambition, lusts and desires, things of this world, pride, etc.), the world will never see the real Jesus. When we die, we will bear much fruit!

II. Word Definitions For Faithful, Faithfully, Faithfulness

    A. Hebrew

        1. *Emunah* – Firmness, security, moral fidelity, stability, steady, true, established, trustworthiness

        2. *Aman* – To build up or support, to foster as a parent or nurse, to be firm, to be permanent, to be true or certain, assurance, to go to the right hand (blessing), to be faithful of long continuance, steadfast or sure, nursing father, trust verified

    B. Greek word, *Pistos* – Trustworthy, sure, true; it comes from a root, *peitho* – to convince, to conciliate, to rely because of inward certainty

    C. Dictionary Definitions

        1. Steadfast in keeping promises or in fulfilling duties; steady, firm, dependable, allegiance or devotion, loyal, unswerving adherence to an oath, to a promise, or to a person; a firm resistance to any temptation to desert or betray; constant, steadfast, a loyal follower.

        2. Bible dictionary definition – commitment to a relationship with God or human beings; devotion and service seen in your life; a steadfast commitment, unwavering loyalty.

III. Faithful Unto Death

    A. Scriptures exhorting us to die (to our soulish man)

        1. Psalms 116:12-19 – "*12What shall I render unto the LORD for all his benefits toward me? 13I will take the cup of salvation, and call upon the name of the LORD. 14I will pay my vows unto the LORD now in the presence of all his people. 15<u>Precious in the sight of the LORD is the death of his saints</u>. 16O LORD, truly I am thy servant; I am thy servant, and the son of thine handmaid: thou hast loosed my bonds. 17I will offer to thee the sacrifice of thanksgiving, and will call upon the name of the LORD. 18I will pay my vows unto the LORD now in the presence of all his people, 19In the courts of the LORD's house, in the midst of thee, O Jerusalem. Praise ye the LORD.*" – We gain the crown for faithfulness by receiving all of God's salvation, continuing to call upon His name (character), being His servant, and honoring every vow we make to Him in the presence of God's people. We also prove our faithfulness by worshipping when it's a sacrifice. All of these actions ultimately culminates in our death, be it in our souls or bodies. This is precious to Him.

        2. I Corinthians 15:31 – "*I protest by your rejoicing which I have in Christ Jesus our Lord, <u>I die daily</u>.*" – We see then this dying to ourselves is a life long experience. It would be easy to die once as a martyr; but much harder to die as we continue to live.

        3. Job 14:14 – "*If a man die, shall he live again? all the days of my appointed time will I wait, till my change come.*" – We shall live again, but as Ecclesiastes says "to everything there is a season" (Ecclesiastes 3:1). There is an appointed time given by God for us to walk in this death until it changes us.

        4. Romans 6:6-14 – "*6Knowing this, that our old man is crucified with him, that the body of sin might be destroyed, that henceforth we should not serve sin. 7<u>For he that is dead is freed from sin</u>. 8Now if we be dead with Christ, we believe that we shall also live with him: 9Knowing that Christ being raised from the dead dieth no more; death hath no more dominion over him. 10For in that he died, he died unto sin once: but in that he liveth, he liveth unto God. 11Likewise <u>reckon ye also yourselves to be dead indeed unto sin</u>, but alive unto God through Jesus Christ our Lord.*

¹²Let not sin therefore reign in your mortal body, that ye should obey it in the lusts thereof. ¹³Neither yield ye your members as instruments of unrighteousness unto sin: but yield yourselves unto God, as those that are alive from the dead, and your members as instruments of righteousness unto God. ¹⁴For sin shall not have dominion over you: for ye are not under the law, but under grace." – You cannot tempt, harm, or charm, or hurt a dead man. We need to be dead to the world.

5. II Corinthians 4:7-12 – "*⁷But we have this treasure in earthen vessels, that the excellency of the power may be of God, and not of us. ⁸We are troubled on every side, yet not distressed; we are perplexed, but not in despair; ⁹Persecuted, but not forsaken; cast down, but not destroyed; ¹⁰Always bearing about in the body the dying of the Lord Jesus, that the life also of Jesus might be made manifest in our body. ¹¹For we which live are alway delivered unto death for Jesus' sake, that the life also of Jesus might be made manifest in our mortal flesh. ¹²So then death worketh in us, but life in you.*" – We are never really dying to just ourselves. What is happening is we bless others through our deaths.

6. II Corinthians 6:4-10 – "*⁴But in all things approving ourselves as the ministers of God, in much patience, in afflictions, in necessities, in distresses, ⁵In stripes, in imprisonments, in tumults, in labours, in watchings, in fastings; ⁶By pureness, by knowledge, by longsuffering, by kindness, by the Holy Ghost, by love unfeigned, ⁷By the word of truth, by the power of God, by the armour of righteousness on the right hand and on the left, ⁸By honour and dishonour, by evil report and good report: as deceivers, and yet true; ⁹As unknown, and yet well known; as dying, and, behold, we live; as chastened, and not killed; ¹⁰As sorrowful, yet alway rejoicing; as poor, yet making many rich; as having nothing, and yet possessing all things.*" – One of the main traits of a minister is the ability to die to himself so that others might live.

a. Hebrews 11:21 – "*By faith Jacob, when he was a dying, blessed both the sons of Joseph; and worshipped, leaning upon the top of his staff.*"

b. John 12:24 – "*Verily, verily, I say unto you, Except a corn of wheat fall into the ground and die, it abideth alone: but if it die, it bringeth forth much fruit.*

c. II Timothy 2:10-12 – "*¹⁰Therefore I endure all things for the elect's sakes, that they may also obtain the salvation which is in Christ Jesus with eternal glory. ¹¹It is a faithful saying: For if we be dead with him, we shall also live with him: ¹²If we suffer, we shall also reign with him: if we deny him, he also will deny us:*"

7. Job 14:7-9 – "*⁷For there is hope of a tree, if it be cut down, that it will sprout again, and that the tender branch thereof will not cease. ⁸Though the root thereof wax old in the earth, and the stock thereof die in the ground; ⁹Yet through the scent of water it will bud, and bring forth boughs like a plant.*"

8. Revelation 14:12-13 – "*¹²Here is the patience of the saints: here are they that keep the commandments of od, and the faith of Jesus. ¹³And I heard a voice from heaven saying unto me, Write, Blessed are the dead which die in the Lord from henceforth: Yea, saith the Spirit, that they may rest from their labours; and their works do follow them*

9. John 11:44 – "*And he that was dead came forth, bound hand and foot with graveclothes: and his face was bound about with a napkin. Jesus saith unto them, Loose him, and let him go.*" – Lazarus, by dying, was loosed from his bondages.

a. Psalms 23:4 – "*Yea, though I walk through the valley of the shadow of death, I will fear no evil: for thou art with me; thy rod and thy staff they comfort me. Thou preparest a table before me in the presence of mine enemies: thou anointest my head with oil; my cup runneth over. Surely goodness and mercy shall follow me all the days of my life: and I will dwell in the house of the LORD for ever.*"

10. Philippians 3:10-15 – "*[10]That I may know him, and the power of his resurrection, and the fellowship of his sufferings, being made conformable unto his death; [11]If by any means I might attain unto the resurrection of the dead. [12]Not as though I had already attained, either were already perfect: but I follow after, if that I may apprehend that for which also I am apprehended of Christ Jesus. [13]Brethren, I count not myself to have apprehended: but this one thing I do, forgetting those things which are behind, and reaching forth unto those things which are before, [14]I press toward the mark for the prize of the high calling of God in Christ Jesus. [15]Let us therefore, as many as be perfect, be thus minded: and if in any thing ye be otherwise minded, God shall reveal even this unto you.*" – By dying we obtain the prize

    a. Colossians 3:1-4 – "*[1]If ye then be risen with Christ, seek those things which are above, where Christ sitteth on the right hand of God. [2]Set your affection on things above, not on things on the earth. [3]For ye are dead, and your life is hid with Christ in God. [4]When Christ, who is our life, shall appear, then shall ye also appear with him in glory.*"

11. Ezekiel 37:1-14 – the army of dead bones
12. Revelation 12:4 – "*And they overcame him by the blood of the Lamb, and by the word of their testimony; and they loved not their lives unto the death*"

IV. God Is Looking For Faithfulness

A. There seems to be a lack of true faithfulness

    1. Proverbs 20:6 – "*Most men will proclaim every one his own goodness: but a faithful man who can find?*"
    2. Isaiah 1:21-24 – "*[21]How is the faithful city become an harlot! it was full of judgment; righteousness lodged in it; but now murderers. [22]Thy silver is become dross, thy wine mixed with water: [23]Thy princes are rebellious, and companions of thieves: every one loveth gifts, and followeth after rewards: they judge not the fatherless, neither doth the cause of the widow come unto them. [24]Therefore saith the Lord, the LORD of hosts, the mighty One of Israel, Ah, I will ease me of mine adversaries, and avenge me of mine enemies:*"
    3. Psalms 12:1 – "*Help, LORD; for the godly man ceaseth; for the faithful fail from among the children of men.*"
    4. Psalms 5:8-10 – "*[8]Lead me, O LORD, in thy righteousness because of mine enemies; make thy way straight before my face. [9]For there is no faithfulness in their mouth; their inward part is very wickedness; their throat is an open sepulchre; they flatter with their tongue. [10]Destroy thou them, O God; let them fall by their own counsels; cast them out in the multitude of their transgressions; for they have rebelled against thee.*"

B. God is looking for faithfulness

    1. I Corinthians 4:2 – "*Moreover it is required in stewards, that a man be found faithful.*"
    2. Psalms 101:6 – "*Mine eyes shall be upon the faithful of the land, that they may dwell with me: he that walketh in a perfect way, he shall serve me.*"
    3. Revelation 17:14 – "*These shall make war with the Lamb, and the Lamb shall overcome them: for he is Lord of lords, and King of kings: and they that are with him are called, and chosen, and faithful.*"
    4. Hosea 2:14-20 – "*...[19]And I will betroth thee unto me for ever; yea, I will betroth thee unto me in righteousness, and in judgment, and in lovingkindness, and in mercies. [20]I will even betroth thee unto me in faithfulness: and thou shalt know the LORD.*"
    5. Luke 12:42-48 – "*[42]And the Lord said, Who then is that faithful and wise steward, whom his lord shall make ruler over his household, to give them their portion of meat in due season?*

43Blessed is that servant, whom his lord when he cometh shall find so doing. 44Of a truth I say unto you, that he will make him ruler over all that he hath..."

6. II Timothy 2:2 – *"And the things that thou hast heard of me among many witnesses, the same commit thou to faithful men, who shall be able to teach others also."* – Faithfulness in discipleship

    a. I Corinthians 4:17 – *"For this cause have I sent unto you Timotheus, who is my beloved son, and faithful in the Lord, who shall bring you into remembrance of my ways which be in Christ, as I teach every where in every church."*
    b. Philippians 2:20-23 – *"20For I have no man likeminded, who will naturally care for your state. 21For all seek their own, not the things which are Jesus Christ's. 22But ye know the proof of him, that, as a son with the father, he hath served with me in the gospel. 23Him therefore I hope to send presently, so soon as I shall see how it will go with me."*

7. Luke 16:10-12 – *"10He that is faithful in that which is least is faithful also in much: and he that is unjust in the least is unjust also in much. 11If therefore ye have not been faithful in the unrighteous mammon, who will commit to your trust the true riches? 12And if ye have not been faithful in that which is another man's, who shall give you that which is your own?"*

C. Examples in Scripture of faithful people and the definitions of their names

1. Abraham – Father of a multitude, Father of many nations, Father of mercy

    a. Galatians 3:9 – *"So then they which be of faith are blessed with faithful Abraham."*
    b. Nehemiah 9:7-8 – *"7Thou art the LORD the God, who didst choose Abram, and broughtest him forth out of Ur of the Chaldees, and gavest him the name of Abraham; 8And foundest his heart faithful before thee, and madest a covenant with him to give the land of the Canaanites, the Hittites, the Amorites, and the Perizzites, and the Jebusites, and the Girgashites, to give it, I say, to his seed, and hast performed thy words; for thou art righteous:"*

2. Moses – Taken out of the water, drawn out, a son

    a. Numbers 12:7 – *"My servant Moses is not so, who is faithful in all mine house."*
    b. Hebrews 3:2, 5 – *"2Who was faithful to him that appointed him, as also Moses was faithful in all his house...5And Moses verily was faithful in all his house, as a servant, for a testimony of those things which were to be spoken after;"*

3. Samuel – Heard of God, asked of God, offering of God, appointed by God, to hear God, His name is of God

    a. I Samuel 2:35 – *"And I will raise me up a faithful priest, that shall do according to that which is in mine heart and in my mind: and I will build him a sure house; and he shall walk before mine anointed for ever."*

4. David – Beloved; his name comes from a root word that means – to boil in love towards

    a. I Samuel 22:14 – *"Then Ahimelech answered the king, and said, And who is so faithful among all thy servants as David, which is the king's son in law, and goeth at thy bidding, and is honourable in thine house?"*

5. *Hanani* – Graciously given of the Lord, gracious to me, the mercy of God

     a.   Nehemiah 7:1-2 – "*1Now it came to pass, when the wall was built, and I had set up the doors, and the porters and the singers and the Levites were appointed, 2That I gave my brother Hanani, and Hananiah the ruler of the palace, charge over Jerusalem: for he was a faithful man, and feared God above many.*"

6.   Daniel – Judge of God, my judge is God, one who delivers judgment in the name of God, God is my Judge, He that judges

     a.   Daniel 6:4 – "*Then the presidents and princes sought to find occasion against Daniel concerning the kingdom; but they could find none occasion nor fault; forasmuch as he was faithful, neither was there any error or fault found in him.*"

7.   Judah – Praised, the Lord be praised, object of praise, praise of the Lord, He shall be praised

     a.   Hosea 11:12 – "*Ephraim compasseth me about with lies, and the house of Israel with deceit: but Judah yet ruleth with God, and is faithful with the saints.*"

8.   Lydia – bending, brought forth, to firebrand, travailing

     a.   Acts 16:14-16 – "*14And a certain woman named Lydia, a seller of purple, of the city of Thyatira, which worshipped God, heard us: whose heart the Lord opened, that she attended unto the things which were spoken of Paul. 15And when she was baptized, and her household, she besought us, saying, If ye have judged me to be faithful to the Lord, come into my house, and abide there. And she constrained us. 16And it came to pass, as we went to prayer, a certain damsel possessed with a spirit of divination met us, which brought her masters much gain by soothsaying:*"

9.   Priests – Levites and Scribes

     a.   Nehemiah 13:13 – "*And I made treasurers over the treasuries, Shelemiah the priest, and Zadok the scribe, and of the Levites, Pedaiah: and next to them was Hanan the son of Zaccur, the son of Mattaniah: for they were counted faithful, and their office was to distribute unto their brethren.*"

10.   Tychicus – Fortuitous, fortunate

     a.   Ephesians 6:21 – "*But that ye also may know my affairs, and how I do, Tychicus, a beloved brother and faithful minister in the Lord, shall make known to you all things:*"

     b.   Colossians 4:7 – "*All my state shall Tychicus declare unto you, who is a beloved brother, and a faithful minister and fellowservant in the Lord:*"

11.   Epaphras – Commended, charming, foamy

     a.   Colossians 1:7 – "*As ye also learned of Epaphras our dear fellowservant, who is for you a faithful minister of Christ*"

12.   Onesimus – Profitable

     a.   Colossians 4:9 – "*With Onesimus, a faithful and beloved brother, who is one of you. They shall make known unto you all things which are done here.*"

13.   Paul – Little, love slave

      a.   I Timothy 1:12 – *"And I thank Christ Jesus our Lord, who hath enabled me, for that he counted me faithful, putting me into the ministry;"*

      b.   I Corinthians 7:25 – *"Now concerning virgins I have no commandment of the Lord: yet I give my judgment, as one that hath obtained mercy of the Lord to be faithful."*

14. Silvanus – Lover of words, of the forest

      a.   I Peter 5:12 – *"By Silvanus, a faithful brother unto you, as I suppose, I have written briefly, exhorting, and testifying that this is the true grace of God wherein ye stand."*

15. Timothy – Honoring God, honored of God, worshipping God, valued of God, zealot

      a.   I Corinthians 4:17 – *"For this cause have I sent unto you Timotheus, who is my beloved son, and faithful in the Lord, who shall bring you into remembrance of my ways which be in Christ, as I teach every where in every church."*

      b.   Philippians 2:20-23 – *"20For I have no man likeminded, who will naturally care for your state. 21For all seek their own, not the things which are Jesus Christ's. 22But ye know the proof of him, that, as a son with the father, he hath served with me in the gospel. 23Him therefore I hope to send presently, so soon as I shall see how it will go with me."*

16. Jesus – Jehovah is salvation, saviour, Jehovah my salvation, the Lord saves

      a.   Revelation 1:5 – *"And from Jesus Christ, who is the faithful witness, and the first begotten of the dead, and the prince of the kings of the earth. Unto him that loved us, and washed us from our sins in his own blood,"*

      b.   Revelation 3:14 – *"And unto the angel of the church of the Laodiceans write; These things saith the Amen, the faithful and true witness, the beginning of the creation of God;"*

      c.   Hebrews 3:1-5 – *"1Wherefore, holy brethren, partakers of the heavenly calling, consider the Apostle and High Priest of our profession, Christ Jesus; 2Who was faithful to him that appointed him, as also Moses was faithful in all his house. 3For this man was counted worthy of more glory than Moses, inasmuch as he who hath builded the house hath more honour than the house. 4For every house is builded by some man; but he that built all things is God. 5And Moses verily was faithful in all his house, as a servant, for a testimony of those things which were to be spoken after;"*

      d.   Revelation 19:11 – *"And I saw heaven opened, and behold a white horse; and he that sat upon him was called Faithful and True, and in righteousness he doth judge and make war."*

      e.   II Timothy 2:13 – *"If we believe not, yet he abideth faithful: he cannot deny himself."*

      f.   Hebrews 10:23 – *"Let us hold fast the profession of our faith without wavering; (for he is faithful that promised;)"*

      g.   Hebrews 2:17 – *"Wherefore in all things it behoved him to be made like unto his brethren, that he might be a merciful and faithful high priest in things pertaining to God, to make reconciliation for the sins of the people."*

      h.   I Thessalonians 5:24 – *"Faithful is he that calleth you, who also will do it."*

V. God Is Faithful

God never requires something of us that He is not willing to do Himself. If He demands or is looking for faithfulness in His people, you can be sure that He is faithful. Because He is the personification of faithfulness, He will give us the desire and ability to be faithful ourselves.

    A.   Faithfulness is essentially who God is

1. Deuteronomy 7:9 – *"Know therefore that the LORD thy God, he is God, the faithful God, which keepeth covenant and mercy with them that love him and keep his commandments to a thousand generations;"*

    a. Other translations:
    "...the steadfast God..."
    "...a trustworthy God..."

2. Isaiah 49:7 – *"...because of the LORD that is faithful, and the Holy One..."*
3. I Corinthians 1:9 – *"God is faithful, by whom ye were called unto the fellowship of his Son Jesus Christ our Lord."*
4. I Corinthians 10:13 – *"There hath no temptation taken you but such as is common to man: but God is faithful, who will not suffer you to be tempted above that ye are able; but will with the temptation also make a way to escape..."*
5. I Thessalonians 5:24 – *"Faithful is he that calleth you, who also will do it."*
6. 2 Thessalonians 3:3 – *"But the Lord is faithful, who shall stablish you, and keep you from evil."*
7. II Timothy 2:13 – *"If we believe not, yet he abideth faithful: he cannot deny himself."*
8. Hebrews 2:17 – *"Wherefore in all things it behoved him to be made like unto his brethren, that he might be a merciful and faithful high priest in things pertaining to God, to make reconciliation for the sins of the people."*
9. Hebrews 3:1-4 – *"...consider the Apostle and High Priest of our profession, Christ Jesus; Who was faithful to him that appointed him, as also Moses was faithful in all his house. For this man was counted worthy of more glory than Moses, inasmuch as he who hath builded the house hath more honour than the house. For every house is builded by some man; but he that built all things is God."*
10. Hebrews 10:23 – *"Let us hold fast the profession of our faith without wavering; (for he is faithful that promised;)"*
11. Hebrews 11:11 – *"Through faith also Sara herself received strength to conceive seed, and was delivered of a child when she was past age, because she judged him faithful who had promised."* (Psalms 143:1)
12. I Peter 4:19 – *"...let them that suffer according to the will of God commit the keeping of their souls to him in well doing, as unto a faithful Creator."*
13. I John 1:9 – *"If we confess our sins, he is faithful and just to forgive us our sins, and to cleanse us from all unrighteousness."*
14. Revelation 1:5 – *"And from Jesus Christ, who is the faithful witness, and the first begotten of the dead..."* (Revelation 3:14)
15. Revelation 19:11 – *"And I saw heaven opened, and behold a white horse; and he that sat upon him was called Faithful and True, and in righteousness he doth judge and make war."*
16. Psalms 36:5 – *"Thy mercy, O LORD, is in the heavens; and thy faithfulness reacheth unto the clouds."*
17. Psalms 40:10 – *"I have not hid thy righteousness within my heart; I have declared thy faithfulness and thy salvation..."*

18. Psalms 89:1-2 – *"I will sing of the mercies of the LORD for ever: with my mouth will I make known thy faithfulness to all generations. For I have said, Mercy shall be built up for ever: thy faithfulness shalt thou establish in the very heavens."*

    a. Psalms 89:5, 8
    b. Psalms 92:2

19. Psalms 89:24 – *"But my faithfulness and my mercy shall be with him: and in my name shall his horn be exalted."*

20. Psalms 89:33 – *"Nevertheless my lovingkindness will I not utterly take from him, nor suffer my faithfulness to fail."*
21. Psalms 119:75 – *"I know, O LORD, that thy judgments are right, and that thou in faithfulness hast afflicted me."*
22. Psalms 119:90 – *"Thy faithfulness is unto all generations: thou hast established the earth, and it abideth."*
23. Isaiah 11:5 – *"And righteousness shall be the girdle of his loins, and faithfulness the girdle of his reins."*
24. Lamentations 3:23 – *"...great is thy faithfulness."*
25. Hosea 2:19-20 – *"...I will even betroth thee unto me in faithfulness: and thou shalt know the LORD."*

B. Other Scriptural Principles That Show His Great Faithfulness

1. God will not forsake His people

    a. Genesis 28:15 – *"...behold, I am with thee, and will keep thee in all places whither thou goest, and will bring thee again into this land; for I will not leave thee, until I have done that which I have spoken to thee of."*
    b. Hebrews 13:5 – *"...for he hath said, I will never leave thee, nor forsake thee."*
    c. Deuteronomy 4:31 – *"...he will not forsake thee, neither destroy thee, nor forget the covenant..."*
    d. I Samuel 12:22 – *"For the LORD will not forsake his people for his great name's sake..."*
    e. I Chronicles 28:20 – *"...for the LORD God, even my God, will be with thee; he will not fail thee, nor forsake thee, until thou hast finished all the work..."*
    f. Ezra 9:9 – *"For we were bondmen; yet our God hath not forsaken us in our bondage..."*
    g. Psalms 9:10 – *"...for thou, LORD, hast not forsaken them that seek thee."*
    h. Psalms 37:28 – *"For the LORD loveth judgment, and forsaketh not his saints; they are preserved for ever..."*
    i. Psalms 94:14 – *"For the LORD will not cast off his people, neither will he forsake his inheritance."*
    j. Psalms 121:3-4 – *"He will not suffer thy foot to be moved..."*
    k. Isaiah 42:16 – *"...These things will I do unto them, and not forsake them."*
    l. Isaiah 44:21 – *"...O Israel, thou shalt not be forgotten of me."*
    m. Jeremiah 51:5 – *"For Israel hath not been forsaken, nor Judah of his God..."*
    n. Romans 11:2 – *"God hath not cast away his people which he foreknew..."*
    o. Romans 11:29 – *"For the gifts and calling of God are without repentance."*

2. God keeps His covenant with His people

    a. Psalms 105:8 – *"He hath remembered his covenant for ever..."*
    b. Psalms 111:5 – *"...he will ever be mindful of his covenant."*
    c. Isaiah 54:9-10 – *"...neither shall the covenant of my peace be removed, saith the LORD that hath mercy on thee."*
    d. Jeremiah 32:40 – *"And I will make an everlasting covenant with them, that I will not turn away from them, to do them good..."*
    e. II Samuel 23:5 – *"Although my house be not so with God; yet he hath made with me an everlasting covenant, ordered in all things, and sure..."*
    f. Genesis 9:15-16 – Rainbow symbolic of God's covenant
    g. Leviticus 26:44
    h. Psalms 89:34 – *"My covenant will I not break, nor alter the thing that is gone out of my lips."*

3. God faithfully keeps His promises

   a. I Kings 8:56 – *"Blessed be the LORD, that hath given rest unto his people Israel, according to all that he promised: there hath not failed one word of all his good promise, which he promised by the hand of Moses..."*
   b. Joshua 23:14 – *"...ye know in all your hearts and in all your souls, that not one thing hath failed of all the good things which the LORD your God spake concerning you..."*
   c. Jeremiah 33:14 – *"Behold, the days come, saith the LORD, that I will perform that good thing which I have promised..."*
   d. Titus 1:2 – *"In hope of eternal life, which God, that cannot lie, promised before the world began;"*
   e. Hebrews 6:10-19
   f. II Peter 3:9 – *"The Lord is not slack concerning his promise..."*
   g. Jeremiah 29:10
   h. Genesis 21:1 – *"And the LORD visited Sarah as he had said, and the LORD did unto Sarah as he had spoken."* (Hebrews 11:11)
   i. Acts 13:32-33
   j. II Corinthians 1:20 – *"For all the promises of God in him are yea, and in him Amen, unto the glory of God by us."*

4. God's Word is always faithful

   a. Psalms 119:86 – *"All thy commandments are faithful..."*
   b. Psalms 119:138 – *"Thy testimonies that thou hast commanded are righteous and very faithful."*
   c. Isaiah 25:1 – *"...thy counsels of old are faithfulness and truth."*
   d. Deuteronomy 9:5 – *"...that he may perform the word which the LORD sware unto thy fathers, Abraham, Isaac, and Jacob."*
   e. II Samuel 7:28 – *"And now, O Lord GOD, thou art that God, and thy words be true, and thou hast promised this goodness unto thy servant:"*
   f. Nehemiah 9:8 – *"...and hast performed thy words; for thou art righteous:"*
   g. Matthew 24:34-35 – *"Verily I say unto you, This generation shall not pass, till all these things be fulfilled. Heaven and earth shall pass away, but my words shall not pass away."*

5. God does not and can not lie

   a. Numbers 23:19 – *"God is not a man, that he should lie; neither the son of man, that he should repent..."*
   b. Romans 3:4 – *"God forbid: yea, let God be true, but every man a liar; as it is written..."*
   c. John 3:33 – *"He that hath received his testimony hath set to his seal that God is true."*
   d. II Timothy 2:13 – *"If we believe not, yet he abideth faithful: he cannot deny himself."*
   e. Titus 1:2 – *"In hope of eternal life, which God, that cannot lie, promised before the world began;"*
   f. Hebrews 6:18 – *"That by two immutable things, in which it was impossible for God to lie..."*
   g. Job 36:4 – *"For truly my words shall not be false: he that is perfect in knowledge is with thee."*
   h. Revelation 19:11 – *"...he that sat upon him was called Faithful and True..."*
   i. I John 5:20 – *"And we know that the Son of God is come, and hath given us an understanding, that we may know him that is true, and we are in him that is true, even in his Son Jesus Christ. This is the true God, and eternal life."*
   j. James 1:17 – *"...with whom is no variableness, neither shadow of turning."*
   k. II Corinthians 1:18 – *"But as God is true (faithful)..."*

l. I Samuel 15:29 – *"And also the Strength of Israel will not lie nor repent: for he is not a man, that he should repent."*

m. Psalms 89:35 – *"Once have I sworn by my holiness that I will not lie unto David."*

n. John 2:21 – *"I have not written unto you because ye know not the truth, but because ye know it, and that no lie is of the truth."*

VI. What Is A Faithful Man?

A. Characteristics of a faithful man

1. Proverbs 11:13 – *"A talebearer revealeth secrets: but he that is of a faithful spirit concealeth the matter."*

   a. Psalms 5:9 – *"For there is no faithfulness in their mouth; their inward part is very wickedness; their throat is an open sepulchre; they flatter with their tongue."*

2. Proverbs 13:17 –One who brings life – The Hebrew root word for health is *rapha* which means – a cure, medicine, sound, wholesome, yielding.

3. Proverbs 14:5 – Doesn't lie.

4. I Timothy 3:11 – Faithful in all things.

5. II Samuel 23:11-12 –Faithful in the least.

   a. Luke 16:10 – *"He that is faithful in that which is least is faithful also in much..."*
   b. Matthew 25:21
   c. Acts 6:2-5, 8
   d. Luke 12:43

6. Faithful in that which is another man's

   a. Luke 16:12 – *"And if ye have not been faithful in that which is another man's, who shall give you that which is your own?"*
   b. 2 Timothy 2:2 – *"And the things that thou hast heard of me among many witnesses, the same commit thou to faithful men, who shall be able to teach others also."*
   c. He's a servant.

7. Being faithful is not seeking your own.

   a. Philippians 2:19-23
   b. John 5:30
   c. John 7:18 – *"He that speaketh of himself seeketh his own glory: but he that seeketh his glory that sent him, the same is true, and no unrighteousness is in him."*
   d. I Corinthians 13:5 – *"Doth not behave itself unseemly, seeketh not her own, is not easily provoked, thinketh no evil;"*
   e. I Corinthians 10:24, 33

B. Faithfulness is a requirement for leadership.

1. Luke 12:41-44 – *"Then Peter said unto him, Lord, speakest thou this parable unto us, or even to all? 42And the Lord said, Who then is that faithful and wise steward, whom his lord shall make <u>ruler over his household</u>, to give them their portion of meat in due season? 43Blessed is that servant, whom his lord when he cometh shall find so doing. 44Of a truth I say unto you, that he will make him ruler over all that he hath."*

      a.   I Samuel 16:11
      b.   1 Timothy 1:12 – Paul
      c.   1 Samuel 2:35 – Samuel
      d.   II Chronicles 19:9 – Judges appointed by Jehoshaphat.
      e.   Nehemiah 7:2 – Nehemiah's appointees.
      f.   Acts 6:2-5, 8 – Stephen
      g.   Joshua 1:1 – Joshua
      h.   II Kings 3:11 – Elisha
      i.   I Corinthians 4:17 – Timothy (Philippians 2:20-23)
      j.   Colossians 1:17 – Timothy
      k.   Colossians 4:7-9 – Tychicus and Onesimus

VII.   Blessing for Being Faithful

    A.   Scriptural examples

        1.   Proverbs 28:20 – *"A faithful man shall abound with blessings..."*
        2.   Psalms 31:23 – *"...for the Lord preserveth the faithful..."*
        3.   Revelation 2:10 – *"...be thou faithful and I will give thee a crown of life."*

    B.   God will help us to be faithful.

        1.   I Corinthians 7:25 – *"...one that hath obtained mercy of the Lord to be faithful."*

VIII.   Faithful Man – Psalms 101:6 – *"Mine eyes shall be upon the faithful of the land, that they may dwell with me: he that walketh in a perfect way, he shall serve me."*

    A.   A faithful man is a servant

        1.   James 1:1 – *"James, a servant of God and of the Lord Jesus Christ..."*
        2.   Jude 1
        3.   II Peter 1:1
        4.   Titus 1:1

        5.   Examples of Paul

            a.   I Corinthians 9:19 – *"...yet have I made myself servant unto all..."*
            b.   I Corinthians 3:4-7, 21-23

    B.   Jesus is our example of faithfulness

        1.   Philippians 2:7 – *"But made himself of no reputation, and took upon him the form of a servant, and was made in the likeness of men:"*
        2.   Hebrews 2:17 – *"...in all things it behoved him to be made like unto his brethren, that he might be a merciful and faithful high priest in things pertaining to God..."*
        3.   I Thessalonians 5:24 – *"Faithful is he that calleth you, who also will do it."*
        4.   Hebrews 10:23 – *"Let us hold fast the profession of our faith without wavering; (for he is faithful that promised;)"*
        5.   II Timothy 2:13 – *"If we believe not, yet he abideth faithful: he cannot deny himself."*
        6.   Hebrews 3:2

    C.   God wants us to be servants, Matthew 20:25-29

IX. Aspects of a Faithful Man

    A. Luke 12:41-44 – Ruler

        1. Genesis 41:33-43

        2. Matthew 25:14 – Meat – gives proper food – must know what kind of food they need.

            a. I Peter 3:2
            b. John 21:15
            c. II Samuel 5:2
            d. Acts 20:28
            e. Proverbs 31:15
            f. Deuteronomy 32:1

        3. Due Season

            a. Proverbs 15:23 – *"...a word spoken in due season, how good is it"*
            b. Proverbs 25:11 – *"A word fitly spoken is like apples of gold in pictures of silver."*
            c. Isaiah 50:4
            d. Ecclesiastes 12:10

    B. Hard to find a faithful man.

        1. Proverbs 20:6 – *"...a faithful man who can find?"*
        2. Proverbs 31:10 – *"Who can find a virtuous woman?"*
        3. Psalms 12:1

        4. Paul was able to find some.

            a. I Corinthians 4:17
            b. Colossians 1:7, 4:7-9

Lesson 16
GOD'S PLACE FOR US

I.   II Samuel 7:10-16 – He appoints a place. God has a specific place in the body in a local church for all of us.

"*10Moreover <u>I will appoint a place</u> for my people Israel, and will plant them, that they may dwell in a place of their own, and move no more; neither shall the children of wickedness afflict them any more, as beforetime, 11And as since the time that I commanded judges to be over my people Israel, and have caused thee to rest from all thine enemies. Also the LORD telleth thee that he will make thee an house. 12And when thy days be fulfilled, and thou shalt sleep with thy fathers, I will set up thy seed after thee, which shall proceed out of thy bowels, and I will establish his kingdom. 13He shall build an house for my name, and I will stablish the throne of his kingdom for ever. 14I will be his father, and he shall be my son. If he commit iniquity, I will chasten him with the rod of men, and with the stripes of the children of men: 15But my mercy shall not depart away from him, as I took it from Saul, whom I put away before thee. 16And thine house and thy kingdom shall be established for ever before thee: thy throne shall be established for ever.*"

A.   Word Definitions

1.   Place in Hebrew – A standing, a spot, a locality. A condition of the mind and body; An open place, room, space; From a root word – to abide, to accomplish, to be clear, to be confirmed, to lift up.
2.   Plant in Hebrew – to strike (as if to hammer in), to fix, to fasten.
3.   Appoint in Hebrew – to put, to bring, to call a name, to care, to cast in, to change, to ordain, to wholly work in.

B.   Other Translations:

1.   "*And I will provide a place for my people Israel, and I will plant them, so that they can have a home of their own, and no longer be disturbed, wicked people will not oppress them anymore, as they did at the beginning. I will give you rest from your enemies.*"
2.   "*...Neither shall the sons of perversion, humiliate them anymore.*"
3.   "*...violent men shall no more distress them.*"
4.   "*...they shall never be troubled by evil men, as before.*"
5.   "*I will establish a place...*"
6.   "*...they shall inhabit their place, and be unsettles no more...*"
7.   "*...be disquieted no more...*"
8.   "*...there will be no more disturbance*"

II.   Understanding the Passage – II Samuel 7:10-16

A.   Verse 10

1.   "*...I will appoint a place...*" – God appoints our place not us or others

a.   I Corinthians 12:18 – "*But now hath God set the members every one of them in the body, as it hath pleased him.*"
b.   Deuteronomy 12:5-7 – "*5But unto the place which the LORD your God shall choose out of all your tribes to put his name there, even unto his habitation shall ye seek, and thither thou shalt come: 6And thither ye shall bring your burnt offerings, and your sacrifices, and your tithes, and heave offerings of your hand, and your vows, and your freewill offerings, and the firstlings of your herds and of your flocks: 7And there ye shall eat before the LORD*"

your God, and ye shall rejoice in all that ye put your hand unto, ye and your households, wherein the LORD thy God hath blessed thee."

c.   Deuteronomy 14:23 – *"And thou shalt eat before the LORD thy God, in the place which he shall choose to place his name there, the tithe of thy corn, of thy wine, and of thine oil, and the firstlings of thy herds and of thy flocks; that thou mayest learn to fear the LORD thy God always."* (Deuteronomy 16:2, 6, 15)

d.   Deuteronomy 18:6 – *"And if a Levite come from any of thy gates out of all Israel, where he sojourned, and come with all the desire of his mind unto the place which the LORD shall choose;"*

e.   Deuteronomy 31:11 – *"When all Israel is come to appear before the LORD thy God in the place which he shall choose, thou shalt read this law before all Israel in their hearing."*

f.   Psalms 24:3 – *"Who shall ascend into the hill of the LORD? or who shall stand in his holy place?"*

g.   I Chronicles 17:9 – *"Also I will ordain a place for my people Israel, and will plant them, and they shall dwell in their place, and shall be moved no more; neither shall the children of wickedness waste them any more, as at the beginning,"*

h.   Mark 6:39-40 – *"³⁹And he commanded them to make all sit down by companies upon the green grass. ⁴⁰And they sat down in ranks, by hundreds, and by fifties."*

i.   John 14:2 – *"In my Father's house are many mansions: if it were not so, I would have told you. I go to prepare a place for you."*

j.   Numbers 2:17 – *"Then the tabernacle of the congregation shall set forward with the camp of the Levites in the midst of the camp: as they encamp, so shall they set forward, every man in his place by their standards."*

k.   Hosea 11:11 – *"They shall tremble as a bird out of Egypt, and as a dove out of the land of Assyria: and I will place them in their houses, saith the LORD."*

l.   Ephesians 2:19-22 – *"In whom all the building fitly framed together groweth unto an holy temple in the Lord: In whom ye also are builded together for an habitation of God..."*

m.   Ephesians 4:11-16 – *"From whom the whole body fitly joined together and compacted by that which every joint supplieth, according to the effectual working in the measure of every part, maketh increase of the body unto the edifying of itself in love."*

2.   Facts about the place

a.   Ezekiel 43:7 – *"...place of my throne, and the place of the soles of my feet, where I will dwell in the midst of the children of Israel for ever, and my holy name, shall the house of Israel no more defile..."*

b.   Haggai 2:9 – *"...in this place will I give peace, saith the LORD of hosts..."* – There will be peace in God's place. There will be security and rest in God's place

c.   Malachi 1:11 – *"...in every place incense shall be offered unto my name..."*

d.   Proverbs 15:3 – *"The eyes of the LORD are in every place..."*

e.   Isaiah 22:23-25 – *"And I will fasten him as a nail in a sure place; and he shall be for a glorious throne..."*

f.   Isaiah 33:21 – *"But there the glorious LORD will be unto us a place of broad rivers and streams..."*

g.   Isaiah 60:13 – *"...and I will make the place of my feet glorious."*

h.   Jeremiah 17:12 – *"A glorious high throne from the beginning is the place of our sanctuary."*

3.   We should never leave our place.

a.   Hebrews 10:22-25 – *"...Not forsaking the assembling of ourselves together..."*

b.   I Corinthians 1:10 – *"...there be no divisions among you; but that ye be perfectly joined together..."*

    c.   Proverbs 27:8 – *"As a bird that wandereth from her nest, so is a man that wandereth from his place."*

    d.   Ecclesiastes 10:4 – *"...leave not thy place..."*

    e.   Job 27:13-23 – *"...storm hurl him out of his place."*

    f.   Ecclesiastes 8:10 – *"...gone from the place of the holy..."*

    g.   Proverbs 14:12 – *"There is a way which seemeth right unto a man, but the end thereof are the ways of death."*

    h.   Job 14:14 – *"...all the days of my appointed time will I wait, till my change come..."*

4.   The Glory of being in His place

    a.   II Samuel 9:1-13

    b.   Exodus 33:12-23

    c.   Genesis 28:10-22

    d.   Ephesians 1:3 – in heavenly places (Ephesians 2:6 – *"And hath raised us up together, and made us sit together in heavenly places in Christ Jesus:"*)

    e.   Zechariah 3:6-10

    f.   Micah 4:1-8

5.   There will be unity in God's place

    a.   Psalms 133 – *"[1]Behold, how good and how pleasant it is for brethren to dwell together in unity! [2]It is like the precious ointment upon the head, that ran down upon the beard, even Aaron's beard: that went down to the skirts of his garments; [3]As the dew of Hermon, and as the dew that descended upon the mountains of Zion: for there the LORD commanded the blessing, even life for evermore."*

    b.   Acts 2:44 – *"And all that believed were together, and had all things common;"*

    c.   II Chronicles 5:11-14

    d.   I Corinthians 1:10 – *"Now I beseech you, brethren, by the name of our Lord Jesus Christ, that ye all speak the same thing, and that there be no divisions among you; but that ye be perfectly joined together in the same mind and in the same judgment."*

    e.   Ephesians 1:10 – *"That in the dispensation of the fulness of times he might gather together in one all things in Christ, both which are in heaven, and which are on earth; even in him:"*

    f.   Joel 2:7 – *"They shall run like mighty men; they shall climb the wall like men of war; and they shall march every one on his ways, and they shall not break their ranks:"*

6.   There will be commitment and a sense of community and family in God's place. We are now yoke-follows

    a.   Acts 2:44-45 – *"[44]And all that believed were together, and had all things common; [45]And sold their possessions and goods, and parted them to all men, as every man had need."*

    b.   Philippians 4:3 – *"And I intreat thee also, true yokefellow, help those women which laboured with me in the gospel, with Clement also, and with other my fellowlabourers, whose names are in the book of life."*

    c.   Ephesians 2:19 – *"Now therefore ye are no more strangers and foreigners, but fellowcitizens with the saints, and of the household of God;"*

    d.   Ephesians 3:6 – *"That the Gentiles should be fellowheirs, and of the same body, and partakers of his promise in Christ by the gospel:"*

    e.   John 11:16 – *"Then said Thomas, which is called Didymus, unto his fellowdisciples..."*

    f.   I Peter 3:8 – *"Finally, be ye all of one mind, having compassion one of another, love as brethren, be pitiful, be courteous..."*

    g.   I John 3:14-18

     h.   I Corinthians 10:24 – *"Let no man seek his own, but every man another's wealth."*

    7. *"...and will plant them..."*
    8. *"...that they may dwell in a place of their own..."* (Genesis 26:17-25)
    9. *"...and move no more..."*
  10. *"...neither shall the children of wickedness afflict them anymore..."* – Finding our place brings deliverance from the enemy. As we begin to fulfill God's call on our life and begin to function, becoming a fruitful member of our own local body and the general body of Christ at large, the devil will have no place in our lives. The key is to be humble, meek, and submissive but willing and bold. God will see fit to bring forth that which He has ordained for us.

B.   Verse 11 – Other translations

    1. *"...have cause thee to rest..."*
    2. *"...from all thine enemies..."*
    3. *"...he will make thee an house"*

C.   Verse 12

    1. *"...thy days be fulfilled..."*
    2. *"...I will set up thy seed after thee..."*
    3. *"...I will establish his kingdom"*

D.   Verse 13

    1. *"He will build an house for my name..."*
    2. *"I will stablish the throne* (authority) *of his kingdom for ever."*

E.   Verse 14

    1. *"I will be his father..."*
    2. *"...he shall be my son..."*

F.   Verse 15

    1. *"But my mercy shall not depart from him..."*

III. We Are Members Now In The body of Christ

A.   Scriptures showing our entrance into the body of Christ

    1. I Corinthians 12:12-17
    2. Acts 2:36-47
    3. Acts 4:32-35
    4. Acts 5:11-17
    5. Acts 11:19-26
    6. Matthew 16:13-20

B.   The foundation of the church

    1. Greek for church – *Ekklesia*, called out ones, assembly gathered together. We have found a new family, Matthew 12:48-50
    2. When it was established, Acts 2:1-4, 41-47

3. Who can become members of the church? How do they become members?

    a. Acts 2:41
    b. Acts 5:14
    c. Acts 11:21-24
    d. Acts 8:5-8, 12, 17

4. How they come to be called Christians

    a. Acts 11:26 – Greek meaning for *Antioch* – driven against

        1) Isaiah 62:1-3
        2) Isaiah 65:11-16

5. We are now brethren and should address each other as such. Greek meaning for *brother* – neighbor, fellow countryman.

    a. Acts 9:17
    b. Acts 21:20

    c. We should call each other *brother* – Hebrews 2:11-12

        1) I Thessalonians 5:26
        2) Revelation 19:10
        3) I John 3:16
        4) I Peter 3:8
        5) I Peter 1:22
        6) Acts 6:3
        7) I Corinthians 16:20
        8) Ephesians 6:23
        9) Philippians 4:1, 8
        10) Colossians 4:15
        11) I Thessalonians 2:14

6. Christ is the Head of the Church

    a. Ephesians 1:22
    b. Ephesians 5:23
    c. Colossians 1:18

7. The Church is the Body of Christ

    a. Ephesians 1:22-23
    b. Colossians 1:24
    c. I Corinthians 12:12-27   *Ge. 3:14*

IV. The Meaning of the Word *"Church"*

The New Testament Greek Word for church, "ecclesia" is used some one hundred and nine times, and over ninety times this word refers to the *local church*. Many local churches are named in the Scriptures, such as the seven churches of Asia, the church at the house of Priscilla and Aquila, the church at Rome, the church at Corinth, etc. Thus the local church patterns and teaching occupy most of the New Testament references to the church.

Ecumenicalism may bring all denominations together. When Babylon is thus solidified, it will be clear to every believer that the unscriptural basis of anything, except the local church of the New Testament.

V.   The Church Is the Body of Jesus Christ (Colossians 1:18, 24; I Corinthians 12:12; Ephesians 1:21-23)

From all of the above given references, we see that church membership in the New Testament church is a spiritual status and a spiritual relationship.

Lesson 17
GUIDANCE

I. We need Guidance in our lives

A. Scriptures

1. Proverbs 14:12 – *"There is a way which seemeth right unto a man, but the end thereof are the ways of death."*
2. Ecclesiastes 10:15 – *"The labour of the foolish wearieth every one of them, because he knoweth not how to go to the city."*
3. Isaiah 53:6 – *"All we like sheep have gone astray; we have turned every one to his own way; and the LORD hath laid on him the iniquity of us all."*
4. Acts 2:40 – *"And with many other words did he testify and exhort, saying, Save yourselves from this untoward generation."*

II. We should go to God for Guidance

A. Scriptures

1. Job 23:10 – *"But he knoweth the way that I take: when he hath tried me, I shall come forth as gold."*
2. Psalms 37:5 – *"Commit thy way unto the LORD; trust also in him; and he shall bring it to pass."*
3. Psalms 1:6 – *"For the LORD knoweth the way of the righteous: but the way of the ungodly shall perish."*
4. Proverbs 3:5-7
5. Jeremiah 6:16 – *"Thus saith the LORD, Stand ye in the ways, and see, and ask for the old paths, where is the good way, and walk therein, and ye shall find rest for your souls. But they said, We will not walk therein."*
6. James 1:5 – *"If any of you lack wisdom, let him ask of God, that giveth to all men liberally, and upbraideth not; and it shall be given him."*
7. Isaiah 46:10 – *"Declaring the end from the beginning, and from ancient times the things that are not yet done, saying, My counsel shall stand, and I will do all my pleasure"*:

III. Where should we <u>not</u> go for Guidance?

A. Scriptures

1. Exodus 20:2-3 – *"I am the LORD thy God, which have brought thee out of the land of Egypt, out of the house of bondage. Thou shalt have no other gods before me."*
2. Deuteronomy 18:9-13
3. Psalms 1:1 – *"Blessed is the man that walketh not in the counsel of the ungodly, nor standeth in the way of sinners, nor sitteth in the seat of the scornful."*
4. Acts 19:14 – *"And there were seven sons of one Sceva, a Jew, and chief of the priests, which did so."*
5. I Samuel 28:3-21

IV. To receive guidance we must first have a yielded or teachable spirit

A. Scriptures

1. Psalms 25:9 – *"The meek will he guide in judgment: and the meek will he teach his way."*

2. Psalms 61:2 – *"From the end of the earth will I cry unto thee, when my heart is overwhelmed: lead me to the rock that is higher than I."*
3. James 1:21 – *"Wherefore lay apart all filthiness and superfluity of naughtiness, and receive with meekness the engrafted word, which is able to save your souls."*
4. I Peter 3:4 – *"But let it be the hidden man of the heart, in that which is not corruptible, even the ornament of a meek and quiet spirit, which is in the sight of God of great price."*
5. Psalms 51:17 – *"The sacrifices of God are a broken spirit: a broken and a contrite heart, O God, thou wilt not despise."*

V. We need to know how God guides us because:

    A. Scriptures

        1. I Corinthians 14:10 – *"There are, it may be, so many kinds of voices in the world, and none of them is without signification."*
        2. John 4:1 – *"Beloved, believe not every spirit, but try the spirits whether they are of God: because many false prophets are gone out into the world."*
        3. Matthew 22:29 – *"Jesus answered and said unto them, Ye do err, not knowing the scriptures, nor the power of God."*

VI. All must be balanced by the Word.

    A. Scriptures

        1. II Corinthians 11:4 – *"For if he that cometh preacheth another Jesus, whom we have not preached, or if ye receive another spirit, which ye have not received, or another gospel, which ye have not accepted, ye might well bear with him."*
        2. Galatians 1:6-10
        3. I Timothy 3:5-8
        4. I Timothy 6:3-5
        5. II Timothy 3:14-17
        6. Titus 1:9-12
        7. Titus 2:1 – *"But speak thou the things which become sound doctrine"*:
        8. Revelation 22:18-20
        9. Deuteronomy 4:2 – *"Ye shall not add unto the word which I command you, neither shall ye diminish ought from it, that ye may keep the commandments of the LORD your God which I command you."*
     10. Proverbs 30:6 – *"Add thou not unto his words, lest he reprove thee, and thou be found a liar."*
     11. John 8:31-31
     12. II John 9-12
     13. John 17:17 – *"Sanctify them through thy truth: thy word is truth."*
        God will never speak anything contrary to his Word. The word is our plumb line.

VII. God's Forms of Guidance

    A. We can receive guidance from all of these three separately. But, they all <u>should</u> agree.

        1. **Word**

           a. Psalms 19:7-11
           b. Proverbs 6:20-24
           c. Psalms 119:98 – *"Thou through thy commandments hast made me wiser than mine enemies: for they are ever with me."*

THE DOCTRINE OF FIRST THINGS

d. Psalms 119:104-105

e. Psalms 119:130 – *"The entrance of thy words giveth light; it giveth understanding unto the simple."*

f. Hebrews 2:2 – *"For if the word spoken by angels was stedfast, and every transgression and disobedience received a just recompence of reward"*;

g. Acts 20:32 – *"And now, brethren, I commend you to God, and to the word of his grace, which is able to build you up, and to give you an inheritance among all them which are sanctified."*

h. II Timothy 3:15-17

2. **Spirit** – or inward witness

a. 1 John 5:10 – *"He that believeth on the Son of God hath the witness in himself: he that believeth not God hath made him a liar; because he believeth not the record that God gave of his Son."*

b. 1 John 2:20 – *"But ye have an unction from the Holy One, and ye know all things"*

c. 1 John 2:27 – *"But the anointing which ye have received of him abideth in you, and ye need not that any man teach you: but as the same anointing teacheth you of all things, and is truth, and is no lie, and even as it hath taught you, ye shall abide in him."*

d. 1 John 5:6 – *"This is he that came by water and blood, even Jesus Christ; not by water only, but by water and blood. And it is the Spirit that beareth witness, because the Spirit is truth."*

e. John 14:26 – *"But the Comforter, which is the Holy Ghost, whom the Father will send in my name, he shall teach you all things, and bring all things to your remembrance, whatsoever I have said unto you."*

f. John 16:13 – *"Howbeit when he, the Spirit of truth, is come, he will guide you into all truth: for he shall not speak of himself; but whatsoever he shall hear, that shall he speak: and he will shew you things to come."*

g. Job 32:8 – *"But there is a spirit in man: and the inspiration of the Almighty giveth them understanding."*

h. Nehemiah 9:20 – *"Thou gavest also thy good spirit to instruct them, and withheldest not thy manna from their mouth, and gavest them water for their thirst."*

i. Isaiah 30:21 – *"And thine ears shall hear a word behind thee, saying, This is the way, walk ye in it, when ye turn to the right hand, and when ye turn to the left."*

j. Luke 1:39-49

3. God given leaders or counselors

a. Proverbs 1:5 – *"A wise man will hear, and will increase learning; and a man of understanding shall attain unto wise counsels"*

b. Proverbs 9:9 – *"Give instruction to a wise man, and he will be yet wiser: teach a just man, and he will increase in learning."*

c. Proverbs 11:14 – *"Where no counsel is, the people fall: but in the multitude of counsellers there is safety."*

d. Proverbs 12:15 – *"The way of a fool is right in his own eyes: but he that hearkeneth unto counsel is wise."*

e. Proverbs 15:22 – *"Without counsel purposes are disappointed: but in the multitude of counsellers they are established."*

f. Proverbs 19:20 – *"Hear counsel, and receive instruction, that thou mayest be wise in thy latter end."*

g. Proverbs 20:18 – *"Every purpose is established by counsel: and with good advice make war."*

h. Proverbs 24:6 – "*For by wise counsel thou shalt make thy war: and in multitude of counsellers there is safety.*"

i. 1 Peter 5:5 – "*Likewise, ye younger, submit yourselves unto the elder. Yea, all of you be subject one to another, and be clothed with humility: for God resisteth the proud, and giveth grace to the humble.*"

j. Hebrews 13:17 – "*Obey them that have the rule over you, and submit yourselves: for they watch for your souls, as they that must give account, that they may do it with joy, and not with grief: for that is unprofitable for you.*"

k. Galatians 2:2 –"*And I went up by revelation, and communicated unto them that gospel which I preach among the Gentiles, but privately to them which were of reputation, lest by any means I should run, or had run, in vain.*"

Lesson 18
KNOWING HIM

I. Hebrew and Greek Word Definitions of *Know, Knew*

   A. Hebrew word, *yada* – to know (properly, to ascertain by seeing); this word
   B. Greek, *ginosko* - to know absolutely, to understand completely; it means to understand in a present tense.

II. Knowing Him should be the cry of our hearts

   A. Found throughout the Scriptures

      1. Exodus 33:13 – Moses, *"Now therefore, I pray thee, if I have found grace in thy sight, shew me now thy way, that I may know thee, that I may find grace in thy sight: and consider that this nation is thy people."*
      2. Philippians 3:8-10 – Paul, *"Yea doubtless, and I count all things but loss for the excellency of the knowledge of Christ Jesus my Lord: for whom I have suffered the loss of all things, and do count them but dung, that I may win Christ, ⁹And be found in him, not having mine own righteousness, which is of the law, but that which is through the faith of Christ, the righteousness which is of God by faith: ¹⁰That I may know him, and the power of his resurrection, and the fellowship of his sufferings, being made conformable unto his death;"*
      3. Psalms 46:10 – God wants us to know Him, *"Be still, and know that I am God: I will be exalted among the heathen, I will be exalted in the earth."*

         a. Jeremiah 9:23-24 – *"Thus saith the LORD, Let not the wise man glory in his wisdom, neither let the mighty man glory in his might, let not the rich man glory in his riches: ²⁴But let him that glorieth glory in this, that he understandeth and knoweth me, that I am the LORD which exercise lovingkindness, judgment, and righteousness, in the earth: for in these things I delight, saith the LORD."*
         b. Psalms 103:7 – *"He made known his ways unto Moses, his acts unto the children of Israel."*
         c. John 17:3 – *"And this is life eternal, that they might know thee the only true God, and Jesus Christ, whom thou hast sent."*
         d. Hebrews 3:10 – *"Wherefore I was grieved with that generation, and said, They do alway err in their heart; and they have not known my ways."*
         e. II Peter 3:18 – *"But grow in grace, and in the knowledge of our Lord and Saviour Jesus Christ. To him be glory both now and for ever. Amen."*
         f. I John 5:20 – *"And we know that the Son of God is come, and hath given us an understanding, that we may know him that is true, and we are in him that is true, even in his Son Jesus Christ. This is the true God, and eternal life."*

   B. Sadly this is not the case for many of God's people

      1. Isaiah 1:2-3 – *"Hear, O heavens, and give ear, O earth: for the LORD hath spoken, I have nourished and brought up children, and they have rebelled against me. ³The ox knoweth his owner, and the ass his master's crib: but Israel doth not know, my people doth not consider."*
      2. Jeremiah 2:8, 31-32 – *"⁸The priests said not, Where is the LORD? and they that handle the law knew me not: the pastors also transgressed against me, and the prophets prophesied by Baal, and walked after things that do not profit...³¹O generation, see ye the word of the LORD. Have I been a wilderness unto Israel? a land of darkness? wherefore say my people, We are lords; we will come no more unto thee? ³²Can a maid forget her ornaments, or a bride her attire? yet my people have forgotten me days without number..."*
      3. Song of Solomon 5:1-9

4. Matthew 7:21-23 – *"Not every one that saith unto me, Lord, Lord, shall enter into the kingdom of heaven; but he that doeth the will of my Father which is in heaven. ²²Many will say to me in that day, Lord, Lord, have we not prophesied in thy name? and in thy name have cast out devils? and in thy name done many wonderful works? ²³And then will I profess unto them, I never knew you: depart from me, ye that work iniquity."*

Somehow we begin well but end up bad. We start out desiring the Lord only, but then get swallowed up in desiring everything and anything but Him. We become religious.

C. You can be surrounded by the things of God and yet still not know Him

1. I Samuel 3:7 *"Now Samuel did not yet know the LORD, neither was the word of the LORD yet revealed unto him."*
2. Ezekiel 44:9-17
3. John 21:4 – *"But when the morning was now come, Jesus stood on the shore: but the disciples knew not that it was Jesus."*
4. John 5:39 – *"Search the scriptures; for in them ye think ye have eternal life: and they are they which testify of me."*

Consider the Pharisees who knew so much; they knew the Scriptures; they knew the law; they had their religious artifacts; but they didn't have or know Jesus.

D. Some want a place, not Him

1. Genesis 32:26 – *"And he said, Let me go, for the day breaketh. And he said, I will not let thee go, except thou bless me."*
2. Matthew 19:27 – *"Then answered Peter and said unto him, Behold, we have forsaken all, and followed thee; what shall we have therefore?"* Many ask like the disciples here, "what am I going to get?" or "What will I become?" We should simply want Him!
3. Matthew 20:20-24

E. Just wanting Him

1. Psalms 42:1-3 – *"¹As the hart panteth after the water brooks, so panteth my soul after thee, O God. ²My soul thirsteth for God, for the living God: when shall I come and appear before God? ³My tears have been my meat day and night, while they continually say unto me, Where is thy God?"*
2. John 12:1-8

III. Aspects of Knowing Him

A. A day is coming when all will know Him

1. Hebrews 8:10-13
2. Jeremiah 31:31-34

B. Levels of knowing

1. Knowing Him as a child

a. I John 2:13 – *"I write unto you, fathers, because ye have known him that is from the beginning. I write unto you, young men, because ye have overcome the wicked one. I write unto you, little children, because ye have known the Father."*

    b.   I Corinthians 13:11 – *"When I was a child, I spake as a child, I understood as a child, I thought as a child: but when I became a man, I put away childish things."*

    c.   Proverbs 22:15 – *"Foolishness is bound in the heart of a child; but the rod of correction shall drive it far from him."*

    d.   Ecclesiastes 11:10 – *"Therefore remove sorrow from thy heart, and put away evil from thy flesh: for childhood and youth are vanity."*

    e.   Ephesians 4:14 – *"That we henceforth be no more children, tossed to and fro, and carried about with every wind of doctrine, by the sleight of men, and cunning craftiness, whereby they lie in wait to deceive;"*

    f.   I John 2:1, 12 – *"My little children, these things write I unto you, that ye sin not. And if any man sin, we have an advocate with the Father, Jesus Christ the righteous...12I write unto you, little children, because your sins are forgiven you for his name's sake."*

    g.   I John 3:7 – *"Little children, let no man deceive you: he that doeth righteousness is righteous, even as he is righteous."*

2.   Knowing Him as a father

    a.   I John 2:13 – *"I write unto you, fathers, because ye have known him that is from the beginning. I write unto you, young men, because ye have overcome the wicked one. I write unto you, little children, because ye have known the Father."*

    b.   Hebrews 5:13-14 – *"13For every one that useth milk is unskilful in the word of righteousness: for he is a babe. 14But strong meat belongeth to them that are of full age, even those who by reason of use have their senses exercised to discern both good and evil."*

    c.   I Corinthians 3:1-3 – *"1And I, brethren, could not speak unto you as unto spiritual, but as unto carnal, even as unto babes in Christ. 2I have fed you with milk, and not with meat: for hitherto ye were not able to bear it, neither yet now are ye able. 3For ye are yet carnal: for whereas there is among you envying, and strife, and divisions, are ye not carnal, and walk as men?"*

    d.   I Corinthians 4:15 – *"For though ye have ten thousand instructors in Christ, yet have ye not many fathers: for in Christ Jesus I have begotten you through the gospel."*

    e.   Ephesians 6:4 – *"And, ye fathers, provoke not your children to wrath: but bring them up in the nurture and admonition of the Lord."*

    f.   Job 42:5 – *"I have heard of thee by the hearing of the ear: but now mine eye seeth thee."*

    g.   Romans 11:33 – *"O the depth of the riches both of the wisdom and knowledge of God! how unsearchable are his judgments, and his ways past finding out!"*

3.   Knowing Him as a bride knows her Husband

    a.   Genesis 4:1 – *"And Adam knew Eve his wife; and she conceived, and bare Cain, and said, I have gotten a man from the LORD."*

    b.   Hosea 2:14-20 – *"14Therefore, behold, I will allure her, and bring her into the wilderness, and speak comfortably unto her. 15And I will give her her vineyards from thence, and the valley of Achor for a door of hope: and she shall sing there, as in the days of her youth, and as in the day when she came up out of the land of Egypt. 16And it shall be at that day, saith the LORD, that thou shalt call me Ishi; and shalt call me no more Baali. 17For I will take away the names of Baalim out of her mouth, and they shall no more be remembered by their name. 18And in that day will I make a covenant for them with the beasts of the field, and with the fowls of heaven, and with the creeping things of the ground: and I will break the bow and the sword and the battle out of the earth, and will make them to lie down safely. 19And I will betroth thee unto me for ever; yea, I will betroth thee unto me in righteousness, and in judgment, and in lovingkindness, and in mercies. 20I will even betroth thee unto me in faithfulness: and thou shalt know the LORD."*

     c.   Isaiah 54:5 – *"For thy Maker is thine husband; the LORD of hosts is his name; and thy Redeemer the Holy One of Israel; The God of the whole earth shall he be called."*

     d.   Ephesians 5:22-32

     e.   Isaiah 62:5 – *"For as a young man marrieth a virgin, so shall thy sons marry thee: and as the bridegroom rejoiceth over the bride, so shall thy God rejoice over thee."*

C.   Out of this knowing will come great things

1. Daniel 11:32 – *"...but the people that do know their God shall be strong, and do exploits."*

2. II Timothy 1:12 – *"For the which cause I also suffer these things: nevertheless I am not ashamed: for I know whom I have believed, and am persuaded that he is able to keep that which I have committed unto him against that day."*

3. I Chronicles 28:9 – *"And thou, Solomon my son, know thou the God of thy father, and serve him with a perfect heart and with a willing mind: for the LORD searcheth all hearts, and understandeth all the imaginations of the thoughts: if thou seek him, he will be found of thee; but if thou forsake him, he will cast thee off for ever."*

4. Philippians 3:10-11 – *"[10]That I may know him, and the power of his resurrection, and the fellowship of his sufferings, being made conformable unto his death; [11]If by any means I might attain unto the resurrection of the dead."*

5. Exodus 33:13-14 – *"[13]Now therefore, I pray thee, if I have found grace in thy sight, shew me now thy way, that I may know thee, that I may find grace in thy sight: and consider that this nation is thy people. [14]And he said, My presence shall go with thee, and I will give thee rest."*

Lesson 19
LOVING ONE ANOTHER

I.   God Sets the Standard

A.   He loves not only us but the whole world

1.   Greek definitions of love

a.   *Phileo* – To be a friend of, fond of, to have affection for
b.   *Agape* – Affection or benevolence, a love feast.

B.   Scriptures declaring His love

1.   John 3:16 – "*...For God so loved the world he gave us...*"
2.   Titus 3:4 – "*...love of God our Saviour toward man...*"
3.   John 13:1 – "*...having loved his own which were in the world, he loved them unto the end...*"
4.   John 13:34-35 – "*A new commandment I give unto you, that ye love one another as I have loved you, that ye also love one another by this shall all men know that ye are my disciples, if ye have love one to another...*"
5.   Ephesians 5:25 – "*...as Christ loved the church and gave himself for it...*"

C.   We are all His offspring

1.   Revelation 5:9 – "*...redeemed us to God by the blood of every kindred and tongue, people and nation.*"
2.   Romans 12:4-5 – "*...many members in one body...so we being many are one body in Christ and everyone members of another...*"
3.   1 John 4:7-21
4.   I John 3:11-18
5.   Ephesians 3:17-19 (all saints)
6.   Ephesians 2:13-22 (His household)
7.   Song of Solomon 4:7 – "*...thou art all fair my love, there is no spot in thee...*"
8.   Psalms 22:27-28
9.   Psalms 57:9
10. Psalms 66:7
11. Psalms 72:11-17
12. Psalms 82:8
13. Psalms 86:9
14. Psalms 117:1
15. Isaiah 2:2-9
16. Zechariah 2:8-11
17. Matthew 28:19
18. Mark 13:10
19. Acts 2:38-39
20. Isaiah 52:10
21. Isaiah 66:18-19
22. Micah 4:1-4

II.   We Are To Forget Our Own Heritages and Now Love Our Brothers

A.   Scriptures

1. Matthew 10:34-37 – "...*He that loveth Father or mother more than me...*"
2. Psalms 45:10 – "...*hearken O daughter and consider and incline thine ear: forget also thine own people and thy father's house...*"

III. He Commands Us to Love One Another

A. Scriptures

1. Leviticus 19:18 – "...*thou shalt love thy neighbour as thyself...*"
2. Leviticus 19:33-34 – "...*And if a stranger sojourn with thee in your land, ye shall not vex him. But the stranger that dwelleth with you shall be unto you as one born among you, and thou shalt love him as thyself; for ye were strangers in the land of Egypt: I am the LORD your God.*"
3. Micah 6:8 – "...*He hath shewed thee, O man, what is good; and what doth the LORD require of thee, but to do justly, and to love mercy, and to walk humbly with thy God?*"
4. John 13:34-35 – "...*That ye love one another; as I have loved you, that ye also love one another. By this shall all men know that ye are my disciples, if ye have love one to another...*"
5. John 15:12-13 – "*This is my commandment, That ye love one another, as I have loved you. Greater love hath no man than this, that a man lay down his life for his friends.*"
6. Acts 9:10-17
7. Acts 10:28 – "...*but God hath shewed me that I should not call any man common or unclean.*"
8. Acts 11:1-18 – contention because of the circumcision
9. Romans 5:5 – "...*because the love of God is shed abroad in our hearts by the Holy Ghost which is given unto us.*"
10. Romans 12:3-5 – "...*so we, being many, are one body in Christ, and every one members one of another.*"
11. Romans 12:9-10 – "*Let love be without dissimulation (without hyprocracy, sincere, genuine)... be kindly affectioned one to another with brotherly love; in honour preferring one another;*"
12. Proverbs 17:17 – "...*A friend loveth at all times, and a brother is born for adversity.*"
13. Romans 13:10 – "*Love worketh no ill to his neighbour: therefore love is the fulfilling of the law.*"
14. Luke 6:27-36
15. Galatians 5:13-14 – "...*but by love serve one another. For all the law is fulfilled in one word, even in this; Thou shalt love thy neighbour as thyself.*"
16. Philippians 1:9 – "*And this I pray, that your love may abound yet more and more in knowledge and in all judgment;*"
17. Colossians 1:4 – "*Since we heard of your faith in Christ Jesus, and of the love which ye have to all the saints,*"
18. Colossians 2:2 – "...*being knit together in love, and unto all riches of the full assurance of understanding...*"
19. I Thessalonians 3:12 – "*And the Lord make you to increase and abound in love one toward another, and toward all men, even as we do toward you:*"
20. I Thessalonians 4:9 – "*But as touching brotherly love ye need not that I write unto you: for ye yourselves are taught of God to love one another.*"
21. Hebrews 13:1-3 – "*Let brotherly love continue. Be not forgetful to entertain strangers: for thereby some have entertained angels unawares. Remember them that are in bonds, as bound with them; and them which suffer adversity, as being yourselves also in the body.*"
22. I Peter 1:22 – "*Seeing ye have purified your souls in obeying the truth through the Spirit unto unfeigned love of the brethren, see that ye love one another with a pure heart fervently:*"
23. I Peter 2:17 – "*Honour all men. Love the brotherhood. Fear God. Honour the king.*"
24. I Peter 3:8 – "*Finally, be ye all of one mind, having compassion one of another, love as brethren, be pitiful, be courteous:*"

25. I John 2:9-10 – "*He that saith he is in the light, and hateth his brother, is in darkness even until now. He that loveth his brother abideth in the light, and there is none occasion of stumbling in him.*"
26. I John 3:11-18
27. I Timothy 4:12 – "*...but be thou an example of the believers, in word, in conversation, in charity, in spirit, in faith, in purity.*"

B. Concerns of the last days

1. II Timothy 3:1-14
2. I Timothy 4:1-11

Lesson 20
Our Salvation Is Eternal

I.   The Scriptures Speak For Themselves

Whenever the Bible states unequivocally that something is so, and it does it over and over again – when there are many clear and obvious statements that something is so, we do not throw hundreds of obvious, easily understood passages away because of a few that *seem* to speak contrarily. We should always go where the weight of evidence lies. We then must wait for the Holy Spirit to give light on the misunderstood passages. We may find that these can easily be understood, in the context of the passage, in the meaning of the Greek or Hebrew words, or by comparing Scripture with other Scripture. Also, where the Bible is silent, we should not try to make it say something it doesn't. God has made sure that if we seek His Word and are willing, we will know of the doctrine, whether it is of God or not (John 7:17). Also, He has made it quite plain that out of the mouth of two or three witnesses let everything be established (II Corinthians 13:1).

A.   Scriptures that declare our salvation is forever.

   1.   Hebrews 13:5 – "*...I will never leave thee or forsake thee...*"

      a.   Deuteronomy 4:31 – "*(For the LORD thy God is a merciful God;) he will not forsake thee, neither destroy thee, nor forget the covenant of thy fathers which he sware unto them.*"
      b.   Deuteronomy 31:6, 8
      c.   Joshua 1:5 – "*There shall not any man be able to stand before thee all the days of thy life: as I was with Moses, so I will be with thee: I will not fail thee, nor forsake thee.*"
      d.   1 Samuel 12:22 – "*For the LORD will not forsake his people for his great name's sake: because it hath pleased the LORD to make you his people.*"
      e.   Isaiah 42:16 – "*And I will bring the blind by a way that they knew not; I will lead them in paths that they have not known: I will make darkness light before them, and crooked things straight. These things will I do unto them, and not forsake them.*"
      f.   Isaiah 62:4, 12

   2.   Psalms 89:24-37 – "*...My covenant will I not break...*"

      a.   Isaiah 54:10
      b.   Psalms 105:8-10
      c.   Psalms 111:5-9
      d.   II Samuel 23:5

   3.   John 10:27-31 – "*...No man is able to pluck them out of mine hand.*"
   4.   Psalms 77:5-13
   5.   Isaiah 49:13-16

   6.   Ecclesiastes 3:14 – "*I know that, whatsoever God doeth, it shall be for ever...*"

      a.   Isaiah 32:17
      b.   Isaiah 51:6-8
      c.   Hosea 2:19
      d.   Hebrews 10:12, 14
      e.   Hebrews 12:28
      f.   Psalms 37:23-28
      g.   I Peter 1:3-5, 23

7. Hebrews 5:9 – Jesus, the Author of Eternal Salvation

   a. John 10:28 – Amplified Translation – *"And I give them eternal life and they shall never lose it, or perish throughout the ages, to all eternity they shall never by any means be destroyed. And no one is able to snatch them out my hand."*
   b. Romans 6:23 – the gift of God is eternal life.
   c. Hebrews 9:11-15 – Jesus obtained eternal redemption for us.
   d. John 5:24

8. Romans 17:29—God doesn't change His mind.

   a. Malachi 3:6
   b. James 1:17
   c. Numbers 23:19
   d. Luke 14:28-33

9. Psalms 138:8 – He finishes what He starts.

   a. Philippians 1:6
   b. Genesis 28:15
   c. Isaiah 46:4
   d. Zechariah 4:9
   e. Isaiah 66:9

10. I Kings 8:56 – His promise never fails.

    a. Psalms 77:7-14
    b. Joshua 21:45
    c. Matthew 24:35
    d. Psalms 105:42
    e. II Corinthians 1:20
    f. Hebrews 10:23
    g. Romans 4:21
    h. Jeremiah 33:14

Lesson 21
OUR TRUE INHERITANCE

I.   Hebrews 6:12 – *"That ye be not slothful, but followers of them who through faith and patience inherit the promises."*

We have been called of God to obtain an inheritance. This does not mean heaven. Heaven was secured for us through the cross of Jesus. The inheritance we speak of is our reward for going on with God and being faithful to His call.

A.   Word definitions of "inherit"

1.   Hebrew

a.   *Yarash* – to occupy by driving out the previous tenants and possessing in their place, to take possession
b.   *Nachal* – to inherit, to occupy, an estate, a portion

2.   Greek, *Kleronomeo* – to be an heir to; from a root, *kleronomos* – a sharer by lot, inheritor, a possessor; from a root, *kleros* – a portion, heritage, inheritance

II.   What Our Inheritance Consists Of

A.   The Lord Himself

1.   Psalms 16:5 – *"The LORD is the portion of mine inheritance..."*
2.   Deuteronomy 10:8-9 – *"At that time the LORD separated the tribe of Levi, to bear the ark of the covenant of the LORD, to stand before the LORD to minister unto him, and to bless in his name, unto this day. Wherefore Levi hath no part nor inheritance with his brethren; the LORD is his inheritance, according as the LORD thy God promised him."*

a.   Deuteronomy 18:1-2 – *"The priests the Levites, and all the tribe of Levi, shall have no part nor inheritance with Israel: they shall eat the offerings of the LORD made by fire, and his inheritance. Therefore shall they have no inheritance among their brethren: the LORD is their inheritance, as he hath said unto them."*
b.   Numbers 18:20 – *"And the LORD spake unto Aaron, Thou shalt have no inheritance in their land, neither shalt thou have any part among them: I am thy part and thine inheritance..."*
c.   Ezekiel 44:28 – *"And it shall be unto them for an inheritance: I am their inheritance: and ye shall give them no possession in Israel: I am their possession."*
d.   Joshua 13:33 – *"But unto the tribe of Levi Moses gave not any inheritance: the LORD God of Israel was their inheritance, as he said unto them."*

B.   Other definitions of our inheritance given to God's holy remnant, His overcomers, His chosen, His elect.

1.   Revelation 21:7 – *"He that overcometh shall inherit all things; and I will be his God, and he shall be my son."*
2.   Proverbs 8:21 – *"That I may cause those that love me to inherit substance; and I will fill their treasures."*
3.   Proverbs 3:35 – *"The wise shall inherit glory..."*
4.   Isaiah 65:9 – *"And I will bring forth a seed out of Jacob, and out of Judah an inheritor of my mountains: and mine elect shall inherit it, and my servants shall dwell there."*

5. Matthew 25:31-34 – "*...And before him shall be gathered all nations: and he shall separate them one from another, as a shepherd divideth his sheep from the goats: And <u>he shall set the sheep on his right hand</u>, but the goats on the left. Then shall the King say unto them on his right hand, Come, ye blessed of my Father, inherit the kingdom prepared for you from the foundation of the world:*"

C. Facts about this inheritance

1. Ephesians 1:11-14, 19
2. Colossians 1:12 – "*Giving thanks unto the Father, which hath made us meet to be partakers of the inheritance of the saints in light:*"
3. I Peter 1:4 – "*To an inheritance incorruptible, and undefiled, and that fadeth not away, reserved in heaven for you*"
4. Psalms 47:3-4 – "*He shall subdue the people under us, and the nations under our feet. He shall choose our inheritance for us, the excellency of Jacob whom he loved. Selah.*"
5. Psalms 2:8 – "*Ask of me, and I shall give thee the heathen for thine inheritance, and the uttermost parts of the earth for thy possession.*"

III. Those that despise their inheritance in God

A. Scriptural examples

1. Hebrews 12:15-22

   a. Esau sold his birthright
   b. He was supposed to inherit the firstborn blessing, but was rejected (Genesis 25:34 – Esau despised his birthright)

2. Luke 15:12-13 – "*And the younger of them said to his father, Father, give me the portion of goods that falleth to me. And he divided unto them his living. And not many days after the younger son gathered all together, and took his journey into a far country, and there wasted his substance with riotous living.*"

   a. Proverbs 12:27 – "*The slothful man roasteth not that which he took in hunting: but the substance of a diligent man is precious.*"
   b. Proverbs 8:21 – "*That I may cause those that love me to inherit substance; and I will fill their treasures.*"

3. Matthew 19:27 – "*Then answered Peter and said unto him, Behold, we have forsaken all, and followed thee; what shall we have therefore?*" – Everyone wants to know what I am going to get out of following Jesus. The answer simply is Jesus. Is He enough for you? Or do you need more than just Him? Let's be satisfied with Him.

   a. Satisfied with Jesus

      1) Philippians 3:7-15
      2) Psalms 27:4

Never forget the admonition in Deuteronomy 32:9, "*For the LORD's portion is his people...*"

Lesson 22
PEACE: THE INWARD WITNESS

I. Peace: The Inward Witness of the Holy Ghost

   A. Moving in peace

      1. I John 5:10 – *"He that believeth on the Son of God hath the witness in himself..."*
      2. Luke 1:40-45
      3. I John 2:20, 27 – *"...ye have an unction from the Holy One, and ye know all things..."*
      4. John 14:26-28 – *"Peace I leave with you, my peace I give unto you..."*
      5. James 3:16-17 – *"...wisdom that is from above is first pure, then peaceable..."*
      6. Romans 8:6 – *"...to be spiritually minded is life and peace."*
      7. Jeremiah 30:5
      8. Philippians 4:6-8 – *"...And the peace of God...shall keep your hearts and minds..."*
      9. Colossians 3:15 – *"...let the peace of God rule in your hearts..."*
      10. Isaiah 55:12 – *"For ye shall...be led forth with peace..."*
      11. Isaiah 48:17-19
      12. Isaiah 30:15
      13. II Corinthians 2:13
      14. Acts 11:12
      15. Luke 1:79

   B. Keeping our peace

      1. I Thessalonians 5:13 – *"...And be at peace among yourselves."*
      2. Isaiah 26:3 – *"Thou wilt keep him in perfect peace, whose mind is stayed on thee: because he trusteth in thee."*
      3. Psalms 119:165 – *"Great peace have they which love thy law..."*
      4. 1 Timothy 2:2 – *"For kings, and for all that are in authority; that we may lead a quiet and peaceable life in all godliness and honesty."*
      5. Isaiah 48:22 – *"There is no peace, saith the LORD, unto the wicked."*
      6. Galatians 5:22 – *"But the fruit of the Spirit is love, joy, peace..."*

   C. What is peace?

      1. Isaiah 53:5 – *"...the chastisement of our peace was upon him..."*
      2. Romans 5:1 – *"...we have peace with God through our Lord Jesus Christ:"*
      3. Jeremiah 6:16 – *"Thus saith the LORD, Stand ye in the ways, and see, and ask for the old paths, where is the good way, and walk therein, and ye shall find rest for your souls. But they said, We will not walk therein."*
      4. Isaiah 32:17 – *"And the work of righteousness shall be peace..."*
      5. Romans 14:17 – *"For the kingdom of God is not meat and drink; but righteousness, and peace, and joy in the Holy Ghost."*
      6. Galatians 5:22 – *"But the fruit of the Spirit is love, joy, peace, longsuffering, gentleness, goodness, faith,"*
      7. Luke 1:79 – *"...to guide our feet into the way of peace."*

Lesson 23
POWER IN THE NAME OF JESUS

This will be a simple yet powerful study on the name of Jesus. In this lesson, we will see the importance of His great name. This will certainly not be exhaustive, for that would take many lessons, but we will confine ourselves to just the basic truths revealed in Scripture concerning the name of Jesus. The hope is that all of us see the great power and authority that His name will bring to our lives, and that we would begin to walk in it and use it for the glory of God!

I. Distinctive Names Given To Jesus and Their Definitions:

    A. **Jesus** – Jehovah is salvation, Jehovah my salvation (Matthew 1:21)

    B. **Emmanuel** – God with us (Matthew 1:23, Isaiah 7:14)

    C. **Christ** – Anointed One (Luke 2:11, Matthew 16:16)

    D. **Saviour** – Deliverer, preserver, controller; it comes from a root word that means – heal, save, deliver, make whole (Acts 5:31, John 4:42)

    E. **Lord** – Supreme authority (Luke 24:3, Acts 2:36, Revelation 11:61, Matthew 23:9, John 13:14)

    F. **Master** – Instructor, teacher; from a root word that means – to cause to learn (Matthew 26:18, Luke 6:40)

    G. **Alpha and Omega** – The beginning and the end (Revelation 1:8, 21:6, 22:13)

    H. **I Am** – I will be that I will be, I am because I am, I will become whosoever I please (Exodus 3:14, John 8:58)

    I. **King** – Foundation of power, a sovereign (Matthew 21:5, John 18:39, I Timothy 3:15)

    J. **Messiah** – The Anointed (Daniel 9:25-26, John 1:41)

    K. **The Word** – The expression of though or of something said (John 1:1, 14)

    L. **God** – Deity, Supreme Divinity (Luke 4:41, John 10:36)

II. Powerful Truths Concerning The Name Of Jesus

    A. His name is excellent, far above every name

        1. Psalms 8:1, 9 – *"¹O LORD our Lord, how excellent is thy name in all the earth! who hast set thy glory above the heavens..."*

        2. Hebrews 1:1-4 – *"¹God, who at sundry times and in divers manners spake in time past unto the fathers by the prophets, ²Hath in these last days spoken unto us by his Son, whom he hath appointed heir of all things, by whom also he made the worlds; ³Who being the brightness of his glory, and the express image of his person, and upholding all things by the word of his power, when he had by himself purged our sins, sat down on the right hand of the Majesty on high; ⁴Being made so much better than the angels, as he hath by inheritance obtained a more excellent name than they."*

        3. Philippians 2:9-11 – *"⁹Wherefore God also hath highly exalted him, and given him a name which is above every name: ¹⁰That at the name of Jesus every knee should bow, of things in heaven, and things in earth, and things under the earth; ¹¹And that every tongue should confess that Jesus Christ is Lord, to the glory of God the Father."*

        4. Ephesians 1:20-21 – *"²⁰Which he wrought in Christ, when he raised him from the dead, and set him at his own right hand in the heavenly places, ²¹Far above all principality, and power, and might, and dominion, and every name that is named, not only in this world, but also in that which is to come:"*

        5. Acts 4:12, 17-18 – *"¹²Neither is there salvation in any other: for there is none other name under heaven given among men, whereby we must be saved..."*

        6. Colossians 3:17 – *"And whatsoever ye do in word or deed, do all in the name of the Lord Jesus, giving thanks to God and the Father by him."*

7. Acts 10:43 – *"To him give all the prophets witness, that through his name whosoever believeth in him shall receive remission of sins."*

B. His name has been given to us; it is all we have, but it is more than enough

1. Acts 3:3-6, 16 – *"³Who seeing Peter and John about to go into the temple asked an alms. ⁴And Peter, fastening his eyes upon him with John, said, Look on us. ⁵And he gave heed unto them, expecting to receive something of them. ⁶Then Peter said, Silver and gold have I none; but such as I have give I thee: In the name of Jesus Christ of Nazareth rise up and walk...¹⁶And his name through faith in his name hath made this man strong, whom ye see and know: yea, the faith which is by him hath given him this perfect soundness in the presence of you all."*
2. Matthew 1:21-23 – *"²¹And she shall bring forth a son, and thou shalt call his name JESUS: for he shall save his people from their sins. ²²Now all this was done, that it might be fulfilled which was spoken of the Lord by the prophet, saying, ²³Behold, a virgin shall be with child, and shall bring forth a son, and they shall call his name Emmanuel, which being interpreted is, God with us."*
3. I Corinthians 6:11 – *"And such were some of you: but ye are washed, but ye are sanctified, but ye are justified in the name of the Lord Jesus, and by the Spirit of our God."*

C. Prayers answered in the name of Jesus

1. John 16:23-24 – *"²³And in that day ye shall ask me nothing. Verily, verily, I say unto you, Whatsoever ye shall ask the Father in my name, he will give it you. ²⁴Hitherto have ye asked nothing in my name: ask, and ye shall receive, that your joy may be full."*
2. John 14:13-14 – *"¹³And whatsoever ye shall ask in my name, that will I do, that the Father may be glorified in the Son. ¹⁴If ye shall ask any thing in my name, I will do it."*
3. Matthew 18:19-20 – *"¹⁹Again I say unto you, That if two of you shall agree on earth as touching any thing that they shall ask, it shall be done for them of my Father which is in heaven. ²⁰For where two or three are gathered together in my name, there am I in the midst of them."*
4. John 15:16 – *"Ye have not chosen me, but I have chosen you, and ordained you, that ye should go and bring forth fruit, and that your fruit should remain: that whatsoever ye shall ask of the Father in my name, he may give it you."*

D. Authority over the devil in His name

1. I John 3:23 – *"And this is his commandment, That we should believe on the name of his Son Jesus Christ, and love one another, as he gave us commandment."*
2. Acts 16:16-18 – *"¹⁶And it came to pass, as we went to prayer, a certain damsel possessed with a spirit of divination met us, which brought her masters much gain by soothsaying: ¹⁷The same followed Paul and us, and cried, saying, These men are the servants of the most high God, which shew unto us the way of salvation. ¹⁸And this did she many days. But Paul, being grieved, turned and said to the spirit, I command thee in the name of Jesus Christ to come out of her. And he came out the same hour."*
3. Mark 16:16-17 – *"¹⁶He that believeth and is baptized shall be saved; but he that believeth not shall be damned. ¹⁷And these signs shall follow them that believe; In my name shall they cast out devils; they shall speak with new tongues;"*
4. Luke 10:17 – *"And the seventy returned again with joy, saying, Lord, even the devils are subject unto us through thy name."*

E. Faith in His name

1. I John 3:23 – *"And this is his commandment, That we should believe on the name of his Son Jesus Christ, and love one another, as he gave us commandment."*

2. Acts 3:16 – *"And his name through faith in his name hath made this man strong, whom ye see and know: yea, the faith which is by him hath given him this perfect soundness in the presence of you all."*

F. Our worship affected by the name

1. Hebrews 13:15 – *"By him therefore let us offer the sacrifice of praise to God continually, that is, the fruit of our lips giving thanks to his name."*
2. Ephesians 5:20 – *"Giving thanks always for all things unto God and the Father in the name of our Lord Jesus Christ;"*
3. Malachi 1:11 – *"For from the rising of the sun even unto the going down of the same my name shall be great among the Gentiles; and in every place incense shall be offered unto my name, and a pure offering: for my name shall be great among the heathen, saith the LORD of hosts."*
4. Matthew 6:9 – *"After this manner therefore pray ye: Our Father which art in heaven, Hallowed be thy name."*
5. Psalms 48:10 – *"According to thy name, O God, so is thy praise unto the ends of the earth: thy right hand is full of righteousness."*
6. Psalms 149:3 – *"Let them praise his name in the dance: let them sing praises unto him with the timbrel and harp."*
7. Psalms 69:30 – *"I will praise the name of God with a song, and will magnify him with thanksgiving."*
8. Psalms 99:3 – *"Let them praise thy great and terrible name; for it is holy."*
9. Psalms 103:1 – *"Bless the LORD, O my soul: and all that is within me, bless his holy name."*

G. The name used in baptism, Acts 2:38 – *"Then Peter said unto them, Repent, and be baptized every one of you in the name of Jesus Christ for the remission of sins, and ye shall receive the gift of the Holy Ghost."*

H. Our preaching of the great commission done in His name

1. Matthew 28:18-20 – *"[18]And Jesus came and spake unto them, saying, All power is given unto me in heaven and in earth. [19]Go ye therefore, and teach all nations, baptizing them in the name of the Father, and of the Son, and of the Holy Ghost: [20]Teaching them to observe all things whatsoever I have commanded you: and, lo, I am with you alway, even unto the end of the world. Amen."*
2. Mark 16:17 – *"And these signs shall follow them that believe; In my name shall they cast out devils; they shall speak with new tongues;"*
3. Luke 24:47 – *"And that repentance and remission of sins should be preached in his name among all nations, beginning at Jerusalem."*

I. We are to gather in His name, Matthew 18:20 – *"For where two or three are gathered together in my name, there am I in the midst of them."*

J. We will be hated for His name's sake

1. Matthew 10:22 – *"And ye shall be hated of all men for my name's sake: but he that endureth to the end shall be saved."*
2. John 15:20-21 – *"[20]Remember the word that I said unto you, The servant is not greater than his lord. If they have persecuted me, they will also persecute you; if they have kept my saying, they will keep yours also. [21]But all these things will they do unto you for my name's sake, because they know not him that sent me."*
3. Acts 15:26 – *"Men that have hazarded their lives for the name of our Lord Jesus Christ."*

4. I Peter 4:14 – *"If ye be reproached for the name of Christ, happy are ye; for the spirit of glory and of God resteth upon you: on their part he is evil spoken of, but on your part he is glorified."*
5. Matthew 24:9 – *"Then shall they deliver you up to be afflicted, and shall kill you: and ye shall be hated of all nations for my name's sake."*

K. We are to have His name in our minds

1. Revelation 14:1 – *"And I looked, and, lo, a Lamb stood on the mount Sion, and with him an hundred forty and four thousand, having his Father's name written in their foreheads."*
2. Revelation 22:4 – *"And they shall see his face; and his name shall be in their foreheads."*

L. We are to walk in the name of Jesus our God

1. Micah 4:5 – *"For all people will walk every one in the name of his god, and we will walk in the name of the LORD our God for ever and ever."*
2. Colossians 3:17 – *"And whatsoever ye do in word or deed, do all in the name of the Lord Jesus, giving thanks to God and the Father by him."*
3. Zechariah 10:12 – *"And I will strengthen them in the LORD; and they shall walk up and down in his name, saith the LORD."*
4. Malachi 3:16 – *"Then they that feared the LORD spake often one to another: and the LORD hearkened, and heard it, and a book of remembrance was written before him for them that feared the LORD, and that thought upon his name."*

M. Suffering for His name

1. Acts 5:41 – *"And they departed from the presence of the council, rejoicing that they were counted worthy to suffer shame for his name."*
2. Acts 9:16 – *"For I will shew him how great things he must suffer for my name's sake."*

N. His name is as ointment, Song of Solomon 1:13 – *"A bundle of myrrh is my wellbeloved unto me; he shall lie all night betwixt my breasts."*

O. Our help is in His name, Psalms 124:8 – *"Our help is in the name of the LORD, who made heaven and earth."*

Lesson 24
THE PRINCIPLE OF PATIENCE

If there is one characteristic or virtue in life most of us lack, it is patience. So as we search the Scriptures concerning the "principle of patience", we will let the Word of God define it for us. Patience is not a gift. It is something that must be learned through discipline and trials, but what it produces is something rather remarkable. Our God is a God of patience, and we want to be like Him, so let's see how we can be an "imitator of Him" and learn the beauty and joy of patience.

I.   Defining The Word Patience

A.   Dictionary

1.   Bearing pains or trials calmly or without complaint, being kindly and tolerant, not hasty or impetuous, steadfast despite opposing difficulty or adversity. The capacity or <u>habit</u> of being patient. Calmly tolerating delay, diligent preserving, calm endurance.

B.   Hebrew

1.   *Arek* – Longsuffering, slow to anger. From a root – To draw out, to lengthen, to make long.
2.   *Qavah* – To bind together by twisting, to look patiently, to tarry, to wait.

C.   Greek

1.   *Makrothumeo* – To be long spirited, forbearing, to be longsuffering, patiently endure, fortitude, lenient, long enduring.
2.   *Hupomeno* – To stay under, to remain, to have fortitude, to persevere, to bear trials, to abide or endure.
3.   *Hupmone* – Cheerful, endurance, constancy, patient continuance.
4.   *Epieikes* – Mild, gentle, moderation.

D.   These same Hebrew and Greek words translated differently in the KJV Bible

1.   Hebrew – *Longsuffering, slow to anger, wait*
2.   Greek – *Suffer, suffereth, endure, endured, gentle, moderation*

II.   Our God Is A Patient God

A.   The Father

1.   Exodus 34:5-6 – *"And the LORD descended in the cloud, and stood with him there, and proclaimed the name of the LORD. And the LORD passed by before him, and proclaimed, The LORD, The LORD God, merciful and gracious, <u>longsuffering</u>, and abundant in goodness and truth."*
2.   Numbers 14:18 – *"The LORD is <u>longsuffering</u>, and of great mercy, forgiving iniquity and transgression, and by no means clearing the guilty, visiting the iniquity of the fathers upon the children unto the third and fourth generation."*
3.   Psalms 86:15 – *"But thou, O Lord, art a God full of compassion, and gracious, <u>longsuffering</u>, and plenteous in mercy and truth."*
4.   Psalms 103:8 – *"The LORD is merciful and gracious, <u>slow</u> to anger, and plenteous in mercy."*
5.   Joel 2:13 – *"And rend your heart, and not your garments, and turn unto the LORD your God: for he is gracious and merciful, <u>slow</u> to anger, and of great kindness, and repenteth him of the evil."*

6. Nahum 1:3 – "*The LORD is <u>slow</u> to anger, and great in power, and will not at all acquit the wicked...*"

7. Romans 15:5 – "*Now the God of <u>patience</u> and consolation grant you to be likeminded one toward another according to Christ Jesus*"

8. James 3:17 – "*But the wisdom that is from above is first pure, then peaceable, <u>gentle</u>, and easy to be intreated, full of mercy and good fruits, without partiality, and without hypocrisy.*"

9. Romans 2:4 – "*Or despisest thou the riches of his goodness and forbearance and <u>longsuffering</u>; not knowing that the goodness of God leadeth thee to repentance?*"

10. I Peter 3:20 – "*Which sometime were disobedient, when once the <u>longsuffering</u> of God waited in the days of Noah, while the ark was a preparing, wherein few, that is, eight souls were saved by water.*"

11. II Peter 3:9 – "*The Lord is not slack concerning his promise, as some men count slackness; but is <u>longsuffering</u> to us-ward, not willing that any should perish, but that all should come to repentance.*"

B. Jesus

1. James 5:7 – "*...Behold, the husbandman waiteth for the precious fruit of the earth, and hath long <u>patience</u> for it, until he receive the early and latter rain.*"

2. Hebrews 12:2 – "*Looking unto Jesus the author and finisher of our faith; who for the joy that was set before him <u>endured</u> the cross, despising the shame, and is set down at the right hand of the throne of God.*"

3. II Peter 3:15 – "*And account that the <u>longsuffering</u> of our Lord is salvation...*"

4. Matthew 17:17 – "*Then Jesus answered and said, O faithless and perverse generation, how long shall I be with you? how long shall I <u>suffer</u> you?...*"

5. I Timothy 1:16 – "*Howbeit for this cause I obtained mercy, that in me first Jesus Christ might shew forth all <u>longsuffering</u>, for a pattern to them which should hereafter believe on him to life everlasting.*"

III. What The Scriptures Declare About Patience

A. God requires it of His people

1. Colossians 1:11 – "*Strengthened with all might, according to his glorious power, unto all <u>patience</u> and <u>longsuffering</u> with joyfulness;*"

2. I Thessalonians 5:14 – "*...be <u>patient</u> toward all men.*"

3. James 5:8 "*Be ye also <u>patient</u>; stablish your hearts: for the coming of the Lord draweth nigh.*"

4. I Timothy 6:11 – "*But thou, O man of God, flee these things; and follow after righteousness, godliness, faith, love, <u>patience</u>, meekness.*"

5. Hebrews 12:1 – "*Wherefore seeing we also are compassed about with so great a cloud of witnesses, let us lay aside every weight, and the sin which doth so easily beset us, and let us run with <u>patience</u> the race that is set before us,*"

6. II Peter 1:5-7 – "*And beside this, giving all diligence, add to your faith virtue; and to virtue knowledge; And to knowledge temperance; and to temperance <u>patience</u>; and to patience godliness; And to godliness brotherly kindness; and to brotherly kindness charity.*"

7. Philippians 4:5 – "*Let your <u>moderation</u> be known unto all men. The Lord is at hand.*"

8. Galatians 5:22-23 – "*But the fruit of the Spirit is love, joy, peace, <u>longsuffering</u>, gentleness, goodness, faith, Meekness, temperance: against such there is no law.*"

9. Proverbs 16:32 – "*He that is <u>slow</u> to anger is better than the mighty; and he that ruleth his spirit than he that taketh a city.*"

10. James 5:10-11 – "*Take, my brethren, the prophets, who have spoken in the name of the Lord, for an example of suffering affliction, and of <u>patience</u>. Behold, we count them happy which*

endure. Ye have heard of the <u>patience</u> of Job, and have seen the end of the Lord; that the Lord is very pitiful, and of tender mercy."

11. Colossians 3:12 – *"Put on therefore, as the elect of God, holy and beloved, bowels of mercies, kindness, humbleness of mind, meekness, <u>longsuffering</u>;"*

12. Ephesians 4:1-3 – *"I therefore, the prisoner of the Lord, beseech you that ye walk worthy of the vocation wherewith ye are called, With all lowliness and meekness, with <u>longsuffering</u>, forbearing one another in love; Endeavouring to keep the unity of the Spirit in the bond of peace."*

B. God requires of leaders patience

1. I Timothy 3:2-3 – *"A bishop then must be blameless...but patient, not a brawler, not covetous;"*

2. II Timothy 2:24 – *"And the servant of the Lord must not strive; but be gentle unto all men, apt to teach, <u>patient</u>,"*

3. II Corinthians 6:4 – *"But in all things approving ourselves as the ministers of God, in much <u>patience</u>..."*

4. Titus 2:2 – *"That the aged men be sober, grave, temperate, sound in faith, in charity, in <u>patience</u>."*

5. II Corinthians 12:12 – *"Truly the signs of an apostle were wrought among you in all <u>patience</u> (perseverance), in signs, and wonders, and mighty deeds."*

6. II Timothy 4:2 – *"Preach the word; be instant in season, out of season; reprove, rebuke, exhort with all <u>longsuffering</u> and doctrine."*

7. II Timothy 3:10 – *"But thou hast fully known my doctrine, manner of life, purpose, faith, <u>longsuffering</u>, charity, <u>patience</u>,"*

8. James 5:7 – *"Be <u>patient</u> therefore, brethren, unto the coming of the Lord. Behold, the husbandman <u>waiteth</u> for the precious fruit of the earth, and hath long <u>patience</u> for it, until he receive the early and latter rain."*

IV. What Brings The Fruit Of Patience Into Our Lives?

It is said that patience is the quality of forbearance and self control which shows itself particularly in a willingness to wait upon God and His will. Believers are called upon to be patient in their expectations of God's actions, and in their relationships one with another.

A. Tribulation, adversity, persecution, and trials of faith

1. Romans 5:3 – *"...knowing that tribulation worketh <u>patience</u>;"*

2. James 1:3-4 – *"Knowing this, that the trying of your faith worketh (produces) <u>patience</u>. But let <u>patience</u> have her perfect work, that ye may be perfect and entire, wanting nothing."*

3. James 1:12 – *"Blessed is the man that <u>endureth</u> temptation: for when he is tried, he shall receive the crown of life, which the Lord hath promised to them that love him."*

4. James 5:10-11 – *"Take, my brethren, the prophets, who have spoken in the name of the Lord, for an example of suffering affliction, and of <u>patience</u>. Behold, we count them happy which endure. Ye have heard of the patience of Job, and have seen the end of the Lord; that the Lord is very pitiful, and of tender mercy."*

5. II Thessalonians 1:4 – *"...for your <u>patience</u> and faith in all your persecutions and tribulations that ye endure:"*

6. Romans 12:12 – *"Rejoicing in hope; <u>patient</u> in tribulation; continuing instant in prayer;"*

7. Hebrews 12:7 – *"If ye <u>endure</u> chastening, God dealeth with you as with sons; for what son is he whom the father chasteneth not?"*

8. I Peter 2:20 – *"For what glory is it, if, when ye be buffeted for your faults, ye shall take it patiently? but if, when ye do well, and suffer for it, ye take it <u>patiently</u>, this is acceptable with God."*

       9.   Revelation 1:9 – *"I John, who also am your brother, and companion in tribulation, and in the kingdom and <u>patience</u> of Jesus Christ…"*

   B.   Waiting on the Lord

       1.   Isaiah 40:31 – *"But they that <u>wait</u> upon the LORD shall renew their strength; they shall mount up with wings as eagles; they shall run, and not be weary; and they shall walk, and not faint."*

       2.   Lamentations 3:25-26 – *"The LORD is good unto them that <u>wait</u> for him, to the soul that seeketh him. It is good that a man should both hope and quietly wait for the salvation of the LORD."*

       3.   II Thessalonians 3:5 – *"And the Lord direct your hearts into the love of God, and into the <u>patient</u> waiting for Christ."*

       4.   Psalms 37:7 – *"Rest in the LORD, and <u>wait patiently</u> for him…"*

       5.   Psalms 40:1 – *"I <u>waited patiently</u> for the LORD; and he inclined unto me, and heard my cry."*

       6.   I Thessalonians 1:3 – *"Remembering without ceasing your work of faith, and labour of love, and <u>patience</u> of hope in our Lord Jesus Christ…"*

       7.   Romans 8:25 – *"But if we hope for that we see not, then do we with <u>patience</u> wait for it."*

   C.   The Holy Scriptures

       1.   Romans 15:4 – *"For whatsoever things were written aforetime were written for our learning, that we through <u>patience</u> and comfort of the scriptures might have hope."*

       2.   Revelation 14:12 – *"Here is the <u>patience</u> of the saints: here are they that keep the commandments of God, and the faith of Jesus."*

       3.   Psalms 130:5 – *"I <u>wait</u> for the LORD, my soul doth <u>wait</u>, and in his word do I hope."*

   D.   Faith and patience working together

       1.   Hebrews 6:12 – *"That ye be not slothful, but followers of them who through faith and <u>patience</u> inherit the promises."*

       2.   Hebrews 10:36 – *"For ye have need of <u>patience</u>, that, after ye have done the will of God, ye might receive the promise."*

       3.   Revelation 13:10 – *"…Here is the <u>patience</u> and the faith of the saints."*

       4.   Revelation 2:19 – *"I know thy works, and charity, and service, and faith, and thy <u>patience</u>, and thy works; and the last to be more than the first."*

       5.   II Peter 1:5-8 – *"…add to your faith…patience…"*

       6.   II Thessalonians 1:4 – *"So that we ourselves glory in you in the churches of God for your <u>patience</u> and faith in all your persecutions and tribulations that ye endure:"*

V.   What the fruit of patience yields

   A.   Scriptures

       1.   Luke 21:19 – *"In your <u>patience</u> possess ye your souls."*

           a.   Ecclesiastes 7:8
           b.   Proverbs 16:32

       2.   Hebrews 6:15 – *"And so, after he had <u>patiently</u> endured, he obtained the promise."*

           a.   Hebrews 10:36

3. Psalms 27:14 – "*Wait* on the LORD: be of good courage, and he shall strengthen thine heart: *wait*, I say, on the LORD."
4. Revelation 3:10 – "*Because thou hast kept the word of my <u>patience</u>, I also will keep thee from the hour of temptation, which shall come upon all the world…*"
5. James 1:4 – "*But let <u>patience</u> have her perfect work, that ye may be perfect and entire, wanting nothing.*"
6. I Corinthians 13:4 – "*Charity <u>suffereth</u> long…*"
7. II Timothy 2:12 – "*If we <u>suffer</u>, we shall also reign with him…*"
8. James 1:12 – "*Blessed is the man that <u>endureth</u> temptation: for when he is tried, he shall receive the crown of life, which the Lord hath promised…*"
9. Romans 2:7 – "*To them who by <u>patient</u> continuance in well doing seek for glory and honour and immortality, eternal life:*"
10. Luke 8:15 – "*But that on the good ground are they, which in an honest and good heart, having heard the word, keep it, and bring forth fruit with <u>patience</u>.*"
11. Proverbs 14:29 – "*He that is <u>slow</u> to wrath is of great understanding…*"
12. Proverbs 15:18 – "*A wrathful man stirreth up strife: but he that is <u>slow</u> to anger appeaseth strife.*"

Lesson 25
THE PRINCIPLE OF YIELDING

I. As Defined By The Scriptures – Ecclesiastes 10:4 – *"If the spirit of the ruler rise up against thee, leave not thy place; for yielding pacifieth great offences."*

A. Word definitions for yielding

   1. Dictionary definition – to surrender or submit, to give way under pressure, to not be stiff, to bend, flexible.
   2. Hebrew – *marpe* – curative, a medicine, health, remedy, deliverance; from a root word, *raphah* – to mend or physician.
   3. Greek – *paristemi* – to stand beside

B. Other places in Scripture where the above Hebrew word is found (underlined word below). All of these places combined define this principle for us.

   1. Proverbs 14:30 – *"A sound heart is the life of the flesh..."* – To yield is a sound thing to do.
   2. Proverbs 15:4 – *"A wholesome tongue is a tree of life..."* – To yield is the wholesome thing to do.

   3. II Chronicles 36:16 – *"...till there was no remedy."* – Yielding brings a remedy to any situation.

      a. Proverbs 6:15
      b. Proverbs 29:1

   4. Proverbs 4:22 – *"...health to all their flesh."* – To yield is the healthy thing to do.

      a. Proverbs 12:18
      b. Proverbs 13:17
      c. Proverbs 16:24
      d. Jeremiah 8:15
      e. Jeremiah 14:19

   5. Malachi 4:2 – *"...the Sun of righteousness arise with healing in his wings..."* – Isn't this what we are looking for!

C. Other translations of Ecclesiastes 10:4

   "...for submission pacifieth great offenses."
   "...for gentleness allayeth great offenses."
   "...for a reconciliation will mollify great offenses."
   "...great harm by the healing touch may yet be assuaged."
   "...defer to him and you will pacify."

D. Other passages in Scripture which speak of this

   1. Daniel 3:28 – When we yield, we don't serve nor worship the God of self. We can go through the fire by yielding.

      a. Ephesians 4:21-27 – By not yielding we give *"...place to the devil"*

2. II Chronicles 30:7-9 – The opposite of yielding is being stiff-necked. If we yield, we enter into His presence, and then our children find compassion, and the Lord will not turn His face from us.

3. Romans 6:11-17, 19 – We are to "...*yield yourselves unto God...*" as those who are true believers. And in so doing, "...*sin shall not have dominion over you...*" In times past we all have yielded to the flesh rather than to God. Paul encourages us to "...*now yield your members servants to righteousness unto holiness.*"

II. Most of Our Warfare Is Because We Will Not Yield

A. God then must move in and help us.

1. I Samuel 2:3-9 – God will begin to send circumstances our way that will cause us to decide one way or the other.
2. Jeremiah 1:10

B. The whole purpose of this is to bring us to perfection or to grow us up

1. Job 5:17-19
2. Hosea 6:1-3
3. Psalms 66:8-12
4. Psalms 138:8 – God wants to perfect us and in doing so He cannot leave us alone.

C. Satan cries out constantly to God that all we care about is ourselves

1. Job 2:4 – God must somewhere find a group of people who like Job will not consider their own life. This is the way to overcome the devil; love not their own life.

III. Our Answer Is To Simply Yield

A. As we yield, life springs forth. It is a paradox, but it is the truth. Nothing can be that important that it is worth sacrificing the presence and favor of God.

1. John 12:24-25 – "...*Except a corn of wheat fall into the ground and die, it abideth alone: but if it die, it bringeth forth much fruit...*" – As we allow our own earthly opinion and desire to die purposely, it will bring God's fruit into our lives. This is true in:

   a. Ministry – John 3:25-31
   b. Family – Philemon 14-15, Genesis 37:3, 42:36-38 – The very thing we try so hard to preserve, if we would just surrender and let go, we would not only preserve it but gain more in the process.

2. Luke 17:33
3. Job 14:7-9, 14
4. II Corinthians 4:10-12

B. God desires the death of our old nature

1. I John 3:16 – Laying down our life doesn't always mean your physical life; it could and many times does mean your own wants and desires.
2. Psalms 116:15 – "*Precious in the sight of the LORD is the death of his saints.*"
3. Matthew 10:39

       4.   Matthew 6:24-25 – Our problem is self-preservation. We are concerned about the big number one.

       5.   Judges 16:30 – We can do more in our death than in our life

C.   Jesus had to do it – He is our example.

       1.   Philippians 2:5-13
       2.   Hebrews 2:14
       3.   John 10:15-18
       4.   Galatians 5:1-2

D.   God requires this of us

       1.   Examples in Scripture

           a.   I Corinthians 15:31 – Paul
           b.   II Corinthians 11:23 – Paul
           c.   II Samuel 16:5-14 – David
           d.   Genesis 50:20 - Joseph

       2.   Our testimony

           a.   John 21:18
           b.   Galatians 2:20

E.   Simple yielding guidelines from Scripture

       1.   Ephesians 4:31-32 – *"Let all bitterness, and wrath, and anger, and clamour, and evil speaking, be put away from you, with all malice: And be ye kind one to another, tenderhearted, forgiving one another, even as God for Christ's sake hath forgiven you."*
       2.   Proverbs 15:1 – *"A soft answer turneth away wrath..."*
       3.   Romans 12:18 – *"If it be possible...live peaceably with all men."*
       4.   Revelation 12:11 – *"And they overcame him by the blood of the Lamb, and by the word of their testimony; and they loved not their lives unto the death."*
       5.   Matthew 5:11-12
       6.   Romans 12:21 – *"Be not overcome of evil, but overcome evil with good."*
       7.   Ephesians 6:12 – *"For we wrestle not against flesh and blood..."*
       8.   I Corinthians 4:12-14

F.   To yield we must see as God sees

       1.   Matthew 5:8 – *"Blessed are the pure in heart: for they shall see God."*
       2.   Proverbs 29:18 – *"Where there is no vision, the people perish..."*

G.   Quotations from others concerning yielding

       1.   A Chinese proverb says – to yield is to preserve oneself
       2.   Forgiveness is the fragrance of the flower that clings to the heel that crushed it.
       3.   Some say I will forgive, but not forget, and say I won't have anything more to do with him or her. How Spirit grieving and self-defeating they are! Remember Song of Solomon 2:15 – it's the <u>little</u> foxes that spoil the vine.
       4.   No man is able to force me so low as to make me hate him.
       5.   You can tell a man's character by how he treats those who can do nothing for him.

6. A young Christian asked an elderly Christian, what are the three Christian virtues, which are indispensable to the Christian walk? The answer – the first is humility, the second is humility, and the third is humility.

7. In matters controversial, my prescription is very fine – I always see both sides of things, the one that is wrong and then mine.

8. Self preservation may be the first law of nature, but self-denial is the first law of grace.

If we yield, we set in motion the cure, the remedy, soundness, the wholesome answer, and we will bring health to the situation!

Lesson 26
PURE HEARTS

I.   Keeping Our Hearts – I Samuel 16:7 – *"...the LORD seeth not as man seeth; for man looketh on the outward appearance, but the LORD looketh on the heart."*

   A.   Causes for heart problems

      1.   Proverbs 28:14 – *"...but he that hardeneth his heart shall fall into mischief."*
      2.   Proverbs 28:25 – *"He that is of a proud heart stirreth up strife..."*
      3.   Deuteronomy 8:14 – *"Then thine heart be lifted up, and thou forget the LORD thy God..."*
      4.   II Samuel 6:16
      5.   I Kings 11:1-10
      6.   Psalms 24:4 – *"...who hath not lifted up his soul unto vanity, nor sworn deceitfully."*
      7.   Psalms 95:8
      8.   James 3:14
      9.   Psalms 78:37 – *"For their heart was not right with him, neither were they stedfast in his covenant."*

   B.   Effects

      1.   Proverbs 23:7 – *"For as he thinketh in his heart, so is he..."*
      2.   Proverbs 14:10 – *"The heart knoweth his own bitterness..."*
      3.   Matthew 12:34-35 – *"...an evil man out of the evil treasure bringeth forth evil things."*
      4.   Matthew 15:16 – *"And Jesus said, Are ye also yet without understanding?"*
      5.   Matthew 6:21 – *"For where your treasure is, there will your heart be also."*

   C.   What our hearts should be doing.

      1.   Proverbs 4:23 – *"Keep thy heart with all diligence; for out of it are the issues of life."*
      2.   Matthew 5:8 – *"Blessed are the pure in heart: for they shall see God."*
      3.   II Kings 22:19
      4.   Psalms 34:18 – *"The LORD is nigh unto them that are of a broken heart..."*
      5.   Hebrews 13:9
      6.   Psalms 12:7-8
      7.   I Samuel 2:1
      8.   Ephesians 4:32 – *"And be ye kind one to another, tenderhearted..."*
      9.   Psalms 57:7 – *"My heart is fixed, O God, my heart is fixed: I will sing..."*
      10. I Kings 8:61 – *"Let your heart therefore be perfect with the LORD our God, to walk in his statutes, and to keep his commandments, as at this day."*

   D.   How can we get help?

      1.   Psalms 51:7, 10
      2.   Job 23:16 – *"For God maketh my heart soft, and the Almighty troubleth me:"*
      3.   Psalms 66:18 – *"If I regard iniquity in my heart, the Lord will not hear me:"*
      4.   Psalms 119:11, 80
      5.   James 4:8
      6.   I Kings 3:9
      7.   I Samuel 10:9 – *"...God gave him another heart..."*

II. Examples of Heart Problems

A. Saul – I Samuel 15:23
B. Cain – Genesis 4:6 – *"And the LORD said unto Cain, Why art thou wroth? and why is thy countenance fallen?"*
C. Judas – John 13:26, John 12:3-9

III. Examples of Those Who Repented!

A. Peter – Luke 22:31-38, John 21:15, Luke 22:55-63
B. David – Psalms 51:10-19, II Samuel 11:2-27
C. Paul – Acts 15:37-41, Acts 13:13, II Timothy 4:11
D. Hezekiah – II Kings 20:1-6

Lesson 27
PURPOSE

I. <u>Purpose</u> Is a Requirement for True Disciples – We must have a place to go toward.

A. We are in a race

1. I Corinthians 9:25-27 – "*25And every man that striveth for the mastery is temperate in all things. Now they do it to obtain a corruptible crown; but we an incorruptible. 26I therefore so run, not as uncertainly; so fight I, not as one that beateth the air: 27But I keep under my body, and bring it into subjection: lest that by any means, when I have preached to others, I myself should be a castaway.*"
2. Hebrews 12:1-3 – "*1Wherefore seeing we also are compassed about with so great a cloud of witnesses, let us lay aside every weight, and the sin which doth so easily beset us, and let us run with patience the race that is set before us...*"
3. Ecclesiastes 9:11

B. This race is called many things, but at the end there is one prize.

1. II Timothy 4:7 – "*I have fought a good fight, I have finished my course, I have kept the faith:*"
2. Matthew 7:14 – "*Because strait is the gate, and narrow is the way, which leadeth unto life, and few there be that find it.*"
3. Isaiah 35:8
4. Proverbs 4:18 – Don't hurry it. It will come to pass as we keep our hearts right.

C. Reasons for having a purpose. We need to know where we are going and how to get there.

1. Proverbs 29:18 – "<u>*Where there is no vision*</u>, *the people perish: but he that keepeth the law, happy is he.*" Other translations:

    "*...no redemptive revelations...*"
    "*...no prophecy...*"
    "*without a vision a people is made naked*"
    "*where there is no vision the people are unrestrained*"
    "*the people cast off restraint*"
    "*do not accept divine guidance, they run wild*"
    "*without revelation people are uncontrolled*"

2. Habakkuk 2:1-4 – "*...Write the vision, and make it plain upon tables, that he may run that readeth it. 3For the vision is yet for an appointed time, but at the end it shall speak, and not lie: though it tarry, wait for it; because it will surely come, it will not tarry...*" – *Vision* in Hebrew– a mental sight, a dream, a revelation; from a root – to gaze, to contemplate, to perceive with pleasure

3. Ecclesiastes 10:15 – "*The labour of the foolish wearieth every one of them, because he knoweth not how to go to the city.*"

    a. *Labor* in Hebrew – wearing effort; from a root, to toil, work severely with irksomeness; anguish, troublesome work
    b. *Foolish* in Hebrew – fat, stupid or silly
    c. *Wearieth* in Hebrew – to gasp, to be exhausted, to faint

4.   Ephesians 5:14-16 – "*14Wherefore he saith, Awake thou that sleepest, and arise from the dead, and Christ shall give thee light. 15See then that ye walk circumspectly, not as fools, but as wise, 16Redeeming the time, because the days are evil.*" Other translations:

"*...see then, you walk without stumbling...*"
"*...take great care, how you live...*"
"*...look, therefore carefully how ye walk...*"
"*...live life, then, with a since of responsibility...*"
"*...not unwisely, but wisely...*"
"*...not thoughtlessly, but thoughtfully...*"
"*...buying up opportunities...*"
"*...making the most of every opportunity...*"
"*...make the best use of your time...*"

5.   I Corinthians 9:25-27 – "*...26I therefore so run, not as uncertainly; so fight I, not as one that beateth the air...*" Other translations:

"*...so I run straight to the goal, with purpose in every step...*"
"*...so I run with a clear goal ahead of me...*"
"*...I fight to win, I'm not playing around...*"
"*...I'm no shadow boxer, I really fight...*"

6.   Acts 2:40 – "*...Save yourselves from this untoward generation.*" Untoward in Greek – warped, winding, perverse, curved; from a root, to parch through leanness
7.   Ephesians 4:14 – not to be children tossed to and fro
8.   I Samuel 3:1
9.   Isaiah 28:7
10. Micah 3:5-8

D.   Word studies – Hebrew and Greek words for *purpose*

1.   Hebrew – pleasure, desire, valuable thing; from a root, to incline, to delight in
2.   Greek – a setting forth, intention; from a root to place before

E.   Purposes found in Scripture

1.   God has an *eternal* purpose for the earth

a.   Ephesians 1:9-12
b.   II Timothy 1:9-11
c.   Ephesians 3:9-11, 16-19
d.   I John 3:8 – "*He that committeth sin is of the devil; for this purpose the Son of God was manifested, that he might destroy the works of the devil.*"

2.   God has a *corporate* purpose for His people

a.   Romans 8:28-30 – We are to be conformed into His image
b.   Ephesians 3:9-10

3.   God has a *personal* purpose for each individual person

a.   There are two types of "personal purpose"

1) Enduring (lasting, this does not change)
2) Temporary, seasonal or proceeding

b. Enduring

1) Acts 26:16-19
2) II Timothy 3:10 – *"But thou hast fully known my doctrine, manner of life, purpose, faith, longsuffering, charity, patience,..."*
3) Jeremiah 29:11 – *"For I know the thoughts that I think toward you, saith the Lord, thoughts of peace, and not of evil, to give you an expected end."*
4) Habakkuk 2:1-4

c. Temporary

1) Matthew 4:4 – proceeding word – *"But he answered and said, It is written, Man shall not live by bread alone, but by every word that proceedeth out of the mouth of God."*
2) Ecclesiastes 3:1 – *"To everything there is a season, and a time to every purpose under the heaven:"*
3) Acts 19:21
4) Acts 20:3
5) Romans 1:13

d. Every purpose has a time. When you see it you must run after it; timing related to our purpose

1) Ecclesiastes 3:1
2) Ecclesiastes 3:17
3) Ecclesiastes 8:6

F. Counsel is needed

1. Proverbs 15:22 – *"Without counsel purposes are disappointed: but in the multitude of counsellers they are established."*
2. Proverbs 20:18 – *"Every purpose is established by counsel: and with good advice make war."*
3. Ruth 2:16 – *"And let fall also some of the <u>handfuls of purpose</u> for her, and leave them, that she may glean them, and rebuke her not."* Other translations: *"...drop something for her on purpose and let them be..."*, *"...Indeed pull out some bunches..."*, *"...See you pull up after ears of corn from the bundles and let them fall..."*
4. Romans 8:28-30

5. When God has a purpose it will be fulfilled

a. Isaiah 14:24
b. Isaiah 46:11
c. Jeremiah 51:29
d. Jeremiah 4:28

G. We must make a decision to do it

1. I Kings 5:5 – *"And, behold, I purpose to build an house unto the name of the LORD my God, as the LORD spake unto David my father, saying, Thy son, whom I will set upon thy throne in thy room, he shall build an house unto my name."*

2. Acts 11:23 – *"Who, when he came, and had seen the grace of God, was glad, and exhorted them all, that with purpose of heart they would cleave unto the Lord."*
3. Isaiah 46:11 – *"Calling a ravenous bird from the east, the man that executeth my counsel from a far country: yea, I have spoken it, I will also bring it to pass; I have purposed it, I will also do it."*
4. Psalms 27:4
5. Daniel 1:8
6. Psalms 17:3
7. II Corinthians 9:7
8. Acts 26:19

H. There will be adversaries trying to overthrow our purpose

1. Psalms 140:4 – *"Keep me, O LORD, from the hands of the wicked; preserve me from the violent man; who have purposed to overthrow my goings."*
2. Job 17:11 – *"My days are past, my purposes are broken off, even the thoughts of my heart."*
3. Ezra 4:4-5 – *"⁴Then the people of the land weakened the hands of the people of Judah, and troubled them in building, ⁵And hired counsellers against them, to frustrate their purpose, all the days of Cyrus king of Persia, even until the reign of Darius king of Persia."* Other translations: *"...the people of the country set out to dishearten and frighten the people...", "...hired counselors...to defeat their purpose..."*

I. Our purpose will sustain us through any hardship, affliction, wilderness, trial, etc.

II. The Cause

A. Our lives are meant to have a cause or a vision to run after.

1. I Samuel 17:22-31 – *"...²⁹And David said, What have I now done? Is there not a cause?..."*

   a. Cause in Hebrew – a word, or matter
   b. Other Translations: *"Was it not laid upon me?", "Was it not a word?"*
   c. Enemies to our vision, Genesis 37:3-11, 18-20 – *"And Joseph dreamed a dream, and he told it his brethren: and they hated him yet the more. ⁶And he said unto them, Hear, I pray you, this dream which I have dreamed:"*

2. Acts 26:19 – *"Whereupon, O king Agrippa, I was not disobedient unto the heavenly vision:"*

   a. Vision in Greek – something gazed upon that's supernatural, to discern clearly
   b. Vision in Hebrew – sight, to gaze upon mentally, to dream

3. Habakkuk 2:2-3 – *"And the LORD answered me, and said, Write the vision, and make it plain upon tables, that he may run that readeth it. ³For the vision is yet for an appointed time, but at the end it shall speak, and not lie: though it tarry, wait for it; because it will surely come, it will not tarry."*
4. I Samuel 3:1 – No open vision - *"And the child Samuel ministered unto the LORD before Eli. And the word of the LORD was precious in those days; there was no open vision."*
5. Proverbs 29:18 – *"Where there is no vision, the people perish: but he that keepeth the law, happy is he."*
6. Ecclesiastes 5:3 – *"For a dream cometh through the multitude of business; and a fool's voice is known by multitude of words."* – A dream comes through a multitude of business.

   a. Business in Hebrew – employment – from a root word that means to humble oneself

b. Hebrews 12:1 – run with patience
c. I Corinthians 9:24-27 – keep my body under discipline
d. Luke 12:48-51 – ignore family
e. I Samuel 17:18-20 – friends

8. Genesis 28:10-19 – Jacob's vision of heaven; Luz – Perverse to Bethel – House of God
9. Matthew 7:13-14 – *"...Narrow is the way that leads to life."*
10. II Timothy 4:7-8 – *"I have fought a good fight, I have finished my course, I have kept the faith: ⁸Henceforth there is laid up for me a crown of righteousness..."*

    a. Matthew 25:23 – *"Well done thou good and faithful servant."*
    b. Proverbs 13:19 – *"The desire accomplished is sweet to the soul"*
    c. Proverbs 12:24 – *"The hand of the diligent shall bear rule: but the slothful shall be under tribute."*
    d. Job 19:23-27 – *"Oh that my words were now written! oh that they were printed in a book! ²⁴That they were graven with an iron pen and lead in the rock for ever! ²⁵For I know that my redeemer liveth, and that he shall stand at the latter day upon the earth: ²⁶And though after my skin worms destroy this body, yet in my flesh shall I see God: ²⁷Whom I shall see for myself, and mine eyes shall behold, and not another; though my reins be consumed within me."*
    e. Psalms 17:15 – *"As for me, I will behold thy face in righteousness: I shall be satisfied, when I awake, with thy likeness."*

Lesson 28
Psalms 23:1
The Lord Is My Shepherd

I.   Psalms 23:1 – *"The LORD is my shepherd; I shall not want."*

  A.   *"The LORD is…"*

  1.   Word definition of LORD, *Yehovah* – Jehovah, the self existent one, the eternal, ever loving one, I am that I am
  2.   He just is what His name means.

  B.   *"…my shepherd…"*

  1.   My – Refers to having a personal and intimate relationship with Him.

  2.   Shepherd

   a.   Word definition – From the root word *Rohi* – to shepherd, to feed, to lead to pasture, to tend a flock, to rule, to associate with (as a friend), a companion.

   b.   Defining Scriptures – Remember, He is all of this to us!

   1)   Psalms 80:1 – *"Give ear, O Shepherd of Israel, thou that leadest Joseph like a flock; thou that dwellest between the cherubims, shine forth."*
   2)   Ecclesiastes 12:11 – *"The words of the wise are as goads, and as nails fastened by the masters of assemblies, which are given from one shepherd."* All Words of God come from Him
   3)   Isaiah 40:11 – Feed, gather His lambs in His arms; carry them in His bosom; gently lead
   4)   Ezekiel 34
   5)   John 10:7-16 – Door; came to give us life (*Zoe*) and more abundantly; good; gives His life; knows His sheep, and they know Him; other sheep He will bring (Gentiles).
   6)   Hebrews 13:20 – The resurrected great shepherd
   7)   I Peter 2:25 – *"…Shepherd and Bishop of your souls."*

  C.   *"…I shall not want."*

  1.   Hebrew definition for "want" – to lack, to fail, to lessen, to abate, to bereave, to decrease, to make lower.

  2.   Defining Scriptures about "want"

   a.   Psalms 34:9-10
   b.   Proverbs 6:11
   c.   Proverbs 13:25 – *"The righteous eateth to the satisfying of his soul: but the belly of the wicked shall want."*
   d.   Luke 15:14 – Want from being backslidden
   e.   James 1:4 – Dealings of God bring us to a place where we want nothing

   f.   II Corinthians 8:14 – Body provides

   1)   II Corinthians 9:12

D.   Other translations of Psalms 23:1

"The Lord shepherds me, therefore can I lack nothing."
"The Lord shepherds me, I shall never be in need."
"The Lord takes care of me as His sheep, I will not be without any good thing."
"Because the Lord is my Shepherd, I have everything I need."

E.   Other compatible Scriptures

1.   II Peter 1:3 – *"According as his divine power hath given unto us all things that pertain unto life and godliness..."*

2.   Philippians 4:19 – *"But my God shall supply all your need according to his riches in glory by Christ Jesus."*

   a.   *"Need"* in Greek – Employment, that which the occasion demands, requirement, lack, necessities.
   b.   *"Supply"* in Greek – To cram (a net full), to level up a hollow, to furnish, to satisfy. From a root word – to give a major portion to, to complete.

3.   Psalms 37:23-26 – *"I have been young, and now am old; yet have I not seen the righteous forsaken, nor his seed begging bread. He is ever merciful, and lendeth; and his seed is blessed."*
4.   Luke 22:35 – When He sends us, we lack nothing (Deuteronomy 2:7)
5.   Psalms 34:10 – *"...they that seek the LORD shall not want any good thing."*
6.   Psalms 84:11 – *"...no good thing will he withhold from them that walk uprightly."*

7.   Proverbs 28:27 – When we give, we lack nothing

   a.   Luke 6:38 – *"Give, and it shall be given unto you..."*

Lesson 29
HUMILITY

I.   What God's Word Says About Being Humble

    A.   Hebrew and Greek words

        1.   Hebrew

            a.   *Anah* – to depress, look down, to abase – Deuteronomy 8:2, Exodus 10:3

            b.   *Kawnah* – to bend the knee, to humiliate, to vanquish –
II Chronicles 7:14, II Kings 22:19

            c.   *Shaphel* – to depress or sink – Proverbs 16:19, Psalms 113:6, Isaiah 2:9

            d.   *Anauah* – condescension, divine gentleness

            e.   *Tsona* – lowly – Micah 6:8

        2.   Greek

            a.   *Tapeinos* – depressed, humiliated – James 4:6 – other translations:

                "God set Himself against the haughty but to the lowly He shows grace."
                "God opposes a haughty person, but He blesses humble minded ones."

            b.   *Tapeinophrosure* – humiliation of mind, modesty, lowliness – Acts 20:19, I Peter 5:5

            c.   *Tapeinoo* – to depress, to abase in condition or heart – Luke 14:11, Philippians 2:8, I Peter 5:6, Matthew 18:4

        3.   Definition of humility

            a.   Not proud or arrogant, modest, a modest sense of one's importance.

            b.   A bending or bowing attitude of the heart.

            c.   Lowly, gentle, meek of heart

            d.   An understanding of who Jesus is and who we really are. It is seeing our own helplessness apart form His ability.

            e.   Acting just like Jesus; not thinking more highly of yourself than you ought to (example: Moses – Exodus 34:29)

II. God Wants Us To Walk In Humility

    A.   It is actually a command

        1.   Micah 6:8 – *"He hath shewed thee, O man, what is good; and what doth the LORD require of thee, but to do justly, and to love mercy, and to walk humbly with thy God?"* – One of the three things God requires of us is humility. Other translations:

            "...only doing what is right, and loving mercy, & walking without pride before God."
            "...only to ask justly, to love loyalty, to walk wisely before God."

        2.   I Peter 5:5-6 – *"...be clothed with humility..."* – Other translations:

            "...Indeed, all of your should wrap yourselves in the garment of humility towards each other..."
            "...bow down then before the strong hand of God..."

3.   Colossians 3:12 – "*Put on therefore, as the elect of God, holy and beloved, bowels of mercies, kindness, humbleness of mind, meekness, longsuffering;*" – Here He says to put it on. He will not force us. It is our choice – Other translations:

"*...tenderness of heart, kindness, self humiliation...*"
"*...be merciful in action, kindly in heart, humble in mind...*"
"*...tender affections of compassion, graciousness...*"

B.   Jesus is our great example

1.   Matthew 11:29 – "*...learn of me; for I am meek and lowly in heart...*"

a.   Zechariah 9:9 – Jesus' nature is one of humility, gentleness, meekness. He is not arrogant or proud. He knows who he is, but he was always acknowledging God as the author of the work he was doing. He gave the glory to God.

2.   Philippians 2:5-11 – "*...let this mind* (attitude*) be in you...*" – Notice that exaltation, promotion, etc, comes out of real humility. We must first learn what it means to be abased – Other translations:

"*...He finally humiliated Himself in obedience...*"
"*...He humbled Himself and even stooped to die...*"

3.   Isaiah 57:15 – "*For thus saith the high and lofty One that inhabiteth eternity, whose name is Holy; I dwell in the high and holy place, with him also that is of a contrite and humble spirit, to revive the spirit of the humble, and to revive the heart of the contrite ones.*" – He dwells with those of a humble spirit

C.   God's attitude toward humility

1.   Isaiah 66:2 – "*...to this man will I look...*" – Other translations:

"*...But this is the man to whom I will look and have regard, he who is humble...*"
"*...But my eyes are drawn to the man of a humbled and contrite spirit...*"
"*...for him who is humbled and smitten in spirit...*"

2.   James 4:6 – "*...God resisteth the proud, but giveth grace unto the humble.*"

a.   Proverbs 3:34
b.   I Peter 5:5

3.   Luke 14:11 – Exaltation comes out of humility

a.   Luke 18:14
b.   Philippians 2:5-11

4.   Proverbs 15:33 – "*...before honour is humility.*"

a.   Proverbs 18:12
b.   Proverbs 29:23

5.   Psalms 9:12 – "*...he forgetteth not the cry of the humble.*"

       a.   Psalms 10:17
       b.   Psalms 138:6
       c.   Psalms 18:27

6.   Proverbs 16:19 – *"Better it is to be of an humble spirit..."*
7.   Proverbs 11:2 – *"...with the lowly is wisdom."*
8.   Proverbs 22:4 – Humility has a reward

III. What God is Bringing Forth

A.   Zephaniah 3:11-20 – Other translation, *"I will leave in the midst of you, a people humble and lowly. They shall seek refuge in the name of the Lord."*

The day is coming when God is going to remove out of the body of Christ those that are proud and haughty in spirit. What He will leave will be an afflicted (from the Hebrew root word for humble) and poor (needy) people. Those who make it into God's great company of overcomers will be those who are walking in humility and those who see their desperate need for Him.

1.   God is bringing forth a people of humility

    a.   Matthew 5:3 – The kingdom belongs to the humble of mind and heart.

       Other translations:

       "...the poor in spirit (the humble, rating themselves insignificant)"
       "...those who feel their spiritual need."
       "...how happy are the humble minded."

    b.   Psalms 51:17 – Sacrifices of God – broken spirit, contrite heart
    c.   Psalms 86:1 – *"...I am poor and needy."* – David was one of the richest men ever. He is referring to his need for God.
    d.   Proverbs 20:6 – *"Most men will proclaim every one his own goodness..."*
    e.   Isaiah 66:2

    f.   I Corinthians 1:26-29 – God hath chosen these:

       1)   Foolish – because the world doesn't understand their testimony

           a)   I Corinthians 1:18, 21
           b)   I Corinthians 2:14, 4:10

       2)   Weak – because they know it's by His strength. They are totally dependent on Him.
       3)   Base – they see themselves as insignificant; they are not impressed with themselves, only with Him.
       4)   Despised – because they don't fit into religion's plans. They are only concerned with His plans.
       5)   The are nots – because they have no pride. They have surrendered their ambitions and identity to receive the identity of the body of Christ.

IV. God Is Not Looking For People Who Exalt Themselves

A.   Jeremiah 45:5 – *"...seekest thou great things for thyself? seek them not..."*

1. Romans 12:3
2. Proverbs 25:6-8
3. Proverbs 30:32
4. Luke 14:7-11 – It is all in the attitude of the heart. Are we ambitious to be seen and approved of by men? Is all our striving that we might become something? This is not the Lord.
5. Luke 18:9-14 – If what we've done causes us to think we can judge others, we are very wrong. That is a subtle form of pride.
6. Matthew 18:1-4 – *"Who is the greatest in the kingdom of heaven?..."* is so far below God's great purpose for us. Let's be delivered from this kind of thinking and strive to be like Jesus who walked in humility.

V.   God Resists The Proud

A.   God's heart toward pride

1.   James 4:6-10 (I Peter 5:5) – Other translations:

"God sets himself against the proud"
"God opposes haughty persons."

a.   What pride cause:

1)   Rebellion (won't submit)
2)   The devil is involved with us
3)   We're far from God
4)   We're in sin
5)   Our hearts are impure
6)   We are double-minded

2.   Proverbs 6:16-17 – God hates pride
3.   Proverbs 21:4 – God says it is sin
4.   I John 2:16 – Pride is not of God the Father, it is born and bred by the world.
5.   Proverbs 14:3 – Only in the mouth of a fool will you find pride
6.   Proverbs 16:18-19, Proverbs 11:2 – Pride brings shame. Pride and haughtiness come before destruction and falling away from the Lord.
7.   Proverbs 28:25, Proverbs 13:10 – Only those with a proud heart are involved in strife. Pride breeds strife.

B.   Examples of some caught in pride

1.   Daniel 4:28-37 – Nebuchadnezzar

a.   Verse 30 – All he could see was how great he was. He didn't acknowledge God. Destruction came and stayed until he learned that all glory belongs to God.

b.   He is able to abase

1)   Acts 12:21-23
2)   Daniel 4:37
3)   Job 40:12

2. I Samuel 15:17-23 – Saul (I Samuel 13:7-9) – Saul forgot who he was, and in his pride, he disobeyed God. He became big in his own eyes. The only one big in the universe is Jesus. The result for Saul was the kingdom was taken from him.

3. II Chronicles 26:1-22 – Once he became strong, he felt he didn't need God anymore.

4. Deuteronomy 8:7-19 – We're not really tested until God blesses us. It's then that we find out what kind of person we really are. We must remember whatever we have, we've received from Him (I Corinthians 4:7).

5. Ezekiel 28:14-19 (Isaiah 14:12-16) – This is a sad story of Lucifer. Who knows how many eons he remained faithful? But one day his heart was lifted up with pride. Notice the horrible destruction that followed. It could happen to anyone.

VI. Either We Will Humble Ourselves or God Will Humble Us

A. His best is that we humble ourselves

1. II Chronicles 7:1-14

a. I Peter 5:6
b. James 4:10
c. Luke 14:11
d. Isaiah 58:5 – Fasting is one way to humble yourself. The word afflict here is the Hebrew word for humble.
e. Leviticus 23:27

B. If He has no other choice, God will humble us

1. Daniel 4:37
2. Proverbs 15:25
3. Isaiah 5:11-17
4. Deuteronomy 8:2-3

C. God knows how to deal with us

1. Hosea 6:1-2
2. Job 5:11-27
3. Jeremiah 18:1-10
4. I Samuel 2:6-11

D. We need to be thankful that He will do this

1. Psalms 119:67, 71, 75

Lesson 30
INTEGRITY

I. Definition of Integrity

    A. Hebrew word for integrity, *tom* – completeness, innocence, perfection
    B. Dictionary definition – state or quality of being complete, undivided, or unbroken, soundness, purity, moral soundness, honesty, uprightness.

II. Eight Things That Characterize a Man of Integrity

    A. Not given to change – not double-minded.

        1. Proverbs 24:21-22 – *"My son, fear thou the LORD and the king: and meddle not with them that are given to change: For their calamity shall rise suddenly; and who knoweth the ruin of them both?"*
        2. James 1:8 – *"A double minded man is unstable in all his ways."*

            a. Ephesians 4:14 – Indicative of children
            b. Isaiah 54:11

        3. I Chronicles 12:33 – *"...they were not of double heart."*
        4. I Kings 9:4-5 – If we walk in integrity of heart, God will establish

    B. Don't forsake loyalties – God can be trusted

        1. Job 2:3-11

            a. Job 13:15 – *"Though he slay me, yet will I trust in him: but I will maintain mine own ways before him."*

        2. People will forsake men.

            a. John 16:32 (Matthew 26:31-35)
            b. II Timothy 3:4 – Traitor in the Greek – surrender, betrayer.
            c. I Samuel 30:1-6

    C. Will always try to do what's right.

        1. Proverbs 20:7 – *"The just man walketh in his integrity..."*

            a. Proverbs 11:3 – *"The integrity of the upright shall guide them..."*
            b. Psalms 26:1, 11
            c. Psalms 7:8
            d. Job 31:6 – *"Let me be weighed in an even balance, that God may know mine integrity."*

        2. Even when we miss it, if we're walking in integrity, God will cover us.

            a. Genesis 20:5-6 (Hebrews 4:12)

                1) Psalms 25:21 – *"Let integrity and uprightness preserve me..."*
                2) Psalms 41:12 – *"...thou upholdest me in mine integrity..."*

D. One who stands up for truth. He will not turn from what is right no matter what the cost.

    1. Proverbs 19:1 – *"Better is the poor that walketh in his integrity..."* (Proverbs 23:3)
    2. Proverbs 28:6
    3. Psalms 78:72

E. When adversity comes he will stand and not run (you can count on him).

    1. Proverbs 24:10 – *"If thou faint in the day of adversity, thy strength is small."*
    2. Job 27:5 – *"...till I die I will not remove mine integrity from me."*

    3. Examples:

        a. Daniel 3 – Fiery furnace.
        b. Daniel 6:4-24 – Lion's den.

4. Revelation 12:11 – *"And they overcame him by the blood of the Lamb, and by the word of their testimony; and they loved not their lives unto the death."*

F. When proven wrong, will repent – Is free to receive instruction.

    1. Proverbs 6:23 – *"...reproofs of instruction are the way of life:"*

        a. Proverbs 17:10 – *"A reproof entereth more into a wise man than an hundred stripes into a fool."*
        b. Proverbs 19:25
        c. Proverbs 15:31-32

    2. Those that aren't open to correction err.

        a. Proverbs 10:17 – *"...but he that refuseth reproof erreth."*
        b. Proverbs 12:1
        c. Proverbs 15:5, 10

G. Keeps his word.

    1. Psalms 15:4 – *"...He that sweareth to his own hurt, and changeth not."*
    2. Deuteronomy 23:21-23

    3. Importance of our words:

        a. Proverbs 6:2
        b. Psalms 139:4
        c. Matthew 12:37 – *"For by thy words thou shalt be justified, and by thy words thou shalt be condemned."*
        d. Daniel 10:12

H. Always exalts Jesus above all.

    1. Proverbs 20:6
    2. Philippians 2:19-23
    3. Genesis 41:16 – *"And Joseph answered Pharaoh, saying, It is not in me: God shall give Pharaoh an answer of peace."*

Lesson 31
I WAS BROUGHT LOW AND HE HELPED ME

I.   Psalms 116:6 – *"The LORD preserveth the simple: I was brought low, and he helped me."*

A.   Other translations:

"The Lord preserves the simple; I was brought low, and He helped and saved me." (Amplified)
"A preserver of the simple [is] Jehovah, I was low, and to me He giveth salvation." (Young's)
"The LORD protects the simplehearted; when I was in great need, he saved me." (NIV)
"The Lord protects those of childlike faith; I was facing death, and he saved me." (NLT)
"God takes the side of the helpless; when I was at the end of my rope, he saved me." (Message)
"The Lord watches over the foolish; when I was helpless, he saved me." (NCV)
"The Lord protects the untrained; I was in serious trouble and he delivered me." (NET Bible)
"The LORD protects defenseless people. When I was weak, he saved me." (God's Word)
"The Lord keeps the simple; I was made low, and he was my saviour." (BBE)
"The Lord is the keeper of little ones: I was humbled, and he delivered me." (Douay-Rheims)
"The LORD guards the inexperienced; I was helpless, and He saved me." (HCSB)

B.   Definition of *low* in Hebrew – to slacken or be feeble, to be oppressed; it is also translated *dry up, be emptied, be not equal, fail, be impoverished, be made thin.*

II.   We Need To Understand The Ways Of God

A.   Ways of God

1.   Psalms 103:7 – *"He made known his ways unto Moses, his acts unto the children of Israel."*
2.   Deuteronomy 10:12 – *"And now, Israel, what doth the LORD thy God require of thee, but to fear the LORD thy God, to walk in all his ways, and to love him, and to serve the LORD thy God with all thy heart and with all thy soul,"*
3.   Job 26:14 – *"Lo, these are parts of his ways: but how little a portion is heard of him? but the thunder of his power who can understand?"*
4.   Micah 4:2 – *"And many nations shall come, and say, Come, and let us go up to the mountain of the LORD, and to the house of the God of Jacob; and he will teach us of his ways, and we will walk in his paths: for the law shall go forth of Zion, and the word of the LORD from Jerusalem."*
5.   Psalms 145:17 – *"The LORD is righteous in all his ways, and holy in all his works."*
6.   Romans 11:33-36 – *"³³O the depth of the riches both of the wisdom and knowledge of God! how unsearchable are his judgments, and his ways past finding out! ³⁴For who hath known the mind of the Lord? or who hath been his counsellor? ³⁵Or who hath first given to him, and it shall be recompensed unto him again? ³⁶For of him, and through him, and to him, are all things: to whom be glory for ever. Amen."*

III.   Being Brought Low – One Of God's Ways

A.   Scriptures

1.   I Samuel 2:6-10 – *"⁶The LORD killeth, and maketh alive: he bringeth down to the grave, and bringeth up. ⁷The LORD maketh poor, and maketh rich: he bringeth low, and lifteth up. ⁸He raiseth up the poor out of the dust, and lifteth up the beggar from the dunghill, to set them among princes, and to make them inherit the throne of glory: for the pillars of the earth are the LORD's, and he hath set the world upon them. ⁹He will keep the feet of his saints, and the wicked shall be silent in darkness; for by strength shall no man prevail. ¹⁰The adversaries of the LORD*

shall be broken to pieces; out of heaven shall he thunder upon them: the LORD shall judge the ends of the earth; and he shall give strength unto his king, and exalt the horn of his anointed."

2. Ecclesiastes 10:6-7 – *"⁶Folly is set in great dignity, and the rich sit in low place. ⁷I have seen servants upon horses, and princes walking as servants upon the earth."*

3. Isaiah 40:2-5 – *"²Speak ye comfortably to Jerusalem, and cry unto her, that her warfare is accomplished, that her iniquity is pardoned: for she hath received of the LORD's hand double for all her sins. ³The voice of him that crieth in the wilderness, Prepare ye the way of the LORD, make straight in the desert a highway for our God. ⁴Every valley shall be exalted, and every mountain and hill shall be made low: and the crooked shall be made straight, and the rough places plain: ⁵And the glory of the LORD shall be revealed, and all flesh shall see it together: for the mouth of the LORD hath spoken it."*

4. Ezekiel 17:24 – *"And all the trees of the field shall know that I the LORD have brought down the high tree, have exalted the low tree, have dried up the green tree, and have made the dry tree to flourish: I the LORD have brought down the high tree, have exalted the low tree, have dried up the green tree, and have made the dry tree to flourish: I the LORD have spoken and have done it."*

5. James 1:9-10 – *"⁹Let the brother of low degree rejoice in that he is exalted: ¹⁰But the rich, in that he is made low: because as the flower of the grass he shall pass away."*

B. Why are we brought low?

   1. Psalms 106:39-48
   2. Psalms 107:31-43
   3. Proverbs 29:23 – *"A man's pride shall bring him low: but honour shall uphold the humble in spirit."*
   4. Isaiah 2:12-17

C. He will help us

   1. Job 5:6-11
   2. Psalms 79:8-13
   3. Psalms 136:23-26
   4. Luke 1:46-54
   5. Isaiah 38:14-20
   6. Psalms 142:1-6

Lesson 32
HAVING A RIGHT HEART

I. The Importance of Having a Right Heart

   A. Scriptural examples

      1. Proverbs 4:23 – *"Keep thy heart with all diligence; for out of it are the issues of life."*

         a. Matthew 15:16-20 – *"...those things which proceed out of the mouth come forth from the heart; and they defile the man..."*
         b. Matthew 12:23, 25
         c. Proverbs 23:7 – *"For as he thinketh in his heart, so is he..."*
         d. Proverbs 14:30 – *"A sound heart is the life of the flesh..."*

      2. Matthew 5:8 – *"Blessed are the pure in heart: for they shall see God."*
      3. I Samuel 16:7 – *"...the LORD seeth not as man seeth; for man looketh on the outward appearance, but the LORD looketh on the heart."*
      4. Mark 4:15

   B. Purity of heart

      1. Matthew 5:8 – *"Blessed are the pure in heart: for they shall see God"* – pure in Greek – clean, clear

         a. II Samuel 22:27 – *"With the pure thou wilt shew thyself pure..."*

      2. Psalms 24:2 – Hebrew word for pure here means – beloved, empty, choice, clean, clear; it comes from a root word – to clarify, brighten, examine, or select.

         a. Malachi 1:11 – *"...in every place incense shall be offered unto my name, and a pure offering..."*
         b. II Timothy 2:22 – *"Flee also youthful lusts: but follow righteousness, faith, charity, peace, with them that call on the Lord out of a pure heart."* – This Greek word means – clean, fair

      3. I Timothy 1:5 – Other translation – *"The aim or your instruction must be love that springs from a pure heart and from a good conscience and from a sincere faith."*
      4. I Timothy 3:9 – Other translation – *"Holding the divine truth of the faith in a clear conscience."*
      5. I Timothy 5:22 – *"...keep thyself pure."*
      6. I Peter 1:22 – *"...see that ye love one another with a pure heart fervently."*
      7. I John 3:3 (Revelation 22:1)

      8. Proverbs 22:11 – Other translation – *"The Lord loves the pure in heart. And he who is gracious in speech, the king is his friend."*

         a. Proverbs 15:26
         b. Proverbs 21:8

      9. Luke 8:15 – *"But that on the good ground are they, which in an honest and good heart, having heard the word, keep it, and bring forth fruit with patience."*

   C. Some bad conditions of the heart as found in Scripture

1. Proverbs 28:14 – **hardened**
   (Psalms 95:8, Mark 3:5, John 12:40)
2. Proverbs 28:25 – **proud**
3. II Samuel 6:16 – **despising**
4. Deuteronomy 8:14 – **lifted up**
   (Ezekiel 28:2, Daniel 5:20)
5. Psalms 78:37 – **not right**
6. James 3:14-15 – **bitter, envy, and strife**
7. John 14:1 – **troubled**
8. Ephesians 4:18 – **blindness**
9. Hebrews 3:7-19 – **evil, unbelieving**
10. James 1:26 – **deceived**
11. Hosea 10:2 – **divided**
12. Jeremiah 17:5-10 – **departing, deceitful**
13. I Kings 11:1-10 – **turned away**
14. Proverbs 14:10 – **bitter**
15. James 4:8 – **double minded (hearted)**
    (Psalms 12:2, I Chronicles 12:33)
16. Proverbs 31:6 – **heavy or depressed** (Psalms 104:15-16, 42:5, 90:3)
17. Romans 1:21 – **foolish, darkened**
18. Matthew 13:15 – **waxed gross**
19. Jeremiah 5:20-24 – **rebellious**
20. Ezekiel 16:30 – **weak**
21. Proverbs 6:14 – **forward or perverse**
    (Proverbs 17:20)
22. Psalms 38:8 – **disquieted**
    (Psalms 42:5)
23. Ezekiel 25:15 – **despiteful, vengeful**

D. How do these bad conditions above fill our heart?

1. Hebrews 10:39 – *"But we are not of them who draw back unto perdition; but of them that believe to the saving of the soul."* – Hebrews 6:1 – *"Therefore leaving the principles of the doctrine of Christ, let us go on unto perfection..."*

The truth is, we are either going on unto perfection or drawing back unto perdition. There is no middle ground. If we are not going on unto perfection, then we are drawing back and allow our hearts to depart from the Lord. By doing this we have to fill them with other things. There is no vacuum in our hearts.

2. Mark 4:18-19 – *"[18]And these are they which are sown among thorns; such as hear the word, [19]And the cares of this world, and the deceitfulness of riches, and the lusts of other things entering in, choke the word, and it becometh unfruitful."*
3. Matthew 13:15 – *"For this people's heart is waxed gross, and their ears are dull of hearing, and their eyes they have closed; lest at any time they should see with their eyes, and hear with their ears, and should understand with their heart, and should be converted, and I should heal them."*
4. Romans 1:21 – *"Because that, when they knew God, they glorified him not as God, neither were thankful; but became vain in their imaginations, and their foolish heart was darkened."*
5. Jeremiah 5:20-29
6. Jeremiah 17:5-10
7. Matthew 18:23-34 – **unforgiveness**
8. I Kings 11:1-10 – *"[1]But king Solomon loved many strange women..."*
9. Proverbs 7 – *"...[9]In the twilight, in the evening, in the black and dark night..."*

E.   Double hearted (double minded)

1.   These are one and the same

   a.   Hosea 10:2 – *"Their heart is divided; now shall they be found faulty: he shall break down their altars, he shall spoil their images."* – divided in Hebrew means – to apportion or separate

   b.   James 4:8 – *"Draw nigh to God, and he will draw nigh to you. Cleanse your hands, ye sinners; and purify your hearts, ye double minded."* – double minded in Greek means – two spirited, vacillating in opinion or purpose

   c.   James 1:7-8 – *"⁷For let not that man think that he shall receive any thing of the Lord. ⁸A double minded man is unstable in all his ways."*

   d.   Genesis 1:4 – *"And God saw the light, that it was good: and God divided the light from the darkness."*

   e.   Psalms 12:2 – *"They speak vanity every one with his neighbour: with flattering lips and with a double heart do they speak."*

   f.   I Chronicles 12:33 – *"Of Zebulun, such as went forth to battle, expert in war, with all instruments of war, fifty thousand, which could keep rank: they were not of double heart."*

   g.   I Timothy 3:8 – *"Likewise must the deacons be grave, not doubletongued, not given to much wine, not greedy of filthy lucre;"*

   h.   Matthew 12:25-26 – *"²⁵And Jesus knew their thoughts, and said unto them, Every kingdom divided against itself is brought to desolation; and every city or house divided against itself shall not stand: ²⁶And if Satan cast out Satan, he is divided against himself; how shall then his kingdom stand?"*

   i.   II Timothy 2:25 – *"In meekness instructing those that oppose themselves; if God peradventure will give them repentance to the acknowledging of the truth;"*

2.   To be double hearted is to be tossed

   a.   Ephesians 4:14 – *"That we henceforth be no more children, tossed to and fro, and carried about with every wind of doctrine, by the sleight of men, and cunning craftiness, whereby they lie in wait to deceive;"*

   b.   Isaiah 54:11-14 – *"¹¹O thou afflicted, tossed with tempest, and not comforted, behold, I will lay thy stones with fair colours, and lay thy foundations with sapphires..."*

   c.   James 1:6 – *"But let him ask in faith, nothing wavering. For he that wavereth is like a wave of the sea driven with the wind and tossed."*

3.   God wants us to have a single heart

   a.   Matthew 6:22 – *"The light of the body is the eye: if therefore thine eye be single, thy whole body shall be full of light."*

   b.   Acts 2:42-47 – *"⁴²And they continued stedfastly in the apostles' doctrine and fellowship, and in breaking of bread, and in prayers. ⁴³And fear came upon every soul: and many wonders and signs were done by the apostles. ⁴⁴And all that believed were together, and had all things common; ⁴⁵And sold their possessions and goods, and parted them to all men, as every man had need. ⁴⁶And they, continuing daily with one accord in the temple, and breaking bread from house to house, did eat their meat with gladness and singleness of heart, ⁴⁷Praising God, and having favour with all the people. And the Lord added to the church daily such as should be saved."*

   c.   Ephesians 6:5 – *"Servants, be obedient to them that are your masters according to the flesh, with fear and trembling, in singleness of your heart, as unto Christ;"*

    d.   Colossians 3:22 – *"Servants, obey in all things your masters according to the flesh; not with eyeservice, as menpleasers; but in singleness of heart, fearing God:"*

    e.   Psalms 86:11 – *"Teach me thy way, O LORD; I will walk in thy truth: unite my heart to fear thy name."*

    f.   Jeremiah 32:39 – *"And I will give them one heart, and one way, that they may fear me for ever, for the good of them, and of their children after them:"*

    g.   Song of Solomon 4:1 – *"Behold, thou art fair, my love; behold, thou art fair; thou hast doves' eyes within thy locks: thy hair is as a flock of goats, that appear from mount Gilead."*

F.   Having a soft heart

1.   Job 23:16 – *"For God maketh my heart soft, and the Almighty troubleth me"* – The Hebrew word here for soft is also translated tender

2.   II Chronicles 34:27 – *"Because thine heart was tender, and thou didst humble thyself before God, when thou heardest his words against this place, and against the inhabitants thereof, and humbledst thyself before me, and didst rend thy clothes, and weep before me; I have even heard thee also, saith the LORD."*

3.   Ephesians 4:29 – *"Let no corrupt communication proceed out of your mouth, but that which is good to the use of edifying, that it may minister grace unto the hearers."*

4.   Matthew 11:29 – *"Take my yoke upon you, and learn of me; for I am meek and lowly in heart: and ye shall find rest unto your souls."*

5.   Psalms 51:17 – *"The sacrifices of God are a broken spirit: a broken and a contrite heart, O God, thou wilt not despise."*

6.   Acts 13:22 – *"And when he had removed him, he raised up unto them David to be their king; to whom also he gave testimony, and said, I have found David the son of Jesse, a man after mine own heart, which shall fulfil all my will."* (I Samuel 2:35, 13:14)

7.   Ezekiel 11:19-20 – *"[19]And I will give them one heart, and I will put a new spirit within you; and I will take the stony heart out of their flesh, and will give them an heart of flesh: [20]That they may walk in my statutes, and keep mine ordinances, and do them: and they shall be my people, and I will be their God."* – Flesh in Hebrew comes from a root word that means – to be fresh, full (rosy, cheerful), to announce glad news.

    a.   I Samuel 10:1, 6, 9

G.   Having a merry heart

1.   Ephesians 5:17-22 – *"[17]Wherefore be ye not unwise, but understanding what the will of the Lord is. [18]And be not drunk with wine, wherein is excess; but be filled with the Spirit; [19]Speaking to yourselves in psalms and hymns and spiritual songs, singing and making melody in your heart to the Lord..."* – Melody in the Greek means to rub or touch the surface, to twitch, or twang (i.e. to play on a stringed instrument).

2.   Proverbs 15:15 – *"...he that is of a merry heart hath a continual feast."*

3.   Proverbs 17:22 – *"A merry heart doeth good like a medicine: but a broken spirit drieth the bones."* – Merry here means in Hebrew – blithe or gleeful; it comes from a root word that means – to brighten up, to cheer up, to make glad

4.   Luke 15:32 – *"It was meet that we should make merry, and be glad: for this thy brother was dead, and is alive again; and was lost, and is found."*

5.   II Chronicles 7:10 – *"And on the three and twentieth day of the seventh month he sent the people away into their tents, glad and merry in heart for the goodness that the LORD had shewed unto David, and to Solomon, and to Israel his people."*

6.   Acts 26:2 – *"I think myself happy, king Agrippa, because I shall answer for myself this day before thee touching all the things whereof I am accused of the Jews"* – Happy in Greek – supremely blessed, well off, fortunate

7. Psalms 144:15 – "*Happy is that people, that is in such a case: yea, happy is that people, whose God is the LORD.*"

8. Deuteronomy 33:29 – "*Happy art thou, O Israel: who is like unto thee, O people saved by the LORD, the shield of thy help, and who is the sword of thy excellency! and thine enemies shall be found liars unto thee; and thou shalt tread upon their high places.*"

9. Psalms 146:5 – "*Happy is he that hath the God of Jacob for his help, whose hope is in the LORD his God:*"

10. I Samuel 2:1 – "*And Hannah prayed, and said, My heart rejoiceth in the LORD, mine horn is exalted in the LORD: my mouth is enlarged over mine enemies; because I rejoice in thy salvation.*" A rejoicing heart

11. Psalms 57:7-11 – "*[7]My heart is fixed, O God, my heart is fixed: I will sing and give praise. [8]Awake up, my glory; awake, psaltery and harp: I myself will awake early. [9]I will praise thee, O Lord, among the people: I will sing unto thee among the nations. [10]For thy mercy is great unto the heavens, and thy truth unto the clouds. [11]Be thou exalted, O God, above the heavens: let thy glory be above all the earth.*"

Lesson 33
HAVING DONE ALL, STAND

I.   Ephesians 6:13-18 – *"...that ye may be able to withstand in the evil day, and having done all, to stand. Stand therefore..."*

   A.   Normally when facing adversity, we think we should be doing something. (I Samuel 12:7)

       1.   Philippians 2:12 – *"...work out your own salvation with fear and trembling."*
       2.   Philippians 4:13 – *"I can do all things through Christ which strengtheneth me."*
       3.   Colossians 1:29 – *"Whereunto I also labour, striving according to his working..."*
       4.   I Timothy 6:12 – *"Fight the good fight of faith, lay hold on eternal life..."*
       5.   James 2:17, 20 – *"Even so faith, if it hath not works, is dead..."*

II. Standing According To The Scriptures

   A.   Word meanings

       1.   Greek – *histemi* – to make to stand, establish, set, abide, hold up
       2.   Hebrew – *yatsab* – to place anything so as to stay, to continue, to station.

   B.   How and what are we to stand in and with?

       1.   Exodus 14:13 – *"...Fear ye not, stand still, and see the salvation of the LORD..."*
       2.   Galatians 5:1 – *"Stand fast therefore in the liberty wherewith Christ hath made us free..."*
       3.   I Thessalonians 3:8 (Philippians 4:1) – *"For now we live, if ye stand fast in the Lord."*

       4.   II Corinthians 1:24 – *"...for by faith ye stand."*

          a.   I Corinthians 16:13 – *"Watch ye, stand fast in the faith, quit you like men, be strong."*
          b.   Romans 11:20

       5.   I Corinthians 7:37 – *"Nevertheless he that standeth stedfast in his heart..."*
       6.   Colossians 4:12 – *"...that ye may stand perfect and complete in all the will of God."*
       7.   I Peter 5:12 – *"...testifying that this is the true grace of God wherein ye stand."*
       8.   I Corinthians 15:1 – *"Moreover, brethren, I declare unto you the gospel which I preached unto you, which also ye have received, and wherein ye stand"*
       9.   Mark 11:25 – *"And when ye stand praying, forgive..."*
   10. Philippians 1:27 – *"...that ye stand fast in one spirit, with one mind striving together for the faith of the gospel"*

Lesson 34
HEARING GOD'S VOICE

I. It Takes Faith to Hear God's Voice and Know His Will

    A. A Problem in Hearing

        1. Job 33:14 – *"For God speaketh once, yea twice, yet man perceiveth it not."*

        2. John 12:28-29 – *"28Father, glorify thy name. Then came there a voice from heaven, saying, I have both glorified it, and will glorify it again. 29The people therefore, that stood by, and heard it, said that it thundered: others said, An angel spake to him."*

        3. I Corinthians 14:8 – *"For if the trumpet give an uncertain sound, who shall prepare himself to the battle?"*

        4. I Samuel 3:4-10

        5. I Corinthians 14:10-11 – *"10There are, it may be, so many kinds of voices in the world, and none of them is without signification. 11Therefore if I know not the meaning of the voice, I shall be unto him that speaketh a barbarian, and he that speaketh shall be a barbarian unto me."*

    B. God Wants Us to Hear and Know

        1. John 10:2-4, 27 – *"2But he that entereth in by the door is the shepherd of the sheep. 3To him the porter openeth; and the sheep hear his voice: and he calleth his own sheep by name, and leadeth them out. 4And when he putteth forth his own sheep, he goeth before them, and the sheep follow him: for they know his voice...27My sheep hear my voice, and I know them, and they follow me:"*

        2. Ephesians 5:17 – *"Wherefore be ye not unwise, but understanding what the will of the Lord is."*

        3. John 15:15 – *"Henceforth I call you not servants; for the servant knoweth not what his lord doeth: but I have called you friends; for all things that I have heard of my Father I have made known unto you."*

        4. I John 5:20 – *"And we know that the Son of God is come, and hath given us an understanding, that we may know him that is true, and we are in him that is true, even in his Son Jesus Christ. This is the true God, and eternal life."*

        5. Psalms 32:8-9 – *"8I will instruct thee and teach thee in the way which thou shalt go: I will guide thee with mine eye. 9Be ye not as the horse, or as the mule, which have no understanding: whose mouth must be held in with bit and bridle, lest they come near unto thee."*

        6. Daniel 2:23 – *"I thank thee, and praise thee, O thou God of my fathers, who hast given me wisdom and might, and hast made known unto me now what we desired of thee: for thou hast now made known unto us the king's matter."*

        7. Acts 22:14 – *"And he said, The God of our fathers hath chosen thee, that thou shouldest know his will, and see that Just One, and shouldest hear the voice of his mouth."*

        8. Isaiah 30:30 – *"And the LORD shall cause his glorious voice to be heard..."* It is God's responsibility to speak. He will make sure we hear. The question is will we be able to discern His voice?

    C. What Is God's Voice Like? To the degree we have the written Word of God in our hearts, will determine the degree we hear God's supernatural voice. His voice must have a foundation. That foundation is His Word

        1. James 3:17 – *"But the wisdom that is from above is first pure, then peaceable, gentle, and easy to be intreated, full of mercy and good fruits, without partiality, and without hypocrisy."*

        2. John 6:63 – *"It is the spirit that quickeneth; the flesh profiteth nothing: the words that I speak unto you, they are spirit, and they are life."*

3. Isaiah 45:19 – *"I have not spoken in secret, in a dark place of the earth: I said not unto the seed of Jacob, Seek ye me in vain: I the LORD speak righteousness, I declare things that are right."*
4. Psalms 29:3-9
5. Psalms 68:33 – *"To him that rideth upon the heavens of heavens, which were of old; lo, he doth send out his voice, and that a mighty voice."*

D. God speaks to us in six ways

1. In His Word
2. Prophetically
3. Through people
4. Through God ordained leadership (pastors, teachers)
5. Through situations
6. To us privately – by the Spirit

E. How does God speak to us supernaturally? He speaks to our spirit, but first we must realize God is a Spirit (John 4:24). God is a Spirit being and communicates on a spiritual level. Man's spirit is where the Lord speaks.

1. Man's spirit – God's speaking place

   a. Proverbs 20:27 – *"The spirit of man is the candle of the LORD, searching all the inward parts of the belly."*
   b. Genesis 2:7 – *"And the LORD God formed man of the dust of the ground, and breathed into his nostrils the breath of life; and man became a living soul."*
   c. Matthew 16:17 – *"And Jesus answered and said unto him, Blessed art thou, Simon Barjona: for flesh and blood hath not revealed it unto thee, but my Father which is in heaven."*
   d. Job 32:8 – *"But there is a spirit in man: and the inspiration of the Almighty giveth them understanding."*

2. When we are born again and filled with the Spirit, God then comes and lives in our spirit.

   a. I Corinthians 6:17 – *"But he that is joined unto the Lord is one spirit."*
   b. John 14:23 – *"Jesus answered and said unto him, If a man love me, he will keep my words: and my Father will love him, and we will come unto him, and make our abode with him."*
   c. Revelation 3:20 – *"Behold, I stand at the door, and knock: if any man hear my voice, and open the door, I will come in to him, and will sup with him, and he with me."*

3. And because of that we can know all things and hear His voice. He is inside of us. We hear the voice of God inwardly. We must learn to hear the voice of God inside of us.

   a. I John 5:10 – *"He that believeth on the Son of God hath the witness in himself..."*
   b. I John 2:20, 27 – *"20But ye have an unction from the Holy One, and ye know all things...27But the anointing which ye have received of him abideth in you, and ye need not that any man teach you: but as the same anointing teacheth you of all things, and is truth, and is no lie, and even as it hath taught you, ye shall abide in him."*
   c. I Corinthians 2:9-12 – *"9But as it is written, Eye hath not seen, nor ear heard, neither have entered into the heart of man, the things which God hath prepared for them that love him. 10But God hath revealed them unto us by his Spirit: for the Spirit searcheth all things, yea, the deep things of God. 11For what man knoweth the things of a man, save the spirit of man which is in him? even so the things of God knoweth no man, but the Spirit of God. 12Now we*

have received, not the spirit of the world, but the spirit which is of God; that we might know the things that are freely given to us of God."

    d.   Job 36:4 – "...he that is perfect in knowledge is with thee."

    e.   Job 6:13 – "Is not my help in me? and is wisdom driven quite from me?"

    f.   Luke 24:32 – "And they said one to another, Did not our heart burn within us, while he talked with us by the way, and while he opened to us the scriptures?"

    g.   Luke 1:41 – "And it came to pass, that, when Elisabeth heard the salutation of Mary, the babe leaped in her womb; and Elisabeth was filled with the Holy Ghost:"

    h.   Genesis 3:8 – "And they heard the voice of the LORD God walking in the garden in the cool of the day..."

II.   How Can We Hear When He Speaks?

    A.   Get quiet on the inside

        1.   Psalms 46:10 – "Be still, and know that I am God: I will be exalted among the heathen, I will be exalted in the earth."

        2.   Job 37:2 – "Hear attentively the noise of his voice, and the sound that goeth out of his mouth."

        3.   Isaiah 30:7, 15

        4.   I Kings 19:9-19

    B.   Then simply ask

        1.   James 4:2 – "Ye lust, and have not: ye kill, and desire to have, and cannot obtain: ye fight and war, yet ye have not, because ye ask not."

        2.   James 1:5 – "If any of you lack wisdom, let him ask of God, that giveth to all men liberally, and upbraideth not; and it shall be given him."

        3.   John 16:23-24 – "23And in that day ye shall ask me nothing. Verily, verily, I say unto you, Whatsoever ye shall ask the Father in my name, he will give it you. 24Hitherto have ye asked nothing in my name: ask, and ye shall receive, that your joy may be full."

        4.   Proverbs 2:2-6

        5.   I Kings 3:5-14

    C.   When we ask we must believe – There is no point in asking if you don't really believe there is going to be an answer. Prayer to seek God can be very religious and become a dead work if we don't have a vibrant, living faith that when we come to Him He hears and answers.

        1.   Hebrews 11:6 – "But without faith it is impossible to please him: for he that cometh to God must believe that he is, and that he is a rewarder of them that diligently seek him."

        2.   Philippians 4:6-7 – "6Be careful for nothing; but in every thing by prayer and supplication with thanksgiving let your requests be made known unto God. 7And the peace of God, which passeth all understanding, shall keep your hearts and minds through Christ Jesus."

        3.   James 1:5-8 – "5If any of you lack wisdom, let him ask of God, that giveth to all men liberally, and upbraideth not; and it shall be given him. 6But let him ask in faith, nothing wavering. For he that wavereth is like a wave of the sea driven with the wind and tossed. 7For let not that man think that he shall receive any thing of the Lord. 8A double minded man is unstable in all his ways."

        4.   Proverbs 3:5 – "Trust in the LORD with all thine heart; and lean not unto thine own understanding."

        5.   I John 5:14-15 – "14And this is the confidence that we have in him, that, if we ask any thing according to his will, he heareth us: 15And if we know that he hear us, whatsoever we ask, we know that we have the petitions that we desired of him." – We must know He hears before we can know He answers

D. What happens when we ask and believe?

1. Isaiah 30:21 – *"And thine ears shall hear a word behind thee, saying, This is the way, walk ye in it, when ye turn to the right hand, and when ye turn to the left."*
2. Jeremiah 33:3 – *"Call unto me, and I will answer thee, and shew thee great and mighty things, which thou knowest not."*
3. Isaiah 65:24 – *"And it shall come to pass, that before they call, I will answer; and while they are yet speaking, I will hear."*

E. Once you've heard from God – remember these things

1. Galatians 1:15-16 – *"15But when it pleased God, who separated me from my mother's womb, and called me by his grace, 16To reveal his Son in me, that I might preach him among the heathen; immediately I conferred not with flesh and blood:"*

    a. Nehemiah 2:12 – We don't have to tell everything that God shares with us. Some people may not receive it or they may not be able to understand. Be sensitive.
    b. Deuteronomy 29:29

2. Don't let the knowledge of good and evil in.

    a. Genesis 2:17 – *"But of the tree of the knowledge of good and evil, thou shalt not eat of it: for in the day that thou eatest thereof thou shalt surely die."*, Genesis 3:1-13

Man no longer would be living on the voice of God, but he would be living by reason. The Word of God brings life, faith, vision. Man's mind can never attain that. This is the first thing the devil did; he tried to convince man God really didn't mean what He said, and he made man reason about what the Lord said. The minute man did, he died – he was cut off. Even the knowledge of good is bad, because immediately when you know what's good you realize what's bad or evil. Any knowledge that exalts itself over God's Word whether good or bad is error. Man's soul, at this point, became preeminent and he began to digress to where now the intellect is given great honor.

F. There are two trees

1. The Tree of Life – This is what man had originally in the beginning. God was his source. This is God's best, that man would allow God to live through him, to lead him, to instruct him, to take care of him, and to let God be his source. If man will do this he then has all that God has at his command. It's a place of dominion. God wants us to live like this.

    a. Psalms 87:7 – *"As well the singers as the players on instruments shall be there: all my springs are in thee."*
    b. Romans 8:14 – *"For as many as are led by the Spirit of God, they are the sons of God."*
    c. Galatians 2:20 – *"I am crucified with Christ: nevertheless I live; yet not I, but Christ liveth in me: and the life which I now live in the flesh I live by the faith of the Son of God, who loved me, and gave himself for me."*
    d. Habakkuk 2:4 – *"Behold, his soul which is lifted up is not upright in him: but the just shall live by his faith."*
    e. John 15:4-7 – *"4Abide in me, and I in you. As the branch cannot bear fruit of itself, except it abide in the vine; no more can ye, except ye abide in me. 5I am the vine, ye are the branches: He that abideth in me, and I in him, the same bringeth forth much fruit: for without me ye can do nothing. 6If a man abide not in me, he is cast forth as a branch, and is withered; and men gather them, and cast them into the fire, and they are burned. 7If ye*

abide in me, and my words abide in you, ye shall ask what ye will, and it shall be done unto you."

2. The Tree of the Knowledge of Good and Evil – This is the tree of reason, of man's wisdom. It cuts you off from your life-giving source. There is no right or wrong! There is only God's voice (His Word).

III. Enemies that keep us from hearing or walking in God's voice

A. Mark 4:15 – *"And these are they by the way side, where the word is sown; but when they have heard, Satan cometh immediately, and taketh away the word that was sown in their hearts."* Satan comes to steal – how does he do this?

1. Mark 4:17-19 – *"17And have no root in themselves, and so endure but for a time: afterward, when affliction or persecution ariseth for the word's sake, immediately they are offended. 18And these are they which are sown among thorns; such as hear the word, 19And the cares of this world, and the deceitfulness of riches, and the lusts of other things entering in, choke the word, and it becometh unfruitful."*

    a. Affliction
    b. Persecution
    c. Cares of the World
    d. Lust of other things
    e. Deceitfulness of riches

2. Genesis 27:22 – *"And Jacob went near unto Isaac his father; and he felt him, and said, The voice is Jacob's voice, but the hands are the hands of Esau."* – Going by feelings instead of God's voice. God doesn't pressure us, He speaks and then it's up to us. God makes sure we hear His voice but then it's up to us what happens.

    a. I Samuel 16:1, 3, 6-13
    b. John 20:14-16 – She couldn't tell by His appearance but she knew the voice.
    c. Luke 24:13-16, 30-32 – They could hear the voice, but were led by what they saw. If we will spend more time with Jesus, we will become accustomed to hearing Him.

Lesson 35
HEART OF A LION

In the last days, God is bringing forth a people who have the heart of a lion. They will be fearless in the face of the enemy. They will have a heart like the Lord Jesus.

I.   A Look Into The Scriptures Concerning This

A.   The lamb and the lion nature of our Lord

1.   Revelation 5:5-7 – "*⁵And one of the elders saith unto me, Weep not: behold, the Lion of the tribe of Juda, the Root of David, hath prevailed to open the book, and to loose the seven seals thereof. ⁶And I beheld, and, lo, in the midst of the throne and of the four beasts, and in the midst of the elders, stood a Lamb as it had been slain, having seven horns and seven eyes, which are the seven Spirits of God sent forth into all the earth. ⁷And he came and took the book out of the right hand of him that sat upon the throne.*"

To be complete in Him, we must have both aspects of God's nature working in us. There is a time for everything (Ecclesiastes 3:1), and we must discern properly the right nature for the right time. For instance, in counseling, the lamb nature would be the normal flow, but in public ministry (leading worship, preaching, teaching, prophesying, etc) the lion nature seems to be more effective.

We must have the lion nature operating in us to overcome, to run off and cast out the devil and his cohorts, as well as get rid of all religion and traditions of men.

It takes a confident (in the Lord), secure, and broken (humble) person to fill this bill. This one must have God's authority working with them and through them.

a.   Lamb nature of our Lord

1)   His response to children
2)   His care for the poor and needy
3)   His concern for the sick
4)   His ability to forgive and show mercy
5)   Matthew 11:29

b.   Lion nature of our Lord

1)   Casting out the money changers
2)   Rebuking the religious Pharisees
3)   His way of ministering to some people
4)   Dealing with the devil
5)   Revelation 5:5

B.   Lions symbolic of people in Scripture

1.   Proverbs 28:1 – "*The wicked flee when no man pursueth: but the righteous are bold as a lion.*" Other translations:

"*...the righteous are fearless...*"
"*...like a lion are confident...*"
"*...uncompromising...*"

2. Revelations 4:6-11 (Ezekiel 1:10)

    a. Four – Number for creation (new creation man)
    b. Face of a lion and a man
    c. Six wings – Six is the number for man

3. Micah 5:8 – *"And the remnant of Jacob shall be among the Gentiles in the midst of many people as a lion among the beasts of the forest, as a young lion among the flocks of sheep: who, if he go through, both treadeth down, and teareth in pieces, and none can deliver."*
4. Numbers 23:24 – *"Behold, the people shall rise up as a great lion, and lift up himself as a young lion: he shall not lie down until he eat of the prey, and drink the blood of the slain."*
4. Numbers 23:24 (Numbers 24:9)
5. Young lions of Judah

C. Who and what they are like

1. Proverbs 28:1 – *"The wicked flee when no man pursueth: but the righteous are bold as a lion."*

    a. Bold
    b. Secure
    c. Fearless
    d. Confident

2. I Chronicles 12:8 – *"And of the Gadites there separated themselves unto David into the hold to the wilderness men of might, and men of war fit for the battle, that could handle shield and buckler, whose faces were like the faces of lions, and were as swift as the roes upon the mountains;"*

    a. Men of might
    b. Men of war
    c. Fit for battle
    d. Could handle shield and buckler
    e. Upon the mountains

3. Micah 5:8 – *"And the remnant of Jacob shall be among the Gentiles in the midst of many people as a lion among the beasts of the forest, as a young lion among the flocks of sheep: who, if he go through, both treadeth down, and teareth in pieces, and none can deliver."*

    a. These are the remnant
    b. Among the gentiles (nations)
    c. Midst of many people (not secluded)
    d. Treads down
    e. Teareth in pieces
    f. None can deliver

4. Revelation 5:5 – *"And one of the elders saith unto me, Weep not: behold, the Lion of the tribe of Juda, the Root of David, hath prevailed to open the book, and to loose the seven seals thereof."*

    a. Prevailed
    b. To open (door opener)
    c. Root of David (One of David's line, like Paul)
    d. The ability to loose
    e. Of the tribe of Judah

5. Deuteronomy 33:20-22 – "*20And of Gad he said, Blessed be he that enlargeth Gad: he dwelleth as a lion, and teareth the arm with the crown of the head. 21And he provided the first part for himself, because there, in a portion of the lawgiver, was he seated; and he came with the heads of the people, he executed the justice of the LORD, and his judgments with Israel. 22And of Dan he said, Dan is a lion's whelp: he shall leap from Bashan.*"

   a. Teareth the arm with the crown of the head – This means to destroy the works by the authority of God.
   b. Executed judgment of the Lord
   c. Leap from Bashan – Psalms 22:12

6. Revelation 4:6-7 – "*6And before the throne there was a sea of glass like unto crystal: and in the midst of the throne, and round about the throne, were four beasts full of eyes before and behind. 7And the first beast was like a lion, and the second beast like a calf, and the third beast had a face as a man, and the fourth beast was like a flying eagle.*"

   a. Full of eyes within – Able to judge yourself, to be objective and discern your own heart and motives.
   b. Holy, holy, holy – They are worshippers
   c. Lord, God Almighty, who was, and is and is to come – They have a revelation of the Godhead
   d. They are pioneers and leaders. Others follow what they do. All of heaven responds to their worship. Others enter in because of them.

D. Their exploits

   1. II Samuel 23:8-23 – This is the list of the supernatural deeds performed by David's mighty men. These men had the heart of a lion.
   2. I Samuel 17:33-39
   3. Hebrews 11:33-39
   4. Judges 14:5-14
   5. Daniel 6:4-28
   6. Daniel 3:12-30

Lesson 36
HIS TREASURE IN US

I.   His Treasure In Us, II Corinthians 4:7 – *"But we have this treasure in earthen vessels, that the excellency of the power may be of God, and not of us."*

A.   Other translations:

"But we have this treasure in jars of clay to show that this all surpassing power is from God and not from us"
"If you only look at us, you might well miss the brightness. We carry this precious message around in the unadorned clay pots of our ordinary lives. That's to prevent anyone from confusing God's incomparable power with us"
"But this precious treasure, this light and power that now shines within us, is held in a perishable container, that is, in our weak bodies. Everyone can see that the glorious power within us must be from God, and is not our own"
"But we have this wealth in vessels of earth, so that it may be seen that the power comes not from us but God"
"But we have this treasure (the reflection of the knowledge of the glory of God in the face of Christ) in earthen ware containers in order that the super excellence of the power might be from God as a source, and not from us"
"Yet we who have this spiritual treasure are like common clay pots, in order to show that the supreme power belongs to God, not to us"
"frail vessel of earth"

B.   Word definitions for "Treasure"

1.   Greek, *thesauros* – a deposit, wealth literally and figuratively

2.   Hebrew words

a.   *Owtsar* – a depositary, storehouse; it comes from a root, *atsar* – to store up
b.   *Chocen* – wealth, riches, strength, to hoard or lay up treasures

C.   Vessels of Clay – Process of water into wine, John 2:1-10

"*1And the <u>third day</u> there was a <u>marriage</u> in Cana of Galilee; and the mother of Jesus was there: 2And both <u>Jesus was called, and his disciples, to the marriage</u>. 3And when they wanted wine, the mother of Jesus saith unto him, They have no wine. 4Jesus saith unto her, Woman, what have I to do with thee? mine hour is not yet come. 5 His mother saith unto the servants, Whatsoever he saith unto you, do it. 6 And there were set there six waterpots of stone, after the manner of the purifying of the Jews, containing two or three firkins apiece. 7 Jesus saith unto them, Fill the waterpots with water. And they filled them up to the brim. 8And he saith unto them, Draw out now, and bear unto the governor of the feast. And they bare it. 9 When the ruler of the feast had tasted the water that was made wine, and knew not whence it was: (but the servants which drew the water knew;) the governor of the feast called the bridegroom, 10And saith unto him, Every man at the beginning doth set forth good wine; and when men have well drunk, then that which is worse: but thou hast <u>kept the good wine until now</u>. 11This <u>beginning of miracles</u> did Jesus in Cana of Galilee, and <u>manifested forth his glory</u>; and his disciples believed on him.*"

1.   Six waterpots – 6 is the number in Scripture for man which is a type here of his people (earthen vessels)
2.   Fill them with water – type of Word and Holy Ghost
3.   Governor – type of the world
4.   Water that was made wine – Holy Ghost

D.   Other corresponding Scriptures

1.   Proverbs 21:20 – *"There is treasure to be desired and oil in the dwelling of the wise; but a foolish man spendeth it up."*

2.   Proverbs 15:6 – *"In the house of the righteous is much treasure: but in the revenues of the wicked is trouble."*

3.   Job 36:4 – *"For truly my words shall not be false: he that is perfect in knowledge is with thee."*

4.   Philemon 6 – *"That the communication of thy faith may become effectual by the acknowledging of every good thing which is in you in Christ Jesus."*

5.   John 14:10-12 – *"[10]Believest thou not that I am in the Father, and the Father in me? the words that I speak unto you I speak not of myself: but the Father that dwelleth in me, he doeth the works. [11]Believe me that I am in the Father, and the Father in me: or else believe me for the very works' sake. [12]Verily, verily, I say unto you, He that believeth on me, the works that I do shall he do also; and greater works than these shall he do; because I go unto my Father."*

6.   Romans 7:18 – *"[18]For I know that in me (that is, in my flesh,) dwelleth no good thing: for to will is present with me; but how to perform that which is good I find not."*

7.   Galatians 1:15-16 – *"[15]But when it pleased God, who separated me from my mother's womb, and called me by his grace, [16]To reveal his Son in me, that I might preach him among the heathen; immediately I conferred not with flesh and blood:"*

8.   Galatians 2:20 – *"I am crucified with Christ: nevertheless I live; yet not I, but Christ liveth in me: and the life which I now live in the flesh I live by the faith of the Son of God, who loved me, and gave himself for me."*

9.   Colossians 1:27-29 – *"[27]To whom God would make known what is the riches of the glory of this mystery among the Gentiles; which is Christ in you, the hope of glory: [28]Whom we preach, warning every man, and teaching every man in all wisdom; that we may present every man perfect in Christ Jesus: [29]Whereunto I also labour, striving according to his working, which worketh in me mightily."*

10. I Corinthians 4:7 – *"For who maketh thee to differ from another? and what hast thou that thou didst not receive? now if thou didst receive it, why dost thou glory, as if thou hadst not received it?"*

11. Acts 3:12 – *"And when Peter saw it, he answered unto the people, Ye men of Israel, why marvel ye at this? or why look ye so earnestly on us, as though by our own power or holiness we had made this man to walk?"*

12. II Chronicles 5:1 – *"Thus all the work that Solomon made for the house of the LORD was finished: and Solomon brought in all the things that David his father had dedicated; and the silver, and the gold, and all the instruments, put he among the treasures of the house of God."*

13. II Timothy 2:19-21 – *"[19]Nevertheless the foundation of God standeth sure, having this seal, The Lord knoweth them that are his. And, Let every one that nameth the name of Christ depart from iniquity. [20]But in a great house there are not only vessels of gold and of silver, but also of wood and of earth; and some to honour, and some to dishonour. [21]If a man therefore purge himself from these, he shall be a vessel unto honour, sanctified, and meet for the master's use, and prepared unto every good work."*

Lesson 37
HOLDING ONTO OUR PEACE

Proverbs 17:28 – *"Even a fool, when he holdeth his peace, is counted wise: and he that shutteth his lips is esteemed a man of understanding."*

This is more than just being quiet. You can be quiet and not talk, but no have peace within. This is holding on to your peace within, no matter the external circumstances. Once we let go of our peace, we take up the problem while turmoil and torment begins.

I.   Holding Our Peace

    A.   Scriptures

        1.   Job 33:33 – *"...hold thy peace, and I shall teach thee wisdom."*
        2.   Mark 14:61 – *"But he held his peace, and answered nothing..."*

What does this mean? It means staying in faith, staying full of the Spirit, staying in the holy place, and staying in the secret place in God. No matter what is going on outside of us, no matter how much garbage is taking place. Inside there will be peace.

        3.   It's living in God, Psalms 46:1-7 – *"[1]God is our refuge and strength, a very present help in trouble. [2]Therefore will not we fear, though the earth be removed, and though the mountains be carried into the midst of the sea; [3]Though the waters thereof roar and be troubled, though the mountains shake with the swelling thereof. Selah. [4]There is a river, the streams whereof shall make glad the city of God, the holy place of the tabernacles of the most High. [5]God is in the midst of her; she shall not be moved: God shall help her, and that right early. [6]The heathen raged, the kingdoms were moved: he uttered his voice, the earth melted. [7]The LORD of hosts is with us; the God of Jacob is our refuge. Selah."*

           1)   Isaiah 66:12 – *"For thus saith the LORD, Behold, I will extend peace to her like a river, and the glory of the Gentiles like a flowing stream: then shall ye suck, ye shall be borne upon her sides, and be dandled upon her knees."*
           2)   Philippians 4:7 – *"And the peace of God, which passeth all understanding, shall keep your hearts and minds through Christ Jesus."*

    B.   Peace has been purchased for us

        1.   Romans 5:1 – *"...we have peace with God through our Lord Jesus Christ:"*
        2.   Isaiah 53:5 – *"...the chastisement of our peace was upon him..."*
        3.   Romans 14:17 – *"...kingdom of God is not meat and drink; but righteousness, and peace, and joy in the Holy Ghost."*
        4.   John 14:27 – *"Peace I leave with you, my peace I give unto you..."*

II.   How Do We Hold Our Peace?

    A.   Scriptures

        1.   Colossians 3:15 – *"And let the peace of God rule in your hearts..."*
        2.   Isaiah 26:3 – *"Thou wilt keep him in perfect peace, whose mind is stayed on thee: because he trusteth in thee."*
        3.   Exodus 14:14 – *"The LORD shall fight for you, and ye shall hold your peace."*
        4.   Job 22:21 – *"Acquaint now thyself with him, and be at peace..."*

Lesson 38
HOLDING ONTO OUR VISION

I. Habakkuk 2:2-3 – "*²And the LORD answered me, and said, Write the vision, and make it plain upon tables, that he may run that readeth it. ³For the vision is yet for an appointed time, but at the end it shall speak, and not lie: though it tarry, wait for it; because it will surely come, it will not tarry.*"

A. God has given us all a vision, both personally and corporately

1. Matthew 4:4 – "*But he answered and said, It is written, Man shall not live by bread alone, but by every word that proceedeth out of the mouth of God.*"
2. II Peter 1:12 – "*Wherefore I will not be negligent to put you always in remembrance of these things, though ye know them, and be established in the present truth.*"
3. Proverbs 29:18 – "*Where there is no vision, the people perish: but he that keepeth the law, happy is he.*" Hebrew for vision – a mental sight, a dream, a revelation, an oracle; comes from a root – to gaze at mentally, to contemplate with pleasure, prophesy
4. Acts 26:19 – "*Whereupon, O king Agrippa, I was not disobedient unto the heavenly vision:*"

B. Once we see it, we must run after it.

1. Genesis 22:4 – "*Then on the third day Abraham lifted up his eyes, and saw the place afar off.*"
2. I Corinthians 9:24 – "*Know ye not that they which run in a race run all, but one receiveth the prize? So run, that ye may obtain.*"
3. Philippians 3:14 – "*I press toward the mark for the prize of the high calling of God in Christ Jesus.*"

C. We must count the cost and know we won't do it in our own ability

1. Luke 14:28-30 – "*²⁸For which of you, intending to build a tower, sitteth not down first, and counteth the cost, whether he have sufficient to finish it? ²⁹Lest haply, after he hath laid the foundation, and is not able to finish it, all that behold it begin to mock him, ³⁰Saying, This man began to build, and was not able to finish.*"
2. I Kings 19:7 – "*And the angel of the LORD came again the second time, and touched him, and said, Arise and eat; because the journey is too great for thee.*"
3. Ecclesiastes 9:11 – "*I returned, and saw under the sun, that the race is not to the swift, nor the battle to the strong, neither yet bread to the wise, nor yet riches to men of understanding, nor yet favour to men of skill; but time and chance happeneth to them all.*"
4. Acts 20:24 – "*But none of these things move me, neither count I my life dear unto myself, so that I might finish my course with joy, and the ministry, which I have received of the Lord Jesus, to testify the gospel of the grace of God.*"
5. Revelation 12:11 – "*And they overcame him by the blood of the Lamb, and by the word of their testimony; and they loved not their lives unto the death.*"
6. Zechariah 4:6 – "*Then he answered and spake unto me, saying, This is the word of the LORD unto Zerubbabel, saying, Not by might, nor by power, but by my spirit, saith the LORD of hosts.*"

D. If God gave it, He will finish it

1. Genesis 28:15 – "*And, behold, I am with thee, and will keep thee in all places whither thou goest, and will bring thee again into this land; for I will not leave thee, until I have done that which I have spoken to thee of.*"
2. Isaiah 55:11 – "*So shall my word be that goeth forth out of my mouth: it shall not return unto me void, but it shall accomplish that which I please, and it shall prosper in the thing whereto I sent it.*"

3. Isaiah 46:11 – *"Calling a ravenous bird from the east, the man that executeth my counsel from a far country: yea, I have spoken it, I will also bring it to pass; I have purposed it, I will also do it."*
4. Ezekiel 36:36 – *"Then the heathen that are left round about you shall know that I the LORD build the ruined places, and plant that that was desolate: I the LORD have spoken it, and I will do it."*

E.   There is an appointed time in which God's Word will be fulfilled

1. Job 14:14 – *"If a man die, shall he live again? all the days of my appointed time will I wait, till my change come."*
2. Psalms 105:19 – *"Until the time that his word came: the word of the LORD tried him."*
3. Ecclesiastes 3:1 – *"To every thing there is a season, and a time to every purpose under the heaven:"* (Ecclesiastes 3:17, 8:6)
4. Luke 1:20 – *"And, behold, thou shalt be dumb, and not able to speak, until the day that these things shall be performed, because thou believest not my words, which shall be fulfilled in their season."*

F.   Hold fast and have faith in God

1. Hebrews 10:35-36 – *"Cast not away therefore your confidence, which hath great recompence of reward. For ye have need of patience, that, after ye have done the will of God, ye might receive the promise."*
2. Hebrews 6:12 – *"That ye be not slothful, but followers of them who through faith and patience inherit the promises."*
3. Hebrews 10:23 – *"Let us hold fast the profession of our faith without wavering; (for he is faithful that promised;)"*

G.   God will bring our vision to pass

1. Jeremiah 29:11 – *"For I know the thoughts that I think toward you, saith the LORD, thoughts of peace, and not of evil, to give you an expected end."*
2. Zechariah 4:9 – *"The hands of Zerubbabel have laid the foundation of this house; his hands shall also finish it; and thou shalt know that the LORD of hosts hath sent me unto you."*

Lesson 39
HONORING GOD

I. Word Definitions For Honour, Honoureth, Honourable. Both the Hebrew and Greek Words for honour are also translated glory.

A. Hebrew words

1. *Kabod* – Weight, glory, splendor
2. *Kabed* – Heavy, to make weighty, abounding with more
3. *Hadar* – Magnificence, ornament or splendor. It comes from a root – to swell, to favor or honor, to be high.

B. Greek words

1. *Doxa* – Glory, dignity, praise
2. *Time* – Money paid, valuables, esteem of the highest degree, dignity

C. Basic definitions

It would seem then to give God honor is to give Him glory, weight praise, telling Him of His magnificence, splendor, and to serve Him like there is no one higher in the universe (He can count on us). It would seem when God gives us honour it means dignity, esteem of the highest degree, something valuable beyond words; we have His favor, we receive His glory.

II. God Is To Be Honoured

A. Scriptures

1. I Samuel 2:30 – "*...for them that honour me I will honour, and they that despise me shall be lightly esteemed.*"
2. Malachi 1:6 – "*...if then I be a father, where is mine honour? and if I be a master, where is my fear? saith the Lord of hosts unto you, O priests, that despise my name...*"
3. John 12:26 – "*...if any man serve me, him will my Father honour.*"
4. John 5:23 – "*That all men should honour the Son, even as they honour the Father. He that honoureth not the Son honoureth not the Father which hath sent him.*"
5. Isaiah 43:18-21

III. God Is Worthy Of Honor

A. Scriptures

1. Psalms 96:6 – "*Honour and majesty are before him: strength and beauty are in his sanctuary.*"
2. Psalms 104:1 – "*...O LORD my God, thou art very great; thou art clothed with honour and majesty.*"
3. Psalms 111:3 – "*His work is honourable and glorious: and his righteousness endureth for ever.*"
4. Psalms 145:5 – "*I will speak of the glorious honour of thy majesty, and of thy wondrous works.*"
5. I Timothy 1:17 – "*Now unto the King eternal, immortal, invisible, the only wise God, be honour and glory for ever and ever. Amen.*"
6. I Chronicles 16:27 – "*Glory and honour are in his presence; strength and gladness are in his place.*"
7. Hebrews 2:9 – "*But we see Jesus, who was made a little lower than the angels for the suffering of death, crowned with glory and honour...*"

8. I Timothy 6:16 – *"...to whom be honour and power everlasting. Amen."*

B. Especially in worship

1. Psalms 149:6-9 – *"Let the high praises of God be in their mouth...this honour have all his saints. Praise ye the LORD."*
2. Psalms 66:2 – *"Sing forth the honour of his name: make his praise glorious."*
3. Revelation 4:10-11
4. Revelation 5:12-14
5. Daniel 4:34-37
6. Revelation 21:24-26
7. Revelation 7:9-12

IV. The Scriptural Ways We Are Told How To Honour God

How we honour God is by giving the reverence and respect to Him which is His due. All God's people have a duty to honour Him in every aspect to their lives. With great respect the creation is called upon to revere Him as its Creator. Since human beings are made in the image of God, they should also respect and revere one another. Even unbelievers can also honour Him.

A. By walking in humility

1. Proverbs 15:33 – *"...before honour is humility."* (Proverbs 18:12)
2. Proverbs 29:23 – *"...honour shall uphold the humble in spirit."*
3. Micah 6:8 – *"He hath shewed thee, O man, what is good; and what doth the LORD require of thee, but to do justly, and to love mercy, and to walk humbly with thy God?"*
4. Proverbs 22:4

B. By Fearing The Lord

1. Proverbs 22:4 – *"By humility and the fear of the LORD are riches, and honour, and life."*
2. Psalms 15:4 – *"...but he honoureth them that fear the LORD..."*
3. Psalms 34:9 – *"O fear the LORD, ye his saints: for there is no want to them that fear him."*
4. Ecclesiastes 12:13 – *"...Fear God, and keep his commandments: for this is the whole duty of man."*

C. By giving tithes and offerings

1. Proverbs 3:9 – *"Honour the LORD with thy substance, and with the firstfruits of all thine increase:"*
2. Deuteronomy 26:1-11 – *"...I have brought the firstfruits of the land..."*
3. Malachi 3:10-12 – *"Bring ye all the tithes into the storehouse..."*
4. II Corinthians 9:6-15 – *"...He which soweth sparingly shall reap also sparingly; and he which soweth bountifully shall reap also bountifully..."*
5. Isaiah 60:9 – *"...to bring thy sons from far, their silver and their gold with them, unto the name of the LORD thy God, and to the Holy One of Israel, because he hath glorified thee."*
6. Psalms 112:9 – *"He hath dispersed, he hath given to the poor...his horn shall be exalted with honour."*
7. Luke 6:38 – *"Give, and it shall be given unto you; good measure, pressed down..."*

D. Ceasing from strife

1. Proverbs 20:3 – *"It is an honour for a man to cease from strife..."*

2. James 3:14-16 – *"...For where envying and strife is, there is confusion and every evil work."*
3. Philippians 2:3 – *"Let nothing be done through strife or vainglory..."*
4. Galatians 5:20 – Strife is a fruit of the flesh.

E. By searching the Scriptures

1. Proverbs 25:2 – *"It is the glory of God to conceal a thing: but the honour of kings is to search out a matter."*
2. Acts 17:11 – *"...searched the scriptures daily, whether those things were so."*
3. I Peter 3:15 – *"...be ready always to give an answer to every man that asketh you a reason of the hope that is in you with meekness and fear:"*
4. Psalms 119:80 – *"Let my heart be sound in thy statutes; that I be not ashamed."*
5. II Timothy 2:15 – *"Study to shew thyself approved unto God, a workman that needeth not to be ashamed, rightly dividing the word of truth."*
6. John 5:39 – *"Search the scriptures..."*

F. By waiting on the Lord

1. Proverbs 27:18 – *"...so he that waiteth on his master shall be honoured."*
2. Isaiah 40:31 – *"But they that wait upon the LORD shall renew their strength..."*
3. Psalms 27:14 – *"Wait on the LORD: be of good courage, and he shall strengthen thine heart: wait, I say, on the LORD."*
4. Psalms 130:5 – *"I wait for the Lord, my soul doth wait, and in his word do I hope."*

G. By following after righteousness

1. Proverbs 21:21 – *"He that followeth after righteousness and mercy findeth life, righteousness, and honour"*
2. Matthew 6:33 – *"But seek ye first the kingdom of God, and his righteousness; and all these things shall be added unto you."*
3. Zephaniah 2:3 – *"...seek righteousness, seek meekness..."*
4. I Corinthians 15:34 – *"Awake to righteousness, and sin not..."*
5. II Timothy 2:22 – *"Flee also youthful lusts: but follow righteousness, faith, charity, peace, with them that call on the Lord out of a pure heart."*

H. By receiving reproof

1. Proverbs 13:18 – *"Poverty and shame shall be to him that refuseth instruction: but he that regardeth reproof shall be honoured."*
2. Proverbs 15:5 – *"...he that regardeth reproof is prudent."*
3. Proverbs 15:31-32 – *"...he that heareth reproof getteth understanding."*
4. Proverbs 6:23 – *"...reproofs of instruction are the way of life:"*
5. Proverbs 8:33 – *"Hear instruction, and be wise, and refuse it not."*
6. II Chronicles 1:11-12 – Solomon asked for wisdom and not riches and God gave him wisdom, riches, and honour.

I. By loving the Lord

1. Psalms 91:14-15 – *"Because he hath set his love upon me...I will deliver him, and honour him."*
2. John 21:15-17 – *"...lovest thou me more than these?..."*
3. Psalms 31:23 – *"O love the LORD, all ye his saints..."*
4. Psalms 116:1 – *"I love the LORD, because he hath heard my voice and my supplications."*

J.   Possessing our vessel in sanctification (walking in purity)

1.   I Thessalonians 4:3-4 – *"For this is the will of God, even your sanctification, that ye should abstain from fornication: That every one of you should know how to possess his vessel in sanctification and honour;"*
2.   Romans 6:19 – *"...even so now yield your members servants to righteousness unto holiness."*
3.   II Corinthians 7:1 – *"Having therefore these promises, dearly beloved, let us cleanse ourselves from all filthiness of the flesh and spirit, perfecting holiness in the fear of God."*
4.   II Timothy 2:20-21 – *"...he shall be a vessel unto honour, sanctified..."*
5.   I Corinthians 6:18-20 – *"...For ye are bought with a price: therefore glorify God in your body, and in your spirit, which are God's."*
6.   Romans 12:1 – *"...present your bodies a living sacrifice, holy, acceptable unto God, which is your reasonable service."*

K.   Allowing the dealings of God in our lives

1.   I Peter 1:7 – *"...the trial of your faith...might be found unto praise and honour..."*
2.   James 1:3 – *"Knowing this, that the trying of your faith worketh patience."*
3.   Romans 5:3 – *"...knowing that tribulation worketh patience;"*
4.   Romans 8:18 – *"For I reckon that the sufferings of this present time are not worthy to be compared with the glory which shall be revealed in us."*
5.   II Corinthians 4:17 – *"For our light affliction, which is but for a moment, worketh for us a far more exceeding and eternal weight of glory;"*

L.   Having mercy on the poor

1.   Proverbs 14:31 – *"He that oppresseth the poor reproacheth his Maker: but he that honoureth him hath mercy on the poor."*
2.   Matthew 10:42 – *"And whosoever shall give to drink unto one of these little ones a cup of cold water...he shall in no wise lose his reward."*
3.   Deuteronomy 26:12-13 – After tithing to the Lord, the Israelits were to give to the poor, the stranger, etc.

V.   The Bride Honours Him

A.   Scriptures

1.   Proverbs 31:25 – *"Strength and honour are her clothing..."*
2.   Revelation 19:7-8 – *"Let us be glad and rejoice, and give honour to him: for themarriage of the Lamb is come, and his wife hath made herself ready..."*
3.   Psalms 45:9 – *"Kings' daughters were among thy honourable women..."*

VI. What We Should Be Seeking

A.   Scriptures

1.   John 5:44 – *"How can ye believe, which receive honour one of another, and seek not the honour that cometh from God only?"*
2.   John 8:54 – *"Jesus answered, If I honour myself, my honour is nothing: it is my Father that honoureth me..."*
3.   John 12:26 – *"If any man serve me, let him follow me; and where I am, there shall also my servant be: if any man serve me, him will my Father honour."*

This is God's great promise to us, that if we would just serve Him faithfully, out of a pure heart, and follow Him, not going our own way, but His, then He proclaims to us, He and His Father will honour us. I know that doing all of the above Scriptures and walking in them, will cost us everything. *"Buy the truth, and sell it not..."* (Proverbs 23:23). However it will bring to us the greatest gift anyone could ever ask for, receiving God's honour and glory. This would be the best gift He could bestow and favor, to be adorned with His honour and glory; which really is Himself, His divine essence! Noting could be more wonderful that that. There is no price too high, no dealing so strong, nor anything more important in this life, but the glory and honour of God, given to us freely because we have sacrificed everything for and to Him. As the apostle Paul so poetically expresses in the book of Philippians 3:7-14, *"But what things were gain to me, those I counted loss for Christ. Yea doubtless, and I count all things but loss for the excellency of the knowledge of Christ Jesus my Lord: for whom I have suffered the loss of all things, and do count them but dung, that I may win Christ, And be found in him, not having mine own righteousness, which is of the law, but that which is through the faith of Christ, the righteousness which is of God by faith: That I may know him, and the power of his resurrection, and the fellowship of his sufferings, being made conformable unto his death; If by any means I might attain unto the resurrection of the dead. Not as though I had already attained, either were already perfect: but I follow after, if that I may apprehend that for which also I am apprehended of Christ Jesus. Brethren, I count not myself to have apprehended: but this one thing I do, forgetting those things which are behind, and reaching forth unto those things which are before, I press toward the mark for the prize of the high calling of God in Christ Jesus."*, or as Jesus' parable in Matthew 13:44, *"Again, the kingdom of heaven is like unto treasure hid in a field; the which when a man hath found, he hideth, and for joy thereof goeth and selleth all that he hath, and buyeth that field."* **Let us honour Him then with our lives**!

Lesson 40
HOPE

I. Definitions of Hope

    A. Hebrew words

        1. *Yachal* – to wait, to be patient
        2. *Tiqvah* – a cord, an attachment, expectancy (same word translated expected or expectation)

    B. Greek word, *elpis* – to anticipate, expectation, or confidence
    C. Dictionary definition – the feeling that what is desired is also possible, or that events may turn out for the best.

II. Scriptural Explanation of Hope

    A. Many times we feel all hope is lost

        1. Ezekiel 37:11 – *"...Our bones are dried, and our hope is lost..."*
        2. Proverbs 13:12 – *"Hope deferred maketh the heart sick..."*
        3. Psalms 42:5, 11
        4. Psalms 130:1-7

    B. But we have hope (in our spirit)

        1. Hebrews 6:19 – *"Which hope we have as an anchor of the soul..."*
        2. I Corinthians 13:13 – *"And now abideth faith, hope, charity..."*

        3. Our hope is in a person – Jesus

            a. Psalms 38:15 – *"For in thee, O LORD, do I hope..."*
            b. Psalms 39:7 – *"...my hope is in thee."*
            c. I Timothy 1:1 – *"...and Lord Jesus Christ, which is our hope."*
            d. Psalms 62:5 – *"...for my expectation is from him."*
            e. Colossians 1:27 – *"...which is Christ in you, the hope of glory."* (Titus 2:13)
            f. Romans 15:13 – He is a God of hope; He will fill us with hope!

    C. We need to exercise our hope

        1. I Corinthians 13:7 – *"...hopeth all things, endureth all things..."*
        2. Psalms 71:14 – *"...I will hope continually, and will yet praise thee more and more."*
        3. I Peter 1:13 – *"...gird up the loins of your mind, be sober, and hope to the end..."*
        4. Lamentations 3:26 – *"It is good that a man should both hope and quietly wait for the salvation of the LORD."*
        5. Psalms 131:3 – *"Let Israel hope in the LORD from henceforth and for ever."*

III. What To Do When Hope Is Lost

    A. Let the Word of God build hope in your heart

        1. Romans 15:4 – *"...we through patience and comfort of the scriptures might have hope."*
        2. Psalms 119:74 – *"...because I have hoped in thy word."*
        3. Psalms 119:147

4. Psalms 119:49 – *"Remember the word unto thy servant, upon which thou hast caused me to hope."*
5. Psalms 130:5 – *"...my soul doth wait, and in his word do I hope."*

B. Let your hope be in God and not in your circumstances

1. Psalms 146:5 – *"Happy is he that hath the God of Jacob for his help, whose hope is in the LORD his God:"*
2. Jeremiah 17:7 – *"Blessed is the man that trusteth in the LORD, and whose hope the LORD is."*
3. Lamentations 3:20-26
4. Job 8:13-15

C. Put on hope as a helmet (to protect your mind)

1. I Thessalonians 5:18 – *"In every thing give thanks..."*
2. Ephesians 6:17 – *"And take the helmet of salvation, and the sword of the Spirit, which is the word of God:"*
3. I Peter 1:13 – *"...gird up the loins of your mind, be sober, and hope to the end..."*

D. Know that even your circumstances are used by God

1. Hosea 2:15 – *"...valley of Achor for a door of hope..."*
2. Romans 5:4 – *"And patience, experience; and experience, hope:"*
3. Zechariah 9:12 – *"...ye prisoners of hope..."*
4. Job 14:7 – *"For there is hope of a tree, if it be cut down, that it will sprout again, and that the tender branch thereof will not cease."*

E. Know that there is an end of hope – when your expectation shall be filled

1. Proverbs 23:18 – *"For surely there is an end; and thine expectation shall not be cut off."*
2. Jeremiah 29:11 – *"...to give you an expected end."*
3. Romans 4:17-22 – *"...And being fully persuaded that, what he had promised, he was able also to perform..."*

F. Be patient in hope

1. Romans 8:25 – *"But if we hope for that we see not, then do we with patience wait for it."*
2. I Thessalonians 1:3 – *"Remembering without ceasing your work of faith, and labour of love, and patience of hope in our Lord Jesus Christ, in the sight of God and our Father."*
3. Hebrews 6:11-12 – *"...you do shew the same diligence to the full assurance of hope unto the end: that ye be not slothful, but followers of them who through faith and patience inherit the promises."*

G. Worship God and allow His presence to save you! – Psalms 42:5 – *"...hope thou in God: for I shall yet praise him for the help of his countenance."* Another translation reads, *"...for His presence is salvation."*

Lesson 41
I Will Restore

I. Joel 2:23-25 – "*23Be glad then, ye children of Zion, and rejoice in the LORD your God: for he hath given you the former rain moderately, and he will cause to come down for you the rain, the former rain, and the latter rain in the first month. 24And the floors shall be full of wheat, and the fats shall overflow with wine and oil. 25And I will restore to you the years that the locust hath eaten, the cankerworm, and the caterpiller, and the palmerworm, my great army which I sent among you.*"

A. Definition for restore

1. To give back
2. To bring back to the first state or condition
3. To recover
4. To heal or cure

B. We need restoration

1. Psalms 51:12 – "*Restore unto me the joy of thy salvation; and uphold me with thy free spirit.*" – Many times our joy, our vision, our hope, or our reason for living needs to be restored.

    a. Lamentations 5:15 – "*The joy of our heart is ceased; our dance is turned into mourning.*"
    b. II Chronicles 15
    c. I Samuel 30:6 – "*And David was greatly distressed; for the people spake of stoning him, because the soul of all the people was grieved, every man for his sons and for his daughters: but David encouraged himself in the LORD his God.*"

C. I will restore

1. Psalms 23:3 – "*He restoreth my soul: he leadeth me in the paths of righteousness for his name's sake.*"
2. Ruth 4:15 – "*And he shall be unto thee a restorer of thy life, and a nourisher of thine old age: for thy daughter in law, which loveth thee, which is better to thee than seven sons, hath born him.*"
3. Jeremiah 30:16-17 – "*Therefore all they that devour thee shall be devoured; and all thine adversaries, every one of them, shall go into captivity; and they that spoil thee shall be a spoil, and all that prey upon thee will I give for a prey. For I will restore health unto thee, and I will heal thee of thy wounds, saith the LORD; because they called thee an Outcast, saying, This is Zion, whom no man seeketh after.*"
4. Isaiah 1:21-26 – "*21How is the faithful city become an harlot! it was full of judgment; righteousness lodged in it; but now murderers. 22Thy silver is become dross, thy wine mixed with water: 23Thy princes are rebellious, and companions of thieves: every one loveth gifts, and followeth after rewards: they judge not the fatherless, neither doth the cause of the widow come unto them. 24Therefore saith the Lord, the LORD of hosts, the mighty One of Israel, Ah, I will ease me of mine adversaries, and avenge me of mine enemies: 25And I will turn my hand upon thee, and purely purge away thy dross, and take away all thy tin: 26And I will restore thy judges as at the first, and thy counsellers as at the beginning: afterward thou shalt be called, The city of righteousness, the faithful city.*"
5. Jeremiah 31:10-14 – "*10Hear the word of the LORD, O ye nations, and declare it in the isles afar off, and say, He that scattered Israel will gather him, and keep him, as a shepherd doth his flock. 11For the LORD hath redeemed Jacob, and ransomed him from the hand of him that was stronger than he. 12Therefore they shall come and sing in the height of Zion, and shall flow together to the goodness of the LORD, for wheat, and for wine, and for oil, and for the young of the flock and of the herd: and their soul shall be as a watered garden; and they shall not sorrow*

any more at all. ¹³*Then shall the virgin rejoice in the dance, both young men and old together: for I will turn their mourning into joy, and will comfort them, and make them rejoice from their sorrow.* ¹⁴*And I will satiate the soul of the priests with fatness, and my people shall be satisfied with my goodness, saith the LORD."*

D.   It may look bad for a while but He knows when we can take no more

1.   Hosea 6:2 – "*After two days will he revive us: in the third day he will raise us up, and we shall live in his sight.*"
2.   Psalms 138:7 – "*Though I walk in the midst of trouble, thou wilt revive me: thou shalt stretch forth thine hand against the wrath of mine enemies, and thy right hand shall save me.*"
3.   Psalms 85:6 – "*Wilt thou not revive us again: that thy people may rejoice in thee?*"
4.   I Peter 5:10 – "*But the God of all grace, who hath called us unto his eternal glory by Christ Jesus, after that ye have suffered a while, make you perfect, stablish, strengthen, settle you.*"

E.   The enemy will have to repay double

1.   Exodus 22:4, 7 – "*If the theft be certainly found in his hand alive, whether it be ox, or ass, or sheep; he shall restore double...If a man shall deliver unto his neighbour money or stuff to keep, and it be stolen out of the man's house; if the thief be found, let him pay double.*"
2.   Isaiah 61:7 – "*For your shame ye shall have double; and for confusion they shall rejoice in their portion: therefore in their land they shall possess the double: everlasting joy shall be unto them.*"
3.   Zechariah 9:12 – "*Turn you to the strong hold, ye prisoners of hope: even to day do I declare that I will render double unto thee;*"
4.   Proverbs 6:31 – "*But if he be found, he shall restore sevenfold; he shall give all the substance of his house.*"
5.   Job 42:10 – "*And the LORD turned the captivity of Job, when he prayed for his friends: also the LORD gave Job twice as much as he had before.*"

Lesson 42
JOY

I. All Things Are Possible

   A. Matthew 19:26 – "*But Jesus beheld them, and said unto them, With men this is impossible; but with God all things are possible.*"
   B. Mark 9:23 – "*Jesus said unto him, If thou canst believe, all things are possible to him that believeth.*"
   C. Mark 14:36 – "*And he said, Abba, Father, all things are possible unto thee; take away this cup from me: nevertheless not what I will, but what thou wilt.*"
   D. Ephesians 3:20 – "*Now unto him that is able to do exceeding abundantly above all that we ask or think, according to the power that worketh in us,*"
   E. Romans 8:32 – "*He that spared not his own Son, but delivered him up for us all, how shall he not with him also freely give us all things?*"

II. It's Gods Desire For All Christians To Have Joy

   A. Romans 14:17 – "*For the kingdom of God is not meat and drink; but righteousness, and peace, and joy in the Holy Ghost.*"
   B. John 15:11 – "*These things have I spoken unto you, that my joy might remain in you, and that your joy might be full.*" – John 16:24 – 1 John 1:4
   C. Galatians 5:22 – "*But the fruit of the Spirit is love, joy, peace, longsuffering, gentleness, goodness, faith,*"
   D. Psalms 144:15 – "*Happy is that people, that is in such a case: yea, happy is that people, whose God is the LORD.*" – Psalms 146:5
   E. Isaiah 51:3 – "*For the LORD shall comfort Zion: he will comfort all her waste places; and he will make her wilderness like Eden, and her desert like the garden of the LORD; joy and gladness shall be found therein, thanksgiving, and the voice of melody.*"

III. God is not interested in us walking around with our hands hanging down and our faces full of frowns. He delivered us from Egypt so that:

   A. Psalms 105:43 – "*And he brought forth his people with joy, and his chosen with gladness:*"
   B. Isaiah 55:12 – "*For ye shall go out with joy, and be led forth with peace: the mountains and the hills shall break forth before you into singing, and all the trees of the field shall clap their hands.*"
   C. Jeremiah 31:11-15
   D. Psalms 30:11 – "*Thou hast turned for me my mourning into dancing: thou hast put off my sackcloth, and girded me with gladness;*"

IV. We Can Have Joy Even In Hard Places

   A. I Thessalonians 1:6 – "*And ye became followers of us, and of the Lord, having received the word in much affliction, with joy of the Holy Ghost:*"
   B. II Corinthians 8:2 – "*How that in a great trial of affliction the abundance of their joy and their deep poverty abounded unto the riches of their liberality.*"
   C. James 1:2 – "*My brethren, count it all joy when ye fall into divers temptations;*"
   D. John 16:33 – "*These things I have spoken unto you, that in me ye might have peace. In the world ye shall have tribulation: but be of good cheer; I have overcome the world.*"

   E. How can we be joyful in hard places?

       1. James 1:3 – "*Knowing this, that the trying of your faith worketh patience.*"

2. Hebrews 12:2 – *"Looking unto Jesus the author and finisher of our faith; who for the joy that was set before him endured the cross, despising the shame, and is set down at the right hand of the throne of God."*
3. Psalms 66:9-13 – wealthy place
4. Psalms 30:5 – *"For his anger endureth but a moment; in his favour is life: weeping may endure for a night, but joy cometh in the morning."*

V.   Joy Is Part Of Our Inheritance, God Gave It To Us.

A.   John 16:22 – Don't let anyone take it, stay in the presence of the Lord.
B.   Psalms 16:11 – *"Thou wilt shew me the path of life: in thy presence is fulness of joy; at thy right hand there are pleasures for evermore."*
C.   Nehemiah 8:10 – *"Then he said unto them, Go your way, eat the fat, and drink the sweet, and send portions unto them for whom nothing is prepared: for this day is holy unto our Lord: neither be ye sorry; for the joy of the LORD is your strength."*

VI.   Reasons People Do Not Experience Joy

A.   Psalms 68:6 – *"...the rebellious dwell in a dry land."*
B.   Jeremiah 5:25 – *"Your iniquities have turned away these things, and your sins have withholden good things from you."*
C.   Proverbs 13:15 – *"...but the way of the transgressors is hard."*
D.   Isaiah 1:19-20

VII.   What To Do

A.   Galatians 6:1 – *"Brethren, if a man be overtaken in a fault, ye which are spiritual, restore such an one in the spirit of meekness; considering thyself, lest thou also be tempted."*
B.   II Timothy 2:25
C.   Matthew 10:16 – (II Samuel 16:5, 13)
D.   Jude 21 – *"Keep yourselves in the love of God, looking for the mercy of our Lord Jesus Christ unto eternal life."*
E.   I Thessalonians 3:12 – John 13:34-35

Lesson 43
KNOWING ABOUT WORDS

I.   The Importance of Words

A.   There is more power than we know in our mouths.

1.   Proverbs 18:21 – *"Death and life are in the power of the tongue: and they that love it shall eat the fruit thereof."* (James 3:1-13)
2.   Matthew 12:34-37
3.   Proverbs 12:14 – *"A man shall be satisfied with good by the fruit of his mouth..."*
4.   Proverbs 21:23 – *"Whoso keepeth his mouth and his tongue keepeth his soul from troubles."*
5.   Proverbs 6:3 – *"...humble thyself, and make sure thy friend."*
6.   Proverbs 13:3 – *"He that keepeth his mouth keepeth his life: but he that openeth wide his lips shall have destruction."*

II. The Force of Good or Right Words

A.   Words are carriers of power

1.   Job 6:25 – There is a force behind every word – whether it is good or bad; and it carries with it the power to accomplish its task.

2.   Mark 11:23 – We must make sure that what we are saying is in line with God's word.

a.   Lamentations 3:37 – Here we see it may come to pass if it's not in line with God's word simply because of the power of words; but God was not pleased, we shouldn't say anything he isn't or hasn't said.

3.   Proverbs 15:1, 4

4.   Proverbs 12:18 – *"...but the tongue of the wise is health."*

a.   Proverbs 16:24 – *"Pleasant words are as an honeycomb, sweet to the soul, and health to the bones."*

5.   Proverbs 12:6 – *"...the mouth of the upright shall deliver them."*
6.   Proverbs 12:25 – *"...a good word maketh it glad."*
7.   I Kings 12:7

B.   The force of wrong words

1.   Job 19:2 – Words can wound and destroy.
2.   Proverbs 11:9 – *"An hypocrite with his mouth destroyeth his neighbour..."*
3.   Psalms 64:3
4.   Proverbs 15:1 – *"...grievous words stir up anger."*

5.   Proverbs 18:8 – *"The words of a talebearer are as wounds, and they go down into the innermost parts of the belly."*

a.   Proverbs 26:22

6. Proverbs 26:28 – *"A lying tongue hateth those that are afflicted by it; and a flattering mouth worketh ruin."*

III. A Time to Keep Silent

A. We must learn the balance of speaking and not speaking

1. Ecclesiastes 3:7 – *"...a time to keep silence, and a time to speak;"*
2. I Thessalonians 4:11 – *"And that ye study to be quiet..."*
3. Proverbs 17:27 – *"He that hath knowledge spareth his words..."*
4. Proverbs 10:19 – *"In the multitude of words there wanteth not sin: but he that refraineth his lips is wise."*
5. Psalms 46:10

B. Example of Jesus

1. Isaiah 53:7 – This is so unlike us – Job 13:19
2. Matthew 27:11-14
3. I Timothy 6:13
4. Luke 23:8
5. Matthew 26:59-63

C. We should be slow to speak – Think before speaking

1. James 1:19 – *"...let every man be swift to hear, slow to speak, slow to wrath:"*

   a. Job 7:11
   b. Psalms 106:33 – *"...he spake unadvisedly with his lips."*

2. Proverbs 29:20
3. Ecclesiastes 5:1, 2, 4-6
4. I Samuel 3:19

IV. Other Aspects about Our Words

A. Words of authority

1. Ecclesiastes 8:4 –Words of authority do not have to be loud words

   a. Ecclesiastes 9:17 – *"The words of wise men are heard in quiet more than the cry of him that ruleth among fools."*

2. Jesus spoke with authority

   a. John 7:46 – *"The officers answered, Never man spake like this man."*
   b. Matthew 7:28-29 – *"...he taught them as one having authority..."*

B. Words for a right season

1. Isaiah 50:4 – *"...I should know how to speak a word in season..."*
2. Proverbs 15:23 – *"...a word spoken in due season, how good is it!"*
3. Proverbs 25:11 – *"A word fitly spoken is like apples of gold in pictures of silver."*
4. Ecclesiastes 12:10 – *"The preacher sought to find out acceptable words..."*

C.   We must hold fast our confession of faith

    1.   Hebrews 4:14 – *"...let us hold fast our profession."*
    2.   Hebrews 10:23 – The word profession is the same word as confession.

V.   What Should Be Our Attitude Toward The Way We Speak?

A.   That Jesus <u>must</u> help us

    1.   Psalms 141:3 – *"Set a watch, O Lord, before my mouth; keep the door of my lips."*

        a.   James 3:8 – No man can tame his tongue

    2.   Psalms 19:14 – *"Let the words of my mouth...be acceptable in thy sight, O Lord..."*
    3.   Colossians 3:17
    4.   Psalms 17:2-3 – Sentence came forth from thy presence.
    5.   Psalms 34:13 – *"Keep thy tongue from evil, and thy lips from speaking guile."*
    6.   Proverbs 31:26 – Law of kindness in her tongue.
    7.   II Timothy 1:13
    8.   I Peter 3:10
    9.   Psalms 75:5 – Don't speak with a stiff neck.

B.   What should be coming out of our mouths?

    1.   Psalms 119:46 – *"I will speak of thy testimonies also before kings..."*
    2.   Psalms 119:72 – *"The law of thy mouth is better unto me than thousands of gold and silver."*
    3.   Psalms 29:9 – *"...in his temple doth every one speak of his glory."*
    4.   Psalms 145:21 – *"My mouth shall speak the praise of the LORD..."*
    5.   Psalms 34:1 – *"...I will bless the LORD at all times: his praise shall continually be in my mouth."*
    6.   Psalms 40:3 – *"...he hath put a new song in my mouth, even praise unto our God..."*
    7.   Psalms 51:15 – *"O Lord, open thou my lips; and my mouth shall shew forth thy praise."*
    8.   Psalms 71:8 – *"Let my mouth be filled with thy praise and with thy honour all the day."*
    9.   Psalms 89:1 – *"...with my mouth will I make known thy faithfulness to all generations."*
    10. Psalms 107:2 – *"Let the redeemed of the LORD say so..."*

Lesson 44
LUSTS OF THE FLESH

I.   Defining and Understanding the Principles of the Flesh

    A.   Word Definitions – English, Hebrew and Greek

        1.   English

            a.   The soft substance of an animal or human body, consisting of muscle and fat.
            b.   The body, especially as distinguished from the spirit or soul.
            c.   Man's physical or animal nature, as distinguished from his moral or spiritual nature.
            d.   Present before one's eyes: in person, something seen.
            e.   To enflame the ardor or passions of by subjecting to a foretaste.
            f.   To fill with flesh or fleshly enjoyments; surfeiting glut.
            g.   The word "fleshly" means – pertaining to the body, corporeal, physical. It also means carnal or sensual, worldly rather than spiritual.

        2.   Hebrew, *Basar* – flesh, meat, meaty part plus the skin of men. From a root that means – to be fresh, full
        3.   Greek, *Sarx* – flesh, the substance of the body; the weaker element in human nature, the unregenerate state of man, the seat of sin in man – but this is not the same thing as the body.

        4.   Our definition of the flesh is two-fold:

It obviously speaks of the body or skin and bones of a creature. It also speaks of how that body can inspire unlawful and carnal desires in someone. But I believe what it really means is the soulish, carnal, adamic nature in man's soul that is allowed free reign. The physical body will do whatever the human spirit (where Jesus dwells in the lives of believers) or the soul (mind, emotions, will, intellect, and reasoning) tells it to do. The question is which part of us is ruling: the soulish nature or our spirit (which flows with the life of God). It is our choice.

The essence of sin is self-centeredness, and self will exercised against the will of God; hence pride. Pride means inordinate self esteem, conceit, vanity, and self-exaltation.

II.   Understanding Man

    A.   Man is a three-fold being:

        1.   Spirit, Soul, Body

            a.   Hebrews 4:12   e.   Deuteronomy 6:5
            b.   I Thessalonians 5:23   f.   Isaiah 53:5
            c.   Genesis 2:7   g.   Job 10:11-12
            d.   Psalms 84:2   i.   Psalms 146:4

        2.   Hebrew and Greek words for our triune being:

            a.   Hebrew

                1)   *Ruach* – spirit
                2)   *Nepesh* – soul
                3)   *Beten* or *Geshem* – body

      b.   Greek

         1) *Pneuma* – spirit
         2) *Psueche* – soul
         3) *Soma* – body

3. Man's spirit is either the dwelling place of God for believers or the dwelling place for a demon in an unbeliever's life:

  a.   Believers

    1) Proverbs 20:27 – "*The spirit of man is the candle of the Lord...*"
    2) Job 32:8 – "*...there is a spirit in man, and the inspiration...*"
    3) Psalms 42:7 – "*...deep calleth unto deep...*"
    4) I John 2:20, 27 – "*But ye have an unction...the anointing...*"
    5) I John 5:10 – "*...hath the witness in himself...*"
    6) Psalms 51:6 – "*...inward parts...hidden part...*"
    7) John 7:38 – "*belly*" here means womb or hollow – Other translation – "*Out from his innermost being springs and rivers of living water shall flow continuously*"
    8) I Peter 3:4 – "*...hidden man of the heart...*"
    9) Romans 1:9
    10) Romans 8:9, 15, 16
    11) I Corinthians 2:10-12
    12) I Corinthians 6:17

  b.   Unbelievers

    1) I John 5:19
    2) Ephesians 2:2
    3) Colossians 1:13
    4) Death and sin passed upon all men, likewise sin.

      a) Romans 5:12   f) Romans 3:23
      b) Psalms 51:5   g) I Kings 8:46
      c) Psalms 14:2-3   h) Isaiah 53:6
      d) Isaiah 48:8   i) Romans 7:5
      e) Romans 7:14

4. Man's soul is the place of our mind and reasoning capabilities, our emotions, our will, feelings, desires, passions, etc.

This is the true place and part of our lives as believers that still has within it the old adamic nature. Original sin is inherited from Adam (we should consider that having been in the loins of Adam, we would have done the same thing in his place). Actual sin is what each man commits when he falls. Man is sinful in nature, therefore he is also sinful in acts. Man sins because he is a sinner. He does what he does because of who he is. However, once we are saved we have become a new creation (species), which takes place in our spirit. After salvation, a man is no longer simply "a sinner", but the old Adamic nature and the "*motions of sin*" still live in his soul – this is where and why he must be sanctified everyday.

  a.   Different aspects of the soul

    1) Mind

       a)   Reasonings (doubt and unbelief) – Mark 2:6
       b)   Our will – Psalms 143: 8
       c)   Imaginations – II Corinthians 10:5

   2)   Emotions

       a)   Affections – Colossians 3:2
       b)   Desires – Ephesians 2:3
       c)   Feelings (passions) – James 5:17

   3)   Intellect

       a)   Thought life – Philemon 4:8
       b)   Intelligence – I Corinthians 1:26
       c)   Cares – I Peter 5:7

  b.   What we once were

   1)   Romans 7:5 – Other translation: *"When we were living in the flesh (mere physical lives), the sinful passions that were awakened and aroused up by (what) the Law (makes sin) were constantly operating in our natural powers (in our bodily organs, in the sensitive appetites and wills of the flesh), so that we bore fruit for death."*
   2)   Ephesians 2:1-5
   3)   Genesis 6:5, 12
   4)   I John 2:15-17
   5)   Ephesians 4:17-22
   6)   Romans 1:20-32

5.   Our souls are now the battleground. It is the place of warfare in our lives.

  a.   Defining the soul of man

   1)   Hebrew, Greek and dictionary definitions of "soul"

       a)   Hebrew – *Nephesh* – a breathing creature; from the root – to breathe
       b)   Greek – *Psueche* – breath
       c)   Bible Dictionary – life itself, the man himself, the individual
       d)   General definition – the principle of life, feeling, thought, and actions in humans regarded as a distinct entity, separate from the body.

   2)   What, then, is the soul of man?

The soul is the "self conscious part of man". The soul is the part of our triune body that connects the spirit and body. It is truly very important because it is the deciding factor in what we choose to do or not do. It is the part of our being where sanctification is taking place. Justification (the aspect of our salvation for our spirit) and glorification (the aspect of our salvation for our new body) are one time experiences, separated by our life times. Sanctification, however, takes a lifetime: it is the daily aspect of our salvation. **MAN IS ESSENTIALLY A SPIRIT, WHO HAS A SOUL THAT LIVES IN A BODY.**

       a)   Genesis 2:7
       b)   I Thessalonians 5:23
       c)   Psalms 84:2

       d)   Hebrews 4:12
       e)   Isaiah 26:9
       f)   Luke 1:46
       g)   Deuteronomy 6:5

3)   Our soul is the part of us that is our responsibility. Our spirit and our body belong to the Lord (I Corinthians 6:20)

       a)   It's in our hands, to do with as we please

            (1)   Psalms 119:109
            (2)   I Peter 4:19
            (3)   Deuteronomy 4:9

       b)   We must give it to God

            (1)   Psalms 25:1
            (2)   Psalms 143:8
            (3)   Lamentations 3:40-41

       c)   III John 2
       d)   Psalms 35:13 – "*...I humbled my soul...*"

4)   It is the place of warfare in our lives; it is the battleground

       a)   I Peter 2:11 – "*...abstain from fleshly lusts, which war against the soul*"
       b)   James 4:1-3
       c)   I Peter 1:13-14
       d)   Romans 8:6-8
       e)   Romans 1:24
       f)   Hebrews 12:3 – "*...faint in your minds.*" (see Psalms 27:13)
       g)   Psalms 143:3 – "*...enemy hath persecuted my soul...*"
       h)   Job 24:12 – "*...soul of the wounded crieth out.*"
       i)   John 12:27 – "*...Now is my soul troubled...*"
       j)   I Samuel 25:29 – "*...man is risen...to seek thy soul...*"
       k)   II Kings 4:27 – "*...her soul is vexed within her...*" (see also – I Samuel 1:16)
       l)   Job 10:1 – "*My soul is weary of my life...*"
       m)   Psalms 57:4 – "*My soul is among lions...*"
       n)   Psalms 88:3 – "*...my soul is full of troubles...*"
       o)   Matthew 26:38 – "*...My soul is exceedingly sorrowful, even unto death...*"
       p)   Judges 16:16 – "*...his soul was vexed unto death.*"

5)   Our souls need to be changed

       a)   II Corinthians 3:18
       b)   Romans 12:2

            (1)   Hebrews 10:16
            (2)   Hebrews 8:10

       c)   James 1:21
       d)   Psalms 19:7
       e)   Psalms 23:3

    f) Psalms 34:22 (Psalms 71:23)
    g) Psalms 6:4
    h) Psalms 124:7 (John 8:30-32)
    i) James 4:8 (James 1:8)
    j) I Peter 1:13-14
    k) Ephesians 4:23
    l) Romans 8:6-14
    m) Psalms 142:7
    n) Luke 21:19

6. Our Bodies – As we have said before, our bodies will obey either the will of God through the Holy Spirit living in our human spirit, or it will obey the will of our souls, with its appetite for evil desires, lusts, passions, etc.

  a. James 1:14-17 – *"...drawn away of our own lusts...do not err..."*
  b. Romans 6:12 – *"Let not sin reign in your mortal body..."*
  c. Galatians 5:24 – *"...live in the spirit...walk in the spirit..."*
  d. Galatians 5:16-25
  e. Romans 8:4 – *"...who walk not after the flesh..."*
  f. I Peter 2:11 – *"...abstain from fleshly lusts..."*
  g. Romans 13:12-14 – *"...cast off the works of darkness...put on armor of light."*
  h. Hebrews 10:22 – *"Let us draw near...our bodies washed with pure water."*
  i. I Corinthians 6:20 – ye are bought with a price, therefore glorify God in your bodies
  j. I Corinthians 9:27 – *"I keep under my body, and bring it into subjection..."*
  k. Romans 12:1 – *"...present your bodies a living sacrifice..."*

III. Understanding the Term "Flesh" In Scripture

 A. God is the Creator of all flesh

  1. Numbers 16:22 – *"...the God of the spirits of all flesh..."*
  2. Numbers 27:16 – *"...the God of the spirits of all flesh..."*
  3. Job 10:11 – *"Thou hast clothed me with skin and flesh..."*
  4. Jeremiah 32:27 – *"Behold, I am the Lord, the God of all flesh..."*

 B. He understands us and why we do the things we do:

  1. Psalms 103:14 – *"For he knoweth our frame: he remembereth that we are dust."*
  2. Psalms 78:39 – *"...he remembered that they were but flesh..."*
  3. Genesis 6:3 – *"...for that he also is flesh..."*
  4. Matthew 26:41 – *"...the spirit indeed is willing, but the flesh is weak."*
  5. Romans 8:3-4 – *"...God sending His own Son in the likeness of sinful flesh..."*
  6. Psalms 139:1-17
  7. Psalms 130:1-5
  8. Hebrews 4:15-16 – He can be touched with the feelings of our weaknesses
  9. Isaiah 26:19
  10. Isaiah 52:2
  11. Isaiah 65:25

  12. Psalms 113:7

    a. I Samuel 2:8

C. This is why Jesus became flesh – Only He could be the perfect overcomer and show us how to overcome our sins and how to walk in the Spirit.

1. I Peter 3:18
2. John 1:14
3. I Peter 4:1
4. I Timothy 3:16
5. Hebrews 2:14

6. Hebrews 10:20
7. John 6:51-56
8. Romans 8:3
9. Ephesians 2:15
10. Colossians 1:22

D. It affects and uses our minds:

1. II Corinthians 1:12
2. Colossians 2:16-23
3. Matthew 16:17
4. John 8:15 – *"Ye judge after the flesh..."*
5. Ephesians 4:17-20 – *"...as other Gentiles walk, in the vanity of their mind."*

E. Men use our flesh:

1. Galatians 6:8, 12
2. Philippians 3:1-4-12
3. II Chronicles 32:7-8
4. Psalms 56:1-9

5. II Peter 2:9-22
6. Galatians 6:12-13
7. II Corinthians 11:18
8. I Corinthians 1:23-26

F. It sullies us

1. Jude 23
2. Jude 8, 12-24
3. I Peter 3:21
4. Genesis 6:9-13
5. Exodus 16:3 – flesh pots
6. Jeremiah 17:5-12

IV. What Flesh Is According To Scripture

A. Scriptures

1. Romans 7:5 – *"For when we were in the flesh, the motions of sins...did work in our members..."*
2. John 3:6 – *"That which is born of the flesh is flesh..."*
3. John 6:63 – *"...the flesh profiteth nothing..."*
4. Galatians 4:29 – *"...he that was born after the flesh persecuted him that was born after the Spirit, even so it is now."*
5. Galatians 5:17 – *"For the flesh lusteth against the Spirit, and the Spirit against the flesh: and these are contrary the one to the other: so that ye cannot do the things that ye would."*
6. Galatians 5:19-21 – *"...Adultery, fornication, uncleanness, lasciviousness, Idolatry, witchcraft, hatred, variance, emulations, wrath, strife, seditions, heresies, Envyings, murders, drunkenness, revellings, and such like..."* – Amplified translation – *"Now the practices of the flesh are clear (obvious): immorality, impurity, indecency, idolatry, sorcery, enmity, strife, jealousy, anger (ill temper), selfishness, divisions, dissensions, party spirit, factions, sects, with peculiar opinions, heresies, envy, drunkenness, carousing and the like."*
7. Romans 4:1-7 – *"...Now to him that worketh is the reward not reckoned of grace, but of debt..."*
8. Colossians 2:11-23
9. Romans 7:18 – *"For I know that in me (that is, in my flesh) dwelleth no good thing..."*

10. Matthew 26:41 – "...*but the flesh is weak.*" (Psalms 73:26)
11. I Corinthians 15:39
12. I Corinthians 15:50 – "...*flesh and blood cannot inherit the kingdom of God; neither doth corruption inherit incorruption.*"
13. Job 7:5 – "*My flesh is clothed with worms and clods of dust...*"
14. Romans 8:5-8 – "*For they that are after the flesh do mind the things of the flesh...to be carnally minded is death...the carnal mind is enmity against God...so then they that are in the flesh cannot please God.*"
15. Romans 7:14-25, 8:1-17
16. Leviticus 17:11, 14

B. Flesh and our lusts

 1. Word definitions for "lust"

   a. Hebrew

    1) *avah* – to wish for; to covet; to desire
    2) *nephesh* – a breathing creature (This is the same Hebrew word for soul. We can see then, that our flesh is controlled by our soulish nature.)
    3) *shriyrawth* – twisted; firm; obstinancy; imagination; from a root – to be hostile; an enemy
    4) *taavah* – a longing; satisfaction; greedy; exceedingly lusting

   b. Greek, *epithumia* – a longing; craving; stresses the lust or desire for what is usually forbidden; a craving for mostly evil desires

 2. The scriptures concerning lust and flesh

   a. I John 2:16
   b. I Peter 2:10-11, 21 – "...*abstain from fleshly lusts which war against...*"
   c. II Peter 3:3 – "...*in the last days scoffers, walking after their own lusts.*"
   d. Ephesians 2:1-6
   e. II Peter 2:10 – "...*them that walk after the flesh in the lust of uncleanness, and despise government. Presumptuous are they, selfwilled, they are not afraid to speak evil of dignitaries.*"
   f. Galatians 5:16 – "...*Walk in the Spirit, and ye shall not fulfil the lust of the flesh.*"
   g. James 1:13-15
   h. Jude 17-21

 3. Examples in Scripture

   a. Psalms 78:18
   b. Romans 1:18-32
   c. Psalms 106:13-16

 4. The origin of lust (the entrance of sin into the universe): It all began with Lucifer, and he continues even now to torment and tempt men in their fallen nature.

   a. Isaiah 14:12-14 – This story begins with Satan's lustful desire to be like the Most High. He was beautiful (God had made him so) and became proud. This led to deception and the exaltation of selfishness, and self-will ignoring the great and holy will of God. Notice the five "I wills":

1) *"I will ascend into heaven"*
2) *"I will exalt my throne above the stars of God"*
3) *"I will sit upon the mount of the congregation"*
4) *"I will ascend above the heights of the clouds"*
5) *"I will be like the Most High"*

   b. Ezekiel 28:11-19
   c. Luke 10:18
   d. Hebrews 2:6
   e. John 8:44

5. How Satan works to tempt, condemn, and destroy us

   a. Luke 22:31 – Sift as wheat
   b. I Peter 5:8 – Devour
   c. II Corinthians 2:11 – Wicked devices
   d. Ephesians 6:16 – Fiery darts
   e. Matthew 4:1-5 – Tempter
   f. Revelation 12:9 – Deception
   g. Revelation 12:10 – Accuser
   h. Job 1:6-19
   i. Job 2:1-7
   j. Genesis 3:4 – He lies
   k. Luke 4:13 – original Greek – *"...for a more opportune time..."*
   l. Proverbs 7:6-23 – Appearances
   m. Genesis 3:13 – Beguiler
   n. II Corinthians 4:4
   o. Ephesians 2:2 – Evil spirits make us disobedient
   p. I Thessalonians 3:5

6. Adam's fall

   a. Genesis 3:1-6 (Matthew 4:3)
   b. I John 2:16 – temptation

     1) Body – lust of the flesh – tree good for food
     2) Soul – tree pleasant to the eyes
     3) Spirit – to become wise; to be like God

   c. Satan always seeks to exploit and pervert our God-given senses

     1) Taste – gluttony, sensual desires
     2) Smell – distorted perfumes (Psalms 45:8 – myrrh, aloes, and cassia – Jesus, versus Proverbs 7:17 – myrrh aloes and cinnamon – Religion), drugs, and other unholy enticements
     3) Touch – perverted touching, touching unholy things, sensual feelings
     4) Hear – listening to ungodly things, lies, gossip
     5) Sight – Satan seeks to cause us to look upon those things that God has commanded us not to.

7. Effects of the Fall

a. Genesis 2:23-24 and chapter 3:

    1) Verse 7 – Naked – shame
    2) Fig leaves – False covering, religion
    3) Verse 8 – Hiding from voice – rebellion
    4) Hid from His presence – running away form their very present help
    5) Verse 9 – *"Where art thou?"* – Deception, not seeing where you're really at
    6) Verse 10 – *"I was afraid"* – fear
    7) Verse 12 – *"The woman thou gavest me"*, "The serpent beguiled me" – blaming someone or anything for your sin
    8) Verse 19 – The curse of labor and sweat
    9) Verse 24 – Driven out of God's presence

b. Romans 5:12, 16, 19

    1) Death and sin now are passed onto all men
    2) Condemnation
    3) Disobedience

c. Man's spirit thrust into darkness, Proverbs 20:27
d. Titus 1:15 – Conscience is defiled
e. II Timothy 2:25-26 – We now oppose ourselves, and are snared by the devil

f. Matthew 4:8-9 – Satan is now in control of this earthly kingdom

    1) II Corinthians 4:4 – He has become the god of this world (greek – age)

g. Genesis 6:5, 12

    1) Imaginations and thoughts of men now are only evil continually
    2) Man has corrupted his way

h. Ephesians 4:17-20
i. Jeremiah 17:9
j. Psalms 39:5
k. Mark 7:20-23 – That which is in man's heart now
l. Galatians 5:19-21 – Works of the flesh
m. Romans 3:23 – All sin and all come short of the glory

n. Romans 6:23 – physical death (man was intended to be immortal)

    1) Ecclesiastes 12:7   5) Ezekiel 18:20
    2) Psalms 90:7-12   6) Numbers 16:29
    3) Genesis 2:17   7) Hebrews 9:27
    4) Jeremiah 31:30

o. Spiritual death

    1) John 5:24
    2) Ephesians 2:5
    3) Romans 5:12, 21

p. Corruption, II Peter 1:4

q.   Titus 3:3

1)   Foolish
2)   Disobedient
3)   Deceived
4)   Serving divers lusts and pleasures
5)   Living in malice
6)   Envy
7)   Hateful
8)   Hating one another

r.   II Timothy 2:22 – Lust is now in all of us and we are to flee from it
s.   I Peter 4:3

1)   Walked in lasciviousness (sensual pleasure)
2)   Lusts
3)   Excess of wine
4)   Reveling: rioting, wild parties
5)   Banqueting: drunkenness
6)   Abominable idolatries: worship of idols

t.   Ephesians 2:1-3
u.   James 4:1-6

8.   How does lust happen? Everyone is tempted

a.   Jesus

1)   Hebrews 4:15
2)   Matthew 4:1-6
3)   Luke 22:28

b.   All men

1)   Luke 8:13   5)   Genesis 22:1
2)   I Peter 5:9   6)   James 1:2
3)   Hebrews 3:8   7)   I Peter 1:6
4)   Revelation 3:10

9.   How it happens

a.   James 1:14-15   g.   Ephesians 4:17-20
b.   Matthew 5:28   h.   I Timothy 6:9-11
c.   I John 2:16   i.   I Timothy 3:1-7
d.   Galatians 5:17   j.   II Peter 2:18-22
e.   Mark 4:19   k.   Proverbs 11:17
f.   John 8:44   l.   Ephesians 5:6

10. Examples in Scripture (illustrating the progression of sin):

a.   II Samuel 11:1-5, 8-13, 15

        1) Should have gone to battle
        2) Idle instead of doing the work and will of God
        3) Evening
        4) Should have been resting in God
        5) Lusted from rooftop
        6) Tries to deceive and make Uriah sin
        7) Commits murder

    b. II Samuel 13:1-16 – The sin of Ammon against his sister.
    c. I Samuel 15:1-31 – The sad story of the fall of Saul.

11. We should and need to learn how to deal with lust

    a. I Corinthians 10:6
    b. Galatians 5:16
    c. Romans 6:12
    d. Romans 13:14
    e. Galatians 5:24
    f. Ephesians 4:21-32
    g. I Peter 2:11
    h. I Peter 4:2
    i. Titus 2:11-14
    j. I Timothy 6:11-12
    k. I Timothy 5:22
    l. II Corinthians 10:5
    m. I John 3:3

    n. Don't look

        1) Proverbs 6:23-35
        2) Job 31:1

    o. II Timothy 2:22 – flee
    p. Psalms 119:9-11
    q. John 8:31-34

12. Sin is not to have dominion over us

    a. Romans 6:14
    b. Titus 2:14
    c. Micah 7:19
    d. Zechariah 13:9
    e. Zechariah 14:20-21
    f. Psalms 65:3 – "...as for our transgressions, thou shalt purge them away."
    g. Hebrews 9:14
    h. I Thessalonians 5:23 – "...sanctify you wholly..."
    i. Hebrews 6:1 – "...let us go on to perfection..."
    j. Philippians 3:13
    k. Proverbs 24:3-4 – "...And by knowledge shall the chambers be filled with all precious and pleasant riches."
    l. Ezekiel 16:3-15
    m. Job 11:14-19 – "...thou shalt lift up thy face without spot..."
    n. Isaiah 4:4-6 – "When the Lord shall have washed away the filth..."

o. Obadiah 17 – *"But upon Mt. Zion shall be deliverance..."*
p. Joel 2:32
q. II Corinthians 1:10 – *"Who delivered us from so great a death, and doth deliver: in whom we trust that He will yet deliver us."*

V. How God Feels About Wrong Desires

A. Scriptural Examples

1. Ecclesiastes 6:9 – Wandering desires are vanity and will bring vexation to your spirit. The grass is not greener anywhere else. Better the sight of what God has given you than some foolish desire
2. Job 36:20 – Desire not the night. The night speaks of all that is darkness, in other words, all that is of the devil. What happens to you is you are "cut off" from God and you lose your place.
3. Ephesians 2:1-3 – We have been quickened from the desires of the flesh and from walking according to how the devil wants us to.
4. James 4:1-2 – Wars and fighting within and without are a result of evil desires.
5. Proverbs 23:3-8 – Desire not his (the devil's) doctrines. They are deceitful.

B. We need to desire Jesus

1. Isaiah 26:8-9 – We need to desire Him, even in the night (the place of darkness), He must be our desire.

   a. Psalms 73:25 – Nothing on earth should take His place. He is to be the pearl of great price.
   b. Psalms 27:4 – His beauty surpasses all others. This is the one thing we should give our lives for and seek after.
   c. II Samuel 23:5 – His everlasting covenant should be our desire.
   d. Proverbs 8:11

C. Only He can satisfy the deep longings of our souls

1. Psalms 87:7 – "springs" in the Hebrew – sources of satisfaction. Everything we are, all that we want, all that we do is to Him.
2. Psalms 107:9 – He will satisfy the longing soul.
3. Psalms 145:14-19

D. God will help us in our hour of temptation:

1. He gives us a way out

   a. I Corinthians 10:13
   b. Revelation 3:10
   c. II Peter 2:9

E. We must die to ourselves and all unrighteous desires:

This will happen as we see something greater than what we are longing for: we must see Jesus – therein lies our deliverance.

1. We must crucify our flesh

    a.   Ezekiel 24:15-20 – If we won't kill it, God will.
    b.   Romans 6:11-14
    c.   Galatians 2:20

2.   When we've overcome our temptations, we will receive a reward

    a.   James 1:12
    b.   I Peter 1:6-7

VI. How the Flesh Will Be Conquered

A. God will help us

1.   II Chronicles 32:8 – "*...with us is the Lord our God to help us, and to fight our battles...*"
2.   II Peter 2:9 – "*The Lord knoweth how to deliver the godly out of temptations...*"
3.   Psalms 34:17-19 – "*...Many are the afflictions of the righteous: but the Lord delivereth him out of them all.*"

4.   Psalms 18:2, 50 – He is our deliverer

    a.   Psalms 40:17   e.   II Chronicles 11:14
    b.   Psalms 70:5   f.   Psalms 32:7
    c.   Psalms 144:2   g.   Job 33:24-28
    d.   Psalms 44:4

5.   Job 19:25-26 – "*For I know that my redeemer liveth, and that He shall stand at the latter day upon the earth: And though after my skin worms destroy this body, yet in my flesh shall I see God.*"
6.   Isaiah 49:26 – "*...all flesh shall know that I the LORD am thy Saviour and thy Redeemer, the mighty One of Jacob.*"
7.   Isaiah 66:16 – "*For by fire and by his sword will the LORD plead with all flesh: and the slain of the LORD shall be many.*"
8.   Joel 2:28 – "*...I will pour out my spirit upon all flesh...*"
9.   John 17:2 – "*As thou hast given him power over all flesh...*"
10.   Jude 24 – "*Now unto him that is able to keep you from falling, and to present you faultless before the presence of his glory with exceeding joy.*"

B. It will come through cleansing and sanctification by the Word and the Spirit

1.   The Word

    a.   Psalms 119:9-11
    b.   II Corinthians 7:1
    c.   John 8:31-34
    d.   John 17:17 – "*Sanctify them through thy truth: thy Word is truth.*"
    e.   John 15:3 – "*Now ye are clean through the Word I have spoken...*"

2.   The Spirit

    a.   Leviticus 14:9   g.   Romans 8:11
    b.   Leviticus 16:24-26   h.   Romans 8:26
    c.   Psalms 51:2   i.   II Corinthians 3:17-18

d.	John 13:5-10	j.	Galatians 5:16-18, 25
e.	Hebrews 6:1-3	k.	Ephesians 5:17-20
f.	Romans 8:2		

C. It will come by us ceasing from the desires of the flesh

1. Romans 12:1 – *"...present your bodies a living sacrifice..."*
2. Romans 8:6 – *"...be spiritually minded..."*
3. Romans 13:14 – *"Put ye on the Lord Jesus Christ, and make not provision for the flesh..."*
4. I Peter 4:1 – *"...he that hath suffered in the flesh hath ceased form sin."*
5. Hebrews 12:9 – *"...be in subjection unto the Father of spirits, and live?"*
6. Job 19:26 – Believe – *"...in my flesh I shall see God."*
7. Ecclesiastes 11:10 – *"...remove sorrow from thy heart, and put away evil from thy flesh..."*
8. Isaiah 66:16 – *"...by fire and by His sword will the Lord plead with all flesh."*
9. Zechariah 2:13 – *"Be silent, O all flesh, before the Lord...."*
10. II Corinthians 12:7 – *"...thorn in the flesh..."*
11. Titus 2:11-14 – *"...the grace of God...teaching us that, denying ungodliness and worldly lusts, we should live soberly, righteously, and godly, in this present world..."*
12. Romans 6:19 – *"...yield your members servants to righteousness..."*
13. Galatians 2:20 – *"I am crucified with Christ...the life which I now live in the flesh I live by the faith of the Son of God..."*
14. Romans 8:12-13 – *"...if ye through the Spirit do mortify the deeds of the body..."*
15. Galatians 5:24 – *"...they that are Christ's have crucified the flesh..."*
16. Galatians 6:8 – Don't sow to your flesh.
17. II Corinthians 4:11 – *"...we which live are always delivered unto death for Jesus' sake..."*
18. I Corinthians 5:5 – *"...deliver such an one unto Satan for the destruction of the flesh, that the spirit might be saved..."*
19. Philippians 3:3 – *"...have no confidence in the flesh."*
20. Ephesians 4:20-23 – *"...put off...the old man..."*

D. It will come by having hope

1. Psalms 16:9 – *"...my flesh also shall rest in hope."*
2. Psalms 65:2
3. Job 19:26

E. It will come by crying out for deliverance:

1. Psalms 63:1 – *"...my flesh longeth for thee..."*
2. Psalms 84:2 – *"...my flesh crieth out for the living God."*

F. It will come by mercy and truth

1. Psalms 43:3
2. Psalms 57:3
3. Psalms 61:7
4. Psalms 85:10
5. Psalms 86:15
6. Proverbs 3:3
7. Proverbs 16:6
8. Proverbs 20:28
9. Isaiah 25:1

VII. Ultimately We Will Triumph Over the Flesh

Always remember, however, it will only be by the grace and mercy of our God, and the sanctifying power of His Word and Spirit, with our obedience and willingness.

A. Scriptures

1. Romans 6:14 – *"For sin shall not have dominion over you..."*
2. Psalms 145:21
3. Isaiah 40:5 – *"And the glory of the LORD shall be revealed, and all flesh shall see it together..."*
4. Genesis 6:13 – *"...The end of all flesh is come before me..."*
5. Job 33:25 – *"His flesh shall be fresher than a child's..."*
6. Isaiah 49:26 – *"...all flesh shall know that I the LORD am thy Saviour..."*
7. Isaiah 66:23 – *"...all flesh come to worship before me..."*
8. Ezekiel 20:48
9. Romans 8:20-22 – *"...the creature itself also shall be delivered from the bondage of corruption into the glorious liberty..."*
10. Philippians 3:20
11. Psalms 102:14 – *"...favour the dust thereof."*
12. Romans 7:25 and Romans 8:1 – *"I thank God through Jesus Christ... there is therefore now no condemnation..."*
13. Philippians 1:20 – *"...Christ shall be magnified in my body..."*
14. Luke 3:6 – *"...all flesh shall see the salvation of God."*

B. Other Scriptural ways this will happen

1. The blood of Jesus

   a. Hebrews 9:13-14 – *"...the blood of Christ..."*

      1) I Peter 1:18-19 – *"...redeemed...with the precious blood of Christ"*
      2) I John 1:7-9 – *"...the blood of Jesus Christ his Son cleanseth us from all sin..."*
      3) Revelation 1:5-6 – *"...washed us from our sins in his own blood..."*
      4) Revelation 7:13-17 – *"...made them white in the blood of the lamb..."*
      5) Revelation 12:11 – *"...they overcame him by the blood of the Lamb..."*
      6) Hebrews 9:22 – All things purged with blood

2. Genesis 17:10-14 – The covenant of circumcision spiritually and naturally. This didn't just apply to Israel, for cleanness alone – the spirit of the Word in Genesis 17:11 is also speaking to us to circumcise all flesh.

   a. Joshua 5:2-12
   b. Hebrew for "circumcise" – *muwl* – to cut short, to curtail, to blunt, to destroy, cut down, cut in pieces
   c. As believers, our circumcision is of the soul. The Hebrews cut off their natural body flesh, and we do the same to our old Adamic nature. It's certainly interesting that the part God had Abraham circumcise was man's reproductive and pleasure-giving organ. I think this was on purpose, because He knows our horrible potential for sexual sins.

   d. Ours is a spiritual circumcision
      1) Philippians 3:3
      2) Colossians 2:11

VIII. The Story of Ishmael (Or How Not To Choose the Flesh over the Promises of God)

A. Scriptures

1. Genesis 15:1-6 – God promises Abraham an heir out of his own bowels, and makes a covenant with him and his seed to inherit the land of 10 nations.

   a. Galatians 3:6-9 – And Abram believed God and it was counted unto him for righteousness.

2. Genesis 16:1-5

   a. Definition of names

      1) Abram – exalted father, high and lofty thinker
      2) Sarai – contentious, quarrelsome, my ruler, my princess
      3) Hagar – flight, sojourner, ensnaring (also take note that she was an Egyptian)
      4) Ishmael – he will hear God, he will be heard of God
      5) Canaan – merchants, traders, comes from a root – to be humbled, to subdue, or to be made law
      6) Plain of Mamre – from seeing, from the vision

   b. Points to consider

      1) Neither Abram or Sarai had their names (character) changed yet.
      2) They blamed God for not giving them any children.
      3) Abram hearkened to his wife's counsel rather than God's (Genesis 15:4-6)
      4) They justified their fleshly decision by the fact that God had said the heir would come out of Abram's loins (see how we can pervert the Word to suit us).
      5) As soon as Hagar conceived, she despised Sarai.
      6) Ishmael becomes Abram's first born (he surely loved him dearly).

   c. What really happened?

      1) It may be that their doing this was not based on a Word from God, but rather they were living in pride and needed to be humbled.
      2) Also, they changed the original vision of God (Mamre).
      3) Because they knew better than God ("Abram" – lofty thinker, exalted father).
      4) They thought they would come up with an idea that would make God's promise or Word come to pass sooner.
      5) Sarai, whose name means – quarrelsome and contentious, couldn't wait and she also tried to control Abram (remember, her name also means – my ruler, my princess), and make him listen to her.
      6) How often do we allow impatience and unbelief and controlling people to lead us into trouble? It bears repeating the fact that God had indeed said that Abram's heir would come out of his loins, which makes this a classic example of how we can turn the Word around to force a decision or an issue.
      7) Then we hope God will bless or hear (Ishmael means – God will hear) what we've done and support it.

   d. Ishmael is a product of

      1) Sarai's mind – human reasoning
      2) Abram's loins – human strength
      3) Hagar's body – flight (backsliding); ensnaring (brings us into bondage); an Egyptian (type of the flesh); God cannot bless what He has not called into being.

4) Scriptures concerning flesh

  a) John 3:6 – "*That which is born of the flesh is flesh...*"
  b) Galatians 6:7-8 – "*Be not deceived; God is not mocked: for whatsoever a man soweth, that shall he also reap. For he that soweth to his flesh shall of the flesh reap corruption; but he that soweth to the Spirit shall of the Spirit reap life everlasting.*"
  c) Hosea 8:7 – "*...they have sown the wind, and they shall reap the whirlwind...*"
  d) Romans 8:5 – "*For they that are after the flesh do mind the things of the flesh...*"
  e) Romans 8:8 – "*So then they that are in the flesh cannot please God.*"
  f) Romans 8:13 – "*...if ye live after the flesh, ye shall die...*"
  g) Romans 7:5 – "*...when we were in the flesh, the motions of sins...did work in our members...*"
  h) Romans 7:18 – "*For I know that in me (that is, in my flesh,) dwelleth no good thing...*"
  i) Galatians 5:17 – "*...the flesh lusteth against the Spirit, and the Spirit against the flesh...*"
  j) 1 John 2:16 – "*For all that is in the world, the lust of the flesh, and the lust of the eyes, and the pride of life, is not of the Father, but is of the world.*"
  k) Matthew 26:41 – "*Watch and pray, that ye enter not into temptation: the spirit indeed is willing, but the flesh is weak.*"

e. Isaac was a product of

  1) God's heart and mind – divine wisdom and vision
  2) Sarah's body – (after her character was changed) princess, noblewoman, a (godly) ruler
  3) Abraham's loins – his new name means – father of many nations, Father of mercy
  4) Isaac – his name means – laughter, laughing one – God's promises always to bring joy into our lives

3. Genesis 16:5-6 – Once we recognize we've made a mistake; it can cause us and that which we have created to despise each other. And many times we strike out and hurt something or someone and then try to make it right by abandoning them altogether.

4. Genesis 17:15-22 – Points to consider

  a. God changes their names
  b. He is ready to fulfill His promise, in His timing.
  c. Abraham laughs (at the promise)

  d. "*O that Ishmael might live before thee*"

    1) Other translations: "*...live in your presence*", "*...live by your favor*", "*if only Ishmael might live under your special care*", "*...bless Ishmael...*"

Abraham wanted desperately for God to bless Ishmael. He had grown to love his son and was very attached to him, and cared deeply for him. How many times have we prayed and begged God like this to please let our flesh child live, and let that become His purpose?

  e. God can only bless what is His.

5. Description of who Ishmael will become

      a.   Genesis 16:12

        1)   A wild man – wild in the Hebrew – a wild ass (wild and stubborn)
        2)   His hand will be against every man (always warring).
        3)   Every man's hand against him (always have enemies).
        4)   He will dwell in the presence of all his brethren (this means he will always represent flesh in our lives, or the presence of sin)

           a)   Sin in the camp; trouble by him always present
           b)   Mixture: mixed multitude among us
           c)   Our mistake will live right before our eyes
           d)   Always be reminded of how we blew it
           e)   Truly it will always humble us...but yet, this is used by God as blessing to us – not to condemn, but to teach us what not to do

      b.   Genesis 17:20

        1)   Twelve princes shall he beget – just like Jacob's twelve sons: Israel against the Arab world (Ishmael's descendents became the Arab nation, and most of them are now Muslims who hate Israel with a passion). It makes us think how many people will be affected by our foolishness. We do not live in a vacuum – everything we do has consequences that affect others besides us.
        2)   God does, however, promise to make him fruitful and a great nation.

      c.   Genesis 21:9 – Ishmael mocks God's true heir. (Galatians 4:23-29)
      d.   Genesis 21:10-14 – Even though it will be grievous beyond words, we must cast out that which is not of God and send it away. We must commit our soul and our mistakes in life to God's sovereign cause. (Verse 17-20)

      e.   Genesis 21:20-21

        1)   Ishmael will dwell in the wilderness (type of God's dealings).
        2)   He became an archer (man of the flesh).
        3)   He marries an Egyptian (married to the flesh).

   6.   What can we learn from this?

      a.   1 Peter 4:1 – "...he that hath suffered in the flesh hath ceased from sin."
      b.   II Corinthians 7:1 – "Having therefore these promises, dearly beloved, let us cleanse ourselves from all filthiness of the flesh..."
      c.   Galatians 5:16 – "...Walk in the Spirit, and ye shall not fulfil the lust of the flesh..."
      d.   Psalms 73:26 – "...my flesh and my heart faileth..."
      e.   Matthew 26:41 – "...the flesh is weak."
      f.   Galatians 5:24 – "...they that are Christ's have crucified the flesh with the affections and lusts."
      g.   Philippians 3:3 – "which worship God in the spirit...and have no confidence in the flesh."
      h.   Galatians 2:20 – "...the life which I now live in the flesh I live by the faith of the Son of God..."
      i.   Romans 13:14 – "...put ye on the Lord Jesus Christ, and make not provision for the flesh..."
      j.   Job 19:26 – "...in my flesh shall I see God."

IX.   Lust of the Eyes – I John 2:16

A.   Greek Definition of Eyes – vision, sight, penetrative

1.   Eyes – bad according to Scripture

   a.   Proverbs 27:20 – "...the eyes of man are never satisfied."
   b.   Ecclesiastes 1:8 – "...the eye never satisfied with seeing..."
   c.   Judges 16:16-22 (II Kings 25:7)
   d.   Genesis 3:5-7 – soul represented here in the eyes
   e.   Matthew 6:22-23 – "...light of the body is the eye...
   f.   Matthew 18:9 – "...if thine eye offend thee, pluck it out..."
   g.   Isaiah 3:16-17 – "...daughters of Zion are haughty, and walk with...wanton eyes..."
   h.   Proverbs 12:15 – "The way of a fool is right in his own eyes..."
   i.   I Samuel 3:2 – "...his eyes began to wax dim..."
   j.   Proverbs 30:12-13 – "...There is a generation, O how lofty are their eyes..."
   k.   Genesis 30:41 – stained cattle
   l.   Ecclesiastes 2:10 – "...whatsoever my eyes desired I kept not from them..."

2.   Eyes – good according to Scripture

   a.   Psalms 145:5
   b.   Job 42:5
   c.   Lamentations 3:48-51
   d.   Genesis 22:4, 13
   e.   Psalms 25:15 – "Mine eyes are ever toward the Lord..."
   f.   Psalms 119:18, 37, 82, 123 – we need the Word

3.   What To Do

   a.   Job 31:1
   b.   Ecclesiastes 2:14
   c.   Proverbs 4:20-27 (Proverbs 3:21)
   d.   Song of Solomon 1:5
   e.   Isaiah 11:3
   f.   Acts 9:18
   g.   Revelation 3:18
   h.   Revelation 4:6-8
   i.   Psalms 101:3
   j.   Psalms 121:1-2

X.   Pride of Life – I John 2:16, Ecclesiastes 7:8

A.   Word Definitions of Pride

1.   Hebrew

   a.   Ga'own – arrogance or majesty, ornament, excellency, majesty, pomp swelling, arrogancy
   b.   Ge'ah – lofty, arrogant. From a root – to mount up, to rise up, or to be majestic.

2.   Greek, Huperephania – appearing above others, haughty, comparing ones self with others. From a root – huper – over, above, beyond

B. Scriptures Defining It

1. I Samuel 17:28 – "...*I know thy pride, and the naughtiness of thine heart...*"

2. Job 41:34 – "...*king over all the children of pride.*"

   a. Isaiah 14:6-22 – Hebrew for Leviathan – a serpent, mourning, a symbol of Babylon (dragon)
   b. Ezekiel 28:11-19
   c. Psalms 74:14
   d. Isaiah 27:1

      1) Revelation 12:9
      2) Revelation 20:2

3. Proverbs 8:13 – "...*pride, and arrogancy, and the evil way...*"
4. Proverbs 13:10 – "*Only by pride cometh contention...*"
5. Proverbs 14:3 – "*In the mouth of the foolish is a rod of pride*"
6. Proverbs 16:18 – "*Pride goeth before destruction, and an haughty spirit before a fall.*" (Jeremiah 49:14-16)
7. Proverbs 29:23 – "*A man's pride shall bring him low...*"
8. Daniel 4:30-37 "...*and those that walk in pride he is able to abase.*"
9. Obadiah 1-4 – "*The pride of thine heart...*"
10. Mark 7:17-23 – "...*out of the heart of men, proceed...an evil eye, blasphemy, pride...*"
11. Timothy 3:6 – "...*lest being lifted up with pride...*"
12. I Samuel 2:3 – "*Talk no more so exceeding proudly...*"
13. Jeremiah 50:31-32 – "...*I am against thee, O thou most proud,...And the most proud shall stumble and fall...*"
14. Malachi 4:1 – "...*behold, the day cometh,...and all the proud, yea, and all that do wickedly, shall be stubble...*"
15. Romans 1:28-32 – "...*they did not like to retain God in their knowledge,...Being filled with all unrighteousness,...proud,...*"
16. I Timothy 6:3-6 – "...*He is proud, knowing nothing...*"
17. II Timothy 3:1-7 – "...*in the last days...men shall be lovers of their own selves, covetous, boasters, proud...*"
18. James 4:1-10 – "...*God resisteth the proud, but giveth grace unto the humble...*" (I Pet. 5:5-11)
19. Psalms 101:5 – "...*a proud heart will not I suffer.*"
20. Psalms 138:6 – "...*but the proud he knoweth afar off.*"
21. Proverbs 6:16-19 – "*These six things doth the LORD hate... A proud look...*"
22. Proverbs 15:25 – "*The LORD will destroy the house of the proud...*"
23. Proverbs 16:5 – "*Every one that is proud in heart...shall not be unpunished.*"
24. Proverbs 21:24
25. Proverbs 28:25 – "*He that is of a proud heart stirreth up strife...*" (Isaiah 16:6)

Lesson 45
MEN SENT FROM GOD

A Man Sent from God, John 1:6 – *"There was a man sent from God, whose name was John."*
Other translations:

"God sent a man named John to be His messenger"
"There suddenly appeared a man upon the human scene, sent off as an ambassador from God's presence"

A. Greek words

1. Sent, *apostello* – sent apart, to send out on a mission; an ambassador of the gospel commissioned with miraculous powers; messenger, he that is sent.
2. John – Jehovah as been gracious, Jehovah has graciously given

B. Other places in the New Testament where this Greek word *"sent"* above is used. By looking at these Scriptures, we can better understand and define the word *"sent"*

1. Matthew 10:5 – *"These twelve Jesus sent forth, and commanded them..."*
2. Matthew 10:16-17 – *"16Behold, I send you forth as sheep in the midst of wolves: be ye therefore wise as serpents, and harmless as doves. 17But beware of men: for they will deliver you up to the councils, and they will scourge you in their synagogues;"*
3. Matthew 22:2-14 – *"2The kingdom of heaven is like unto a certain king, which made a marriage for his son, 3And <u>sent forth his servants</u> to call them that were bidden to the wedding..."*
4. Luke 1:5-26 – *"...19And the angel answering said unto him, I am Gabriel, that stand in the presence of God; and am sent to speak unto thee, and to shew thee these glad tidings..."* (of John's birth and mission), *"...26And in the sixth month the angel Gabriel was <u>sent from God</u> unto a city of Galilee, named Nazareth"*

5. Luke 4:18-20 – *"18The Spirit of the Lord is upon me, because he hath anointed me to preach the gospel to the poor; <u>he hath sent me to</u>..."*

    a. Heal the broken hearted
    b. To preach deliverance to the captives
    c. Recovering of sight to the blind
    d. To set at liberty them that are bruised (Greek – crushed)
    e. To preach the acceptable year of the Lord

6. Luke 14:16-24 – *"16Then said he unto him, A certain man made a great supper, and bade many: 17And sent his servant at supper time to say to them that were bidden, Come; for all things are now ready. 18And they all with one consent began to make excuse...23And the lord said unto the servant, Go out into the highways and hedges, and compel them to come in, that my house may be filled..."*
7. John 20:21-22 – *"21Then said Jesus to them again, Peace be unto you: as my Father hath sent me, even so send I you. 22And when he had said this, he breathed on them, and saith unto them, Receive ye the Holy Ghost:"*
8. Romans 10:13-15 – *"...15And how shall they preach, except they be sent?"*

C. The word "Apostle"

1. An apostle is named by the will of God

       a. II Corinthians 1:1 – *"Paul, an apostle of Jesus Christ by the will of God..."* (Ephesians 1:1, Colossians 1:1, II Timothy 1:1)

       b. Galatians 1:1 – *"Paul, an apostle, (not of men, neither by man, but by Jesus Christ, and God the Father, who raised him from the dead;)"*

       c. I Timothy 1:1 – *"Paul, an apostle of Jesus Christ by the commandment of God our Saviour, and Lord Jesus Christ, which is our hope;"*

2. An apostle is called

       a. Romans 1:1 – *"Paul, a servant of Jesus Christ, called to be an apostle, separated unto the gospel of God,"* (I Corinthians 1:1)

       b. I Corinthians 15:9 – *"For I am the least of the apostles, that am not meet to be called an apostle, because I persecuted the church of God."*

       c. II Timothy 1:11 – *"Whereunto I am appointed a preacher, and an apostle, and a teacher of the Gentiles."*

3. An apostle is a servant

       a. Titus 1:1 – *"Paul, a servant of God, and an apostle of Jesus Christ, according to the faith of God's elect, and the acknowledging of the truth which is after godliness;"*

       b. II Peter 1:1 – *"Simon Peter, a servant and an apostle of Jesus Christ..."*

4. Signs of an apostle, I Corinthians 12:12 – *"Truly the signs of an apostle were wrought among you in <u>all patience</u>, <u>in signs</u>, and <u>wonders</u>, and <u>mighty deeds</u>."*

D. We need more men and women sent from God

1. John 20:21 – *"Then said Jesus to them again, Peace be unto you: as my Father hath sent me, even so send I you."*

2. John 17:18 – *"As thou hast sent me into the world, even so have I also sent them into the world."*

II. The Man God Sends As Seen Through the Example of John the Baptist, John 3:26-34

John 3:26-34, *"26And they came unto John, and said unto him, Rabbi, he that was with thee beyond Jordan, to whom thou barest witness, behold, the same baptizeth, and all men come to him. 27John answered and said, A man can receive nothing, except it be given him from heaven. 28Ye yourselves bear me witness, that I said, I am not the Christ, but that I am sent before him. 29He that hath the bride is the bridegroom: but the friend of the bridegroom, which standeth and heareth him, rejoiceth greatly because of the bridegroom's voice: this my joy therefore is fulfilled. 30He must increase, but I must decrease. 31He that cometh from above is above all: he that is of the earth is earthly, and speaketh of the earth: he that cometh from heaven is above all. 32And what he hath seen and heard, that he testifieth; and no man receiveth his testimony. 33He that hath received his testimony hath set to his seal that God is true. 34For he whom God hath sent speaketh the words of God: for God giveth not the Spirit by measure unto him."*

A. Verse 27 – *"John answered and said, A man can receive nothing, except it be given him from heaven."* – He acknowledges everything he has, came from God

1. I Corinthians 4:7 – *"For who maketh thee to differ from another? and what hast thou that thou didst not receive? now if thou didst receive it, why dost thou glory, as if thou hadst not received it?"*

2. James 1:17 – *"Every good gift and every perfect gift is from above, and cometh down from the Father of lights, with whom is no variableness, neither shadow of turning."*

3. John 7:18 – *"He that speaketh of himself seeketh his own glory: but he that seeketh his glory that sent him, the same is true, and no unrighteousness is in him."*

B. Verse 28 – *"Ye yourselves bear me witness, that I said, I am not the Christ, but that I am sent before him."* – We are not <u>the</u> Christ, but witnesses of the light by allowing God's glory to shine through us.

1. Acts 1:8 – *"But ye shall receive power, after that the Holy Ghost is come upon you: and ye shall be witnesses unto me both in Jerusalem, and in all Judaea, and in Samaria, and unto the uttermost part of the earth."*
2. John 1:7-9 – *"7The same came for a witness, to bear witness of the Light, that all men through him might believe. 8He was not that Light, but was sent to bear witness of that Light. 9That was the true Light, which lighteth every man that cometh into the world."*
3. Isaiah 43:10-12 – *"10Ye are my witnesses, saith the LORD, and my servant whom I have chosen: that ye may know and believe me, and understand that I am he: before me there was no God formed, neither shall there be after me. 11I, even I, am the LORD; and beside me there is no saviour. 12I have declared, and have saved, and I have shewed, when there was no strange god among you: therefore ye are my witnesses, saith the LORD, that I am God."*
4. Matthew 24:14 – *"And this gospel of the kingdom shall be preached in all the world for a witness unto all nations; and then shall the end come."*
5. Acts 22:14-15 – Paul's testimony, *"14And he said, The God of our fathers hath chosen thee, that thou shouldest know his will, and see that Just One, and shouldest hear the voice of his mouth. 15For thou shalt be his witness unto all men of what thou hast seen and heard."*
6. Matthew 5:14-16 – *"14Ye are the light of the world. A city that is set on an hill cannot be hid. 15Neither do men light a candle, and put it under a bushel, but on a candlestick; and it giveth light unto all that are in the house. 16Let your light so shine before men, that they may see your good works, and glorify your Father which is in heaven."*
7. Philippians 2:15 – *"That ye may be blameless and harmless, the sons of God, without rebuke, in the midst of a crooked and perverse nation, among whom ye shine as lights in the world;"*
8. I Thessalonians 5:5 – *"Ye are all the children of light, and the children of the day: we are not of the night, nor of darkness."*
9. Ephesians 5:8 – *"For ye were sometimes darkness, but now are ye light in the Lord: walk as children of light:"*
10. Romans 13:12 – *"The night is far spent, the day is at hand: let us therefore cast off the works of darkness, and let us put on the armour of light."*
11. Colossians 1:12 – *"Giving thanks unto the Father, which hath made us meet to be partakers of the inheritance of the saints in light:"*

12. We are to be like Jesus

  a. John 10:34 – *"Jesus answered them, Is it not written in your law, I said, Ye are gods?"*
  b. Psalms 82:6-7 – *"6I have said, Ye are gods; and all of you are children of the most High. 7But ye shall die like men, and fall like one of the princes."*

C. Verse 29 – *"He that hath the bride is the bridegroom: but the friend of the bridegroom, which standeth and heareth him, rejoiceth greatly because of the bridegroom's voice: this my joy therefore is fulfilled."* – We rejoice when Jesus is exalted and His bride recognizes the Husband's voice

1. Philippians 4:1 – *"Therefore, my brethren dearly beloved and longed for, my joy and crown, so stand fast in the Lord, my dearly beloved."*
2. I Thessalonians 2:4-12

D. Verse 30 – *"He must increase, but I must decrease."*

1. Galatians 2:20 – "*I am crucified with Christ: nevertheless I live; yet not I, but Christ liveth in me: and the life which I now live in the flesh I live by the faith of the Son of God, who loved me, and gave himself for me.*"
2. Philippians 3:7-15
3. Job 14:7-9 – "*⁷For there is hope of a tree, if it be cut down, that it will sprout again, and that the tender branch thereof will not cease. ⁸Though the root thereof wax old in the earth, and the stock thereof die in the ground; ⁹Yet through the scent of water it will bud, and bring forth boughs like a plant.*"
4. Judges 16:30 – Samson's testimony, "*...So the dead which he slew at his death were more than they which he slew in his life.*"
5. Psalms 116:15 – "*Precious in the sight of the LORD is the death of his saints.*"
6. John 12:24 – "*Verily, verily, I say unto you, Except a corn of wheat fall into the ground and die, it abideth alone: but if it die, it bringeth forth much fruit.*"
7. I Corinthians 15:31 – "*I protest by your rejoicing which I have in Christ Jesus our Lord, I die daily.*"

E. Verse 34 – "*For he whom God hath sent speaketh the words of God: for God giveth not the Spirit by measure unto him.*"

1. Making sure they are the words of God

   a. Job 12:11 – "*Doth not the ear try words? and the mouth taste his meat?*"
   b. I John 4:1 – "*Beloved, believe not every spirit, but try the spirits whether they are of God: because many false prophets are gone out into the world.*"
   c. I John 5:10 – "*He that believeth on the Son of God hath the witness in himself...*"
   d. Luke 1:44 – "*For, lo, as soon as the voice of thy salutation sounded in mine ears, the babe leaped in my womb for joy.*"
   e. I John 2:20, 27 – "*²⁰But ye have an unction from the Holy One, and ye know all things...²⁷But the anointing which ye have received of him abideth in you, and ye need not that any man teach you: but as the same anointing teacheth you of all things, and is truth, and is no lie, and even as it hath taught you, ye shall abide in him.*"
   f. Job 36:4 – "*...he that is perfect in knowledge is with thee.*"

2. God's Words sent

   a. Psalms 147:15 – "*He sendeth forth his commandment upon earth: his word runneth very swiftly.*"
   b. Psalms 147:18 – "*He sendeth out his word, and melteth them: he causeth his wind to blow, and the waters flow.*"
   c. Isaiah 55:11 – "*So shall my word be that goeth forth out of my mouth: it shall not return unto me void, but it shall accomplish that which I please, and it shall prosper in the thing whereto I sent it.*"
   d. Psalms 107:20 – "*He sent his word, and healed them, and delivered them from their destructions.*"
   e. Jeremiah 20:7-9
   f. Luke 10:38-42 – The process, sitting at Jesus' feet hearing His Word
   g. Isaiah 66:1-2 – Need men who trembleth at His Word (Hosea 13:1)
   h. Jeremiah 1:12 – "*Then said the LORD unto me, Thou hast well seen: for I will hasten my word to perform it.*"
   i. Jeremiah 23:28-29 – Speak His word faithfully; (II Peter 1:19-21)
   j. Psalms 45:1 – "*My heart is inditing a good matter: I speak of the things which I have made touching the king: my tongue is the pen of a ready writer.*"

    k.   Psalms 119:160-162 – "*160Thy word is true from the beginning: and every one of thy righteous judgments endureth for ever. 161Princes have persecuted me without a cause: but my heart standeth in awe of thy word. 162I rejoice at thy word, as one that findeth great spoil.*"

    l.   Psalms 119:89 – "*For ever, O LORD, thy word is settled in heaven.*"

    m.   Psalms 119:140 – "*Thy word is very pure: therefore thy servant loveth it.*"

    n.   Psalms 138:2 – "*...thou hast magnified thy word above all thy name.*"

    o.   Acts 4:29 – "*And now, Lord, behold their threatenings: and grant unto thy servants, that with all boldness they may speak thy word,*"

3.   "*...for God giveth not the Spirit by measure unto him.*"

    a.   John 14:12 – "*Verily, verily, I say unto you, He that believeth on me, the works that I do shall he do also; and greater works than these shall he do; because I go unto my Father.*"

    b.   Mark 11:22-24 – "*22And Jesus answering saith unto them, Have faith in God. 23For verily I say unto you, That whosoever shall say unto this mountain, Be thou removed, and be thou cast into the sea; and shall not doubt in his heart, but shall believe that those things which he saith shall come to pass; he shall have whatsoever he saith. 24Therefore I say unto you, What things soever ye desire, when ye pray, believe that ye receive them, and ye shall have them.*"

    c.   Obadiah 17, 21 – "*17But upon mount Zion shall be deliverance, and there shall be holiness; and the house of Jacob shall possess their possessions...21And saviours shall come up on mount Zion to judge the mount of Esau; and the kingdom shall be the LORD's.*"

    d.   Joel 2:2-11, 32

    e.   Isaiah 60:1-7, 11-22

    f.   Isaiah 62

    g.   I John 4:17 – "*...as he is, so are we in this world.*"

    h.   Matthew 6:10 – "*Thy kingdom come. Thy will be done in earth, as it is in heaven.*"

II.   The Man God Sends As Seen Through the Example of Joseph, Psalms 105:17-22

Psalms 105:17-22, "*17He sent a man before them, even Joseph, who was sold for a servant: 18Whose feet they hurt with fetters: he was laid in iron: 19Until the time that his word came: the word of the LORD tried him. 20The king sent and loosed him; even the ruler of the people, and let him go free. 21He made him lord of his house, and ruler of all his substance: 22To bind his princes at his pleasure; and teach his senators wisdom.*"

A.   Verse 17, "<u>*He sent a man before them, even Joseph, who was sold for a servant*</u>"

    1.   Another translation, "*But He sent a man on ahead: Joseph, sold as a slave*"

    2.   Joseph's names means – may God add, increasing, He shall add

    3.   God sends a man before others:

        a.   II Chronicles 2:3-11 – "*...7Send me now therefore a man cunning to work in gold, and in silver, and in brass, and in iron, and in purple, and crimson, and blue, and that can skill to grave with the cunning men that are with me in Judah and in Jerusalem, whom David my father did provide...*"

            1)   Cunning in Hebrew, *chakam* – wise, intelligent, skillful, artful, subtle, wise hearted; it comes from a root – to be wise in mind, word, or act, one who exceeds, one who can teach wisdom, one who can make wiser

            2)   Wise in doing what

                a)   Gold – working in God's nature, divine character

b) Silver – redemption
c) Brass – judgment
d) Iron – authority (rod of iron)
e) Purple – royalty
f) Crimson – blood, suffering
g) Blue – all things heavenly
h) Skill to grave – ability to engrave upon the hears your wisdom

B. Verse 17-18, *"...who was sold for a servant: ¹⁸Whose feet they hurt with fetters: he was laid in iron"*

In describing God's sent ones though the story of Jesus, we find them yoked by God. Joseph was sold for a servant and his feet hurt with fetters, and he was laid in iron. This all speaks of being imprisoned in the dealings of God and life's circumstances. Remember, all that Joseph went through to bring deliverance was not for himself, but for the then known world.

1. Matthew 26:26 – *"And as they were eating, Jesus took bread, and blessed it, <u>and brake it</u>, and gave it to the disciples, and said, Take, eat; this is my body."*
2. John 21:18 – *"¹⁸Verily, verily, I say unto thee, When thou wast young, thou girdedst thyself, and walkedst whither thou wouldest: but when thou shalt be old, thou shalt stretch forth thy hands, and another shall gird thee, and carry thee whither thou wouldest not."*
3. Acts 9:15-16 – *"¹⁵But the Lord said unto him, Go thy way: for he is a chosen vessel unto me, to bear my name before the Gentiles, and kings, and the children of Israel: ¹⁶For I will shew him how great things he must suffer for my name's sake."*
4. Matthew 11:29-30 – *"²⁹Take my yoke upon you, and learn of me; for I am meek and lowly in heart: and ye shall find rest unto your souls. ³⁰For my yoke is easy, and my burden is light."*
5. Exodus 21:5-6 – *"⁵And if the servant shall plainly say, I love my master, my wife, and my children; I will not go out free: ⁶Then his master shall bring him unto the judges; he shall also bring him to the door, or unto the door post; and his master shall bore his ear through with an aul; and he shall serve him for ever."*
6. Jeremiah 31:16-19 – *"...¹⁷And there is hope in thine end..."*
7. Lamentations 3:18-26 – *"...²⁷It is good for a man that he bear the yoke in his youth..."*
8. Jeremiah 20:7-13
9. I Timothy 6:1-12
10. Psalms 116:1-18 – *"...¹⁵Precious in the sight of the LORD is the death of his saints..."*
11. Psalms 119:67, 71, 75
12. Isaiah 53:7-11 – Example of Jesus, *"⁷He was oppressed, and he was afflicted, yet he opened not his mouth: he is brought as a lamb to the slaughter, and as a sheep before her shearers is dumb, so he openeth not his mouth. ⁸He was taken from prison and from judgment: and who shall declare his generation? for he was cut off out of the land of the living: for the transgression of my people was he stricken. ⁹And he made his grave with the wicked, and with the rich in his death; because he had done no violence, neither was any deceit in his mouth. ¹⁰Yet it pleased the LORD to bruise him; he hath put him to grief: when thou shalt make his soul an offering for sin, he shall see his seed, he shall prolong his days, and the pleasure of the LORD shall prosper in his hand. ¹¹He shall see of the travail of his soul, and shall be satisfied: by his knowledge shall my righteous servant justify many; for he shall bear their iniquities."*
13. Isaiah 63:9 – *"In all their affliction he was afflicted..."*
14. Zephaniah 3:12-17 – *"¹²I will also leave in the midst of thee an afflicted and poor people, and they shall trust in the name of the LORD..."*

C. Verse 19, *"Until the time that his word came: the word of the LORD tried him"*

1. Job 23:8-14 – *"...¹⁰But he knoweth the way that I take: when he hath tried me, I shall come forth as gold..."*

2. Psalms 66:10-12 – "*¹⁰For thou, O God, hast proved us: thou hast tried us, as silver is tried. ¹¹Thou broughtest us into the net; thou laidst affliction upon our loins. ¹²Thou hast caused men to ride over our heads; we went through fire and through water: but thou broughtest us out into a wealthy place.*"

3. Zechariah 13:9 – "*And I will bring the third part through the fire, and will refine them as silver is refined, and will try them as gold is tried: they shall call on my name, and I will hear them: I will say, It is my people: and they shall say, The LORD is my God.*"

4. Hebrews 11:17-19 – "*¹⁷By faith Abraham, when he was tried, offered up Isaac: and he that had received the promises offered up his only begotten son...*"

5. James 1:12 – "*Blessed is the man that endureth temptation: for when he is tried, he shall receive the crown of life, which the Lord hath promised to them that love him.*"

6. I Peter 1:7 – "*That the trial of your faith, being much more precious than of gold that perisheth, though it be tried with fire, might be found unto praise and honour and glory at the appearing of Jesus Christ:*"

7. Revelation 3:14-19 – "*...¹⁸I counsel thee to buy of me gold tried in the fire, that thou mayest be rich; and white raiment, that thou mayest be clothed, and that the shame of thy nakedness do not appear; and anoint thine eyes with eyesalve, that thou mayest see...*"

8. I Peter 4:12-14

9. Mark 4:14-20

10. Job 14:14 – "*If a man die, shall he live again? all the days of my appointed time will I wait, till my change come.*"

D. Verses 20-22, "*The king sent and loosed him; even the ruler of the people, and let him go free. ²¹He made him lord of his house, and ruler of all his substance. ²¹He made him lord of his house, and ruler of all his substance: ²²To bind his princes at his pleasure; and teach his senators wisdom*" The result of the dealings of God:

1. God the Father (type of the king here) loosed him at the appointed time.

2. Made him lord over His house (II Timothy 2:11-13, Matthew 25:14-21)

3. Ruler of all His substance (Key of David – Isaiah 22:15-25, Luke 12:42-43)

4. Bind princes (Psalms 149:6-9)

5. Teach wisdom (teaching priest – II Chronicles 15:3-6)

IV. God Is Seeking the Man

A. Matthew 8:23-27 – "*²³And when he was entered into a ship, his disciples followed him. ²⁴And, behold, there arose a great tempest in the sea, insomuch that the ship was covered with the waves: but he was asleep. ²⁵And his disciples came to him, and awoke him, saying, Lord, save us: we perish. ²⁶And he saith unto them, Why are ye fearful, O ye of little faith? Then he arose, and rebuked the winds and the sea; and there was a great calm. ²⁷But the men marvelled, saying, <u>What manner of man is this</u>, that even the winds and the sea obey him!*"

1. Other translations of verse 27:

"*They were stunned with bewildered wonder and marveled saying, what kind of man is this?*"
"*The disciples were amazed. Who is this man?, they asked*"
"*What sort of man*"
"*Who can this be?*"
"*What sort of person is this?*"
"*The disciples just sat there, awed! Who is this, they asked themselves*"

2. Greek for the word "*manner*", *potapos* – what possible sort; it comes from the root, *pote* – at what time, where, when

3. We were originally created in God's image, Genesis 1:26 – "*And God said, Let us make man in our image, after our likeness: and let them have dominion over the fish of the sea, and over the fowl of the air, and over the cattle, and over all the earth, and over every creeping thing that creepeth upon the earth.*"

    a. Hebrew for *image, tselem* – a phantom, illusion, resemblance, a representative figure
    b. Hebrew for *likeness, demuwth* – resemblance, model, shape, like; it comes from the root word *damah* – to compare, to resemble, to consider how alike they are

4. John 7:46 – "*The officers answered, Never man spake like this man.*"

5. Isaiah 59:16 – "*And he saw that there was no man, and wondered that there was no intercessor: therefore his arm brought salvation unto him; and his righteousness, it sustained him.*" Jesus becomes our link back to the original man through salvation

    a. Ephesians 2:13-14 – "*[13]But now in Christ Jesus ye who sometimes were far off are made nigh by the blood of Christ. [14]For he is our peace, who hath made both one, and hath broken down the middle wall of partition between us;*"
    b. Colossians 1:20 – "*And, having made peace through the blood of his cross, by him to reconcile all things unto himself; by him, I say, whether they be things in earth, or things in heaven.*"
    c. Galatians 4:3-7 – "*[3]Even so we, when we were children, were in bondage under the elements of the world: [4]But when the fulness of the time was come, God sent forth his Son, made of a woman, made under the law, [5]To redeem them that were under the law, that we might receive the adoption of sons. [6]And because ye are sons, God hath sent forth the Spirit of his Son into your hearts, crying, Abba, Father. [7]Wherefore thou art no more a servant, but a son; and if a son, then an heir of God through Christ.*"

B. After the Cross, We Are People Who Live In Two Realms

1. II Corinthians 4:16 – "*For which cause we faint not; but though our outward man perish, yet the inward man is renewed day by day.*"
2. Ephesians 2:6 – "*And hath raised us up together, and made us sit together in heavenly places in Christ Jesus:*"
3. II Corinthians 5:2-5 – "*[2]For in this we groan, earnestly desiring to be clothed upon with our house which is from heaven: [3]If so be that being clothed we shall not be found naked. [4]For we that are in this tabernacle do groan, being burdened: not for that we would be unclothed, but clothed upon, that mortality might be swallowed up of life. [5]Now he that hath wrought us for the selfsame thing is God, who also hath given unto us the earnest of the Spirit.*"
4. Ephesians 4:22-24 – "*[22]That ye put off concerning the former conversation the old man, which is corrupt according to the deceitful lusts; [23]And be renewed in the spirit of your mind; [24]And that ye put on the new man, which after God is created in righteousness and true holiness.*"
5. I Peter 3:3-4 – "*[3]Whose adorning let it not be that outward adorning of plaiting the hair, and of wearing of gold, or of putting on of apparel; [4]But let it be the hidden man of the heart, in that which is not corruptible, even the ornament of a meek and quiet spirit, which is in the sight of God of great price.*"
6. Colossians 3:9 – "*Lie not one to another, seeing that ye have put off the old man with his deeds;*"

C. Becoming this man – we have to mature and put away childish ways

1. I Corinthians 13:9-11 – "*9For we know in part, and we prophesy in part. 10But when that which is perfect is come, then that which is in part shall be done away. 11When I was a child, I spake as a child, I understood as a child, I thought as a child: but when I became a man, I put away childish things.*"

   a. Childish in Greek, *nepios* – an infant, a minor, simple minded person, a babe, an immature Christian; below are examples of this same Greek word

      1) Hebrews 5:13 – "*For every one that useth milk is unskilful in the word of righteousness: for he is a babe.*"
      2) I Corinthians 3:1 – "*And I, brethren, could not speak unto you as unto spiritual, but as unto carnal, even as unto babes in Christ.*"
      3) Ephesians 4:14 – "*That we henceforth be no more children, tossed to and fro, and carried about with every wind of doctrine, by the sleight of men...*"

D. Men as signs

   1. Ezekiel 12:8-11 – "*8And in the morning came the word of the LORD unto me, saying, 9Son of man, hath not the house of Israel, the rebellious house, said unto thee, What doest thou? 10Say thou unto them, Thus saith the Lord GOD; This burden concerneth the prince in Jerusalem, and all the house of Israel that are among them. 11Say, I am your sign: like as I have done, so shall it be done unto them: they shall remove and go into captivity.*" Sign in Hebrew – a miracle, a token; it comes from a root word that means – to be bright, beautiful
   2. Isaiah 8:18 – "*Behold, I and the children whom the LORD hath given me are for signs and for wonders in Israel from the LORD of hosts, which dwelleth in mount Zion.*" Sign in Hebrew – an appearance, a signal like a flag, a beacon, and a monument
   3. Isaiah 55:12-13 – "*12For ye shall go out with joy, and be led forth with peace: the mountains and the hills shall break forth before you into singing, and all the trees of the field shall clap their hands. 13Instead of the thorn shall come up the fir tree, and instead of the brier shall come up the myrtle tree: and it shall be to the LORD for a name, for an everlasting sign that shall not be cut off.*"
   4. I Corinthians 4:9 – "*For I think that God hath set forth us the apostles last, as it were appointed to death: for we are made a spectacle unto the world, and to angels, and to men.*" Spectacle in Greek – a public show
   5. Isaiah 43:10 – "*Ye are my witnesses, saith the LORD, and my servant whom I have chosen: that ye may know and believe me, and understand that I am he: before me there was no God formed, neither shall there be after me.*" Witnesses in Hebrew – a testimony; it comes from a root word that means – to duplicate or repeat
   6. Isaiah 32:1-3
   7. John 7:37-38

   8. John 19:5 – "*Then came Jesus forth, wearing the crown of thorns, and the purple robe. And Pilate saith unto them, Behold the man!*"

      a. I Corinthians 13:11 – "*When I was a child, I spake as a child, I understood as a child, I thought as a child: but when I became a man, I put away childish things.*"
      b. Ephesians 4:11-13

   9. Isaiah 62:3 – "*Thou shalt also be a crown of glory in the hand of the LORD, and a royal diadem in the hand of thy God.*"
   10. Isaiah 60:1-3
   11. Revelation 11:3-12 – Two witnesses

IV. A Few Examples of Sent Ones Found in Scripture and Their Messages

    A. John the Baptist, Mark 1:2-3 – "*²As it is written in the prophets, Behold, I send my messenger before thy face, which shall prepare thy way before thee. ³The voice of one crying in the wilderness, Prepare ye the way of the Lord, make his paths straight.*"

        1. Isaiah 40:1-10 – This was a word both to Israel at Jesus first coming (John) and to us at His second coming (this time a prophetic company)
        2. Malachi 3:1-4

    B. Mark 3:13-15 – "*¹³And he goeth up into a mountain, and calleth unto him whom he would: and they came unto him. ¹⁴And he ordained twelve, that they should be with him, and that he might send them forth to preach, ¹⁵And to have power to heal sicknesses, and to cast out devils:*"

        1. Twelve – number of God's government
        2. First – that they should be with Him
        3. Then sent them to preach
        4. Have power (Greek, *exousia* – "authority") to heal sicknesses
        5. And to cast out devils

    C. Mark 16:15-20 – "*¹⁵And he said unto them, Go ye into all the world, and preach the gospel to every creature. ¹⁶He that believeth and is baptized shall be saved; but he that believeth not shall be damned. ¹⁷And these signs shall follow them that believe; In my name shall they cast out devils; they shall speak with new tongues; ¹⁸They shall take up serpents; and if they drink any deadly thing, it shall not hurt them; they shall lay hands on the sick, and they shall recover. ¹⁹So then after the Lord had spoken unto them, he was received up into heaven, and sat on the right hand of God. ²⁰And they went forth, and preached everywhere, the Lord working with them, and confirming the word with signs following. Amen.*"

        1. Go into all the world and preach the gospel; we are to start doing the work
        2. Signs done in His name shall follow those who are sent

            a. Cast out devils
            b. Speak with new tongues
            c. Take up serpents (the devil – Genesis 3:1-4, Job 26:13, Revelation 12:9)
            d. Nothing they drink shall harm them
            e. Lay hands on the sick and they shall recover
            f. They go forth and preach everything
            g. The Lord working with them
            h. And confirming the Word with signs following

        3. Matthew 10:7-8 – "*⁷And as ye go, preach, saying, The kingdom of heaven is at hand. ⁸Heal the sick, cleanse the lepers, raise the dead, cast out devils: freely ye have received, freely give.*"
        4. Matthew 18:18-20 – "*¹⁸Verily I say unto you, Whatsoever ye shall bind on earth shall be bound in heaven: and whatsoever ye shall loose on earth shall be loosed in heaven. ¹⁹Again I say unto you, That if two of you shall agree on earth as touching any thing that they shall ask, it shall be done for them of my Father which is in heaven. ²⁰For where two or three are gathered together in my name, there am I in the midst of them.*"

    D. God's last day's sent messengers seen in Psalms 110:1-4 – "*¹The LORD said unto my Lord, Sit thou at my right hand, until I make thine enemies thy footstool. ²The LORD shall send the rod of thy strength out of Zion: rule thou in the midst of thine enemies. ³Thy people shall be willing in the day of thy power, in the beauties of holiness from the womb of the morning: thou hast the dew of thy youth. ⁴The LORD hath sworn, and will not repent, Thou art a priest for ever after the order of Melchizedek."* If God is going to do anything in the earth, it will be through His people (Hebrews 10:12-13)

1. Zion sent to teach us to rule

    a. Revelation 12:5 – *"And she brought forth a man child, who was to rule all nations with a rod of iron: and her child was caught up unto God, and to his throne."*

    b. Revelation 2:26-29 – *"²⁶And he that overcometh, and keepeth my works unto the end, to him will I give power over the nations: ²⁷And he shall rule them with a rod of iron; as the vessels of a potter shall they be broken to shivers: even as I received of my Father. ²⁸And I will give him the morning star. ²⁹He that hath an ear, let him hear what the Spirit saith unto the churches."*

    c. Proverbs 12:24 – *"The hand of the diligent shall bear rule: but the slothful shall be under tribute."*

2. Verse 1 – Jesus will use these sent ones to put Satan under God's feet. One of the greatest tools to accomplish this is praise and worship.

    a. Genesis 49:8-10 – *"⁸Judah, thou art he whom thy brethren shall praise: thy hand shall be in the neck of thine enemies; thy father's children shall bow down before thee. ⁹Judah is a lion's whelp: from the prey, my son, thou art gone up: he stooped down, he couched as a lion, and as an old lion; who shall rouse him up? ¹⁰The sceptre shall not depart from Judah, nor a lawgiver from between his feet, until Shiloh come; and unto him shall the gathering of the people be."* Judah means "praise" and is a type of worshippers. (Psalms 76:1-4, Zechariah 10:3-6)

    b. Numbers 10:33-36 – The ark went before them (Psalms 68:1-4

    c. I Samuel 2:1-3 – Hannah's prayer

    d. II Samuel 22:4

    e. II Chronicles 20:1-4, 13-22 – Jehoshaphat's prayer

    f. I Samuel 16:14-19, 23 – David delivering Saul

    g. Psalms 8:2, Matthew 21:16 – Praise defeats the enemy

    h. Psalms 149

    i. Isaiah 66:5-6

    j. Psalms 42:1-5

    k. Zephaniah 3:11-17 – God's remnant

3. Verse 2a, *"The LORD shall send the rod of thy strength out of Zion..."* – Zion is His rod; below are Scriptures about God's rod

    a. Exodus 4:2-4 – *"²And the LORD said unto him, What is that in thine hand? And he said, A rod. ³And he said, Cast it on the ground. And he cast it on the ground, and it became a serpent; and Moses fled from before it. ⁴And the LORD said unto Moses, Put forth thine hand, and take it by the tail. And he put forth his hand, and caught it, and it became a rod in his hand:"* Authority over the serpent

    b. Numbers 17:2-10 – Aaron's rod that budded

    c. Psalms 23:4 – *"Yea, though I walk through the valley of the shadow of death, I will fear no evil: for thou art with me; thy rod and thy staff they comfort me."*

    d. Genesis 49:10 – *"The sceptre shall not depart from Judah, nor a lawgiver from between his feet, until Shiloh come; and unto him shall the gathering of the people be."*

    e. Isaiah 62:1-5

    f. Revelation 2:26-29, Revelation 12:5 – Manchild (overcomers) ruling with rod

4. Verse 2b, *"...rule thou in the midst of thine enemies"*

    a. Proverbs 8:11-16 – *"...15By me kings reign, and princes decree justice. 16By me princes rule, and nobles, even all the judges of the earth"*

    b. Proverbs 12:24 – *"The hand of the diligent shall bear rule..."*

    c. Isaiah 32:1-3 – *"1Behold, a king shall reign in righteousness, and princes shall rule in judgment. 2And a man shall be as an hiding place from the wind, and a covert from the tempest; as rivers of water in a dry place, as the shadow of a great rock in a weary land..."*

    d. II Samuel 23:3 – *"The God of Israel said, the Rock of Israel spake to me, He that ruleth over men must be just, ruling in the fear of God."*

    e. Hosea 11:12 – *"Ephraim compasseth me about with lies, and the house of Israel with deceit: but Judah yet ruleth with God, and is faithful with the saints."*

    f. Psalms 105:17-22 – Joseph made ruler after dealings of God

    g. Matthew 25:21 – *"His lord said unto him, Well done, thou good and faithful servant: thou hast been faithful over a few things, I will make thee ruler over many things: enter thou into the joy of thy lord."*

    h. Luke 12:42-44 – Faithful made ruler over all God has

5. Verse 3, *"Thy people shall be willing in the day of thy power, in the beauties of holiness from the womb of the morning: thou hast the dew of thy youth."*

    a. Willing in Hebrew means – spontaneous

    b. Power in Hebrew means – army, wealth, resources, wealth, valor, strength

6. Verse 4, *"The LORD hath sworn, and will not repent, Thou art a priest for ever after the order of Melchizedek."*

    a. Hebrews 5:5-10 – Jesus our Melchisedec (Hebrews 6:20)

    b. Hebrews 7:11-28 – the order of Melchisedec

    c. Ezekiel 40:46, 44:15-31 – The order (sons) of Zadok

V. After the Glory Hath He Sent Me, Zechariah 2:8-13, Isaiah 66:19

Zechariah 2:8-13 – *"8For thus saith the LORD of hosts; <u>After the glory hath he sent me unto the nations</u> which spoiled you: for he that toucheth you toucheth the apple of his eye. 9For, behold, I will shake mine hand upon them, and they shall be a spoil to their servants: and ye shall know that the LORD of hosts hath sent me. 10Sing and rejoice, O daughter of Zion: for, lo, I come, and I will dwell in the midst of thee, saith the LORD. 11And many nations shall be joined to the LORD in that day, and shall be my people: and I will dwell in the midst of thee, and thou shalt know that the LORD of hosts hath sent me unto thee. 12And the LORD shall inherit Judah his portion in the holy land, and shall choose Jerusalem again. 13Be silent, O all flesh, before the LORD: for he is raised up out of his holy habitation."* Other translations of Zechariahs 2:8:

"After a period of glory, the Lord of heavens armies sent me, against the nations who plundered you..."
"For Adonai-Tzva'ot has sent me on a glorious mission to the nations..."
"For the Lord who rules over all says to me that for His own glory He has sent me to the nations..."
"Afterwards, the Glory sent me to the nations who looted you..."
"The Lord of Glory has sent me..."
"For this is what the Lord of Armies has said: In the way of glory He has sent me to the nations..."

Isaiah 66:19 – *"And I will set a sign among them, and I will send those that escape of them unto the nations, to Tarshish, Pul, and Lud, that draw the bow, to Tubal, and Javan, to the isles afar off, that have not heard my fame, neither have seen my glory; and they shall declare my glory among the Gentiles."*

A. God's eyes are on the nations

1. Psalms 66:7 – "*He ruleth by his power for ever; his eyes behold the nations...*"
2. Psalms 22:27-28 – "*27All the ends of the world shall remember and turn unto the LORD: and all the kindreds of the nations shall worship before thee. 28For the kingdom is the LORD's: and he is the governor among the nations.*"
3. Psalms 113:4 – "*The LORD is high above all nations, and his glory above the heavens.*"
4. Isaiah 2:2-4 – "*2And it shall come to pass in the last days, that the mountain of the LORD's house shall be established in the top of the mountains, and shall be exalted above the hills; and all nations shall flow unto it...*"
5. Isaiah 40:13-15, 17-18 – Nations are as a drop in the bucket
6. Haggai 2:6-9 – "*6For thus saith the LORD of hosts; Yet once, it is a little while, and I will shake the heavens, and the earth, and the sea, and the dry land; 7And I will shake all nations, and the desire of all nations shall come: and I will fill this house with glory, saith the LORD of hosts...*"

B. We are to possess the nations by His grace

1. Deuteronomy 11:22-25 – "*22For if ye shall diligently keep all these commandments which I command you, to do them, to love the LORD your God, to walk in all his ways, and to cleave unto him; 23Then will the LORD drive out all these nations from before you, and ye shall possess greater nations and mightier than yourselves. 24Every place whereon the soles of your feet shall tread shall be yours: from the wilderness and Lebanon, from the river, the river Euphrates, even unto the uttermost sea shall your coast be. 25There shall no man be able to stand before you: for the LORD your God shall lay the fear of you and the dread of you upon all the land that ye shall tread upon, as he hath said unto you.*"
2. Isaiah 55:1-5
3. Micah 7:16-17
4. Revelation 2:26-28, Revelation 12:5
5. Psalms 2:8 – "*Ask of me, and I shall give thee the heathen for thine inheritance, and the uttermost parts of the earth for thy possession.*"

C. We are to reach the nations with the gospel

1. Matthew 24:14 – "*And this gospel of the kingdom shall be preached in all the world for a witness unto all nations; and then shall the end come.*"
2. Matthew 28:19-20 – "*19Go ye therefore, and teach all nations, baptizing them in the name of the Father, and of the Son, and of the Holy Ghost: 20Teaching them to observe all things whatsoever I have commanded you: and, lo, I am with you alway, even unto the end of the world. Amen.*"
3. John 4:35 – "*...behold, I say unto you, Lift up your eyes, and look on the fields; for they are white already to harvest.*"

Lesson 46
MERCY

I. Word Definitions for Mercy, Mercies, Merciful

A. Hebrew words

1. *Chanan* – To bend or stoop in kindness to an inferior, to bestow favor, to have pity upon, to show graciousness to, to make supplication for
2. *Rachuwn* – Full of compassion
3. *Racham* – To fondle, to love, to have compassion upon, to have pity
4. *Racham* – Compassion, as cherishing the fetus in the womb, tender love, bowels of compassion, great pity.
5. *Kaphar* – To cover, to expiate, to placate or cancel, to appease, to make atonement for, to cleanse, pacify, pardon, to disannul, to purge away, to make reconciliation.
6. *Checed* – Kindness, beauty; It comes from a root word, *chacad* – To bow the neck in courtesy, to be kind.

B. Greek words

1. *Hileos* – Cheerful, propitious, God's graciousness in averting some calamity
2. *Oiktirmon* – Pity; it comes from a root, *oikteiro* – To exercise pity, to have compassion on
3. *Eleemon* – Actively compassionate and merciful; It comes from a root word, *eleeo* – To have compassion by divine grace, to show mercy upon

C. Other words translated differently in the King James Version, but the same word translated mercy

The words lovingkindness and kindness, though translated differently are the same Hebrew word. You can use these words interchangeably because they mean the same thing. Why the translators chose to translate the same Hebrew word differently, we will never know.

II. Our God Is Merciful

A. He is mercy

1. II Corinthians 1:3 – "*Blessed be God, even the Father of our Lord Jesus Christ, the Father of mercies, and the God of all comfort;*"

a.	Daniel 9:9	j.	Exodus 25:22
b.	Exodus 33:19-23 34:5-6	k.	I Chronicles 21:13
c.	Deuteronomy 4:23-31-37	l.	Psalms 116:5
d.	Nehemiah 9:30-32	m.	Psalms 62:12
e.	Psalms 37:25	n.	Psalms 130
f.	Matthew 5:7	o.	Romans 11:32
g.	Psalms 25:10	p.	James 5:11
h.	Psalms 103:7-8	q.	Jeremiah 33:11
i.	Ephesians 2:4	r.	Micah 7:18-19

2. He is kind (His loving kindness)

3. Proverbs 20:28 – Other Translations:

"...His throne is sustained by mercy..."
"...His throne is founded on kindness..."
"...the seat of His power is based on upright acts..."
"...His throne is established by mercy..."

4. Isaiah 16:5

5. The mercy seat – Exodus 25:17-22

   a. Pure gold – God's nature
   b. Length and breadth but no height or depth. His mercy is unfathomable; it reaches to the sky (height) and goes to the deepest valley (depth) to help us.
   c. Four cubits total – number for creation (mercy over all His works)
   d. Two cherubim – (His glory is guarded by mercy)
   e. Even the cherubim look toward the mercy seat.
   f. Mercy over ark (mercy over law)
   g. He meets and has communion with us from the mercy seat.

6. Zechariah 7:9 – Other translation – *"...Apply the law fairly and practice kindness."*
7. Psalms 103:10-11
8. Hosea 12:6

9. Habakkuk 3:2 – Other translations:

   "...for all your wrath, remember to be merciful..."
   "...and though we have earned thy anger, be think thee of mercy still."

10. II Samuel 23:3
11. Psalms 101:1

12. Psalms 119:156

    a. Isaiah 54:8, 10 (Psalms 89:33)
    b. Jeremiah 9:23-24
    c. Jeremiah 31:3
    d. Nehemiah 9:17
    e. Psalms 117:2
    f. Isaiah 63:7
    g. Psalms 63:3
    h. Psalms 103:4

II. We Are To Be Like Him

   A. We are to be merciful

      1. Luke 6:36

      2. Proverbs 31:26 (the Bride)

         a. Malachi 2:5-7
         b. Colossians 3:12-14

      3. Micah 6:8

        a.   Ephesians 4:32

        b.   II Peter 1:4-9

    4.   Zechariah 7:8-9

    5.   Luke 10:25-36

B.   Those who show mercy, receive mercy

    1.   Matthew 5:7

    2.   Psalms 18:25

    3.   Proverbs 11:17

    4.   James 2:13

III.   Mercy and Judgment

A.   Mercy rejoices over judgment

    1.   James 2:13 – Other translations:

        "...mercy triumphs over judgment..."
        "...mercy glories in the face of judgment..."
        "...mercy boasteth over judgment..."

    2.   Proverbs 20:28

B.   Other related passages

    1.   Psalms 25:5-11

    2.   Psalms 51:1

    3.   Psalms 145:9

C.   Examples of mercy rejoicing over judgment

    1.   John 8:1-11

    2.   Jonah 3:10

    3.   II Samuel 12:13,14

    4.   Luke 23:39-43

    5.   I Samuel 25:32-35

    6.   Jeremiah 30:12-20

IV. Mercy and Truth

A.   The combination of these two delivers us from iniquity

    1.   Proverbs 16:6 – *"By mercy and truth iniquity is purged: and by the fear of the LORD men depart from evil."*

    2.   Psalms 61:7 – *"He shall abide before God for ever: O prepare mercy and truth, which may preserve him."*

        a.   Psalms 40:11 – *"Withhold not thou thy tender mercies from me, O LORD: let thy lovingkindness and thy truth continually preserve me."*

3. Psalms 85:10 – *"Mercy and truth are met together; righteousness and peace have kissed each other."*
4. Psalms 57:3 – *"...God shall send forth his mercy and his truth."*
5. Ephesians 4:15 – *"But speaking the truth in love, may grow up into him in all things, which is the head, even Christ:"*
6. Exodus 34:5-8
7. Psalms 25:5-6 – *"Lead me in thy truth, and teach me: for thou art the God of my salvation; on thee do I wait all the day. Remember, O LORD, thy tender mercies and thy lovingkindnesses; for they have been ever of old."*

B. The Lord is a God of mercy and truth

1. Psalms 86:15 – *"But thou, O Lord, art a God full of compassion, and gracious, longsuffering, and plenteous in mercy and truth."*

    a. Proverbs 20:28 – *"Mercy and truth preserve the king: and his throne is upholden by mercy."*
    b. Psalms 115:1 – *"Not unto us, O LORD, not unto us, but unto thy name give glory, for thy mercy, and for thy truth's sake."*
    c. II Samuel 2:6 – *"And now the LORD shew kindness and truth unto you..."*

C. He wants us to walk in it

    a. Proverbs 3:3 – *"Let not mercy and truth forsake thee: bind them about thy neck; write them upon the table of thine heart:"*
    b. Proverbs 14:22 – *"Do they not err that devise evil? but mercy and truth shall be to them that devise good."*

III. Defining the Mercy Of God

A. Sure mercies

1. Hebrew for sure, *aman* – To build up or support, to foster as a parent or nurse, to be firm or faithful, to morally be true or certain, to guard, to protect.

2. Examples in Scripture of the sure mercies of David

    a. Isaiah 55:3 – *"Incline your ear, and come unto me: hear, and your soul shall live; and I will make an everlasting covenant with you, even the sure mercies of David."*
    b. Acts 13:34 – *"And as concerning that he raised him up from the dead, now no more to return to corruption, he said on this wise, I will give you the sure mercies of David."*

3. Other passages with this Hebrew word sure

    a. Deuteronomy 7:9 – *"Know therefore that the LORD thy God, he is God, the faithful (Hebrew, aman) God, which keepeth covenant and mercy with them that love him and keep his commandments to a thousand generations"*
    b. I Samuel 25:28 (Abigail – Nabal's wife) – *"...for the LORD will certainly make my lord a sure house; because my lord fighteth the battles of the LORD..."*
    c. Psalms 93:5 – *"Thy testimonies are very sure: holiness becometh thine house, O LORD, for ever."*

    d.   Isaiah 22:20-25 – (Key of David to Eliakim) – *"...And the key of the house of David will I lay upon his shoulder; so he shall open, and none shall shut; and he shall shut, and none shall open. And I will fasten him as a nail in a <u>sure</u> place..."*

    e.   II Samuel 23:5 – *"Although my house be not so with God; yet he hath made with me an everlasting covenant, ordered in all things, and <u>sure</u>: for this is all my salvation, and all my desire..."*

    f.   Psalms 89:27-36 – *"Also I will make him my firstborn, higher than the kings of the earth. My mercy will I keep for him for evermore, and my covenant <u>shall stand fast</u> (Hebrew, aman) with him. His seed also will I make to endure for ever, and his throne as the days of heaven. If his children forsake my law, and walk not in my judgments; If they break my statutes, and keep not my commandments; Then will I visit their transgression with the rod, and their iniquity with stripes. Nevertheless my lovingkindness will I not utterly take from him, nor suffer my faithfulness to fail. My covenant will I not break, nor alter the thing that is gone out of my lips. Once have I sworn by my holiness that I will not lie unto David. His seed shall endure forever, and his throne as the sun before me."*

4.   Lamentations 3:22-25 – *"...It is of the LORD's mercies that we are not consumed, because his compassions fail not. They are new every morning: great is thy faithfulness. The LORD is my portion, saith my soul; therefore will I hope in him. The LORD is good unto them that wait for him..."*

B.   Tender mercies

1.   Hebrew for tender, *racham* – Compassion in the plural, like cherishing the fetus in the womb.

2.   Psalms 25:6 – *"Remember, O LORD, thy <u>tender mercies</u> and thy lovingkindnesses; for they have been ever of old."*

3.   Psalms 40:11 – *"Withhold not thou thy <u>tender mercies</u> from me, O LORD: let thy lovingkindness and thy truth continually preserve me."*

4.   Psalms 51:1 – *"Have mercy upon me, O God, according to thy lovingkindness: according unto the <u>multitude of thy tender mercies</u> blot out my transgressions."*

5.   Psalms 69:16 – *"Hear me, O LORD; for thy lovingkindness is good: turn unto me according to the <u>multitude of thy tender mercies</u>."*

6.   Psalms 77:9-10 – *"Hath God forgotten to be gracious? hath he in anger shut up <u>his tender mercies</u>? Selah. And I said, This is my infirmity: but I will remember the years of the right hand of the most High."* (Psalms 66:18-20)

7.   Psalms 79:8 – *"O remember not against us former iniquities: let thy <u>tender mercies</u> speedily prevent us: for we are brought very low."*

8.   Psalms 103:4 – *"...who crowneth thee with lovingkindness and <u>tender mercies</u>;"*

9.   Psalms 119:77 – *"Let <u>thy tender mercies</u> come unto me, that I may live: for thy law is my delight."*

10.   Psalms 119:156 – *"<u>Great are thy tender mercies</u>, O LORD: quicken me according to thy judgments"*

11.   Psalms 145:9 – *"The LORD is good to all: and <u>his tender mercies are over all his works</u>."*

12.   Luke 1:78 – *"Through the <u>tender mercy of our God</u>; whereby the dayspring from on high hath visited us,"*

13.   James 5:11 – *"...Ye have heard of the patience of Job, and have seen the end of the Lord; that the Lord is very pitiful, and of <u>tender mercy</u>."*

C.   Plenteous in mercy

1.   Hebrew for plenteous, *rab* – Abundant in size, quantity and quality

2.   Psalms 86:5 – *"For thou, Lord, art good, and ready to forgive; and <u>plenteous in mercy</u> unto all them that call upon thee."*

3. Psalms 86:15 – "*But thou, O Lord, art a God full of compassion, and gracious, longsuffering, and* <u>*plenteous in mercy and truth*</u>."
4. Psalms 103:8 – "*The LORD is merciful and gracious, slow to anger, and* <u>*plenteous in mercy*</u>."
5. Psalms 130:7 – "*Let Israel hope in the LORD: for with the LORD there is* <u>*mercy*</u>*, and with him is* <u>*plenteous redemption*</u>."

D. Great mercy

1. Hebrew for great, *rab* – Abundant in size, quantity, and quality
2. Numbers 14:18 – "*The LORD is longsuffering, and of* <u>*great mercy*</u>*, forgiving iniquity and transgression...*"
3. I Samuel 12:22 – "*For the LORD will not forsake his people for his* <u>*great name's sake*</u>*: because it hath pleased the LORD to make you his people.*"
4. II Samuel 24:14 – "*...let us fall now into the hand of the LORD; for* <u>*his mercies are great*</u>*...*"
5. I Kings 3:6 – "*And Solomon said, Thou hast shewed unto thy servant David my father* <u>*great mercy*</u>*, according as he walked before thee in truth, and in righteousness, and in uprightness of heart with thee; and thou hast kept for him this* <u>*great kindness*</u>*, that thou hast given him a son to sit on his throne, as it is this day.*"
6. Psalms 31:19 – "*Oh how* <u>*great is thy goodness*</u>*, which thou hast laid up for them that fear thee...*"
7. Psalms 86:13 – "*For* <u>*great is thy mercy toward me*</u>*: and thou hast delivered my soul from the lowest hell.*"
8. Psalms 103:11 – "*For as the heaven is high above the earth,* <u>*so great is his mercy*</u> *toward them that fear him.*"
9. Psalms 108:4 – "*For* <u>*thy mercy is great above the heavens*</u>*: and thy truth reacheth unto the clouds.*"
10. Psalms 117:2 – "*For his* <u>*merciful kindness is great*</u> *toward us...*"
11. Psalms 119:156 – "<u>*Great are thy tender mercies*</u>*, O LORD: quicken me according to thy judgments*"
12. Psalms 145:8 – "*The LORD is gracious, and full of compassion; slow to anger, and of* <u>*great mercy*</u>."
13. Psalms 69:16 – "*Hear me, O LORD; for thy lovingkindness is good: turn unto me according to the* <u>*multitude of thy tender mercies*</u>."
14. Isaiah 54:7 – "*For a small moment have I forsaken thee; but with* <u>*great mercies*</u> *will I gather thee.*"

E. New every morning

1. Lamentations 3:22-23 – Other translations:

"*Hope comes with each dawn*"
"*New things for the mornings*"
"*His loving kindness begins afresh each day*"

2. Psalms 42:8 – "*Yet the LORD will command his lovingkindness in the daytime, and in the night his song shall be with me...*"
3. Psalms 92:2 – "*To shew forth thy lovingkindness in the morning, and thy faithfulness every night,*"
4. Psalms 143:8 – "*Cause me to hear thy lovingkindness in the morning...*"
5. Isaiah 33:2 – "*O LORD, be gracious unto us; we have waited for thee: be thou their arm every morning, our salvation also in the time of trouble.*"

F. Excellent

1. Hebrew word – valuable; brightness, costly, fat; it comes from a root – to be heavy, rare, valuable

    a. Psalms 36:7 – *"How excellent is thy lovingkindness, O God! therefore the children of men put their trust under the shadow of thy wings."*
    b. Psalms 17:7 – *"Shew thy marvellous lovingkindness, O thou that savest by thy right hand..."*

G. Forever

    1. Psalms 37:26 – *"He is ever merciful, and lendeth; and his seed is blessed."*
    2. Psalms 77:7-11 – He's merciful, we forget
    3. Psalms 100:5 – *"For the LORD is good; his mercy is everlasting..."*
    4. Psalms 23:6 – *"Surely goodness and mercy shall follow me all the days of my life: and I will dwell in the house of the LORD for ever."*
    5. Psalms 136 – *"...for his mercy endureth for ever..."*
    6. I Chronicles 16:34 – *"O give thanks unto the LORD; for he is good; for his mercy endureth for ever."*
    7. II Samuel 7:15 – *"But my mercy shall not depart away from him..."*
    8. II Chronicles 5:13
    9. II Chronicles 7:3-5

H. Abundant

    1. I Peter 1:3 – *"Blessed be the God and Father of our Lord Jesus Christ, which according to his abundant mercy hath begotten us again unto a lively hope by the resurrection of Jesus Christ from the dead,"*

Lesson 47
OUR JOURNEY WITH GOD

I Kings 19:7 – "*...Arise and eat; because the journey is too great for thee.*"

For each one of us after we are born again by the blood of Jesus and the Word of God, we begin for each of us a unique journey with God. Though no one's journey is the same, all are different in that they are tailored by the sovereign God for each of us individually, and if we truly "follow on to know the Lord", we will see in the Scriptures a pattern that all will experience. It is imperative that true disciples learn these patterns so they can be prepared and know what is coming and how to respond. By knowing what the Word of God says, we can have hope in whatever situation we find ourselves in. It is my sincerest hope that by showing these Scriptural patterns about our journey with God, many lives will be spared from disappointment, hopelessness, and defeat, to having an understanding of the ways of God, knowing that in the end His desire for us is that we be victorious, that we be overcomers, and like Enoch have a true walk with God.

I. Word Definitions

    A. Definitions of "journey"

        1. Hebrew words

            a. *Derek* – A course of life, a trodden road, a mode of action; from a root, *darak*, that means to tread, to walk, to string a bow.
            b. *Naca* – To pull up the tent pins, to start on a journey, to cause to blow, to go forward, onward, forth, and to march

        2. Greek words

            a. *Hodos* – A road, a progress, a mode or means
            b. *Euodoo* – To help on the road, to succeed in reaching, to have a prosperous journey.
            c. *Apodemeo* – To go abroad, to visit a foreign land, to travel to a far country

II. God's Special Road for His People

There are many roads in life that any of us can take. This is true even for Christians, but God has a particular road for His true believers. It is a special path.

    A. Two roads, **one of God** and **the other not of God**

        1. Not of God, the froward way – Matthew 7:13 – "*...for wide is the gate, and broad is the way, that leadeth to destruction, and many there be which go in thereat.*"

            a. Proverbs 14:12 – "*There is a way which seemeth right unto a man, but the end thereof are the ways of death.*" (Proverbs 16:25)
            b. Proverbs 5:7-14 – "*Hear me now therefore, O ye children, and depart not from the words of my mouth. Remove thy way far from her, and come not nigh the door of her house: Lest thou give thine honour unto others, and thy years unto the cruel: Lest strangers be filled with thy wealth; and thy labours be in the house of a stranger; And thou mourn at the last, when thy flesh and thy body are consumed, And say, How have I hated instruction, and my heart despised reproof; And have not obeyed the voice of my teachers, nor inclined mine ear to them that instructed me! I was almost in all evil in the midst of the congregation and assembly.*"

c. I Samuel 26:21 – "...*I have played the fool, and have erred exceedingly.*"
d. Proverbs 15:19 – "*The way of the slothful man is as an hedge of thorns...*"
e. Proverbs 22:5 – "*Thorns and snares are in the way of the froward: he that doth keep his soul shall be far from them.*"
f. Luke 15:13 – "*...the younger son gathered all together, and took his journey into a far country, and there wasted his substance with riotous living.*"
g. Job 8:13-15 – "*So are the paths of all that forget God; and the hypocrite's hope shall perish: Whose hope shall be cut off, and whose trust shall be a spider's web. He shall lean upon his house, but it shall not stand: he shall hold it fast, but it shall not endure.*"
h. Psalms 1:6 – "*...the way of the ungodly shall perish.*"
i. Proverbs 12:15 – "*The way of a fool is right in his own eyes: but he that hearkeneth unto counsel is wise.*"
j. Proverbs 21:2 – "*Every way of a man is right in his own eyes: but the LORD pondereth the hearts.*"
k. Proverbs 13:15 – "*...the way of transgressors is hard.*"
l. Proverbs 4:19 – "*The way of the wicked is as darkness: they know not at what they stumble.*"
m. Jude 10-19
n. II Peter 2:9-22
o. Jeremiah 18:15-16 – "*Because my people hath forgotten me, they have burned incense to vanity, and they have caused them to stumble in their ways from the ancient paths, to walk in paths, in a way not cast up; To make their land desolate...*"
p. Judges 2:17-19
q. Deuteronomy 9:12, 16
r. Genesis 35:16-19 – Rachel died in the way because of stolen images (Genesis 31:34)
s. Ezekiel 33:17-20 – "*...The way of the Lord is not equal: but as for them, their way is not equal...*"

2. The Godly road – Matthew 7:14 – "*Because strait is the gate, and narrow is the way, which leadeth unto life, and few there be that find it.*"

a. Psalms 23:3 – "*...he leadeth me in the paths of righteousness for his name's sake.*"
b. Psalms 65:11 – "*Thou crownest the year with thy goodness; and thy paths drop fatness (abundance).*"
c. Job 23:10-11
d. Psalms 32:8 – "*I will instruct thee and teach thee in the way which thou shalt go...*"
e. Psalms 25:10 – "*All the paths of the LORD are mercy and truth unto such as keep his covenant and his testimonies.*"
f. Proverbs 16:17 – "*The highway of the upright is to depart from evil: he that keepeth his way preserveth his soul.*"
g. Song of Solomon 1:7-8 – "*Tell me, O thou whom my soul loveth, where thou feedest, where thou makest thy flock to rest at noon: for why should I be as one that turneth aside by the flocks of thy companions? If thou know not, O thou fairest among women, go thy way forth by the footsteps of the flock, and feed thy kids beside the shepherds' tents.*"
h. Isaiah 2:3 – "*...Come ye, and let us go up to the mountain of the LORD, to the house of the God of Jacob; and he will teach us of his ways, and we will walk in his paths: for out of Zion shall go forth the law, and the word of the LORD from Jerusalem.*"
i. Isaiah 30:21 – "*...thine ears shall hear a word behind thee, saying, This is the way, walk ye in it...*"
j. Genesis 24:27 – "*And he said, Blessed be the LORD God of my master Abraham, who hath not left destitute my master of his mercy and his truth: I being in the way, the LORD led me...*"

     k.   Exodus 13:21 – *"And the LORD went before them by day in a pillar of a cloud, to lead them the way; and by night in a pillar of fire, to give them light; to go by day and night"*

     l.   Exodus 18:19-20 – *"Hearken now unto my voice, I will give thee counsel, and God shall be with thee: Be thou for the people to Godward, that thou mayest bring the causes unto God: And thou shalt teach them ordinances and laws, and shalt shew them the way wherein they must walk, and the work that they must do."*

     m.   Deuteronomy 1:32-33 – *"...Who went in the way before you, to search you out a place to pitch your tents in..."*

     n.   II Samuel 22:31-33 – *"As for God, his way is perfect..."*

B. We must want God's way

    1. Examples of this cry throughout the Scripture

       a.   Exodus 33:13 – *"...shew me now thy way, that I may know thee..."*

          1)   Psalms 103:7 – *"He made known his ways unto Moses, his acts unto the children of Israel."*

       b.   Ezra 8:21 – *"Then I proclaimed a fast there, at the river of Ahava, that we might afflict ourselves before our God, to seek of him a right way for us, and for our little ones, and for all our substance."*

       c.   Psalms 27:11 – *"Teach me thy way, O LORD, and lead me in a plain path, because of mine enemies."*

       d.   Psalms 25:4-5, 9-10 – *"Shew me thy ways, O LORD; teach me thy paths. Lead me in thy truth, and teach me: for thou art the God of my salvation; on thee do I wait all the day...The meek will he guide in judgment: and the meek will he teach his way. All the paths of the LORD are mercy and truth unto such as keep his covenant and his testimonies."*

       e.   Psalms 86:11 – *"Teach me thy way, O LORD; I will walk in thy truth: unite my heart to fear thy name."*

       f.   Psalms 143:8 – *"...cause me to know the way wherein I should walk..."*

C. Some of the titles of God's way

    1. Matthew 7:14 – *"Because strait is the gate, and <u>narrow is the way</u>, which leadeth unto life, and few there be that find it."*

    2. Jeremiah 6:16 – *"... Stand ye in the ways, and see, and ask for the <u>old paths</u>, where is the <u>good way</u>, and walk therein, and ye shall find rest for your souls..."*

    3. Isaiah 35:8-10 – *"And an highway shall be there, and a way, and it shall be called The <u>way of holiness</u>; the unclean shall not pass over it; but it shall be for those: the wayfaring men, though fools, shall not err therein. No lion shall be there, nor any ravenous beast shall go up thereon, it shall not be found there; but the redeemed shall walk there: And the ransomed of the LORD shall return, and come to Zion with songs and everlasting joy upon their heads: they shall obtain joy and gladness, and sorrow and sighing shall flee away."*

    4. Proverbs 4:18 – *"But the <u>path of the just</u> is as the shining light..."*

    5. Psalms 16:11 – *"Thou wilt shew me the <u>path of life</u>: in thy presence is fulness of joy..."*

    6. Job 28:7-8 – *"There is <u>a path</u> which no fowl knoweth, and which the vulture's eye hath not seen: The lion's whelps have not trodden it, nor the fierce lion passed by it."*

    7. Jeremiah 50:5 – *"They shall ask <u>the way to Zion</u> with their faces thitherward, saying, Come, and let us join ourselves to the LORD in a perpetual covenant..."*

    8. Psalms 77:13 – *"<u>Thy way, O God, is in the sanctuary</u>: who is so great a God as our God?"*

    9. II Peter 2:2 – *"...by reason of whom the <u>way of truth</u> shall be evil spoken of."*

    10. I Kings 8:36 – *"...teach them the <u>good way</u> wherein they should walk..."*

11. I Samuel 12:23 – "...teach you the good and the right way"
12. Numbers 20:17 – "...we will go by the king's high way..."
13. John 8:12, 23

III. We Are In a Race

After salvation we all begin to run the divine race. The end of this race is not heaven. Heaven is just the gate in. The finish line is the prize of the high calling of God which is the manifestation of the sons of God, being conformed to the image of Christ, and our full inheritance. This is what we spend our entire Christian life running after. God's way is always onward and upward. We are either "going on to perfection" (Hebrews 6:1), or "drawing back unto perdition" (Hebrews 10:39).

A. The race

1. Hebrews 12:1 – "...let us lay aside every weight, and the sin which doth so easily beset us, and let us run with patience the race that is set before us"
2. I Corinthians 9:24-27 – "Know ye not that they which run in a race run all, but one receiveth the prize? So run, that ye may obtain..."
3. Ecclesiastes 9:11 – "I returned, and saw under the sun, that the race is not to the swift, nor the battle to the strong, neither yet bread to the wise, nor yet riches to men of understanding, nor yet favour to men of skill; but time and chance happeneth to them all."
4. Philippians 3:14 (Living Bible Translation) – "I strain to reach the end of the race and receive the prize for which God is calling us up to heaven because of what Christ Jesus did for us."

B. How God moves us in this race

"To every thing there is a season, and a time to every purpose under the heaven", Solomon said (Ecclesiastes 3:1). Jesus said in Matthew 4:4, "Man shall not live by bread alone, but by every word that proceedeth out of the mouth of God." The angel Gabriel, speaking for God said, "...my words, which shall be fulfilled in their season." The Lord will speak a proceeding word to the lives of His people, which will begin a season. A season will last as long as it takes for that word to be performed in a person's life. As we complete each season, a new proceeding word will come from the Lord, moving us forward. As you and I fulfill each season, we continue moving down this race, entering into a new level of glory, strength, faith, revelation, etc, until our entire vessel is emptied with the old carnal nature and filled with God's Word, His character and glory.

1. II Corinthians 3:18 – "But we all, with open face beholding as in a glass the glory of the Lord, are changed into the same image from glory to glory, even as by the Spirit of the Lord."
2. Psalms 84:7 – "They go from strength to strength, every one of them in Zion appeareth before God."
3. Romans 1:17 – "For therein is the righteousness of God revealed from faith to faith: as it is written, The just shall live by faith."
4. Jeremiah 48:11 – "Moab hath been at ease from his youth, and he hath settled on his lees, and hath not been emptied from vessel to vessel, neither hath he gone into captivity: therefore his taste remained in him, and his scent is not changed."

5. Proverbs 4:18 – "But the path of the just is as the shining light, that shineth more and more unto the perfect day."

a. Psalms 71:14 – "But I will hope continually, and will yet praise thee more and more."
b. Psalms 115:14 – "The LORD shall increase you more and more..."
c. Philippians 1:9 – "And this I pray, that your love may abound yet more and more in knowledge and in all judgment"

    d.   I Thessalonians 4:1 – *"Furthermore then we beseech you, brethren, and exhort you by the Lord Jesus, that as ye have received of us how ye ought to walk and to please God, so ye would abound more and more."*

C.   God's way of dealing with us

This is the pattern of growth that God has for us. His way is to bless us abundantly, then deal with us to remove the things in our lives that shouldn't be there. This pattern is found throughout the Scriptures.

The Seasonal Balance of God's Dealings and Blessings

Scripture Reference	God's Dealings	God's Blessings
Song of Solomon 2:6	Left hand – Judgment	Right hand – Blessing
Ecclesiastes 7:14	Adversity	Prosperity
Philippians 4:12	Abased Hungry Suffer need	Abound Full Abound
Luke 24:50 – Bethany	"House of adversity or affliction"	"House of figs or fruitfulness"
Psalms 66:10-12	Affliction, Caused men to ride over our heads, fire and water	A wealthy place
Hosea 6:1	Torn Smitten	Heal us Bind us up
Psalms 34:19	Many are the afflictions of the righteous	The Lord delivereth him out of all
Psalms 90:3	Thou (God) turnest man to destruction ("depression")	And sayest, Return, ye children of men
Genesis 8:22	Seedtime Cold Winter Night	Harvest Heat Summer Day
Job 42:10-12	Captivity	Double Portion
Psalms 116:6	Brought low	He helped me
Joshua 8:34	Cursings	Blessings
Deut. 28:47-48	In want of all things	The abundance of all things

IV. A Scriptural Look at How Our Journey in God Takes Us (Patterns of Journeys)

    A.   II Kings 2:1-15 – Journey of Elisha ("my God is salvation") obtaining double portion from Elijah ("my God is God")

        1.   Verse 1 – Gilgal

            a.   Gilgal means – Rolling away, a cutting away of flesh

The first place on their journey was a place of circumcision and a place of God cutting away the flesh in their life. Elisha was given a choice to stay, but a journey means you keep going. Elisha would not stop here. Many stop and remain at Gilgal because they can't handle the circumcision that God is requiring of them.

        2.   Verses 2-3 – Bethel

      a.   Bethel means – House of God

The next place they went was the House of God. Some people are content just to be saved and go to church, and nothing more. We can't stop here either. Elisha is pushed again to make a choice to keep going. Bethel can also represent a place of God's dealings and our interactions with His people, learning to love one another, etc.

    3.   Verses 4-5 – Jericho

      a.   Jericho means – Fragrant place, the moon city

Jericho represents to us a good place. Moon in Scripture represents the bride of Christ. In Jericho, you find yourself in a place of revelation of the bride, a place of worship and intimacy, and it is a nice place. But you and I cannot stay here either. Once again, Elisha has to make the choice again to keep moving on. It is interesting to note that there are many people in each place, having a revelation of what God was doing, but never followed Elijah themselves. We will find that at every place in our journey there will be people content and deciding to not go on any further. But for Elisha and those who want a double portion, we can't stay in Jericho.

    4.   Verses 6-8 – Jordan

      a.   Jordan means – Descending

Jordan speaks of a place of humility and a place of descending. For many it is hard to leave the fragrant place of Jericho and go to Jordan, but this is part of our journey. To ultimately ascend and fulfill the call of God in our lives we must first descend. The bride in the Song of Solomon is found in the wilderness before the day of her showing (Song of Solomon 3:6, 8:5). The same applied to John the Baptist (Luke 1:80). True change ultimately comes in a place of descending.

    5.   Verses 13-15

After taking up Elijah's mantle, Elisha has to cross the Jordan again, but this time alone. God uses this for all to see that Elisha has the anointing now!

B.   Deuteronomy 10:6-9 – *"And the children of Israel took their journey..."*

    1.   *"...from Beeroth of the children of Jaakan..."*

      a.   Beeroth – Wells
      b.   Jaakin – Intelligent, one who turns

    2.   *"...to Mosera..."*

      a.   Mosera – Bonds
      b.   Aaron, the high priest dies here. Aaron's name means – Light, a shining light, a mountain of strength
      c.   Eleazar, Aaron's son, ministered in his place. Eleazar's name means – Who God helps or aids, God is helper

    3.   *"...From thence they journeyed unto Gudgodah..."*

      a.   Gudgodah – The slashing place, cavern of thunder

4. *"...to Jotbath..."*

   a. Jotbath – Goodness, pleasant; it comes from a root – To be good, to please, to do well to
   b. It was a land of rivers of waters

5. Verse 8

   a. At that time (of what was spoken of above)
   b. The Lord separated
   c. The tribe of Levi – Joined – One out of 12 tribes separated, i.e. a remnant
   d. To bear the Ark of the Covenant (i.e. the manifest presence of God)
   e. To stand before the Lord (to wait on God)
   f. To minister unto Him (worshipers)
   g. And to bless in His name – You can't bless in His name unless you have done all that is prior to it.

6. Verse 9

   a. Levi hath no part

      1) Principle of aloneness
      2) This is the cost of ministry

   b. No inheritance with his brethren – We, as His ministering tribe, never to enjoy what others enjoy
   c. The Lord is his inheritance – God is our only reward. Is God enough for you?

7. Verse 11 – Now Moses, you can take them into their inheritance

C. Ezekiel 47:1-9

This story is not only a typical one concerning our journey in God, but is also a type of the last great move of God on the earth. It may be that this journey in God will determine who participates in that great move of the Spirit and who for whatever reason cannot seem to finish this journey.

1. The principle of our seasons in God

   a. Ecclesiastes 3:1, 17 – *"To every thing there is a season, and a time to every purpose under the heaven...for there is a time there for every purpose and for every work."*
   b. I Chronicles 29:30 – *"With all his reign and his might, and the times that went over him, and over Israel, and over all the kingdoms of the countries."*
   c. Psalms 1:3 – *"And he shall be like a tree planted by the rivers of water, that bringeth forth his fruit in his season..."*
   d. Psalms 145:15 – *"The eyes of all wait upon thee; and thou givest them their meat in due season."*
   e. Ezekiel 34:26 – *"...and I will cause the shower to come down in his season..."*
   f. Luke 1:20 – *"...my words, which shall be fulfilled in their season."*
   g. II Timothy 4:2 – *"...be instant in season, out of season..."*
   h. Galatians 6:9 – *"...for in due season we shall reap, if we faint not."*

2. He has set our determined times

   a. Psalms 31:15 – *"My times are in thy hand..."*

    b.   Job 14:5 – *"Seeing his days are determined, the number of his months are with thee…"*

    c.   Job 24:1 – *"Why, seeing times are not hidden from the Almighty, do they that know him not see his days?"*

    d.   Ecclesiastes 3:11 – *"He hath made every thing beautiful in his time…"*

    e.   Acts 17:26 – *"…and hath determined the times before appointed, and the bounds of their habitation"*

    f.   Deuteronomy 32:8 – *"When the most High divided to the nations their inheritance, when he separated the sons of Adam, he set the bounds of the people according to the number of the children of Israel."*

    g.   Daniel 2:21 – *"And he changeth the times and the seasons…"*

3.   The Lord is sovereign and knows everything

    a.   Isaiah 46:10 – *"Declaring the end from the beginning, and from ancient times the things that are not yet done…"*

    b.   Revelation 21:6 – *"…I am Alpha and Omega, the beginning and the end…"*

    c.   Job 28:10 – *"…his eye seeth every precious thing."*

    d.   Psalms 37:18 – *"The LORD knoweth the days of the upright…"*

    e.   Psalms 139:2, 4 – *"Thou knowest my downsitting and mine uprising…"*

    f.   Daniel 4:32 – *"…until thou know that the most High ruleth in the kingdom of men…"*

4.   Verses 1-2

    a.   Ezekiel brought to the door of the house of the Lord

    b.   At this time the door will be shut

        1)   Principle of a shut door

            a)   Matthew 25:10 – *"And while they went to buy, the bridegroom came; and they that were ready went in with him to the marriage: and the door was shut."*

            b)   Luke 13:25-27 – *"When once the master of the house is risen up, and hath shut to the door, and ye begin to stand without, and to knock at the door, saying, Lord, Lord, open unto us; and he shall answer and say unto you, I know you not whence ye are: Then shall ye begin to say, We have eaten and drunk in thy presence, and thou hast taught in our streets. But he shall say, I tell you, I know you not whence ye are; depart from me, all ye workers of iniquity."*

            c)   Isaiah 26:20 – *"Come, my people, enter thou into thy chambers, and shut thy doors about thee: hide thyself as it were for a little moment, until the indignation be overpast."*

            d)   Genesis 6:16 – Noah's ark

    c.   Waters issued out from under the threshold – This will be the time of the "manifestation of the sons of God", when God's glory shall arise upon them and through them (Isaiah 60:1-3)

    d.   Waters came down from the altar – This is the golden altar of incense, the place of high and holy worship

    e.   There ran out waters on the right side – There will be so much glory in this house, it is squeezing out from under the threshold.

5.   Verse 3

    a.   God is measuring His people

1) Revelation 11:1-2
2) Zechariah 2:1-4
3) Ezekiel 40:3-49

b. Thousand in Scripture is the number for rest and perfect fruitfulness. This speaks of one level, dimension, or season or time of glory, light, strength, faith, etc. We stay in this particular place until we've completed what God wanted in us.

1) Steps in God

a) Song of Solomon 2:14 – "...*the secret places of the stairs...*" – Each stair is a dimension in God. We stay there until we are ready to move on.
b) Genesis 28:12 – Jacob's ladder – Each rung on the ladder is also a dimension in God. It ultimately leads to the door of heaven (Revelation 4:1)

c. "...*brought me through the waters...*" – This speaks of the dealings of God in that particular place or dimension in God.
d. "...*to the ankles.*" – This speaks of our walk with God being strong and stable

6. Verse 4

a. Once again we are measured until we have come to rest and perfect fruitfulness in the particular dimension. We can't go on until God's living Word to us has been fulfilled. Our walk must have been stabilized by going through the waters, the dealings of God.
b. "...*to the knees...*" – This speaks of our will being broken, our pride humbled and that the dealings of God have made us submissive to the will and purpose of God.
c. "...*and he brought me through...*" – Once again God's faithfulness to deliver and bring us through (Isaiah 43:5)
d. "...*to the loins.*" – This speaks of God gaining control naturally of our sexual desires and wants. Also, it speaks of our ability to reproduce ourselves. It will not be man made or religious, but it will be the seed of God produced through our loin spiritually.

7. Verse 5

a. Thousand once again means rest and perfect fruitfulness. We must reach maturity in all these places in God.
b. "...*it was a river that I could not pass over...*" – Only God can do this, human strength will accomplish nothing.
c. "...*for the waters were risen...*" – Our feet are no longer on the bottom, we now have no control, we must let go and let God. At this point we cease to be important. Jesus is our all in all. We have decreased and He has increased. It is no longer us that live but Christ living in us. We have gone through every phase, every season, and have overcome. Now we are in total submission to Him.
d. "...*waters to swim in, a river that could not be passed over.*" – We are now in over our heads in the things of God. We have "launched out into the deep", but He is holding us up. These waters are a river of glory. The type is II Chronicles 5:14 where the priests could not stand to minister by reason of the glory cloud.

D. Psalms 42:5-8

"Why art thou cast down, O my soul? and why art thou disquieted in me? hope thou in God: for I shall yet praise him for the help of his countenance. O my God, my soul is cast down within me: therefore will I

remember thee from the land of Jordan, and of the Hermonites, from the hill Mizar. Deep calleth unto deep at the noise of thy waterspouts: all thy waves and thy billows are gone over me. Yet the LORD will command his lovingkindness in the daytime, and in the night his song shall be with me, and my prayer unto the God of my life."

1. Verse 6 – The pattern

   a. Soul cast down (depressed)
   b. *"I will remember thee..."* – During these times we must force ourselves to remember God always and what He's done for us before.
   c. Jordan – Descending
   d. Hermonites – Devoted, a prominent summit of a mountain
   e. The hill Mizar – Smallness, diminutive, young

E. John 4:3-7

"He left Judaea, and departed again into Galilee. And he must needs go through Samaria. Then cometh he to a city of Samaria, which is called Sychar, near to the parcel of ground that Jacob gave to his son Joseph. Now Jacob's well was there. Jesus therefore, being wearied with his journey, sat thus on the well: and it was about the sixth hour. There cometh a woman of Samaria to draw water: Jesus saith unto her, Give me to drink."

1. *"He left Judaea..."* – Judaea means land of praise
2. *"...departed again to Galilee..."* – Galilee means circuit as enclosed, revolving
3. *"...must needs go through Samaria..."* – Samaria means a place of watching, to watch intensely
4. Sychar – Drunken, to be tipsy
5. *"...being wearied with his journey, sat thus on the well..."*
6. Jesus gives prophetic insight to the woman and a whole town is saved

F. I Kings 18:46 – I Kings 19:3-10

1. Verse 46 (I Kings 18) – Jezreel – God sows, have a numerous progeny, the Lord sows, he will be sown of God; from a root – To plant, to be made fruitful

2. Verse 3 (I Kings 19)

   a. Elijah runs for his life
   b. Beersheba – The well of the oath
   c. Judah – Praise
   d. He leaves his servant there

3. Verse 4

   a. Day's journey into the wilderness – Place of God's dealings
   b. Sat down under a juniper tree – Gave up trying
   c. Asked God to die
   d. *"I am not better than my fathers"* – Too much introspection, condemnation

4. Verse 5

   a. Goes to sleep – Not a resting in God, but slothfulness
   b. God sends him a messenger (angel)
   c. The angel awoke him and said, *"arise and eat"*

5. Verses 6-7

    a. Cake baking on the coals – A living Word, a fresh Word from God
    b. Cruise of water – A type of the Holy Ghost
    c. At his head – Type of his soulish man, where most of our warfare is
    d. Eats and drinks, and lays down again
    e. Messenger comes a second time – Two is the number for witness and separation
    f. Arise and eat – Shake yourself and believe God's Word
    g. Because the journey is too great for thee

6. Verse 8

    a. He arose and did eat and drink – He obeyed the messenger's word
    b. This meat gave him strength – This is what happens when we eat the Word of God
    c. Forty days and nights – 40 is the number for trial, testing, chastening, probation. The living Word and living presence will keep us during the times of testing and trial.
    d. Come to Horeb, the mount of God – Horeb – Waster, desert, desolation; from a root – to dry up, to lie waste, to be destroyed

7. Verse 9

    a. Came to a cave and lodged there – Cave in Hebrew – To be made bare or naked – When we face some trials, they will make us seem to be naked or laid bare for everyone to see.
    b. And the Word of the Lord came to him
    c. *"What doest thou here Elijah?"*
    d. He hears the voice of the Lord.

8. Verse 10 – This is pure selfishness and an exalted opinion of himself. He has let what he has been through cloud his judgment. He thinks he is the only person serving God faithfully.

9. Verses 11-12

    a. Go forth
    b. And stand upon the mount (Horeb – waster) before the Lord
    c. There is so much turmoil in his life it's hard for him to discern the voice of God.
    d. God sends a rushing mighty wind that shakes up everything in our lives
    e. God then blows away all that Elijah thought might be God
    f. God wasn't in the wind, or the earthquake, or the fire
    g. After all these distractions comes the voice of the Lord in a "still small voice"

10. Verses 13-16

    a. Elijah wraps his face (his heart, his soul)
    b. In his mantle (symbolic of God's call and anointing) – In times like these we must wear the mantle of God, to keep us from deception
    c. He repeats his words from earlier, about how all Israel had forsaken God and he alone was left, the only one who remained faithful
    d. God sends him back to the place he ran from
    e. To another wilderness
    f. Damascus – Activity, moist with blood, sackcloth
    g. It is time to anoint another king and another prophet
    h. Elijah's ministry was coming to a close

        i.   God spoke of His coming judgment that Elijah would not have to face.

    11.   Verses 17-19

        a.   There was at least seven thousand (a remnant) left in Israel who were faithful
        b.   And so Elijah departs

G.   Genesis 35:1-12

    1.   Verses 1-5

        a.   Arise Jacob and go to Bethel (the house of God)
        b.   But before this can happen, all the idols (strange Gods – type of demons) must be put away.
        c.   The easier will be afraid of these, who are so devoted to God.

    2.   Verse 6

        a.   Luz – Perverse
        b.   Canaan – Merchants, servant; It comes from a root – To be humbled, to be subdued, to be brought low

    3.   Verse 7

        a.   As he builds an altar to God, the perverse, humbling place becomes El Bethel (God of the house of God), not just to the house of God (which can become religious), but to the God <u>of</u> the house of God.

    4.   Verse 8

        a.   There will be some dying here
        b.   We must bury Deborah – Eloquent, her speaking
        c.   Allon-bachuth – Oak of weeping; It comes from a root – To flow by drops.
        d.   It is time to bury all that may have been eloquent for us though we may weep.

    5.   Verses 9-11

        a.   God will appear again unto Jacob
        b.   We must come out of:
        c.   Padanaram – The ransom is high
        d.   The price we pay here is high, but even though we must sacrifice what we love, God will meet with us again.
        e.   Jacob experiences a name change, or in type a character change
        f.   Jacob – Deceiver, supplanter
        g.   Israel – Prince with God, champion, a God ruled man.
        h.   Be fruitful and multiply
        i.   And kings shall come forth out of thee

Lesson 48
OVERCOMING TEMPTATIONS

I. Understanding What Temptations Are All About

   A. Hebrew and Greek words

      1. Hebrew – *Nacah* – to test, to prove.
      2. Hebrew – *Maccah* – a testing, trial, temptation
      3. Greek – *Peira* – root word meaning a test, experience, trial
      4. Greek – *Peirazo* – to test, examine, try
      5. Greek – *Peirasmos* – putting to proof by experiment of evil or good.

   B. There ARE going to be temptations in our lives

      1. James 1:13 – When he is tempted.
      2. I Corinthians 10:13 – Temptations are common.
      3. Hebrews 11:37 – Old Testament prophets tempted.

      4. Mark 4:1 – Jesus was tempted.

         a. Hebrews 4:15
         b. Luke 22:28

   C. We need to see they never stop

      1. Luke 22:28
      2. I Peter 1:6-7

   D. We need to be tempted, proven, and tested

      1. Luke 8:13
      2. Hebrews 3:8

II. Who Tempts Us?

   A. God tests us

      1. Genesis 22:1 – *"...that God did tempt Abraham..."*
      2. Hebrews 17:15
      3. James 1:12-14 – God does not tempt us with evil, He tests us.
      4. Matthew 6:13 – Greek – *peirasmos*

   B. Satan tempts us. He can only tempt us as the Lord allows (Job 1 and 2).

      1. Luke 4:2 – *"Being forty days tempted of the devil..."*
      2. I Corinthians 7:5
      3. I Thessalonians 3:5

   C. Other People

      1. Matthew 22:18
      2. Proverbs 7:6-23

D. We bring it on ourselves. How?

    1. James 1:14 – *"But every man is tempted, when he is drawn away of his own lust, and enticed."*
    2. Galatians 6:1
    3. I Timothy 6:9
    4. Matthew 26:36-46 – Sleeping
    5. Ecclesiastes 10:18

III. What Do We Do When Tempted?

A. Count it all joy

    1. James 1:2 – *"My brethren, count it all joy when ye fall into divers temptations;"*
    2. I Peter 1:6

B. Endure it

    1. James 1:12
    2. I Corinthians 10:13

C. Trust God

    1. Hebrews 11:37-39
    2. Psalms 34:19
    3. II Peter 2:9

D. Don't harden your heart

    1. Hebrews 3:8
    2. Luke 8:13

E. Keep doing the will of God.

    1. Revelation 3:10
    2. Psalms 119:67-71
    3. Psalms 119:92

F. Look for God's way of escape

    1. I Corinthians 10:13
    2. Luke 4:4, 8, 12

III. Remember, Jesus Will Always Be There To Understand and Help

A. Hebrews 2:14-18
B. Hebrews 4:15 – *"For we have not an high priest which cannot be touched with the feeling of our infirmities; but was in all points tempted like as we are, yet without sin."*
C. Hebrews 7:25 – *"...seeing he ever liveth to make intercession for them."*

Lesson 49
PATTERN OF THE EARLY CHURCH

I.   Pattern of the Early Church, Acts 2:41-47

Acts 2:41-47 – "*41Then they that gladly received his word were baptized: and the same day there were added unto them about three thousand souls. 42And they continued stedfastly in the apostles' doctrine and fellowship, and in breaking of bread, and in prayers. 43And fear came upon every soul: and many wonders and signs were done by the apostles. 44And all that believed were together, and had all things common; 45And sold their possessions and goods, and parted them to all men, as every man had need. 46And they, continuing daily with one accord in the temple, and breaking bread from house to house, did eat their meat with gladness and singleness of heart, 47Praising God, and having favour with all the people. And the Lord added to the church daily such as should be saved.*"

A.   Verse 41 – They were not coerced into following Jesus. They came to Him gladly

B.   They continued steadfastly

   1.   Luke 24:53 – "*And were continually in the temple, praising and blessing God. Amen.*"
   2.   Proverbs 8:34 – "*Blessed is the man that heareth me, watching daily at my gates, waiting at the posts of my doors.*"
   3.   I Corinthians 15:58 – "*Therefore, my beloved brethren, be ye stedfast, unmoveable, always abounding in the work of the Lord, forasmuch as ye know that your labour is not in vain in the Lord.*"
   4.   Hebrews 3:14 – "*For we are made partakers of Christ, if we hold the beginning of our confidence stedfast unto the end;*"

C.   In the Apostle's doctrine

   1.   Acts 19:9-11 – "*9But when divers were hardened, and believed not, but spake evil of that way before the multitude, he departed from them, and separated the disciples, disputing daily in the school of one Tyrannus. 10And this continued by the space of two years; so that all they which dwelt in Asia heard the word of the Lord Jesus, both Jews and Greeks. 11And God wrought special miracles by the hands of Paul:*"
   2.   Acts 5:42 – "*And daily in the temple, and in every house, they ceased not to teach and preach Jesus Christ.*"
   3.   Luke 19:47 – "*And he taught daily in the temple. But the chief priests and the scribes and the chief of the people sought to destroy him,*" (Luke 22:53)
   4.   Acts 17:11, 17 – "*11These were more noble than those in Thessalonica, in that they received the word with all readiness of mind, and searched the scriptures daily, whether those things were so…17Therefore disputed he in the synagogue with the Jews, and with the devout persons, and in the market daily with them that met with him.*"
   5.   Acts 6:4 – "*But we will give ourselves continually to prayer, and to the ministry of the word.*"
   6.   John 8:31 – "*Then said Jesus to those Jews which believed on him, If ye continue in my word, then are ye my disciples indeed*"

   7.   Exodus 16:4 – "*Then said the LORD unto Moses, Behold, I will rain bread from heaven for you; and the people shall go out and gather a certain rate every day, that I may prove them, whether they will walk in my law, or no.*"

      a.   Luke 11:3 – "*Give us day by day our daily bread.*"
      b.   Luke 4:4 – "*And Jesus answered him, saying, It is written, That man shall not live by bread alone, but by every word of God.*"

D. And fellowship – Greek word for fellowship, *koinonia* – communion, sharing in common, partnership, participation, interaction

1. Hebrews 10:23-25 – "*23Let us hold fast the profession of our faith without wavering; (for he is faithful that promised;) 24And let us consider one another to provoke unto love and to good works: 25Not forsaking the assembling of ourselves together, as the manner of some is; but exhorting one another: and so much the more, as ye see the day approaching.*"
2. Hebrews 3:13 – "*But exhort one another daily, while it is called To day; lest any of you be hardened through the deceitfulness of sin.*"
3. I Thessalonians 5:11 – "*Wherefore comfort yourselves together, and edify one another, even as also ye do.*"
4. Malachi 3:16 – "*Then they that feared the LORD spake often one to another: and the LORD hearkened, and heard it, and a book of remembrance was written before him for them that feared the LORD, and that thought upon his name.*"

E. Breaking of bread (The Lord's supper)

1. I Corinthians 11:23-26 – "*23For I have received of the Lord that which also I delivered unto you, That the Lord Jesus the same night in which he was betrayed took bread: 24And when he had given thanks, he brake it, and said, Take, eat: this is my body, which is broken for you: this do in remembrance of me. 25After the same manner also he took the cup, when he had supped, saying, This cup is the new testament in my blood: this do ye, as oft as ye drink it, in remembrance of me. 26For as often as ye eat this bread, and drink this cup, ye do shew the Lord's death till he come.*"

F. Prayers

1. Colossians 4:2 – "*Continue in prayer, and watch in the same with thanksgiving;*"
2. Ephesians 6:18 – "*Praying always with all prayer and supplication in the Spirit, and watching thereunto with all perseverance and supplication for all saints;*"
3. I Thessalonians 5:17 – "*Pray without ceasing.*"
4. Luke 18:1 – "*And he spake a parable unto them to this end, that men ought always to pray, and not to faint;*"

Lesson 50
PREPARATION

I.   Preparation in Being Taught

A.   God is a God of preparation

1.   Hosea 6:3 – *"Then shall we know, if we follow on to know the LORD: his going forth is prepared as the morning; and he shall come unto us as the rain, as the latter and former rain unto the earth."*
2.   Psalms 80:9 – *"Thou preparedst room before it, and didst cause it to take deep root, and it filled the land."*
3.   Psalms 147:8 – *"Who covereth the heaven with clouds, who prepareth rain for the earth, who maketh grass to grow upon the mountains."*
4.   Psalms 74:16 – *"The day is thine, the night also is thine: thou hast prepared the light and the sun."*
5.   Psalms 65:9-11 – *"9Thou visitest the earth, and waterest it: thou greatly enrichest it with the river of God, which is full of water: thou preparest them corn, when thou hast so provided for it. 10Thou waterest the ridges thereof abundantly: thou settlest the furrows thereof: thou makest it soft with showers: thou blessest the springing thereof. 11Thou crownest the year with thy goodness; and thy paths drop fatness."*
6.   Psalms 68:10 – *"Thy congregation hath dwelt therein: thou, O God, hast prepared of thy goodness for the poor."*
7.   Hebrews 10:10 – *"By the which will we are sanctified through the offering of the body of Jesus Christ once for all."*

B.   Things God has prepared

1.   I Corinthians 2:9 – *"But as it is written, Eye hath not seen, nor ear heard, neither have entered into the heart of man, the things which God hath prepared for them that love him."*
2.   Jonah 1:17, 4:6-8
3.   Psalms 23:5 – *"Thou preparest a table before me in the presence of mine enemies: thou anointest my head with oil; my cup runneth over."*
4.   John 14:1-3 – *"1Let not your heart be troubled: ye believe in God, believe also in me. 2In my Father's house are many mansions: if it were not so, I would have told you. I go to prepare a place for you. 3And if I go and prepare a place for you, I will come again, and receive you unto myself; that where I am, there ye may be also."*
5.   Matthew 25:34 – *"Then shall the King say unto them on his right hand, Come, ye blessed of my Father, inherit the kingdom prepared for you from the foundation of the world:"*
6.   Hebrews 11:16 – *"But now they desire a better country, that is, an heavenly: wherefore God is not ashamed to be called their God: for he hath prepared for them a city."*
7.   Matthew 25:41 – *"Then shall he say also unto them on the left hand, Depart from me, ye cursed, into everlasting fire, prepared for the devil and his angels:"*
8.   Matthew 20:23 – *"And he saith unto them, Ye shall drink indeed of my cup, and be baptized with the baptism that I am baptized with: but to sit on my right hand, and on my left, is not mine to give, but it shall be given to them for whom it is prepared of my Father."*
9.   Exodus 23:20 – *"Behold, I send an Angel before thee, to keep thee in the way, and to bring thee into the place which I have prepared."*

II. How Does God Prepare Us? Matthew 26:26 – *"And as they were eating, Jesus took bread, and blessed it, and brake it, and gave it to the disciples, and said, Take, eat; this is my body."*

A.   God calls us – *"Jesus took bread..."*

1. John 15:16 – *"Ye have not chosen me, but I have chosen you, and ordained you, that ye should go and bring forth fruit, and that your fruit should remain: that whatsoever ye shall ask of the Father in my name, he may give it you."*
2. I Peter 2:9-10 – *"⁹But ye are a chosen generation, a royal priesthood, an holy nation, a peculiar people; that ye should shew forth the praises of him who hath called you out of darkness into his marvellous light: ¹⁰Which in time past were not a people, but are now the people of God: which had not obtained mercy, but now have obtained mercy."*
3. Psalms 139:13 – *"For thou hast possessed my reins: thou hast covered me in my mother's womb."*
4. Ephesians 1:4 – *"According as he hath chosen us in him before the foundation of the world, that we should be holy and without blame before him in love:"*
5. Ezekiel 16:5-8

B. He blesses us – *"...and blessed it..."*

1. Ezekiel 16:7-14 – He blesses us in everyway possible
2. Ephesians 1:3 – *"Blessed be the God and Father of our Lord Jesus Christ, who hath blessed us with all spiritual blessings in heavenly places in Christ:"*
3. Psalms 103:2-7
4. Psalms 10:17 – *"LORD, thou hast heard the desire of the humble: thou wilt prepare their heart, thou wilt cause thine ear to hear:"*
5. Psalms 132:13-16
6. Genesis 12:1-3

C. He breaks us – *"...and brake it..."*

1. Isaiah 40:3 – *"The voice of him that crieth in the wilderness, Prepare ye the way of the LORD, make straight in the desert a highway for our God."* – He breaks us in the wilderness; the desert is a time of proving and taking the things prepared and having them become "bone of our bone".
2. Deuteronomy 8:2-3 – *"²And thou shalt remember all the way which the LORD thy God led thee these forty years in the wilderness, to humble thee, and to prove thee, to know what was in thine heart, whether thou wouldest keep his commandments, or no. ³And he humbled thee, and suffered thee to hunger, and fed thee with manna, which thou knewest not, neither did thy fathers know; that he might make thee know that man doth not live by bread only, but by every word that proceedeth out of the mouth of the LORD doth man live."*
3. Luke 4:1 – *"And Jesus being full of the Holy Ghost returned from Jordan, and was led by the Spirit into the wilderness,"* – This is where most Christians in training back off
4. Job 23:8-11 – We must wait until He is finished; if not, we won't really be ready.

D. The taking, blessing, and breaking, is for one purpose – He gives us, *"...and gave it"*

1. I Peter 5:10 – *"But the God of all grace, who hath called us unto his eternal glory by Christ Jesus, after that ye have suffered a while, make you perfect, stablish, strengthen, settle you."*
2. John 15:16 – *"Ye have not chosen me, but I have chosen you, and ordained you, that ye should go and bring forth fruit, and that your fruit should remain: that whatsoever ye shall ask of the Father in my name, he may give it you."*
3. Isaiah 40:1-5

III. Other Aspects of God's Preparation

A. We need to understand that there is a season time element

1. Ecclesiastes 3:1 – *"To every thing there is a season, and a time to every purpose under the heaven:"*
2. Habakkuk 2:2-3 – *"²And the LORD answered me, and said, Write the vision, and make it plain upon tables, that he may run that readeth it. ³For the vision is yet for an appointed time, but at the end it shall speak, and not lie: though it tarry, wait for it; because it will surely come, it will not tarry."*
3. Luke 1:20
4. Galatians 4:4
5. Acts 7:17
6. Acts 2:1 – *"And when the day of Pentecost was fully come, they were all with one accord in one place."*

B. Preparing ourselves

1. Proverbs 16:1 – *"The preparations of the heart in man, and the answer of the tongue, is from the LORD."* – God will prepare us
2. I Chronicles 29:17 – *"I know also, my God, that thou triest the heart, and hast pleasure in uprightness. As for me, in the uprightness of mine heart I have willingly offered all these things: and now have I seen with joy thy people, which are present here, to offer willingly unto thee."* – How much we're prepared is determined by us
3. Proverbs 24:27 – *"Prepare thy work without, and make it fit for thyself in the field; and afterwards build thine house."*
4. Exodus 15:2 – *"...I will prepare him an habitation; my father's God..."*
5. II Timothy 2:20-21 – *"²⁰But in a great house there are not only vessels of gold and of silver, but also of wood and of earth; and some to honour, and some to dishonour. ²¹If a man therefore purge himself from these, he shall be a vessel unto honour, sanctified, and meet for the master's use, and prepared unto every good work."*
6. Ezra 7:10 – *"For Ezra had prepared his heart to seek the law of the LORD, and to do it, and to teach in Israel statutes and judgments."*
7. II Timothy 3:16-17 – Word of God prepares and perfects us
8. Job 11:13-19 – What happens when we prepare our heart
9. II Chronicles 19:3 – Prepared just to seek God (II Chronicles 12:14 – Rehoboam prepared not)
10. II Chronicles 8:16 – *"Now all the work of Solomon was prepared unto the day of the foundation of the house of the LORD, and until it was finished. So the house of the LORD was perfected."* – Preparation never stops
11. Proverbs 21:31 – *"The horse is prepared against the day of battle: but safety is of the LORD."* – We prepare, but victory ultimately comes from the Lord

C. Some go before they are prepared

1. II Samuel 18:19-32
2. Proverbs 20:21 – *"An inheritance may be gotten hastily at the beginning; but the end thereof shall not be blessed."* (Luke 15:12)
3. Proverbs 25:8 – *"Go not forth hastily to strive, lest thou know not what to do in the end thereof, when thy neighbour hath put thee to shame."*
4. Luke 14:28-33

5. God's preparation doesn't happen overnight. It takes many, many years. Below are Scriptural examples of preparation

   a. Jesus – 30 years

       b.   Moses – 40 years

       c.   David – 17 years

       d.   Paul – 14 years

       e.   Joshua – 40 years

       f.   Joseph – 13 years

       g.   Noah – 100 years

       h.   Elisha under Elijah during entire life

IV.   God Is Preparing a People to Be His Army in the Last Days

    A.   Relevant Scriptures

        1.   Joel 2:1-14

        2.   Isaiah 6:1-8

        3.   Psalms 110:2-3

        4.   Matthew 9 37-38

        5.   Ezekiel 37:1-10

    B.   The question is who will prepare themselves to go?

        1.   Isaiah 6:7-8 – "*7And he laid it upon my mouth, and said, Lo, this hath touched thy lips; and thine iniquity is taken away, and thy sin purged. 8Also I heard the voice of the Lord, saying, Whom shall I send, and who will go for us? Then said I, Here am I; send me.*"

        2.   Ezekiel 22:30 – "*And I sought for a man among them, that should make up the hedge, and stand in the gap before me for the land, that I should not destroy it: but I found none.*"

        3.   Exodus 32:26 – "*Then Moses stood in the gate of the camp, and said, Who is on the LORD's side? let him come unto me. And all the sons of Levi gathered themselves together unto him.*"

        4.   II Chronicles 7:14 – "*If my people, which are called by my name, shall humble themselves, and pray, and seek my face, and turn from their wicked ways; then will I hear from heaven, and will forgive their sin, and will heal their land.*"

    C.   God needs a people who will prepare themselves and be ready

        1.   Proverbs 24:27 – "*Prepare thy work without, and make it fit for thyself in the field; and afterwards build thine house.*"

        2.   Exodus 15:2 – "*The LORD is my strength and song, and he is become my salvation: he is my God, and I will prepare him an habitation; my father's God, and I will exalt him.*"

        3.   Joel 3:9 – "*Proclaim ye this among the Gentiles; Prepare war, wake up the mighty men, let all the men of war draw near; let them come up:*"

        4.   Luke 1:17 – "*...to make ready a people prepared for the Lord.*"

        5.   Revelation 21:2 – "*And I John saw the holy city, new Jerusalem, coming down from God out of heaven, prepared as a bride adorned for her husband.*"

        6.   Job 11:13-19

        7.   II Timothy 2:15 – "*Study to shew thyself approved unto God, a workman that needeth not to be ashamed, rightly dividing the word of truth.*"

        8.   I Peter 3:15 – "*But sanctify the Lord God in your hearts: and be ready always to give an answer to every man that asketh you a reason of the hope that is in you with meekness and fear:*"

        9.   Hebrews 5:12-14, Hebrews 6:1-3

    C.   Who will take this challenge? Where are the valiant men?

        1.   Jeremiah 9:3 – "*...but they are not valiant for the truth upon the earth; for they proceed from evil to evil, and they know not me, saith the LORD.*"

2. II Samuel 23:17 – *"...is not this the blood of the men that went in jeopardy of their lives?"*
3. Hebrews 11:24-38
4. Job 29:18 – *"Then I said, I shall die in my nest, and I shall multiply my days as the sand."*
5. Psalms 90:9-12 – *"...¹²So teach us to number our days, that we may apply our hearts unto wisdom."*
6. Isaiah 64:7 – *"And there is none that calleth upon thy name, that stirreth up himself to take hold of thee..."*
7. Matthew 26:46 – *"Rise, let us be going..."*

Lesson 51
PEARL OF GREAT PRICE

I.   Pearl of Great Price, Matthew 13:45-46 – "*45Again, the kingdom of heaven is like unto a merchant man, seeking goodly pearls: 46Who, when he had found one pearl of great price, went and sold all that he had, and bought it.*"

    A.   Salvation is a free gift

        1.   Ephesians 2:8-9 – "*8For by grace are ye saved through faith; and that not of yourselves: it is the gift of God: 9Not of works, lest any man should boast.*"
        2.   Titus 3:5-6 – "*5Not by works of righteousness which we have done, but according to his mercy he saved us, by the washing of regeneration, and renewing of the Holy Ghost; 6Which he shed on us abundantly through Jesus Christ our Saviour;*"
        3.   Romans 3:20-28, 4:14-16

    B.   God has called us to holiness and to be like Him

        1.   II Peter 1:4 – "*Whereby are given unto us exceeding great and precious promises: that by these ye might be partakers of the divine nature, having escaped the corruption that is in the world through lust.*"
        2.   Hebrews 12:10 – "*For they verily for a few days chastened us after their own pleasure; but he for our profit, that we might be partakers of his holiness.*"
        3.   Romans 8:29 – "*For whom he did foreknow, he also did predestinate to be conformed to the image of his Son, that he might be the firstborn among many brethren.*"
        4.   Leviticus 20:7 – "*Sanctify yourselves therefore, and be ye holy: for I am the LORD your God*" (I Peter 1:16)
        5.   Matthew 5:48 – "*Be ye therefore perfect, even as your Father which is in heaven is perfect.*"

Salvation, the Holy Ghost, divine healing, prosperity, etc. are all free gifts because Jesus paid the price, but there is a price for us now to pay to "*go on unto perfection*" (Hebrews 6:1). For this to happen, we must change and change always costs us something.

    C.   Paying the price

        1.   Proverbs 23:23 – "*Buy the truth, and sell it not; also wisdom, and instruction, and understanding.*"
        2.   II Samuel 24:24 – "*...I will surely buy it of thee at a price: neither will I offer burnt offerings unto the LORD my God of that which doth cost me nothing...*"
        3.   I Chronicles 11:15-19 – Mighty men going in the jeopardy of their lives
        4.   Hebrews 11:32-40 – Those who paid the price, "*...Of whom the world was not worthy...*"
        5.   John 12:23-28 – "*...Verily, verily, I say unto you, Except a corn of wheat fall into the ground and die, it abideth alone: but if it die, it bringeth forth much fruit...*"
        6.   Micah 6:8 – "*He hath shewed thee, O man, what is good; and what doth the LORD require of thee, but to do justly, and to love mercy, and to walk humbly with thy God?*"
        7.   Luke 14:26 – "*If any man come to me, and hate not his father, and mother, and wife, and children, and brethren, and sisters, yea, and his own life also, he cannot be my disciple.*"
        8.   Deuteronomy 10:12 – "*And now, Israel, what doth the LORD thy God require of thee, but to fear the LORD thy God, to walk in all his ways, and to love him, and to serve the LORD thy God with all thy heart and with all thy soul,*"
        9.   Luke 14:28 – We must count the cost, "*For which of you, intending to build a tower, sitteth not down first, and counteth the cost, whether he have sufficient to finish it?*"

D. The Pearl of Great Price is Jesus – why was the man so willing to sell all that he had and pay the price? He had found the pearl, who is Jesus. The end justifies the journey, because in the end we get Him (Genesis 15:1)! If we'll be so caught up and in love with Jesus, we won't be bothered by the price.

1. Philippians 3:7-14 – "*7But what things were gain to me, those I counted loss for Christ. 8Yea doubtless, and I count all things but loss for the excellency of the knowledge of Christ Jesus my Lord: for whom I have suffered the loss of all things, and do count them but dung, <u>that I may win Christ</u>, 9And be found in him, not having mine own righteousness, which is of the law, but that which is through the faith of Christ, the righteousness which is of God by faith: 10That I may know him, and the power of his resurrection, and the fellowship of his sufferings, being made conformable unto his death; 11If by any means I might attain unto the resurrection of the dead. 12Not as though I had already attained, either were already perfect: but I follow after, if that I may apprehend that for which also I am apprehended of Christ Jesus. 13Brethren, I count not myself to have apprehended: but this one thing I do, forgetting those things which are behind, and reaching forth unto those things which are before, 14I press toward the mark for the prize of the high calling of God in Christ Jesus.*"

2. Song of Solomon 5 – "*...9What is thy beloved more than another beloved, O thou fairest among women? what is thy beloved more than another beloved, that thou dost so charge us?...*"

3. Proverbs 8:35 – "*For whoso findeth me findeth life, and shall obtain favour of the LORD.*"

4. Colossians 3:1-3 – "*1If ye then be risen with Christ, seek those things which are above, where Christ sitteth on the right hand of God. 2Set your affection on things above, not on things on the earth. 3For ye are dead, and your life is hid with Christ in God.*"

5. Hebrews 12:1-2 – "*1Wherefore seeing we also are compassed about with so great a cloud of witnesses, let us lay aside every weight, and the sin which doth so easily beset us, and let us run with patience the race that is set before us, 2Looking unto Jesus the author and finisher of our faith; who for the joy that was set before him endured the cross, despising the shame, and is set down at the right hand of the throne of God.*"

Lesson 52
KNOWING THE TIMES

I.   Knowing the Times

    A.   We are to know the time

        1.   Romans 13:11-14 – "*[11]And that, knowing the time, that now it is high time to awake out of sleep: for now is our salvation nearer than when we believed. [12]The night is far spent, the day is at hand: let us therefore cast off the works of darkness, and let us put on the armour of light. [13]Let us walk honestly, as in the day; not in rioting and drunkenness, not in chambering and wantonness, not in strife and envying. [14]But put ye on the Lord Jesus Christ, and make not provision for the flesh, to fulfil the lusts thereof.*"

        2.   Ecclesiastes 8:5-6 – "*[5]Whoso keepeth the commandment shall feel no evil thing: and a wise man's heart discerneth both time and judgment. [6]Because to every purpose there is time and judgment, therefore the misery of man is great upon him.*"

        3.   I Chronicles 12:32 – "*And of the children of Issachar, which were men that had understanding of the times, to know what Israel ought to do...*"

        4.   Ecclesiastes 3:1-8, 17 – "*To every thing there is a season, and a time to every purpose under the heaven...*"

        5.   Job 24:1 – "*Why, seeing times are not hidden from the Almighty, do they that know him not see his days?*"

    B.   Not knowing your day of visitation, Luke 19:35-44

"*[35]And they brought him to Jesus: and they cast their garments upon the colt, and they set Jesus thereon. [36]And as he went, they spread their clothes in the way. [37]And when he was come nigh, even now at the descent of the mount of Olives, the whole multitude of the disciples began to rejoice and praise God with a loud voice for all the mighty works that they had seen; [38]Saying, Blessed be the King that cometh in the name of the Lord: peace in heaven, and glory in the highest. [39]And some of the Pharisees from among the multitude said unto him, Master, rebuke thy disciples. [40]And he answered and said unto them, I tell you that, if these should hold their peace, the stones would immediately cry out. [41]And when he was come near, <u>he beheld the city, and wept over it,</u> [42]Saying, If thou hadst known, even thou, at least in this thy day, the things which belong unto thy peace! but now they are hid from thine eyes. [43]For the days shall come upon thee, that thine enemies shall cast a trench about thee, and compass thee round, and keep thee in on every side, [44]And shall lay thee even with the ground, and thy children within thee; and they shall not leave in thee one stone upon another; <u>because thou knewest not the time of thy visitation.</u>*"

        1.   This was His promised and glorious entrance into Jerusalem

        2.   Oh how His heart must have soared knowing that the people loved and worshipped Him so.

        3.   They finally had a revelation of who Jesus was.

        4.   In answering the Pharisees, one must think they had to be surrounded in a deluge of glory.

        5.   But yet, He weeps over the city and people who should know Him, but most had rejected Him.

        6.   He wept because they had no true revelation of His purpose and what He wanted for them.

        7.   He weeps over their coming judgment

        8.   He weeps because they knew not the time of their visitation when they should have.

    C.   God's rebuke for not knowing

        1.   Matthew 16:3 – "*...O ye hypocrites, ye can discern the face of the sky; but can ye not discern the signs of the times?*"

2. Hebrews 5:12 – *"For when for the time ye ought to be teachers, ye have need that one teach you again which be the first principles of the oracles of God; and are become such as have need of milk, and not of strong meat."*

3. Esther 4:14 – *"For if thou altogether holdest thy peace at this time, then shall there enlargement and deliverance arise to the Jews from another place; but thou and thy father's house shall be destroyed: and who knoweth whether thou art come to the kingdom for such a time as this?"*

D. We need to realize our time is short

1. Psalms 89:47 – *"Remember how short my time is: wherefore hast thou made all men in vain?"*

2. Psalms 90:12 – *"So teach us to number our days, that we may apply our hearts unto wisdom."*

Lesson 53
GOD'S PICTURES OF HIS PEOPLE

I.   The Twelve sons of Jacob, A Type

A.   The twelve sons of Jacob are representative or typical of the household of faith.
B.   Twelve is the number of divine government. This would represent the whole of God's sons.
C.   We can perhaps find out where we fit in, what our characteristics are, and whom they relate to, and by doing so, spare ourselves the pitfalls these sons faced, as well as realize our destiny and march towards it.

1.   We are also the sons of Jacob.

a.   Genesis 49:1-2 – Notice the term, *"in the last days."* I believe he is speaking of His people (Jew or Gentile believers or types of His people in the end times.)
b.   Psalm 77:14-15 – *"Thy people"*
c.   Isaiah 65:9 – A seed out of Jacob

d.   Obadiah 17, 18, 27

1)   Mount Zion – All His remnant
2)   House of Jacob shall possess

2.   Micah 5:7-8 – The remnant of Jacob is you and me

3.   Jacob represents us (so does Israel)

a.   Jacob – Deceiver, supplanter, our old nature
b.   Israel – Prince with God, champion – our new nature

4.   Israel 9:8 – This speaks of how the word of God changes us from that old, deceiving nature into champions.

5.   Song of Solomon 3:8 – Valiant men of Israel made up of all God's remnant

a.   Psalm 22:3 – We are Israel

6.   Romans 9:6-8 – Children of promise are the Israel spoken of here

a.   Romans 2:28-29
b.   Galatians 6:12-16
c.   Hebrews 12:18-23
d.   Galatians 4:22-29

7.   Galatians 3:26-29 – "*...And if ye be Christ's, then are ye Abraham's seed, and heirs according to the promise.*"
8.   Ephesians 2:11-22 – He hath made both one
9.   Acts 15:8-9 – Put no difference between us
10. Romans 10:12-13 – No difference between Jew and Greek

II. The Twelve sons of Jacob

A. Genesis 49:1-2 – In this chapter, Jacob does several important things that are typical of what the Lord will do in the last days.

1. Calls all his sons
2. Asks them to "gather together" in unity
3. So that He can tell them what will happen to them in the last days
4. He asks them to listen to their Father (Malachi 4:6)
5. And to do (hearken) to what he says and consider what he reveals to them

B   Rueben

1. Rueben – His name in Hebrew means – Behold a son, vision of a son
2. Eldest son of Jacob – responsibility

3. Born to Leah – Genesis 29:30-32

    a. Born to a mother and father who were having problems in their marriage
    b. Leah was trying to please her husband, make him love her by having children
    c. Leah was hated by Jacob (Genesis 29:25)
    d. Rueben had to grow up into this despised atmosphere

4. During wheat harvest found mandrakes and gave them to his mother of which she used to bargain for Jacob's affections. He was taught to bargain for love. How sad. Genesis 30:14
5. Committed adultery with his father's concubine. Genesis 35:22 – perverse nature
6. Did save his brother from death, but went along with the mob (his brothers). Showed no leadership or willingness to sacrifice for his brother (Genesis 37:21)

7. He was the firstborn and was to receive the birthright blessing (Deuteronomy 21:17), the double portion, which he did not, it went to:

    a. Birthright – Manasseh and Ephraim
    b. Kingdom Blessing went to Judah
    c. Priesthood – Levi

8. Genesis 42:37 – He did show some admirable qualities here, in that he offered his two sons as a guarantee he would return with Benjamin

9. He was to be the vision of a true son (manifested son of God), Genesis 49:3 he was to be (typically see this)

    a. Jacob's firstborn
    b. His might
    c. The beginning of his strength – This is translated elsewhere, "*my first fruits*"
    d. Excellency of dignity
    e. The Excellency of power – How sad that Rueben didn't make it. He did not fulfill his great potential. He missed his destiny. He was still a son but not the double portion son he was intended to be.

10. Unstable as water – He was double-minded (James 1:8) – Unstable in Hebrew – to froth, seething, overflowing or outburst of passion or anger. Some say it means he was full of lust
11. Thou shalt not excel – Excel in Hebrew – to put over, to exceed, or to remain or be left. I believe this means he didn't make it into the remnant.

12. Because he went up to his father's bed – His perversion cost him greatly. We must receive from this that he never repented for his sin of incest.

13. Deuteronomy 33:6 – Let Rueben live and not die. Let not his men be few – God still blessed him by sparing his life and giving him children. And his tribe received the first parcel of land when it was divided.

14. Numbers 32:5 – Here his family wants the land on this side of the Jordan and Moses reacts angrily in verse 6 and says, basically that they:

    a. Are thinking of themselves
    b. Want to let their brothers go to war while they sit and watch
    c. They brought discouragement to the rest of Israel. It looks like his children received some of his bad traits.
    d. I Chronicles 5:1

C. Simeon

1. His name means – hearkening, hearing with acceptance, hears to obey (also possibly "a little hyena beast").
2. Simeon and Levi will be forever linked together because of their plotting together and massacre of the Hivites of Shechem.
3. He was the second (witness and separation = 2) of Leah and Jacob.
4. Genesis 29:33 – His birth – Because Leah was hated, Simeon, like Rueben grew up in a household of hostility.
5. Genesis 42:24 – Simeon was the brother, Joseph kept as security when he allowed his brothers to leave Egypt. (He was obviously not esteemed by his other brothers)
6. Genesis 46:10 – One of his sons was born of a "Canaanitish" woman, a union of which God was not pleased.

7. Genesis 49:5-7

    a. Things said about Simeon

        1) Instrument of cruelty in his habitation. This is found in Genesis 34:25:31

            a) Things that happened here

                1) All the males
                2) Took all the possessions

        2) Genesis 49:6

            a) He was cruel
            b) He was vindictive
            c) He was given to anger
            d) Self willed
            e) Headstrong
            f) Couldn't wait for God's justice
            g) They dug down a wall – tore at the fabric of his own soul bringing him down to a level of sin that had the wall remained he wouldn't have fallen in to

        3) God's judgment on Simeon

        a)   Divided

        b)   Scattered

The sad thing is, there are these types of people in the Kingdom. They may not actually kill someone, but they hate their brothers, or they are angry, self-willed, vindictive, cruel, etc. God, deliver us from these characteristics.

D.   Levi – Genesis 49:5-7

    1.   Word Definitions

        a.   Hebrew – Attached; from a root that means to twine, to unite, to remove; it basically means joined

    2.   Important aspects of Levi's life

        a.   He was the third son of Jacob and Leah. Three is the number of resurrection and Godhead.

        b.   Genesis 29:34 – "*Now will my husband be joined...*" (Root of the word Levi). "*Now I'll have true love and intimacy with my husband because...*" Once again Leah's sons struggle with their father's love and acceptance. Henceforth their security and identity is hindered.

        c.   Born in Horan – Horan in Hebrew – very dry; place parched with sun, from a root – to be dry, to kindle, to burn; grievous. Hence, Levi's origins are ones of dryness, thirst, and grievousness.

        d.   Genesis 34:25-30 – A murderous slaughter of a people. This is the character of Levi.

        e.   Genesis 37:3, 4, 18

            1)   He hated his brother, couldn't speak peaceably to him
            2)   Conspired against Joseph to kill him

        f.   Genesis 49:5-7

            1)   Instruments of cruelty
            2)   Into their secret – They plotted together in secret
            3)   Anger
            4)   Self will
            5)   Cruel wrath

        g.   Moses was a Levite – Exodus 2:1-3, 10-11
        h.   Exodus 32:26 – All Levi joined Moses
        i.   Deuteronomy 10:6-10 – Other translation:

"*Then the Eternal set apart the clan of Levi to carry the ark of the Eternal's compact, to serve the Eternal as His ministers and to bless others in His name as they do this day. Levi therefore enjoys no property or possessions like his brothers; his possession is the Eternal...*"

This is the story of the children of Levi, their deliverance, and their entering into their calling and destiny. It tells of what they had to go through to finally fulfill what God wanted in Levi.

            1)   Beeroth – Wells (wells of salvation)
            2)   Jaakan – Bands (confinement, bands)
            3)   Gudgodah – The slashing place

4) Jotbath – Rivers of water

Levi – Joined truly now, separated now, to the Lord.

E. Judah – Genesis 49:8-12

1. Judah's name means – Praise
2. Fourth son of Jacob and Leah – Four is the number for creation ("new creation")

3. Founder of the family out of which the Messiah would come (Matthew 1:16) – Called to bring forth the delivered, to manifest the Son

   a. Matthew 1:1-16
   b. Hebrews 7:14
   c. Revelation 5:5
   d. Matthew 2:6

4. Genesis 29:35 – Leah decides it doesn't matter anymore what her husband thinks. *"Now, will I praise the Lord."* Because she was now delivered from men, Judah was free from the opinions of men. He could praise without inhibitions.
5. Saved Joseph's life, Genesis 37:26-28 – By suggesting they sell him, appealing to their beast instincts.
6. Genesis 43:8-10 – He was willing to become the surety guarantor of his brother's life, and take all the blame.
7. Geneses 44:14-31 – Judah confesses and tells most of the truth and offers himself as a slave to Joseph in exchange for his brother.

8. Judah appears to be the leader of Jacob's sons, though he is "not the oldest".

   a. Genesis 46:28 – He was sent before Jacob into Egypt
   b. Genesis 44:11 – He appears to be the spokesperson for the brothers.
   c. Genesis 49:8-10 – He received His father's blessing

   d. Genesis 49:8

      1) Your brothers shall praise you
      2) Thy father's children shall bow down before you

   e. Genesis 49:10 – The scepter given to him.

F. Zebulun

1. Definition of name – Wished for habitation, elevated dwelling. The revelation is – a place people want to be.
2. Jacob's 10th son – Ten is the number for law

3. Genesis 30:20

   a. Leah's 6th son – Human perfection – not enough
   b. *"Now my husband will dwell with me"*
   c. Zebulun used as a pawn to make someone dwell with them. We can never be good enough to please anyone.

4. Tribe placed on the east side of the Tabernacle. East – coming of the Lord.

5. Genesis 46:14

    a. His fruit – Three sons

        1) Sered – Stubbornness, subdued, fear, to tremble
        2) Elon – Magnificent oak, strong, might
        3) Jahleel – Hope of God, God waits. All of these seeds lie in Zebulun, waiting to come forth.

6. Genesis 49:13

    a. "*A haven of ships*" – A comfortable place for people to dwell
    b. Border of Zidon – Fishing, plenty of fish – revival takes place here; the world loves Zebulun.

G. Issachar

    1. Definition of name – He is wages, he is fired, reward, hireling
    2. Jacob's 9th son – Nine is the number for finality, fruits of the Spirit
    3. Genesis 30:16-18 – Issachar was payment for mandrakes – Once again, forced love created this child.
    4. Leah's 5th son – Five is the number of grace

    5. Issachar fathered four sons

        a. Tola – Little worm, scarlet
        b. Shimron – Vigilant guardian, watchful
        c. Puah – Mouth utterance, a blast, from a root – to blow away or scatter into corners.
        d. Job – Hated, persecuted, ever returning to God

    6. Issachar was located on the east side of the Tabernacle. East represents the coming of the Lord.

    7. Genesis 49:14-15 – Other translations:

        "*Issachar is a big boned donkey*"
        "*Lying down between the sheepfolds*"
        "*...desired earnestly what was good, halting between two choices*"
        "*stretched out among the flocks*"
        "*lounging among thieves*"

        a. A strong ass – Stubborn and strong – Mark 11:2
        b. Couching down – Love of comfort or rest, hiding
        c. Two burdens – The Lord's or men?
        d. Rest was good – Slothful
        e. Become a servant – Rather than being a leader, he took the path of least resistance.

    8. His fruit

        a. I Chronicles 17:5 – Valiant men of might

        b.   I Chronicles 12:32

            1)   They had "understanding of the times"
            2)   They knew "what Israel ought to do"

This is what we can become; as we follow on to know the Lord

H.   Dan

1. Definition of name – Judging, judge, from a root word – to rule, to execute judgment, to contend.
2. Fifth son of Jacob – Five is the number for grace and spiritual ministry

3. First son born to Rachel's handmaid Bilhah

    a.   Bilhah means – Timidity, in weakness, from a root word – to terrify, to trouble, in languishing, decrepit.

    b.   Genesis 30:1-6

        1)   Envied Leah
        2)   Give me children, or else I die
        3)   Jacob angry with her
        4)   Gave him Bilhah (this is never a good thing)
        5)   God judged me for what I've don. Dan was born into mess.

4. Dan had one son – He had two names (he obviously had two natures or characters)

    a.   Hushim – Genesis 46:23 – Those who hasten their birth, those who make haste
    b.   Shuham – Numbers 26:42 – Pit digger, depression, from a root word – to bow down.

5. They were given land occupied by the Philistines (Joshua 13:3), but failed to conquer it. Later migrated north and conquered Laish – Lion, old lion.
6. Worshipped an idol – Judges 18:30-31
7. Dan was always a small tribe and never exercised significant influence in Israel.
8. Most prominent individual to come out of Dan – Samson, Judges 13:2, 24 – Stilling, fighting the Philistines

9. Genesis 49:16-18

    a.   Dan shall judge his people
    b.   Shall be a serpent
    c.   By the way in the path
    d.   Waiting for God's salvation

10. Dan was on the north side of the Tabernacle of Moses – North means judgment.
11. Deuteronomy 33:22 – Lead from Bashan. Bashan means sandy soil

I.   Gad

1. Definition – Good fortune, good luck, from a root word – to gather in troops, to cut through.
2. Seventh son of Jacob – Seven is the number for perfection

3. Zilpah's first born – This was Leah's handmaid (this is never a good thing). Zilpah's name means a dropping, drop, flippant mouth.

4. Gad had seven sons

   a. Ziphion – Earnest, expectation; root – intense longing
   b. Haggi – Exultation, festive, my feast
   c. Shuni – Tranquility, quiet, calm, my rest
   d. Ezbon – Great beauty, splendor, hastening
   e. Eri – Watcher of the Lord, worshipper of Jehovah
   f. Arodi – Wild ass
   g. Areli – Lion of God, heroic, valiant

5. They were on the south side of the Tabernacle of Moses. South means blessing.

6. Deuteronomy 33:20-21

   a. Blessed are these who bless Gad
   b. Gad tears the arm (strength, works) with the crown (authority) of the head (Jesus).
   c. Ate the first part of himself
   d. Leadership (herds of people)
   e. Executed justice

7. Genesis 49:19

   a. Overcome
   b. But overcomes at last

8. Numbers 32:1-7, 14-23

J. Asher

1. Definition of name – Fortunate, happy, fortress, from a root word – to be straight, to be level, to be honest.
2. He was the eighth son of Jacob. Eight is the number of new beginnings.
3. Second son of Leah's maidservant Zilpah – Two is the number of witness and separation.
4. Genesis 30:13 – This time, surprisingly, Leah says, *"happy am I"*. She feels differently about Asher.
5. Asher was on the north side of the Tabernacle of Moses – North means judgment.

6. Asher has five children

   a. Four sons

      1) Jimnah – Prosperity, he allots success, right handed, he will number.
      2) Ishuah – He will be equal, alike, self satisfaction, level, from a root word – to be even, to be level.
      3) Isui – Level
      4) Beriah – In calamity, in evil, unfortunate

   b. One daughter

      1) Serah – abundance, the prince breathed

231

7. Asher could not drive out the Canaanites and had to live among them (Joshua 19:24-31, Judges 1:31-32)
8. Asher's greatest hero was Anna the prophetess – Luke 2:36-38

9. Deuteronomy 33:24-25

   a. Blessed with children (spiritual and natural)
   b. Accepted by his brethren
   c. Foot in oil – A walk in the anointing
   d. Shoes iron and brass – A walk of judgment

10. Genesis 49:20

   a. Bread fat – Rich provision
   b. Royal dainties – Food for a king

K. Naphtali

1. Definition of name – A struggle, my wrestling, my twisting,
2. The sixth son of Jacob – Six is the number for man or Satan
3. Genesis 30:7-8 – This son was also born out of envy and spite, Rachel wrestling with Leah.
4. Second son of Bilhah – Two is the number of witness and separation

5. Naphtali had four sons – Genesis 46:24

   a. Jahzeel – He will allot of God, whom God allots, God apportions, and God divides, from a root word – to divide.
   b. Guni – My garden, protected, painted with colors
   c. Jezer – Frame, form, anything made, or his parents, from a root word – To form, to fashion.
   d. Sillem – Recompense, retribution

6. Isaiah 9:1-2 – Prophecy that the Messiah, Jesus, would visit Nephtali's land.
7. Naphtali was on the north side of the Tabernacle of Moses. North means judgment.
8. Judges 5:18 – Naphtali risked their lives on behalf of Israel

9. Deuteronomy 33:23

   a. Satisfied with favor (blessed)
   b. Possesses the west (backsliding) and south (blessing, prosperity)

10. Genesis 49:21

   a. Let loose – liberated, free
   b. Giveth good words – ministers the good Word of God

L. Joseph

1. Definition of name – May God add, he shall add, increasing, adding.
2. Eleventh son of Jacob – eleven is the number for incompleteness, disorganization (one short of twelve – government).

3. Genesis 30:22-24 – Rachel is finally delivered from her wrestlings, envy, and hostility as well as has a breakthrough with God. Now her womb is opened.
4. Rachel's first child – One is the number for God and unity.
5. Genesis 37:3 – Favorite son of his father – knew he was loved
6. Joseph was a dreamer, a visionary – Genesis 37:5
7. Envied of his brothers, ultimately sold out by them – Genesis 37:11, 18-20, 28
8. Genesis 39:7-20 – Unjustly accused. He was accused of sexual impropriety. If they can't get you in your walk, then they will accuse you falsely.
9. Joseph prospers no matter what – Genesis 9:3-4, 21-23
10. All this blessing, however, did seem to feed Joseph's ego, and he needed to be humbled.
11. Genesis 41:16 – Now he is humbled
12. Genesis 41:39-44 – Elevated to highest place in the kingdom, next to pharaoh
13. Genesis 45:3-8 – A revelation of the sovereignty of God – didn't blame or hold grudges against anyone and forgave his brothers.
14. Genesis 45:3 – Saw that he was a pioneer – one sent before
15. A great administrator, ruler, gifts of government, preparation, etc.

16. Father of two sons – Genesis 41:50-52

    a. Manasseh – one who causes to forget, forgetting
    b. Ephraim – twofold increase, doubly fruitful

17. Genesis 49:22-26

    a. Fruitful bough by a well – Psalms 1:3
    b. Verse 23 – Persecuted
    c. Verse 24 – Made strong by God
    d. Verse 25 – Blessed of brethren, etc.
    e. Verse 26 – Separate from his brethren – remnant

18. Psalms 105:17-22
19. Psalms 81:5-6

M. Benjamin

1. Definition of name – Son of my right hand, son of my days, son of old age, son of the south.
2. Benjamin was camped on the west side of the Tabernacle of Moses. West in Scripture speaks of backsliding, going away from the coming of the Lord. Standing afar off from a revelation of Jesus; the sun setting.
3. Benjamin was the only full blooded brother of Joseph.

4. They had a reputation as men of war

    a. Judges 5:14
    b. Judges 20:12-16 – They could sling stones on hairs breadth and not miss.
    c. Genesis 49:27

5. Benjamin was left handed

    a. Judges 20:16
    b. Judges 3:15 – The revelation of the left hand is – judgment.

6. Benjamin's greatest names

    a.   Saul – Israel's first king – I Samuel 9:1

    b.   Paul – The apostle – Romans 11:1, Philippians 3:5

7.   Shimei – man who cursed David (II Samuel 16:5-13) – a Benjamite.

8.   Of all the children of Jacob he alone was born in Palestine. He was born between Ephrath (fruitful, ash heap) and Bethel (house of God).

9.   Benjamin became part of the southern part of Judah, when Israel was divided into two nations – I Kings 12:21, Ezra 4:1

10.   Benjamin supported Saul over David – II Samuel 2:9, 15, I Chronicles 12:29

11.   Jacob had two favorite sons – Joseph (a type of Jesus) and Benjamin (a type of the sons of God).

12.   Benjamin had five sons (Numbers 26:38-41). Five is the number for grace:

    a.   Belah – Devouring, swallowing, destruction

    b.   Ahirah – Brother of height, to lift up oneself

    c.   Ashbel – Vain fire, fire of old age, to waste away

    d.   Shupham – Their barrenness, serpent

    e.   Hupham – Inhabitants of the sea, protected

13.   His birth

    a.   Genesis 35:16-19

        1)   Rachel travailed to bring forth a son (body of Christ is travailing to bring forth a son).

        2)   It was hard labor just outside the city.

        3)   Rachel had to die to birth this son.

        4)   She called him Benoni (son of my sorrows)

        5)   Jacob called him Benjamin (son of my right hand) – Right hand is the hand of blessing. God had already spoken to Jacob of this boy (Genesis 35:10-11).

14.   Genesis 43:29-30, 34

    a.   God be gracious

    b.   Joseph (Jesus) yearned for his brother and wept.

    c.   Benjamin's mess (food, provision) was five times more than his brothers.

15.   Genesis 44:2 – Silver cup in Benjamin's sack – silver represents redemption.

16.   Genesis 44:30 – The father's life is bound up in Benjamin's.

17.   Genesis 45:14 – Specifically fell on Benjamin's neck first and wept, when the revelation of who he really was came to pass.

18.   Genesis 45:22

    a.   Benjamin received five times the clothing (speaks of righteousness and holiness and what we've attained in our walk with God).

    b.   Three hundred is the number for the faithful remnant.

19.   Genesis 49:27

    a.   Ravin – to pluck off, to pull to pieces, to supple with food (speaks of being a warrior, provide).

    b.   In the morning (resurrection time) he shall devourer the prey (the devil ultimately defeated by the sons of God).

    c.   At night (during dark times) he will be sharing the spoil.

20.   Deuteronomy 33:12

    a.   Other translation – *"Of Benjamin he said he is the beloved of the Lord with Him he dwells securely. He ever encircles him and has established His abode between his shoulders."*

    b.   He's beloved of the Lord

    c.   He shall dwell in safety, by the Lord

    d.   Shall be covered by the Lord all day

    e.   Benjamin shall dwell between God's shoulders

        1)   Mind of Christ

        2)   Carried by the Lord

21.   Psalms 68:27 – There is little Benjamin in the sanctuary of God with the ruler.

22.   Obadiah 19 – Benjamin shall possess Gilead (perpetual fountain, heap of testimony, a witness). Benjamin shall possess al of these.

23.   The son of the right hand

    a.   Psalms 45:9

    b.   Matthew 20:20-24

Lesson 54
GOD'S PROMISE OF PROSPERITY

I.   Genesis 22:14 – *"And Abraham called the name of that place Jehovah-jireh: as it is said to this day, In the mount of the LORD it shall be seen."*

  A.   Jehovah-Jireh

   1.   Hebrew definition – the Lord will provide, the Lord will see, the Lord will give a means of deliverance.

  B.   God's heart for our prosperity, according to Scripture

   1.   Philippians 4:19 – *"But my God shall supply all your need according to his riches in glory by Christ Jesus."*

    a.   *Supply* in Greek – to cram in, to fill, to cover over, to compute
    b.   *Need* in Greek – employment, lack, necessity, occasion demands
    c.   *Riches* in Greek – wealth, money, possessions, abundance

   2.   Psalms 35:27 – *"Let the Lord be magnified, which hath pleasure in the prosperity of his servant."*
   3.   III John 2 – *"Beloved, I wish above all things that thou mayest prosper and be in health, even as thy soul prospereth."* – *Prosper* in Greek – help on the road, to succeed in reaching
   4.   Psalms 132:13-15 – *"For the Lord hath chosen Zion; he hath desired it for his habitation. This is my rest for ever: here will I dwell; for I have desired it. I will abundantly bless her provision..."*
   5.   Zechariah 8:11-13 – *"...For the seed shall be prosperous; the vine shall give her fruit..."* – *Prosperous* in Hebrew – *shalom* – peace, wholeness, well being
   6.   Nehemiah 2:20 – *"...The God of heaven, he will prosper us; therefore we his servants will arise and build..."*
   7.   Psalms 78:19-25 – *"...Can God furnish a table in the wilderness? Behold, he smote the rock, that the waters gushed out, and the streams overflowed; can he give bread also? can he provide flesh for his people?..."*
   8.   Ezekiel 16:13 – *"...thou didst prosper into a kingdom."*

II.   Scriptural Ways to Prosperity

  A.   The Word of God

   1.   Joshua 1:7-8 – *"...This book of the law shall not depart out of thy mouth; but thou shalt meditate therein day and night, that thou mayest observe to do...for then thou shalt make thy way prosperous, and then thou shalt have good success."*
   2.   Psalms 1:2-3 – *"But his delight is in the law of the Lord...and whatsoever he doeth shall prosper."*
   3.   Deuteronomy 29:9 – *"Keep therefore the words of this covenant, and do them, that ye may prosper in all that ye do."*
   4.   I Kings 2:3 – *"...to keep his statutes, and his commandments, and his judgments, and his testimonies, as it is written in the law of Moses, that thou mayest prosper in all that thou doest..."*

  B.   Prophetic Utterance

    1. Ezra 6:14 – *"And the elders of the Jews builded, and they prospered through the prophesying of Haggai the prophet and Zechariah the son of Iddo..."*

    2. II Chronicles 20:20 – *" ...Believe in the Lord your God, so shall ye be established; believe his prophets, so shall ye prosper."*

C. Giving (Tithing and First- fruits Offerings, Sacrificial Giving)

    1. Luke 6:38 – *"Give, and it shall be given unto you; good measure, pressed down, and shaken together, and running over, shall men give into your bosom. For with the same measure that ye mete withal it shall be measured to you again."*

    2. Proverbs 3:9-10 – *"Honour the LORD with thy substance, and with the firstfruits of all thine increase: So shall thy barns be filled with plenty, and thy presses shall burst out with new wine."*

    3. Ecclesiastes 11:1-6 – *"Cast thy bread upon the waters: for thou shalt find it after many days. Give a portion to seven, and also to eight; for thou knowest not what evil shall be upon the earth. If the clouds be full of rain, they empty themselves upon the earth: and if the tree fall toward the south, or toward the north, in the place where the tree falleth, thee it shall be. He that observeth the wind shall not sow; and he that regardeth the clouds shall not reap...In the morning sow thy seed, and in the evening withhold not thine hand: for thou knowest not whether shall prosper..."*

    4. Malachi 3:10-11 – *"Bring ye all the tithes into the storehouse, that there may be meat in mine house, and prove me now herewith, saith the LORD of hosts, if I will not open you the windows of heaven, and pour you out a blessing..."*

D. Loving, Praying and Supporting Natural Israel

    1. Psalms 122:6 – *"Pray for the peace of Jerusalem: they shall prosper that love thee."*

E. Serving with All of Our Hearts

    1. II Chronicles 31:21 – *"And in every work that he (Hezekiah) began in the service of the house of God, and in the law, and in the commandments, to seek his God, he did it with all his heart, and prospered."*

    2. Job 36:11 – *"If they obey and serve him, they shall spend their days in prosperity, and their years in pleasures."*

III. Send Now Prosperity

A. Psalms 118:25 – *"Save now, I beseech thee, O Lord: O Lord, I beseech thee, send now prosperity."*

    1. Hebrew for *prosperity* in this passage – to push forward, to break out, to mightily go over.

Lesson 55
GOING ON OR GOING BACK

I.   Hebrews 10:38-39 – *"Now the just shall live by faith: but if any man draw back, my soul shall have no pleasure in him. But we are not of them who draw back unto perdition; but of them that believe to the saving of the soul."*

    A.   We are either going on with Jesus or going back (backsliding). The Christian life is full of decisions and we're constantly deciding either way.

        1.   There is no middle ground
        2.   Perhaps some of us have drawn back

II.   God's Desire for Us is to Go On – Our Pursuit after Jesus

    A.   When we are born again, we immediately enter a race.

        1.   Hebrews 12:1 – *"...let us run with patience the race that is set before us,"*
        2.   I Corinthians 9:24-27 – *"...So run, that ye may obtain..."*
        3.   Proverbs 4:18
        4.   Ecclesiastes 9:11

    B.   God is calling us upward

        1.   Song of Solomon 2:10 – *"...Rise up, my love, my fair one, and come away."*
        2.   Psalms 61:2 – *"...lead me to the rock that is higher than I."*
        3.   Revelation 4:1 – *"...the first voice which I heard...which said, Come up hither..."*
        4.   Hebrews 3:1 – *"...partakers of the heavenly calling..."*

    C.   As we begin to go after Jesus, our heart is crying for more of Him

        1.   Mark 1:16-21
        2.   Psalms 27:4 – *"One thing have I desired of the LORD, that will I seek after..."*
        3.   Philippians 3:14
        4.   Psalms 42:1 – *"...so panteth my soul after thee, O God."*
        5.   Song of Solomon 1:1-4

    D.   God wants continual growth

        1.   I Peter 3:18 – *"...grow in grace, and in the knowledge of our Lord and Saviour..."*
        2.   Hebrews 6:1 – *"...let us go on unto perfection..."*
        3.   Matthew 4:19 – *"...Follow me, and I will make you fishers of men."*
        4.   I Corinthians 9:24 – *"Know ye not that they which run in a race run all..."*
        5.   Song of Solomon 2:10 – *"...Rise up, my love, my fair one, and come away."*
        6.   Hebrews 12:1 – *"...let us lay aside every weight, and the sin which doth so easily beset us, and let us run with patience the race that is set before us"*
        7.   Philippians 3:14 – *"I press toward the mark for the prize..."*

    E.   We move in seasons

        1.   Ecclesiastes 3:1 – *"To every thing there is a season..."*
        2.   Ecclesiastes 8:6 – *"Because to every purpose there is time and judgment..."*

F. God gives us a proceeding word

    1.   God gives the word, and then we grow up into it. And when we've sufficiently done that, we move again. This should be the normal Christian life.

        a.   II Corinthians 3:18 – "*...changed into the same image from glory to glory...*"
        b.   Romans 1:17 – "*...the righteousness of God revealed from faith to faith...*"
        c.   Psalms 84:7 – "*They go from strength to strength...*"
        d.   Proverbs 4:18 – "*...the path of the just is as the shining light, that shineth more and more unto the perfect day.*"
        e.   Isaiah 40:31

G. There comes a time when a word is accomplished and to stay there any longer would be unfruitful.

    1.   Isaiah 28:20 – Example of a bed
    2.   I Samuel 2:18-19 – Example of a coat
    3.   Deuteronomy 2:1-3 – "*...Ye have compassed this mountain long enough...*"
    4.   Exodus 40:34-38 – Example of the cloud
    5.   Luke 1:20 – "*...my words, which shall be fulfilled in their season.*"

III. We must not turn or look back.

A. Scriptural exhortations

    1.   Luke 9:62 – "*...No man, having put his hand to the plough, and looking back, is fit for the kingdom of God.*"
    2.   Acts 7:39 – "*...and in their hearts turned back again into Egypt*"

    3.   In this last hour the devil wants many to fall and turn back.

        a.   Mark 13:14-16
        b.   I Timothy 4:1-3 (II Timothy 3:1-5)
        c.   Matthew 24:12
        d.   II Timothy 4:10

B. What happens to those who look back?

    1.   Luke 9:62 – Not fit
    2.   Genesis 19:26 – You become a pillar of salt
    3.   Luke 17:31-37 – Lose reward
    4.   John 6:66 – Walked no more
    5.   Hebrews 11:13-16

C. We should forget the past

    1.   Philippians 3:13
    2.   Isaiah 43:18

D. There is a temptation just to settle down and take it easy

    1.   Ecclesiastes 10:18
    2.   Proverbs 6:10-11

       3.   Proverbs 6:16-24

  E.   There is a temptation to let what other people are doing affect us

       1.   John 21:22
       2.   Galatians 2:11-15
       3.   Joshua 24:15
       4.   Hebrews 6:4-10

IV. But What if Someone Doesn't Grow?

  A.   What happens to those who resist growth?

       1.   Jeremiah 48:10-12

           a.   Stink (Exodus 16:4, 20)
           b.   You lose what you had.

       2.   II Peter 1:5-11

           a.   Blind – stumbles in darkness
           b.   Cannot see afar off – loses vision
           c.   Forgets his righteousness
           d.   Loses that abundant entrance

       3.   Our hearts become hard – I Timothy 4:1-2
       4.   We become religious – I Timothy 4:3
       5.   Our revelation of Jesus and His presence is limited

       6.   We believe the old was better than what is before us

           a.   Luke 5:36-39 – "*...No man also having drunk old wine straightway desireth new: for he saith, The old is better.*"
           b.   Isaiah 43:18 – "*...neither consider the things of old.*"
           c.   Ecclesiastes 7:10

       7.   We are not conformed into His image

           a.   Romans 8:29
           b.   I John 3:2

       8.   Of course, with all of this, God is not pleased

           a.   Hebrews 10:38
           b.   Hebrews 11:6

God has called a peculiar people. We need to remember this (Exodus 19:5, Deuteronomy 14:2, Deuteronomy 26:18, Psalms 135:4, Titus 2:14, I Peter 2:9). There will always be those who stay behind.

V. Let's Not Go Back, But Press on to God's High Calling!

  A. Hosea 10:12
  B. Song of Solomon 2:10-13

C. Isaiah 54:2 (I Chronicles 4:9-10)
D. Acts 11:23 – *"...that with purpose of heart they would cleave unto the Lord."*
E. Psalms 63:8 – *"My soul followeth hard after thee..."*
F. Isaiah 55:6 – *"Seek ye the LORD..."*

Lesson 56
GUARDING OURSELVES AGAINST THE ENEMY

I. Job 4:11 – "*The old lion perisheth for lack of prey...*"

A. The devil should not find anything in us to feast on

1. John 14:30 – "*Hereafter I will not talk much with you: for the prince of this world cometh, and hath nothing in me.*"
2. Ephesians 4:21-27 – "*²¹If so be that ye have heard him, and have been taught by him, as the truth is in Jesus: ²²That ye put off concerning the former conversation the old man, which is corrupt according to the deceitful lusts; ²³And be renewed in the spirit of your mind; ²⁴And that ye put on the new man, which after God is created in righteousness and true holiness. ²⁵Wherefore putting away lying, speak every man truth with his neighbour: for we are members one of another. ²⁶Be ye angry, and sin not: let not the sun go down upon your wrath: ²⁷Neither give place to the devil.*"
3. Job 28:7-8 – "*There is a path which no fowl knoweth, and which the vulture's eye hath not seen: The lion's whelps have not trodden it, nor the fierce lion passed by it.*"
4. Isaiah 35:8-10 – "*And an highway shall be there, and a way, and it shall be called The way of holiness; the unclean shall not pass over it; but it shall be for those: the wayfaring men, though fools, shall not err therein. No lion shall be there, nor any ravenous beast shall go up thereon, it shall not be found there; but the redeemed shall walk there: And the ransomed of the LORD shall return, and come to Zion with songs and everlasting joy upon their heads: they shall obtain joy and gladness, and sorrow and sighing shall flee away.*"

B. Scriptural ways to make sure this happens

1. James 4:7 – "*<u>Submit yourselves</u> therefore to God. <u>Resist the devil</u>, and he will flee from you.*"
2. I John 5:18 – "*We know that whosoever is born of God sinneth not; but he that is begotten of God <u>keepeth</u> (Greek – guard) <u>himself</u>, and that wicked one toucheth him not.*"
3. II Samuel 7:10 – "*Moreover I will appoint a place for my people Israel, and will plant them, that they may dwell in a place of their own, and move no more; neither shall the children of wickedness afflict them any more, as beforetime,*" – we need to stay in God's ordained place (local church)
4. Isaiah 54:13-14 – "*And all thy children shall be taught of the LORD; and great shall be the peace of thy children. In righteousness shalt thou be established: thou shalt be far from oppression; for thou shalt not fear: and from terror; for it shall not come near thee.*" – We need to be taught of the Lord and be established in righteousness.
5. I John 3:8 – "*He that committeth sin is of the devil; for the devil sinneth from the beginning. For this purpose the Son of God was manifested, that he might destroy the works of the devil.*" – having a revelation of God's purpose
6. Ephesians 6:10-18 – "*¹⁰Finally, my brethren, be strong in the Lord, and in the power of his might. ¹¹<u>Put on the whole armour of God</u>, that ye may be able to stand against the wiles of the devil. ¹²For we wrestle not against flesh and blood, but against principalities, against powers, against the rulers of the darkness of this world, against spiritual wickedness in high places. ¹³Wherefore take unto you the whole armour of God, that ye may be able to withstand in the evil day, and having done all, to stand. ¹⁴Stand therefore, having your loins girt about with truth, and having on the breastplate of righteousness; ¹⁵And your feet shod with the preparation of the gospel of peace; ¹⁶Above all, taking the shield of faith, wherewith ye shall be able to quench all the fiery darts of the wicked. ¹⁷And take the helmet of salvation, and the sword of the Spirit, which is the word of God: ¹⁸Praying always with all prayer and supplication in the Spirit, and watching thereunto with all perseverance and supplication for all saints;*"

7. II Corinthians 2:11 – *"Lest Satan should get an advantage of us: for <u>we are not ignorant of his devices</u>."*

   a. Luke 4:13 – *"And when the devil had ended all the temptation, he departed from him for a season* (other translation – *"for a more opportune time"*)."

8. Revelation 12:11 – *"And they overcame him by the blood of the Lamb, and by the word of their testimony; and they loved not their lives unto the death."*

9. Ecclesiastes 10:8 – *"He that diggeth a pit shall fall into it; and whoso breaketh an hedge, a serpent shall bite him."*

10. Matthew 12:43-45 – *"When the unclean spirit is gone out of a man, he walketh through dry places, seeking rest, and findeth none. Then he saith, I will return into my house from whence I came out; and when he is come, he findeth it empty, swept, and garnished. Then goeth he, and taketh with himself seven other spirits more wicked than himself, and they enter in and dwell there: and the last state of that man is worse than the first. Even so shall it be also unto this wicked generation."* – We must fill our chambers with the Word of God and His Presence.

11. Proverbs 1:17 – *"Surely in vain the net is spread in the sight of any bird."* – We must stay seated in heavenly places.

12. Luke 22:31-32 – *"And the Lord said, Simon, Simon, behold, Satan hath desired to have you, that he may sift you as wheat: But I have prayed for thee, that thy faith fail not: and when thou art converted, strengthen thy brethren."* – We must always keep our faith alive.

13. II Timothy 2:25-26 – *"In meekness instructing those that oppose themselves; if God peradventure will give them repentance to the acknowledging of the truth; And that they may recover themselves out of the snare of the devil, who are taken captive by him at his will."* – don't oppose ourselves

14. I Peter 5:8-9 – *"Be sober, be vigilant; because your adversary the devil, as a roaring lion, walketh about, seeking whom he may devour: Whom <u>resist stedfast in the faith</u>, knowing that the same afflictions are accomplished in your brethren that are in the world."*

15. Ephesians 4:2, 27 – *"With all lowliness and meekness, with longsuffering, forbearing one another in love…Neither give place to the devil."*

Lesson 57
HANDLING BETRAYAL

I.   Definitions

   A.   Betray

      1.   Dictionary – to give over to an enemy by treachery or fraud; to be unfaithful, to betray a trust.
      2.   Greek – to deliver over to another; it comes from a root word – near, beside.
      3.   Hebrew – to hurt, to shoot, to betray as causing one to fall.

II.   Who Can Betray Us?

   A.   Only those who are truly close to us can hurt us.

      1.   Psalms 41:9 – *"Yea, mine own familiar friend, in whom I trusted, which did eat of my bread, hath lifted up his heel against me."*
      2.   Psalms 55:12-14 – *"For it was not an enemy that reproached me...But it was thou, a man mine equal, my guide, and mine acquaintance. We took   sweet counsel together, and walked unto the house of God in company."*
      3.   Psalms 7:4 – *"...rewarded evil unto him that was at peace with me..."*
      4.   Zechariah 13:6 – *"...I was wounded in the house of my friends."*

   B.   This is why the Scriptures tell us not to trust in people of any kind.

      1.   Jeremiah 17:5-6 – Men and flesh in general

         a.   Psalms 118:8 – *"It is better to trust in the LORD than to put confidence in man."*

      2.   Psalms 146:3 – Princes or leaders

         a.   Psalms 118:9 – *"It is better to trust in the LORD than to put confidence in princes."*

      3.   Jeremiah 9:4-5 – Neighbors and brothers
      4.   Micah 7:5 – Friend, guide, wife (or husband)
      5.   II Corinthians 1:9 – Ourselves

         a.   Jeremiah 17:9 – *"The heart is deceitful above all things, and desperately wicked..."*

III.   What Happens To Us When We Are Betrayed?

   A.   Proverbs 26:22 – *"The words of a talebearer are as wounds, and they go down into the innermost parts of the belly."*
   B.   Proverbs 18:14 – *"...a wounded spirit who can bear?"*
   C.   Job 24:12 – *"...the soul of the wounded crieth out..."* Hebrew for wound – pierced, polluted, to bore, to dissolve
   D.   Matthew 11:2-6 – *"...And blessed is he, whosoever shall not be offended in me."*
   E.   Proverbs 18:19 – *"A brother offended is harder to be won than a strong city..."*

IV.   What Is The Scriptural Way To Handle Betrayal?

   A.   We need to forgive and have an awareness that God has purposely allowed this to happen.

1. Jesus' response

    a. I Corinthians 11:23 – "*...the Lord Jesus the same night in which he was betrayed took bread.*"
    b. Luke 22:47-51 – "*...And Jesus answered and said, Suffer ye thus. And he touched his ear, and healed him.*"
    c. Matthew 26:49-50 – "*...Jesus said unto him, Friend, wherefore art thou come?...*"
    d. John 18:3-11
    e. John 13:1-5 – Washed the disciples' feet

2. Luke 21:16-19 – Us – "*And ye shall be betrayed...In your patience possess ye your souls.*"
3. Hosea 2:5-23

4. Joseph

    a. Genesis 45:1-13
    b. Genesis 50:15-21

5. David

    a. II Samuel 15:2-14
    b. II Samuel 16:5-14

Lesson 58
HOW GOD MOVES

I.   How God Moves, Luke 19:44, Genesis 28:16, John 12:28-30

   A.   Some examples in Scripture how He moves

      1.   Moses, Exodus 1:13-2:11
      2.   Samuel, I Samuel 2:12-18
      3.   John, Luke 3:1-3, Matthew 11:7-11
      4.   Jesus, Isaiah 53:1-3, Luke 2:7
      5.   Day of Pentecost, Acts 2

   B.   People God uses

      1.   I Corinthians 1:26-31
      2.   Ezekiel 44:9-18
      3.   Ecclesiastes 9:14-16
      4.   Luke 16:10-11

   C.   Persecution from other believers – Just because God is moving doesn't mean there won't be persecution

      1.   Genesis 26:17-23 – Striving against Isaac
      2.   I Kings 2:1-9, 13-15 – As we set our hearts to believe God for a move of God, we must not turn back, become embarrassed, or ashamed.
      3.   I Samuel 1:1-12

   D.   There is a price to pay to see God move

      1.   Proverbs 23:23 – *"Buy the truth, and sell it not; also wisdom, and instruction, and understanding."*
      2.   Hebrews 11:13-17, 33-40

   E.   How can we prepare for God moving?

      1.   Understand His timing

         a.   Galatians 4:4 – *"But when the fulness of the time was come, God sent forth his Son, made of a woman, made under the law"*
         b.   Luke 1:20 – *"And, behold, thou shalt be dumb, and not able to speak, until the day that these things shall be performed, because thou believest not my words, which shall be fulfilled in their season."*
         c.   Acts 2:1 – *"And when the day of Pentecost was fully come, they were all with one accord in one place."*

      2.   Travail to bring to birth

         a.   Isaiah 66:8 – *"Who hath heard such a thing? who hath seen such things? Shall the earth be made to bring forth in one day? or shall a nation be born at once? for as soon as Zion travailed, she brought forth her children."*

      3.   Humility

      a.   Psalms 51:17 – *"The sacrifices of God are a broken spirit: a broken and a contrite heart, O God, thou wilt not despise."*

      b.   Isaiah 57:15 – *"For thus saith the high and lofty One that inhabiteth eternity, whose name is Holy; I dwell in the high and holy place, with him also that is of a contrite and humble spirit, to revive the spirit of the humble, and to revive the heart of the contrite ones."*

4.   Keeping a right heart

      a.   Proverbs 22:11 – *"He that loveth pureness of heart, for the grace of his lips the king shall be his friend."*

      b.   Matthew 5:8 – *"Blessed are the pure in heart: for they shall see God."*

5.   True worship

      a.   John 4:23-25 – *"²³But the hour cometh, and now is, when the true worshippers shall worship the Father in spirit and in truth: for the Father seeketh such to worship him. ²⁴God is a Spirit: and they that worship him must worship him in spirit and in truth. ²⁵The woman saith unto him, I know that Messias cometh, which is called Christ: when he is come, he will tell us all things."*

6.   Not seeking things for yourself

      a.   Jeremiah 45:5 – *"And seekest thou great things for thyself? seek them not: for, behold, I will bring evil upon all flesh, saith the LORD: but thy life will I give unto thee for a prey in all places whither thou goest."*

      b.   Psalms 34:10 – *"The young lions do lack, and suffer hunger: but they that seek the LORD shall not want any good thing."*

7.   Be valiant for the truth

      a.   Jeremiah 9:3 – *"And they bend their tongues like their bow for lies: but they are not valiant for the truth upon the earth; for they proceed from evil to evil, and they know not me, saith the LORD."*

8.   Be listening – He will show us things to come

      a.   John 16:13 – *"Howbeit when he, the Spirit of truth, is come, he will guide you into all truth: for he shall not speak of himself; but whatsoever he shall hear, that shall he speak: and he will shew you things to come."*

      b.   Isaiah 42:9 – *"Behold, the former things are come to pass, and new things do I declare: before they spring forth I tell you of them."*

      c.   Isaiah 43:19 – *"Behold, I will do a new thing; now it shall spring forth; shall ye not know it? I will even make a way in the wilderness, and rivers in the desert."*

II.   The Move Is On – God is going to pour out His glory in the last days, will you be ready?

A.   We're in a race

1.   John 1:43 – *"The day following Jesus would go forth into Galilee, and findeth Philip, and saith unto him, Follow me."*

2. Hebrews 12:1 – *"Wherefore seeing we also are compassed about with so great a cloud of witnesses, let us lay aside every weight, and the sin which doth so easily beset us, and let us run with patience the race that is set before us,"*

3. I Corinthians 9:24 – *"Know ye not that they which run in a race run all, but one receiveth the prize? So run, that ye may obtain."*

4. Ecclesiastes 9:11 – *"I returned, and saw under the sun, that the race is not to the swift, nor the battle to the strong, neither yet bread to the wise, nor yet riches to men of understanding, nor yet favour to men of skill; but time and chance happeneth to them all."*

B. We end up having to make a decision – go on or stay

1. Exodus 32:26 – *"Then Moses stood in the gate of the camp, and said, Who is on the LORD's side? let him come unto me. And all the sons of Levi gathered themselves together unto him."*

2. John 6:66-67 – *"⁶⁶From that time many of his disciples went back, and walked no more with him. ⁶⁷Then said Jesus unto the twelve, Will ye also go away?"*

3. Matthew 4:4 – *"But he answered and said, It is written, Man shall not live by bread alone, but by every word that proceedeth out of the mouth of God."*

C. What happens when we don't move on?

1. Jeremiah 48:11 – *"Moab hath been at ease from his youth, and he hath settled on his lees, and hath not been emptied from vessel to vessel, neither hath he gone into captivity: therefore his taste remained in him, and his scent is not changed."*

2. Exodus 16:19-22 – *"¹⁹And Moses said, Let no man leave of it till the morning. ²⁰Notwithstanding they hearkened not unto Moses; but some of them left of it until the morning, and it bred worms, and stank: and Moses was wroth with them. ²¹And they gathered it every morning, every man according to his eating: and when the sun waxed hot, it melted..."*

3. Ecclesiastes 9:8 – *"Let thy garments be always white; and let thy head lack no ointment."*

D. In God's will is divine provision

1. Philippians 4:19 – *"But my God shall supply all your need according to his riches in glory by Christ Jesus."*

2. Matthew 6:33 – *"But seek ye first the kingdom of God, and his righteousness; and all these things shall be added unto you."*

3. I Kings 17:1-17

4. Exodus 16:12-19

E. God doesn't want us to get comfortable

1. Hebrews 11:8-10 – *"⁸By faith Abraham, when he was called to go out into a place which he should after receive for an inheritance, obeyed; and he went out, not knowing whither he went. ⁹By faith he sojourned in the land of promise, as in a strange country, dwelling in tabernacles with Isaac and Jacob, the heirs with him of the same promise: ¹⁰For he looked for a city which hath foundations, whose builder and maker is God."*

2. Ecclesiastes 10:15 – *"The labour of the foolish wearieth every one of them, because he knoweth not how to go to the city."*

F. How do we know when God moves?

1. II Samuel 5:24 – *"And let it be, when thou hearest the sound of a going in the tops of the mulberry trees, that then thou shalt bestir thyself: for then shall the LORD go out before thee, to smite the host of the Philistines."*

2. Exodus 13:20-22 – "*20And they took their journey from Succoth, and encamped in Etham, in the edge of the wilderness. 21And the LORD went before them by day in a pillar of a cloud, to lead them the way; and by night in a pillar of fire, to give them light; to go by day and night: 22He took not away the pillar of the cloud by day, nor the pillar of fire by night, from before the people.*"

3. Word of God

   a. Psalms 119:105 – "*Thy word is a lamp unto my feet, and a light unto my path.*"
   b. Psalms 119:130 – "*The entrance of thy words giveth light; it giveth understanding unto the simple.*"

4. Witness of the Spirit within us

   a. I John 5:10 – "*He that believeth on the Son of God hath the witness in himself: he that believeth not God hath made him a liar; because he believeth not the record that God gave of his Son.*"
   b. Luke 24:32 – "*And they said one to another, Did not our heart burn within us, while he talked with us by the way, and while he opened to us the scriptures?*"
   c. I John 2:20, 27 – "*20But ye have an unction from the Holy One, and ye know all things...27But the anointing which ye have received of him abideth in you, and ye need not that any man teach you: but as the same anointing teacheth you of all things, and is truth, and is no lie, and even as it hath taught you, ye shall abide in him.*"

5. If it comes to pass, Deuteronomy 18:19-22 – "*19And it shall come to pass, that whosoever will not hearken unto my words which he shall speak in my name, I will require it of him. 20But the prophet, which shall presume to speak a word in my name, which I have not commanded him to speak, or that shall speak in the name of other gods, even that prophet shall die. 21And if thou say in thine heart, How shall we know the word which the LORD hath not spoken? 22When a prophet speaketh in the name of the LORD, if the thing follow not, nor come to pass, that is the thing which the LORD hath not spoken, but the prophet hath spoken it presumptuously: thou shalt not be afraid of him.*"

6. Multitude of counselors

   a. Proverbs 11:14 – "*Where no counsel is, the people fall: but in the multitude of counsellers there is safety.*"
   b. Proverbs 24:6 – "*For by wise counsel thou shalt make thy war: and in multitude of counsellers there is safety.*"
   c. Proverbs 15:22 – "*Without counsel purposes are disappointed: but in the multitude of counsellers they are established.*"

G. The Word of the Lord to us

   1. Isaiah 60:1 – "*Arise, shine; for thy light is come, and the glory of the LORD is risen upon thee.*"
   2. Romans 13:11-12 – "*11And that, knowing the time, that now it is high time to awake out of sleep: for now is our salvation nearer than when we believed. 12The night is far spent, the day is at hand: let us therefore cast off the works of darkness, and let us put on the armour of light.*"
   3. Psalms 110:3 – "*Thy people shall be willing in the day of thy power, in the beauties of holiness from the womb of the morning: thou hast the dew of thy youth.*"
   4. Hebrews 10:35-39

Lesson 59
HOLY LAUGHTER

I. Word Definitions

    A. Laughter, Laugh

        1. Hebrew words

            a. *Tsechoq* – laughter; from a root, *tsachaq* – to laugh outright
            b. *Sachaq* – to laugh in pleasure or merriment

        2. Greek word, *gelao* – to laugh as a sign of joy or satisfaction

    B. Joy

        1. Hebrew words

            a. *Simchah* – blithesomeness or glee, from a root, *samach* – to brighten up, to cheer up
            b. *Sasown* – cheerfulness; from a root, *suws* – to be bright, cheerful, glad

        2. Greek word, *chara* – cheerfulness, calm delight; from a root, *chairo* – to be cheerful, calmly happy or well-off

II. Genesis 21:6 – "*And Sarah said, <u>God hath made me to laugh</u>, so that all that hear will laugh with me.*"

    A. God laughs

        1. Psalms 2:4 – "*He that sitteth in the heavens shall laugh: the Lord shall have them in derision.*"
        2. Psalms 37:13 – "*The Lord shall laugh at him: for he seeth that his day is coming.*"
        3. Psalms 59:8 – "*But thou, O LORD, shalt laugh at them; thou shalt have all the heathen in derision.*"
        4. Proverbs 1:26 – "*I also will laugh at your calamity; I will mock when your fear cometh;*"
        5. Zephaniah 3:17 – "*The LORD thy God in the midst of thee is mighty; he will save, he will rejoice over thee with joy; he will rest in his love, he will joy over thee with singing.*"

    B. It is God's will for us to laugh and have joy

        1. Isaiah 65:18-19 – "*But be ye glad and rejoice for ever in that which I create: for, behold, I create Jerusalem a rejoicing, and her people a joy. And I will rejoice in Jerusalem, and joy in my people: and the voice of weeping shall be no more heard in her, nor the voice of crying.*"
        2. Isaiah 35:10 – "*And the ransomed of the LORD shall return, and come to Zion with songs and everlasting joy upon their heads: they shall obtain joy and gladness, and sorrow and sighing shall flee away.*"
        3. John 15:11 – "*These things have I spoken unto you, that my joy might remain in you, and that your joy might be full.*"
        4. John 16:24 – "*Hitherto have ye asked nothing in my name: ask, and ye shall receive, that your joy may be full.*"
        5. Ecclesiastes 8:15 – "*Then I commended mirth, because a man hath no better thing under the sun, than to eat, and to drink, and to be merry: for that shall abide with him of his labour the days of his life, which God giveth him under the sun.*"
        6. Ecclesiastes 9:7 – "*Go thy way, eat thy bread with joy, and drink thy wine with a merry heart; for God now accepteth thy works.*"

7. Ecclesiastes 5:18-19 – "*Behold that which I have seen: it is good and comely for one to eat and to drink, and to enjoy the good of all his labour that he taketh under the sun all the days of his life, which God giveth him: for it is his portion. Every man also to whom God hath given riches and wealth, and hath given him power to eat thereof, and to take his portion, and to rejoice in his labour; this is the gift of God.*"

8. Ecclesiastes 2:24-26

C. Laughter is good for us

1. Proverbs 17:22 – "*A merry heart doeth good like a medicine: but a broken spirit drieth the bones.*"
2. Proverbs 15:13, 15 – "*A merry heart maketh a cheerful countenance: but by sorrow of the heart the spirit is broken...All the days of the afflicted are evil: but he that is of a merry heart hath a continual feast.*"
3. Nehemiah 8:10 – "*Then he said unto them, Go your way, eat the fat, and drink the sweet, and send portions unto them for whom nothing is prepared: for this day is holy unto our Lord: neither be ye sorry; for the joy of the LORD is your strength.*"
4. Galatians 5:22 – "*But the fruit of the Spirit is love, joy, peace, longsuffering, gentleness, goodness, faith,*"

D. God fills us with laughter

1. Psalms 105:43 – "*And he brought forth his people with joy, and his chosen with gladness:*"
2. Psalms 126:1-3 – "*¹When the LORD turned again the captivity of Zion, we were like them that dream. ²Then was our mouth filled with laughter, and our tongue with singing: then said they among the heathen, The LORD hath done great things for them. ³The LORD hath done great things for us; whereof we are glad.*"
3. Job 8:20-21 – "*Behold, God will not cast away a perfect man, neither will he help the evil doers: Till he fill thy mouth with laughing, and thy lips with rejoicing.*"
4. Nehemiah 12:43 – "*Also that day they offered great sacrifices, and rejoiced: for God had made them rejoice with great joy: the wives also and the children rejoiced: so that the joy of Jerusalem was heard even afar off.*"

E. His presence brings it

1. Psalms 16:11 – "*Thou wilt shew me the path of life: in thy presence is fulness of joy; at thy right hand there are pleasures for evermore.*"
2. Psalms 42:7 – "*Deep calleth unto deep at the noise of thy waterspouts: all thy waves and thy billows are gone over me.*"
3. Acts 2:1-19

III. Ecclesiastes 3:4 – "*A time to weep, and a time to laugh; a time to mourn, and a time to dance;*"

A. Principle of laughing in the face of difficulties

1. James 1:2-3 – "*My brethren, count it all joy when ye fall into divers temptations; Knowing this, that the trying of your faith worketh patience.*"
2. Psalms 52:6 – "*The righteous also shall see, and fear, and shall laugh at him:*"
3. Job 5:22 – "*At destruction and famine thou shalt laugh: neither shalt thou be afraid of the beasts of the earth.*"

B. Principle of laughter after sorrow

1. Psalms 30:5, 11 – *"For his anger endureth but a moment; in his favour is life: weeping may endure for a night, but joy cometh in the morning...Thou hast turned for me my mourning into dancing: thou hast put off my sackcloth, and girded me with gladness;"*
2. Psalms 126:5 – *"They that sow in tears shall reap in joy."*
3. Luke 6:21 – *"Blessed are ye that hunger now: for ye shall be filled. Blessed are ye that weep now: for ye shall laugh."*
4. Isaiah 61:3 – *"To appoint unto them that mourn in Zion, to give unto them beauty for ashes, the oil of joy for mourning, the garment of praise for the spirit of heaviness; that they might be called trees of righteousness, the planting of the LORD, that he might be glorified."*
5. Jeremiah 31:10-17

C. A look at God's people and their corporate gatherings

1. Acts 2:1-19
2. Ezra 3:10-13 – *"10And when the builders laid the foundation of the temple of the LORD, they set the priests in their apparel with trumpets, and the Levites the sons of Asaph with cymbals, to praise the LORD, after the ordinance of David king of Israel. 11And they sang together by course in praising and giving thanks unto the LORD; because he is good, for his mercy endureth for ever toward Israel. And all the people shouted with a great shout, when they praised the LORD, because the foundation of the house of the LORD was laid. 12But many of the priests and Levites and chief of the fathers, who were ancient men, that had seen the first house, when the foundation of this house was laid before their eyes, wept with a loud voice; and many shouted aloud for joy: 13So that the people could not discern the noise of the shout of joy from the noise of the weeping of the people: for the people shouted with a loud shout, and the noise was heard afar off."*
3. Nehemiah 12:43 – *"Also that day they offered great sacrifices, and rejoiced: for God had made them rejoice with great joy: the wives also and the children rejoiced: so that the joy of Jerusalem was heard even afar off."*
4. I Chronicles 15:16 – *"And David spake to the chief of the Levites to appoint their brethren to be the singers with instruments of musick, psalteries and harps and cymbals, sounding, by lifting up the voice with joy."*
5. Psalms 149:5 – *"Let the saints be joyful in glory: let them sing aloud upon their beds."*
6. Isaiah 56:7 – *"Even them will I bring to my holy mountain, and make them joyful in my house of prayer: their burnt offerings and their sacrifices shall be accepted upon mine altar; for mine house shall be called an house of prayer for all people."*
7. Psalms 122:1 – *"I was glad when they said unto me, Let us go into the house of the LORD."*
8. Psalms 27:6 – *"And now shall mine head be lifted up above mine enemies round about me: therefore will I offer in his tabernacle sacrifices of joy; I will sing, yea, I will sing praises unto the LORD."*
9. Psalms 42:4 – *"When I remember these things, I pour out my soul in me: for I had gone with the multitude, I went with them to the house of God, with the voice of joy and praise, with a multitude that kept holyday."*
10. Jeremiah 33:7-11
11. Luke 15:23-24, 32 – *"...32It was meet that we should make merry, and be glad: for this thy brother was dead, and is alive again; and was lost, and is found."*

Lesson 60
RADICAL DESIRE

I. Isaiah 40:3-8 – Before His Coming, There Is Preparation

"The voice of him that crieth in the wilderness, Prepare ye the way of the LORD, make straight in the desert a highway for our God. Every valley shall be exalted, and every mountain and hill shall be made low: and the crooked shall be made straight, and the rough places plain: And the glory of the LORD shall be revealed, and all flesh shall see it together: for the mouth of the LORD hath spoken it..."

A. Psalms 63:1-8 – There should be such a Holy zeal and desire, hunger and thirst for God and His presence that nothing else matters – Psalms 27:4, 42:1-2

1. If we want more, we must bring it by our desire.

a. Matthew 11:12 – *"And from the days of John the Baptist until now the kingdom of heaven suffereth violence, and the violent take it by force."*
b. Isaiah 66:8 – *"...for as soon as Zion travailed, she brought forth her children."*

2. There must be tremendous determination. We won't settle for anything less than a move a God.

a. Genesis 32:24-30
b. Matthew 15:21-28
c. Luke 11:5-10
d. Mark 10:46-52

3. We should never be satisfied until we have His presence.

a. Psalms 17:15 – *"As for me, I will behold thy face in righteousness: I shall be satisfied, when I awake, with thy likeness."*
b. Matthew 5:6 – *"Blessed are they which do hunger and thirst after righteousness: for they shall be filled."*
c. Romans 8:19-23

4. Revelation 22:17-20

Lesson 61
SHOUTING UNTO GOD

The Bible is very clear about shouting unto the Lord with thanksgiving. There is the shout of joy, the shout of battle, the shout of praise and worship, and the shout of thanksgiving. The Scriptures say *"The dead praise not the LORD, neither any that go down into silence"* (Psalms 115:17). It also says *"Let every thing that hath breath praise the LORD. Praise ye the LORD"* (Psalms 150:6). We are actually commanded to *"make the voice of his praise to be heard"* (Psalms 66:8). So really there is no excuse for not using shouting as a part of our worship. It is simply the overflow of our hearts giving thanks for His greatness, love, mercy, power, etc. If we can shout at athletic events, then why can't we shout in praise to our God? What we do or don't do should be founded on what the Scriptures say, not on the traditions of men, denominations, etc. If we are going to be people of the Word, then let us obey it and enter into it without fear or doubting. We all don't have to shout the same, but we must at least be willing. Our God is so great who can't help but shout!

I.   Word Definitions for Shout

   A.   Hebrew words

      1.   *Teruw'ah* – clamor, acclamation of joy, a battle cry, loud noise, rejoicing
      2.   *Ruwa* – to split the ears with sound
      3.   *Rinnah* – a creaking or shrill sound, gladness, rejoicing, shout of triumph
      4.   *Ranan* – to creak or emit a stridulous (harsh in sound) sound, shout for joy

   B.   Greek word, *Keleusma* – a cry of incitement, to hail, or command

II. Word Definition for Roar

   A.   Hebrew word, *Sha'ag* – to rumble or moan, to shout mightily, to moo

III. We Should Shout As the Scriptures Declare For Us To

   A.   Scriptures

      1.   Psalms 47:1 – *"...shout unto God with the voice of triumph."*
      2.   Numbers 23:21 – *"He hath not beheld iniquity in Jacob, neither hath he seen perverseness in Israel: the LORD his God is with him, and the shout of a king is among them."*
      3.   Psalms 32:11 – *"Be glad in the LORD, and rejoice, ye righteous: and shout for joy, all ye that are upright in heart."*
      4.   Psalms 35:27 – *"Let them shout for joy, and be glad, that favour my righteous cause: yea, let them say continually, Let the LORD be magnified, which hath pleasure in the prosperity of his servant."*
      5.   Zephaniah 3:14 – *"Sing, O daughter of Zion; shout, O Israel; be glad and rejoice with all the heart, O daughter of Jerusalem."*
      6.   Jeremiah 31:7 – *"For thus saith the LORD; Sing with gladness for Jacob, and shout among the chief of the nations: publish ye, praise ye, and say, O LORD, save thy people, the remnant of Israel."*

IV. Why We Should Shout

   A.   Because Of His Presence

1. I Samuel 4:5 – *"And when the ark of the covenant of the LORD came into the camp, all Israel shouted with a great shout, so that the earth rang again."*
2. II Samuel 6:15 – *"So David and all the house of Israel brought up the ark of the LORD with shouting, and with the sound of the trumpet."*
3. Leviticus 9:24 – *"And there came a fire out from before the LORD, and consumed upon the altar the burnt offering and the fat: which when all the people saw, they shouted, and fell on their faces."*
4. Numbers 23:21 – *"...the LORD his God is with him, and the shout of a king is among them."*

B. For Battle

1. Joshua 6:5, 10, 20 – *"⁵And it shall come to pass, that when they make a long blast with the ram's horn, and when ye hear the sound of the trumpet, all the people shall shout with a great shout; and the wall of the city shall fall down flat, and the people shall ascend up every man straight before him...¹⁰And Joshua had commanded the people, saying, Ye shall not shout, nor make any noise with your voice, neither shall any word proceed out of your mouth, until the day I bid you shout; then shall ye shout...²⁰So the people shouted when the priests blew with the trumpets: and it came to pass, when the people heard the sound of the trumpet, and the people shouted with a great shout, that the wall fell down flat, so that the people went up into the city, every man straight before him, and they took the city."*
2. II Chronicles 13:15 – *"Then the men of Judah gave a shout: and as the men of Judah shouted, it came to pass, that God smote Jeroboam and all Israel before Abijah and Judah."*
3. Amos 1:14 – *"But I will kindle a fire in the wall of Rabbah, and it shall devour the palaces thereof, with shouting in the day of battle, with a tempest in the day of the whirlwind:"*
4. Amos 2:2 – *"But I will send a fire upon Moab, and it shall devour the palaces of Kerioth: and Moab shall die with tumult, with shouting, and with the sound of the trumpet:"*

C. Because of God's Greatness and Goodness

1. Isaiah 12:6 – *"Cry out and shout, thou inhabitant of Zion: for great is the Holy One of Israel in the midst of thee."*
2. Ezra 3:11-13 – *"¹¹And they sang together by course in praising and giving thanks unto the LORD; because he is good, for his mercy endureth for ever toward Israel. And all the people shouted with a great shout, when they praised the LORD, because the foundation of the house of the LORD was laid. ¹²But many of the priests and Levites and chief of the fathers, who were ancient men, that had seen the first house, when the foundation of this house was laid before their eyes, wept with a loud voice; and many shouted aloud for joy: ¹³So that the people could not discern the noise of the shout of joy from the noise of the weeping of the people: for the people shouted with a loud shout, and the noise was heard afar off."*
3. Psalms 5:11 – *"But let all those that put their trust in thee rejoice: let them ever shout for joy, because thou defendest them: let them also that love thy name be joyful in thee."*
4. Psalms 132:9, 16 – *"Let thy priests be clothed with righteousness; and let thy saints shout for joy...I will also clothe her priests with salvation: and her saints shall shout aloud for joy."*
5. Zechariah 9:9 – *"Rejoice greatly, O daughter of Zion; shout, O daughter of Jerusalem: behold, thy King cometh unto thee: he is just, and having salvation; lowly, and riding upon an ass, and upon a colt the foal of an ass."*
6. Proverbs 11:10 – *"When it goeth well with the righteous, the city rejoiceth: and when the wicked perish, there is shouting."*

V. God Himself Shouts

A. Scriptures

1. Psalms 47:5 – *"God is gone up with a shout, the LORD with the sound of a trumpet."*
2. Amos 1:2 – *"And he said, The LORD will roar from Zion, and utter his voice from Jerusalem; and the habitations of the shepherds shall mourn, and the top of Carmel shall wither."*
3. Hosea 11:10 – *"They shall walk after the LORD: he shall roar like a lion: when he shall roar, then the children shall tremble from the west."*
4. Jeremiah 25:30 – *"Therefore prophesy thou against them all these words, and say unto them, The LORD shall roar from on high, and utter his voice from his holy habitation; he shall mightily roar upon his habitation; he shall give a shout, as they that tread the grapes, against all the inhabitants of the earth."*
5. Isaiah 42:13 – *"The LORD shall go forth as a mighty man, he shall stir up jealousy like a man of war: he shall cry, yea, roar; he shall prevail against his enemies."*

Lesson 62
STIRRING UP OURSELVES

I. Stirring Up Ourselves, Isaiah 64:7 – *"And there is none that calleth upon thy name, that stirreth up himself to take hold of thee: for thou hast hid thy face from us, and hast consumed us, because of our iniquities."*

A. God wants people who are stirred up!

1. Exodus 35:21 – *"And they came, every one whose heart stirred him up, and every one whom his spirit made willing, and they brought the LORD's offering to the work of the tabernacle of the congregation, and for all his service, and for the holy garments."*
2. Exodus 36:2 – *"And Moses called Bezaleel and Aholiab, and every wise hearted man, in whose heart the LORD had put wisdom, even every one whose heart stirred him up to come unto the work to do it:"*

B. We're not serving a dead God – we should be alive and full of worship

1. Psalms 115:17 – *"The dead praise not the LORD, neither any that go down into silence."*
2. Psalms 33:3 – *"Sing unto him a new song; play skilfully with a loud noise."*
3. Psalms 98:4 – *"Make a joyful noise unto the LORD, all the earth: make a loud noise, and rejoice, and sing praise."*
4. II Chronicles 20:19 – *"And the Levites, of the children of the Kohathites, and of the children of the Korhites, stood up to praise the LORD God of Israel with a loud voice on high."*
5. Nehemiah 12:43 – *"Also that day they offered great sacrifices, and rejoiced: for God had made them rejoice with great joy: the wives also and the children rejoiced: so that the joy of Jerusalem was heard even afar off."*
6. Psalms 66:8 – *"O bless our God, ye people, and make the voice of his praise to be heard:"*
7. Psalms 30:11-12 – *"11Thou hast turned for me my mourning into dancing: thou hast put off my sackcloth, and girded me with gladness; 12To the end that my glory may sing praise to thee, and not be silent. O LORD my God, I will give thanks unto thee for ever."*

C. How we stayed stirred

1. Galatians 5:1 – *"Stand fast therefore in the liberty wherewith Christ hath made us free, and be not entangled again with the yoke of bondage."* We need to stand fast in our liberty
2. Jude 20 – *"But ye, beloved, building up yourselves on your most holy faith, praying in the Holy Ghost,"* Speaking in tongues keeps us stirred and builds up our faith
3. II Peter 1:13, 31 – *"13Yea, I think it meet, as long as I am in this tabernacle, to stir you up by putting you in remembrance..."* Remembering what God has done
4. Psalms 119:92-93 – *"92Unless thy law had been my delights, I should then have perished in mine affliction. 93I will never forget thy precepts: for with them thou hast quickened me."* – The Word of God keeps us stirred
5. Isaiah 61:3 – *"To appoint unto them that mourn in Zion, to give unto them beauty for ashes, the oil of joy for mourning, the garment of praise for the spirit of heaviness; that they might be called trees of righteousness, the planting of the LORD, that he might be glorified."*
6. Acts 17:16-17 – *"16Now while Paul waited for them at Athens, his spirit was stirred in him, when he saw the city wholly given to idolatry. 17Therefore disputed he in the synagogue with the Jews, and with the devout persons, and in the market daily with them that met with him."* Seeing others in trouble

Lesson 63
WORSHIPPERS

I.   The Call to Worship

    A.   Definitions of worship

        1.   Hebrew – To prostrate, bow down, stoop
        2.   Greek – To prostrate, adore, to kiss, like a dog licking his master's hand

    B.   Man's call from God is to worship

        1.   Genesis 2:7 – Man was formed not called into being. He is of a higher state – Man was created to worship God of his own free will
        2.   Isaiah 43:21 – *"This people have I formed for myself; they shall shew forth my praise."*
        3.   1 Peter 2:9
        4.   Psalms 102:18
        5.   Revelation 5:9-14 – This is what we'll be doing throughout eternity.
        6.   John 4:23 – God is seeking such to worship Him.
        7.   Revelation 4:11 – We were created to worship God.

    C.   A kingdom of priests – God has called forth a priesthood to minister unto Him.

        1.   Exodus 19:6 – *"And ye shall be unto me a kingdom of priests…"*

            a.   I Peter 2:5, 9
            b.   Revelation 1:6
            c.   Revelation 5:10
            d.   Hebrews 13:15 – *"By him therefore let us offer the sacrifice of praise to God continually…"*
            e.   Revelation 20:6

II. Understanding Worship

    A.   John 4:19-24

        1.   Verses 20 and 21 – Building or place have nothing to do with it.
        2.   Verse 22 – *"Ye worship ye know not what…"*

            a.   What is worshipping?

                1)   Psalms 45:11 – *"…for he is thy Lord; and worship thou him."*
                2)   Isaiah 44:6
                3)   Isaiah 57:15
                4)   Psalms 92:8
                5)   Psalms 91:9

        3.   Verse 23 – True worshippers – There is a difference between worshippers and true worshippers explained by the rest of the verse. True worshippers worship in spirit and in truth.

            a.   What does it mean to worship *"…in spirit…"*?

                1)   Spirit of man – Spirit of God

    2)   Why in spirit? Verse 24 – God is a spirit

    3)   The Word says they must.

    4)   Worship should always begin out of a man's spirit.

    5)   Worshipping with the Spirit of God – using all the tools the Spirit has given, such as tongues.

  b.   Worshipping *"...in truth..."*

    1)   Worship biblically – using the Bible as our guideline to worship – *"...thy Word is truth."* (John 17:17)

    2)   To worship in reality – not hypocrisy (what we do must be real to us – not just ritual or form).

III.   What Happens When We Worship?

  A.   God inhabits our worship – He reveals Himself.

    1.   Psalms 22:3 – *"But thou art holy, O thou that inhabitest the praises of Israel."*

    2.   Psalms 76:1 – *"In Judah is God known..."*

    3.   Exodus 34:5-8

    4.   Isaiah 64:5 – *"Thou meetest him that rejoiceth..."*

    5.   James 4:8 – *"Draw nigh to God, and he will draw nigh to you..."*

    6.   II Chronicles 5:11-14

    7.   Ephesians 5:18-19

IV.   Worship Defeats the Enemy

  A.   The devil despises worship because when we worship he is overcome.

    1.   Psalms 8:2, Matthew 21:6 – Praise = strength

    2   Psalms 149:6-9

    3   I Samuel 2:1 – *"...mouth is enlarged over mine enemies; because I rejoice thy salvation."*

    4.   II Samuel 22:4 – *"I will call on the LORD, who is worthy to be praised: so shall I be saved from mine enemies."*

    5.   II Chronicles 20:22 – *"And when they began to sing and to praise, the LORD set ambushments against the children of Ammon, Moab, and mount Seir, which were come against Judah; and they were smitten."*

    6.   Acts 16:25 – *"And at midnight Paul and Silas prayed, and sang praises unto God: and the prisoners heard them."*

    7.   Psalms 68:1 – *"Let God arise, let his enemies be scattered..."*

V.   How Do We Worship?

  A.   Biblical ways to worship

    1.   Psalms 47:1 – Clapping our hands

    2.   Psalms 63:5 – Singing with joyful lips

    3.   Psalms 63:4 – Lifting up of our hands (Psalms 134:2)

    4.   Psalms 95:6 – Bowing and kneeling

    5.   Isaiah 12:6 – Shouting unto the Lord

      a.   Psalms 47:1 – *"...shout unto God with the voice of triumph."*

      b.   II Samuel 6:15 – *"...all the house of Israel brought up the ark of the LORD with shouting..."*

      c.   Ezra 1:11-13
      d.   Psalms 132:9 – "*...let thy saints shout for joy.*"

VI.   Should Worship Be Quiet And Soft?

    A.   Psalms 33:3 – "*Sing unto him a new song; play skilfully with a loud noise.*"
    B.   Psalms 98:4
    C.   II Chronicles 20:19
    D.   II Chronicles 30:21
    E.   Nehemiah 12:43
    F.   Psalms 66:8 – "*O bless our God, ye people, and make the voice of his praise to be heard:*"
    G.   Psalms 30:11

VII.   Prostrate Before the Lord, Job 1:20 – "*Then Job arose, and rent his mantle, and shaved his head, and fell down upon the ground, and worshipped,*"

VIII. Stand Up and Bless the Lord, Nehemiah 9:5 – "*...Stand up and bless the LORD your God for ever and ever: and blessed be thy glorious name, which is exalted above all blessing and praise.*"

IX.   In the Dance – Psalms 149:3 – "*Let them praise his name in the dance...*"

    A.   Exodus 15:20 – "*...all the women went out after her with timbrels and with dances.*"
    B.   II Samuel 6:14 – "*And David danced before the LORD with all his might...*"
    C.   Psalms 30:11 – "*Thou hast turned for me my mourning into dancing...*"
    D.   Luke 15:25 – "*Now his elder son was in the field: and as he came and drew nigh to the house, he heard musick and dancing.*"
    E.   Psalms 150:4 – "*Praise him with the timbrel and dance...*"

X.   Weeping before the Lord, Ezra 3:12 – "*...wept with a loud voice; and many shouted aloud for joy:*"

XI.   With a Song (There Are Three Types of Songs)

    A.   Ephesians 5:18-19 – "*...be filled with the Spirit; Speaking to yourselves in psalms and hymns and spiritual songs, singing and making melody in your heart to the Lord;*"
    B.   Colossians 3:16 – "*...admonishing one another in psalms and hymns and spiritual songs, singing with grace in your hearts to the Lord.*"
    C.   Psalms 28:7 – "*...and with my song will I praise him.*"

    D.   The three types:

        1.   Psalms – These are songs taken from the Bible, Scriptural choruses.
        2.   Hymns – These are songs written about God and His work.
        3.   Spiritual Songs – These are supernatural songs. The Greek word for spiritual means ethereal or supernatural, the Greek word for song is an "ode" or a "chant." So, it is obvious this is singing in a supernatural chant or in the spirit (tongues).

Lesson 64
REVIVAL

I believe if someone is in need of reviving, they are dead either physically, soulishly, or spiritually. The word revive itself gives the impression of having to activate or set something in motion again, to restore to life or consciousness, to bring back, to renew, to return to life, to restore, or to be quickened. It seems that only that which is dead needs reviving. In Christianity, we hear the term "revival" used often to express a series of meetings at a church or religious happening. It doesn't seem to be clear to anyone that for that to happen, the church or people had to have been in a state of deadness. We will see what the Scriptures say about his term and then if we find ourselves in this condition, that is in need of revival, perhaps we will have discovered the way back to life and also to stay in a vibrant state of well being, spirit, soul, and body so that we no longer need to be revived because we are staying and living in God's constant stream of life. In view of the frequent modern use of the term "revive and revival", it is worthy of notice that Paul addressed Timothy in II Timothy 1:6 saying *"I put thee in remembrance that thou stir up the gift of God, which is in thee"*. Perhaps Timothy like us had forgotten or let slip his passion, zeal, and heart for God and His purposes, and like too many, had fallen into a slothful sleep that leads to a spiritual death. May God show us through His holy Word, not only what this term "revive or revival" means, but also reveal to us the way to stay away, alive, fresh, and vibrant in Him by His Word and Spirit, so that we never again need to use the term revival, for the flame of God's Spirit and Word forever and continually burns hot and deep within us.

I.   Word Definitions for "Revive, Revived, Reviving" In Scripture

    A.   Hebrew words

        1.   *Chayah* – to live literally or figuratively, to quicken, to recover, to restore to life, to repair, to nourish up, to preserve alive, to surely be whole

        2.   *Michyah* – preservation of life, sustenance, recover selves; this word is also translated - *preserve life, quick, recover*

    B.   Greek word

        1.   *Anazao* – to recover life literally or figuratively, to live again; this word is also translated – *"is alive again"*

II. Defining the Term Revival in Scripture

    A.   Too often we have need of revival

        1.   Psalms 85:6 – *"Wilt thou not revive us again: that thy people may rejoice in thee?"*

        2.   Isaiah 57:15 – *"For thus saith the high and lofty One that inhabiteth eternity, whose name is Holy; I dwell in the high and holy place, with him also that is of a contrite and humble spirit, to revive the spirit of the humble, and to revive the heart of the contrite ones."*

        3.   Habakkuk 3:2 – *"O LORD, I have heard thy speech, and was afraid: O LORD, revive thy work in the midst of the years, in the midst of the years make known; in wrath remember mercy."*

    B.   This happens to us because of slothfulness and a backing off from our walk in God

        1.   Proverbs 6:10-11 – *"Yet a little sleep, a little slumber, a little folding of the hands to sleep: So shall thy poverty come as one that travelleth, and thy want as an armed man."*

        2.   Nahum 3:18 – *"Thy shepherds slumber, O king of Assyria: thy nobles shall dwell in the dust: thy people is scattered upon the mountains, and no man gathereth them."*

3. Matthew 25:5-12 – "*⁵While the bridegroom tarried, they all slumbered and slept. ⁶And at midnight there was a cry made, Behold, the bridegroom cometh; go ye out to meet him. ⁷Then all those virgins arose, and trimmed their lamps. ⁸And the foolish said unto the wise, Give us of your oil; for our lamps are gone out. ⁹But the wise answered, saying, Not so; lest there be not enough for us and you: but go ye rather to them that sell, and buy for yourselves. ¹⁰And while they went to buy, the bridegroom came; and they that were ready went in with him to the marriage: and the door was shut. ¹¹Afterward came also the other virgins, saying, Lord, Lord, open to us. ¹²But he answered and said, Verily I say unto you, I know you not.*"

4. Proverbs 18:9 – "*He also that is slothful in his work is brother to him that is a great waster.*"
5. Proverbs 21:25 – "*The desire of the slothful killeth him; for his hands refuse to labour.*"
6. Proverbs 12:24 – "*The hand of the diligent shall bear rule: but the slothful shall be under tribute.*"
7. Proverbs 24:30-34 – "*³⁰I went by the field of the slothful, and by the vineyard of the man void of understanding; ³¹And, lo, it was all grown over with thorns, and nettles had covered the face thereof, and the stone wall thereof was broken down. ³²Then I saw, and considered it well: I looked upon it, and received instruction. ³³Yet a little sleep, a little slumber, a little folding of the hands to sleep: ³⁴So shall thy poverty come as one that travelleth; and thy want as an armed man.*"
8. Matthew 25:26-28 – "*His lord answered and said unto him, Thou wicked and slothful servant, thou knewest that I reap where I sowed not, and gather where I have not strawed: Thou oughtest therefore to have put my money to the exchangers, and then at my coming I should have received mine own with usury. Take therefore the talent from him, and give it unto him which hath ten talents.*"
9. Hebrews 6:12 – "*That ye be not slothful, but followers of them who through faith and patience inherit the promises.*"

III. Scriptural Ways to Stay In a Constant State of Revival

A. We must stir ourselves up

1. Exodus 35:21, 26 – "*And they came, every one whose heart stirred him up, and every one whom his spirit made willing, and they brought the LORD's offering to the work of the tabernacle of the congregation, and for all his service, and for the holy garments...And all the women whose heart stirred them up in wisdom spun goats' hair.*"
2. Exodus 36:2 – "*And Moses called Bezaleel and Aholiab, and every wise hearted man, in whose heart the LORD had put wisdom, even every one whose heart stirred him up to come unto the work to do it:*"
3. II Timothy 1:6 – "*Wherefore I put thee in remembrance that thou stir up the gift of God, which is in thee by the putting on of my hands.*"
4. Isaiah 64:7 – "*And there is none that calleth upon thy name, that stirreth up himself to take hold of thee: for thou hast hid thy face from us, and hast consumed us, because of our iniquities.*"
5. Romans 12:11 – "*Not slothful in business; fervent in spirit; serving the Lord;*"

B. We must stay in the Word of God

1. Deuteronomy 8:3 – "*And he humbled thee, and suffered thee to hunger, and fed thee with manna, which thou knewest not, neither did thy fathers know; that he might make thee know that man doth not live by bread only, but by every word that proceedeth out of the mouth of the LORD doth man live.*"
2. Deuteronomy 4:1 – "*Now therefore hearken, O Israel, unto the statutes and unto the judgments, which I teach you, for to do them, that ye may live, and go in and possess the land which the LORD God of your fathers giveth you.*"

3. Psalms 119:25, 40, 50, 77, 93, 116, 154, 159 – "*25My soul cleaveth unto the dust: quicken thou me according to thy word. 40Behold, I have longed after thy precepts: quicken me in thy righteousness. 50This is my comfort in my affliction: for thy word hath quickened me. 77Let thy tender mercies come unto me, that I may live: for thy law is my delight. 93I will never forget thy precepts: for with them thou hast quickened me. 116Uphold me according unto thy word, that I may live: and let me not be ashamed of my hope. 154Plead my cause, and deliver me: quicken me according to thy word. 159Consider how I love thy precepts: quicken me, O LORD, according to thy lovingkindness.*"

4. Proverbs 4:4 – "*He taught me also, and said unto me, Let thine heart retain my words: keep my commandments, and live.*"

5. Proverbs 7:2 – "*Keep my commandments, and live; and my law as the apple of thine eye.*"

6. Isaiah 55:3 – "*Incline your ear, and come unto me: hear, and your soul shall live; and I will make an everlasting covenant with you, even the sure mercies of David.*"

C. We must allow the Holy Spirit to rain continually in our lives

1. Ezekiel 37:3-10

"*3And he said unto me, Son of man, can these bones live? And I answered, O Lord GOD, thou knowest. 4Again he said unto me, Prophesy upon these bones, and say unto them, O ye dry bones, hear the word of the LORD. 5Thus saith the Lord GOD unto these bones; Behold, I will cause breath to enter into you, and ye shall live: 6And I will lay sinews upon you, and will bring up flesh upon you, and cover you with skin, and put breath in you, and ye shall live; and ye shall know that I am the LORD. 7So I prophesied as I was commanded: and as I prophesied, there was a noise, and behold a shaking, and the bones came together, bone to his bone. 8And when I beheld, lo, the sinews and the flesh came up upon them, and the skin covered them above: but there was no breath in them. 9Then said he unto me, Prophesy unto the wind, prophesy, son of man, and say to the wind, Thus saith the Lord GOD; Come from the four winds, O breath, and breathe upon these slain, that they may live. 10So I prophesied as he commanded me, and the breath came into them, and they lived, and stood up upon their feet, an exceeding great army.*"

2. II Kings 13:21 – "*And it came to pass, as they were burying a man, that, behold, they spied a band of men; and they cast the man into the sepulchre of Elisha: and when the man was let down, and touched the bones of Elisha, he revived, and stood up on his feet.*"

3. Ezekiel 47:9 – "*And it shall come to pass, that every thing that liveth, which moveth, whithersoever the rivers shall come, shall live: and there shall be a very great multitude of fish, because these waters shall come thither: for they shall be healed; and every thing shall live whither the river cometh.*"

4. Judges 15:19 – "*But God clave an hollow place that was in the jaw, and there came water thereout; and when he had drunk, his spirit came again, and he revived...*"

5. Jude 20 – "*But ye, beloved, building up yourselves on your most holy faith, praying in the Holy Ghost,*"

D. We must repent

1. Luke 15:20-24 – "*...And the son said unto him, Father, I have sinned against heaven, and in thy sight, and am no more worthy to be called thy son. But the father said to his servants...this my son was dead, and is alive again; he was lost, and is found. And they began to be merry.*"

2. Ezekiel 33:11 – "*Say unto them, As I live, saith the Lord GOD, I have no pleasure in the death of the wicked; but that the wicked turn from his way and live: turn ye, turn ye from your evil ways; for why will ye die, O house of Israel?*"

3. Ezekiel 18:32 – "*For I have no pleasure in the death of him that dieth, saith the Lord GOD: wherefore turn yourselves, and live ye.*"

E. We must make Godly choices

 1. Deuteronomy 30:19 – *"I call heaven and earth to record this day against you, that I have set before you life and death, blessing and cursing: therefore choose life, that both thou and thy seed may live:"*

F. We must wait on God

 1. Job 14:14 – *"If a man die, shall he live again? all the days of my appointed time will I wait, till my change come."*

G. We must stay in faith

 1. Habakkuk 2:4 – *"Behold, his soul which is lifted up is not upright in him: but the just shall live by his faith."*
 2. Hebrews 10:38-39 – *"Now the just shall live by faith: but if any man draw back, my soul shall have no pleasure in him. But we are not of them who draw back unto perdition; but of them that believe to the saving of the soul."*

H. We must stay in His presence

 1. Hosea 14:7 – *"They that dwell under his shadow shall return; they shall revive as the corn, and grow as the vine: the scent thereof shall be as the wine of Lebanon."*
 2. Lamentations 4:20 – *"The breath of our nostrils, the anointed of the LORD, was taken in their pits, of whom we said, Under his shadow we shall live among the heathen."*
 3. Psalms 16:11 – *"Thou wilt shew me the path of life: in thy presence is fulness of joy; at thy right hand there are pleasures for evermore."*
 4. Psalms 27:4 – *"One thing have I desired of the LORD, that will I seek after; that I may dwell in the house of the LORD all the days of my life, to behold the beauty of the LORD, and to inquire in his temple."*

I. We must walk in God's ways

 1. Deuteronomy 5:33 – *"Ye shall walk in all the ways which the LORD your God hath commanded you, that ye may live, and that it may be well with you, and that ye may prolong your days in the land which ye shall possess."*
 2. Deuteronomy 16:20 – *"That which is altogether just shalt thou follow, that thou mayest live, and inherit the land which the LORD thy God giveth thee."*
 3. Proverbs 9:6 – *"Forsake the foolish, and live; and go in the way of understanding."*

J. We must seek God

 1. Psalms 22:26 – *"The meek shall eat and be satisfied: they shall praise the LORD that seek him: your heart shall live for ever."*
 2. Psalms 80:18 – *"So will not we go back from thee: quicken us, and we will call upon thy name."*
 3. Amos 5:4, 6 – *"For thus saith the LORD unto the house of Israel, Seek ye me, and ye shall live...Seek the LORD, and ye shall live..."*

K. We must endure the dealings of God

 1. Hosea 6:1-3 – *"Come, and let us return unto the LORD: for he hath torn, and he will heal us; he hath smitten, and he will bind us up. After two days will he revive us: in the third day he will raise us up, and we shall live in his sight. Then shall we know, if we follow on to know the LORD:*

his going forth is prepared as the morning; and he shall come unto us as the rain, as the latter and former rain unto the earth."

2. Psalms 138:7 – *"Though I walk in the midst of trouble, thou wilt revive me: thou shalt stretch forth thine hand against the wrath of mine enemies, and thy right hand shall save me."*

3. Psalms 71:20 – *"Thou, which hast shewed me great and sore troubles, shalt quicken me again, and shalt bring me up again from the depths of the earth."*

4. Deuteronomy 32:39 – *"See now that I, even I, am he, and there is no god with me: I kill, and I make alive; I wound, and I heal: neither is there any that can deliver out of my hand."*

5. I Samuel 2:6 – *"The LORD killeth, and maketh alive: he bringeth down to the grave, and bringeth up."*

6. The life of Joseph

   a. Genesis 45:5 – *"Now therefore be not grieved, nor angry with yourselves, that ye sold me hither: for God did send me before you to preserve life."*

   b. Genesis 50:20 – *"But as for you, ye thought evil against me; but God meant it unto good, to bring to pass, as it is this day, to save much people alive."*

L. We must experience resurrection power

1. I Kings 17:22 – *"And the LORD heard the voice of Elijah; and the soul of the child came into him again, and he revived."* (II Kings 8:1)

2. Isaiah 26:19 – *"Thy dead men shall live, together with my dead body shall they arise. Awake and sing, ye that dwell in dust: for thy dew is as the dew of herbs, and the earth shall cast out the dead."*

3. Ezekiel 16:6 – *"And when I passed by thee, and saw thee polluted in thine own blood, I said unto thee when thou wast in thy blood, Live; yea, I said unto thee when thou wast in thy blood, Live."*

Lesson 65
SATAN HAS BEEN DEFEATED

I. Corresponding Scriptures

   A. Colossians 2:15 – *"And having spoiled principalities and powers, he made a shew of them openly, triumphing over them in it."* – Spoiled in Greek- to divest wholly oneself; It comes from a root word that means – to undress.

   B. Hebrews 2:14 – *"Forasmuch then as the children are partakers of flesh and blood, he also himself likewise took part of the same; that through death he might destroy him that had the power of death, that is, the devil."* – Destroy in Greek – to disannul, make inactive or useless

   C. I John 3:8 – *"He that committeth sin is of the devil; for the devil sinneth from the beginning. For this purpose the Son of God was manifested, that he might destroy the works of the devil."*

   1. Destroy in Greek – to loosen, breakup, dissolve or melt
   2. Jesus

      a. Matthew 28:18 – *"And Jesus came and spake unto them, saying, All power is given unto me in heaven and in earth."*
      b. Revelation 1:18 – *"I am he that liveth, and was dead; and, behold, I am alive for evermore, Amen; and have the keys of hell and of death."*
      c. Revelation 5:1-8 – *"...⁵And one of the elders saith unto me, Weep not: behold, the Lion of the tribe of Juda, the Root of David, hath prevailed to open the book, and to loose the seven seals thereof..."*

   D. Romans 16:20 – *"And the God of peace shall bruise Satan under your feet shortly. The grace of our Lord Jesus Christ be with you. Amen."*

   1. Bruise in Greek – to crush completely, to shatter, to break in pieces or broken to shivers
   2. Genesis 3:15 – *"And I will put enmity between thee and the woman, and between thy seed and her seed; it shall bruise thy head, and thou shalt bruise his heel."*

   E. Nahum 1:13 – *"For now will I break his yoke from off thee, and will burst thy bonds in sunder."*

   1. Isaiah 10:27 – *"And it shall come to pass in that day, that his burden shall be taken away from off thy shoulder, and his yoke from off thy neck, and the yoke shall be destroyed because of the anointing."*

   F. Colossians 1:13 – *"Who hath delivered us from the power of darkness, and hath translated us into the kingdom of his dear Son."*

   1. Ephesians 6:10-18
   2. I Peter 2:9 – *"But ye are a chosen generation, a royal priesthood, an holy nation, a peculiar people; that ye should shew forth the praises of him who hath called you out of darkness into his marvellous light:"*

   G. Deuteronomy 33:27 – *"The eternal God is thy refuge, and underneath are the everlasting arms: and he shall thrust out the enemy from before thee; and shall say, Destroy them."*

   1. Deuteronomy 9:1-3 – *"Hear, O Israel: Thou art to pass over Jordan this day, to go in to possess nations greater and mightier than thyself, cities great and fenced up to heaven, A people great and tall, the children of the Anakims, whom thou knowest, and of whom thou hast heard say, Who can stand before the children of Anak! Understand therefore this day,*

that the LORD thy God is he which goeth over before thee; as a consuming fire he shall destroy them, and he shall bring them down before thy face: so shalt thou drive them out, and destroy them quickly, as the LORD hath said unto thee."

    a.   Jordan – going down, descending

    b.   Anakims – giants

H.   Esther 7:4-10

    1.   Haman – Hebrew = alone, solitary, a rioter, the rager (a type of Satan)

I.   Job 4:11 – *"The old lion perisheth for lack of prey, and the stout lion's whelps are scattered abroad."*

    1.   Ephesians 4:26-27 – *"Be ye angry, and sin not: let not the sun go down upon your wrath: Neither give place to the devil."*

    2.   Revelation 12:7-11 - *"...And they overcame him by the blood of the Lamb, and by the word of their testimony; and they loved not their lives unto the death."*

    3.   Revelation 15:2 – *"And I saw as it were a sea of glass mingled with fire: and them that had gotten the victory over the beast, and over his image, and over his mark, and over the number of his name, stand on the sea of glass, having the harps of God."*

    4.   James 4:7 – *"Submit yourselves therefore to God. Resist the devil, and he will flee from you."*

    5.   Luke 10:19 – *"Behold, I give unto you power to tread on serpents and scorpions, and over all the power of the enemy: and nothing shall by any means hurt you."*

    6.   Mark 16:17 – *"And these signs shall follow them that believe; In my name shall they cast out devils; they shall speak with new tongues;"*

    7.   1 John 5:18-20 – *"We know that whosoever is born of God sinneth not; but he that is begotten of God keepeth himself, and that wicked one toucheth him not"*

    8.   2 Corinthians 10:3-5 – *"For though we walk in the flesh, we do not war after the flesh: (For the weapons of our warfare are not carnal, but mighty through God to the pulling down of strong holds;) Casting down imaginations, and every high thing that exalteth itself against the knowledge of God, and bringing into captivity every thought to the obedience of Christ;"*

    9.   1 Peter 5:8-9 – *"Be sober, be vigilant; because your adversary the devil, as a roaring lion, walketh about, seeking whom he may devour: Whom resist stedfast in the faith,..."*

    10.   Psalms 8:2 – *"Out of the mouth of babes and sucklings hast thou ordained strength because of thine enemies, that thou mightest still the enemy and the avenger."* (Mt.21:16)

    11.   Psalms 17:4 – *"Concerning the works of men, by the word of thy lips I have kept me from the paths of the destroyer."*

J.   Acts 10:38 – *"How God anointed Jesus of Nazareth with the Holy Ghost and with power: who went about doing good, and healing all that were oppressed of the devil; for God was with him."*

K.   Romans 8:37-39 – *"Nay, in all these things we are more than conquerors through him that loved us. For I am persuaded, that neither death, nor life, nor angels, nor principalities, nor powers, nor things present, nor things to come, Nor height, nor depth, nor any other creature, shall be able to separate us from the love of God, which is in Christ Jesus our Lord."*

Lesson 66
RESPONDING TO SUFFERING

I. A Look at What the Scriptures Declare – Isaiah 48:10 – "*...I have chosen thee in the furnace affliction.*"

   A. Examples

      1. Job 1:6-19 – Job's calamites; Job 1:20-22 – Job's response

         a. Rent his mantle – his righteousness could only come from God
         b. Shaved his head – no covering other than the Lord
         c. Fell down on the ground – Submission to the will of God
         d. And worshipped – honoring God in spite of his circumstances
         e. The Lord gave and then took away, yet blessed be the name (character) of the Lord

      2. Job 2:1-9 – Job's calamites; Job 2:10 – Job's response

         a. He rebuked his wife
         b. He knew God controled the interplay of good and evil

      3. II Samuel 11-12:1-9 – David's calamites; II Samuel 12:20 – David's response

         a. Arose from the earth – arose from the flesh
         b. Washed – applied the blood
         c. Anointed himself – refilled with the Holy Spirit
         d. Changed apparel – put on God's righteousness
         e. Came to the house of the Lord – went to church
         f. Worshipped – honoring God in spite of his circumstances

      4. Acts 16:16-24 – Paul's calamites; Acts 16:25-32 – Paul's response

         a. Midnight – darkest hour
         b. Prayed – sought God and didn't complain
         c. Sang praises – worshipped in spite of his circumstance
         d. Other prisoners heard him – Paul's testimony in his affliction brought salvation

      5. Genesis 37-50 – Joseph's calamities; Genesis 50:20 – Joseph's response

         a. Acknowledged God did it
         b. Joseph was just a vessel to save not only his brothers, but the then known world

   B. This is the way God works

      1. Hosea 6:1-3 – "*Come, and let us return unto the LORD: for he hath torn, and he will heal us; he hath smitten, and he will bind us up. After two days will he revive us: in the third day he will raise us up, and we shall live in his sight. Then shall we know, if we follow on to know the LORD: his going forth is prepared as the morning; and he shall come unto us as the rain, as the latter and former rain unto the earth.*"

      2. Job 5:17-20 – "*Behold, happy is the man whom God correcteth: therefore despise not thou the chastening of the Almighty: For he maketh sore, and bindeth up: he woundeth, and his hands make whole. He shall deliver thee in six troubles: yea, in seven there shall no evil touch thee.In famine he shall redeem thee from death: and in war from the power of the sword.*"

3. I Samuel 2:6-8 – *"The LORD killeth, and maketh alive: he bringeth down to the grave, and bringeth up. The LORD maketh poor, and maketh rich: he bringeth low, and lifteth up. He raiseth up the poor out of the dust, and lifteth up the beggar from the dunghill, to set them among princes, and to make them inherit the throne of glory: for the pillars of the earth are the LORD's, and he hath set the world upon them."*

4. Isaiah 45:7 – *"I form the light, and create darkness: I make peace, and create evil: I the LORD do all these things."*

5. Romans 11:22 – *"Behold therefore the goodness and severity of God: on them which fell, severity; but toward thee, goodness, if thou continue in his goodness: otherwise thou also shalt be cut off."*

6. Ecclesiastes 7:14 – *"In the day of prosperity be joyful, but in the day of adversity consider: God also hath set the one over against the other, to the end that man should find nothing after him."*

7. I Peter 5:10 – *"But the God of all grace, who hath called us unto his eternal glory by Christ Jesus, after that ye have suffered a while, make you perfect, stablish, strengthen, settle you."*

8. Song of Solomon 4:16 – *"Awake, O north wind; and come, thou south; blow upon my garden, that the spices thereof may flow out. Let my beloved come into his garden, and eat his pleasant fruits."*

9. Genesis 8:22 – *"While the earth remaineth, seedtime and harvest, and cold and heat, and summer and winter, and day and night shall not cease."*

10. Jeremiah 1:10 – *"See, I have this day set thee over the nations and over the kingdoms, to root out, and to pull down, and to destroy, and to throw down, to build, and to plant."*

11. Song of Solomon 2:6 – *"His left hand is under my head, and his right hand doth embrace me."*

12. Ecclesiastes 3:3-4 – *"A time to kill, and a time to heal; a time to break down, and a time to build up; A time to weep, and a time to laugh; a time to mourn, and a time to dance;"*

13. Luke 24:50 – *"And he led them out as far as to Bethany, and he lifted up his hands, and blessed them."*

14. Psalms 66:10-12 – *"For thou, O God, hast proved us: thou hast tried us, as silver is tried. Thou broughtest us into the net; thou laidst affliction upon our loins. Thou hast caused men to ride over our heads; we went through fire and through water: but thou broughtest us out into a wealthy place."*

15. Job 14:7-9 – *"For there is hope of a tree, if it be cut down, that it will sprout again, and that the tender branch thereof will not cease. Though the root thereof wax old in the earth, and the stock thereof die in the ground; Yet through the scent of water it will bud, and bring forth boughs like a plant."*

16. II Timothy 2:11-12 – *"It is a faithful saying: For if we be dead with him, we shall also live with him: If we suffer, we shall also reign with him: if we deny him, he also will deny us:"*

17. John 12:24 – *"Verily, verily, I say unto you, Except a corn of wheat fall into the ground and die, it abideth alone: but if it die, it bringeth forth much fruit."*

18. Psalms 71:20-21 – *"Thou, which hast shewed me great and sore troubles, shalt quicken me again, and shalt bring me up again from the depths of the earth. Thou shalt increase my greatness, and comfort me on every side."*

19. Philippians 3:9-12 – *"And be found in him, not having mine own righteousness, which is of the law, but that which is through the faith of Christ, the righteousness which is of God by faith: That I may know him, and the power of his resurrection, and the fellowship of his sufferings, being made conformable unto his death; If by any means I might attain unto the resurrection of the dead. Not as though I had already attained, either were already perfect: but I follow after, if that I may apprehend that for which also I am apprehended of Christ Jesus."*

20. Romans 8:28 – *"And we know that all things work together for good to them that love God, to them who are the called according to his purpose."*

C.   What suffering ultimately leads to

1. Romans 8:18 – "*For I reckon that the sufferings of this present time are not worthy to be compared with the glory which shall be revealed in us.*"
2. II Corinthians 4:17 – "*For our light affliction, which is but for a moment, worketh for us a far more exceeding and eternal weight of glory;*"
3. Luke 24:26 – "*Ought not Christ to have suffered these things, and to enter into his glory?*"
4. Job 23:10 – "*But he knoweth the way that I take: when he hath tried me, I shall come forth as gold.*"
5. James 1:2-4 – "*My brethren, count it all joy when ye fall into divers temptations; Knowing this, that the trying of your faith worketh patience. But let patience have her perfect work, that ye may be perfect and entire, wanting nothing.*"

Lesson 67
SCRIPTURAL HAPPINESS

I. Dictionary Definitions

A. *"Happiness"*, (a pronouncing happy, a declaring blessing)

1. Translations

Happiness and blessedness are synonyms in English Semantics. The Greek word *makarismos* is translated into one or the other, (happiness or blessedness) depending on the translator's preference. The word is used only three times in the New Testament, by Paul in Romans 4:6, 9 and Galatians 4:15. It is not translated, "happiness" in either the Revised Standard Version or the King James Version, but in New English Bible it is translated "happiness" in Romans and "happy" in Galatians. Phillips translates it "happy state" (Romans 4:6), "happiness" (Romans 4:9), and "that fine spirit" (Galatians 4:15). In the King James Version it is translated "blessedness" in all three instances. In the Revised Standard Version it is "blessing" in the Roman Reference, and "the satisfaction you felt" in the Galatians reference. Consequently, the Biblical concept of happiness may be derived from these translations of the word *makarismos*.

2. Applications

Two related ideas are seen in Paul's use of this Greek word. In the first instance, Paul describes happiness as the state of the just. He said, *"In the same sense David speaks of the happiness of the man whom God 'counts' as just … 'Happy are they', he says, 'whose lawless deeds are forgiven…happy is the man whose sins the Lord does not count against him'"* (Romans 4:6-8 New English Bible). Nor is being a Jew a sole requisite for "this happiness," as seen in Abraham's righteousness by faith (Romans 4:9). The other use of "happiness" is that of an emotional experience of delight or joy in the presence of a person loved, as the Galatians' happiness in having Paul with them (Galatians 4:15). BIBLIOGRAPHY, E. S. Jones, Abundant Living (1942), 331; E. V. Pierce, the Supreme Beatitude (1947), 13-27. G. B. Funderburk

B. Word Definitions

The words *happy, happiness, bless* and *blessedness* are the same Hebrew and Greek words, just translated differently. We will look at all of the correct Hebrew and Greek words, translated differently so that you will know which ones are actually the same.

1. We will be looking in the Scriptures: Happiness, Joy and Laughter.
2. Why? So we can see what God's will really is for our lives, according to the Scriptures.
3. What brings true happiness? Joy? Laughter in our lives?
4. There are 32 Biblical causes for happiness, and we will look at them all. Thirty-two is the number in the Bible that means **covenant**.
5. We will define how we can be happy, why we <u>should</u> be happy, and hopefully put an end to depression, oppression and sorrow in our lives.
6. Let's put happiness on the board, and define it as we look at this first lesson. As we see what each word means and its accompanying translations, we can know then what the Bible means when it speaks of happiness.

7. What does happiness mean?

   a. Happiness and blessed are the same Greek word and many of the Old Testament words for blessed mean happiness.

      1) Blessed

2) Happy state
3) That fine spirit
4) The state of the just
5) Emotional experience, delight or joy in the presence of a person loved
6) Pronounced happy
7) Declared blessed
8) Prosperity
9) To be straight, to be level
10) To be right
11) To go forward
12) To be honest
13) Supremely blessed
14) Fortunate
15) Well off
16) Beautification
17) A declaration of blessing
18) To pronounce fortunate or call blessed.

    b.   Hebrew Words:

1) *Escher* – happiness, how happy, blessed. Twenty-six occurrences of this word appear in the book of the Psalms, and eight in Proverbs. It connotes the state of prosperity or happiness, when a superior bestows his favor or blessing on one. In most passages the one bestowing the favor is God Himself. This word comes from a root word "*ashar*" which means – to be straight, to be level, to be right, to go forward, to be honest, and to prosper.

    c.   Greek Words:

1) *Makarios* – supremely blessed, fortunate, well off, happy. This word is used in the beatitudes of Matthew 5 and Luke 6. It is especially frequent in the Book of Luke and is found seven times in Revelation.
2) *Makarismos* – beautification, good fortune, a declaration of blessing. It comes from a root word – *Makariso* – to pronounce or esteem fortunate, to call blessed, to count happy. It also comes from a root that means – large, lengthy.

II.   Understanding Happiness According to the Scriptures.

   A.   God is a happy God.

      1.   Psalms 72:17
      2.   I Timothy 1:11
      3.   I Timothy 6:15

      4.   God's nature is a happy one

         a.   He laughs

            1)   Psalms 2:4
            2)   Psalms 37:13
            3)   Psalms 59:8

      5.   He has joy

      a. Nehemiah 8:10
      b. Nehemiah 12:43
      c. Psalms 16:11
      d. Psalms 48:2
      e. Isaiah 61:3
      f. Isaiah 65:19
      g. Psalms 89:15
      h. John 17:13, John 15:11
      i. Zephaniah 3:17

6. Psalms 45.7
7. God is merry – Luke 15:32, 7&10
8. Jeremiah 33:11

B. Happiness is a result of our covenant with God.

  1. Deuteronomy 33:29

      a. Happy art thou Israel
      b. Who is like unto thee?
      c. People saved by the Lord
      d. The shield of they help
      e. Sword of thy Excellency
      f. Your enemies shall be found liars
      g. Thou shalt tread upon their high places

C. Look at what we have as a result of our covenant with God

  1. Defining these spiritually

      a. Because of God's grace, we have become a happy people, not a sad people.

          1) Isaiah 61:1-3
          2) Jeremiah 31:10-14
          3) Isaiah 51:11
          4) Isaiah 44:21-24
          5) Isaiah 43:1-21
          6) Psalms 107:1-22
          7) Isaiah 49:13-17
          8) Isaiah 54:1-15

      b. Happy are the people whose **God is the Lord!** – Psalms 144:9-15

          1) Deuteronomy 4:29-39
          2) Deuteronomy 32:36-43
          3) II Samuel 22:31-51
          4) Isaiah 45:5-13
          5) Revelation 4:6-11
          6) Revelation 11:15-18
          7) Revelation 15:1-6
          8) John 20:24-31
          9) John 14:1-14

10) Psalms 68:19
11) Psalms 103:1-14

c. We are happy now because of our relationship with God. He has become our hope and our refuge. – Psalms 146:5

1) He is our help and we can surely hope in Him.
2) Psalms 33:18-22
3) Psalms 42:5
4) Psalms 46:1-11
5) Isaiah 41:10-20
6) Hebrews 13:6
7) Psalms 116:1-9

d. We are a blessed people because we proclaim Jesus as our Lord and we are the people whom He has chosen for His own inheritance. (Psalms 33:1) We are His chosen ones and nothing can compare to knowing we each are one of His chosen.

1) We are his chosen
2) Revelation 17:14
3) I Peter 2:4, 9
4) John 15:16, 19
5) I Corinthians 1:27-28
6) Psalms 132:13-18

Lesson 68
SECRET SIN

I.   God Wants to Deliver Us from Secret Sin

A.   We do not live unto ourselves.

No Christian has been created by God to live alone, to be separated from God's people. On the contrary, in the last days, we are to be gathering together more and more. Everything we do literally affects those around us. God is delivering us from the secret hidden things in our life; because the longer we hang onto these it not only hinders us but those that God has joined us to. We must confess and forsake the hidden things in our life.

1.   In these last days God is drawing us together in Him.

a.   Ephesians 1:10 – *"That in the dispensation of the fulness of times he might gather together in one all things in Christ..."*
b.   Isaiah 2:1-5
c.   Isaiah 60:1-5 – He is gathering us into one in unity unto Him to glorify Him. As we come together, His purposes will be finally carried out in the earth.

d.   Gathered unto Him

1)   Song of Solomon 5:16
2)   Genesis 49:10 – *"...unto him shall the gathering of the people be."*
3)   John 12:32 – *"And I, if I be lifted up from the earth, will draw all men unto me."*

e.   Example of the early church

1)   Acts 2:44
2)   Acts 4:32

f.   John 17:20-23 – In this hour we are not to be doing our own thing. We need to be concerned with what God is doing and He is gathering His people together in Him.

2.   There are some who don't want to come together. We need to ask, why?

a.   Hebrews 10:24-27 – We are not to forsake assembling together. There is a reason people don't, and the answer is simple – hidden sins (either outward or of the heart). Some try to use the old excuse about everybody's a hypocrite, but that's unscriptural.
b.   Psalms 75:2 (I John 4:20-21) – When we receive the congregation, our brothers, regardless of their condition, we judge uprightly. The truth is, if someone is on the out most of the time (there are sometimes when God will require us to go outside the camp) it's because of something in them, rather than others.

3.   The reason is secret sin

a.   I John 1:7-10 – When we are walking in the light, it's no problem fellowshipping with others. It's only when I have transgressed from the light and haven't repented that I don't seek the fellowship of my brothers and sisters. The reason is simply that darkness cannot fellowship with light because if it stays there long enough, it is going to get exposed.
b.   John 3:19-21

    c.   Isaiah 6:1, 5 – When we come into God's presence, His light, we will either be repenting or rejoicing. Isaiah said, *"Woe is me."*

    d.   Genesis 3:8 (Job 31:33 – *"If I covered my transgressions as Adam, by hiding mine iniquity in my bosom."*) – Here we see Adam and Eve hiding away, not fellowshipping because of secret sin.

B.   Secret sin and its effects

   1.   Secret sins – there are secret things in the lives of God's people. This is obvious and the Scriptures bear it out.

      a.   Psalms 19:12 – *"...cleanse thou me from secret faults."*

      b.   Psalms 90:8 – *"...our secret sins..."*

      c.   Obadiah 6 – *"How are the things of Esau searched out! how are his hidden things sought up!"*

      d.   II Kings 17:9 – *"And the children of Israel did secretly those things that were not right against the LORD their God..."*

      e.   Ezekiel 8:12 – We think of these things as secret but the Lord sees them. The things that we do in the dark, in the chambers of our imagery (minds), God sees them.

      f.   Proverbs 9:16-18 – *"...Stolen waters are sweet, and bread eaten in secret is pleasant..."*

      g.   II Corinthians 4:2 – *"...the hidden things of dishonesty..."*

      h.   Job 24:13-17

      i.   Isaiah 3:16-17 – *"Moreover the Lord saith, Because the daughters of Zion are haughty, and walk with stretched forth necks and wanton eyes, walking and mincing as they go, and making a tinkling with their feet: Therefore the Lord will smite with a scab the crown of the head of the daughters of Zion, and the Lord will discover their secret parts."*

   2.   How it affects the whole body

      a.   I Chronicles 21:1, 7, 8, 14 – Here, David foolishly numbers Israel. It was his sin, but notice, the affect on the rest of the body. Seventy thousand Israelites died.

      b.   Joshua 7:1-16 – Notice when one man sins, God says (verses 1-11) Israel has sinned. Our sin, no matter how little we think it is, is so important because it can be the very thing holding back the rest of God's people; or it may be the reason why some have fallen into the hand of the enemy. In this case, Achan's sin caused thirty-six people along with Achan's family who were stoned with him to die. What a waste, when all we need do is repent.

      c.   Ezra 9, 10:1-12

      d.   I Corinthians 5:6 – The church of Jesus Christ is only as strong corporately as it is individually.

C.   God will, and must expose it

   1.   God sees everything

      a.   Proverbs 15:3 – *"The eyes of the Lord are in every place, beholding the evil and the good."*

      b.   Psalms 90:8 – *"Thou hast set our iniquities before thee, our secret sins in the light of thy countenance."*

      c.   Hebrews 4:13 – *"Neither is there any creature that is not manifest in his sight: but all things are naked and opened unto the eyes of him with whom we have to do."*

      d.   Jeremiah 16:17 – *"For mine eyes are upon all their ways: they are not hid from my face, neither is their iniquity hid from mine eyes."*

e. Job 34:21-22 – *"For his eyes are upon the ways of man, and he seeth all his goings. There is no darkness, nor shadow of death, where the workers of iniquity may hide themselves."*

f. Ezekiel 11:5 – *"...Thus saith the Lord...O house of Israel: for I know the things that come into your mind, every one of them."*

g. Hosea 7:2 – *"And they consider not in their hearts that I remember all their wickedness: now their own doings have beset them about; they are before my face."*

h. Jeremiah 23:24 – *"Can any hide himself in secret places that I shall not see him? Saith the Lord. Do not I fill heaven and earth? saith the Lord."*

i. Psalms 139:1-2 – *"O LORD, thou hast searched me, and known me. Thou knowest my downsitting and mine uprising, thou understandest my thought afar off."*

2. He must do this before we destroy ourselves and others.

   a. Acts 5:1-5
   b. II Samuel 12:12
   c. Ecclesiastes 12:14
   d. I Corinthians 4:5 – God will bring to light the hidden things of darkness; every secret thing will be brought into judgment.
   e. Numbers 32:23 – Be <u>sure</u> your sin will find you out. If we would repent and judge ourselves, we would not be exposed or judged openly.
   f. Luke 12:2 – If we think we can stay hidden and don't repent, God will uncover us.
   g. Proverbs 26:23-26
   h. Acts 8:18-24 – Simon

3. Even if God doesn't expose it in this life, He will in the next.

   a. I Corinthians 5:10
   b. Ecclesiastes 8:11-13
   c. I Timothy 5:24-25

D. What should we do? Repent and go on with God

1. I Thessalonians 5:4-9 – *"...But let us, who are of the day, be sober, putting on the breastplate of faith and love; and for an helmet, the hope of salvation..."*

   a. Mark 13:34-37
   b. Luke 21:36

2. Hebrews 10:25 – *"Not forsaking the assembling of ourselves together, as the manner of some is..."*

3. Proverbs 28:13 – *"He that covereth his sins shall not prosper: but whoso confesseth and forsaketh them shall have mercy."* – Don't cover sin

4. II Corinthians 7:1 – *"Having therefore these promises, dearly beloved, <u>let us cleanse ourselves</u> from all filthiness of the flesh and spirit..."*

5. Psalms 119:9-11

6. Romans 13:11-12 – *"...The night is far spent, the day is at hand: let us therefore <u>cast off the works of darkness</u>, and let us put on the armour of light."*

7. II Corinthians 4:2 – *"But have renounced the hidden things of dishonesty, not walking in craftiness, nor handling the word of God deceitfully; but by manifestation of the truth commending ourselves to every man's conscience in the sight of God."* – Renounce hidden things

8. Ephesians 5:1-16

9. Psalms 19:12, 14

       10. I John 1:7
       11. I John 3:3
       12. Romans 12:1-2
       13. Psalms 139:23-24 – Search me

II.   We Must Trust in the Grace, Mercy & Forgiveness of God

    A.   His Grace is Always Sufficient

        1.   We can find grace in His loving eyes

           a.   Genesis 6:6 – Noah found grace in the eyes
           b.   Exodus 33:12 – Moses found grace in His sight
           c.   Ruth 2:10 – Ruth found grace in Boaz's eyes

        2.   The Lord gives grace

           a.   Ps 84:11 – "...*the Lord will give grace and glory...*"
           b.   Zechariah 12:10 – grace poured upon the inhabitants of Jerusalem
           c.   Acts 20:32 – Ephesus elders commended to God and the word of His grace.
           d.   Romans 5:2
           e.   II Corinthians 12:9 – "...*My grace is sufficient for thee...*"
           f.   Ephesians 2:5 – "...*by grace ye are saved.*"
           g.   Ephesians 4:7 – "*But unto every one of us is given grace ...*"
           h.   I Timothy 1:14 – "*And the grace of our Lord was exceeding   abundant...*"
           i.   I Peter 5:5 – "...*giveth grace to the humble.*"
           j.   I Peter 1:13 – "...*the grace that is to be brought unto you at the revelation of Jesus Christ*"
           k.   James 4:6 – "...*He giveth more grace....*"
           l.   Hebrews 12:28 – "...*let us have grace, whereby we may serve God acceptably...*"
           m.   John 1:16 – "*And of his fulness have all we received, and grace for grace.*"

        3.   Other great truths about God's grace toward us

           a.   II Peter 3:18 – we are to grow in grace
           b.   II Peter 1:2
           c.   I Peter 5:12 – we stand in grace (Romans 5:15)
           d.   Hebrews 13:9 – "...*For it is a good thing that the heart be established with grace...*"
           e.   Hebrews 12:15 – "*Looking diligently lest any man fail of the grace of God...*"
           f.   Hebrews 4:16 – "*Let us therefore come boldly unto the throne of grace, that we may obtain mercy, and find grace to help in time of need.*"
           g.   Titus 3:7 – "*That being justified by his grace, we should be made heirs...*"
           h.   Titus 2:11-14 – "*For the grace of God that bringeth salvation...*" – Grace teaches us to deny ungodliness and worldly lusts and to live soberly, righteously, and godly in this present world. Grace encourages us to look for the blessed hope and the glorious appearing of the great God and our saviour Jesus Christ.
           i.   II Timothy 2:1 – we are to be strong in the grace that is in Christ Jesus.
           j.   John 1:17 – grace and truth came by Jesus Christ
           k.   Romans 3:24 – being justified freely by His grace

    B.   Our God Is Merciful

        1.   He is mercy

      a.   II Corinthians 1:3
      b.   Daniel 9:9
      b.   Exodus 33:19-23 and Exodus 34:5,6
      c.   Deuteronomy 4:23-31-37
      d.   Nehemiah 9:30-32
      e.   Psalms 37:25
      f.   Matthew 5:7
      g.   Psalms 25:10
      h.   Psalms 103:7-8
      i.   Ephesians 2:4
      j.   Micah 7:18-19
      k.   Exodus 25:22
      l.   I Chronicles 21:13
      m.   Psalms 116:5
      n.   Psalms 62:12
      o.   Psalms 130
      p.   Romans 11:32
      q.   James 5:11
      r.   Jeremiah 33:11
      s.   Proverbs 20:28 (Isaiah 16:5)

2.   He is kind (His loving kindness)

Note, the words mercy, loving kindness, and kindness are the same Hebrew word. You can use them inter-changeably. They mean the same thing. Why the translators used different words to translate the same Hebrew word, I don't understand.

3.   Other translations of Proverbs 20:28

"...His throne is sustained by mercy..."
"...His throne is founded on kindness..."
"...the seat of His power is based on upright acts..."
"...His throne is established by mercy..."

4.   Isaiah 16:5

5.   The mercy seat – Exodus 25:17-22

      a.   Pure gold – God's nature
      b.   Length and breadth but no height or depth. His mercy is unfathomable, it reaches to the sky (height) and goes to the deepest valley (depth) to help us
      c.   Four cubits total – number for creation (mercy over all His works)
      d.   Two cherubim – (His glory is guarded by mercy)
      e.   Even the cherubim look toward the mercy seat
      f.   Mercy over ark (mercy over law)
      g.   He meets and has communion with us from the mercy seat.

6.   Zechariah 7:9 – Other translation - *"...Apply the law fairly and practice kindness."*
7.   Psalms 103:10-11
8.   Hosea 12:6
9.   Habakkuk 3:2 – Other translations – *"...for all your wrath, remember to be merciful..."*, *"...and though we have earned thy anger, be think thee of mercy still."*
10. II Samuel 23:3

11. Psalms 101:1

12. Psalms 119:156

    a. Isaiah 54:8, 10 (Psalms 89:33)
    b. Jeremiah 9:23-24
    c. Jeremiah 31:3
    d. Nehemiah 9:17
    e. Psalms 117:2
    f. Isaiah 63:7
    g. Psalms 63:3
    h. Psalms 103:4

C. Mercy rejoices over judgment

1. James 2:13

    a. Other translations

       "...mercy triumphs over judgment..."
       "...mercy glories in the face of judgment..."
       "...mercy boasteth over judgment..."

2. Proverbs 20:28

3. Other Passages

    a. Psalms 25:5-11
    b. Psalms 51:1
    c. Psalms 145:9

4. Examples of mercy rejoicing over judgment

    a. John 8:1-11
    b. Jonah 3:10
    c. II Samuel 12:13,14
    d. Luke 23:39-43
    e. I Samuel 25:32-35
    f. Jeremiah 30:12-20

D. The combination of mercy and truth delivers us from iniquity

1. Proverbs 16:6
2. Psalms 6:7 (Psalms 40:11)
3. Psalms 85:10
4. Psalms 57:3
5. Ephesians 4:15
6. Exodus 34:5-8
7. Psalms 25:5,6

E. The Lord is a God of mercy and truth

1. Psalms 86:15

      a.   Proverbs 20:28

      b.   Psalms 115:1

      c.   II Samuel 2:6

F.   Defining the mercy of God

    1.   Sure

        a.   Isaiah 55:3 (Acts 13:34) Sure in Hebrew – To build up, to support, firm; to hedge, to guard, to protect

        b.   Isaiah 54:8, 10

        c.   Psalms 89:33

        d.   II Samuel 23:5

    2.   Tender (Hebrew for tender – a twig, a plant, a sprout)

        a.   Psalms 103:4

        b.   Psalms 145:9

        c.   Psalms 69:16

        d.   Psalms 79:8

        e.   Psalms 25:6

    3.   New every morning

        a.   Lamentations 3:22, 23

           1)   Other translations

               "Hope comes with each dawn"
               "New things for the mornings"
               "His loving kindness begins afresh each day"

        b.   Psalms 42:8

        c.   Psalms 92:2

        d.   Psalms 143:8

        e.   Isaiah 33:2

    4.   Plenteous – Plenteous in Hebrew – abundant in quantity or size; comes from a root word which means to multiply; to increase.

        a.   Psalms 86:5

        b.   Psalms 103:8

    5.   Great – from a root that means to trust, to be or make large

        a.   Isaiah 54:7

        b.   Psalms 117:2

        c.   Numbers 14:18-19

        d.   Psalms 145:8

        e.   Psalms 69:16 – multitude

6. Excellent – Hebrew word – valuable; brightness, costly, fat; from a root – to be heavy, rare, valuable

    a. Psalms 36:7
    b. Psalms 17:7 – marvelous

7. Forever

    a. Psalms 37:26
    b. Psalms 77:7-11 – He's merciful, we forget
    c. Psalms 100:5
    d. Psalms 23:6
    e. Psalms 136
    f. I Chronicles 16:30
    g. II Samuel 7:15

G. God's Great Forgiveness

1. Psalms 86:5-7 – "*For thou, Lord, art good, and ready to forgive…*"
2. I Kings 8:30-40 – Solomon's prayer for forgiveness
3. Daniel 9:4-9 – Daniel's prayer
4. Psalms 130 – "*…But there is forgiveness with thee, that thou mayest be feared…*"
5. Colossians 1:14 – "*In whom we have redemption through his blood, even the forgiveness of sins*"

    a. Ephesians 1:7
    b. Colossians 2:13 – "*…having forgiven you all trespasses*"

6. I John 2:12 – "*I write unto you, little children, because your sins are forgiven you for his name's sake.*"
7. I John 1:9 – "*If we confess our sins, he is faithful and just to forgive us our sins, and to cleanse us from all unrighteousness.*" (Psalms 32:1-2, 5)
8. Matthew 9:1-9 – The man sick of the palsy
9. Luke 7:36-50 – "*…Her sins, which are many, are forgiven; for she loved much…*"

10. Luke 6:36-37 – "*…forgive, and ye shall be forgiven.*"

    a. Ephesians 4:32 – "*And be ye kind one to another, tenderhearted, forgiving one another, even as God for Christ's sake hath forgiven you.*"
    b. Matthew 6:12-15 – "*And forgive us our debts, as we forgive our debtors…*"
    c. Mark 11:25-26 – "*And when ye stand praying, forgive…*"
    d. Colossians 3:13
    e. Matthew 18:21-35

11. Psalms 99:8 – "*…thou wast a God that forgavest them…*"

Lesson 69
SEEING THE LORD

I.   Word Definitions for "See"

A.   Hebrew – *Raah* – To Observe, to perceive, to examine, look after, get acquainted with

B.   Greek

1.   *Optanomai* – To gaze with wide open eyes, as at something remarkable
2.   *Blepo* – To take heed, look at, behold, discern, observe, perceive
3.   *Eido* – To know by perception (it suggests fullness of knowing)

II.   John 12:21 – "*...Sir, we would see Jesus.*"

A.   The word "*see*" in this verse is the Greek word "*Eido*" above – Other translations:

"*...Sir, we wish to see Jesus.*"
"*...We want to become acquainted with Jesus.*"
"*...We would like to meet Jesus.*"

B.   Exodus 33:20 – "*...Thou canst not see my face: for there shall no man see me, and live.*"

1.   Other translations:

"*...Thou art unable to see...*"
"*...No man can see my face and live.*"
"*...No man can see my face and survive.*"
"*...Mortal man cannot see my face and live to tell of it.*"
"*...For no son of earth...*"

2.   It is clear that no MAN, no MORTAL man, no son of EARTH can see Him, but the Bible is full of people who've seen Him and lived to tell about it.

a.   You have to be "*in the Spirit*" (Revelation 1:10-19)
b.   You have to be more than just a man. God is bringing forth the remnant of "God-men" who can and shall see Him. We will prove this by looking at the many Scriptures that admonish us as to HOW we can see the Lord.

III. There Have Been Those Who Have Seen the Lord

A.   Examples in the Scriptures – The Hebrew word for <u>appear</u> is the same word <u>see</u> in the O.T (*raah*)

1.   Abram in Genesis 12:7 – "*And the LORD appeared unto Abram, and said, Unto thy seed will I give this land: and there builded he an altar unto the LORD, who appeared unto him.*" – Abram is given a promise is verses 1-3, and he obeyed (verse 4).

2.   Abram in Genesis 17:1-22

a.   Ninety nine – ninety nine means sealed; it is one short of 100 (imperfect by trying)
b.   "Almighty God" – El Shaddai which means breasty one
c.   Abram was commanded to walk before Him

    d.   Abram and Sarai both had name changes (meaning a character change)

        1)   Abram – exalted father; Abraham – father of nations
        2)   Sarai – contentious, quarrelsome, my ruler; Sarah – princess, noble lady, to lead

    e.   Instructions about His covenant and Abraham was obedient in circumcision (vs. 23-27)

3.   Abraham in Genesis 18:1-8

    a.   Mamre means – seeing the vision
    b.   Sat in the tent door – expectant
    c.   ran to meet them and bowed himself toward the ground
    e.   served them

4.   Abraham in Genesis 18:17-19

    a.   He will command his children and household
    b.   Keep the way of the Lord
    c.   Do justice and judgment
    d.   More than anything He knew Abraham would

5.   Abraham in Genesis 18:23-33 – interceded for the people
6.   Isaac in Genesis 26:2-6 – Isaac was told not to go into Egypt because of the oath he sware unto Abraham and Isaac obeyed.
7.   Jacob in Genesis 28:10-22 – Vision of Jacob's ladder
8.   Genesis 35:9 – "And <u>God appeared unto Jacob again</u>, when he came out of Padan-aram, and blessed him."
9.   Moses in Exodus 3:2 – "And the angel of the LORD appeared unto him in a flame of fire out of the midst of a bush: and he looked, and, behold, the bush burned with fire, and the bush was not consumed."
10. Moses in Exodus 24:1-3
11. Gideon in Judges 6:12 – "And the angel of the LORD appeared unto him, and said unto him, The LORD is with thee, thou mighty man of valour."
12. Manoah's wife in Judges 13:3, 10 – "And the angel of the LORD appeared unto the woman, and said unto her, Behold now, thou art barren, and bearest not: but thou shalt conceive, and bear a son..."
13. I Kings 3:5 – "In Gibeon the <u>LORD appeared to Solomon</u> in a dream by night: and God said, Ask what I shall give thee."
14. I Kings 9:2 – "That the <u>LORD appeared to Solomon the second time</u>, as he had appeared unto him at Gibeon."
15. I Chronicles 21:18-19 – "Then the angel of the LORD commanded Gad to say to David, that David should go up, and set up an altar unto the LORD in the threshingfloor of Ornan the Jebusite. And David went up at the saying of Gad, which he spake in the name of the LORD."
16. II Chronicles 3:1 – "Then Solomon began to build the house of the LORD at Jerusalem in mount Moriah, where the LORD appeared unto David his father, in the place that David had prepared in the threshingfloor of Ornan the Jebusite."
17. Paul in Acts 9:3-9, 17

B.   One must understand that the Hebrew word translated presence is also translated face. In fact this Hebrew word, *paniym* translated presence means – the face that turns.

    1.   We are to see, know, and enjoy His presence (face)

a. Exodus 33:13-18 – "*¹³Now therefore, I pray thee, if I have found grace in thy sight, shew me now thy way, that I may know thee, that I may find grace in thy sight: and consider that this nation is thy people. ¹⁴And he said, My presence shall go with thee, and I will give thee rest. ¹⁵And he said unto him, If thy presence go not with me, carry us not up hence. ¹⁶For wherein shall it be known here that I and thy people have found grace in thy sight? is it not in that thou goest with us? so shall we be separated, I and thy people, from all the people that are upon the face of the earth. ¹⁷And the LORD said unto Moses, I will do this thing also that thou hast spoken: for thou hast found grace in my sight, and I know thee by name. ¹⁸And he said, I beseech thee, shew me thy glory.*"

b. Psalms 16:11 – "*Thou wilt shew me the path of life: in thy presence is fulness of joy; at thy right hand there are pleasures for evermore.*"

c. I Chronicles 16:27 – "*Glory and honour are in his presence; strength and gladness are in his place.*"

d. Psalms 51:11 – "*Cast me not away from thy presence; and take not thy holy spirit from me.*"

e. Psalms 95:2 – "*Let us come before his presence with thanksgiving, and make a joyful noise unto him with psalms.*"

f. Psalms 100:2 – "*Serve the LORD with gladness: come before his presence with singing.*"

g. Psalms 139:7 – "*Whither shall I go from thy spirit? or whither shall I flee from thy presence?*"

h. Psalms 140:13 – "*Surely the righteous shall give thanks unto thy name: the upright shall dwell in thy presence.*"

i. I Chronicles 16:33 – "*Then shall the trees of the wood sing out at the presence of the LORD, because he cometh to judge the earth.*"

2. God does hide himself at times

a. Proverbs 25:2 – "*It is the glory of God to conceal a thing: but the honour of kings is to search out a matter.*"

b. Job 26:9 – "*He holdeth back the face of his throne, and spreadeth his cloud upon it.*"

c. Psalms 30:7 – "*LORD, by thy favour thou hast made my mountain to stand strong: thou didst hide thy face, and I was troubled.*"

d. Psalms 104:29 – "*Thou hidest thy face, they are troubled: thou takest away their breath, they die, and return to their dust.*"

e. Isaiah 45:15 – "*Verily thou art a God that hidest thyself, O God of Israel, the Saviour.*"

f. Habakkuk 3:4 – "*And his brightness was as the light; he had horns coming out of his hand: and there was the hiding of his power.*"

g. Isaiah 8:17 – "*And I will wait upon the LORD, that hideth his face from the house of Jacob, and I will look for him.*"

h. Isaiah 54:8 – "*In a little wrath I hid my face from thee for a moment; but with everlasting kindness will I have mercy on thee, saith the LORD thy Redeemer.*"

3. We can only endure and truly live by seeing Him.

a. Psalms 27:13 – "*I had fainted, unless I had believed to see the goodness of the LORD in the land of the living.*"

b. Hebrews 11:27 – "*By faith he forsook Egypt, not fearing the wrath of the king: for he endured, as seeing him who is invisible.*"

c. Job 24:1 – "*Why, seeing times are not hidden from the Almighty, do they that know him not see his days?*"

d. I Corinthians 13:12 – "*For now we see through a glass, darkly; but then face to face: now I know in part; but then shall I know even as also I am known.*"

e. Proverbs 16:15 – *"In the light of the king's countenance is life; and his favour is as a cloud of the latter rain."*

f. Psalms 89:15-16 – *"Blessed is the people that know the joyful sound: they shall walk, O LORD, in the light of thy countenance. In thy name shall they rejoice all the day: and in thy righteousness shall they be exalted."*

g. Psalms 51:9-12 – *"⁹Hide thy face from my sins, and blot out all mine iniquities. ¹⁰Create in me a clean heart, O God; and renew a right spirit within me. ¹¹Cast me not away from thy presence; and take not thy holy spirit from me. ¹²Restore unto me the joy of thy salvation; and uphold me with thy free spirit."*

C. One thing is certain – a day is coming when we shall see Him, whether good or bad.

1. Good

a. Numbers 24:17 – *"I shall see him, but not now: I shall behold him, but not nigh: there shall come a Star out of Jacob, and a Sceptre shall rise out of Israel, and shall smite the corners of Moab, and destroy all the children of Sheth."*

b. Job 19:25-26 – *"For I know that my redeemer liveth, and that he shall stand at the latter day upon the earth: And though after my skin worms destroy this body, yet in my flesh shall I see God:"*

c. Revelation 1:7 – *"Behold, he cometh with clouds; and every eye shall see him, and they also which pierced him: and all kindreds of the earth shall wail because of him. Even so, Amen."*

d. Revelation 22:4 – *"And they shall see his face; and his name shall be in their foreheads."*

2. Bad – the coming judgment

a. Exodus 16:7 – *"And in the morning, then ye shall see the glory of the LORD; for that he heareth your murmurings against the LORD: and what are we, that ye murmur against us?"*

b. Luke 8:28 – *"When he saw Jesus, he cried out, and fell down before him, and with a loud voice said, What have I to do with thee, Jesus, thou Son of God most high? I beseech thee, torment me not."*

c. Revelation 20:11 – *"And I saw a great white throne, and him that sat on it, from whose face the earth and the heaven fled away; and there was found no place for them."*

d. Deuteronomy 32:37-43

e. Mark 14:60-63

f. Psalms 97:1-6

g. Amos 9:1-9

IV. Scriptural Ways We Can See God

A. Listed here are the things which we must do or have working in our lives to see Him.

1. Matthew 5:8 – *"Blessed are the <u>pure in heart</u>: for they shall see God."*

2. Hebrews 12:14 – *"<u>Follow peace with all men</u>, and <u>holiness</u>, without which no man shall see the Lord:"*

3. I John 3:2-3 – *"Beloved, now are we the sons of God, and it doth not yet appear what we shall be: but we know that, when he shall appear, <u>we shall be like him</u>; for we shall see him as he is. And every man that hath this hope in him <u>purifieth himself</u>, even as he is pure."*

4. Isaiah 6:1 – *"In the year that king Uzziah died I saw also the Lord sitting upon a throne, high and lifted up, and his train filled the temple."* – The Uzziah's in our life must die; Uzziah means – strength of the Lord, might of Jehovah; our dependence on men must eventually die and then we shall see.

5. Numbers 24:16 – "*He hath said, which <u>heard the words of God</u>, and <u>knew the knowledge of the most High</u>, which saw the vision of the Almighty, falling into a trance, but having his eyes open:*"

6. Daniel 3:25 – "*He answered and said, Lo, I see four men loose, walking in the midst of the fire, and they have no hurt; and the form of the fourth is like the Son of God.*" – We will see Him in the fire.

7. Ezekiel 1:1 – "*Now it came to pass in the thirtieth year, in the fourth month, in the fifth day of the month, as I was among the captives by the river of Chebar, that the heavens were opened, and I saw visions of God.*" – 30 is the number for preparation in ministry, 4 is the number for creation or the new creation man, 5 is the number for grace and the five fold ministry, Chebar means – as is made clear. The revelation is that even though we might be captive, God, in this time of preparation, is creating by His grace a new man. Even in captivity we can still have an open heaven and see the Lord.

8. John 11:40 – "*Jesus saith unto her, Said I not unto thee, that, <u>if thou wouldest believe</u>, thou shouldest see the glory of God?*"

9. Psalms 24:3-6 – "*³Who shall ascend into the hill of the LORD? or who shall stand in his holy place? ⁴He that hath <u>clean hands</u>, and a <u>pure heart</u>; who <u>hath not lifted up his soul unto vanity, nor sworn deceitfully</u>. ⁵He shall receive the blessing from the LORD, and righteousness from the God of his salvation. ⁶This is the generation of them that seek him, that seek thy face, O Jacob. Selah.*"

10. Revelation 3:17-18 – "*Because thou sayest, I am rich, and increased with goods, and have need of nothing; and knowest not that thou art wretched, and miserable, and poor, and blind, and naked: I counsel thee to buy of me gold tried in the fire, that thou mayest be rich; and white raiment, that thou mayest be clothed, and that the shame of thy nakedness do not appear; and anoint thine eyes with eyesalve, that thou mayest see.*" – We will see the Lord as we buy God's character in our lives and become pure.

11. Isaiah 33:13-17 – "*¹³Hear, ye that are far off, what I have done; and, ye that are near, acknowledge my might. ¹⁴The sinners in Zion are afraid; fearfulness hath surprised the hypocrites. Who among us shall dwell with the devouring fire? who among us shall dwell with everlasting burnings? ¹⁵He that <u>walketh righteously</u>, and <u>speaketh uprightly</u>; he that <u>despiseth the gain of oppressions</u>, that <u>shaketh his hands from holding of bribes</u>, that <u>stoppeth his ears from hearing of blood</u>, and <u>shutteth his eyes from seeing evil</u>; ¹⁶He shall dwell on high: his place of defence shall be the munitions of rocks: bread shall be given him; his waters shall be sure. ¹⁷Thine eyes shall see the king in his beauty: they shall behold the land that is very far off.*"

12. Psalms 17:15 – "*As for me, I will behold thy face in righteousness: I shall be satisfied, <u>when I awake, with thy likeness</u>.*"

13. Exodus 14:13 – "*And Moses said unto the people, <u>Fear ye not</u>, <u>stand still</u>, and <u>see the salvation of the LORD</u>, which he will shew to you to day: for the Egyptians whom ye have seen to day, ye shall see them again no more for ever.*"

14. Exodus 33:21-23 – "*²¹And the LORD said, Behold, <u>there is a place by me</u>, and thou shalt <u>stand upon a rock</u>: ²²And it shall come to pass, while my glory passeth by, that I will put thee <u>in a clift of the rock</u>, and will <u>cover thee with my hand</u> while I pass by: ²³And I will take away mine hand, and thou shalt see my back parts: but my face shall not be seen.*"

15. Luke 8:9-10 – "*And his disciples asked him, saying, What might this parable be? And he said, Unto you it is given to know the mysteries of the kingdom of God: but to others in parables; that seeing they might not see, and hearing they might not understand.*" – Disciple should see and know

16. Job 33:24-30 – "*²⁴Then he is <u>gracious unto him</u>, and saith, <u>Deliver him</u> from going down to the pit: I have found a ransom. ²⁵His flesh shall be fresher than a child's: he shall return to the days of his youth: ²⁶He shall <u>pray unto God, and he will be favourable unto him</u>: and he shall see his face with joy: for he will render unto man his righteousness. ²⁷He looketh upon men, and if any say, I have sinned, and perverted that which was right, and it profited me not; ²⁸He will deliver his soul from going into the pit, and his life shall see the light. ²⁹Lo, all these things worketh God*"

oftentimes with man, 30To bring back his soul from the pit, to be enlightened with the light of the living."

17. Exodus 24:1-3, 6-9, 12, 15-18

18. Genesis 18:1-4 – "*1And the LORD appeared unto him in the plains of Mamre: and <u>he sat in the tent door</u> <u>in the heat of the day</u>; 2And he <u>lift up his eyes and looked</u>, and, lo, three men stood by him: and when he saw them, <u>he ran to meet them</u> from the tent door, and <u>bowed himself toward the ground</u>, 3And said, My Lord, if now I have found favour in thy sight, pass not away, I pray thee, from <u>thy servant</u>: 4Let a little water, I pray you, be fetched, and wash your feet, and rest yourselves under the tree:*"

19. Revelation 1:9-19 – John saw the Lord during his persecution on the isle of Patmos; Patmos means – my killing

20. Acts 7:2-60 – "*...56And said, Behold, I see the heavens opened, and the Son of man standing on the right hand of God.*" – Stephen saw the Lord while speaking the truth, being full of the Word of God, while being persecuted and attacked, while having a forgiving heart.

21. Acts 22:12-14 – Being chosen by God

22. Luke 19:1-11 – Zacchaeus seeing the Lord

23. Matthew 25:31-46 – seeing Jesus as the stranger, naked, sick, or in prison

    a. I Corinthians 11:26-33 – not discerning the Lord's body

24. II Corinthians 3:18 – "*But we all, <u>with open face</u> <u>beholding as in a glass the glory of the Lord</u>, are changed into the same image from glory to glory, even as by the Spirit of the Lord.*" As we have an unveiled face as we look into the Word of God (glass) we will see and behold Jesus.

Lesson 70
SEEKING THE LORD

I.   Seeking the Lord

A.   God longs for us to seek Him – In seeking, we find Him. God's promise to us is whenever we get serious and seek Him with our <u>whole</u> heart, we will find Him.

    1.   II Chronicles 15:3-4 – "*3Now for a long season Israel hath been without the true God, and without a teaching priest, and without law. 4But when they in their trouble did turn unto the LORD God of Israel, and sought him, he was found of them.*"

    2.   Jeremiah 29:13 – "*And ye shall seek me, and find me, when ye shall search for me with all your heart.*"

    3.   Isaiah 55:6 – "*...6Seek ye the LORD while he may be found, call ye upon him while he is near:*"

    4.   Matthew 7:7 – "*Ask, and it shall be given you; seek, and ye shall find; knock, and it shall be opened unto you:*"

    5.   Proverbs 8:17 – "*I love them that love me; and those that seek me early shall find me.*"

    6.   Hebrews 11:6 – "*But without faith it is impossible to please him: for he that cometh to God must believe that he is, and that he is a rewarder of them that diligently seek him.*"

    7.   Deuteronomy 4:25-31

    8.   I Chronicles 28:9 – "*And thou, Solomon my son, know thou the God of thy father, and serve him with a perfect heart and with a willing mind: for the LORD searcheth all hearts, and understandeth all the imaginations of the thoughts: if thou seek him, he will be found of thee; but if thou forsake him, he will cast thee off for ever.*"

    9.   James 4:8 – "*Draw nigh to God, and he will draw nigh to you. Cleanse your hands, ye sinners; and purify your hearts, ye double minded.*"

B.   What do we seek? – Our problem is we get our eyes on the wrong thing

    1.   Philippians 2:21 – "*For all seek their own, not the things which are Jesus Christ's.*"

    2.   I Corinthians 10:24 – "*Let no man seek his own, but every man another's wealth.*"

    3.   Romans 3:11 – "*There is none that understandeth, there is none that seeketh after God.*"

    4.   Isaiah 55:1-3 – "*1Ho, every one that thirsteth, come ye to the waters, and he that hath no money; come ye, buy, and eat; yea, come, buy wine and milk without money and without price. 2Wherefore do ye spend money for that which is not bread? and your labour for that which satisfieth not? hearken diligently unto me, and eat ye that which is good, and let your soul delight itself in fatness. 3Incline your ear, and come unto me: hear, and your soul shall live; and I will make an everlasting covenant with you, even the sure mercies of David.*"

    5.   Matthew 6:31-33 – "*31Therefore take no thought, saying, What shall we eat? or, What shall we drink? or, Wherewithal shall we be clothed? 32(For after all these things do the Gentiles seek:) for your heavenly Father knoweth that ye have need of all these things. 33But seek ye first the kingdom of God, and his righteousness; and all these things shall be added unto you.*"

    6.   Jeremiah 45:5 – "*And seekest thou great things for thyself? seek them not: for, behold, I will bring evil upon all flesh, saith the LORD: but thy life will I give unto thee for a prey in all places whither thou goest.*"

    7.   Isaiah 58:2 – "*Yet they seek me daily, and delight to know my ways, as a nation that did righteousness, and forsook not the ordinance of their God: they ask of me the ordinances of justice; they take delight in approaching to God.*"

    8.   Colossians 3:1-4 – "*1If ye then be risen with Christ, seek those things which are above, where Christ sitteth on the right hand of God. 2Set your affection on things above, not on things on the earth. 3For ye are dead, and your life is hid with Christ in God. 4When Christ, who is our life, shall appear, then shall ye also appear with him in glory.*"

C. What happens when we don't seek God?

    1. Hosea 5:2-15
    2. Jeremiah 29:4 – *"Thus saith the LORD of hosts, the God of Israel, unto all that are carried away captives, whom I have caused to be carried away from Jerusalem unto Babylon;"*
    3. II Chronicles 15:2-6

D. Our great love for Him should be our motivation for seeking Him

    1. Song of Solomon 3:1-4 – *"¹By night on my bed I sought him whom my soul loveth: I sought him, but I found him not. ²I will rise now, and go about the city in the streets, and in the broad ways I will seek him whom my soul loveth: I sought him, but I found him not. ³The watchmen that go about the city found me: to whom I said, Saw ye him whom my soul loveth? ⁴It was but a little that I passed from them, but I found him whom my soul loveth: I held him, and would not let him go, until I had brought him into my mother's house, and into the chamber of her that conceived me."*
    2. Psalms 27:4-8 – *"⁴One thing have I desired of the LORD, that will I seek after; that I may dwell in the house of the LORD all the days of my life, to behold the beauty of the LORD, and to inquire in his temple...⁸When thou saidst, Seek ye my face; my heart said unto thee, Thy face, LORD, will I seek."*
    3. Psalms 111:2 – *"The works of the LORD are great, sought out of all them that have pleasure therein."*
    4. Luke 19:1-10

E. How long should we seek Him?

    1. I Chronicles 16:11 – *"Seek the LORD and his strength, seek his face <u>continually</u>."*
    2. I Chronicles 22:17-19 – *"¹⁷David also commanded all the princes of Israel to help Solomon his son, saying, ¹⁸Is not the LORD your God with you? and hath he not given you rest on every side? for he hath given the inhabitants of the land into mine hand; and the land is subdued before the LORD, and before his people. ¹⁹Now set your heart and your soul to seek the LORD your God; arise therefore, and build ye the sanctuary of the LORD God, to bring the ark of the covenant of the LORD, and the holy vessels of God, into the house that is to be built to the name of the LORD."* – Not only when we're in trouble, but even in times of great peace and rest.
    3. Hebrews 11:13-16

F. What happens when we seek?

    1. Amos 5:4-6 – *"⁴For thus saith the LORD unto the house of Israel, Seek ye me, and ye shall live..."*
    2. Psalms 22:26 – *"The meek shall eat and be satisfied: they shall praise the LORD that seek him: your heart shall live for ever."*
    3. Ezra 8:22 – *"...The hand of our God is upon all them for good that seek him; but his power and his wrath is against all them that forsake him."*
    4. Lamentations 3:25 – *"The LORD is good unto them that wait for him, to the soul that seeketh him."*
    5. Psalms 34:4, 10 – *"⁴I sought the LORD, and he heard me, and delivered me from all my fears...¹⁰The young lions do lack, and suffer hunger: but they that seek the LORD shall not want any good thing."*
    6. Psalms 9:10 – *"And they that know thy name will put their trust in thee: for thou, LORD, hast not forsaken them that seek thee."*
    7. Proverbs 28:5 – *"Evil men understand not judgment: but they that seek the LORD understand all things."*

8. Psalms 16:11 – "*Thou wilt shew me the path of life: in thy presence is fulness of joy; at thy right hand there are pleasures for evermore.*"

9. Hosea 10:12 – "*Sow to yourselves in righteousness, reap in mercy; break up your fallow ground: for it is time to seek the LORD, till he come and rain righteousness upon you.*"

II. Keeping Our Flow of Strength

A. Our problem many times is we don't seek Him – If we don't seek Him, we run out of divine strength

   1. Isaiah 1:2-3 – "*²Hear, O heavens, and give ear, O earth: for the LORD hath spoken, I have nourished and brought up children, and they have rebelled against me. ³The ox knoweth his owner, and the ass his master's crib: but Israel doth not know, my people doth not consider.*"

   2. Hosea 8:14 – "*For Israel hath forgotten his Maker, and buildeth temples; and Judah hath multiplied fenced cities: but I will send a fire upon his cities, and it shall devour the palaces thereof.*"

   3. Jeremiah 2:32 – "*Can a maid forget her ornaments, or a bride her attire? yet my people have forgotten me days without number.*"

   4. Jeremiah 2:13 – "*For my people have committed two evils; they have forsaken me the fountain of living waters, and hewed them out cisterns, broken cisterns, that can hold no water.*"

B. God is our life source

   1. Philippians 4:19 – "*But my God shall supply all your need according to his riches in glory by Christ Jesus.*"

   2. Psalms 145:15-16 – "*¹⁵The eyes of all wait upon thee; and thou givest them their meat in due season. ¹⁶Thou openest thine hand, and satisfiest the desire of every living thing.*"

   3. Psalms 87:7 – "*...all my springs are in thee.*"

C. We must seek the Lord for strength

   1. Jesus is our example

      a. Mark 1:35 – "*And in the morning, rising up a great while before day, he went out, and departed into a solitary place, and there prayed.*"

      b. Mark 6:46 – "*And when he had sent them away, he departed into a mountain to pray.*"

      c. Hebrews 5:7 – "*Who in the days of his flesh, when he had offered up prayers and supplications with strong crying and tears unto him that was able to save him from death, and was heard in that he feared;*"

   2. Proverbs 8:34-35 – "*³⁴Blessed is the man that heareth me, watching daily at my gates, waiting at the posts of my doors. ³⁵For whoso findeth me findeth life, and shall obtain favour of the LORD.*"

D. Our strength is to sit still

   1. Isaiah 30:7, 15 – "*⁷For the Egyptians shall help in vain, and to no purpose: therefore have I cried concerning this, Their strength is to sit still...¹⁵For thus saith the Lord GOD, the Holy One of Israel; In returning and rest shall ye be saved; in quietness and in confidence shall be your strength: and ye would not.*"

   2. Exodus 14:15 – "*And the LORD said unto Moses, Wherefore criest thou unto me? speak unto the children of Israel, that they go forward:*"

3. I Samuel 12:7 – *"Now therefore stand still, that I may reason with you before the LORD of all the righteous acts of the LORD, which he did to you and to your fathers."*
4. Psalms 46:10 – *"Be still, and know that I am God: I will be exalted among the heathen, I will be exalted in the earth."*

Lesson 71
SERVING ONE ANOTHER

I.   We Serve One Another Because We Love – We love because God first loved us and spread that love abroad in our hearts by the Holy Spirit. Love requires a corresponding action (John 3:16). Serving is action motivated by love.

A.   We are commanded to do it.

1.   Galatians 5:13 – *"For, brethren...by love serve one another."*

a.   John 15:12 – *"This is my commandment, That ye love one another, as I have loved you."* Jesus is the greatest example of one who serves by love.
b.   I John 4:7, 21 – If we love God we love our brother and this is a prerequisite to serving.
c.   Hebrews 10:24 – *"And let us consider one another to provoke unto love and to good works:"* By considering (loving) my brother I can then serve him.

B.   We need to learn to care for our brothers and sisters more than ourselves.

1.   Philippians 2:3-5 – *"...but in lowliness of mind let each esteem other better than themselves..."*

a.   Philippians 2:20-22 – *"For I have no man likeminded, who will naturally care for your state..."*
b.   I Corinthians 12:25 – *"...that the members should have the same care one for another."*
c.   Luke 10:30-36 – This passage shares how the majority of believers (priest, Levite) pass on by. But God is bringing forth a people in this hour that will have compassion and take care of their brothers. In doing this they act just like Jesus.

C.   Being a servant is one of the highest calls on a believer's life.

1.   Matthew 20:27 – *"And whosoever will be chief among you, let him be your servant:"*
2.   Matthew 23:11 – *"But he that is greatest among you shall be your servant."*

To serve God's family is a high and holy privilege that God calls us to walk in.

D.   What the scriptures declare we are to do for one another.

1.   Ephesians 4:2 – Forbearing one another
2.   Ephesians 4:32 – Kind to one another
3.   Ephesians 5:21 – Submitting to one another
4.   1 Thessalonians 4:18 – Comfort one another
5.   1 Thessalonians 5:11 – Edify one another
6.   Hebrews 3:13 – Exhort one another
7.   Hebrews 10:24-25 – Consider one another
8.   James 5:16 – Confess and pray for one another
9.   1 Peter 4:9 – Use hospitality one to another
10. 1 Peter 3:8 – Show compassion to one another
11. 1 Peter 5:5 – Be subject one to another
12. 1 Peter 4:10 – Minister the gifts one to another

II. John 13:16-17 – *"Verily, verily, I say unto you, The servant is not greater than his lord; neither he that is sent greater than he that sent him. If ye know these things, happy are ye if ye do them."*

Lesson 72
SHEPHERDING

I. What a Shepherd Should Be

   A. II Samuel 23:3 – *"The God of Israel said, the Rock of Israel spake to me, He that ruleth over men must be just, ruling in the fear of God."*

   1. Acts 20:28 – *"Take heed therefore unto yourselves, and to all the flock, over the which the Holy Ghost hath made you overseers, to feed the church of God, which he hath purchased with his own blood."*
   2. I Peter 5:1-5 – *"[1]The elders which are among you I exhort, who am also an elder, and a witness of the sufferings of Christ, and also a partaker of the glory that shall be revealed: [2]Feed the flock of God which is among you, taking the oversight thereof, not by constraint, but willingly; not for filthy lucre, but of a ready mind; [3]Neither as being lords over God's heritage, but being ensamples to the flock. [4]And when the chief Shepherd shall appear, ye shall receive a crown of glory that fadeth not away. [5]Likewise, ye younger, submit yourselves unto the elder. Yea, all of you be subject one to another, and be clothed with humility: for God resisteth the proud, and giveth grace to the humble."*
   3. Titus 1:7-9 – *"[7]For a bishop must be blameless, as the steward of God; not selfwilled, not soon angry, not given to wine, no striker, not given to filthy lucre; [8]But a lover of hospitality, a lover of good men, sober, just, holy, temperate; [9]Holding fast the faithful word as he hath been taught, that he may be able by sound doctrine both to exhort and to convince the gainsayers."*
   4. I Corinthians 9:19-23 – *"[19]For though I be free from all men, yet have I made myself servant unto all, that I might gain the more. [20]And unto the Jews I became as a Jew, that I might gain the Jews; to them that are under the law, as under the law, that I might gain them that are under the law; [21]To them that are without law, as without law, (being not without law to God, but under the law to Christ,) that I might gain them that are without law. [22]To the weak became I as weak, that I might gain the weak: I am made all things to all men, that I might by all means save some. [23]And this I do for the gospel's sake, that I might be partaker thereof with you."*
   5. I Corinthians 4 – The whole chapter
   6. John 10:2-5, 11-14
   7. II Corinthians 11:7-13, 23-30

      a. II Corinthians 13:10
      b. I Samuel 12:1-5

   8. II Corinthians 12:5-19
   9. Ezekiel 34:1-9
         10 Proverbs 27:23 (Romans 12:8)

   11. I Thessalonians 2:1-12, 19

   B. Problems with rebellious people

   1. Acts 20:29-30
   2. III John 9-12
   3. Jude 3-5, 8, 10-20
   4. I Corinthians 3:1-7
   5. II Timothy 4:14-15
   6. Numbers 16 – The whole chapter

       7.   Deuteronomy 31:27-29

C.   What should be done to the causers of strife and division?

       1.   Romans 16:17-19 – Mark them
       2.   I Timothy 5:19-21 – Rebuke before all
       3.   Titus 1:9-11, 15-16 – Whose mouths must be stopped
       4.   Jude 11-23 – Execute judgment, some have compassion, others save by pulling them out of the fire
       5.   Proverbs 22:10 – Cast out the scorners
       6.   Ecclesiastes 10:4-14 – Fall into a pit, serpent will bite him
       7.   Galatians 2:4-6, 11-16 – We gave place not for an hour

       8.   Ephesians 5:6-11 – Deceivers with vain word (have no fellowship)

            a.   James 3
            b.   Proverbs 16:27-30
            c.   Proverbs 17:9-13

       9.   II Timothy 3:1-10, 13-14
     10. I Corinthians 5:1-6, 11-14

D.   What God thinks of these and what He will do

       1.   What He thinks

            a.   Proverbs 6:16-18 – Hates them
            b.   I Samuel 16:1 – Fill your horn and stop mourning
            c.   Jeremiah 7:16 – Pray not for this people
            d.   I Samuel 15:23 – Rebellion is as witchcraft

       2.   What He will do

            a.   Ezekiel 20:38 – I will purge out the rebels from among you
            b.   Hosea 7:11-16 – I will bring them down, I will chastise them
            c.   Isaiah 63:8-10 – He turned to be their enemy

E.   What a congregation's response should be?

       1.   I Timothy 5:1-17, 19
       2.   Hebrews 13:7, 17-18
       3.   I Peter 5:5-10
       4.   Romans 16:17 – Mark them
       5.   Ephesians 5:6-7, 11 – No fellowship
       6.   Matthew 26:31 – Smite the shepherd
       7.   Psalms 105:15 – Touch not mine anointed

Lesson 73
SLOTHFULNESS

I.   Word Meanings For Slothful

    A.   Hebrew for slothful:

        1.   *Atsel* – indolent (avoiding exertion); from a root that means to lean idly; also translated sluggard
        2.   *Raphah* – to slacken, abate, cease (to draw towards evening), to fail
        3.   *Rmyah* – treachery, false, guile, idle; from a root that means to betray or delude

    B.   Greek for slothful:

        1.   *Nothros* – sluggish, lazy, stupid, dull; from a root that means illegitimate son, bastard
        2.   *Okneros* – tardy, irksome, grievous; from a root that means hesitation, to be slow

    C.   Dictionary definition for slothful – habitual disinclination to exertion
    D.   Hebrew for Idleness, *shipluwth*" – idleness; from a root that means to depress or sink

II. Scriptural definition of Slothfulness

    A.   What it does to you:

        1.   Proverbs 19:15 – "*Slothfulness casteth into a deep sleep; and an idle soul shall suffer hunger.*"
        2.   Ecclesiastes 10:18 – "*By much slothfulness the building decayeth; and through idleness of the hands the house droppeth through.*"
        3.   I Timothy 5:13 – "*And withal they learn to be idle, wandering about from house to house; and not only idle, but tattlers also and busybodies, speaking things which they ought not.*"
        4.   Proverbs 12:24 – "*The hand of the diligent shall bear rule: but the slothful shall be under tribute.*"
        5.   Proverbs 15:19 – "*The way of the slothful man is as an hedge of thorns: but the way of the righteous is made plain.*"
        6.   Proverbs 19:24, 26:15
        7.   Proverbs 26:13-16
        8.   Proverbs 13:4 – "*The soul of the sluggard desireth, and hath nothing: but the soul of the diligent shall be made fat.*"
        9.   Proverbs 20:4 – "*The sluggard will not plow by reason of the cold; therefore shall he beg in harvest, and have nothing.*"
      10. Proverbs 6:6-11
      11. Proverbs 21:25-26

    B.   Defined even more clearly.....

        1.   Proverbs 24:30-34 – "*[30]I went by the field of the slothful, and by the vineyard of the man void of understanding; [31]And, lo, it was all grown over with thorns, and nettles had covered the face thereof, and the stone wall thereof was broken down. [32]Then I saw, and considered it well: I looked upon it, and received instruction. [33]Yet a little sleep, a little slumber, a little folding of the hands to sleep: [34]So shall thy poverty come as one that travelleth; and thy want as an armed man.*"
        2.   Proverbs 12:27 – "*The slothful man roasteth not that which he took in hunting: but the substance of a diligent man is precious.*"
        3.   Proverbs 18:9 – "*He also that is slothful in his work is brother to him that is a great waster.*"

4. Romans 12:11 – *"Not slothful in business; fervent in spirit; serving the Lord"*;
5. Proverbs 10:26 – *"As vinegar to the teeth, and as smoke to the eyes, so is the sluggard to them that send him."*

C. Scriptural admonition against slothfulness

1. Hebrews 6:12 – *"That ye be not slothful, but followers of them who through faith and patience inherit the promises."*
2. Judges 18:9 – *"And they said, Arise, that we may go up against them: for we have seen the land, and, behold, it is very good: and are ye still? be not slothful to go, and to enter to possess the land.*
3. Matthew 25:24-30
4. Matthews 20:1-6
5. Proverbs 31:27 – *"She looketh well to the ways of her household, and eateth not the bread of idleness."*

Lesson 74
STRONG IN THE LORD

I.   A Strange Challenge

A.   Joshua 1:9 – *"Have not I commanded thee? Be strong and of a good courage..."*

1.   I Corinthians 16:13 – *"Watch ye, stand fast in the faith, quit you like men, be strong."*
2.   Isaiah 35:4 – *"Say to them that are of a fearful heart, Be strong, fear not..."*

These scriptures offer what seemingly is a very bold challenge, "Be Strong". To one who is weak and desperate those words might seem strange. He might ask "How can I be strong"? That's a good question. The answer is: God will never command us to do something He doesn't give us the wherewithal to do. The Bible gives us a clear definition of how we can be strong. Of course I would be the first to admit, that human beings will always be limited in strength, but once we are born again, we step into the strength of the unlimited God! We can be <u>strong in the Lord</u>!

B.   God knows we have limitations.

1.   We will never prevail in our own strength.

a.   I Samuel 2:9 – *"...for by strength shall no man prevail."*
b.   Isaiah 30:7 – *"For the Egyptians shall help in vain, and to no purpose..."*
c.   Psalms 33:16 – *"...a mighty man is not delivered by much strength."*

2.   It's only as we look to Him in our weakness that we will altogether be delivered.

a.   Psalms 147:10-11 – *"...The LORD taketh pleasure in them that fear him, in those that hope in his mercy."*
b.   II Corinthians 12:9 – *"...for my strength is made perfect in weakness. Most gladly therefore will I rather glory in my infirmities, that the power of Christ may rest upon me."*
c.   Hebrews 11:34 – *"...out of weakness were made strong..."*

3.   If we are strong, it's because we are strong in Him.

a.   Jeremiah 9:23-24
b.   Psalms 84:5 – *"Blessed is the man whose strength is in thee..."*
c.   Psalms 71:16 – *"I will go in the strength of the Lord GOD..."*
d.   Philippians 4:13 – *"I can do all things through Christ which strengtheneth me."*
e.   Isaiah 40:29 – *"He giveth power to the faint; and to them that have no might he increaseth strength."*
f.   Ephesians 6:10 – If we overcome anything, win any battle, it's because He helped us.

g.   He works with us.

1)   Mark 16:20 – *"...the Lord working with them, and confirming the word with signs following."*
2)   1 Corinthians 3:9 – *"...we are labourers together with God..."*
3)   Acts 15:4

God instantly delivers us from some things, others He expects us to do our part. If He delivered us instantly from everything, we would never overcome anything. He gives us the ability, and then we must accomplish the task.

          4)   He works in us, and then we do.

             a)   Philippians 2:13
             b)   Hebrews 13:21

    4.   He is our strength

        a.   Psalms 27:1 – *"...the LORD is the strength of my life..."*
        b.   Exodus 15:2 – *"The LORD is my strength and song..."*
        c.   I Samuel 15:29 – *"...the Strength of Israel..."*
        d.   Psalms 46:1 – *"...God is our refuge and strength..."*
        e.   Psalms 81:1
        f.   Habakkuk 3:19

II.   Now that we know our strength is in and through Him, and that we can't do it on our own, we must realize however, there are things we can do to be strong.

A.   Our confession

    1.   Joel 3:10 – We need to let the word of God come out of our mouth. Not how we feel or look.

B.   Praise and Worship

    1.   Psalms 8:2 (Matthew 21:16) – Strength comes as we begin to praise and worship Him. We can stay strong by continually doing those things.

C.   Waiting on the Lord – This could correctly be called, spending time with Him.

    1.   Isaiah 40:31 – *"But they that wait upon the LORD shall renew their strength; they shall mount up with wings as eagles; they shall run, and not be weary; and they shall walk, and not faint."*
    2.   Daniel 11:32 – As we spend time with Him, we come to know Him.

D.   The joy of the Lord

    1.   Nehemiah 8:10 – Joy is not a feeling; it is a fact. I can be full of the joy of the Lord regardless of circumstances

E.   Praying In Tongues

    1.   Jude 20 – *"...building up yourselves on your most holy faith, praying in the Holy Ghost,"*
    2.   I Corinthians 14:4 – *"He that speaketh in an unknown tongue edifieth himself..."*

Lesson 75
THE GOD OF ALL COMFORT

This will be one of my favorite lessons. The reason is that I have experienced this revelation so many times personally; our wonderful, loving, precious God has comforted me in every sense possible. Believe me when I say my own personal image of God has been formed over years and years of studying the Word of God, being in His glorious presence, pastoring people and seeing how our wonderful Father is always so dear, so near and comforting to His people when they need Him the most. As Paul declared II Timothy 1:12 *"For the which cause I also suffer these things: nevertheless I am not ashamed: for I know whom I have believed, and am persuaded that he is able to keep that which I have committed unto him against that day."*

I have seen His hand gently helping me and countless others through the most difficult circumstances. I have heard His voice tenderly and lovingly speaking to me in others in the hour of their greatest needs. I have watched as people going through horrible circumstances have found Him and His abiding and loving presence. I have seen how Jesus our true and great Sheppard of the sheep carries His lambs in His arms when necessary. I can honestly say like David in Psalms 37:25 *"I have been young, and now am old; yet have I not seen the righteous forsaken, nor his seed begging bread."* This has been my life story, my God has never failed me, never forsaken me, never yelled or got angry with me even when I deserved all of these things. He has remained the most constant thing in my life. He is faithful, generous, kind, merciful, loving in all situations and in all of life's circumstances and always there as my dearest and closest friend! Each one of us however must hew this out of the rock in our own lives. One thing is absolutely certain as David declared is Psalms 56:9 *"When I cry unto thee, then shall mine enemies turn back: this I know; for God is for me."* I can testify that for almost an entire generation He has proven this to me.

My hope as we search the Scriptures concerning the God of all comfort is that you will receive this revelation, believe it and act on it by allowing Him to simply do what the Word says, and what His great heart desires to do for you. Jesus said in John 16:32 *"Behold, the hour cometh, yea, is now come, that ye shall be scattered, every man to his own, and shall leave me alone: and yet I am not alone, because the Father is with me."* You will clearly see that the Scriptures bear this out not just for Jesus but for you as well. Not only will you be comforted but you will learn and know how to share His comfort with others. It is certainly a privilege to be God's servant but even more so when you know and have a true Biblical image of Him in your heart, knowing how loving, kind, merciful, generous, caring and comforting He is and always has been. As you study, I hope you fall even that much more in love with Him. Never forget Isaiah 51:3 *"For the LORD shall comfort Zion: he will comfort all her waste places; and he will make her wilderness like Eden, and her desert like the garden of the LORD; joy and gladness shall be found therein, thanksgiving, and the voice of melody."* This is His heart. We are never alone or without comfort for He is always near!

I. II Corinthians 1:3-4 – *"...the Father of mercies, and the God of all comfort; who comforteth us in all our tribulation..."*

    A. Word definitions

        1. General – The consolation and reassurance of those who are in distress, anxiety or need. Such comfort is an essential aspect of the human condition. Scripture declares that God comforts His people in times of distress.

        2. Hebrew, *Nacham* – To sigh, to breathe strongly, to ease, to be sorry in a favorable sense, to console, to give solace, compassion, consolation.

        3. Greek, *Parakaleo* – To call near, to be of good comfort, to give consolation, to exhort, to implore.

II. Our God Is the God of All Comfort

    A. Scriptures declaring this

1. Isaiah 40:1 – *"Comfort ye, comfort ye my people, saith your God."*
2. Isaiah 66:12-13 – *"As one whom his mother comforteth, so will I comfort you; and ye shall be comforted in Jerusalem."*
3. Isaiah 51:3 – *"For the Lord shall comfort Zion: He will comfort all her waste places..."*
4. Isaiah 51:11-12-16 – *"...I, even I, am He that comforteth you..."*
5. Isaiah 52:9 – *"Break forth into joy, sing together, ye waste places of Jerusalem: for the Lord hath comforted His people..."*
6. Isaiah 49:13 – *"...for the Lord hath comforted His people, and will have mercy upon His afflicted."*
7. Psalms 71:21 – *"Thou shalt increase my greatness, and comfort me on every side."*
8. Zechariah 1:17 – *"...My cities through prosperity shall yet be spread abroad; and the Lord shall yet comfort Zion, and shall yet choose Jerusalem."*
9. II Thessalonians 2:16-17 – *"Now our Lord Jesus Christ Himself, and God, even our Father...Comfort your hearts..."*
10. Psalms 94:17-19 – *"...thy comforts delight my soul."*
11. Isaiah 57:15-18 – *"...I have seen his ways, and will heal him: I will lead him also, and restore comforts unto him and to his mourners."*
12. Matthew 5:4 – *"Blessed are they that mourn: for they shall be comforted."*

B. The Holy Spirit given as our comforter

1. Greek definition – *parakletos* – comforter, one called alongside to help, advocator, intercessor.

   a. John 15:26 – *"But when the Comforter is come, whom I will send unto you from the Father..."*
   b. John 14:16-17 – *"...and He shall give you another Comforter..."*
   c. John 14:26 – *"But the Comforter, which is the Holy Ghost..."*
   d. John 16:7-14
   e. Acts 9:31 – *"...walking in the fear of the Lord, and in the comfort of the Holy Ghost..."*
   f. Isaiah 61:2 – *"...to comfort all that mourn."*

III. Our Condition

A. It's hard for us to believe in a God of comfort

1. Jeremiah 8:18 – *"When I would comfort myself against sorrow, my heart is faint in me."*
2. Isaiah 49:14-16 – *"[14]But Zion said, The LORD hath forsaken me, and my Lord hath forgotten me. [15]Can a woman forget her sucking child, that she should not have compassion on the son of her womb? yea, they may forget, yet will I not forget thee. [16]Behold, I have graven thee upon the palms of my hands; thy walls are continually before me."*
3. Psalms 77:1-15 – *"...my soul refused to be comforted..."*
4. Psalms 119:82 – *"Mine eyes fail for Thy Word, saying, When wilt thou comfort me?"*
5. Lamentations 1:20-21 – *"...there is none to comfort me..."*
6. Genesis 37:34-35 – *"And Jacob...refused to be comforted..."*
7. Isaiah 54:11 – *"O thou afflicted, tossed with tempest, and not comforted, behold, I will lay thy stones with fair colours..."*

B. We have seen such a lack of comfort

1. Job 16:2 – *"...miserable comforters are ye all."*

2. Job 21:34 – *"How then comfort ye me in vain, seeing in your answers there remaineth falsehood?"*
3. Psalms 69:20 – *"...I looked for some to take pity, but there was none; and for comforters, but I found none."*
4. Ecclesiastes 4:1 – *"So I returned, and considered all the oppressions that are done under the sun: and behold the tears of such as were oppressed, and they had no comforter; and on the side of their oppressors there was power; but they had no comforter."*
5. Lamentations 1:8-10, 16-17
6. Zechariah 10:2 – *"...the idols have spoken vanity, and the diviners have seen a lie, and have told false dreams; they comfort in vain...because there was no shepherd."*
7. Isaiah 51:15-23
8. Job 2:9 – Job's wife said, *"...curse God, and die."*

C. He will not leave us comfortless

1. John 14:18
2. II Corinthians 7:6 – *"Nevertheless God, that comforteth those that are cast down..."*
3. Jeremiah 31:10-14
4. Hosea 2:14 – *"I will allure her...and speak comfortably to her."*

IV. Ways God Comforts Us

A. In Scripture

1. Psalms 23:4 – Rod and staff
2. Psalms 119:50 – His Word (Romans 15:4)
3. Psalms 119:76 – His mercy
4. Song of Solomon 2:5 – His presence
5. I Corinthians 14:3, 31 – Prophetic utterance
6. I Thessalonians 5:11, 14 – One another (I Thessalonians 4:18)

B. People

1. Genesis 5:29 – Noah
2. Genesis 18:5 – Abraham
3. Genesis 37:35 – Jacob's sons and daughters
4. Ephesians 6:22 – Tychicus (Colossians 4:18)
5. I Thessalonians 3:2 – Timothy
6. Job 42:11 – Our families

C. We must encourage ourselves

1. I Samuel 30:6 – *"...but David encouraged himself in the LORD his God."*
2. Psalms 103:1-2 – *"Bless the LORD, O my soul..."*
3. Psalms 104:1, 35 – *"...Bless thou the LORD, O my soul. Praise ye the LORD."*
4. Psalms 42:5-11
5. Acts 16:22-34
6. Isaiah 40:13
7. Isaiah 52:1-2 – *"Awake, awake; put on thy strength, O Zion; put on thy beautiful garments, O Jerusalem, the holy city: for henceforth there shall no more come into thee the uncircumcised and the unclean. Shake thyself from the dust; arise, and sit down, O Jerusalem: loose thyself from the bands of thy neck, O captive daughter of Zion."*
8. Isaiah 64:7 – *"...stirreth up himself to take hold of thee..."*

V. What We Should Do In Times When We Need Comfort

  A. Scriptures

   1. Psalms 61:1 – *"Hear my cry, O God; attend unto my prayer."*
   2. Psalms 62:8 – *"Trust in Him at all times..."*
   3. Psalms 91
   4. Psalms 56:3 – *"What time I am afraid, I will trust in Thee."*
   5. Isaiah 41:10 – *"Fear thou not; for I am with thee: be not dismayed..."*

Lesson 76
THE IMPORTANCE OF THE NAME OF JESUS

I. Jesus is the Name of the Godhead

    A. Scriptural definition

        1. Zechariah 14:9   6. John 8:58
        2. Colossians 1:19   7. Matthew 1:21-23
        3. Colossians 2:9   8. John 5:43
        4. Matthew 28:19   9. John 10:25
        5. Ephesians 1:20-21   10. John 17:25-26

Jesus came in the name of name of the Father, Son, and Holy Spirit. God is not a name, but God has a name, and that name is the <u>Lord Jesus Christ</u> !

    B. Jesus manifested the name of the Godhead

        1. John 17: 6, 26 – Jesus declared the name of the triune God and walked in His divine nature. He revealed God's character as He walked and ministered on the earth.

           a. John 14:7, 9
           b. Colossians 1:15
           c. Colossians 2:9

        2. Hebrews 1:2-3 – Jesus is the brightness of His glory and the express image of His person.

           a. Philippians 2:9-11 – The Godhead has given us His name, and it is exalted above all, and that name is Jesus.
           b. Colossians 3:17
           c. Colossians 1:15-19
           d. Ephesians 1:20-21
           e. Psalms 22:22

II. The Power and Authority of the Name JESUS

    A. All the things scripturally associated with His name

        1. What we can do in His name and what His name does for us

           a. Psalms 20:1 – It defends us
           b. Psalms 20:5 – Set up our banners
           c. Psalms 44:5 – Tread down our enemies

               1) Psalms 118:11-12

           d. Romans 10:13 – Salvation in His name

               1) Acts 10:43   5) Acts 2:21
               2) Psalms 54:1   6) I John 2:12
               3) Luke 1:31   7) I Corinthians 6:11
               4) Joel 2:32   8) Luke 24:47

  e. Psalms 91:14 – We are set on high
  f. Psalms 124:8 – Our help is in His name
  g. Proverbs 18:10 – A strong tower from the enemy
  h. John 17:12 – Kept by His name

  i. Mark 16:17 – Cast out devils

   1) Mark 9:38
   2) Acts 16:18
   3) Mark 16:17

  j. Mark 16:17 – Heal the sick in His name

   1) James 5:14
   2) Acts 4:30
   3) Acts 3:6

  k. Deuteronomy 18:18-22 – Prophesy in His name
  l. Luke 10:17 – Devils are subject to us in his name
  m John 20:31 – Life is in His name

  n Acts 4:30 – Signs, wonders, miracles, done in His name

   1) Mark 16:17

  o. Psalms 63:4 – Our ability to worship
  p. Psalms 124:8 – Protection in His name

   1) Psalms 91:10
   2) Psalms 20:1
   3) Psalms 89:36
   4) Psalms 91:14

III. All the Other Aspects of the Name

 A. Awesome is the name of Jesus

  1. Philippians 2:9-10   6. Psalms 111:9
  2. Psalms 99:3   7. Acts 19:17
  3. Hebrews 1:4   8. Ephesians 1:21
  4. Malachi 1:11, 14   9. Acts 4:12
  5. Isaiah 42:8

 B. His name can be trusted

  1. Psalms 33:21
  2. Zechariah 3:12
  3. Matthew 12:21

 C. His name is to be given glory

  1. Psalms 29:2
  2. John 12:28

3.   II Thessalonians 1:12

D.   His name is to be praised

1.   Hebrews 13:15   10.   Psalms 75:1
2.   Psalms 9:2   11.   Psalms 89:6
3.   Psalms 18:49   12.   Psalms 92:1
4.   Psalms 54:6   13.   Psalms 96:2
5.   Psalms 61:8   14.   Psalms 105:1, 3
6.   Psalms 69:30   15.   Psalms 142:7
7.   Psalms 66:2,4   16.   Psalms 149:3
8.   Psalms 68:4   17.   Isaiah 12:4
9.   Psalms 74:21

E.   His name is to be known

1.   Psalms 9:10
2.   Isaiah 52:6

F.   His name is to be remembered

1.   Psalms 20:7
2.   Psalms 119:55
3.   Malachi 3:16
4.   Isaiah 26:8

G.   His name is to be feared

1.   Psalms 61:5
2.   Psalms 86:11
3.   Malachi 4:2
4.   Revelation 11:18

H.   His name is to be exalted

1.   Psalms 34:3
2.   Psalms 138:2
3.   Isaiah 12:4

I.   His name is to be loved

1.   Psalms 69:36
2.   Psalms 119:132

J.   His name is excellent

1.   Psalms 81:9
2.   Psalms 148:13

K.   His name is not to be polluted

1.   Isaiah 48:11   6.   Leviticus 18:21
2.   Jeremiah 34:16   7.   Ezekiel 36:21-23

3. I Timothy 6:1
4. Ezekiel 20:39
5. Ezekiel 43:8

8. Romans 2:24
9. James 2:7

L. His name will endure

1. Psalms 72:17
2. Psalms 135:13
3. Isaiah 63:16

M. His name not to be taken in vain

1. Exodus 20:7

N. His name is the highest

1. Ephesians 1:21
2. Ephesians 3:15
3. Deuteronomy 28:58

4. II Samuel 7:13, 23
5. I Chronicles 16:10, 29
6. I Chronicles 29:13

O. His name is to be delighted in

1. Psalms 5:11
2. Psalms 9:2
3. Psalms 34:3

4. Psalms 48:10
5. Psalms 66:2
6. Psalms 18:49

P. His name is holy

1. Isaiah 57:15
2. Matthew 6:9
3. Luke 1:49

Q. Religion hates His name

1. Acts 4:18
2. Acts 5:28, 40
3. Matthew 10:22
4. Matthew 24:9
5. Luke 21:12, 17

6. Acts 9:16
7. Acts 4:17
8. Acts 9:29
9. John 15:20-21

R. His name is to be seen

1. Micah 6:9

S. His name is to be in the place of His choosing; in His city, upon His people

1. Exodus 20:24
2. I Kings 8:20, 29, 43
3. Deuteronomy 12:21
4. I Chronicles 13:6
5. II Samuel 6:2

6. I Kings 9:7
7. II Chronicles 7:20
8. II Chronicles 7:14
9. Jeremiah 7:12, 14

T. His name is blessed

      1.   Job 1:21

U.   We are to gather in His name

      1.   Matthew 18:20

V.   His name alone is worthy

      1.   Psalms 83:18
      2.   Psalms 113:2
      3.   Psalms 111:9

IV.   What We Are To Do With His Name

    A.   Ask in His name

      1.   John 14:13-14
      2.   John 15:16
      3.   John 16:23-24

    B.   We are to have faith in His name

      1.   Acts 3:16   4.   John 3:18
      2.   John 1:12   5.   John 20:31
      3.   John 2:23   6.   I John 3:23

    C.   His name is to be written in our minds

      1.   Revelation 14:1
      2.   Revelation 22:4
      3.   Revelation 3:12
      4.   II Thessalonians 1:12

    D.   We are to glorify His name in tribulation

      1.   Isaiah 24:15

    E.   Preach in His name

      1.   Acts 9:21
      2.   Acts 4:30

    F.   We must be willing to suffer and die for His name

      1.   Acts 9:16   6.   Acts 5:40-41
      2.   Acts 21:13   7.   Acts 15:26
      3.   Acts 5:41   8.   Mark 3:13
      4.   I Peter 4:14   9.   Hebrews 13:13-15
      5.   Matthew 19:29

    G.   We are to hold fast to His name

1. Revelation 2:13
2. Revelation 3:8

H. We are to walk in His name

1. Micah 4:5
2. Zechariah 10:12

I. We are to do things for His name's sake

1. I Samuel 12:22
2. Psalms 106:8
3. Revelation 2:3
4. III John 7
5. Mark 13:13
6. Acts 9:16
7. Isaiah 48:9

J. We are to make mention of His name – Isaiah 26:13
K. Everything we do we do in His name – Colossians 3:17

Lesson 77
THE NEED FOR MEEKNESS

Psalms 25:9-10 – *"The meek will he guide in judgment: and the meek will he teach his way. All the paths of the Lord are mercy and truth unto such as keep his covenant and his testimonies."*

I.   Definitions of meek

    A.   Hebrew – depressed (abased) in mind, humble, lowly.
    B.   Greek – mild, gentle, humble.
    C.   Dictionary – humbly patient, submissive, gentle, kind.
    D.   Composite Definition – teachable, one who has an ability to receive, not a know-it-all, peaceable.

II.   Meekness is an attribute to be desired by all of God's people.

    A.   God desires meekness

        1.   Zephaniah 2:3 – *"Seek the Lord (inquire for Him, inquire of Him, and require Him as the foremost necessity of your life) all you humble of the land who have acted in compliance with His revealed will and have kept His commandments; seek righteousness, seek humility (inquire for them, require them as vital). It may be that you will be hidden in the day of the Lord's anger."* (Amplified) – The Lord says here to seek meekness that we might be delivered from His anger.

            a.   Psalms 76:9

        2.   I Peter 3:4 – *"But let it be the inward adorning and beauty of the hidden person of the heart, with the incorruptible and unfading charm of a gentle and peaceful spirit, which (is not anxious or wrought up, but) is very precious in the sight of God."* (Amplified) – Meekness is of great price in His sight. It is the ornament God wants His people to wear. It cannot be corrupted.

        3.   Ephesians 4:2 – *"Living as becomes you, with complete lowliness of mind (humility) and meekness (unselfishness, gentleness, mildness), with patience, bearing with one another and making allowances because you love one another."* (Amplified) – One way to walk worthy of our calling is to walk in meekness. By doing so, we can keep the unity of the Spirit, avoiding pride and strife and divisions.

            a.   Titus 3:2 – *"To speak evil of no man, to be no brawlers, but gentle, shewing all meekness unto all men"*

        4.   Galatians 5:23-26 – Meekness is one of the fruits of the Spirit, so if we're filled with the Spirit, meekness should be operating in us. God wants us to be like Him, *"meek and lowly of heart"*.
        5.   Matthew 11:29 – *"Take My yoke upon you and learn of Me, for I am gentle (meek) and humble (lowly) in heart..."* (Amplified) – This, more than any other reason shows us that God desires meekness. We are being conformed into His image. Therefore, we will be meek like Him.

    B.   Meekness is a requirement for ministry.

        1.   I Timothy 6:11 – The man of God here is instructed to flee the desire of riches and wealth and run after godly qualities like meekness.

        2.   II Timothy 2:24-26 – *"And the servant of the Lord must not be quarrelsome (fighting and contending). Instead, he must be kindly to everyone and mild tempered (preserving the bond of*

peace); he must be a skilled and suitable teacher, patient and forbearing and willing to suffer wrong. He must correct his opponents with courtesy and gentleness, in the hope that God may grant that they will repent..." (Amplified) – The servant of God must not strive with those that oppose themselves, but respond with meekness. The thought here is if he doesn't they may not get out of bondage because he didn't lead them gently.

    a.   Instructing in meekness

        1) Galatians 6:1
        2) II Corinthians 10:1 – "*Now I Paul myself beseech you by the meekness and gentleness of Christ...*"

A good definition here of meekness is to always be considering yourself. We all have the potential of falling into sin. A true minister knows the only way to minister to people who have trouble backsliding is to deal gently with them. By letting them know you and Jesus still love them, you give them hope. Only in extreme cases are we to deal harshly with God's people (I Corinthians 4:21 – "*What will ye? shall I come unto you with a rod, or in love, and in the spirit of meekness?*")

        3) I Peter 3:15 – "*But sanctify the Lord God in your hearts: and be ready always to give an answer to every man that asketh you a reason of the hope that is in you with meekness and fear...*"

We are to always be ready to give an answer to anyone who asks about the Lord or His Word in meekness. We are not to talk like know-it-alls, for "*what do we have that we haven't received from the Lord?*" (See John 3:27, I Corinthians 4:6-7).

        4) James 3:13 – "*Who is there among you who is wise and intelligent? Then let him by his noble living show forth his good works with the unobtrusive humility, which is the proper attitude of true wisdom.*" (Amplified)
        5) II Timothy 2:24-25 – "*And the servant of the Lord must not strive; but be gentle unto all men, apt to teach, patient, In meekness instructing those that oppose themselves; if God peradventure will give them repentance to the acknowledging of the truth...*"

  3. Examples of Meekness

    a.   Numbers 12:3 – "*(Now the man Moses was very meek, above all the men which were upon the face of the earth.)*"
    b.   Matthew 21:5 – "*Tell ye the daughter of Sion, Behold, thy King cometh unto thee, meek, and sitting upon an ass, and a colt the foal of an ass.*"

C. Meekness is a requirement for receiving the Word and being taught.

  1. James 1:21 – "*So get rid of all uncleanness and the rampant outgrowth of wickedness, and in a humble (gentle, modest) spirit receive and welcome the Word which implanted and rooted (in your hearts) contains the power to save your souls.*" (Amplified) – We must receive the Word with meekness if we expect to receive its benefits.
  2. Psalms 25:9 – "*The meek will he guide in judgment: and the meek will he teach his way.*"
  3. Isaiah 66:2 – "*For all those things hath mine hand made, and all those things have been, saith the Lord: but to this man will I look, even to him that is poor and of a contrite spirit, and trembleth at my word.*" – God will teach those who are teachable.
  4. Luke 8:15 – "*But that on the good ground are they, which in an honest and good heart, having heard the word, keep it, and bring forth fruit with patience.*"
  5. Matthew 11:29 – If we are to learn of Him who is meek, we must also be.

D. The blessings of meekness

1. Psalms 22:26 – *"The meek shall eat and be satisfied: they shall praise the LORD that seek him: your heart shall live for ever."* – They always have their provision.
2. Psalms 147:6 – *"The Lord lifteth up the meek: he casteth the wicked down to the ground."* – The Lord lifts them out of every situation.
3. Psalms 149:4 – *"For the Lord taketh pleasure in his people: he will beautify the meek with salvation."* – They enjoy all the provisions of their salvation.
4. Isaiah 29:19 – *"The meek also shall increase their joy in the Lord, and the poor among men shall rejoice in the Holy One of Israel."*
5. Matthew 11:29 – Find rest for their souls
6. Psalms 37:11 and Matthew 5:5 – Dominion will be theirs again. The overcomers will surely reign with Jesus, but they will be gentle, compassionate rulers like He is.

   a. Psalms 37:29 – *"The righteous shall inherit the land, and dwell therein for ever."*
   b. Matthew 5:5 – *"Blessed (happy, blithesome, joyous, spiritually prosperous – with life-joy and satisfaction in God's favor and salvation, regardless of their outward conditions) are the meek (the mild, patient, long suffering), For they shall inherit the earth!"* (Amplified)
   c. Psalms 37:11 – *"But the meek (in the end) shall inherit the earth, and shall delight themselves in the abundance of peace."* (Amplified)
   d. Psalms 37:29 – *"Then the consistently righteous shall inherit the land and dwell upon it forever."* (Amplified)

Lesson 78
THE OPEN AND CLOSED BOOK ON WHY JESUS CAME

I.   Luke 4:16-22 – "*16And he came to Nazareth, where he had been brought up: and, as his custom was, he went into the synagogue on the sabbath day, and stood up for to read. 17And there was delivered unto him the book of the prophet Esaias. And when he had opened the book, he found the place where it was written, 18The Spirit of the Lord is upon me, because he hath anointed me to preach the gospel to the poor; he hath sent me to heal the brokenhearted, to preach deliverance to the captives, and recovering of sight to the blind, to set at liberty them that are bruised, 19To preach the acceptable year of the Lord. 20And he closed the book, and he gave it again to the minister, and sat down. And the eyes of all them that were in the synagogue were fastened on him. 21And he began to say unto them, This day is this scripture fulfilled in your ears. 22And all bare him witness, and wondered at the gracious words which proceeded out of his mouth. And they said, Is not this Joseph's son?*"

A.   Verse 16

1.   This is taking place where Jesus had been brought up
2.   Nazareth in Greek – branch, preservation
3.   He was accustomed to being called on to read the Scriptures

B.   Verse 17

1.   It just so happened (supernaturally) He was handed the book of Isaiah
2.   He opened (revelation) the book – Opened in Greek means – to unroll
3.   He turned to the exact passage He wanted

C.   Verse 18

1.   He gives the reason for why the "Spirit of the Lord" was upon Him.
2.   "*he hath anointed me to preach*" – "*for he has consecrated me to preach*"
3.   "*preach the gospel to the poor*" – "*good news to the poor*", "*to tell glad tidings to the destitute*"
4.   "*to heal the brokenhearted*"
5.   "*to preach deliverance to the captives*" – "*to proclaim to captives a release*", "*to announce to prisoners, you are free*"
6.   "*a recovering of sight to the blind*" – "*to the blind, you will see again*", "*to give new eyes to the blind*"
7.   "*to set at liberty them that are bruised*" – "*to let the broken victims go free*", "*setting the shattered free*", "*to free those who are oppressed*", "*to liberate the downtrodden*", "*to free those whom tyranny has crushed*"

D.   Verse 19

1.   "*To preach the acceptable year of the Lord*" – "*the year of the Lord's favor*", "*that the year of the Lord's good pleasure has come*", "*to proclaim a year when men may find acceptance with the Lord*"

E.   Verse 20

1.   "*And he closed the book...and sat down*" – "*And he closed the book (signifying this is done)*", "*rolling up the book*"
2.   "*And the eyes of all them that were in the synagogue were fastened on him*" – "*And the eyes of the whole congregation were riveted upon Him*"

    F.   Verse 21

        1.   *"This day is this scripture fulfilled in your ears"* – *"Today while you're listening, what is written here has come true"*, *"In your hearing this text is come true"*

    G.   Verse 22

        1.   *"And all bare him witness, and wondered at the gracious words which proceeded out of his mouth"* – *"There was a general stir of admiration, they were surprised that words of such grace should fall from His lips"*, *"they were astonished at the beautiful words that feel from His lips"*

        2.   *"Is not this Joseph's son?"* – This was asked because He was claiming to be more than just a man.

II.   Isaiah 61:1-3 – *"¹The Spirit of the Lord GOD is upon me; because the LORD hath anointed me to preach good tidings unto the meek; he hath sent me to bind up the brokenhearted, to proclaim liberty to the captives, and the opening of the prison to them that are bound; ²To proclaim the acceptable year of the LORD, and the day of vengeance of our God; to comfort all that mourn; ³To appoint unto them that mourn in Zion, to give unto them beauty for ashes, the oil of joy for mourning, the garment of praise for the spirit of heaviness; that they might be called trees of righteousness, the planting of the LORD, that he might be glorified."*

    A.   Verse 1

        a.   *"because the Lord hath anointed me"* – *"the reason God has consecrated me"*
        b.   *"to preach good <u>tidings</u>* (Hebrew- fresh, full, rosy, cheerful) *unto the meek"* – *"to bring good news to the lowly"*
        c.   Meek in Hebrew – lowly, humble, poor
        d.   *"<u>bind</u>* (Hebrew – to wrap fully like a turban) *up the brokenhearted"* – *"to bind up hearts that are broken"*
        e.   *"to proclaim liberty to the captives"* – *"to tell prisoners they are free"*
        f.   *"the <u>opening</u>* (Hebrew – double opening from jail) *of the prison to them that bound"* – *"to release those in prison"*, *"to tell captives they are released"*

    B.   Verse 2

        a.   *"To proclaim the <u>acceptable</u>* (Hebrew – delight, favor, good pleasure) *year of the Lord"* – *"the year of the Lord's favor"*, *"The Year of acceptance of Jehovah"*
        b.   *"the day of vengeance of our God"* – *"the day of God's avenging"*
        c.   *"to <u>comfort</u>* (Hebrew – to sigh with, to be sorry for) *all that mourn"*

    C.   Verse 3

        a.   *"To appoint unto them that mourn in Zion"* – *"comfort for every mourner"*
        b.   *"to give unto them <u>beauty</u>* (Hebrew – to cause to gleam, to embellish) *for <u>ashes</u>* (Hebrew – to scatter the dust)*, the oil of joy for mourning, the <u>garment</u>* (Hebrew – mantle, wrap, or covering) *of <u>praise</u>* (to be clamorously foolish) *for the spirit of <u>heaviness</u>* (Hebrew – dejection, fainthearted, to be weak, to be dark as dull)*"*
        c.   *"that they may be called <u>trees</u>* (Hebrew – strength, chief, an oak) *of righteousness"* – *"oaks of justice"*, *"sturdy oaks of greatness"*, *"lofty, strong and magnificent trees distinguished for their uprightness"*
        d.   *"the planting of the LORD, that he might be glorified."* – *"that He will get the glory for their deliverance."*

Lesson 79
THE POWER OF THE ATONING BLOOD

I.   A Look at the Blood And Its Power

A.   Blood speaks – The word *blood* occurs 447 times in Scripture. Especially in Leviticus which deals with how we can approach God, and our way into the holiest. In the book of Hebrews, the *blood* is spoken of nearly 100 times, almost always a commentary on Leviticus.

    1.   Blood contains the essence of human and animal life.

    2.   The life of our flesh is in (or carried by) the blood.

        a.   Leviticus 17:11 – *"For the life of the flesh is in the blood: and I have given it to you upon the altar to make an atonement for your souls: for it is the blood that maketh an atonement for the soul."*

When God created man, He molded his body out of the ground. He then breathed into man the breath of life. He somehow breathed into His creation, His own spiritual life and that life was held in the substance we call blood. Blood is not life; it carries life. We humans can only live if this ingredient flows through our veins. Life itself is spiritual, but it must be carried by something natural.

        b.   I John 5:8 – *"And there are three that bear witness in earth, the spirit, and the water, and the blood: and these three agree in one."* – Three witnesses on earth, the water, spirit and blood; The Word by the Holy Spirit is effectual in those who received Him. The blood witnesses to the Father we are now justified. Atonement has been made.

    3.   Leviticus 17:11-14 – God counts blood as a sacred thing, which He gave to both man and animal. It was forbidden to eat flesh from which the blood had not been removed completely. This was so important to the Lord that the penalty for it was being, "cut off from among his people". This penalty of lost fellowship was very strong.

    4.   Genesis 4:10 – *"The Lord said, what hast thou done? The voice of thy brother's blood crieth unto me from the ground."* This tells us that the life that was in Abel's blood did not cease after he was murdered. Abel's blood was crying out for vengeance.

        a.   Hebrews 12:24 – *"...the blood of sprinkling that speaketh better things than that of Abel..."* Abel's blood cried out for justice. Jesus' blood cries out for mercy. This is such a powerful truth, to know that the incorruptible, spotless, pure, and precious blood of Christ Jesus will never stop crying out. Not until this world ends, will it stop crying out to the Father as the Lamb of God for mercy for His creation. The blood is still crying from the mercy seat today because Jesus *"...ever liveth to make intercession for us."*

B.   History of blood sacrifices

    1.   It started way back in the beginning when Adam and Eve sinned

        a.   Genesis 3:21

Adam and Eve tried to use fig leaves to cover their nakedness (Verse 7). The King James Version of the Bible uses the word *apron*, which in the Hebrew means, a belt, girdle, armour. It comes from a root word that means to gird on, to be afraid, or to restrain on every side. This was the beginning of religion. Man trying to do only what God can do. Only blood can make atonement for your soul. He made them skins.

1) Leviticus 17:11
2) Hebrews 9:22 – "...*without shedding of blood is no remission.*" – Greek word for remission means – freedom, paid on, forgiveness or release from bondage – it comes from a root that means to send off; Other translations:

"...*unless blood is shed, there is no forgiveness to be obtained*..."
"...*unless blood is poured out, nothing is forgiven*..."
"...*there is neither release from sin and its guilt nor the remission of the due and merited punishment from sins*..."
"...*no blood shed, no remission of sin*..."

2. Genesis 4:2-4 – Abel, having learned from his Father about sacrificing and himself being a shepherd, offered a lamb and the best parts of the lamb as an offering. The Bible says, "...*God had respect unto Abel and his offering*..." – The Hebrew word for offering means – to apportion, bestow, a donation; other translations:

"...*The Lord looked with favor*..."
"...*took notice of Abel*..."
"...*approved of Abel*..."
"...*the Lord was pleased*..."

God respected it because sacrificing and the shedding of blood is a God ordained principle. How sad it is that those who walk and try to please God are persecuted by their brothers. It has been and always will be this way.

3. Genesis 8:20-22

Noah offered these blood sacrifices to the Lord once the ark rested. What the Bible says here is very important, "...*and the Lord smelled a sweet savour: and the Lord said in his heart*..."

This obviously touched God very deeply. After having judged the earth and wiping all of them out, with the exception of Noah and his family, this offering of repentance and thanksgiving caused God to say, "...*neither will I again smite any more every living thing*..." Blood atones and blood changes things. This principle was being established now on the earth. If man wanted to repent or bless God, this was the way he should do it.

You might ask why? Remember Jesus is the "*Lamb slain from the foundation of the world*..." (Revelation 13:8) God had already set the precedent, and those that would love Him and walk with Him understood this was His principle. In Genesis 22, when God called upon Abraham to offer Isaac, this principle was further validated. When God saw that Abraham was willing, He poured out His blessing upon him. Hebrews 11:19 tells us Abraham believed God would raise him up from the dead. Now a people were beginning to understand that God requires a sacrifice. He requires that blood be shed. The truth is that God never asks a man to do something that He isn't prepared to do also. He was hinting to the earth that a lamb had already been slain for them.

4. The Passover

a. Exodus 12:1-11 – A lamb for a house

b. Exodus 12:13-14

1) Blood shall be a token
2) When I see the blood

           3)   I will pass over you

     c.   Exodus 12:21-24

          1)   Bunch of hyssop
          2)   Dip it in the blood
          3)   Strike the lintel and door post
          4)   When He seeth the blood
          5)   The Lord will pass over
          6)   And will not suffer the destroyer to come into your houses to smite you.

Here we see that the blood not only connects us with God (a blood covenant), but also delivers us from death. The blood brings protection from God to all that have this revelation. He also established this as a feast, a memorial for them to do from then on.

    5.   Exodus 23:18 – *"Thou shalt not offer the blood of my sacrifice with unleavened bread; neither shall the fat of my sacrifice remain until the morning."*

The Lord is saying here, *"the blood of my sacrifice"*. In other words, God required this shedding of blood. It belongs to Him. What was set in motion here was to be a continual thing throughout Israel's history. God required blood from them, and they would sacrifice animals unto Him.

    6.   Blood of bulls and goats – Exodus 24:3-8

Moses poured half of the blood, shed from burnt offering, on the altar, and then he sprinkled the people. Israel and God had just made a blood covenant. This was before the Tabernacle had been built. It showed Israel that blood and a sacrifice were required by God. Thus the beginning for the principle of blood sacrifices to the Lord. Blood will be the way. Blood must be shed.

    7.   Exodus 29:1-3, 10-29 – Cleansing the priests; the blood shed here was to reveal things.

     a.   *"to hallow them"* – Hallow in Hebrew means – to be or make clean, to sanctify
     b.   *"Aaron and his sons shall put their hands upon the head of the bullock."* – This was for forgiveness of their sins.

     c.   Blood was put on:

          1)   The horns of the altar – This speaks of the blood covering the whole earth as well as sanctifying the priests to minister at the altar.
          2)   The rest of the blood was poured out at the bottom of the altar.

     d.   Then a ram was brought and Aaron and his sons laid their hands upon the head of the ram.
     e.   The blood was then sprinkled around and on the altar.
     f.   The other ram was brought and Aaron and his sons, once again laid their hands on it.
     g.   The ram was then killed.

     h.   Blood was to be placed upon the:

          1)   Tip of the right ear
          2)   Thumb of right hand
          3)   Upon the great toe of right foot
          4)   Then sprinkled upon the altar round about

5) Then a mixture of blood and oil sprinkled on the priests and their garments
6) Then God says they shall be holy

We see that no one can speak or minister for or to Him without blood being shed and placed upon our ear, (to be able to hear from the Lord), on the thumb (to be able to do the work of the Lord), on the toe (to be able to walk with the Lord), and then sprinkled all around the altar (signifying that the altar, or the place they were standing, spiritually speaking, was sanctified). It is not just the blood but blood mixed with oil, (later oil is to be placed on the priests' ear, thumb and toe). It takes the blood of Jesus and the anointing of the Holy Ghost to hallow, or make us holy.

8. Exodus 29:36 – This was to happen every day. They offered a bullock for a sin offering for atonement and cleansing. Atonement in Hebrew means – to cover over, to propitiate, to condone, reconcile

9. Atonement for Israel obtained by blood

   a. Leviticus 1:2-5

      1) Israel was to bring of the herd or flock an animal without blemish (symbolically this is speaking of the Lamb of God without spot)
      2) Then they were to put their hands on the head of the animal and kill it. It then made atonement for him. This blood indicated the substitution of the animal's blood for that of the sinner.

   10. Joshua 2:4, 9-17, 18 (Joshua 6:23-24)

This is the story of Rahab, the harlot who helped Israel. When Israel came to attack, they promised that neither she nor any of her family would be hurt as long as she placed in the window the piece of <u>scarlet</u> thread. Scarlet is blood red; this is a type of the blood. God spared this lowly harlot because she believed in him. Deliverance truly comes through the blood.

   11. I Kings 8:5 – As Solomon was preparing to dedicate the temple, he and all of the children of Israel were sacrificing before the Ark of the Covenant. They were sacrificing sheep and oxen that could not be numbered for multitude. Other translations:

"...sacrificing sheep and oxen, so many they could not be numbered or counted."

The revelation for us is that at the dedication of God's final house (which Solomon's temple represents), blood will be everywhere. So this tells us that when the last days are fully come, there will be a remembrance of His blood. We come in desperate and needy for blood (Adam). We will go out a people purchased by the precious blood of Christ. A people who will ever be thankful for what our Precious Lord did. Jesus is our one and only saviour. Throughout eternity we will ever be praising Him.

II. The Blood of the Lamb of God

Though Israel had to do this often, and it only covered their sins, it was pointing to a day when the Messiah would come and redeem them.

   A. John 1:29 – Jesus was the Lamb of God, given to "...*taketh away the sin of the world*..." For Jesus, in one offering, has obtained eternal redemption for us.

      1. Hebrews 9:11-14

Neither by the blood of bulls and goats and calves, but by His own blood had he entered once into the holy place, having obtained eternal redemption for us! How much more shall the blood of Christ, "...*offered himself without spot to God, purge your conscience.*"

The blood of animals was now no longer acceptable. Only the one time sacrifice of Jesus, the shedding of His blood is acceptable.

2.   Hebrews 10:1-4

   a.   The law was a shadow (or a type).
   b.   Those sacrifices which were offered year by year could never make them perfect.
   c.   It is not possible for the blood of an animal to take away sins. If so, they would not have been conscience of their sins.

3.   Hebrews 10:5-10

   a.   God was not interested any more in sacrifice and offerings that were offered by the law.
   b.   But he had prepared the body of his own son.
   c.   We are sanctified through the offering of the body of Jesus Christ <u>once for all</u>.

4.   Hebrews 10:14-22

   a.   By one offering he hath perfected for ever them that are sanctified.
   b.   This is the new covenant.
   c.   Because of Jesus' sacrifice, he will never remember our sins and iniquities any more.
   d.   Where remission of these is, there is no more need for sacrifice and offering for sin.
   e.   We can now enter boldly into the most holy place by the blood of Jesus.
   f.   We can draw near now because our hearts have been sprinkled from an evil conscience by his blood.

5.   I Peter 1:19

The Greek word for *precious* means – valuable, costly, honored and esteemed. It comes from a root that means value, money paid. We have not been redeemed by corruptible things. But with the precious blood of Christ.

   a.   I Corinthians 6:20

We have been bought with a price. The great substitution sacrifice of our blessed and wonderful Lord, on the cross is the price for our salvation. It's hard to even read or write this because when we consider His precious blood, it overwhelms us. All we can do is worship and thank Him. So, as Paul says, the way we can thank Him is to glorify God in our lives.

   b.   I Corinthians 7:23

6.   Joel 3:21 – He has kept His promise to cleanse our blood, with His own blood.

7.   Romans 3:23-25

   a.   All have sinned and fallen short of His glory.
   b.   Being justified freely through the redemption that is in Jesus Christ.

   c.   Whom God sat forth to be a propitiation.

1) Propitiation in Greek means an atoning victim. It is used in Hebrews 9:5, as the mercy seat. He was the atoning victim. His blood stands for the voluntary giving up of His life, by the shedding of His blood in expiatory sacrifice under divine judgment righteously due to us as sinners. He simply took our place.

   a) I John 2:2 – *"He is the propitiation for our sins: and not for ours only, but also for the sins of the whole world."*

   (1) Other translations

"...the one who made personal atonement for our sins..."
"...and he is Himself the atoning sacrifice for our sins..."
"...He in his own person, is the atonement for our sins..."

   b) I John 4:10 – *"Herein is love, not that we loved God, but that He loved us, and sent his Son to be the propitiation for our sins."*

   (1) Other translations

"...and sending his Son as an atoning sacrifice for our sins..."
"...to make personal atonement..."

8. I Peter 1:2 – *"...sprinkling of the blood of Jesus Christ..."*

9. Matthew 26:28 (I Corinthians 10:16) – This was the last supper. Here He foretold us of His cross, where his blood will be shed for many for the remission of sins.

   a. I Corinthians 11:25-27 – This is why the communion table is so very important. We remember Him there.

10. John 6:53-56

   a. Without symbolically drinking His blood and eating His flesh, we have no life in us.
   b. *"He that eateth my flesh and drinketh my blood, dwelleth in me, and I in him."*

11. Acts 20:28 – The church was purchased by His own blood.
12. Ephesians 1:7 – Redemption through His blood, the forgiveness of sins
13. Ephesians 2:13 – We who were far off are made nigh by the blood of Christ (Colossians 1:14)

14. Hebrews 13:12, 20

"...that he might sanctify the people with His own blood..." (verse 12)
"...through the blood of the everlasting covenant..." (verse 20)

15. I John 1:7 – *"...if we walk in light, as he...and the blood of Jesus Christ his Son cleanseth us from all sin."*
16. I John 5:6-8
17. Revelation 1:5 – *"...unto him that loved us and washed us from our sins in his own blood..."*
18. Colossians 1:20 – Peace has come through the blood of Jesus

B. The future of the Blood of Jesus

1. Revelation 19:13 – When the heavens open He is coming again in a vesture dipped in blood on which is written, "King of Kings and Lord of Lords." Truly he has earned these titles as well as the vesture because of his great and marvelous sacrifice.

2. Zechariah 13:1 – In the last days, a fountain will be opened to God's people. The word *fountain* in Hebrew means, something dug, a source of blood, water or tears. I believe that just as we believe the feasts of Passover, Pentecost, and Tabernacles are to be experienced spiritually, so also shall the Day of Atonement. For all those who have struggled against sin, as long as they kept fighting and repenting, the day will come when, as His people before His coming, will experience deliverance totally from sin. (Proverbs 24:16)

3. Revelation 12:9 – "...*And they overcame him (*satan*) by the blood of the Lamb, and by the word of their testimony.*" – Other translations

"...because of the blood..."
"...and they conquered him by the blood of the lamb."
"...they defeated him by the blood of the lamb."
"...their victory was due to the blood of the lamb."

Lesson 80
THE WORKINGS AND DEALINGS OF GOD

I.   Genesis 8:22 – *"While the earth remaineth, seedtime and harvest, and cold and heat, and summer and winter, and day and night shall not cease."*

   After this judgment (Noah's flood), God decided how He would work and deal with His people.

   A.   God controls and has established all the times of our lives

      1.   Acts 17:26 – *"And hath made of one blood all nations of men for to dwell on all the face of the earth, and hath determined the times before appointed, and the bounds of their habitation"*

      2.   Job 14:5 – *"Seeing his days are determined, the number of his months are with thee, thou hast appointed his bounds that he cannot pass"*

         a.   Other translations:

"Whether the course of his life on earth be one day, or months be numbered out for him, he cometh to the term thou has set, but cannot pass it."
"Since mans days are already determined and the number of his months is wholly in your control, and he cannot pass the bounds of his allotted time"
"Since man's days are measured out, since his tale of months, depends on you. Since you assign him bounds he cannot pass."

         b.   Job 23:14

      3.   Acts 1:7 – *"...It is not for you to know the times or the seasons, which the Father hath put in his own power."*

         a.   Psalms 104:19-24

      4.   Deuteronomy 32:8 – *"When the most High divided to the nations their inheritance, when he separated the sons of Adam, he set the bounds of the people according to the number of the children of Israel."*

      5.   Psalms 74:16-17 – *"The day is thine, the night also is thine: thou hast prepared the light and the sun. Thou hast set all the borders of the earth: thou hast made summer and winter."*

         a.   Jeremiah 33:19-26
         b.   Jeremiah 5:24
         c.   Daniel 2:19-23

      6.   Psalms 31:15 – *"My times are in thy hand..."*

         Other translation, *"My destiny is under your control..."*

         a.   Job 24:1 – *"Why, seeing times are not hidden from the Almighty, do they that know him not see his days?"*
         b.   I Chronicles 12:32
         c.   I Timothy 6:15

II.   A Scriptural Look at How God Works and Deals with His People

A. Ecclesiastes 3:1-8, 11, 17

   1. Philippians 4:12-13 – *"I know both how to be abased, and I know how to abound: every where and in all things I am instructed both to be full and to be hungry, both to abound and to suffer need..."*

   2. Luke 24:50 – *"And he led them out as far as to Bethany, and he lifted up his hands, and blessed them."* Bethany in Greek – House of figs or fruitfulness, house of affliction

   3. Romans 11:22 – *"Behold therefore the goodness and severity of God..."*

   4. Ecclesiastes 7:14 – *"In the day of prosperity be joyful, but in the day of adversity consider: God also hath set the one over against the other, to the end that man should find nothing after him."*

   5. Psalms 66:12 – *"Thou hast caused men to ride over our heads; we went through fire and through water: but thou broughtest us out into a wealthy place."*

   6. John 19:41 – *"Now in the place where he was crucified there was a garden..."* Other translation, *"There was a garden near the place he was crucified..."*

   7. Hosea 6:1 – *"Come, and let us return unto the LORD: for he hath torn, and he will heal us; he hath smitten, and he will bind us up."*

   8. Deuteronomy 32:39 – *"See now that I, even I, am he, and there is no god with me: I kill, and I make alive; I wound, and I heal: neither is there any that can deliver out of my hand."*

   9. I Samuel 2:6-8 – *"The LORD killeth, and maketh alive: he bringeth down to the grave, and bringeth up. The LORD maketh poor, and maketh rich: he bringeth low, and lifteth up. He raiseth up the poor out of the dust, and lifteth up the beggar from the dunghill, to set them among princes, and to make them inherit the throne of glory: for the pillars of the earth are the LORD's, and he hath set the world upon them."*

  10. Psalms 90:3 – *"Thou turnest man to destruction* (Hebrew – depression)*; and sayest, Return, ye children of men."* – Other translation, *"Thou turnest man back to the dust and sayest, turn back O children of men"*

  11. Jeremiah 18:2-4 – *"Arise, and go down to the potter's house, and there I will cause thee to hear my words. Then I went down to the potter's house, and, behold, he wrought a work on the wheels. And the vessel that he made of clay was marred* (Hebrew ruined) *in the hand of the potter: so he made it again another vessel, as seemed good to the potter to make it."*

      a. The two hands of God

         1) Right – blessing
         2) Left – judgment

  12. Isaiah 45:7 – *"I form the light, and create darkness: I make peace, and create evil: I the LORD do all these things."*

  13. Isaiah 61:3 – *"To appoint unto them that mourn in Zion, to give unto them beauty for ashes, the oil of joy for mourning, the garment of praise for the spirit of heaviness; that they might be called trees of righteousness, the planting of the LORD, that he might be glorified."*

  14. Job 14:7-9

B. All is working according to His plan

   1. Romans 8:28 – *"And we know that all things work together for good to them that love God, to them who are the called according to his purpose."*

2. Job 23:14 – *"For he performeth the thing that is appointed for me: and many such things are with him."* Other translations:

"For he will complete what he appoints for me"
"He will carry out what He has planned for me."

C. The principle of dying to bring forth life

1. John 12:24-25 – *"...Except a corn of wheat fall into the ground and die, it abideth alone: but if it die, it bringeth forth much fruit. He that loveth his life shall lose it; and he that hateth his life in this world shall keep it unto life eternal."*
2. Romans 6:4-5 – *"Therefore we are buried with him by baptism into death: that like as Christ was raised up from the dead by the glory of the Father, even so we also should walk in newness of life..."*
3 I Corinthians 15:36 – *"Thou fool, that which thou sowest is not quickened, except it die"*
4. II Corinthians 4:10
5. II Corinthians 6:9

Lesson 81
UNITY

Unity does not mean agreeing with everything, but it does mean flowing together toward a common goal. (Jeremiah 31:12 – "*Therefore they shall come and sing in the height of Zion, and shall flow together to the goodness of the LORD...*")

I. What Is God Doing?

    A. Ephesians 1:10 – "*That in the dispensation of the fulness of times he might gather together in one all things in Christ, both which are in heaven, and which are on earth; even in him:*"

    B. Isaiah 60:1-6

    C. Ezekiel 37:1-10

II. This Unity Has Always Been In The Heart Of God.

    A. John 17:18-23 – "[18]*As thou hast sent me into the world, even so have I also sent them into the world.* [19]*And for their sakes I sanctify myself, that they also might be sanctified through the truth.* [20]*Neither pray I for these alone, but for them also which shall believe on me through their word;* [21]*That they all may be one; as thou, Father, art in me, and I in thee, that they also may be one in us: that the world may believe that thou hast sent me.* [22]*And the glory which thou gavest me I have given them; that they may be one, even as we are one:* [23]*I in them, and thou in me, that they may be made perfect in one; and that the world may know that thou hast sent me, and hast loved them, as thou hast loved me.*"

    B. Genesis 2:23-25 – They had unity with God and with each other until Satan came.

    C. Philippians 2:1-3

    D. I Corinthians 1:10 – "*...that there be no divisions among you; but that ye be perfectly joined together in the same mind and in the same judgment.*"

    E. Acts 2:41-47

III. Satan's Desire is to Divide and Separate

    A. Ezra 4:1-6

    B. I Corinthians 3:3

    C. Proverbs 6:19 – Discord – Judge

IV. Blessings of Unity

    A. Psalms 133 – "[1]*Behold, how good and how pleasant it is for brethren to dwell together in unity!* [2]*It is like the precious ointment upon the head, that ran down upon the beard, even Aaron's beard: that went down to the skirts of his garments;* [3]*As the dew of Hermon, and as the dew that descended upon the mountains of Zion: for there the LORD commanded the blessing, even life for evermore.*"

        1. Good
        2. Pleasant
        3. Anointing
        4. God commands His blessings
        5. Life

    B. II Chronicles 5:11-14 – "*...[13]It came even to pass, as the trumpeters and singers were as one, to make one sound to be heard in praising and thanking the LORD; and when they lifted up their voice with the trumpets and cymbals and instruments of musick, and praised the LORD, saying, For he is good; for his mercy endureth for ever: that then the house was filled with a cloud, even the house of* *the LORD; 14So that the priests could not stand to minister by reason of the cloud: for the glory of the LORD had filled the house of God."*

    1.   The Glory of God filled the house
    2.   Priests were slain in the spirit

C.   Matthew 18:19-20 – *"19Again I say unto you, That if two of you shall agree on earth as touching any thing that they shall ask, it shall be done for them of my Father which is in heaven. 20For where two or three are gathered together in my name, there am I in the midst of them."*

    1.   Prayers answered
    2.   He is in the midst of unity

D.   Genesis 11:1-9 – Nothing that they had vision for would be restrained from them as long as they were in unity!

V.   How Then Can We Have Unity?

A.   Lift up Jesus

    a.   Genesis 49:10 – *"The sceptre shall not depart from Judah, nor a lawgiver from between his feet, until Shiloh come; and unto him shall the gathering of the people be."*
    b.   Isaiah 60:1-5
    c.   John 12:32 – *"And I, if I be lifted up from the earth, will draw all men unto me."*

B.   By realizing we don't have it all

    a.   Isaiah 65:5 – *"Which say, Stand by thyself, come not near to me; for I am holier than thou. These are a smoke in my nose, a fire that burneth all the day."*
    b.   I Corinthians 3:1-9 – God hates a sectarian spirit.

C.   Everybody has a part, and without it we won't make it

    a.   I Corinthians 12:12-27
    b.   Ephesians 4:11-16
    c.   Song of Solomon 5:16
    d.   Joel 2:7-8

D.   Be willing to humble ourselves and flow

    a.   Jeremiah 31:10-14 – *"10Hear the word of the LORD, O ye nations, and declare it in the isles afar off, and say, He that scattered Israel will gather him, and keep him, as a shepherd doth his flock. 11For the LORD hath redeemed Jacob, and ransomed him from the hand of him that was stronger than he. 12Therefore they shall come and sing in the height of Zion, and shall flow together to the goodness of the LORD, for wheat, and for wine, and for oil, and for the young of the flock and of the herd: and their soul shall be as a watered garden; and they shall not sorrow any more at all. 13Then shall the virgin rejoice in the dance, both young men and old together: for I will turn their mourning into joy, and will comfort them, and make them rejoice from their sorrow. 14And I will satiate the soul of the priests with fatness, and my people shall be satisfied with my goodness, saith the LORD."*

Lesson 82
WALKING IN LOVE

I.   God Wants Us to Walk in Love

   A.   Ephesians 5:1-3 – "*Be ye therefore followers of God, as dear children; And walk in love, as Christ also hath loved us, and hath given himself for us an offering and a sacrifice to God for a sweetsmelling savour...*"
   B.   Ephesians 4:1-4
   C.   I John 4:7, 11, 19
   D.   I John 3:9-18
   E.   I Thessalonians 4:9-10 – "*... ye yourselves are taught of God to love one another....but we beseech you, brethren, that ye increase more and more;*"
   F.   Hebrews 13:1 – "*Let brotherly love continue.*"

II. How Can We Do This? By Realizing We Are ONE BODY

   A.   I Corinthians 12:12-14
   B.   I Peter 2:17 – "*Honour all men. Love the brotherhood. Fear God. Honour the king.*"
   C.   I Peter 1:22 – "*Seeing ye have purified your souls in obeying the truth through the Spirit unto unfeigned love of the brethren, see that ye love one another with a pure heart fervently:*"
   D.   Galatians 6:10 – "*As we have therefore opportunity, let us do good unto all men, especially unto them who are of the household of faith.*"
   E.   Ephesians 2:19 – "*Now therefore ye are no more strangers and foreigners, but fellowcitizens with the saints, and of the household of God;*"

III. Following Jesus' Example

   A.   I Samuel 16:7 – "*...but the LORD looketh on the heart.*"
   B.   I Peter 2:21-24
   C.   Ephesians 2:4-5 – "*...God, who is rich in mercy, for his great love wherewith he loved us...*"
   D.   Matthew 21:5 – "*...thy King cometh unto thee, meek, and sitting upon an ass...*"
   E.   John 7:18
   F.   Proverbs 18:24 – "*A man that hath friends must shew himself friendly: and there is a friend that sticketh closer than a brother.*"
   G.   Isaiah 53:7 – "*He was oppressed, and he was afflicted, yet he opened not his mouth...*"
   H.   Matthew 11:29 – "*Take my yoke upon you, and learn of me; for I am meek and lowly in heart: and ye shall find rest unto your souls.*"

IV. God Wants Meek People

   A.   Isaiah 57:15 – "*...I dwell.with him also that is of a contrite and humble spirit...*"
   B.   Psalms 25:9 – "*The meek will he guide in judgment: and the meek will he teach his way.*"
   C.   I Peter 3:4
   D.   Matthew 5:5 – "*Blessed are the meek: for they shall inherit the earth.*"

V.   Allow the Holy Ghost to Move Through Us

   A.   Galatians 5:23
   B.   Colossians 3:12 – "*Put on therefore, as the elect of God, holy and beloved, bowels of mercies, kindness, humbleness of mind, meekness, longsuffering;*"
   C.   Romans 5:5 – "*...the love of God is shed abroad in our hearts by the Holy Ghost which is given unto us.*"

VI.   What Not To Do.

    A.   Luke 9:51-56

    B.   John 7:24 – *"Judge not according to the appearance, but judge righteous judgment."*

    C.   Luke 6:32 – *"For if ye love them which love you, what thank have ye? for sinners also love those that love them."*

    D.   Luke 18:10-15 – Parable

VII.   What To Do

    A.   Galatians 6:1 – *"Brethren, if a man be overtaken in a fault, ye which are spiritual, restore such an one in the spirit of meekness; considering thyself, lest thou also be tempted."*

    B.   II Timothy 2:25 – *"In meekness instructing those that oppose themselves..."*

    C.   Matthew 10:16 – *"...be ye therefore wise as serpents, and harmless as doves."* (II Samuel 16:5, 13)

    D.   Jude 21 – *"Keep yourselves in the love of God..."*

    E.   I Corinthians 13:4-8

    F.   I Thessalonians 3:12 – *"And the Lord make you to increase and abound in love one toward another, and toward all men, even as we do toward you:"* – John 13:34-35

VIII.   I Peter 1:22 – *"Seeing ye have purified your souls in obeying the truth through the Spirit unto unfeigned love of the brethren, see that ye love one another with a pure heart fervently:"* (Matt 24:12)

    A.   Hebrews 10:24-26

        1.   Romans 13:8-13

    B.   Why should we love and care?

        1.   God commands us to.

            a.   I John 4:21 – *"...this commandment have we from him, That he who loveth God love his brother also"*

            b.   I Peter 2:17 – *"Honour all men. Love the brotherhood. Fear God..."*

            c.   Hebrews 13:1 – *"Let brotherly love continue."*

            d.   I Peter 3:8 – *"Finally, be ye all of one mind, having compassion one of another, love as brethren, be pitiful, be courteous:"*

    C.   Because God loved us in spite of ourselves and expects the same out of us.

        1.   John 15:12 – *"...love one another, as I have loved you."*

        2.   I John 4:7-10

        3.   Ephesians 5:2 – *"And walk in love, as Christ also hath loved us, and hath given himself for us..."*

        4.   I John 3:16 – *"Hereby perceive we the love of God, because he laid down his life for us: and we ought to lay down our lives for the brethren."*

        5.   I Thessalonians 2:4-10

IX.   God Is Tired Of Our Excuses

    A.   John 13:35 – *"By this shall all men know that ye are my disciples, if ye have love one to another."*

    B.   I John 3:17, 19

    C.   Matthew 25:34-40

D. Luke 10:34 – *"And went to him, and bound up his wounds, pouring in oil and wine, and set him on his own beast, and brought him to an inn, and took care of him."*

X. **Why Does God Call Us Into Covenant?**

A. I Peter 4:8 – *"And above all things have fervent charity among yourselves: for charity shall cover the multitude of sins."*
B. Ecclesiastes 4:9-13
C. I Corinthians 12:14-28

D. Galatians 6:2 – *"Bear ye one another's burdens, and so fulfil the law of Christ."*

1. I Thessalonians 5:14 – Support the weak.
2. Romans 15:1 – We ought to bear the infirmities of the weak.
3. Acts 20:35

E. Song of Solomon 5:16 – *"His mouth is most sweet: yea, he is altogether lovely. This is my beloved, and this is my friend, O daughters of Jerusalem."*

We are in this together

1. I Samuel 30:9-10, 21, 25
2. Colossians 2:2 – *"That their hearts might be comforted, being knit together in love..."*
3. Acts 2:41-47

XI. **What Manner Of Love Is This?**

A. Laying down your life.

1. John 15:13 – *"Greater love hath no man than this, that a man lay down his life for his friends."*
2. II Corinthians 12:14-16
3. I Thessalonians 2:4-10

B. Philippians 2:20-21 – Unselfish

1. Numbers 14:11-22

C. Romans 12:9 – I Peter 1:22 – Without hypocrisy

D. Being hospitable

1. I Peter 4:9 – *"Use hospitality one to another without grudging.*
2. Romans 12:13 – *"Distributing to the necessity of saints; given to hospitality."*

E. Care for someone – I Corinthians 12:25 – *"...members should have the same care one for another."*
F. Speak not evil
G. I Corinthians 13:4-8 – God's love

Lesson 83
WALKING IN TRUTH

I. Jeremiah 9:3 – Isaiah 59:9-15

    A. What about man? Is he basically honest?

        1. Psalms 39:5 – *"...verily every man at his best state is altogether vanity. Selah."*
        2. John 2:23-25 – *"...But Jesus did not commit himself unto them, because he knew all men..."*
        3. Jeremiah 17:9 – *"The heart is deceitful above all things..."* (Romans 7:18)
        4. Jeremiah 10:23 – (Proverbs 14:12)

    B. Don't trust in men

        1. Jeremiah 9:4-5 – Neighbors and brothers
        2. Micah 7:5 – Friend, guide, wife (or husband)

        3. Proverbs 28:26 – Ourselves

            a. II Corinthians 1:9 – *"...we should not trust in ourselves..."*

        4. Jeremiah 17:5-6 – Men and flesh in general

            a. Psalms 118:8 – *"It is better to trust in the LORD than to put confidence in man."*

        5. Psalms 146:3 – Princes or leaders

            a. Psalms 118:9 – *"It is better to trust in the LORD than to put confidence in princes."*

II. There Are and Will Be A People Walking In Truth.

    A. Examples

        1. II John 4 – *"I rejoiced greatly that I found of thy children walking in truth..."*
        2. III John 3-4

III. Many People Are Talking But Not Walking.

    A. Examples

        1. I John 2:6 – *"He that saith he abideth in him ought himself also so to walk, even as he walked."*
        2. I John 3:18 – *"My little children, let us not love in word, neither in tongue; but in deed and in truth."*
        3. Matthew 23:23
        4. I Samuel 2:3

    B. What we normally do

        1. Romans 1:18 – *"...who hold the truth in unrighteousness;"*
        2. James 3:14 – *"But if ye have bitter envying and strife in your hearts, glory not, and lie not against the truth."*

You can be right about something, but wrong in attitude, (i.e.) saying something that is true to get something (money).

IV. Truth Must Be Bought.

A. Proverbs 23:23 – *"Buy the truth, and sell it not..."*

V. How Can We Walk In Truth?

A. Start by being honest with ourselves

1. Psalms 15:2 – *"...speaketh the truth in his heart."*
2. Psalms 51:6 – *"Behold, thou desirest truth in the inward parts..."*
3. Luke 1:15 – *"For he shall be great in the sight of the Lord..."*
4. I John 1:6-8

We must be honest with ourselves before we can have true fellowship with others.

B. Honest with others

1. Ephesians 4:25 – *"Wherefore putting away lying, speak every man truth with his neighbour: for we are members one of another."*
2. Romans 12:17 – *"...Provide things honest in the sight of all men."*
3. I Thessalonians 4:12 – *"That ye may walk honestly toward them that are without, and that ye may have lack of nothing."*
4. Exodus 18:21

C. Honest with God

1. Joshua 24:14 – *"...fear the LORD, and serve him in sincerity and in truth..."*
2. I Samuel 12:24

D. Examples of not walking in truth

1. Acts 5:1-27
2. 2 Kings 5:20-27
3. Genesis 12:10-20
4. Ezekiel 44:9-20

VI. As We Make Decisions Inwardly, Results Follow Outwardly.

A. Examples

1. John 14:16-17
2. I John 5:6

B. See it in the Word

1. John 17:17 – *"Sanctify them through thy truth: thy word is truth."*
2. John 8:32 – *"And ye shall know the truth, and the truth shall make you free."*

C. In practical terms

      1.   Micah 6:8 – *"He hath shewed thee, O man, what is good; and what doth the LORD require of thee, but to do justly, and to love mercy, and to walk humbly with thy God?"*

      2.   Matthew 5:8 – *"Blessed are the pure in heart: for they shall see God."*

VII. The World Needs Men of Truth

    A.   Examples

      1.   Exodus 18:21

      2.   Psalms 25:5

Lesson 84
THE TREE OF LIFE

I.   The Beginning

A.   Genesis 3:22-24 – Man was denied the tree of life for a reason

   1.   Two trees in the garden

      a.   Tree of life

         1)   Hebrew word for tree means firmness, and it comes from a root word meaning, "to close the eyes shut, to fasten".
         2)   The Hebrew Word for life means, "alive, raw, fresh".
         3)   Definition of the tree of life: a firmness to keep the eyes fastened shut, to be alive, fresh, and raw in God
         4)   Jesus is the tree of life personified.
         5)   Man was originally intended to live from this tree. Ultimately, all men will but because of the fall, a process to prepare us to receive this tree and become this tree had to be started. By eating from the other tree, man now must be purged, etc.

      b.   Tree of knowledge of good and evil

         1)   Genesis 2:16-17

            a)   Not to eat of it
            b)   "Die", literal Hebrew – "in dying thou shalt die"

   2.   Genesis 3:1-5

      a.   Verse 1 – The warfare is over the Word God
      b.   Verse 4 – The first lie (John 8:44)
      c.   Verse 5 – "*...your eyes shall be opened.*"

The tree of life was meant to keep our eyes shut, "to know only God", "to hear only God", "to stay fresh in Him", "to live by His choices", to stay raw or innocent", "to live by Him"

      d.   The opening of the eyes means:

         1)   You make your choices
         2)   You've allowed in good and evil

            a)   What might be good is not necessarily God
            b)   What might be evil is not necessarily not God

         3)   The opening or expanding of the mind (carnal) or soul of man
         4)   The mind or soul of man now will take precedence over the spirit of man or the tree of life.

      e.   Verse 6 – Notice the deception immediately. The woman saw that the tree was:

         1)   Good (not true) – appealed to her flesh
         2)   Pleasant – The enemy always uses disguises

              3)   Desirous – The devil preyed upon her ambition and her trust for soul knowledge

      f.   Verse 7

              1)   Soul (carnal mind) expands and has now become the enemy of the spirit man. The carnal has won.
              2)   Innocence and purity is lost (they knew they were naked)
              3)   Now they start making decisions apart from God (sewed fig leaves, made aprons).
              4)   This is the beginning of religion. Those fig leaves were a false covering – a man-made covering.

      g.   Verse 8

              1)   Now upon hearing His voice, they were condemned.
              2)   They hide and run from that which earlier was their love and life.
              3)   Foolishly amongst the trees (as if God couldn't see)

      h.   Verse 9-13 – Confrontation and excuses
      i.   Verses 14-19 – Curses pronounced
      j.   Verse 15 – Promise of a redeemer
      k.   Verse 22 – Man cannot eat of the tree of life for if he does, he will remain in the state he is in for eternity.
      l.   Verse 24 – Man cast out of paradise

      m.   Verse 24 – Flaming sword placed to turn every way around the tree of life to keep it. The process now begins to prepare man to come back.

              1)   Flaming – the fiery dealings of God
              2)   Sword – the living Word of God

II.   We are to be purged and processed until we are ready to eat of the tree of life and become it.

    A.   Men as trees

      1.   Mark 8:24 – "...I see men as trees, walking."
      2.   Isaiah 61:3
      3.   Psalms 1:3
      4.   Jeremiah 17:7-8
      5.   Matthew 3:10
      6.   Because man ate from the "tree of knowledge", he has become that tree
      7.   But God wants a return to paradise. He still wants a people to live from the tree of life.

    B.   Every tree is known by its fruit, for the seed in itself will produce.

      1.   Genesis 1:10-11 – You will produce from what's inside of you
      2.   Luke 9:43-45 – What is the abundance in our heart? Do we live by the carnal or spiritual man? Whichever tree is in abundance will produce the greater fruit in our life, be it carnal or spiritual.
      3.   Matthew 12:33

    C.   A process of purging has begun

      1.   Genesis 3:24

2. Matthew 7 19
3. Job 14:7-9
4. Matthew 3:10
5. John 15:1-9 – We need to abide in Him

D. Revelation 22:1-7, 14

Lesson 85
WHO CAN SEPARATE US FROM THE LOVE OF GOD?

I. Romans 8:31-39 – "*³¹What shall we then say to these things? If God be for us, <u>who can be against us?</u> ³²He that spared not his own Son, but delivered him up for us all, how shall he not with him also freely give us all things? ³³<u>Who shall lay any thing to the charge of God's elect?</u> It is God that justifieth. ³⁴<u>Who is he that condemneth?</u> It is Christ that died, yea rather, that is risen again, who is even at the right hand of God, who also maketh intercession for us. ³⁵<u>Who shall separate us from the love of Christ?</u> shall tribulation, or distress, or persecution, or famine, or nakedness, or peril, or sword? ³⁶As it is written, For thy sake we are killed all the day long; we are accounted as sheep for the slaughter. ³⁷Nay, in all these things we are more than conquerors through him that loved us. ³⁸For I am persuaded, that neither death, nor life, nor angels, nor principalities, nor powers, nor things present, nor things to come, ³⁹Nor height, nor depth, nor any other creature, shall be able to separate us from the love of God, which is in Christ Jesus our Lord.*"

Who can be against us? Who shall lay a charge against us? Who can condemn us? Who can separate us from the love of Christ? The answer to these questions is: NO ONE OR NOTHING CAN DO THESE THINGS. Verse 31 says "*…If God be for us, who can be against us…*" Verses 37-39 show us that nothing or no one can "*…separate us from the love of God, which is in Christ Jesus our Lord.*" In fact, verse 37 says that "*…we are more than conquerors*" in these things. But if you find the enemy trying to get you to think you can be separated from the love of God, remember Isaiah 54:17 which says "*…every tongue that shall rise against thee in judgment thou shalt condemn.*"

A. Greek word for separate, *choreo* – to give space, to hold; it comes from a root, *chora* which means – empty, expanse, room, a space of territory.

We know the enemy is always seeking to do this. He tries to put space between us and the Lord, space between us and His promises, and space between us and His love. The enemy is not the only one responsible for causing separation. Other people will try. Even our own hearts will try (I John 4:18), but we must know and believe what God says (I John 4:16). We must know God's love is sure and steadfast.

1. Romans 5:8 – "*God commendeth his love toward us, in that, while we were yet sinners, Christ died for us.*"
2. I John 3:1 – "*Behold, what manner of love the Father hath bestowed upon us, that we should be called the sons of God: therefore the world knoweth us not, because it knew him not.*"
3. Hebrews 13:5 – "*Let your conversation be without covetousness; and be content with such things as ye have: for he hath said, I will never leave thee, nor forsake thee.*"

III. The Things Listed In Romans 8:35-39 that try to Separate us from Him

A. Tribulation

1. Tribulation in the Greek, *thlipsis* – pressure, anguish, affliction, trouble; from a root, *thlibo* – to crowd.
2. What God does about tribulation:

a. Deuteronomy 4:30-31 – "*When thou art in tribulation, and all these things are come upon thee, even in the latter days, if thou turn to the LORD thy God, and shalt be obedient unto his voice; (For the LORD thy God is a merciful God;) he will not forsake thee, neither destroy thee, nor forget the covenant of thy fathers which he sware unto them.*"
b. John 16:33 – "*These things I have spoken unto you, that in me ye might have peace. In the world ye shall have tribulation: but be of good cheer; I have overcome the world.*"

c. II Corinthians 1:4 – *"Who comforteth us in all our tribulation, that we may be able to comfort them which are in any trouble, by the comfort wherewith we ourselves are comforted of God."*

d. Acts 14:22 – *"Confirming the souls of the disciples, and exhorting them to continue in the faith, and that we must through much tribulation enter into the kingdom of God."*

e. Matthew 13:20-21 – *"But he that received the seed into stony places, the same is he that heareth the word, and anon with joy receiveth it; Yet hath he not root in himself, but dureth for a while: for when tribulation or persecution ariseth because of the word, by and by he is offended."*

f. Romans 5:3 – *"And not only so, but we glory in tribulations also: knowing that tribulation worketh patience;"*

g. I Thessalonians 3:3-4 – *"That no man should be moved by these afflictions: for yourselves know that we are appointed thereunto. For verily, when we were with you, we told you before that we should suffer tribulation; even as it came to pass, and ye know."* – We also see that tribulation is appointed of God.

h. Revelation 1:9 – *"I John, who also am your brother, and companion in tribulation, and in the kingdom and patience of Jesus Christ, was in the isle that is called Patmos, for the word of God, and for the testimony of Jesus Christ."*

i. II Thessalonians 1:4-5 – *"So that we ourselves glory in you in the churches of God for your patience and faith in all your persecutions and tribulations that ye endure: Which is a manifest token of the righteous judgment of God, that ye may be counted worthy of the kingdom of God, for which ye also suffer:"*

B. Distress

1. Distress in the Greek, *stenochoria* – narrowness of room, calamity, and anguish
2. What God says about distress:

   a. Genesis 35:3 – *"And let us arise, and go up to Bethel; and I will make there an altar unto God, who answered me in the day of my distress, and was with me in the way which I went."*

   b. II Samuel 22:7 – *"In my distress I called upon the LORD, and cried to my God: and he did hear my voice out of his temple, and my cry did enter into his ears."* – We are to call upon Him in our distress.

   c. I Kings 1:29 – *"And the king sware, and said, As the LORD liveth, that hath redeemed my soul out of all distress,"*

   d. Psalms 118:5 – *"I called upon the LORD in distress: the LORD answered me, and set me in a large place."* – God will answer us in our distress.

   e. Isaiah 25:1, 4 – *"O LORD, thou art my God; I will exalt thee, I will praise thy name; for thou hast done wonderful things; thy counsels of old are faithfulness and truth...For thou hast been a strength to the poor, a strength to the needy in his distress, a refuge from the storm, a shadow from the heat, when the blast of the terrible ones is as a storm against the wall."*

   f. Psalms 4:1 – *"Hear me when I call, O God of my righteousness: thou hast enlarged me when I was in distress; have mercy upon me, and hear my prayer."*

   g. Psalms 18:6 – *"In my distress I called upon the LORD, and cried unto my God: he heard my voice out of his temple, and my cry came before him, even into his ears."*

   h. Psalms 120:1 – *"In my distress I cried unto the LORD, and he heard me."*

   i. Psalms 107:6, 19, 28, 13

3. God will give us room – Genesis 26:19-22

4. Distress is appointed of God.

        a.   II Corinthians 6:4 – *"But in all things approving ourselves as the ministers of God, in much patience, in afflictions, in necessities, in distresses,"*

        b.   II Corinthians 12:10 – *"Therefore I take pleasure in infirmities, in reproaches, in necessities, in persecutions, in distresses for Christ's sake: for when I am weak, then am I strong."*

C.   Persecution

1.   Persecution in the Greek, *diogmos* – to pursue, to follow after
2.   What God says about persecution:

    a.   Mark 4:17 – *"And have no root in themselves, and so endure but for a time: afterward, when affliction or <u>persecution ariseth for the word's sake</u>, immediately they are offended."*

    b.   II Timothy 3:12 – *"Yea, and all that will live godly in Christ Jesus shall suffer persecution."*

    c.   II Corinthians 4:9 – *"Persecuted, but not forsaken; cast down, but not destroyed;"*

    d.   Galatians 4:28-29 – *"Now we, brethren, as Isaac was, are the children of promise. But as then he that was born after the flesh persecuted him that was born after the Spirit, even so it is now"* – The children of the flesh always persecute the promised.

    e.   Matthew 5:10-12 – *"Blessed are they which are persecuted for righteousness' sake: for theirs is the kingdom of heaven. Blessed are ye, when men shall revile you, and persecute you, and shall say all manner of evil against you falsely, for my sake. Rejoice, and be exceeding glad: for great is your reward in heaven: for so persecuted they the prophets which were before you."*

    f.   Romans 12:14 – *"Bless them which persecute you: bless, and curse not."*

3.   Persecution is appointed of God.

    a.   John 15:20 – *"Remember the word that I said unto you, The servant is not greater than his lord. If they have persecuted me, they will also persecute you; if they have kept my saying, they will keep yours also."*

    b.   II Thessalonians 1:4-5 – *"So that we ourselves glory in you in the churches of God for your patience and faith in all your persecutions and tribulations that ye endure: Which is a manifest token of the righteous judgment of God, that ye may be counted worthy of the kingdom of God, for which ye also suffer:"*

    c.   II Corinthians 12:10 – *"Therefore I take pleasure in infirmities, in reproaches, in necessities, in persecutions, in distresses for Christ's sake: for when I am weak, then am I strong."*

    d.   I Corinthians 4:9-12 – *"9For I think that God hath set forth us the apostles last, as it were appointed to death: for we are made a spectacle unto the world, and to angels, and to men. 10We are fools for Christ's sake, but ye are wise in Christ; we are weak, but ye are strong; ye are honourable, but we are despised. 11Even unto this present hour we both hunger, and thirst, and are naked, and are buffeted, and have no certain dwellingplace; 12And labour, working with our own hands: being reviled, we bless; being persecuted, we suffer it:"*

D.   Famine

1.   Famine in the Greek, *limos* – destitution, scarcity of food, hunger, dearth
2.   What God says about famine:

    a.   Job 5:20, 22 – *"In famine he shall redeem thee from death: and in war from the power of the sword ...At destruction and famine thou shalt laugh: neither shalt thou be afraid of the beasts of the earth."*

  b. Psalms 33:18-19 – *"Behold, the eye of the LORD is upon them that fear him, upon them that hope in his mercy; To deliver their soul from death, and to keep them alive in famine."*

  c. Ezekiel 36:29 – *"I will also save you from all your uncleannesses: and I will call for the corn, and will increase it, and lay no famine upon you."*

  d. Ruth 1:1-6, 20 – In famine we are tempted to make wrong decisions.

  e. Psalms 37:25-26 – *"I have been young, and now am old; yet have I not seen the righteous forsaken, nor his seed begging bread. He is ever merciful, and lendeth; and his seed is blessed."*

  f. Ecclesiastes 7:14 – *"In the day of prosperity be joyful, but in the day of adversity consider: God also hath set the one over against the other, to the end that man should find nothing after him."* – Famine is appointed of God.

 3. We must rejoice in scarcity and in fullness.

  a. Philippians 4:12-13 – *"I know both how to be abased, and I know how to abound: every where and in all things I am instructed both to be full and to be hungry, both to abound and to suffer need. I can do all things through Christ which strengtheneth me."*

  b. Habakkuk 3:17-19 – *"[17]Although the fig tree shall not blossom, neither shall fruit be in the vines; the labour of the olive shall fail, and the fields shall yield no meat; the flock shall be cut off from the fold, and there shall be no herd in the stalls: [18]Yet I will rejoice in the LORD, I will joy in the God of my salvation. [19]The LORD God is my strength, and he will make my feet like hinds' feet, and he will make me to walk upon mine high places. To the chief singer on my stringed instruments."*

  c. Deuteronomy 8:9-18

E. Nakedness

 1. Nakedness in the Greek, *gumnotes* – absolute nudity, to be uncovered; from a root, *gumniteuo* – to strip.

 2. What God's Word says about nakedness:

  a. Lamentations 1:8 – *"Jerusalem hath grievously sinned; therefore she is removed: all that honoured her despise her, because they have seen her nakedness: yea, she sigheth, and turneth backward."* – Many times when we are uncovered, people see us for what we are and despise us.

  b. Ezekiel 16:8 – *"Now when I passed by thee, and looked upon thee, behold, thy time was the time of love; and I spread my skirt over thee, and covered thy nakedness: yea, I sware unto thee, and entered into a covenant with thee, saith the Lord GOD, and thou becamest mine."*

  c. II Corinthians 11:23-28 – Nakedness is appointed of God

  d. I Corinthians 4:9-11

  e. Revelation 3:17-19 – God allows nakedness so that we might see our shame (bringing us to repentance) and also our need for Him.

  f. John 21:7 – *"Therefore that disciple whom Jesus loved saith unto Peter, It is the Lord. Now when Simon Peter heard that it was the Lord, he girt his fisher's coat unto him, (for he was naked,) and did cast himself into the sea."*

  g. Genesis 3:7-21 – He covers our nakedness.

  h. James 2:14-18 – We need to see the necessity of covering our brothers.

  i. Isaiah 58:7

  j. Matthew 25:38

  k. Genesis 9:22-23

F. Peril

1. Peril in the Greek, *kindunos* – danger
2. What God's Word says about peril:

    a. II Timothy 3:1 – "*This know also, that in the last days perilous times shall come.*"
    b. II Corinthians 11:26 – "*In journeyings often, in perils of waters, in perils of robbers, in perils by mine own countrymen, in perils by the heathen, in perils in the city, in perils in the wilderness, in perils in the sea, in perils among false brethren;*" – Perils are appointed of God. In all of these, God delivers us. He uses these to draw us ever closer to Him and to press us into Him.

G. Sword

1. Sword in the Greek, *machaira* – a knife, war, a battleground, fighting, punishment
2. What God's Word says about sword:

    a. Job 5:20 – "*In famine he shall redeem thee from death: and in war from the power of the sword.*"
    b. Psalms 144:10 – "*It is he that giveth salvation unto kings: who delivereth David his servant from the hurtful sword.*"
    c. Hosea 2:18 – "*And in that day will I make a covenant for them with the beasts of the field, and with the fowls of heaven, and with the creeping things of the ground: and I will break the bow and the sword and the battle out of the earth, and will make them to lie down safely.*"
    d. Joel 2:8 – "*Neither shall one thrust another; they shall walk every one in his path: and when they fall upon the sword, they shall not be wounded.*"
    e. Hebrews 11:34 – "*Quenched the violence of fire, escaped the edge of the sword, out of weakness were made strong, waxed valiant in fight, turned to flight the armies of the aliens.*"

III. Nothing Can Separate Us from the Love of God Because <u>God Is For Us & Not Against Us</u>

A. He is on our side

1. Psalms 118:6 – "*The LORD is on my side; I will not fear: what can man do unto me?*"
2. Psalms 124:1 – "*If it had not been the LORD who was on our side, now may Israel say*"

B. He is for us

1. Nehemiah 4:20 – "*In what place therefore ye hear the sound of the trumpet, resort ye thither unto us: our God shall fight for us.*"
2. Psalms 62:8 – "*Trust in him at all times; ye people, pour out your heart before him: God is a refuge for us.*"
3. Psalms 61:3 – "*For thou hast been a shelter for me, and a strong tower from the enemy.*"
4. Psalms 56:9 – "*When I cry unto thee, then shall mine enemies turn back: this I know; for God is for me.*"
5. Psalms 3:3 – "*But thou, O LORD, art a shield for me; my glory, and the lifter up of mine head.*"

C. God is with us

1. Exodus 33:16 – "*For wherein shall it be known here that I and thy people have found grace in thy sight? is it not in that thou goest with us? so shall we be separated, I and thy people, from all the people that are upon the face of the earth.*"

2. Numbers 14:9 – *"Only rebel not ye against the LORD, neither fear ye the people of the land; for they are bread for us: their defence is departed from them, and the LORD is with us: fear them not."*

3. II Chronicles 32:7-8 – *"Be strong and courageous, be not afraid nor dismayed for the king of Assyria, nor for all the multitude that is with him: for there be more with us than with him: With him is an arm of flesh; but with us is the LORD our God to help us, and to fight our battles. And the people rested themselves upon the words of Hezekiah king of Judah."*

4. II Kings 6:16 – *"And he answered, Fear not: for they that be with us are more than they that be with them."*

5. Psalms 46:7, 11 – *"The LORD of hosts is with us; the God of Jacob is our refuge. Selah...The LORD of hosts is with us; the God of Jacob is our refuge. Selah."*

6. Matthew 1:23 – *"Behold, a virgin shall be with child, and shall bring forth a son, and they shall call his name Emmanuel, which being interpreted is, God with us."*

7. Ezekiel 48:35 – *"It was round about eighteen thousand measures: and the name of the city from that day shall be, The LORD is there."*

Lesson 86
WHERE ARE OUR SIGNS?

Psalms 74:4, 9-10 – "*⁴Thine enemies roar in the midst of thy congregations; they set up their ensigns for signs. ⁹We see not our signs: there is no more any prophet: neither is there among us any that knoweth how long. ¹⁰ O God, how long shall the adversary reproach? shall the enemy blaspheme thy name for ever?*"

The enemies have signs and they're not afraid. Our problem is we can't stop the enemy because we're not having any signs.

I.   God Has Always Had Signs

   A.   **Moses**, Exodus 4:9 – "*And it shall come to pass, if they will not believe also these two signs, neither hearken unto thy voice, that thou shalt take of the water of the river, and pour it upon the dry land: and the water which thou takest out of the river shall become blood upon the dry land.*" (Acts 7:36 – "*He brought them out, after that he had shewed wonders and signs in the land of Egypt, and in the Red sea, and in the wilderness forty years.*")
   B.   **Jesus**, Acts 2:22 – "*Ye men of Israel, hear these words; Jesus of Nazareth, a man approved of God among you by miracles and wonders and signs, which God did by him in the midst of you, as ye yourselves also know:*"
   C.   **Apostles**, Acts 4:30 – "*By stretching forth thine hand to heal; and that signs and wonders may be done by the name of thy holy child Jesus.*"
   D.   **Those that first heard**, Hebrews 2:4 – "*God also bearing them witness, both with signs and wonders, and with divers miracles, and gifts of the Holy Ghost, according to his own will?*"
   E.   **Believers**, Mark 16:17 – "*And these signs shall follow them that believe; In my name shall they cast out devils; they shall speak with new tongues;*"

II.   What are our Signs?

   Mark 16:17-20 – "*And these signs shall follow them that believe; In my name shall they cast out devils; they shall speak with new tongues; ¹⁸They shall take up serpents; and if they drink any deadly thing, it shall not hurt them; they shall lay hands on the sick, and they shall recover. ¹⁹So then after the Lord had spoken unto them, he was received up into heaven, and sat on the right hand of God. ²⁰And they went forth, and preached every where, the Lord working with them, and confirming the word with signs following. Amen.*"

   A.   Cast out Devils

      1.   Mark 10:17-19 – "*And when he was gone forth into the way, there came one running, and kneeled to him, and asked him, Good Master, what shall I do that I may inherit eternal life? ¹⁸And Jesus said unto him, Why callest thou me good? there is none good but one, that is, God. ¹⁹Thou knowest the commandments, Do not commit adultery, Do not kill, Do not steal, Do not bear false witness, Defraud not, Honour thy father and mother.*"
      2.   Matthew 28:18 – "*And Jesus came and spake unto them, saying, All power is given unto me in heaven and in earth.*"
      3.   Luke 9:1 – "*Then he called his twelve disciples together, and gave them power and authority over all devils, and to cure diseases.*"

   B.   Speak with New Tongues

      1.   I Corinthians 14:22 – "*Wherefore tongues are for a sign, not to them that believe, but to them that believe not: but prophesying serveth not for them that believe not, but for them which believe.*"
      2.   Acts 10:46 – "*For they heard them speak with tongues, and magnify God. Then answered Peter*"

C.   Serpents and Deadly Things

1.   Acts 28:3-7 – "*And when Paul had gathered a bundle of sticks, and laid them on the fire, there came a viper out of the heat, and fastened on his hand. And when the barbarians saw the venomous beast hang on his hand, they said among themselves, No doubt this man is a murderer, whom, though he hath escaped the sea, yet vengeance suffereth not to live. And he shook off the beast into the fire, and felt no harm. Howbeit they looked when he should have swollen, or fallen down dead suddenly: but after they had looked a great while, and saw no harm come to him, they changed their minds, and said that he was a god. In the same quarters were possessions of the chief man of the island, whose name was Publius; who received us, and lodged us three days courteously.*"

D.   Lay Hands on the Sick

1.   Genesis 49:24 – "*But his bow abode in strength, and the arms of his hands were made strong by the hands of the mighty God of Jacob; (from thence is the shepherd, the stone of Israel:)*"
2.   Mark 6:2 – "*And when the sabbath day was come, he began to teach in the synagogue: and many hearing him were astonished, saying, From whence hath this man these things? and what wisdom is this which is given unto him, that even such mighty works are wrought by his hands?*"
3.   Hebrews 6:2 – "*Of the doctrine of baptisms, and of laying on of hands, and of resurrection of the dead, and of eternal judgment.*"
4.   Acts 5:12 – "*And by the hands of the apostles were many signs and wonders wrought among the people; (and they were all with one accord in Solomon's porch.*"
5.   Mark 5:24-34

Lesson 87
WHAT GOD IS SEEKING

I.   What God Is Seeking – Examples in Scripture

    A.   I Samuel 13:14 – **A man after His own heart** – "...*the LORD hath sought* him a man *after his own heart*...*" Hebrew word for sought and seeking – To search out, to strive after, to desire, to beseech

    B.   Esther 2:2 – **Virgins** – "...*Let there be fair young virgins sought for the king:*"

        1.   Matthew 25:1-10 – *"Then shall the kingdom of heaven be likened unto ten virgins, which took their lamps, and went forth to meet the bridegroom. And five of them were wise, and five were foolish. They that were foolish took their lamps, and took no oil with them: But the wise took oil in their vessels with their lamps. While the bridegroom tarried, they all slumbered and slept. And at midnight there was a cry made, Behold, the bridegroom cometh; go ye out to meet him. Then all those virgins arose, and trimmed their lamps. And the foolish said unto the wise, Give us of your oil; for our lamps are gone out. But the wise answered, saying, Not so; lest there be not enough for us and you: but go ye rather to them that sell, and buy for yourselves. And while they went to buy, the bridegroom came; and they that were ready went in with him to the marriage: and the door was shut."*
        2.   Song of Solomon 1:3 – *"...therefore do the virgins love thee."*
        3.   Revelation 14:1-5 – *"...and with him an hundred forty and four thousand, having his Father's name written in their foreheads...These are they which were not defiled with women; for they are virgins."*

    C.   Ezekiel 22:30 – **Intercessors** – *"And I sought for a man among them, that should make up the hedge, and stand in the gap before me for the land, that I should not destroy it: but I found none."*

        1.   Ezekiel 36:37 – *"...I will yet for this be inquired of by the house of Israel, to do it for them..."*
        2.   II Chronicles 7:14

    D.   John 4:23 – **Worshippers** – *"But the hour cometh, and now is, when the true worshippers shall worship the Father in spirit and in truth: for the Father seeketh such to worship him."*

    E.   Psalms 27:8 – *"When thou saidst, Seek ye my face; my heart said unto thee, Thy face, LORD, will I seek."*

        1.   His "face" is the Hebrew word also for "presence"
        2.   Psalms 105:4 – *"Seek the LORD, and his strength: seek his face evermore."*

    F.   Isaiah 66:2 – **The Word** – "...*to this man will I look, even to him that is poor and of a contrite spirit, and trembleth at my word.*"

        1.   Isaiah 34:16 – *"Seek ye out of the book of the LORD, and read: no one of these shall fail, none shall want her mate: for my mouth it hath commanded, and his spirit it hath gathered them."*

    G.   Ezekiel 34:16 – **The Lost** – *"I will seek that which was lost, and bring again that which was driven away, and will bind up that which was broken, and will strengthen that which was sick..."*

        1.   Luke 19:10 – *"For the Son of man is come to seek and to save that which was lost."*

H. Exodus 32:26 – **The Lord's Side** – "*Then Moses stood in the gate of the camp, and said, <u>Who is on the LORD's side</u>? <u>let him come unto me</u>. And all the sons of Levi gathered themselves together unto him.*"

I. **A Faithful Man and a Virtuous Woman**

1. Proverbs 20:6 – "*Most men will proclaim every one his own goodness: but a <u>faithful man who can find</u>?*"
2. Proverbs 31:10 – "*<u>Who can find a virtuous woman</u>? for her price is far above rubies.*"

J. Isaiah 6:8 – **Follow His Call** – "*Also I heard the voice of the Lord, saying, <u>Whom shall I send</u>, and <u>who will go for us</u>? Then said I, Here am I; send me.*"

Lesson 88
AFFLICTIONS

Psalms 105:17-24 – "*¹⁷He sent a man before them, even Joseph, who was sold for a servant: ¹⁸Whose feet they hurt with fetters: he was laid in iron: ¹⁹Until the time that his word came: the word of the LORD tried him. ²⁰The king sent and loosed him; even the ruler of the people, and let him go free. ²¹He made him lord of his house, and ruler of all his substance: ²²To bind his princes at his pleasure; and teach his senators wisdom. ²³Israel also came into Egypt; and Jacob sojourned in the land of Ham. ²⁴And he increased his people greatly; and made them stronger than their enemies.*"

Psalms 81:5-6 – "*⁵This he ordained in Joseph for a testimony, when he went out through the land of Egypt: where I heard a language that I understood not. ⁶I removed his shoulder from the burden: his hands were delivered from the pots.*"

Acts 7:10 – "*And delivered him out of all his afflictions, and gave him favour and wisdom in the sight of Pharaoh king of Egypt; and he made him governor over Egypt and all his house.*"

I.   Word Meanings

    A.   Hebrew for affliction, *anah* – to depress or humble
    B.   Greek for affliction, *thlipsis* – pressure. Affliction is the same Greek word as tribulation

II.   Afflictions are not sicknesses

    A.   James 5:13 – "*Is any among you afflicted? let him pray. Is any merry? let him sing psalms.*"

III. They are going to come

    A.   Scriptures

        1.   John 16:33 – "*These things I have spoken unto you, that in me ye might have peace. In the world ye shall have tribulation: but be of good cheer; I have overcome the world.*"
        2.   I Thessalonians 3:3-4 – "*That no man should be moved by these afflictions: for yourselves know that we are appointed thereunto. For verily, when we were with you, we told you before that we should suffer tribulation; even as it came to pass, and ye know.*"

IV.   Are afflictions good?

    A.   Scriptures

        1.   Psalms 119:71 – "*It is good for me that I have been afflicted; that I might learn thy statutes.*"
        2.   Psalms 119:75 – "*I know, O LORD, that thy judgments are right, and that thou in faithfulness hast afflicted me.*"
        3.   Psalms 90:15 – "*Make us glad according to the days wherein thou hast afflicted us, and the years wherein we have seen evil.*"
        4.   Hebrews 11:25-26 – "*Choosing rather to suffer affliction with the people of God, than to enjoy the pleasures of sin for a season; Esteeming the reproach of Christ greater riches than the treasures in Egypt: for he had respect unto the recompence of the reward.*"

V.   Reasons they come

    A.   Sin

1. Psalms 107:17 – "*Fools because of their transgression, and because of their iniquities, are afflicted.*"
2. Psalms 119:67 – "*Before I was afflicted I went astray: but now have I kept thy word.*"
3. Hosea 5:15 – "*I will go and return to my place, till they acknowledge their offence, and seek my face: in their affliction they will seek me early.*"
4. I Kings 8:35-36

B. For the Word's sake – ones that come from God

1. Matthew 4:17 – "*From that time Jesus began to preach, and to say, Repent: for the kingdom of heaven is at hand.*"

C. To gentle us to his yoke

1. Matthew 4:17 – "*From that time Jesus began to preach, and to say, Repent: for the kingdom of heaven is at hand.*"

   a. Jeremiah 31:18-19 – "*I have surely heard Ephraim bemoaning himself thus; Thou hast chastised me, and I was chastised, as a bullock unaccustomed to the yoke: turn thou me, and I shall be turned; for thou art the LORD my God. Surely after that I was turned, I repented; and after that I was instructed, I smote upon my thigh: I was ashamed, yea, even confounded, because I did bear the reproach of my youth.*"

D. To tear down bad in our life and plant good

1. Hosea 6:1-2 – "*Come, and let us return unto the LORD: for he hath torn, and he will heal us; he hath smitten, and he will bind us up. After two days will he revive us: in the third day he will raise us up, and we shall live in his sight.*"
2. Jeremiah 1:10 – "*See, I have this day set thee over the nations and over the kingdoms, to root out, and to pull down, and to destroy, and to throw down, to build, and to plant.*"
3. Job 5:17 – "*Behold, happy is the man whom God correcteth: therefore despise not thou the chastening of the Almighty*":
4. Job 5:18-25

E. Because he loves us and we are his sons (we might be partakers of his holiness)

1. Hebrews 12:5-15

F. It's working something in us

1. Acts 14:22 – "*Confirming the souls of the disciples, and exhorting them to continue in the faith, and that we must through much tribulation enter into the kingdom of God.*"
2. Romans 5:3 – "*And not only so, but we glory in tribulations also: knowing that tribulation worketh patience;*"
3. II Corinthians 4:17-18
4. Psalms 90:15-17

G. It's trying our faith – (so that our faith becomes like gold)

1. Isaiah 48:10 – "*Behold, I have refined thee, but not with silver; I have chosen thee in the furnace of affliction.*"
2. Psalms 55:10-12

3. I Peter 1:6-7
4. Job 23:10 – "*But he knoweth the way that I take: when he hath tried me, I shall come forth as gold.*"
5. Psalms 45:9 – "*Kings' daughters were among thy honourable women: upon thy right hand did stand the queen in gold of Ophir.*"
6. Psalms 45:13 – "*The king's daughter is all glorious within: her clothing is of wrought gold.*"

VI. God doesn't afflict willingly

    A. Scriptures

        1. Lamentations 3:33 – "*For he doth not afflict willingly nor grieve the children of men.*"
        2. Isaiah 63:19 –"*We are thine: thou never barest rule over them; they were not called by thy name.*"

VII. What can keep us while God is doing this?

    A. Scriptures

        1. Psalms 119:50 – "*This is my comfort in my affliction: for thy word hath quickened me.*"
        2. Psalms 119:92 – "*Unless thy law had been my delights, I should then have perished in mine affliction.*"
        3. II Corinthians 1:4-5
        4. Romans 8:35-39
        5. Job 5:27 – "*Lo this, we have searched it, so it is; hear it, and know thou it for thy good.*"

VIII. Afflictions the Devil brings

    A. Scriptures

        1. Luke 13:16 –"*And ought not this woman, being a daughter of Abraham, whom Satan hath bound, lo, these eighteen years, be loosed from this bond on the sabbath day?*"
        2. Acts 10:38 – "*How God anointed Jesus of Nazareth with the Holy Ghost and with power: who went about doing good, and healing all that were oppressed of the devil; for God was with him.*"
        3. John 10:10 – "*The thief cometh not, but for to steal, and to kill, and to destroy: I am come that they might have life, and that they might have it more abundantly.*"
        4. Luke 22:31-34
        5. 1 Peter 5:8 – "*Be sober, be vigilant; because your adversary the devil, as a roaring lion, walketh about, seeking whom he may devour*"
        6. Exodus 1:11-14 – Type of Satan

IX. Affliction man brings on himself

    A. Scriptures

        1. Job 5:7 – "*Yet man is born unto trouble, as the sparks fly upward.*"
        2. Proverbs 14:12 – "*There is a way which seemeth right unto a man, but the end thereof are the ways of death.*"
        3. Proverbs 19:3 – "*The foolishness of man perverteth his way: and his heart fretteth against the LORD.*"
        4. Ecclesiastes 10:8 – "*He that diggeth a pit shall fall into it; and whoso breaketh an hedge, a serpent shall bite him.*"

5. Proverbs 21:16 –*"The man that wandereth out of the way of understanding shall remain in the congregation of the dead."*

6. Proverbs 22:3 – *"A prudent man foreseeth the evil, and hideth himself: but the simple pass on, and are punished."*

7. Proverbs 1:31-31

8. Isaiah 3:8 – *"For Jerusalem is ruined, and Judah is fallen: because their tongue and their doings are against the LORD, to provoke the eyes of his glory"*

9. Proverbs 26:2 –*"As the bird by wandering, as the swallow by flying, so the curse causeless shall not come."*

10. Proverbs 6:27 – *"Can a man take fire in his bosom, and his clothes not be burned?"*

11. Job 4:11 –*"The old lion perisheth for lack of prey, and the stout lion's whelps are scattered abroad."*

X. God always delivers us

A. Scriptures

1. Psalms 34:19 – *"Many are the afflictions of the righteous: but the LORD delivereth him out of them all."*

2. Psalms 54:7 – *"For he hath delivered me out of all trouble: and mine eye hath seen his desire upon mine enemies."*

3. Proverbs 11:8 – *"The righteous is delivered out of trouble, and the wicked cometh in his stead."*

4. Acts 7:10 –*"And delivered him out of all his afflictions, and gave him favour and wisdom in the sight of Pharaoh king of Egypt; and he made him governor over Egypt and all his house."*

Lesson 89
ANGELS WATCHING OVER US

I. Psalms 34:7 – *"The angel of the LORD encampeth round about them that fear him, and delivereth them."*

The Hebrew word for encampeth means – to pitch a tent, and comes from the Hebrew root word which is the Hebrew word for intercession, which means to bend or stoop in kindness to an inferior one. The Hebrew word for delivereth means to pull off or to strip.

    A. Angels are given to us to minister to us and to await their commands.

        1. Hebrews 1:14 – *"Are they not all ministering spirits, sent forth to minister for them who shall be heirs of salvation?"*
        2. Matthew 18:10 – *"Take heed that ye despise not one of these little ones; for I say unto you, That in heaven their angels do always behold the face of my Father which is in heaven."*
        3. Psalms 91:11 – *"For he shall give his angels charge over thee, to keep thee in all thy ways."*
        4. Matthew 4:11 – *"Then the devil leaveth him, and, behold, angels came and ministered unto him."*
        5. Genesis 24:40 – *"And he said unto me, The LORD, before whom I walk, will send his angel with thee, and prosper thy way; and thou shalt take a wife for my son of my kindred, and of my father's house:"* – Abraham's servant
        6. Exodus 23:20-23 – Moses
        7. I Kings 19:5-8 – Elijah fed by an angel
        8. II Kings 6:14-17
        9. Isaiah 63:9
      10. Daniel 6:22 – Lion's den
      11. Daniel 12:1 – Michael

    B. Other passages on angels

        1. Revelation 12:7 – *"And there was war in heaven: Michael and his angels fought against the dragon; and the dragon fought and his angels,"*
        2. Revelation 7:11 – *"And all the angels stood round about the throne, and about the elders and the four beasts, and fell before the throne on their faces, and worshipped God,"*
        3. Revelation 3:5 – *"He that overcometh, the same shall be clothed in white raiment; and I will not blot out his name out of the book of life, but I will confess his name before my Father, and before his angels."*
        4. I Peter 1:12 – *"Unto whom it was revealed, that not unto themselves, but unto us they did minister the things, which are now reported unto you by them that have preached the gospel unto you with the Holy Ghost sent down from heaven; which things the angels desire to look into."*
        5. Hebrews 12:22 – *"But ye are come unto mount Sion, and unto the city of the living God, the heavenly Jerusalem, and to an innumerable company of angels,"*
        6. Hebrews 1:7,13 – *"And of the angels he saith, Who maketh his angels spirits, and his ministers a flame of fire...But to which of the angels said he at any time, Sit on my right hand, until I make thine enemies thy footstool?"*
        7. II Thessalonians 1:7 – *"And to you who are troubled rest with us, when the Lord Jesus shall be revealed from heaven with his mighty angels,"*
        8. John 20:12 – *"And seeth two angels in white sitting, the one at the head, and the other at the feet, where the body of Jesus had lain."*
        9. John 1:51 – *"And he saith unto him, Verily, verily, I say unto you, Hereafter ye shall see heaven open, and the angels of God ascending and descending upon the Son of man."*

10. Luke 16:22 – *"And it came to pass, that the beggar died, and was carried by the angels into Abraham's bosom: the rich man also died, and was buried;"*

11. Luke 15:10 – *"Likewise, I say unto you, there is joy in the presence of the angels of God over one sinner that repenteth."*

12. Mark 12:25 – *"For when they shall rise from the dead, they neither marry, nor are given in marriage; but are as the angels which are in heaven."*

13. Mark 1:13 – *"And he was there in the wilderness forty days, tempted of Satan; and was with the wild beasts; and the angels ministered unto him."*

15. Matthew 13:39-49

16. Psalms 104:4 – *"Who maketh his angels spirits; his ministers a flaming fire:"*

17. Psalms 78:25 – *"Man did eat angels' food: he sent them meat to the full."*

18. Genesis 24:7, 40

19. Numbers 20:16 – *"And when we cried unto the LORD, he heard our voice, and sent an angel, and hath brought us forth out of Egypt: and, behold, we are in Kadesh, a city in the uttermost of thy border:"*

20. Judges 13:16 – *"And the angel of the LORD said unto Manoah, Though thou detain me, I will not eat of thy bread: and if thou wilt offer a burnt offering, thou must offer it unto the LORD. For Manoah knew not that he was an angel of the LORD."*

21. I Samuel 29:9 – *"And Achish answered and said to David, I know that thou art good in my sight, as an angel of God: notwithstanding the princes of the Philistines have said, He shall not go up with us to the battle."*

22. II Samuel 24:16 – *"And when the angel stretched out his hand upon Jerusalem to destroy it, the LORD repented him of the evil, and said to the angel that destroyed the people, It is enough: stay now thine hand. And the angel of the LORD was by the threshingplace of Araunah the Jebusite."*

23. I Chronicles 21:30 – *"But David could not go before it to inquire of God: for he was afraid because of the sword of the angel of the LORD."*

24. Luke 2:13 – *"And suddenly there was with the angel a multitude of the heavenly host praising God, and saying,"*

25. Acts 5:19 – *"But the angel of the Lord by night opened the prison doors, and brought them forth, and said,"*

26. Acts 7:30 – *"And when forty years were expired, there appeared to him in the wilderness of mount Sina an angel of the Lord in a flame of fire in a bush."*

27. Acts 8:26 – *"And the angel of the Lord spake unto Philip, saying, Arise, and go toward the south unto the way that goeth down from Jerusalem unto Gaza, which is desert."*

28. Acts 10:3 – *"He saw in a vision evidently about the ninth hour of the day an angel of God coming in to him, and saying unto him, Cornelius."*

29. Acts 12:7 – *"And, behold, the angel of the Lord came upon him, and a light shined in the prison: and he smote Peter on the side, and raised him up, saying, Arise up quickly. And his chains fell off from his hands."*

C. Angels go before us

1. Exodus 14:19 – *"And the angel of God, which went before the camp of Israel, removed and went behind them; and the pillar of the cloud went from before their face, and stood behind them:"*

2. Exodus 23:20, 23 – *"Behold, I send an Angel before thee, to keep thee in the way, and to bring thee into the place which I have prepared..."*

3. Exodus 32:34 – *"Therefore now go, lead the people unto the place of which I have spoken unto thee: behold, mine Angel shall go before thee: nevertheless in the day when I visit I will visit their sin upon them."*

4. Exodus 33:2

Lesson 90
AS THE DEW

I.   Micah 5:7 – *"And the remnant of Jacob shall be in the midst of many people as a dew from the LORD, as the showers upon the grass, that tarrieth not for man, nor waiteth for the sons of men."*

Hebrew word for dew means to strew over or to cover.
Dictionary meaning - <u>Moisture</u> <u>from</u> <u>the</u> <u>atmosphere</u> <u>condensed</u> <u>by</u> <u>cool</u> <u>bodies</u> <u>upon</u> <u>their</u> <u>surfaces</u>, <u>particularly</u> <u>at</u> <u>night</u>. <u>Figuratively</u>, <u>anything</u> <u>which</u> <u>falls</u> <u>lightly</u> <u>and</u> <u>in</u> <u>a</u> <u>refreshing</u> <u>manner</u>, an <u>emblem</u> <u>of</u> <u>morning</u>, <u>or</u> <u>fresh</u> <u>vigor</u>.

A.   What is the Dew?

    1.   God's hovering manifested presense

        a.   Genesis 27:28 – *"Therefore God give thee of the dew of heaven, and the fatness of the earth, and plenty of corn and wine:"*
        b.   Zechariah 8:12 – *"For the seed shall be osperous; the vine shall give her fruit, and the ground shall give her increase, and the heavens shall give their dew; and I will cause the remnant of this people to possess all these things."*
        c.   Haggai 1:10 – Natural & Spiritual; no fruit – *"Therefore the heaven over you is stayed from dew, and the earth is stayed from her fruit."*

        d.   Song of Solomon 5:2 – *"I sleep, but my heart waketh: it is the voice of my beloved that knocketh, saying, Open to me, my sister, my love, my dove, my undefiled: for my head is filled with dew, and my locks with the drops of the night."*

            1)   Hosea 14:5 – *"I will be as the dew unto Israel: he shall grow as the lily, and cast forth his roots as Lebanon."*

        e.   Proverbs 19:12 – *"The king's wrath is as the roaring of a lion; but his favour is as dew upon the grass."*
        f.   Psalms 133:1-3 – *"¹Behold, how good and how pleasant it is for brethren to dwell together in unity! ²It is like the precious ointment upon the head, that ran down upon the beard, even Aaron's beard: that went down to the skirts of his garments; ³As the dew of Hermon, and as the dew that descended upon the mountains of Zion: for there the LORD commanded the blessing, even life for evermore."*

    2.   Prepares Ground (Hearts) for the Word

        a.   Exodus 16:13-16 – *"And it came to pass, that at even the quails came up, and covered the camp: and in the morning the dew lay round about the host. ¹⁴And when the dew that lay was gone up, behold, upon the face of the wilderness there lay a small round thing, as small as the hoar frost on the ground. ¹⁵And when the children of Israel saw it, they said one to another, It is manna: for they wist not what it was. And Moses said unto them, This is the bread which the LORD hath given you to eat. ¹⁶This is the thing which the LORD hath commanded, Gather of it every man according to his eating, an omer for every man, according to the number of your persons; take ye every man for them which are in his tents."*
        b.   Deuteronomy 32:2 – *"My doctrine shall drop as the rain, my speech shall distil as the dew, as the small rain upon the tender herb, and as the showers upon the grass:"*

    3.   It's our Guide, our Teacher, and the Witness

      a.   I John 2:20, 27

      b.   Judges 6:37-40 – *"Behold, I will put a fleece of wool in the know that thou wilt save Israel by mine hand, as thou hast   said. [38]And it was so: for he rose up early on the morrow, and thrust the fleece together, and wringed the dew out of the fleece, a bowl full of water. [39]And Gideon said unto God, Let not thine anger be hot against me, and I will speak but this once: let me prove, I pray thee, but this once with the fleece; let it now be dry only upon the fleece, and upon all the ground let there be dew. [40]And God did so that night: for it was dry upon the fleece only, and there was dew on all the ground."*

      c.   Daniel 5:21 – *"And he was driven from the sons of men; and his heart was made like the beasts, and his dwelling was with the wild asses: they fed him with grass like oxen, and his body was wet with the dew of heaven; till he knew that the most high God ruled in the kingdom of men, and that he appointeth over it whomsoever he will."*

4.   It Speaks of the Resurrection Morning

      a.   Psalms 110:3 – *"Thy people shall be willing in the day of thy power, in the beauties of holiness from the womb of the morning: thou hast the dew of thy youth."*

      b.   Isaiah 26:19 – *"Thy dead men shall live, together with my dead body shall they arise. Awake and sing, ye that dwell in dust: for thy dew is as the dew of herbs, and the earth shall cast out the dead."*

5.   Dew for the Night – In the night, the Glory falls.

Lesson 91
BEAUTY FOR ASHES

Isaiah 61:3 – "*To appoint unto them that mourn in Zion, <u>to give unto them beauty for ashes</u>, the oil of joy for mourning, the garment of praise for the spirit of heaviness; that they might be called trees of righteousness, the planting of the LORD, that he might be glorified.*"

I. Word Definitions

   A. Beauty in Hebrew, *pe'er* – embellishment, fancy head-dress; from a root, *pa'ar* – to gleam, to beautify self, to shake a tree
   B. Ashes in Hebrew, *epher* – to bestrew, to scatter, to cover over
   C. Another definition of this term "beauty for ashes" based on the definitions above could be – God will beautify or make to shine that which has been scattered over.

II. Scriptural Examples

   A. Judges 14:5-14 – The story of Samson and the young lion – "*...Out of the eater came forth meat, and out of the strong came forth sweetness. And they could not in three days expound the riddle.*" – Out of every bad situation God can and will give beauty if we will let Him.
   B. Job 2:8, 42:10, James 5:11 – The story of Job – "*Job2:8And he took him a potsherd to scrape himself withal; and he sat down among the ashes...Job42:10And the LORD turned the captivity of Job, when he prayed for his friends: also the LORD gave Job twice as much as he had before. James5:11Behold, we count them happy which endure. Ye have heard of the patience of Job, and have seen the end of the Lord; that the Lord is very pitiful, and of tender mercy.*"
   C. Genesis 37:24, 45:8, 50:20 – The story of Joseph – "*24And they took him, and cast him into a pit: and the pit was empty, there was no water in it...8So now it was not you that sent me hither, but God: and he hath made me a father to Pharaoh, and lord of all his house, and a ruler throughout all the land of Egypt...20But as for you, ye thought evil against me; but God meant it unto good, to bring to pass, as it is this day, to save much people alive.*"
   D. I Corinthians 2:8 – Jesus – "*Which none of the princes of this world knew: for had they known it, they would not have crucified the Lord of glory.*"
   E. Psalms 30:11 – "*Thou hast turned for me my mourning into dancing: thou hast put off my sackcloth, and girded me with gladness;*"
   F. II Samuel 12:7-12 – The story of David sinning with Bathsheba and then birthing Solomon.
   G. Romans 8:28 – "*And we know that all things work together for good to them that love God, to them who are the called according to his purpose.*"

   H. Hebrews 9:13 (Numbers 19:9-10, 17) – This is God's way, the ashes or death of one situation led to the purification and life of another.

      1. John 12:24 – "*Verily, verily, I say unto you, Except a corn of wheat fall into the ground and die, it abideth alone: but if it die, it bringeth forth much fruit.*"
      2. II Corinthians 4:10-13 – "*10Always bearing about in the body the dying of the Lord Jesus, that the life also of Jesus might be made manifest in our body. 11For we which live are alway delivered unto death for Jesus' sake, that the life also of Jesus might be made manifest in our mortal flesh. 12So then death worketh in us, but life in you. 13We having the same spirit of faith, according as it is written, I believed, and therefore have I spoken; we also believe, and therefore speak;*"
      3. Philemon 15 – "*For perhaps he therefore departed for a season, that thou shouldest receive him for ever;*"

I.   I Peter 5:10 – *"But the God of all grace, who hath called us unto his eternal glory by Christ Jesus, after that ye have suffered a while, make you perfect, stablish, strengthen, settle you."*

J.   Isaiah 4:2-6 (Isaiah 33:14-17)

III. God Restores That Which Was Ruined

A. Scriptural examples

1. Jeremiah 18:4 – *"And the vessel that he made of clay was marred in the hand of the potter: so he made it again another vessel, as seemed good to the potter to make it."*
2. Amos 9:11 – *"In that day will I raise up the tabernacle of David that is fallen, and close up the breaches thereof; and I will raise up his ruins, and I will build it as in the days of old:"*
3. Ezekiel 36:36 – *"Then the heathen that are left round about you shall know that I the LORD build the ruined places, and plant that that was desolate: I the LORD have spoken it, and I will do it."*
4. Hosea 6:1-3 – *"¹Come, and let us return unto the LORD: for he hath torn, and he will heal us; he hath smitten, and he will bind us up. ²After two days will he revive us: in the third day he will raise us up, and we shall live in his sight. ³Then shall we know, if we follow on to know the LORD: his going forth is prepared as the morning; and he shall come unto us as the rain, as the latter and former rain unto the earth."*
5. Job 14:7-9 – *"⁷For there is hope of a tree, if it be cut down, that it will sprout again, and that the tender branch thereof will not cease. ⁸Though the root thereof wax old in the earth, and the stock thereof die in the ground; ⁹Yet through the scent of water it will bud, and bring forth boughs like a plant."*
6. Job 5:17-19 – *"¹⁷Behold, happy is the man whom God correcteth: therefore despise not thou the chastening of the Almighty: ¹⁸For he maketh sore, and bindeth up: he woundeth, and his hands make whole. ¹⁹He shall deliver thee in six troubles: yea, in seven there shall no evil touch thee."*
7. Psalms 147:2-3 – *"The LORD doth build up Jerusalem: he gathereth together the outcasts of Israel. He healeth the broken in heart, and bindeth up their wounds."*

B. Suffering and Glory

1. Romans 8:18 – *"For I reckon that the sufferings of this present time are not worthy to be compared with the glory which shall be revealed in us."*
2. I Peter 1:11 – *"Searching what, or what manner of time the Spirit of Christ which was in them did signify, when it testified beforehand the sufferings of Christ, and the glory that should follow."*
3. Hebrews 2:10 – *"For it became him, for whom are all things, and by whom are all things, in bringing many sons unto glory, to make the captain of their salvation perfect through sufferings."*
4. II Corinthians 4:17-18 – *"For our light affliction, which is but for a moment, worketh for us a far more exceeding and eternal weight of glory; While we look not at the things which are seen, but at the things which are not seen: for the things which are seen are temporal; but the things which are not seen are eternal."*

Lesson 92
BEGGING THE BODY OF JESUS

I.   Luke 23:50-56 & Matthew 27:57-61

What happens before the Body of Christ enters into their own resurrection?

A.   Verse by verse exposition

   1.   Luke 23:50, Matthew 27:57

      a.   Evening was come
      b.   Greek for Joseph – May God add, increasing, addition
      c.   Arimathaea – lofty or high place
      d.   Jesus' disciple
      e.   A counselor
      f.   Good and just man

There will once again be a Joseph company, to deliver God's people in the last days!

   2.   Luke 23:51

      a.   Joseph did not agree with the Pharisees. He did not agree with the religious people of his day.
      b.   He was waiting for the Kingdom of God.

   3.   Luke 23:52

      a.   Went to Pilate (a type of leadership, those in authority)
      b.   Begged in Greek – to ask, call for, crave, desire, require
      c.   The body of Jesus (Body of Christ, symbolically).
      d.   Commanded the body to be delivered

   4.   Luke 23:53 (Matthew 27:59-61)

      a.   Took it down (humility)
      b.   Wrapped in Greek – to twist, to entwine, to wrap together.
      c.   Clean (holy)
      d.   Linen – Revelation 19:8, Ezekiel 44:17, Ezekiel 16:10
      e.   New tomb – Joseph's own tomb
      f.   Laid it in a grave (symbolic of death)
      g.   Hewn out of the rock (in the dealings of God, to become like Jesus)
      h.   Hewn in stone – I Peter 2:5, Isaiah 54:17, Ephesians 2:19-21
      i.   Never a man was laid there before (especially prepared for this Body)
      j.   Rolled a great stone over it (sealed)
      k.   To the door (to all things heavenly – Revelation 4:1, Isaiah 6:1-5)
      l.   Then departed

      m.   Two Marys sat at sepulchre

         1)   One was a harlot – became a worshipper
         2)   The other always sat at Jesus' feet and heard His Word (Luke 10:38-42)

5. Luke 23:54-55

    a. Friday – preparation day (this will be the last preparation for the Body)
    b. Sabbath is drawing nigh (our rest and deliverance)
    c. Women followed and saw how His body was laid

6. Luke 23:56

    a. Prepared spices and ointments (worship)
    b. Rested – waiting for the Sabbath

7. The Body of Christ

    a. Romans 12:3-5
    b. I Corinthians 11:26-33
    c. I Corinthians 12:12-27
    d. Ephesians 4:4, 11-16
    e. Ephesians 1:10
    f. Psalms 75:2 (Psalms 26:12, 68:26)

8. The principle of love

    a. John 13:34-35
    b. John 15:12-13, 17
    c. I Thessalonians 4:9-10
    d. Hebrews 13:1
    e. I Peter 1:22
    f. I Peter 2:17
    g. I John 4:7-21

Lesson 93
BITTERNESS

I. The Causes and Cure of Bitterness

    A. Defining bitterness

        1. Hebrew – angry, chafed, discontented, to trickle
        2. Greek – To pack or press down

    B. Ruth 1:1-21 – "*...20And she said unto them, Call me not Naomi, call me Mara: for the Almighty hath dealt very bitterly with me. 21I went out full, and the LORD hath brought me home again empty: why then call ye me Naomi, seeing the LORD hath testified against me, and the Almighty hath afflicted me?*"

        1. Famine in God's house (Ecclesiastes 7:14 – temporary)
        2. Sojourned away from Bethlehem Judah – They left the house of bread and praise.
        3. Traveled to Moab – They went outside of God's kingdom
        4. They took heathen wives
        5. Husband and sons die – all fruit disappears
        6. Verse 20 – Call me Mara (bitter) and not Naomi (pleasant) for the Almighty (*El Shaddai*, the great breasty one) hath dealt very bitterly with me.
        7. Other example – Job 9:18

    C. What causes these things?

        1. Deuteronomy 29:10-18
        2. Hebrews 12:15 – "*Looking diligently lest any man fail of the grace of God; lest any root of bitterness springing up trouble you, and thereby many be defiled;*"
        3. James 3:13-16 – "*13Who is a wise man and endued with knowledge among you? let him shew out of a good conversation his works with meekness of wisdom. 14But if ye have bitter envying and strife in your hearts, glory not, and lie not against the truth. 15This wisdom descendeth not from above, but is earthly, sensual, devilish. 16For where envying and strife is, there is confusion and every evil work.*"
        4. Acts 8:23 – "*For I perceive that thou art in the gall of bitterness, and in the bond of iniquity.*"
        5. Lamentations 1:4 – "*The ways of Zion do mourn, because none come to the solemn feasts: all her gates are desolate: her priests sigh, her virgins are afflicted, and she is in bitterness.*"

    D. We can either be made bitter or better

        1. Exodus 15:23 – "*And when they came to Marah, they could not drink of the waters of Marah, for they were bitter: therefore the name of it was called Marah.*"
        2. Proverbs 14:10 – "*The heart knoweth his own bitterness; and a stranger doth not intermeddle with his joy*"

    E. Scripture exhortation to forsake bitterness

        1. Ephesians 4:31-32 – "*Let all bitterness, and wrath, and anger, and clamour, and evil speaking, be put away from you, with all malice: And be ye kind one to another, tenderhearted, forgiving one another, even as God for Christ's sake hath forgiven you.*"

Lesson 94
BROKEN BREAD

Matthew 26:26 – *"And as they were eating, Jesus took bread, and blessed it, and brake it, and gave it to the disciples, and said, Take, eat; this is my body."* – This passage of Scripture, when Jesus is administering the communion bread to His disciples has great revelation for us as Christians. First and foremost, Jesus is our bread of life. He was broken and gave His life for the entire world. But as Christians, we are to follow in His footsteps. We are the body of Christ. Therefore this passage also speaks to us how God deals with His people where He <u>takes us</u>, <u>then He blesses us</u>, <u>then He brakes us</u>, only then to <u>give us away</u>.

I.   He First Takes Us

    A.   Scriptures

        1.   Ezek 16:1-8
        2.   Psalms 116:1-8
        3.   Psalms 78:70 – *"He chose David also his servant, and took him from the sheepfolds"*

Most of us were going nowhere, with no real vision in life. But God has a purpose in taking us. This is the beginning.

II.   Then He Blesses Us

    A.   Scriptures

        1.   Ezek 16:9-14
        2.   Psalms 103:1 – *"A Psalm of David. Bless the LORD, O my soul: and all that is within me, bless his holy name."*
        3.   Psalms 132:13-15 – *"13For the LORD hath chosen Zion; he hath desired it for his habitation. 14This is my rest for ever: here will I dwell; for I have desired it. 15I will abundantly bless her provision: I will satisfy her poor with bread."*
        4.   Romans 8:32 – *"He that spared not his own Son, but delivered him up for us all, how shall he not with him also freely give us all things"?*
        5.   II Peter 1:3 – *"According as his divine power hath given unto us all things that pertain unto life and godliness, through the knowledge of him that hath called us to glory and virtue":*

Many Christians stop here. Even though we believe whole-heartedly in prosperity and how God wants and desires to bless us, this is not the goal of being a Christian. God wants us to grow.

III.   God wants us to Grow!

    A.   Scriptures

        1.   Romans 8:29 – *"For whom he did foreknow, he also did predestinate to be conformed to the image of his Son, that he might be the firstborn among many brethren."*
        2.   Hebrews 6:1 – *"Therefore leaving the principles of the doctrine of Christ, let us go on unto perfection; not laying again the foundation of repentance from dead works, and of faith toward God,"*

        3.   Hebrews 5:12-14

    B.   There different stages of growth:

1. I John 2:12-14 – "*12I write unto you, little children, because your sins are forgiven you for his name's sake. 13I write unto you, fathers, because ye have known him that is from the beginning. I write unto you, young men, because ye have overcome the wicked one. I write unto you, little children, because ye have known the Father. 14I have written unto you, fathers, because ye have known him that is from the beginning. I have written unto you, young men, because ye are strong, and the word of God abideth in you, and ye have overcome the wicked one.*" – From this passage we see there are at least three stages of growth, children, young men, and fathers. Children and young men apply to "taking and blessing", but fathers <u>know</u> Him.

   a. Psalms 103:7 – "*He made known his ways unto Moses, his acts unto the children of Israel.*"
   b. Philippians 3:10 – "*That I may know him, and the power of his resurrection, and the fellowship of his sufferings, being made conformable unto his death*" – The "power of his resurrection" speaks of "taking and blessing." The "fellowship of his sufferings, being made conformable unto his death", speaks of maturing beyond our needs being met and being broken and conformed to his image where we don't just know His acts, but we know His ways. There's more in God.

IV. Then He Breaks us

A. Breaking speaks of our changing or being formed, molded, made into the image of Jesus.

   1. II Corinthians 3:18 – "*But we all, with open face beholding as in a glass the glory of the Lord, are changed into the same image from glory to glory, even as by the Spirit of the Lord.*"
   2. Romans 12:2 – "*And be not conformed to this world: but be ye transformed by the renewing of your mind, that ye may prove what is that good, and acceptable, and perfect, will of God.*"

B. What was Jesus' suffering and death like? We are to have this mind in us which was in Christ Jesus.

   1. Philippians 2:2-8 – "*2Fulfil ye my joy, that ye be likeminded, having the same love, being of one accord, of one mind. 3Let nothing be done through strife or vainglory; but in lowliness of mind let each esteem other better than themselves. 4Look not every man on his own things, but every man also on the things of others. 5Let this mind be in you, which was also in Christ Jesus: 6Who, being in the form of God, thought it not robbery to be equal with God: 7But made himself of no reputation, and took upon him the form of a servant, and was made in the likeness of men: 8And being found in fashion as a man, he humbled himself, and became obedient unto death, even the death of the cross.*"

C. This is where a lot of Christians lose their vision, joy, purpose, desire and God's guidance.

   1. Hosea 6:1-3 – "*1Come, and let us return unto the LORD: for he hath torn, and he will heal us; he hath smitten, and he will bind us up. 2After two days will he revive us: in the third day he will raise us up, and we shall live in his sight. 3Then shall we know, if we follow on to know the LORD: his going forth is prepared as the morning; and he shall come unto us as the rain, as the latter and former rain unto the earth.*"

E. God tears down old ideas, traits, opinions, lifestyles, attitudes, habits, only to make us more like him. If you don't understand this, you miss it.

   1. I Samuel 2:6-9
   2. Job 14:7-10
   3. John 15:2 – "*Every branch in me that beareth not fruit he taketh away: and every branch that beareth fruit, he purgeth it, that it may bring forth more fruit.*"

4. I Corinthians 15:31 – *"I protest by your rejoicing which I have in Christ Jesus our Lord, I die daily."*

5. Romans 6:19 – *"I speak after the manner of men because of the infirmity of your flesh: for as ye have yielded your members servants to uncleanness and to iniquity unto iniquity; even so now yield your members servants to righteousness unto holiness."*

V.   Why does God do this? So He can give us away and others can eat of the fruit of our lives.

A.   Scriptures

1. Matthew 26:26 – *"And as they were eating, Jesus took bread, and blessed it, and brake it, and <u>gave it to the disciples</u>, and said, <u>Take</u>, <u>eat</u>; this is my body."*

2. II Timothy 2:20-21 – *"But in a great house there are not only vessels of gold and of silver, but also of wood and of earth; and some to honour, and some to dishonour. If a man therefore purge himself from these, he shall be a vessel unto honour, sanctified, and meet for the master's use, and prepared unto every good work."*

3. John 12:24 – *"Verily, verily, I say unto you, Except a corn of wheat fall into the ground and die, it abideth alone: but if it die, it bringeth forth much fruit."*

4. John 15:16 – *"Ye have not chosen me, but I have chosen you, and ordained you, that ye should go and bring forth fruit, and that your fruit should remain: that whatsoever ye shall ask of the Father in my name, he may give it you."*

5. John 21:15-19

6. Matthew 4:19 – *"And he saith unto them, Follow me, and I will make you fishers of men."*

7. Psalms 78:70 – *"He chose David also his servant, and took him from the sheepfolds:"*

8. Joseph is a perfect example of this. He was able to feed the then-known world.

Lesson 95
BUILDING FOR PERMANENCE

I. Building for Permanence

    A. What are you building for?

        1. I Corinthians 3:9 – "*...we are labourers together with God; ye are God's husbandry, ye are God's building*"
        2. II Corinthians 4:18 – "*While we look...at the things which are not seen: for...the things which are not seen are eternal.*"
        3. I Timothy 6:19 – "*Laying up in store for themselves a good foundation against the time to come, that they may lay hold on eternal life.*"
        4. Isaiah 61:4 – "*And they shall build the old wastes, they shall raise up the former desolations, and they shall repair the waste cities, the desolations of many generations.*"
        5. II Corinthians 5:1 – "*...we have a building of God, an house not made with hands, eternal in the heavens*"
        6. I Peter 2:5 – "*Ye also, as lively stones, are built up a spiritual house...*"
        7. Colossians 2:7 – "*Rooted and built up in him, and stablished in the faith...*"
        8. I Timothy 4:8 – "*For bodily exercise profiteth little: but godliness is profitable unto all things, having promise of the life that now is, and of that which is to come...*"
        9. I Corinthians 6:3 – "*Know ye not that we shall judge angels?*"

    B. How we are to build? God is a builder and he wants quality, not quantity.

        1. Psalms 127:1 – "*Except the Lord build the house, they labour in vain that build it*"
        2. Luke 14:28 – "*For which of you, intending to build a tower, sitteth not down first, and counteth the cost, whether he have sufficient to finish it?*"
        3. Matthew 7:24-27 – "*Therefore whosoever heareth these sayings of mine, and doeth them, I will liken him unto a wise man, which built his house upon a rock: And the rain descended, and the floods came, and the winds blew, and beat upon that house; and it fell not: for it was founded upon a rock...*"
        4. Proverbs 24:3 – "*Through wisdom is an house builded; and by understanding it is established:*"
        5. Proverbs 9:1 – "*Wisdom hath builded her house, she hath hewn out her seven pillars:*"
        6. Ezra 6:14 – "*And the elders of the Jews builded, and they prospered through the prophesying...*"
        7. I Corinthians 3:9-10 – "*For we are labourers together with God...According to the grace of God which is given unto me, as a wise masterbuilder, I have laid the foundation, and another buildeth thereon. But let every man take heed how he buildeth thereupon.*"
        8. Proverbs 24:27 – "*Prepare thy work without, and make it fit for thyself in the field; and afterwards build thine house.*"
        9. Ephesians 2:20-21 – "*And are built upon the foundation of the apostles and prophets, Jesus Christ himself being the chief corner stone; In whom all the building fitly framed together groweth unto an holy temple in the Lord:*"
      10. Jude 20 – "*...building up yourselves on your most holy faith, praying in the Holy Ghost.*"
      11. II Chronicles 14:7 – "*...because we have sought the LORD our God, we have sought him, and he hath given us rest on every side. So they built and prospered.*"
      12. II Timothy 2:4 – "*No man that warreth entangleth himself with the affairs of this life...*"
      13. John 12:25 – "*...he that hateth his life in this world shall keep it unto life eternal.*"
      14. Proverbs 15:24 – "*The way of life is above to the wise, that he may depart from hell beneath.*"

    C. God has a pattern for building

1. Exodus 25:8-9 – *"And let them make me a sanctuary; that I may dwell among them. According to all that I shew thee, after the pattern of the tabernacle, and the pattern of all the instruments thereof, even so shall ye make it."*
2. I Samuel 2:35 – *"And I will raise me up a faithful priest, that shall do according to that which is in mine heart and in my mind: and I will build him a sure house..."*
3. I Chronicles 28:12 – *"And the pattern of all that he had by the spirit, of the courts of the house of the LORD, and of all the chambers round about, of the treasuries of the house of God, and of the treasuries of the dedicated things:"*
4. Exodus 25:40 – *"And look that thou make them after their pattern, which was shewed thee in the mount."*

D. Adversity in building

1. Ezra 4:4 – *"...people of the land weakened the hands of the people of Judah, and troubled them in building,"*
2. Hebrews 11:25 – *"Choosing rather to suffer affliction with the people of God, than to enjoy the pleasures of sin for a season"*
3. Hebrews 12:11 – *"Now no chastening for the present seemeth to be joyous, but grievous: nevertheless afterward it yieldeth the peaceable fruit of righteousness unto them which are exercised thereby."*
4. Romans 8:18 – *"For I reckon that the sufferings of this present time are not worthy to be compared with the glory which shall be revealed in us."*

E. How not to build

1. Genesis 11:1-8 – *"...And they said one to another, Go to, let us make brick, and burn them throughly. And they had brick for stone, and slime had they for morter. And they said, Go to, let us build us a city and a tower, whose top may reach unto heaven; and let us make us a name..."*
2. Ecclesiastes 10:18 – *"By much slothfulness the building decayeth..."*
3. Psalms 49 – *"...They that trust in their wealth, and boast themselves in the multitude of their riches; None of them can by any means redeem his brother, nor give to God a ransom for him: (For the redemption of their soul is precious, and it ceaseth for ever:) That he should still live for ever, and not see corruption. For he seeth that wise men die, likewise the fool and the brutish person perish, and leave their wealth to others. Their inward thought is, that their houses shall continue for ever, and their dwelling places to all generations; they call their lands after their own names. Nevertheless man being in honour abideth not..."*
4. II Timothy 4:10 – *"...Demas hath forsaken me, having loved this present world..."*
5. John 12:25 – *"He that loveth his life shall lose it..."*

F. God wants the building finished

1. I Kings 6:9 – *"So he built the house, and finished it..."*
2. Galatians 6:9 – *"And let us not be weary in well doing: for in due season we shall reap, if we faint not."*
3. Colossians 4:12 – *"...that ye may stand perfect and complete in all the will of God."*
4. Hebrews 12:2 – *"Looking unto Jesus the author and finisher of our faith..."*
5. Ezra 6:14 – *"...And they builded, and finished it, according to the commandment of the God of Israel..."*

G. Building for permanence

1. Proverbs 10:25 – *"...but the righteous is an everlasting foundation."*

2. Numbers 25:13 – "*And he shall have it, and his seed after him, even the covenant of an everlasting priesthood; because he was zealous for his God...*"
3. II Corinthians 4:18 – "*...the things which are not seen are eternal.*"
4. Ephesians 3:11 – "*According to the eternal purpose which he purposed in Christ Jesus our Lord:*"

H. The end result – What will be left standing?

1. Revelation 6:17 – "*For the great day of his wrath is come; and who shall be able to stand?*"
2. Malachi 3:2 – "*But who may abide the day of his coming? and who shall stand when he appeareth?...*"
3. Hebrews 12:27 – "*...the removing of those things that are shaken, as of things that are made, that those things which cannot be shaken may remain.*"
4. I Corinthians 3:14 – "*If any man's work abide which he hath built thereupon, he shall receive a reward.*"

Lesson 96
THE CALL TO ALONENESS

I.   Isaiah 51:1-3 and I Chronicles 29:1 (Genesis 12:1, Hebrews 11:8-10)

Isaiah 51:1-3 – "*¹Hearken to me, ye that follow after righteousness, ye that seek the LORD: look unto the rock whence ye are hewn, and to the hole of the pit whence ye are digged. ²Look unto Abraham your father, and unto Sarah that bare you: for I called him alone, and blessed him, and increased him. ³For the LORD shall comfort Zion: he will comfort all her waste places; and he will make her wilderness like Eden, and her desert like the garden of the LORD; joy and gladness shall be found therein, thanksgiving, and the voice of melody.*"
I Chronicles 29:1 – "*Furthermore David the king said unto all the congregation, Solomon my son, whom alone God hath chosen, is yet young and tender, and the work is great: for the palace is not for man, but for the LORD God.*"
Genesis 12:1 – "*Now the LORD had said unto Abram, Get thee out of thy country, and from thy kindred, and from thy father's house, unto a land that I will shew thee:*"
Hebrews 11:8-10 – "*⁸By faith Abraham, when he was called to go out into a place which he should after receive for an inheritance, obeyed; and he went out, not knowing whither he went. ⁹By faith he sojourned in the land of promise, as in a strange country, dwelling in tabernacles with Isaac and Jacob, the heirs with him of the same promise: ¹⁰For he looked for a city which hath foundations, whose builder and maker is God.*"

A.   Jesus spent a great amount of time alone

1.   He is our examples, Luke 6:40 – "*A pupil is not superior to his teacher, but everyone when he is completely trained – readjusted, restored, set to rights and perfected – will be like his teacher.*"

a.   Mark 1:35 – He departed to a solitary place and prayed
b.   Luke 5:16 – He withdrew himself into the wilderness and prayed.
c.   Mark 6:47 – The ship was in the midst of the sea, and He was alone on the land.
d.   Matthew 14:23 – When the evening was come, He was there alone.

B.   God's people called to be separated

1.   Israel

a.   Exodus 8:22-23 – "*And I will sever in that day the land of Goshen, in which my people dwell, that no swarms of flies shall be there; to the end thou mayest know that I am the LORD in the midst of the earth. And I will put a division between my people and thy people: to morrow shall this sign be.*"
b.   Numbers 23:9 – "*For from the top of the rocks I see him, and from the hills I behold him: lo, the people shall dwell alone, and shall not be reckoned among the nations.*"
c.   Deuteronomy 33:28 – "*Israel then shall dwell in safety alone: the fountain of Jacob shall be upon a land of corn and wine; also his heavens shall drop down dew.*"
d.   Psalms 135:4 – "*For the LORD hath chosen Jacob unto himself, and Israel for his peculiar treasure.*"

2.   Christians

a.   John 17:16 – "*They are not of the world, even as I am not of the world.*"
b.   Galatians 6:14 – "*...the world is crucified unto me, and I unto the world.*"

C.   The Principle of Aloneness

1.   Jeremiah 15:16-17 – "*...I sat alone because of thy hand...*"

2. Psalms 102:7 – *"I watch, and am as a sparrow alone upon the house top."*
3. Lamentations 3:26-28 – *"...It is good for a man that he bear the yoke in his youth. He sitteth alone and keepeth silence, because he hath borne it upon him."*
4. II Timothy 4:16-17 – *"At my first answer no man stood with me, but all men forsook me... Notwithstanding the Lord stood with me..."*
5. Luke 4:1 – *"And Jesus...was led by the Spirit into the wilderness"*
6. Exodus 24:2 – *"And Moses alone shall come near the LORD: but they shall not come nigh..."*
7. Micah 7:14-16 – *"Feed thy people...which dwell solitarily..."*

D. Things we will be called to be alone in

1. Beyond the veil – Hebrews 9:7 – the high priest alone
2. Repentance – John 8:9 – Jesus was left alone with the woman
3. When people exalt us – John 6:15 – *"When Jesus therefore perceived that they would come and take him by force, to make him a king, he departed again into a mountain himself alone."*
4. After God uses us – Luke 9:36 – *"And when the voice was past, Jesus was found alone..."*
5. Visitation from God – Daniel 10:7-9 – *"...I Daniel alone saw the vision..."* (Acts 9:7)
6. Intercession – Genesis 32:24 – *"...Jacob was left alone; and there wrestled a man with him until the breaking of the day."*
7. Ultimate fruit of our labor – Isaiah 49:20-23
8. Separated from the filthiness of the heathen – Ezra 6:21, II Corinthians 6:17
9. Disciples are always separated – Acts 19:9
10. Desire for the Word – Proverbs 18:1
11. Separated to the Gospel – Romans 1:1, Acts 13:2
12. To minister to God and carry His presence - Deuteronomy 10:8-9
13. The law of separation – Numbers 6:1-21

E. Examples in Scripture

1. David with the sheep
2. Luke 1:80 – John
3. Galatians 2:1 – Paul
4. Psalms 105:17, Genesis 49:26 – Joseph
5. Men of faith – Hebrews 11:32-39
6. I Samuel 2:11, 18, 21, 26; I Samuel 3:1-9, 20-21

F. The truth is we are not really alone

1. He is with us.

   a. John 16:32 – *"...I am not alone, because the Father is with me."*
   b. John 8:16, 29 – *"...And he that sent me is with me: the Father hath not left me alone..."*
   c. Psalms 23:4 – *"...I will fear no evil: for thou art with me..."*
   d. Psalms 46:7 – *"The LORD of hosts is with us; the God of Jacob is our refuge."*

Lesson 97
CAN GOD?

I.   Psalms 78:19 – *"Yea, they spake against God; they said, Can God furnish a table in the wilderness?"*

When things look their hardest and worst and there is no supply, Jesus will supply.

A.   Scriptural Examples

1.   Matthew 14:15-22
2.   I Kings 17:9-17
3.   I Samuel 3:1, 19-21
4.   Mark 5:25-35

5.   John 8:3-12

a.   Psalms 130:3-4 – *"If thou, LORD, shouldest mark iniquities, O Lord, who shall stand? [4]But there is forgiveness with thee, that thou mayest be feared."*

6.   Proverbs 18:24 – *"...there is a friend that sticketh closer than a brother."*

a.   John 14:18 – *"I will not leave you comfortless: I will come to you."*
b.   Isaiah 61:1-4
c.   Joshua 1:9 – *"Have not I commanded thee? Be strong and of a good courage; be not afraid, neither be thou dismayed: for the LORD thy God is with thee whithersoever thou goest."*

7.   Judges 6:24 – *"Then Gideon built an altar there unto the LORD, and called it Jehovah-shalom: unto this day it is yet in Ophrah of the Abi-ezrites."*

a.   John 14:27 – *"Peace I leave with you, my peace I give unto you: not as the world giveth, give I unto you. Let not your heart be troubled, neither let it be afraid."*
b.   Philippians 4:7 – *"And the peace of God, which passeth all understanding, shall keep your hearts and minds through Christ Jesus."*

Lesson 98
CAUSES AND REMEDIES OF REJECTION

I. Judges 6:11-18 – The Story of Gideon

"11And there came an angel of the LORD, and sat under an oak which was in Ophrah, that pertained unto Joash the Abi-ezrite: and his son Gideon threshed wheat by the winepress, to hide it from the Midianites. 12And the angel of the LORD appeared unto him, and said unto him, The LORD is with thee, thou mighty man of valour. 13And Gideon said unto him, Oh my Lord, if the LORD be with us, why then is all this befallen us? and where be all his miracles which our fathers told us of, saying, Did not the LORD bring us up from Egypt? but now the LORD hath forsaken us, and delivered us into the hands of the Midianites. 14And the LORD looked upon him, and said, Go in this thy might, and thou shalt save Israel from the hand of the Midianites: have not I sent thee? 15And he said unto him, Oh my Lord, wherewith shall I save Israel? behold, my family is poor in Manasseh, and I am the least in my father's house. 16And the LORD said unto him, Surely I will be with thee, and thou shalt smite the Midianites as one man. 17And he said unto him, If now I have found grace in thy sight, then shew me a sign that thou talkest with me. 18Depart not hence, I pray thee, until I come unto thee, and bring forth my present, and set it before thee. And he said, I will tarry until thou come again."

A. Causes

1. Experiencing rejection at an early age
2. Having a bad relationship with your father
3. Comparing yourself to others
4. Not loving yourself
5. Demons that inhabit us
6. Expecting more out of yourself than you can actually perform (which breeds a sense of failure)
7. Experiencing rejection even now
8. Not having a revelation of God's care and love for you

B. Remedies

1. Get the revelation of God's care for you. He won't treat you like men do. He accepts you as you are.

    a. Ezekiel 16:4-8 – *"4And as for thy nativity, in the day thou wast born thy navel was not cut, neither wast thou washed in water to supple thee; thou wast not salted at all, nor swaddled at all. 5None eye pitied thee, to do any of these unto thee, to have compassion upon thee; but thou wast cast out in the open field, to the lothing of thy person, in the day that thou wast born. 6And when I passed by thee, and saw thee polluted in thine own blood, I said unto thee when thou wast in thy blood, Live; yea, I said unto thee when thou wast in thy blood, Live. 7I have caused thee to multiply as the bud of the field, and thou hast increased and waxen great, and thou art come to excellent ornaments: thy breasts are fashioned, and thine hair is grown, whereas thou wast naked and bare. 8Now when I passed by thee, and looked upon thee, behold, thy time was the time of love; and I spread my skirt over thee, and covered thy nakedness: yea, I sware unto thee, and entered into a covenant with thee, saith the Lord GOD, and thou becamest mine."*
    b. Ephesians 1:6 – *"To the praise of the glory of his grace, wherein he hath made us accepted in the beloved."*
    c. Ephesians 2:19 – *"Now therefore ye are no more strangers and foreigners, but fellowcitizens with the saints, and of the household of God;"*

2. We need to know that when all others forsake us, He won't

  a.   Psalms 27:10 – *"When my father and my mother forsake me, then the LORD will take me up."*
  b.   Isaiah 49:15 – *"Can a woman forget her sucking child, that she should not have compassion on the son of her womb? yea, they may forget, yet will I not forget thee."*
  c.   Proverbs 18:24 – *"A man that hath friends must shew himself friendly: and there is a friend that sticketh closer than a brother."*

3.   We need to realize we are a new creation

  a.   II Corinthians 5:17 – *"Therefore if any man be in Christ, he is a new creature: old things are passed away; behold, all things are become new."*
  b.   Colossians 3:1-3 – *"¹If ye then be risen with Christ, seek those things which are above, where Christ sitteth on the right hand of God. ²Set your affection on things above, not on things on the earth. ³For ye are dead, and your life is hid with Christ in God."*
  c.   Romans 12:2 – *"And be not conformed to this world: but be ye transformed by the renewing of your mind, that ye may prove what is that good, and acceptable, and perfect, will of God."*

4.   We need to see we are important and unique

  a.   I Corinthians 12:23-24 – *"²³And those members of the body, which we think to be less honourable, upon these we bestow more abundant honour; and our uncomely parts have more abundant comeliness. ²⁴For our comely parts have no need: but God hath tempered the body together, having given more abundant honour to that part which lacked:"*
  b.   Ephesians 4:16 – *"From whom the whole body fitly joined together and compacted by that which every joint supplieth, according to the effectual working in the measure of every part, maketh increase of the body unto the edifying of itself in love."*
  c.   Psalms 139:14-18

5.   We need to accept and love ourselves. If God loves me, I must be worth something.
6.   Don't compare yourself with others – II Corinthians 10:12
7.   Realize your limitations and see that no one can do everything.
8.   Deliverance from spirits of rejection
9.   Face the places and people you feel rejected by
10. As you get lost in the Holy Ghost and in His Word, stick it out and you'll be delivered
11. Make doubly sure you don't reject anyone

Lesson 99
CONDEMNATION

I.   Where Does Condemnation Come From?

    A.   Three Sources

        1.   The Devil

            a.   Isaiah 50:8-9 – *"He is near that justifieth me; who will contend with me? let us stand together: who is mine adversary? let him come near to me. Behold, the Lord GOD will help me; who is he that shall condemn me? lo, they all shall wax old as a garment; the moth shall eat them up."*

            b.   I Peter 5:8 – *"Be sober, be vigilant; because your adversary the devil, as a roaring lion, walketh about, seeking whom he may devour"*

            c.   I Timothy 3:6 – *"Not a novice, lest being lifted up with pride he fall into the condemnation of the devil."*

        2.   We condemn ourselves – our greatest source of condemnation

            a.   I John 3:20-21 – *"For if our heart condemn us, God is greater than our heart, and knoweth all things. Beloved, if our heart condemn us not, then have we confidence toward God."*

            b.   Psalms 66:18 – *"If I regard iniquity in my heart, the Lord will not hear me"*

            c.   Matthew 12:37 – *"For by thy words thou shalt be justified, and by thy words thou shalt be condemned."*

            d.   Romans 14:22 – *"Hast thou faith? have it to thyself before God. Happy is he that condemneth not himself in that thing which he alloweth."*

        3.   Other people condemn us

            a.   Proverbs 17:15 – *"He that justifieth the wicked, and he that condemneth the just, even they both are abomination to the LORD."*

            b.   Job 32:3 – *"Also against his three friends was his wrath kindled, because they had found no answer, and yet had condemned Job."*

            c.   John 8:1-11

            d.   Romans 8:34 – *"Who is he that condemneth? It is Christ that died, yea rather, that is risen again, who is even at the right hand of God, who also maketh intercession for us."*

            e.   Isaiah 54:17 – *"No weapon that is formed against thee shall prosper; and every tongue that shall rise against thee in judgment thou shalt condemn. This is the heritage of the servants of the LORD, and their righteousness is of me, saith the LORD."*

    B.   God does not condemn us

        1.   Romans 8:1 – *"There is therefore now no condemnation to them which are in Christ Jesus, who walk not after the flesh, but after the Spirit."*

        2.   Psalms 37:33 – *"The LORD will not leave him in his hand, nor condemn him when he is judged."*

        3.   John 3:17 – *"For God sent not his Son into the world to condemn the world; but that the world through him might be saved."*

        4.   John 5:24 – *"Verily, verily, I say unto you, He that heareth my word, and believeth on him that sent me, hath everlasting life, and shall not come into condemnation; but is passed from death unto life."*

        5.   I Corinthians 11:32 – *"But when we are judged, we are chastened of the Lord, that we should not be condemned with the world."*

Staying in Jesus Christ keeps us free from condemnation. If you know who justifies you, you are free from condemnation.

C. Who isn't condemned?

1. John 5:24 – "*Verily, verily, I say unto you, He that heareth my word, and believeth on him that sent me, hath everlasting life, and shall not come into condemnation; but is passed from death unto life.*"

    a. Hears word
    b. Believes on Him
    c. Faith is the ability to not feel condemned, but feel confidence to come to God

III. Three reasons why we are condemned

A. Un-repented sin

1. Romans 5:18 – "*Therefore as by the offence of one judgment came upon all men to condemnation; even so by the righteousness of one the free gift came upon all men unto justification of life.*"
2. Matthew 12:41 – "*The men of Nineveh shall rise in judgment with this generation, and shall condemn it: because they repented at the preaching of Jonas; and, behold, a greater than Jonas is here.*"
3. John 3:17-21 – "*[17]For God sent not his Son into the world to condemn the world; but that the world through him might be saved. [18]He that believeth on him is not condemned: but he that believeth not is condemned already, because he hath not believed in the name of the only begotten Son of God. [19]And this is the condemnation, that light is come into the world, and men loved darkness rather than light, because their deeds were evil. [20]For every one that doeth evil hateth the light, neither cometh to the light, lest his deeds should be reproved. [21]But he that doeth truth cometh to the light, that his deeds may be made manifest, that they are wrought in God.*"
4. Titus 3:10-11 – "*A man that is an heretick after the first and second admonition reject; Knowing that he that is such is subverted, and sinneth, being condemned of himself.*"
5. Romans 8:1-2 – "*There is therefore now no condemnation to them which are in Christ Jesus, who walk not after the flesh, but after the Spirit. For the law of the Spirit of life in Christ Jesus hath made me free from the law of sin and death.*"

B. Remembrance of past sin

1. Hebrews 9:14 – "*How much more shall the blood of Christ, who through the eternal Spirit offered himself without spot to God, purge your conscience from dead works to serve the living God*"?
2. Hebrews 10:2 – "*For then would they not have ceased to be offered? because that the worshippers once purged should have had no more conscience of sins.*"
3. Psalms 66:18 – "*If I regard iniquity in my heart, the Lord will not hear me*":
4. II Peter 1:4-9
5. God has forgotten our sin and so should we

    a. Isaiah 38:17 – "*Behold, for peace I had great bitterness: but thou hast in love to my soul delivered it from the pit of corruption: for thou hast cast all my sins behind thy back.*"
    b. Psalms 103:3 – "*Who forgiveth all thine iniquities; who healeth all thy diseases*";

    c.   Psalms 130:3-4 – *"If thou, LORD, shouldest mark iniquities, O Lord, who shall stand? But there is forgiveness with thee, that thou mayest be feared."*

    d.   Micah 7:18-19 – *"Who is a God like unto thee, that pardoneth iniquity, and passeth by the transgression of the remnant of his heritage? he retaineth not his anger for ever, because he delighteth in mercy. He will turn again, he will have compassion upon us; he will subdue our iniquities; and thou wilt cast all their sins into the depths of the sea."*

    e.   Titus 2:14 – *"Who gave himself for us, that he might redeem us from all iniquity, and purify unto himself a peculiar people, zealous of good works.*

    f.   Psalms 32:1 – *"Blessed is he whose transgression is forgiven, whose sin is covered."*

    g.   Philippians 3:13 – *"Brethren, I count not myself to have apprehended: but this one thing I do, forgetting those things which are behind, and reaching forth unto those things which are before"*

C.   Condemning others

    1.   Judging after the law

        a.   James 4:11-12 – *"Speak not evil one of another, brethren. He that speaketh evil of his brother, and judgeth his brother, speaketh evil of the law, and judgeth the law: but if thou judge the law, thou art not a doer of the law, but a judge. There is one lawgiver, who is able to save and to destroy: who art thou that judgest another?"* – Don't use the law (word) to condemn. The exact same message can bring life or death.

        b.   II Corinthians 3:6 – *"Who also hath made us able ministers of the new testament; not of the letter, but of the spirit: for the letter killeth, but the spirit giveth life."*

        c.   Romans 14:13 – *"Let us not therefore judge one another any more: but judge this rather, that no man put a stumblingblock or an occasion to fall in his brother's way."*

        d.   I Corinthians 8:8-13

    2.   Listening to Accusations

        a.   John 8:10 – *"When Jesus had lifted up himself, and saw none but the woman, he said unto her, Woman, where are those thine accusers? hath no man condemned thee?"*

        b.   Revelation 12:10 – *"And I heard a loud voice saying in heaven, Now is come salvation, and strength, and the kingdom of our God, and the power of his Christ: for the accuser of our brethren is cast down, which accused them before our God day and night."*

        c.   Job 32:3 – *"Also against his three friends was his wrath kindled, because they had found no answer, and yet had condemned Job."*

        d.   Isaiah 58:9 – *"Then shalt thou call, and the LORD shall answer; thou shalt cry, and he shall say, Here I am. If thou take away from the midst of thee the yoke, the putting forth of the finger, and speaking vanity"*;

    3.   Judging without mercy

        a.   James 2:12-13 – *"So speak ye, and so do, as they that shall be judged by the law of liberty. For he shall have judgment without mercy, that hath shewed no mercy; and mercy rejoiceth against judgment."*

        b.   Luke 6:36-37 – *"Be ye therefore merciful, as your Father also is merciful. Judge not, and ye shall not be judged: condemn not, and ye shall not be condemned: forgive, and ye shall be forgiven:"*

        c.   Romans 2:1 – *"Therefore thou art inexcusable, O man, whosoever thou art that judgest: for wherein thou judgest another, thou condemnest thyself; for thou that judgest doest the same things."*

4. Holding grudges

    a. James 5:9 – *"Grudge not one against another, brethren, lest ye be condemned: behold, the judge standeth before the door."*
    b. I Peter 4:9 – *"Use hospitality one to another without grudging."*

5. Despising People

    a   Romans 14:16 – *"Let not then your good be evil spoken of"*
    b. Luke 18:9 – *"And he spake this parable unto certain which trusted in themselves that they were righteous, and despised others"*

Lesson 100
CONFRONTATION WITH GOD

I.   It is essential

    A.   Examples in Scripture of how it came about

        1.   Luke 19:1-10

            a.   He sought to see Jesus
            b.   Wanted to know who He was
            c.   He didn't allow his littleness of stature to prevent him
            d.   He didn't allow himself to be stopped because of the presence of the multitude
            e.   He pressed in and Jesus came to his house
            f.   The result of Zachaeus' confrontation:

                1)   Salvation came – verse 9
                2)   Zachaeus became a giver – verse 8
                3)   He made restitution with all of those he had stolen from

All of this happened because he had a confrontation with God.

        2.   Mark 10:46-52 – Blind Bartamaeus

            a.   He began to cry out
            b.   He ignored all those who told him to shut up
            c.   Jesus stood still
            d.   He allowed himself to be naked or exposed before the Lord – verse 50
            e.   He made his request
            f.   Results of Bartemaeus' Confrontation:

                1)   Vision restored – Physical and Spiritual
                2)   He followed Jesus in the way – He went on with God

        5.   I Samuel 3 – Why Samuel?

            a.   Ministered to the Lord – verse 1
            b.   Worshipped
            c.   Results of his confrontation with God

                1)   He was called to be a prophet to his people.
                2)   The Lord appeared again

    B.   Other Confrontations

        1.   Genesis 32:24-30

            a.   Jacob was persistent
            b.   Result – Name or character change; no longer a deceiver, but a prince

        2.   Isaiah 6:1-10

            a.   All earthly representatives must die before confrontation

b.   Results:

1)   A revelation of your sin
2)   Your sin is purged
3)   Hear the voice of the Lord
4)   Revelation of His purpose

3.   Acts 9:1-9

a.   Results

1)   He journeyed
2)   Heard the voice of the Lord
3)   Acknowledged His Lordship
4)   A humbling and willingness to do His will

4.   Judges 6:11-24

a.   Results

1)   A revelation of who <u>God</u> thinks we are
2)   Direction from the Lord

Lesson 101
CORRECTION, INSTRUCTION, REPROOF: A WAY OF LIFE

I. Word Meanings

    A. Instruction and Correction – Hebrew words below are translated both instruction and correction, so to be corrected is to be instructed, and to be instructed is to be corrected.

        1. *Mowcerah* – correction for a fixed time or season
        2. *Sakal* – to be circumspect, intelligent, to be prudent, to act wisely, to give attention to
        3. *Lamad* – to teach, to goad, to cause to learn
        4. *Muwcar* – chastisement, reproof, warning, instruction. This word has a sense of restraint to it, so His chastisement, His punishment will always be restrained.

    B. Counsel

        1. Hebrew word, *Etsah* – advice, prudence, plan. It comes from a root word that means – to advise, to consult.
        2. Greek word, *Boule* – a piece of advice, to give purpose. It comes from a root word that means – to will, or to be willing, to will deliberately. This word simply means an exercise of the will.

    C. Learning

        1. Hebrew words

            a. *Leqaeh* – something received, being instructed
            b. *Limmud* – taught: a disciple or one who is taught. The root word is *lamad* or instruction (as seen in one of the above definitions of instruction)

        2. Greek word, *Manthano* – to learn, to increase one's knowledge. This word is akin to the Greek word for disciple.

    D. Reprove or Reproof

        1. Hebrew words

            a. *Yakack* – to prove; judge, to be right, to correct
            b. *Towkechah* – chastisement, correction

        2. Greek word, *Elegchos* – evidence, proof. It comes from a root word that means – to admonish, to rebuke with the truth.

II. God wants us to receive instruction

    A. Scriptural examples

        1. Proverbs 19:20 – *"Hear counsel, and receive instruction, that thou mayest be wise in thy latter end."*
        2. Proverbs 24:6 – *"...in multitude of counsellers there is safety."*
        3. Proverbs 20:18 – *"Every purpose is established by counsel..."*
        4. Proverbs 1:5 – *"A wise man will hear, and will increase learning; and a man of understanding shall attain unto wise counsels:"*
        5. Proverbs 11:14 – *"Where no counsel is, the people fall..."*

6. Proverbs 4:13 – *"Take fast hold of instruction; let her not go: keep her; for she is thy life."*
7. Proverbs 8:33-35 – *"Hear instruction, and be wise, and refuse it not..."*
8. Proverbs 10:17 – *"He is in the way of life that keepeth instruction: but he that refuseth reproof erreth."*
9. Psalms 32:8 – *"I will instruct thee and teach thee..."*
10. Proverbs 12:1 – *"Whoso loveth instruction loveth knowledge..."*
11. Proverbs 6:23 – *"...reproofs of instruction are the way of life:"*
12. Isaiah 50:4 – *"...he wakeneth mine ear to hear as the learned."*
13. Matthew 11:28-30 – *"...Take my yoke upon you, and learn of me..."*

III. Scriptural examples of God's punishment being restrained

A. Jeremiah 30:11 – *"...I will correct thee in measure, and will not leave thee altogether unpunished."*

    1. Other translations:

"...I will chastise you, but not too hard, though I must punish you."
"...only discipline you in moderation, so as not to let you go quite without punishment."
"...I will correct you justly and will not declare you innocent."
"...Though I punish you as you deserved, I will not sweep you clean away."

    2. Jeremiah 46:28

B. Isaiah 42:1-3 (Matthew 12:19-20 – *"...judgment unto victory."*)

    1. Other translations:

"...He will be gentle, He will not shout or quarrel in the streets..."
"...He will not scream, nor urge with vehemence; nor will His voice be heard abroad in the streets..."
"...He will not shout, nor raise a cry, nor cause his voice to be heard in the street..."
"...He will not shout, nor raise a cry, nor cause his voice to be heart..."

C. Jeremiah 10:24 – *"O LORD, correct me, but with judgment; not in thine anger, lest thou bring me to nothing."*

    1. Other translations:

"Discipline me, O Jehovah yet with moderation; Not in thine anger, lest thou crush me to atoms."
"So correct us, O Eternal One, but not too hard, not in a passion of thine anger."
"Chasten me Lord, but with due measure, kept, not as thy anger demands, or thou will grind me to dust."
"Correct us Yahweh gently, not in your anger, or you will reduce us to nothing."

D. Proverbs 29:21 – *"He that delicately bringeth up his servant from a child shall have him become his son at the length."*

    1. Hebrew for delicately means – not with force or strength
    2. Other translation – *"One brings up his servant tenderly..."*

E. Psalms 18:35 – *"...thy gentleness hath made me great."*

    1. Gentleness in Hebrew – to be humbled, to bow down, afflicted

    2. Other translations:

"...thy loving correction hath made me great."
"...you have stooped to make me great."
"...thy discipline hath made me great."

F.   Proverbs 16:6 – *"By mercy and truth iniquity is purged..."* For most people it is either one or the other and not the combination or the balance of the two.

1.   God mixes mercy and truth together to purge our sin

a.   Proverbs 20:28
b.   Psalms 61:7
c.   Psalms 85:10
d.   Psalms 89:14
e.   Proverbs 3:3
f.   Proverbs 14:22
g.   II Samuel 15:20

2.   He is a merciful God

a.   Psalms 103:8 (Psalms 145:8)
b.   Psalms 25:10
c.   Psalms 86:13
d.   Micah 7:18
e.   James 2:13

f.   Proverbs 20:28 – His throne is upheld in mercy

1)   Isaiah 16:5

g.   Exodus 34:6
h.   Nehemiah 9:17
i.   Psalms 37:26
j.   Genesis 19:19

Lesson 102
DELIVERANCE FROM MEN

I. Our Faith Should Not Stand In the Wisdom of Men

I Corinthians 2:1-5 – "*¹And I, brethren, when I came to you, came not with excellency of speech or of wisdom, declaring unto you the testimony of God. ²For I determined not to know any thing among you, save Jesus Christ, and him crucified. ³And I was with you in weakness, and in fear, and in much trembling. ⁴And my speech and my preaching was not with enticing words of man's wisdom, but in demonstration of the Spirit and of power: ⁵That your faith should not stand in the wisdom of men, but in the power of God.*" – Though we need men and women and God uses them, it can be taken too far. We must remember the balance.

    A.   We need Men and Women (their ministries)

        1.   Ephesians 4:11-13 – "*¹¹And he gave some, apostles; and some, prophets; and some, evangelists; and some, pastors and teachers; ¹²For the perfecting of the saints, for the work of the ministry, for the edifying of the body of Christ: ¹³Till we all come in the unity of the faith, and of the knowledge of the Son of God, unto a perfect man, unto the measure of the stature of the fulness of Christ:*"

        2.   Hebrews 5:12 – "*For when for the time ye ought to be teachers, ye have need that one teach you again which be the first principles of the oracles of God...*"

        3.   II Timothy 2:2 – "*And the things that thou hast heard of me among many witnesses, the same commit thou to faithful men, who shall be able to teach others also.*"

        4.   Matthew 28:19-20 – "*Go ye therefore, and teach all nations, baptizing them in the name of the Father, and of the Son, and of the Holy Ghost: Teaching them to observe all things whatsoever I have commanded you: and, lo, I am with you alway, even unto the end of the world. Amen.*"

        5.   II Chronicles 15:3 – "*Now for a long season Israel hath been without the true God, and without a teaching priest, and without law.*"

        6.   Isaiah 28:9-10 – "*Whom shall he teach knowledge? and whom shall he make to understand doctrine? them that are weaned from the milk, and drawn from the breasts. For precept must be upon precept, precept upon precept; line upon line, line upon line; here a little, and there a little:*"

        7.   John 20:21 – "*Then said Jesus to them again, Peace be unto you: as my Father hath sent me, even so send I you.*"

        8.   Proverbs 11:14 – "*Where no counsel is, the people fall: but in the multitude of counsellers there is safety.*" (Proverbs 24:6)

        9.   Proverbs 20:18 – "*Every purpose is established by counsel: and with good advice make war.*"

    B.   Some foolishly assert we don't need men at all

Many use the passage in I John 2:27 which says, "*But the anointing which ye have received of him abideth in you, and <u>ye need not that any man teach you</u>: but as the same anointing teacheth you of all things, and is truth, and is no lie, and even as it hath taught you, ye shall abide in him.*" As we have brought out in the above passages, I John 2:27 does not mean we don't need men. It simply means the Spirit of God within you will teach you and <u>He will witness to truth</u> (I John 5:10).

They also use Psalms 23:1, "*The Lord is my shepherd...*", but these are not meek and cannot see their need to be taught. This many times is a rebellious spirit. No one is an end unto themselves (III John 5-13).

    C.   The Balance

        1.   Ecclesiastes 12:11 – "*The words of the wise are as goads, and as nails fastened by the masters of assemblies, which are given from one shepherd.*"

2. I Corinthians 3:5, 22-23 – *"Who then is Paul, and who is Apollos, but ministers by whom ye believed, even as the Lord gave to every man...Whether Paul, or Apollos, or Cephas, or the world, or life, or death, or things present, or things to come; all are yours; And ye are Christ's; and Christ is God's."*

3. Acts 26:17 – *"Delivering thee from the people, and from the Gentiles, unto whom now I send thee"*

4. I Corinthians 9:19 – *"For though I be free from all men, yet have I made myself servant unto all, that I might gain the more."*

II. We Should Not Glory in Men – I Corinthians 3:21 – *"Therefore let no man glory in men..."*

A. The error of some is the Over-Dependence on Men

1. I Corinthians 1:12 – *"Now this I say, that every one of you saith, I am of Paul; and I of Apollos; and I of Cephas; and I of Christ."*
2. Galatians 2:4-14
3. Proverbs 29:25 – *"The fear of man bringeth a snare: but whoso putteth his trust in the LORD shall be safe."*
4. Jeremiah 5:31 – *"The prophets prophesy falsely, and the priests bear rule by their means; and my people love to have it so: and what will ye do in the end thereof?"* (Revelation 2:6 – *"But this thou hast, that thou hatest the deeds of the Nicolaitans, which I also hate."*)
5. II Corinthians 11:2 – *"For I am jealous over you with godly jealousy: for I have espoused you to one husband, that I may present you as a chaste virgin to Christ."*

B. Men struggle with one another to be great and to be seen of each other. We think greatness is God.

1. Luke 22:24-27 – *"And there was also a strife among them, which of them should be accounted the greatest. And he said unto them, The kings of the Gentiles exercise lordship over them; and they that exercise authority upon them are called benefactors. But ye shall not be so: but he that is greatest among you, let him be as the younger; and he that is chief, as he that doth serve. For whether is greater, he that sitteth at meat, or he that serveth? is not he that sitteth at meat? but I am among you as he that serveth."*
2. Acts 8:9 – *"But there was a certain man, called Simon, which beforetime in the same city used sorcery, and bewitched the people of Samaria, giving out that himself was some great one:"*
3. Luke 3:1-2 – *"Now in the fifteenth year of the reign of Tiberius Caesar, Pontius Pilate being governor of Judaea, and Herod being tetrarch of Galilee, and his brother Philip tetrarch of Ituraea and of the region of Trachonitis, and Lysanias the tetrarch of Abilene, Annas and Caiaphas being the high priests, the word of God came unto John the son of Zacharias in the wilderness."* – God isn't impressed
4. Job 32:9 – *"Great men are not always wise: neither do the aged understand judgment."*
5. I Samuel 16 – The selection of David; Samuel thought God would choose the others.
6. Proverbs 20:6 – *"Most men will proclaim every one his own goodness: but a faithful man who can find?"*
7. Genesis 11:4 – *"And they said, Go to, let us build us a city and a tower, whose top may reach unto heaven; and let us make us a name, lest we be scattered abroad upon the face of the whole earth."*
8. Job 32:21-22 – *"Let me not, I pray you, accept any man's person, neither let me give flattering titles unto man. For I know not to give flattering titles; in so doing my maker would soon take me away."*
9. John 7:18 – *"He that speaketh of himself seeketh his own glory: but he that seeketh his glory that sent him, the same is true, and no unrighteousness is in him."*

III. Man In General

A. Psalms 39:5 – "...*verily every man at his best state is altogether vanity.*"

1. Ecclesiastes 7:20 – "*For there is not a just man upon earth, that doeth good, and sinneth not.*"
2. II Chronicles 7:14 – Even God's People - "*If my people, which are called by my name, shall humble themselves, and pray, and seek my face, and turn from their wicked ways; then will I hear from heaven, and will forgive their sin, and will heal their land.*"

3. John 2:23-25 – Knew what was in Man – "*Now when he was in Jerusalem at the passover, in the feast day, many believed in his name, when they saw the miracles which he did. 24But Jesus did not commit himself unto them, because he knew all men, 25And needed not that any should testify of man: for he knew what was in man.*"

   a. Romans 7:18 – Matthew 19:16-23
   b. Jeremiah 17:9 – "*The heart is deceitful above all things, and desperately wicked: who can know it?*"
   c. Genesis 8:21 – "*...for the imagination of man's heart is evil from his youth...*"
   d. Jeremiah 10:23 – "*O LORD, I know that the way of man is not in himself: it is not in man that walketh to direct his steps.*"
   e. Proverbs 14:12 – Man's way is Death – "*There is a way which seemeth right unto a man, but the end thereof are the ways of death.*"

B. Man defiled himself

1. Genesis 1:31 – Genesis 3:1-8
    Result – Romans 5:12, 19 and Psalms 51:5

   a. Isaiah 53:6 – "*All we like sheep have gone astray; we have turned every one to his own way; and the LORD hath laid on him the iniquity of us all.*"
   b. Proverbs 20:9 – "*Who can say, I have made my heart clean, I am pure from my sin?*"
   c. Psalms 53:1-3 (Psalm 14:1-3)
   d. Romans 3:10-23

C. Through His grace, however, we've been made righteous

1. Romans 3:24 – "*Being justified freely by his grace through the redemption that is in Christ Jesus:*"
2. Philemon 6 – Something new in Man – "*That the communication of thy faith may become effectual by the acknowledging of every good thing which is in you in Christ Jesus.*" (I John 4:4 – "*...greater is he that is in you, than he that is in the world.*")
3. Ezekiel 36:26-29 – New Heart – "*A new heart also will I give you, and a new spirit will I put within you: and I will take away the stony heart out of your flesh, and I will give you an heart of flesh. 27And I will put my spirit within you, and cause you to walk in my statutes, and ye shall keep my judgments, and do them. 28And ye shall dwell in the land that I gave to your fathers; and ye shall be my people, and I will be your God. 29I will also save you from all your uncleannesses: and I will call for the corn, and will increase it, and lay no famine upon you.*" (I Samuel 10:6-9 – New Man – New heart)
4. II Corinthians 5:17 – "*Therefore if any man be in Christ, he is a new creature: old things are passed away; behold, all things are become new.*"

IV. Beware men – Matthew 10:17 – "*But beware of men: for they will deliver you up to the councils, and they will scourge you in their synagogues;*"

A.   Luke 12:1 – Pharisees – "*In the mean time, when there were gathered together an innumerable multitude of people, insomuch that they trode one upon another, he began to say unto his disciples first of all, Beware ye of the leaven of the Pharisees, which is hypocrisy.*"

B.   Colossians 2:8 – Modern Day Pharisees – "*Beware lest any man spoil you through philosophy and vain deceit, after the tradition of men, after the rudiments of the world, and not after Christ.*"

C.   Luke 20:46-47 – Scribes – "*Beware of the scribes, which desire to walk in long robes, and love greetings in the markets, and the highest seats in the synagogues, and the chief rooms at feasts; ⁴⁷Which devour widows' houses, and for a shew make long prayers: the same shall receive greater damnation.*"

D.   Matthew 7:15 – False Prophets – "*Beware of false prophets, which come to you in sheep's clothing, but inwardly they are ravening wolves.*"

E.   Philippians 3:2 – Evil Workers – "*Beware of dogs, beware of evil workers, beware of the concision.*"

F.   Acts 20:28-31 – Be weary of Men – Drawing Disciples – "*Take heed therefore unto yourselves, and to all the flock, over the which the Holy Ghost hath made you overseers, to feed the church of God, which he hath purchased with his own blood. ²⁹For I know this, that after my departing shall grievous wolves enter in among you, not sparing the flock. ³⁰Also of your own selves shall men arise, speaking perverse things, to draw away disciples after them. ³¹Therefore watch, and remember, that by the space of three years I ceased not to warn every one night and day with tears.*"

G.   II Peter 2:1-3 – False Teachers – "*But there were false prophets also among the people, even as there shall be false teachers among you, who privily shall bring in damnable heresies, even denying the Lord that bought them, and bring upon themselves swift destruction. ²And many shall follow their pernicious ways; by reason of whom the way of truth shall be evil spoken of. ³And through covetousness shall they with feigned words make merchandise of you: whose judgment now of a long time lingereth not, and their damnation slumbereth not.*"

V.   Don't Trust In Men

A.   Jeremiah 17:5-6 – "*Thus saith the LORD; Cursed be the man that trusteth in man, and maketh flesh his arm, and whose heart departeth from the LORD. ⁶For he shall be like the heath in the desert, and shall not see when good cometh; but shall inhabit the parched places in the wilderness, in a salt land and not inhabited.*"

B.   Isaiah 30:1-3 – "*Woe to the rebellious children, saith the LORD, that take counsel, but not of me; and that cover with a covering, but not of my spirit, that they may add sin to sin: ²That walk to go down into Egypt, and have not asked at my mouth; to strengthen themselves in the strength of Pharaoh, and to trust in the shadow of Egypt! ³Therefore shall the strength of Pharaoh be your shame, and the trust in the shadow of Egypt your confusion.*"

C.   Psalms 118:8-9 – Man, Princes – "*It is better to trust in the LORD than to put confidence in man. ⁹It is better to trust in the LORD than to put confidence in princes.*"

D.   Proverbs 25:19 – Unfaithful man – "*Confidence in an unfaithful man in time of trouble is like a broken tooth, and a foot out of joint.*"

E.   Isaiah 2:22 – "*Cease ye from man, whose breath is in his nostrils: for wherein is he to be accounted of?*"

F.   Other examples:

1.   Jeremiah 9:4 – Neighbor, brother - "*Take ye heed every one of his neighbour, and trust ye not in any brother: for every brother will utterly supplant, and every neighbour will walk with slanders.*"

2.   Micah 7:5 – A friend – "*Trust ye not in a friend, put ye not confidence in a guide: keep the doors of thy mouth from her that lieth in thy bosom.*"

3.   Proverbs 28:26- In your own self – "*He that trusteth in his own heart is a fool: but whoso walketh wisely, he shall be delivered.*"

4. II Corinthians 1:9 – *"But we had the sentence of death in ourselves, that we should not trust in ourselves, but in God which raiseth the dead:"*

VI. Why we should not trust

A. All of the above reasons

B. II Corinthians 11:20 – *"For ye suffer, if a man bring you into bondage, if a man devour you, if a man take of you, if a man exalt himself, if a man smite you on the face."*

C. Jeremiah 5:31 – *"The prophets prophesy falsely, and the priests bear rule by their means; and my people love to have it so: and what will ye do in the end thereof?"*

D. Job 32:3 – *"Also against his three friends was his wrath kindled, because they had found no answer, and yet had condemned Job."*

E. II Timothy 3:13 – *"But evil men and seducers shall wax worse and worse, deceiving, and being deceived."*

VII. We should trust God

A. Psalms 146:3-5 – *"Put not your trust in princes, nor in the son of man, in whom there is no help. ⁴His breath goeth forth, he returneth to his earth; in that very day his thoughts perish. ⁵Happy is he that hath the God of Jacob for his help, whose hope is in the LORD his God:"*

B. Jeremiah 17:7-8 – *"Blessed is the man that trusteth in the LORD, and whose hope the LORD is. ⁸For he shall be as a tree planted by the waters, and that spreadeth out her roots by the river, and shall not see when heat cometh, but her leaf shall be green; and shall not be careful in the year of drought, neither shall cease from yielding fruit."*

C. Isaiah 26:4 – *"Trust ye in the LORD for ever: for in the LORD JEHOVAH is everlasting strength:"*

D. Psalms 32:10 – *"Many sorrows shall be to the wicked: but he that trusteth in the LORD, mercy shall compass him about."*

E. Psalms 34:8 – *"O taste and see that the LORD is good: blessed is the man that trusteth in him."*

F. Psalms 62:5-8 – *"My soul, wait thou only upon God; for my expectation is from him. ⁶He only is my rock and my salvation: he is my defence; I shall not be moved. ⁷In God is my salvation and my glory: the rock of my strength, and my refuge, is in God. ⁸Trust in him at all times; ye people, pour out your heart before him: God is a refuge for us. Selah."*

VIII. We should not fear man – Proverbs 29:25 – *"The fear of man bringeth a snare..."*

A. Psalms 27:1 – *"...the LORD is the strength of my life; of whom shall I be afraid?"*

B. Isaiah 51:7, 8, 12, 13

C. Hebrews 13:6 – *"...The Lord is my helper, and I will not fear what man shall do unto me."*

D. Psalms 56:4

E. Hebrews 11:27

F. Acts 5:28-29

IX. Men Will Fail You

A. Job 5:1 – *"Call now, if there be any that will answer thee; and to which of the saints wilt thou turn?"*

1. Job 16:20 – Proverbs 18:24 – Job's test
2. Job 19:14-19

B. Psalms 142:4 – David's test

1. Psalms 102:6-7 – *"I am like a pelican of the wilderness: I am like an owl of the desert. ⁷I watch, and am as a sparrow alone upon the house top."*

2. Psalms 55:12-14 – *"For it was not an enemy that reproached me; then I could have borne it: neither was it he that hated me that did magnify himself against me; then I would have hid myself from him: [13]But it was thou, a man mine equal, my guide, and mine acquaintance. [14]We took sweet counsel together, and walked unto the house of God in company."*

    a. Matthew 10:36 – *"And a man's foes shall be they of his own household."*

3. Examples of people failing David

    a. I Samuel 17:28 – His brother
    b. I Samuel 18:8-9 – His employer
    c. I Samuel 25:10 – His neighbor
    d. I Samuel 30:6 – His people
    e. II Samuel 6:20 – His wife
    f. II Samuel 15:6 – His son
    g. David's reaction to this – II Samuel 16:5-12

X. Other Results of Trusting In Men (Failure)

A. Luke 15:6 – Prodigal's test
B. II Timothy 4:16-17 – Paul's test
C. Mark 14:27, 50 – Jesus' test

    1. John 16:32 – The Father was still there.

XI. God Delivers Us from Men – To Give Us Back

A. Acts 26:17 – I Corinthians 9:19

    1. John 10:17-18
    2. Song of Solomon 4:12-16, 5:1

Lesson 103
DELIVERANCE FROM SPIRITUAL AMBITION

I. Genesis 11:1-10 – "*¹And the whole earth was of one language, and of one speech. ²And it came to pass, as they journeyed from the east, that they found a plain in the land of Shinar; and they dwelt there. ³And they said one to another, Go to, let us make brick, and burn them throughly. And they had brick for stone, and slime had they for morter. ⁴And they said, Go to, let us build us a city and a tower, whose top may reach unto heaven; and let us make us a name, lest we be scattered abroad upon the face of the whole earth. ⁵And the LORD came down to see the city and the tower, which the children of men builded. ⁶And the LORD said, Behold, the people is one, and they have all one language; and this they begin to do: and now nothing will be restrained from them, which they have imagined to do. ⁷Go to, let us go down, and there confound their language, that they may not understand one another's speech. ⁸So the LORD scattered them abroad from thence upon the face of all the earth: and they left off to build the city. ⁹Therefore is the name of it called Babel; because the LORD did there confound the language of all the earth: and from thence did the LORD scatter them abroad upon the face of all the earth. ¹⁰These are the generations of Shem: Shem was an hundred years old, and begat Arphaxad two years after the flood:*"

A. Verse 4 – "*...let us make us a name...*"

1. Proverbs 20:6 – "*Most men will proclaim every one his own goodness...*"

a. Ecclesiastes 2:4-12
b. Genesis 37:1-12
c. I Samuel 13:1-15 – Saul

d. Saul's beginning

1) I Samuel 9:1, 2, 15-17, 21
2) I Samuel 10:1, 6, 9-11, 20-24, 26-27
3) I Samuel 11:5, 6, 7, 12-14
4) I Samuel 13:1-4, 8-14 – A change begins to take place.
5) I Samuel 15:1-32
6) I Samuel 18:5-9, 10-13
7) I Samuel 28:7-9, 14-19
8) I Samuel 26:21 – I have played the fool.

e. II Samuel 15:1-7 – Absalom
f. I Kings 1:5 – Adonijah
g. II Chronicles 26:1-5 15-22 – Uzziah

B. We shouldn't be concerned about our name

1. John 1:23 – John 3:30
2. Hebrews 11:24-26 – Moses
3. Acts 14:12-15 – Paul and Barnabas

4. Job 32:21-22 – "*Let me not, I pray you, accept any man's person, neither let me give flattering titles unto man. For I know not to give flattering titles; in so doing my maker would soon take me away.*"

a. Psalms 49:6-13 – Naming their lands after them
b. Proverbs 22:11 – A name in the eyes of the Lord.
c. John 7:18 – Don't speak of yourself.

II. Mark 10:35-45 – "*35And James and John, the sons of Zebedee, come unto him, saying, Master, we would that thou shouldest do for us whatsoever we shall desire. 36And he said unto them, What would ye that I should do for you? 37They said unto him, Grant unto us that we may sit, one on thy right hand, and the other on thy left hand, in thy glory. 38But Jesus said unto them, Ye know not what ye ask: can ye drink of the cup that I drink of? and be baptized with the baptism that I am baptized with? 39And they said unto him, We can. And Jesus said unto them, Ye shall indeed drink of the cup that I drink of; and with the baptism that I am baptized withal shall ye be baptized: 40But to sit on my right hand and on my left hand is not mine to give; but it shall be given to them for whom it is prepared. 41And when the ten heard it, they began to be much displeased with James and John. 42But Jesus called them to him, and saith unto them, Ye know that they which are accounted to rule over the Gentiles exercise lordship over them; and their great ones exercise authority upon them. 43But so shall it not be among you: but whosoever will be great among you, shall be your minister: 44And whosoever of you will be the chiefest, shall be servant of all. 45For even the Son of man came not to be ministered unto, but to minister, and to give his life a ransom for many.*"

A. Aspiring to be great

   1. Acts 8:9-11, 13, 17-25 – Simon the sorcerer

   2. We need to be delivered of a **Great Man Mentality**

      a. Jeremiah 5:5
      b. Numbers 16:2
      c. I Samuel 14:52

   3. Job 32:9
   4. Luke 3:1-2 – God is not impressed with great men – Psalms 2:1-4
   5. II Kings 5:11

B. Don't desire greatness

   1. Matthew 23:1-11
   2. Jeremiah 45:5 – "*And seekest thou great things for thyself? seek them not...*"
   3. I Corinthians 10:24 – "*Let no man seek his own...*"
   4. Philippians 2:20-21

   5. II Corinthians 12:12-15 – Paul's example

      a. I Corinthians 10:33
      b. I Thessalonians 2:3-8
      c. II Timothy 2:10

   6. Philippians 2:3-4
   7. Luke 16:10-12 – Just be faithful

C. Those whom God chooses

   1. I Corinthians 1:26-29 – Foolish things
   2. I Samuel 2:8 – Poor and beggars
   3. I Samuel 9:21
   4. Judges 6:15 – Gideon
   5. Amos 7:14-15 – A herdsman.

6. Jeremiah 1:6
7. Isaiah 33:23 – Lame takes the prey.
8. Ephesians 3:8 – I Corinthians 15:9 – Paul's opinion.
9. Deuteronomy 7:6-8
10. Luke 9:46-48

III. Isaiah 14:12-16 – "*12How art thou fallen from heaven, O Lucifer, son of the morning! how art thou cut down to the ground, which didst weaken the nations! 13For thou hast said in thine heart, I will ascend into heaven, I will exalt my throne above the stars of God: I will sit also upon the mount of the congregation, in the sides of the north: 14I will ascend above the heights of the clouds; I will be like the most High. 15Yet thou shalt be brought down to hell, to the sides of the pit. 16They that see thee shall narrowly look upon thee, and consider thee, saying, Is this the man that made the earth to tremble, that did shake kingdoms;*"

A. Exalting yourself

1. Lucifer – Ezekiel 28:17, 2 Thessalonians 2:3-4

2. Matthew 23:12 – If you exalt yourself you will be abased.

   a. Daniel 4:30
   b. Acts 12:20-23

3. Jesus was tempted.

   a. Matthew 4:1-11
   b. John 6:15

   He resisted it both times.

B. God wants a humble people. The opposite of pride or self exaltation is humility or self abasement

1. I Peter 5:6 – "*Humble yourselves therefore under the mighty hand of God, that he may exalt you in due time:*"
2. Proverbs 16:19 – "*Better it is to be of an humble spirit with the lowly, than to divide the spoil with the proud.*"
3. Isaiah 57:15 – "*For thus saith the high and lofty One that inhabiteth eternity, whose name is Holy; I dwell in the high and holy place, with him also that is of a contrite and humble spirit, to revive the spirit of the humble, and to revive the heart of the contrite ones.*"
4. James 4:6 – "*But he giveth more grace. Wherefore he saith, God resisteth the proud, but giveth grace unto the humble.*"
5. Colossians 3:12 – "*Put on therefore, as the elect of God, holy and beloved, bowels of mercies, kindness, humbleness of mind, meekness, longsuffering;*"
6. Micah 6:8 – "*He hath shewed thee, O man, what is good; and what doth the LORD require of thee, but to do justly, and to love mercy, and to walk humbly with thy God?*"
7. I Peter 5:5 – "*Likewise, ye younger, submit yourselves unto the elder. Yea, all of you be subject one to another, and be clothed with humility: for God resisteth the proud, and giveth grace to the humble.*"
8. Luke 18:14 – "*I tell you, this man went down to his house justified rather than the other: for every one that exalteth himself shall be abased; and he that humbleth himself shall be exalted.*"

IV. Don't Let Ambition Drive You to Do Something before Your Time

    A.   II Samuel 18:19-32 – Ahimiaz (Romans 12:7)
    B.   II Kings 5:20-27 – Gehazi
    C.   Acts 8:17-19 – Simon

    D.   Genesis 13:5-18 – Abram and lot – Let's realize it's by grace that anything gets done.

        1.   I Corinthians 15:10 – *"But by the grace of God I am what I am..."*
        2.   Philippians 2:13 – *"For it is God which worketh in you both to will and to do of his good pleasure."*

V.   Jesus is the Highest Name...He is exalted in the Highest, He is the greatest – Philippians 2:9-12

Lesson 104
DELIVERANCE FROM YOKES OF BONDAGE

I. Word Definitions

  A. Yoke in Hebrew

    1. An imposed yoke
    2. A heavy pole; or oxbow

  B. Bondage

    1. Hebrew – a chastisement, a restraint
    2. Greek – to be a slave

II. God Has Promised to Break Our Yokes of Bondage

  A. Scriptures

    1. Psalms 116:16 – *"O Lord, truly I am thy servant...thou hast loosed my bonds."*
    2. Nahum 1:13 – *"For now will I break his yoke from off thee, and will burst thy bonds in sunder."*
    3. Jeremiah 30:8 – *"For it shall come to pass in that day, saith the Lord of hosts, that I will break his yoke from off thy neck, and will burst thy bonds..."*
    4. Exodus 2:23-25 – *"...Israel sighed by reason of the bondage, and they cried, and their cry came up unto God by reason of the bondage. And God heard their groaning, and God remembered his covenant with Abraham...And God looked upon the children of Israel, and God had respect unto them."*
    5. Leviticus 26:13 – *"I am the Lord your God, which brought you forth out of the land of Egypt, that ye should not be their bondmen; and I have broken the bands of your yoke, and made you go upright."*

III. How Does He Cause Our Yokes to be Broken?

  A. Scriptures

    1. Isaiah 10:27 – The anointing
    2. Isaiah 58:6 – Through fasting
    3. Galatians 5:1 – Standing fast in His liberty

IV. The Different Kinds of Bondages and Yokes We Fall Into

  A. **Fear**, Romans 8:15 – *"For ye have not received the spirit of bondage again to fear; but ye have received the Spirit of adoption..."*
  B. **Depression**, Exodus 6:9 – *"And Moses spake so unto the children of Israel: but they hearkened not unto Moses for anguish of spirit, and for cruel bondage."*
  C. **Death**, Hebrews 2:15 – *"And deliver them who through fear of death were all their lifetime subject to bondage."*
  D. **Men**, II Corinthians 11:20 – *"For ye suffer, if a man bring you into bondage, if a man devour you, if a man take of you, if a man exalt himself, if a man smite you on the face."*

    1. II Peter 2:19 – *"...for of whom a man is overcome, of the same is he brought in bondage."*
    2. Acts 15:10 – *"...why tempt ye God, to put a yoke upon the neck of the disciples..."*

E. **Religion**, Galatians 2:4 – "...who came in privily to spy out our liberty which we have in Christ Jesus, that they might bring us into bondage:"

F. **Our Sins**, Lamentations 1:14 – "The yoke of my transgressions is bound by his hand: they are wreathed, and come up upon my neck..."

G. **Generational**, Nehemiah 5:5 – "Yet now our flesh is as the flesh of our brethren, our children as their children: and, lo, we bring into bondage our sons and our daughters to be servants, and some of our daughters are brought unto bondage already: neither is it in our power to redeem them; for other men have our lands and vineyards."

H. **Flesh**, Ezekiel 30:18-19 – "...when I shall break there the yokes of Egypt..."

   1. Exodus 1:13-14 – "And the Egyptians made the children of Israel to serve with rigour: And they made their lives bitter with hard bondage..."

I. **The Devil**, Deuteronomy 28:47-48 – "...and he shall put a yoke of iron upon thy neck..."

J. **Corruption**, Romans 8:21 – "Because the creature itself also shall be delivered from the bondage of corruption into the glorious liberty of the children of God."

Lesson 105
DEPRESSION

I.   Psalms 42:5, Numbers 21:4

Psalms 42:5 – *"Why art thou cast down, O my soul? and why art thou disquieted in me? hope thou in God: for I shall yet praise him for the help of his countenance."*
Numbers 21:4 – *"...and the soul of the people was much discouraged because of the way."*

  A.   Word Meanings

    1.   Discouraged (in Hebrew) – to dock or curtail
    2.   Cast down (in Hebrew) – to sink or depress
    3.   Dismayed (in Hebrew) – to prostrate, to break down by violence, confusion, fear

II.   What Brings Depression?

  A.   Scriptural reasons

    1.   Satan – I Samuel 17:11, Mark 5:1-12, Daniel 7:25
    2.   Trials – I Peter 1:6
    3.   Sin – Jeremiah 30:15
    4.   People – Numbers 32:7-9
    5.   Signs of the times – Jeremiah 10:2
    6.   Our journey in God – Numbers 21:4
    7.   Fear – Isaiah 41:10, Joshua 1:9 – fear and discouragement go together
    8.   Unscriptural self image – Numbers 13:30-33
    9.   Inherited traits – Genesis 5:3 – like begets like (curses)

III.   What Happens to Us as We Allow Depression to Rule

  A.   Scriptural conclusions

    1.   Mark 5:5 – We cut and condemn ourselves
    2.   Proverbs 15:13 – Our spirit is broken – we stop pressing on
    3.   II Corinthians 7:10 – It works death in us
    4.   Proverbs 12:25, Psalms 119:28 – Robs us of joy and faith
    5.   Ruth 1:20 – We blame God and complain
    6.   Deuteronomy 1:27-28 – We affect those around us

IV.   How Can We Be Delivered From Depression

  A.   Realize Jesus has already paid the price

    1.   Isaiah 53:4 – *"Surely he hath borne our griefs, and carried our sorrows: yet we did esteem him stricken, smitten of God, and afflicted."*

  B.   Do our best to stay in His manifest presence

    1.   Psalms 42:5 – *"...for I shall yet praise him for the help of his countenance."*
    2.   Proverbs 31:6 – *"Give strong drink unto him that is ready to perish, and wine to those that be of heavy hearts."*
    3.   II Corinthian 3:17-18

    4.   Psalms 104:15-16 – *"...And wine that maketh glad the heart of man..."*

C.   Pour out our heart to God (not to everyone else)

    1.   I Samuel 1:10-15
    2.   Psalms 62:8 – *"...pour out your heart before him: God is a refuge for us."*

D.   Know that no matter what the situation, He will be with us and deliver us

    1.   Isaiah 41:10 – *"Fear thou not; for I am with thee: be not dismayed; for I am thy God: I will strengthen thee; yea, I will help thee..."*
    2.   Joshua 1:9 – *"...Be strong and of a good courage; be not afraid, neither be thou dismayed: for the LORD thy God is with thee whithersoever thou goest."*
    3.   Jeremiah 31:25
    4.   II Chronicles 20:15, 17
    5.   Jeremiah 30:10

E.   Cast down imaginations

    1.   II Corinthians 10:5 – *"Casting down imaginations..."*
    2.   Philippians 4:8
    3.   Colossians 3:1-3 – *"Set your affection on things above, not on things on the earth..."*
    4.   Acts 26:2 – *"I think myself happy..."*

F.   Put on the garments of praise

    1.   Isaiah 61:3 – *"...the garment of praise for the spirit of heaviness..."*
    2.   Jeremiah 31:2-4
    3.   Isaiah 35:10 – *"...come to Zion with songs and everlasting joy upon their heads: they shall obtain joy and gladness, and sorrow and sighing shall flee away."*
    4.   Psalms 8:2 – Matthew 21:16

G.   Encourage yourself in the Lord

    1.   I Samuel 30:1-6
    2.   Psalms 103:1-3
    3.   Habakkuk 3:17-19
    4.   Psalms 77:7-15

H.   Make a decision to arise

    1.   Ezra 9:5 – *"And at the evening sacrifice I arose up from my heaviness; and having rent my garment and my mantle, I fell upon my knees, and spread out my hands unto the LORD my God."*
    2.   II Samuel 12:20 – *"Then David arose from the earth, and washed, and anointed himself, and changed his apparel, and came into the house of the LORD, and worshipped..."*

Lesson 106
DESIRE TO PLEASE THE FATHER

I.   Pleasing the Father

   A.   John 8:29 – *"And he that sent me is with me: the Father hath not left me alone; for I do always those things that please him."*

     1.   We are created to please him.

       a.   Revelation 4:11 – *"Thou art worthy, O Lord, to receive glory and honour and power: for thou hast created all things, and for thy pleasure they are and were created."*
       b.   Psalms 103:21 – *"Bless ye the LORD, all ye his hosts; ye ministers of his, that do his pleasure."*
       c.   I John 3:22 – *"And whatsoever we ask, we receive of him, because we keep his commandments, and do those things that are pleasing in his sight."*
       d.   Proverbs 10:1 – *"...A wise son maketh a glad father..."*

To please the Father means to listen intently to the desires of His heart, and then do all that we can to do it. To believe Him, to put Him first, to give all that we are to see Him, smile, hear Him say well done, and to love Him dearly.

     2.   Examples of pleasing God.

       a.   Hebrews 11:5-6 – *"By faith Enoch was translated that he should not see death; and was not found, because God had translated him: for before his translation he had this testimony, that he pleased God. But without faith it is impossible to please him: for he that cometh to God must believe that he is, and that he is a rewarder of them that diligently seek him."*

       b.   Jesus

         1)   Romans 15:3 – *"For even Christ pleased not himself..."*
         2)   John 6:38 – *"For I came down from heaven, not to do mine own will, but the will of him that sent me."*
         3)   John 5:30
         4)   John 4:34
         5)   Matthew 26:39, 42

       c.   Psalms 123:2 – *"Behold, as the eyes of servants look unto the hand of their masters, and as the eyes of a maiden unto the hand of her mistress; so our eyes wait upon the LORD our God, until that he have mercy upon us."*

         1)   II Samuel 23:14-17
         2)   Isaiah 58:6 – *"Is not this the fast that I have chosen?..."*

       d.   John the Baptist

Lesson 107
DILIGENCE

I. Diligent: Constant in effort to accomplish something; persistent exertion of body, mind or spirit; something done or pursued with persevering attention.

   A. Traits of the diligent.

       1. Proverbs 10:4 – "*...but the hand of the diligent maketh rich.*"
       2. Proverbs 12:24 – "*The hand of the diligent shall bear rule...*"
       3. Proverbs 13:4 – "*...but the soul of the diligent shall be made fat.*"
       4. Proverbs 21:5 – "*The thoughts of the diligent tend only to plenteousness...*"
       5. Proverbs 12:27 – "*...the substance of a diligent man is precious.*"

   B. God requires diligence as it enables us to keep our heart, soul, and His Word.

       1. Deuteronomy 4:9 – "*Only take heed to thyself, and keep thy soul diligently...*"
       2. Proverbs 4:23 – "*Keep thy heart with all diligence...*"
       3. Psalms 119:1-5 – "*...keep his testimonies...keep thy precepts diligently...*"

   C. Traits of the slothful

       1. Proverbs 15:9 – "*The way of the wicked is an abomination unto the LORD...*"
       2. Proverbs 18:9 – "*He also that is slothful in his work is brother to him that is a great waster.*"
       3. Proverbs 19:24 – "*A slothful man hideth his hand in his bosom, and will not so much as bring it to his mouth again.*"
       4. Proverbs 21:25 – "*The desire of the slothful killeth him; for his hands refuse to labour.*"
       5. Proverbs 22:13 – "*The slothful man saith, There is a lion without, I shall be slain in the streets.*"
       6. Proverbs 26:13-17

   D. God's word on slothfulness.

       1. Proverbs 19:15 – "*Slothfulness casteth into a deep sleep; and an idle soul shall suffer hunger.*"
       2. Ecclesiastes 10:18 – "*By much slothfulness the building decayeth; and through idleness of the hands the house droppeth through.*"
       3. Proverbs 19:24 – "*A slothful man hideth his hand in his bosom, and will not so much as bring it to his mouth again.*"
       4. Matthew 25:14-31
       5. Hebrews 6:11-12

II. God Wants Us to be Diligent In Whatever We Do

   A. Ezra 7:23 – "*Whatsoever is commanded by the God of heaven, let it be diligently done for the house of the God of heaven...*"
   B. II Peter 3:14 – "*...be diligent that ye may be found of him in peace, without spot, and blameless.*"

   C. Things to be diligent or continue in.

       1. Proverbs 22:29 – Our business (Romans 12:11 – "*Not slothful in business; fervent in spirit; serving the Lord.*")
       2. Hebrews 11:6 – Seeking the Lord.
       3. John 8:31 – Word of God (James 1:25)

4. Acts 6:4 – Prayer

    a. Colossians 4:2 – *"Continue in prayer..."*
    b. Luke 18:1 – *"...men ought always to pray, and not to faint;"*
    c. 1 Thessalonians 5:17 – *"Pray without ceasing."*
    d. Acts 1:14 – *"These all continued with one accord in prayer and supplication..."*
    e. Acts 2:42 – *"And they continued stedfastly in the apostles doctrine and fellowship, and in breaking of bread, and in prayers."*

5. Hebrews 13:15 – Worship and Praise

    a. Psalms 34:1 – *"...I will bless the LORD at all times: his praise shall continually be in my mouth."*

6. Acts 13:42 – Grace

    a. Hebrews 12:15 – *"Looking diligently lest any man fail of the grace of God..."*
    b. Hebrews 13:9
    c. II Timothy 2:1

7. Hebrews 13:1 – Love
8. Acts 2:42, 26 – Variety (church, fellowship, eating together)
9. Acts 14:22 – The faith

III. What We Must Do To Be Diligent

A. To be diligent – we must be DOERS

1. Matthew 12:48-50
2. John 13:17 – *"If ye know these things, happy are ye if ye do them."*
3. Luke 6:46 – *"And why call ye me, Lord, Lord, and do not the things which I say?"*
4. Matthew 23:3
5. II Peter 1:10 – *"...for if ye do these things, ye shall never fall:"*

B. How can we be diligent? (Or do)

1. Realize in ourselves we can't be diligent

    a. John 5:30 – *"I can of mine own self do nothing..."*
    b. John 15:5 – *"...for without me ye can do nothing."*
    c. Romans 7:18 – *"...how to perform that which is good I find not."*

2. HE must help us – Philippians 2:13 – *"For it is God which worketh in you both to will and to do of his good pleasure."*

    a. Acts 10:38 – *"How God anointed Jesus of Nazareth with the Holy Ghost and with power: who went about doing good..."*
    b. Galatians 2:20 – *"I am crucified with Christ: nevertheless I live; yet not I, but Christ liveth in me..."*
    c. Acts 26:22 – *"Having therefore obtained help of God, I continue unto this day..."*
    d. Philippians 4:13 – *"I can do all things through Christ which strengtheneth me."*

Lesson 108
DO WE REALLY WANT HIM TO SEARCH?

Psalms 139:23-24 – *"Search me, O God, and know my heart: try me, and know my thoughts: nd see if there be any wicked way in me, and lead me in the way everlasting."*
Psalms 26:2 – *"Examine me, O LORD, and prove me; try my reins and my heart."*

I.   Do We Really Want Him To Search?

   A.   Me first (not somebody else)

      1.   Do we really have the courage to ask God to search and deal with us?
      2.   Can we accept what will happen when He does search us?
      3.   Once He exposes our garbage, will we let Him lead us?

   B.   Can we accept the truth about ourselves?

      1.   Job 31:6 – *"Let me be weighed in an even balance, that God may know mine integrity."*
      2.   Matthew 19:16-23 – *"...when the young man heard that saying, he went away sorrowful..."*
      3.   Matthew 26:30-35
      4.   I Samuel 15:1-24

When we won't believe the truth when God shows us, He must let us see it for ourselves.

   C.   God does search and try our hearts

      1.   Jeremiah 17:10 – *"I the LORD search the heart, I try the reins..."*
      2.   Psalms 7:9 – *"...for the righteous God trieth the hearts and reins."*
      3.   Proverbs 17:3 – *"...the LORD trieth the hearts."*
      4.   Jeremiah 20:12 – *"...O LORD of hosts, that triest the righteous, and seest the reins and the heart..."*
      5.   Romans 8:27
      6.   I Thessalonians 2:4
      7.   Revelation 2:23
      8.   Psalms 11:4-5

   D.   Why does God search us?

      1.   Deuteronomy 8:2 – *"And thou shalt remember all the way which the LORD thy God led thee these forty years in the wilderness, to humble thee, and to prove thee, to know what was in thine heart, whether thou wouldest keep his commandments, or no."* – To know what's in our heart, to see if we'll keep His commandments, and to make us know He is our provision.
      2.   I Peter 4:12-13 – *"Beloved, think it not strange concerning the fiery trial which is to try you, as though some strange thing happened unto you: But rejoice, inasmuch as ye are partakers of Christ's sufferings; that, when his glory shall be revealed, ye may be glad also with exceeding joy."*
      3.   I Peter 1:7 – *"That the trial of your faith, being much more precious than of gold that perisheth, though it be tried with fire, might be found unto praise and honour and glory at the appearing of Jesus Christ:"*

Lesson 109
DYING TO SELF

One of the hardest things for anyone to face is death, be it natural, spiritual, or soulish. Spiritual death has been dealt with by the cross of Jesus Christ. If we receive Jesus as our Lord and Saviour, we "*pass from death unto life*" (John 5:24). Natural death has also been dealt with by the cross, for we know that to be "*absent from the body, is to be present with the Lord*" (II Corinthians 5:8). We've been delivered from the fear of death, because Jesus died for us, and we now know heaven waits (Hebrews 2:14-15). But soulish death is not a death like the others. It kills, but in a different way. We simply die to our self, we die to our own selfish ambitions, and we die to the old carnal nature and by doing so we experience life or a resurrection while we are here on earth. Our soulish life is replaced by God's character. Death to our soul is essential to sanctification. As Paul said, "*I am crucified with Christ: nevertheless I live; yet not I, but Christ liveth in me*" (Galatians 2:20). Paul also stated that he "*died daily*" (I Corinthians 15:31). Paul did not physically die, but he died soulishly. He died to the Adamic nature that lives in all of us, but in that dying, life would come forth in his soul, even the divine life; the nature of God. So it is written in Psalms 116:15, "*Precious in the sight of the LORD is the death of his saints.*" We must learn to get used to this type of death, for it will bring to us the true life of God. Jesus said, "*He that loveth his life shall lose it; and he that hateth his life in this world shall keep it unto life eternal*" (John 12:25).

I.   Dying to Self Releases God's Resurrection Power Not Only to us but to others

    A.   II Kings 13:20-21 – "*And Elisha died, and they buried him. And the bands of the Moabites invaded the land at the coming in of the year. And it came to pass, as they were burying a man, that, behold, they spied a band of men; and they cast the man into the sepulchre of Elisha: and when the man was let down, and touched the bones of Elisha, he revived, and stood up on his feet.*"

        1.   John 12:24 – "*Verily, verily, I say unto you, Except a corn of wheat fall into the ground and die, it abideth alone: but if it die, it bringeth forth much fruit.*"

        2.   Job 14:7-9 – "*For there is hope of a tree, if it be cut down, that it will sprout again, and that the tender branch thereof will not cease. Though the root thereof wax old in the earth, and the stock thereof die in the ground; Yet through the scent of water it will bud, and bring forth boughs like a plant.*"

        3.   Judges 16:30 – "*And Samson said, Let me die with the Philistines. And he bowed himself with all his might; and the house fell upon the lords, and upon all the people that were therein. So the dead which he slew at his death were more than they which he slew in his life.*"

        4.   II Corinthians 4:11-12 – "*For we which live are alway delivered unto death for Jesus' sake, that the life also of Jesus might be made manifest in our mortal flesh. So then death worketh in us, but life in you.*"

        5.   John 19:41 – "*Now in the place where he was crucified there was a garden...*"

        6.   II Samuel 14:14 – "*For we must needs die, and are as water spilt on the ground, which cannot be gathered up again; neither doth God respect any person: yet doth he devise means, that his banished be not expelled from him.*"

        7.   Matthew 26:12 – "*For in that she hath poured this ointment on my body, she did it for my burial.*"

        8.   Revelation 12:11 – "*And they overcame him by the blood of the Lamb, and by the word of their testimony; and they loved not their lives unto the death.*"

We need to conquer our fear of death in every realm, spirit, soul, and body, knowing that resurrection and life always follows death. We find then that death is a good thing, not something to resist, but actually something to welcome! If we see this as a means to bring forth life in others, that is, as we die to ourselves then we will truly have the same hurt as Jesus did. Ultimately then, we can say to all our adversaries, "*...Death is swallowed up in victory. O death, where is thy sting? O grave, where is thy victory? ...But thanks be to God, which giveth us the victory through our Lord Jesus Christ.*" (I Corinthians 15:54-57). Of all the hidden truths of the Bible this is one of the most ironic, poignant and glorious. It does, however, go against our nature as well as a lot of present day charismatic teaching. Nonetheless, it is the Word of God. Death is the springboard to all that God wants to do in our lives. Without it there is no true life.

II. Death to the Soul Life is God's Will

    A. Scriptural Examples

        1. Ecclesiastes 3:2 – *"A time to be born, and a time to die; a time to plant, and a time to pluck up that which is planted;"*

        2. Psalms 116:15 – *"Precious in the sight of the LORD is the death of his saints."*

        3. Philippians 3:10 – *"That I may know him, and the power of his resurrection, and the fellowship of his sufferings, being made conformable unto his death;"*

        4. Revelation 12:11 – *"And they overcame him by the blood of the Lamb, and by the word of their testimony; and they loved not their lives unto the death."*

        5. John 12:24-25 – *"Verily, verily, I say unto you, Except a corn of wheat fall into the ground and die, it abideth alone: but if it die, it bringeth forth much fruit. 25He that loveth his life shall lose it; and he that hateth his life in this world shall keep it unto life eternal."*

        6. II Corinthians 4:7-18

        7. II Corinthians 11:23 – *"Are they ministers of Christ? (I speak as a fool) I am more; in labours more abundant, in stripes above measure, in prisons more frequent, in deaths oft."*

        8. I Corinthians 15:31 – *"I protest by your rejoicing which I have in Christ Jesus our Lord, I die daily."*

III. Death Brings Life

    A. Scriptural Examples

        1. Isaiah 26:19-21 – *"Thy dead men shall live, together with my dead body shall they arise. Awake and sing, ye that dwell in dust: for thy dew is as the dew of herbs, and the earth shall cast out the dead. 20Come, my people, enter thou into thy chambers, and shut thy doors about thee: hide thyself as it were for a little moment, until the indignation be overpast. 21For, behold, the LORD cometh out of his place to punish the inhabitants of the earth for their iniquity: the earth also shall disclose her blood, and shall no more cover her slain."*

        2. Job 14:7-9 – *"For there is hope of a tree, if it be cut down, that it will sprout again, and that the tender branch thereof will not cease. 8Though the root thereof wax old in the earth, and the stock thereof die in the ground; 9Yet through the scent of water it will bud, and bring forth boughs like a plant. 14If a man die, shall he live again? all the days of my appointed time will I wait, till my change come."*

        3. 1 Corinthians 15:54 – *"So when this corruptible shall have put on incorruption, and this mortal shall have put on immortality, then shall be brought to pass the saying that is written, Death is swallowed up in victory."*

        4. Revelation 1:18 –*"I am he that liveth, and was dead; and, behold, I am alive for evermore, Amen; and have the keys of hell and of death."*

        5. Revelation 2:10 – *"Fear none of those things which thou shalt suffer: behold, the devil shall cast some of you into prison, that ye may be tried; and ye shall have tribulation ten days: be thou faithful unto death, and I will give thee a crown of life."*

        6. Amos 5:8 – *"Seek him that maketh the seven stars and Orion, and turneth the shadow of death into the morning, and maketh the day dark with night: that calleth for the waters of the sea, and poureth them out upon the face of the earth: The LORD is his name:"*

        7. 2 Samuel 14:14 – *"For we must needs die, and are as water spilt on the ground, which cannot be gathered up again; neither doth God respect any person: yet doth he devise means, that his*

banished be not expelled from him." Though death is painful, if we can endure, we shall see the life of God in the end.

IV.   How to Die – Scriptural Examples

A.   Hebrews 11:21 – *"By faith Jacob, when he was a dying, blessed both the sons of Joseph; and worshipped, leaning upon the top of his staff."* Greek for dying – to die off or away; other Translations:

"...faith enabled Jacob when dying..."
"...prompted by faith, Jacob when dying..."

1.   Bless others – other translation, *"...put his blessing on each of Joseph's sons..."*
2.   Worshipped – other translations, *"...and bowed in worship...", "...and gave God worship..."*
3.   Leaning upon the top of his staff – Greek for leaning – to recline as a corpse or as one at a meal

   a.   John 13:23 – *"Now there was leaning on Jesus' bosom one of his disciples, whom Jesus loved."*
   b.   Song of Solomon 8:5 – *"Who is this that cometh up from the wilderness, leaning upon her beloved? I raised thee up under the apple tree: there thy mother brought thee forth: there she brought thee forth that bare thee."*

4.   Staff – The staff was used for support, as a weapon, and as a symbol of authority, power, and correction; Greek for staff – a stick, cane, or wand or baton of royalty; it comes from a root word which means to slap or smite.

   a.   Mark 6:8 – *"And commanded them that they should take nothing for their journey, save a staff only; no scrip, no bread, no money in their purse:"*
   b.   Psalms 23:4 – *"Yea, though I walk through the valley of the shadow of death, I will fear no evil: for thou art with me; thy rod and thy staff they comfort me."*

B.   Job 21:22-25 – *"Shall any teach God knowledge? seeing he judgeth those that are high. ²³One dieth in his full strength, being wholly at ease and quiet. ²⁴His breasts are full of milk, and his bones are moistened with marrow. ²⁵And another dieth in the bitterness of his soul, and never eateth with pleasure."*

Other Translations of Verse 23:
"...One dies in his full prosperity, wholly at ease and secure..."
"...and again, one man dies in the fullness of his strength, in all possible happiness and ease, sound of body,   wholly confident and at ease..."
"...One man I tell you dies crowned with success, lapped in security and comfort..."

Other Translations of Verse 24:
"...his body full of fat, the marrow of his bones moist..."
"...His loins full of vigor and the marrow juicy in his bones..."
"...His veins are filled with nourishment and the marrow of his bones is fresh..."

Other Translations of Verse 25:
"...one dies in a mood of bitterness..."
"...with a bitter soul..."
"...broken hearted..."

"...another dies with bitterness in his heart..."

C.   Ecclesiastes 10:4 – *"If the spirit of the ruler rise up against thee, leave not thy place; for yielding pacifieth great offences."* – We need to learn the principle of yielding

D.   Proverbs 14:32 – *"The wicked is driven away in his wickedness: but the righteous <u>hath hope in his death</u>."*

   1.   Revelation 21:4 – the end result – *"And God shall wipe away all tears from their eyes; and there shall be no more death, neither sorrow, nor crying, neither shall there be any more pain: for the former things are passed away."*

E.   Job 14:14-15 – *"If a man die, shall he live again? all the days of my appointed time will I wait, till my change come. ¹⁵Thou shalt call, and I will answer thee: thou wilt have a desire to the work of thine hands."* – We must learn to wait through our appointed time till our change (natural and spiritual) comes.

F.   Hebrews 11:13 – *"These all died in faith, not having received the promises, but having seen them afar off, and were persuaded of them, and embraced them, and confessed that they were strangers and pilgrims on the earth."* We need to die in faith.

G.   Psalms 23:4 – death is just a shadow – *"Yea, though I walk through the valley of the shadow of death, I will fear no evil: for thou art with me; thy rod and thy staff they comfort me."*

H.   John 11:1 - Death is sleeping; we should learn to rest in Him while dying – *"Now a certain man was sick, named Lazarus, of Bethany, the town of Mary and her sister Martha."*

V.   We gain much more in death than we ever have in life

A.   Revelation 14:13 – *"And I heard a voice from heaven saying unto me, Write, Blessed are the dead which die in the Lord from henceforth: Yea, saith the Spirit, that they may rest from their labours; and their works do follow them."*

   1.   Judges 16:30 – *"And Samson said, Let me die with the Philistines. And he bowed himself with all his might; and the house fell upon the lords, and upon all the people that were therein. So the dead which he slew at his death were more than they which he slew in his life."*
   2.   Philippians 1:21- to die is gain – *"For to me to live is Christ, and to die is gain."*
   3.   2 Corinthians 4:12 – life in you – *" So then death worketh in us, but life in you."*
   4.   Philippians 3:10 – *"That I may know him, and the power of his resurrection, and the fellowship of his sufferings, being made conformable unto his death;"*
   5.   Hebrews 2:14 – *"Forasmuch then as the children are partakers of flesh and blood, he also himself likewise took part of the same; that through death he might destroy him that had the power of death, that is, the devil;"* It is the same for us as well as we get the victory over Satan.
   6.   Revelation 1:18 – *"I am he that liveth, and was dead; and, behold, I am alive for evermore, Amen; and have the keys of hell and of death."* Jesus has the keys
   7.   Romans 8:38-39 – *"³⁸For I am persuaded, that neither death, nor life, nor angels, nor principalities, nor powers, nor things present, nor things to come, ³⁹Nor height, nor depth, nor any other creature, shall be able to separate us from the love of God, which is in Christ Jesus our Lord."* Nothing will separate us from Him

Lesson 110
FAILURE

I. All Men Fail

   A. Scriptures

     1. Psalms 73:26 – *"My flesh and my heart faileth: but God is the strength of my heart, and my portion for ever."*
     2. Romans 3:23 – *"For all have sinned, and come short of the glory of God;"*
     3. Job 5:7 – *"Yet man is born unto trouble, as the sparks fly upward."*
     4. Isaiah 40:30 – *"Even the youths shall faint and be weary, and the young men shall utterly fall:"*
     5. Isaiah 53:6 – *"All we like sheep have gone astray; we have turned every one to his own way; and the LORD hath laid on him the iniquity of us all."*

II. What causes us to fail or fall?

   A. Scriptures

     1. Proverbs 28:14 – *"Happy is the man that feareth alway: but he that hardeneth his heart shall fall into mischief."*
     2. Proverbs 11:2 – *"When pride cometh, then cometh shame: but with the lowly is wisdom."*
     3. Proverbs 16:18 – *"Pride goeth before destruction, and an haughty spirit before a fall."*
     4. Proverbs 29:23 – *"A man's pride shall bring him low: but honour shall uphold the humble in spirit."*
     5. I Samuel 15:17 – *"And Samuel said, When thou wast little in thine own sight, wast thou not made the head of the tribes of Israel, and the LORD anointed thee king over Israel?"*
     6. I Peter 5:5 – *"Likewise, ye younger, submit yourselves unto the elder. Yea, all of you be subject one to another, and be clothed with humility: for God resisteth the proud, and giveth grace to the humble."*
     7. II Chronicles 26:15-16 – *"And he made in Jerusalem engines, invented by cunning men, to be on the towers and upon the bulwarks, to shoot arrows and great stones withal. And his name spread far abroad; for he was marvellously helped, till he was strong. But when he was strong, his heart was lifted up to his destruction: for he transgressed against the LORD his God, and went into the temple of the LORD to burn incense upon the altar of incense."*

III. God is committed to us even when we fail

   A. Scriptures

     1. II Samuel 14:14 – *"For we must needs die, and are as water spilt on the ground, which cannot be gathered up again; neither doth God respect any person: yet doth he devise means, that his banished be not expelled from him."*
     2. Psalms 112:4 – *"Unto the upright there ariseth light in the darkness: he is gracious, and full of compassion, and righteous."*
     3. Psalms 145:14 – *"The LORD upholdeth all that fall, and raiseth up all those that be bowed down."*
     4. Job 4:4 – *"Thy words have upholden him that was falling, and thou hast strengthened the feeble knees."*
     5. Psalms 37:24 – *"Though he fall, he shall not be utterly cast down: for the LORD upholdeth him with his hand."*
     6. Jude 24 – *"Now unto him that is able to keep you from falling, and to present you faultless before the presence of his glory with exceeding joy"*

7. Psalms 56:13 – *"For thou hast delivered my soul from death: wilt not thou deliver my feet from falling, that I may walk before God in the light of the living?"*

IV. We must face our failures

A. Scriptures

1. Micah 7:8 – *"Rejoice not against me, O mine enemy: when I fall, I shall arise; when I sit in darkness, the LORD shall be a light unto me."*
2. Proverbs 24:16 – *"For a just man falleth seven times, and riseth up again: but the wicked shall fall into mischief."*
3. Psalms 51:6 – *"Behold, thou desirest truth in the inward parts: and in the hidden part thou shalt make me to know wisdom."*

V. We must see God in our failures

A. Scriptures

1. Psalms 139:1-7, 16
2. Romans 8:28 – *"And we know that all things work together for good to them that love God, to them who are the called according to his purpose."*
3. Proverbs 3:6 – *"In all thy ways acknowledge him, and he shall direct thy paths."*
4. Job 23:10 – *"But he knoweth the way that I take: when he hath tried me, I shall come forth as gold."*
5. Isaiah 46:10 – *"Declaring the end from the beginning, and from ancient times the things that are not yet done, saying, My counsel shall stand, and I will do all my pleasure"*
6. Hebrews 12:2 – *"Looking unto Jesus the author and finisher of our faith; who for the joy that was set before him endured the cross, despising the shame, and is set down at the right hand of the throne of God."*

VI. Failure brings success

A. Scriptures

1. Romans 11:11 – *"I say then, Have they stumbled that they should fall? God forbid: but rather through their fall salvation is come unto the Gentiles, for to provoke them to jealousy."*
2. Isaiah 28:13 – *"But the word of the LORD was unto them precept upon precept, precept upon precept; line upon line, line upon line; here a little, and there a little; that they might go, and fall backward, and be broken, and snared, and taken."*
3. Job 14:7-10
4. Hebrews 11:34 – *"Quenched the violence of fire, escaped the edge of the sword, out of weakness were made strong, waxed valiant in fight, turned to flight the armies of the aliens."*
5. John 15:2 – *"Every branch in me that beareth not fruit he taketh away: and every branch that beareth fruit, he purgeth it, that it may bring forth more fruit."*

B. The way up is down

1. John 3:30 – *"He must increase, but I must decrease."*
2. John 12:24 – *"Verily, verily, I say unto you, Except a corn of wheat fall into the ground and die, it abideth alone: but if it die, it bringeth forth much fruit."*
3. I Corinthians 15:31 – *"I protest by your rejoicing which I have in Christ Jesus our Lord, I die daily."*

VII. We must not rejoice over other's failures

A. Scriptures

1. Romans 14:4 – *"Who art thou that judgest another man's servant? to his own master he standeth or falleth. Yea, he shall be holden up: for God is able to make him stand."*

2. Galatians 6:1 – *"Brethren, if a man be overtaken in a fault, ye which are spiritual, restore such an one in the spirit of meekness; considering thyself, lest thou also be tempted."*

3. Romans 2:2 – *"But we are sure that the judgment of God is according to truth against them which commit such things."*

4. Proverbs 24:17-19 – *"Rejoice not when thine enemy falleth, and let not thine heart be glad when he stumbleth: Lest the LORD see it, and it displease him, and he turn away his wrath from him. Fret not thyself because of evil men, neither be thou envious at the wicked;"*

5. II Corinthians 1:4 – *"Who comforteth us in all our tribulation, that we may be able to comfort them which are in any trouble, by the comfort wherewith we ourselves are comforted of God."*

Lesson 111
FAVOR OF GOD

Favor is any free act of kindness toward another person. To find favor means to receive the attention and respect of another. Favor also characterizes strong personal relationships. Lot was granted deliverance from Sodom, because the messengers favored him (Genesis 10:15-23). Jacob sent all kinds of gifts to appease Esau and gain his favor (Genesis 32:5). Joseph was successful, and became greatly favored by Potiphar, and then also the master of the prison (Genesis 39). These three examples indicate a type of relationship in which the party that was favored receives great benefits. Many of the Scriptures translated favor have the word "face" as a component. "To lift up the face" is translated "to win the favor or acceptance of someone". Favor generally means good will or acceptance, and the benefits that flow from these.

I.   The Definition of Favor

    A.   Hebrew words

        1.   *Ratsown* – To delight in, acceptable; it comes from a root, *ratsah* – to be pleased with, to satisfy a debt.
        2.   *Chen* – Graciousness, kindness. This word is used most for the word favor.
        3.   *Chanan* – To bend or stoop in kindness to an inferior. This word is the root of the above word *chen*.
        4.   *Towb* – Good in the widest sense; It comes from a root word, *towb* – to be good, to do or make good in the widest sense.
        5.   *Shalowm* – Safe, well, happy, prosperity, peace; It comes from a root word, *shalam* – to be safe in mind, body, or estate
        6.   *Yatab* – To be or make well, happy, successful, sound, beautiful, right.

These Hebrew words are also translated in the Scriptures as: *accepted, delight, good will, grace, good, better, gracious, mercy, merciful, hath pity upon, peace, prosperity, and pleased.*

    B.   Greek word

        1.   *Charis* – Graciousness, the divine influence upon the heart. This is the New Testament word translated grace.

II.   Defining Favor Scripturally

    A.   What having God's favor does for us

        1.   Psalms 5:12 – *"For thou, LORD, wilt bless the righteous; with favour wilt thou compass him as with a shield."* – The favor of God encompasses the righteous with a shield.
        2.   Psalms 30:5 – *"For his anger endureth but a moment; in his favour is life..."* – Having God's favor brings us life.
        3.   Psalms 45:9-14 – *"...even the rich among the people shall intreat thy favour..."* – The bride has God's favor.

        4.   Psalms 89:15-17 – *"...and in thy favour our horn shall be exalted."*

            a.   Horn in Hebrew, *queren* – A flask, a cornet, a peak of a mountain; it comes from a root, *quaran* – to push or gore, to shoot out, ray of lights. Therefore horn represents our life, our authority, our name. This is what God exalts with His favor.

5. Psalms 41:11 – "*By this I know that thou favourest me, because mine enemy doth not triumph over me.*" – With God's favor, our enemies will never triumph over us.

6. Psalms 106:4 – "*Remember me, O LORD, with the favour that thou bearest unto thy people: O visit me with thy salvation;*" – With God's favor comes salvation.

7. Proverbs 8:34-35 – "*...For whoso findeth me findeth life, and shall obtain favour of the LORD.*" – When we find Him by seeking and waiting for Him, we find life and favor.

8. Proverbs 16:15 – "*In the light of the king's countenance is life; and his favour is as a cloud of the latter rain.*" – To have God's favor means we will enjoy the manifest presence of His glory and be in a move of God.

9. Proverbs 19:12 – "*The king's wrath is as the roaring of a lion; but his favour is as dew upon the grass.*" – With His favor we enjoy His anointing.

10. Isaiah 60:10 – "*...but in my favour have I had mercy on thee.*" -

11. Proverbs 1:8-9 – "*My son, hear the instruction of thy father, and forsake not the law of thy mother: For they shall be an ornament of grace unto thy head, and chains about thy neck.*" – If we will hear His instruction we will have favor on our heads.

12. Psalms 85:1 – "*LORD, thou hast been favourable unto thy land: thou hast brought back the captivity of Jacob.*" – In His favor we find deliverance from our captors.

13. Zechariah 4:6-7 – "*...This is the word of the LORD unto Zerubbabel, saying, Not by might, nor by power, but by my spirit, saith the LORD of hosts. Who art thou, O great mountain? before Zerubbabel thou shalt become a plain: and he shall bring forth the headstone thereof with shoutings, crying, Grace, grace unto it.*" – Favor brings down our mountains.

14. Job 33:24-26 – "*...and he will be favourable unto him: and he shall see his face with joy: for he will render unto man his righteousness.*" – God's favor lets us see His face with joy, and He will give us His righteousness.

15. Psalms 77:7-12 – "*Will the Lord cast off for ever? and will he be favourable no more? Is his mercy clean gone for ever? doth his promise fail for evermore? Hath God forgotten to be gracious? hath he in anger shut up his tender mercies? Selah. And I said, This is my infirmity: but I will remember the years of the right hand of the most High. I will remember the works of the LORD: surely I will remember thy wonders of old. I will meditate also of all thy work, and talk of thy doings.*"

Even though through our own lack of belief, we might ask this question, "*will he be favourable no more?*" The answer will come and say, the truth is He has never removed His favor. This is just a weakness on our part. God never withdraws it; we think He'll forget to show us favor, but He won't.

B. God has given it to His people

1. Exodus 3:21-22 – "*And I will give this people favour in the sight of the Egyptians: and it shall come to pass, that, when ye go, ye shall not go empty: But every woman shall borrow of her neighbour, and of her that sojourneth in her house, jewels of silver, and jewels of gold, and raiment: and ye shall put them upon your sons, and upon your daughters; and ye shall spoil the Egyptians.*"

   a. Exodus 11:3
   b. Exodus 12:36

2. Psalms 5:12 – "*For thou, LORD, wilt bless the righteous; with favour wilt thou compass him as with a shield.*"

3. Psalms 102:13-14 – "*Thou shalt arise, and have mercy upon Zion: for the time to favour her, yea, the set time, is come. For thy servants take pleasure in her stones, and favour the dust thereof.*"

4. James 4:6 – *"But he giveth more grace. Wherefore he saith, God resisteth the proud, but giveth grace unto the humble."*

5. Psalms 84:11 – *"For the LORD God is a sun and shield: the LORD will give grace and glory: no good thing will he withhold from them that walk uprightly."*

6. Daniel 1:9 – *"Now God had brought Daniel into favour and tender love with the prince of the eunuchs."*

7. Zechariah 12:9-10 – *"...And I will pour upon the house of David, and upon the inhabitants of Jerusalem, the spirit of grace and of supplications..."*

8. Proverbs 14:9 – *"...but among the righteous there is favour."*

Let us remember that in the Scriptures, the words grace and favor are the same translated word, especially in the New Testament when it comes to our salvation.

C. The bride of Christ certainly has it. All of these Scriptures whether in type or not refer to the bride.

1. Song of Solomon 8:10 – *"...then was I in his eyes as one that found favour."*
2. Esther 2:15, 17 – Esther in Hebrew means – star, or hidden one
3. Luke 1:28-30

D. How can we learn to walk in it?

1. Proverbs 3:3-4 – *"Let not mercy and truth forsake thee: bind them about thy neck; write them upon the table of thine heart: So shalt thou find favour and good understanding in the sight of God and man."* – Walk in mercy and truth

2. Proverbs 3:34 – *"...but he giveth grace unto the lowly."* – Humility

   a. I Peter 5:5 – *"...God...giveth grace to the humble."*

3. I Peter 5:10 – *"But the God of all grace, who hath called us unto his eternal glory by Christ Jesus, after that ye have suffered a while, make you perfect, stablish, strengthen, settle you."* – Dealings of God

4. Acts 7:46 – *"Who found favour before God, and desired to find a tabernacle for the God of Jacob."* – Desire to build God's house

5. Acts 2:42-47 – Revelation of the whole body of Christ

"42And they continued stedfastly in the apostles' doctrine and fellowship, and in breaking of bread, and in prayers. 43And fear came upon every soul: and many wonders and signs were done by the apostles. 44And all that believed were together, and had all things common; 45And sold their possessions and goods, and parted them to all men, as every man had need. 46And they, continuing daily with one accord in the temple, and breaking bread from house to house, did eat their meat with gladness and singleness of heart, 47Praising God, and having favour with all the people. And the Lord added to the church daily such as should be saved."

6. Luke 2:51-52 – *"And he went down with them, and came to Nazareth, and was subject unto them...And Jesus increased in wisdom and stature, and in favour with God and man."* – Submission to authority

   a. I Peter 5:5 – *"...ye younger, submit yourselves unto the elder. Yea, all of you be subject one to another, and be clothed with humility: for God resisteth the proud, and giveth grace to the humble."*

7. Proverbs 8:34-35 – *"Blessed is the man that heareth me, watching daily at my gates, waiting at the posts of my doors. For whoso findeth me findeth life, and shall obtain favour of the LORD."* – Daily waiting at His doorstep

8. Proverbs 12:2 – *"<u>A good man</u> obtaineth favour of the LORD..."*

9. Proverbs 13:15 – *"<u>Good understanding</u> giveth favour..."*

10. Proverbs 14:35 – *"The king's favour is toward a <u>wise servant</u>..."*

11. Proverbs 18:22 – *"Whoso findeth a wife findeth a good thing, and obtaineth favour of the LORD."* – Finding a wife or husband

12. Proverbs 3:21-22 – *"My son, let not them depart from thine eyes: keep sound wisdom and discretion: So shall they be life unto thy soul, and grace to thy neck."* – Living the Word of God

13. Job 33:26 – *"He shall pray unto God, and he will be favourable unto him: and he shall see his face with joy: for he will render unto man his righteousness."* – Prayer or intercession

14. Hebrews 4:16 – *"Let us therefore come boldly unto the throne of grace, that we may obtain mercy, and find grace to help in time of need."* – By coming boldly to His throne

15. Psalms 84:11 – *"For the LORD God is a sun and shield: the LORD will give grace and glory: no good thing will he withhold from <u>them that walk uprightly</u>."*

Lesson 112
FEAR THE LORD

I.   We Are Commanded To Fear God.

    A.   I Peter 2:17 – *"Honour all men. Love the brotherhood. Fear God. Honour the king."*

    B.   Psalms 96:9 – *"...fear before him, all the earth."*

    C.   Psalms 33:8 – *"Let all the earth fear the LORD: let all the inhabitants of the world stand in awe of him."*

    D.   Ecclesiastes 12:13 – *"Let us hear the conclusion of the whole matter: Fear God, and keep his commandments: for this is the whole duty of man."*

II. What Is The Fear Of God? Who Is A Man That Fears The Lord?

    A.   Give God place

        1.   Exodus 15:2 – *"...I will prepare him an habitation..."*
        2.   Psalms 132:13 – *"For the LORD hath chosen Zion; he hath desired it for his habitation."*
        3.   Matthew 6:33 – *"But seek ye first the kingdom of God..."*
        4.   Colossians 3:1 – *"...seek those things which are above..."*

    B.   Try your best to keep from sin.

        1.   Job 1:8 – *"...an upright man, one that feareth God, and escheweth evil?"*
        2.   Proverbs 16:6 – *"By mercy and truth iniquity is purged: and by the fear of the LORD men depart from evil."*
        3.   Proverbs 8:13 – *"The fear of the LORD is to hate evil: pride, and arrogancy, and the evil way, and the froward mouth, do I hate."*

    C.   Love God because He's God!

        1.   Job 1:19-22
        2.   Genesis 5:24 – Enoch
        3.   Adam had a chance but lost it trying to be his own God.
        4.   Isaiah 65:1-11
        5.   Deuteronomy 7:6-9

    D.   A wise man fears God

        1.   Job 28:28 – *"...Behold, the fear of the Lord, that is wisdom..."*
        2.   Proverbs 1:7 – *"The fear of the LORD is the beginning of knowledge..."*
        3.   Psalms 111:10
        4.   Proverbs 15:33 – *"The fear of the LORD is the instruction of wisdom..."*

    E.   Sacrifice is typical of fearing God

        1.   Genesis 22:1-15
        2.   II Samuel 24:24
        3.   I Peter 5:10

    G.   Confidence

        1.   Proverbs 14:26 – *"...in the fear of the Lord is strong confidence..."*

III. Blessings of Fearing God

    A. Proverbs 19:23 – Satisfied
    B. Psalms 103:13 – The Lord pitieth
    C. Psalms 34:7-9 – Angels Encamp

    D. We're blessed that fear.

        1. Psalms 112:1 – "...*Blessed is the man that feareth the LORD...*"
        2. Psalms 128:1
        3. Proverbs 29:14

IV. What Happens When There Is No Fear Of God?

    A. Genesis 20:11
    B. Romans 3:18 – Sin, emptiness, death
    C. Psalms 36:1 – ...*The transgression of the wicked saith within my heart, that there is no fear of God before his eyes.*"
    D. Ecclesiastes 8:13 – "*But it shall not be well with the wicked, neither shall he prolong his days, which are as a shadow; because he feareth not before God.*"

V. We Can Learn To Fear Him

    A. Deuteronomy 4:10 – Word
    B. Psalms 34:11-15 – Tongue
    C. Psalms 86:11 – Unite our spirit, soul and body.

Lesson 113
FOOLISHNESS OF STRIFE AND DIVISIONS
IN THE BODY OF CHRIST

I. As Seen In the Story of Jephthah

    A. Judges 11:1-3 – "*1Now Jephthah the Gileadite was a mighty man of valour, and he was the son of an harlot: and Gilead begat Jephthah. 2And Gilead's wife bare him sons; and his wife's sons grew up, and they thrust out Jephthah, and said unto him, Thou shalt not inherit in our father's house; for thou art the son of a strange woman. 3Then Jephthah fled from his brethren, and dwelt in the land of Tob: and there were gathered vain men to Jephthah, and went out with him.*"

        1. His name means – He will open, he will set free and liberate
        2. Gilead means – Perpetual fountain, a heap of testimony, a witness, strong

        3. Gilead was known for being a place of refuge

            a. Jacob fled there from Laban – Genesis 31:21
            b. Israelites who feared the Philistines in Saul's days fled there – I Samuel 13:7
            c. Ishbosheth fled there – II Samuel 2:8-9
            d. David – II Samuel 17:22-26 – During Absalom's revolt

        4. Gilead was known for an aromatic gum or resin that had healing virtues ("balm of Gilead")
        5. The tribe of Manasseh lived in this land
        6. Remember Ephraim was the youngest and Manasseh was the oldest of Joseph's sons, but Jacob had chosen Ephraim. So there was extreme jealousy between them. Ephraim did not want Manasseh blessed at all.
        7. They constantly strove with their brothers – They argued with Gideon in Judges 8
        8. They accused the land of Gilead as being just a place of fugitives to demean them

    B. Jephthah

        1. Judges 11:1-33

            a. He was a mighty man of valour
            b. But he was the son of a harlot
            c. Jephthah's brothers threw him out of their house and told him he wouldn't inherit anything from their father because he was a harlot's son.
            d. So he fled from his brethren
            e. He dwelt in the land of Tob which means – good place, to be good
            f. Because he was a man of valour, men joined themselves to him.
            g. The Ammonites began to make war against Israel and the elders of Gilead asked him to be their captain.
            h. He responds by saying you hated me and expelled me from my father's house, why come and ask me to help you now that you are in distress?
            i. They told him you can be head over us now and he became the Gileadite's leader.
            j. After that, he challenged the Ammonites and told them the truth, but they resisted his words, and he had to fight them. The Ammonites had refused Israel passage through their territory during their wilderness experience. In this case, Jephthah had asked the Ephraimites to join him but they did not.
            k. The Spirit of God came upon him and he went to face the Ammonites.
            l. And he made a foolish vow to God (verses 30-31)
            m. The Lord delivered the Ammonites to him. It was a very great slaughter.

2. Judges 11:31-40

    a. He shouldn't have done this.

    b. The Spirit of the Lord had already come upon him.

    c. He still felt he had to offer something to God. This was honorable but an obvious weakness in his faith.

    d. We should learn from this to not make foolish vows we cannot keep, even though he honored it with his daughter's wonderful approval.

    e. The making of vows in Scriptures

       1) Genesis 28:20-22 – *"And Jacob vowed a vow, saying, If God will be with me, and will keep me in this way that I go, and will give me bread to eat, and raiment to put on, So that I come again to my father's house in peace; then shall the LORD be my God: And this stone, which I have set for a pillar, shall be God's house: and of all that thou shalt give me I will surely give the tenth unto thee."*

       2) Numbers 30:2 – *"If a man vow a vow unto the LORD, or swear an oath to bind his soul with a bond; he shall not break his word, he shall do according to all that proceedeth out of his mouth."*

       3) Deuteronomy 23:21 – *"When thou shalt vow a vow unto the LORD thy God, thou shalt not slack to pay it: for the LORD thy God will surely require it of thee; and it would be sin in thee."*

       4) I Samuel 1:11 – *"And she vowed a vow, and said, O LORD of hosts, if thou wilt indeed look on the affliction of thine handmaid, and remember me, and not forget thine handmaid, but wilt give unto thine handmaid a man child, then I will give him unto the LORD all the days of his life, and there shall no rasor come upon his head."*

       5) Psalms 65:1 – *"Praise waiteth for thee, O God, in Sion: and untothee shall the vow be performed"*

       6) Psalms 76:11 – *"Vow, and pay unto the LORD your God..."*

       7) Ecclesiastes 5:4-6 – *"When thou vowest a vow unto God, defer not to pay it; for he hath no pleasure in fools: pay that which thou hast vowed. Better is it that thou shouldest not vow, than that thou shouldest vow and not pay. Suffer not thy mouth to cause thy flesh to sin; neither say thou before the angel, that it was an error: wherefore should God be angry at thy voice, and destroy the work of thine hands?"*

C. Judges 12:1-7

    1. Ephraim angered at not going with them to crush the Ammonites

    2. They say they are going to burn him and his house with fire

    3. He couldn't reason with them.

    4. They called the Gileadite's fugitives – this was a great insult

    5. And so Jephthah destroyed them.

    6. Forty two thousand of them – 42 is the number for antichrist.

    7. Those that tried to escape were cut off at every turn

    8. The Ephraimites couldn't say Shibboleth. Their dialect made them say instead Sibboleth. And so it was easy to know who they were and they were subsequently killed.

    9. This should not have happened and it reminds us of the foolishness in the body of Christ.

    10. It was caused by pride and being offended. How sad.

II. The Divisions within the Body of Christ are started by:

A. Pride

1. Proverbs 8:13 – "*The fear of the LORD is to hate evil: pride, and arrogancy, and the evil way, and the froward mouth, do I hate.*"
2. Proverbs 11:2 – "*When pride cometh, then cometh shame: but with the lowly is wisdom.*"
3. Proverbs 13:10 – "*Only by pride cometh contention: but with the well advised is wisdom.*"
4. Proverbs 14:3 – "*In the mouth of the foolish is a rod of pride: but the lips of the wise shall preserve them.*"
5. Proverbs 16:18 – "*Pride goeth before destruction, and an haughty spirit before a fall.*"
6. Proverbs 29:23 – "*A man's pride shall bring him low: but honour shall uphold the humble in spirit.*"
7. Obadiah 3 – "*The pride of thine heart hath deceived thee, thou that dwellest in the clefts of the rock, whose habitation is high; that saith in his heart, Who shall bring me down to the ground?*"
8. I John 2:16 – "*For all that is in the world, the lust of the flesh, and the lust of the eyes, and the pride of life, is not of the Father, but is of the world.*"
9. Proverbs 6:17 – "*A proud look, a lying tongue, and hands that shed innocent blood,*"
10. Proverbs 16:5 – "*Every one that is proud in heart is an abomination to the LORD: though hand join in hand, he shall not be unpunished.*"
11. Proverbs 28:25 – "*He that is of a proud heart stirreth up strife: but he that putteth his trust in the LORD shall be made fat.*"
12. Romans 1:30 – "*Backbiters, haters of God, despiteful, proud, boasters, inventors of evil things, disobedient to parents,*"
13. II Timothy 3:2 – "*For men shall be lovers of their own selves, covetous, boasters, proud, blasphemers, disobedient to parents, unthankful, unholy,*"
14. James 4:6 – "*But he giveth more grace. Wherefore he saith, God resisteth the proud, but giveth grace unto the humble.*"
15. I Peter 5:5 – "*Likewise, ye younger, submit yourselves unto the elder. Yea, all of you be subject one to another, and be clothed with humility: for God resisteth the proud, and giveth grace to the humble.*"

B. Strife

1. Genesis 13:7-8 – "*And there was a strife between the herdmen of Abram's cattle and the herdmen of Lot's cattle: and the Canaanite and the Perizzite dwelled then in the land. And Abram said unto Lot, Let there be no strife, I pray thee, between me and thee, and between my herdmen and thy herdmen; for we be brethren.*"
2. Proverbs 15:18 – "*A wrathful man stirreth up strife: but he that is slow to anger appeaseth strife.*"
3. Proverbs 16:28 – "*A froward man soweth strife: and a whisperer separateth chief friends.*"
4. Proverbs 17:14 – "*The beginning of strife is as when one letteth out water: therefore leave off contention, before it be meddled with.*"
5. Proverbs 20:3 – "*It is an honour for a man to cease from strife: but every fool will be meddling.*"
6. Proverbs 22:10 – "*Cast out the scorner, and contention shall go out; yea, strife and reproach shall cease.*"
7. Proverbs 26:20-21 – "*Where no wood is, there the fire goeth out: so where there is no talebearer, the strife ceaseth. As coals are to burning coals, and wood to fire; so is a contentious man to kindle strife.*"
8. Luke 22:24 – "*And there was also a strife among them, which of them should be accounted the greatest.*"
9. I Corinthians 3:3 – "*For ye are yet carnal: for whereas there is among you envying, and strife, and divisions, are ye not carnal, and walk as men?*"
10. Philippians 2:3 – "*Let nothing be done through strife or vainglory; but in lowliness of mind let each esteem other better than themselves.*"

11. James 3:14-16 – *"But if ye have bitter envying and strife in your hearts, glory not, and lie not against the truth. This wisdom descendeth not from above, but is earthly, sensual, devilish. For where envying and strife is, there is confusion and every evil work."*

C. Contention

1. Proverbs 13:10 – *"Only by pride cometh contention: but with the well advised is wisdom."*
2. Proverbs 22:10 – *"Cast out the scorner, and contention shall go out; yea, strife and reproach shall cease."*
3. Acts 15:39 – *"And the contention was so sharp between them, that they departed asunder one from the other: and so Barnabas took Mark, and sailed unto Cyprus;"*

D. Envy

1. Job 5:2 – *"For wrath killeth the foolish man, and envy slayeth the silly one."*
2. Proverbs 14:30 – *"A sound heart is the life of the flesh: but envy the rottenness of the bones."*
3. Proverbs 27:4 – *"Wrath is cruel, and anger is outrageous; but who is able to stand before envy?"*
4. Mark 15:10 – *"For he knew that the chief priests had delivered him for envy."*
5. Acts 7:9 – *"And the patriarchs, moved with envy, sold Joseph into Egypt: but God was with him,"*
6. Romans 1:28-32 – *"28 And even as they did not like to retain God in their knowledge, God gave them over to a reprobate mind, to do those things which are not convenient; 29Being filled with all unrighteousness, fornication, wickedness, covetousness, maliciousness; full of envy, murder, debate, deceit, malignity; whisperers, 30Backbiters, haters of God, despiteful, proud, boasters, inventors of evil things, disobedient to parents, 31Without understanding, covenantbreakers, without natural affection, implacable, unmerciful: 32Who knowing the judgment of God, that they which commit such things are worthy of death, not only do the same, but have pleasure in them that do them."*
7. I Timothy 6:3-6 – *"3If any man teach otherwise, and consent not to wholesome words, even the words of our Lord Jesus Christ, and to the doctrine which is according to godliness; 4He is proud, knowing nothing, but doting about questions and strifes of words, whereof cometh envy, strife, railings, evil surmisings, 5Perverse disputings of men of corrupt minds, and destitute of the truth, supposing that gain is godliness: from such withdraw thyself. 6But godliness with contentment is great gain."*
8. Titus 3:3 – *"For we ourselves also were sometimes foolish, disobedient, deceived, serving divers lusts and pleasures, living in malice and envy, hateful, and hating one another."*
9. Romans 13:13 – *"Let us walk honestly, as in the day; not in rioting and drunkenness, not in chambering and wantonness, not in strife and envying."*
10. I Corinthians 3:3 – *"For ye are yet carnal: for whereas there is among you envying, and strife, and divisions, are ye not carnal, and walk as men?"*
11. Galatians 5:26 – *"Let us not be desirous of vain glory, provoking one another, envying one another."*
12. James 3:16 – *"For where envying and strife is, there is confusion and every evil work."*

E. Jealousy

1. Numbers 5:14 – *"And the spirit of jealousy come upon him, and he be jealous of his wife, and she be defiled: or if the spirit of jealousy come upon him, and he be jealous of his wife, and she be not defiled:"* – It is a spirit
2. Song of Solomon 8:6 – *"Set me as a seal upon thine heart, as a seal upon thine arm: for love is strong as death; jealousy is cruel as the grave: the coals thereof are coals of fire, which hath a most vehement flame."*

    F.   This brings divisions

        1.   Romans 16:17 – *"Now I beseech you, brethren, mark them which cause divisions and offences contrary to the doctrine which ye have learned; and avoid them."*

        2.   I Corinthians 1:10 – *"Now I beseech you, brethren, by the name of our Lord Jesus Christ, that ye all speak the same thing, and that there be no divisions among you; but that ye be perfectly joined together in the same mind and in the same judgment."*

        3.   I Corinthians 3:3 – *"For ye are yet carnal: for whereas there is among you envying, and strife, and divisions, are ye not carnal, and walk as men?"*

        4.   I Corinthians 11:18 – *"For first of all, when ye come together in the church, I hear that there be divisions among you; and I partly believe it."*

III.   God Would Rather us to Be Forgiving and Kind and Have a Servant's Heart

    A.   Scriptures

        1.   Mark 10:42-46

"42But Jesus called them to him, and saith unto them, Ye know that they which are accounted to rule over the Gentiles exercise lordship over them; and their great ones exercise authority upon them. 43But so shall it not be among you: but whosoever will be great among you, shall be your minister: 44And whosoever of you will be the chiefest, shall be servant of all. 45For even the Son of man came not to be ministered unto, but to minister, and to give his life a ransom for many. 46And they came to Jericho: and as he went out of Jericho with his disciples and a great number of people, blind Bartimaeus, the son of Timaeus, sat by the highway side begging."

        2.   II Chronicles 10:7 – *"And they spake unto him, saying, If thou be kind to this people, and please them, and speak good words to them, they will be thy servants for ever."*

        3.   Luke 6:35 – *"But love ye your enemies, and do good, and lend, hoping for nothing again; and your reward shall be great, and ye shall be the children of the Highest: for he is kind unto the unthankful and to the evil."*

        4.   I Corinthians 13:4 – *"Charity suffereth long, and is kind; charity envieth not; charity vaunteth not itself, is not puffed up,"*

        5.   Ephesians 4:32 – *"And be ye kind one to another, tenderhearted, forgiving one another, even as God for Christ's sake hath forgiven you."*

        6.   Psalms 141:3 – *"Set a watch, O LORD, before my mouth; keep the door of my lips."*

        7.   Proverbs 31:26 – *"She openeth her mouth with wisdom; and in her tongue is the law of kindness."*

        8.   II Corinthians 6:4-6 – *"But in all things approving ourselves as the ministers of God, in much patience, in afflictions, in necessities, in distresses, In stripes, in imprisonments, in tumults, in labours, in watchings, in fastings; By pureness, by knowledge, by longsuffering, by kindness, by the Holy Ghost, by love unfeigned,"*

        9.   Colossians 3:12 – *"Put on therefore, as the elect of God, holy and beloved, bowels of mercies, kindness, humbleness of mind, meekness, longsuffering;"*

     10.   II Peter 1:7 – *"And to godliness brotherly kindness; and to brotherly kindness charity."*

     11.   Matthew 6:12-15 – *"And forgive us our debts, as we forgive our debtors. And lead us not into temptation, but deliver us from evil: For thine is the kingdom, and the power, and the glory, for ever. Amen. For if ye forgive men their trespasses, your heavenly Father will also forgive you: But if ye forgive not men their trespasses, neither will your Father forgive your trespasses."*

     12.   Matthew 18:21-22 – *"Then came Peter to him, and said, Lord, how oft shall my brother sin against me, and I forgive him? till seven times? Jesus saith unto him, I say not unto thee, Until seven times: but, Until seventy times seven."*

13. Matthew 18:35 – *"So likewise shall my heavenly Father do also unto you, if ye from your hearts forgive not every one his brother their trespasses."*

14. Mark 11:25-26 – *"And when ye stand praying, forgive, if ye have ought against any: that your Father also which is in heaven may forgive you your trespasses. But if ye do not forgive, neither will your Father which is in heaven forgive your trespasses."*

15. Luke 17:3-4 – *"Take heed to yourselves: If thy brother trespass against thee, rebuke him; and if he repent, forgive him. And if he trespass against thee seven times in a day, and seven times in a day turn again to thee, saying, I repent; thou shalt forgive him."*

16. Luke 23:34 – *"Then said Jesus, Father, forgive them; for they know not what they do. And they parted his raiment, and cast lots."*

17. II Corinthians 2:7-11 – *"So that contrariwise ye ought rather to forgive him, and comfort him, lest perhaps such a one should be swallowed up with overmuch sorrow. Wherefore I beseech you that ye would confirm your love toward him. For to this end also did I write, that I might know the proof of you, whether ye be obedient in all things. To whom ye forgive any thing, I forgive also: for if I forgave any thing, to whom I forgave it, for your sakes forgave I it in the person of Christ; Lest Satan should get an advantage of us: for we are not ignorant of his devices."*

Lesson 114
THE FOOLISH

The word foolish is used in Scripture with respect to *moral* rather than *intellectual* deficiencies. The fool is not so much one lacking in mental powers, as one who *misuses* them. A fool is not one who does not reason, but one who reasons wrongfully. The picture which emerges from the Scriptures is quite simple: folly is the opposite of wisdom, and a fool is the opposite of a wise person. We will now look at what the Scriptures define as a fool or foolishness. The dictionary definition of a fool is a person who lacks sense or judgment or lacking in common powers or understanding.

I.   Word definitions

    A.   Hebrew for fool or foolish

        1.   *Nabal* – stupid, wicked, extremely impious. It comes from a root word, *Nabel*, which means – to wilt, to fall away, fail, faint, wicked, to despise, a disgrace.
        2.   *Cakal* – to be silly, make foolish. It comes from a root word, *Kacal*, that means – to be fat, silly, and foolish.
        3.   *Keciyl* – stupid, silly, to be fat, a dull person or stupid fellow.
        4.   *Eviyl* – to be perverse, silly. It describes someone who lacks wisdom, is morally undesirable, one who despises wisdom or discipline, mocks guilt, or is quarrelsome. His only authority is himself.

    B.   Greek for fool or foolish

        1.   *Aphron* – mindless, stupid, ignorant, egotistical, rash, unbelieving, someone without reason, sanity or sobriety.
        2.   *Anoetos* – unintelligent, sensual, not understanding, one who doesn't apply his mind.
        3.   *Moros* – dull, stupid, heedless. It means a blockhead, an absurd person, sluggish, to be silly.

    C.   Foolishness

        1.   Hebrew – *Ivveleth* – silliness, folly, one who is foolish in violating God's law.
        2.   Greek – *Moria* – silliness, absurdity. It comes from a root that means – dull, stupid, heedless, a blockhead.

    D.   Simple in Hebrew, *Pethaiy* – silly, seducible. It comes from a root word, *pathah*, which means – to open, to make roomy in a mental or moral sense, to be simple in a sinister way, to delude, to entice.

II.   Definition of the foolish, fools in Scripture

    A.   God has no joy in the foolish

        1.   Jeremiah 4:22 – *"For my people is foolish, they have not known me..."*
        2.   Psalms 94:8 – "brutish" in Hebrew – stupid
        3.   Proverbs 17:21 – *"...the father of a fool hath no joy."*
        4.   Proverbs 26:10
        5.   Deuteronomy 32:4-6
        6.   Job 2:9-10
        7.   Psalms 74:18, 22
        8.   Proverbs 15:20 – *"...a foolish man despiseth his mother."*
        9.   Proverbs 17:25 – *"A foolish son is a grief to his father..."*

10. Proverbs 19:13 – *"A foolish son is the calamity of his father..."*
11. Ecclesiastes 5:4 – *"...for he hath no pleasure in fools..."*
12. Proverbs 10:1 – *"...A wise son maketh a glad father: but a foolish son is the heaviness of his mother."*
13. Psalms 75:4
14. Proverbs 1:22 – *"How long, ye simple ones, will ye love simplicity?"*
15. Proverbs 8:1-5 – *"...O ye simple, understand wisdom: and, ye fools, be ye of an understanding heart."*
16. Proverbs 9:1-6 – *"...Forsake the foolish, and live; and go in the way of understanding."*

B. Fools always think they know what is right

1. Proverbs 12:15 – *"The way of a fool is right in his own eyes..."*
2. Proverbs 14:15-16 – *"...but the fool rageth, and is confident."*
3. Proverbs 17:10 – *"A reproof entereth more into a wise man than an hundred stripes into a fool."*
4. Proverbs 23:9 – *"...for he will despise the wisdom of thy words."*
5. Proverbs 28:26 – *"He that trusteth in his own heart is a fool..."*
6. Ecclesiastes 10:2-3 – *"...a fool's heart at his left..."*
7. Ecclesiastes 4:5 – *"The fool foldeth his hands together, and eateth his own flesh."*
8. Proverbs 15:5 – *"A fool despiseth his father's instruction..."*
9. Ecclesiastes 2:14 – *"The wise man's eyes are in his head; but the fool walketh in darkness..."*
10. Proverbs 14:8
11. Proverbs 12:23 – *"...but the heart of fools proclaimeth foolishness."*
12. Proverbs 19:3 – *"The foolishness of man perverteth his way: and his heart fretteth against the Lord."*
13. Proverbs 16:22 – *"...but the instruction of fools is folly."*

C. A fool won't receive counsel, correction or discipline

1. Proverbs 27:22 – *"Though thou shouldest bray a fool in a mortar among wheat with a pestle, yet will not his foolishness depart from him."*
2. Proverbs 13:10 – *"Only by pride cometh contention: but with the well advised is wisdom."*
3. Jeremiah 4:1-4
4. Ezekiel 13:3 – *"...Woe unto the foolish prophets, that follow their own spirit..."*
5. Proverbs 1:23-33
6. Luke 24:25 – *"...O fools, and slow of heart to believe all that the prophets have spoken."*
7. Matthew 7:24-27 – *"...26And every one that heareth these sayings of mine, and doeth them not, shall be likened unto a foolish man, which built his house upon the sand: 27And the rain descended, and the floods came, and the winds blew, and beat upon that house; and it fell: and great was the fall of it."*
8. Galatians 3:1-3 – *"O foolish Galatians, who hath bewitched you, that ye should not obey the truth..."*
9. I Samuel 13:5-14 – *"...Thou hast done foolishly: thou hast not kept the commandment of the Lord thy God..."*
10. Proverbs 22:3 (Proverbs 27:12) – *"...the simple pass on, and are punished."*

D. Fools despise correction

1. Proverbs 1:7 – *"...fools despise wisdom and instruction."*
2. Proverbs 1:22 – *"How long, ye simple ones, will ye love simplicity? and the scorners delight in their scorning, and fools hate knowledge?"*

3. Proverbs 18:1-3 – "...[2]*A fool hath no delight in understanding, but that his heart may discover itself...*"

4. Proverbs 17:16 – "*Wherefore is there a price in the hand of a fool to get wisdom, seeing he hath no heart to it?*"

5. Proverbs 24:7 – "*Wisdom is too high for a fool: he openeth not his mouth in the gate.*"

6. Proverbs 12:15 – "*The way of a fool is right in his own eyes: but he that hearkeneth unto counsel is wise.*"

7. Proverbs 15:5 – "*A fool despiseth his father's instruction: but he that regardeth reproof is prudent.*"

8. Proverbs 23:9 – "*Speak not in the ears of a fool: for he will despise the wisdom of thy words.*"

9. Proverbs 16:22 – "*Understanding is a wellspring of life unto him that hath it: but the instruction of fools is folly.*"

E. A fool will not pay the price for wisdom

1. Proverbs 17:16 – "*Wherefore is there a price in the hand of a fool to get wisdom, seeing he hath no heart to it?*"

2. Proverbs 18:2 – "*A fool hath no delight in understanding, but that his heart may discover itself.*"

3. Proverbs 24:7 – "*Wisdom is too high for a fool: he openeth not his mouth in the gate.*"

4. Proverbs 21:20 – "*There is treasure to be desired and oil in the dwelling of the wise; but a foolish man spendeth it up.*"

5. Proverbs 15:5 – "*A fool despiseth his father's instruction: but he that regardeth reproof is prudent.*"

6. Matthew 25:9-10

F. A fool does not keep his mouth or watch his words; fools have a serious problem with their mouths

1. Proverbs 18:6-7 – "*A fool's lips enter into contention...A fool's mouth is his destruction...*"

2. Proverbs 10:18 – "*...he that uttereth a slander, is a fool.*"

3. Proverbs 17:7 – "*Excellent speech becometh not a fool...*"

4. Proverbs 17:28 – "*Even a fool, when he holdeth his peace, is counted wise...*"

5. Proverbs 19:1 – "*...he that is perverse in his lips and is a fool.*"

6. Proverbs 29:11 – "*A fool uttereth all his mind: but a wise man keepeth it in till afterwards.*"

7. Proverbs 26:7-9 – a parable in the mouths of fools

8. Proverbs 10:14 – "*...but the mouth of the foolish is near destruction.*"

9. Proverbs 14:3 – "*In the mouth of the foolish is a rod of pride...*"

10. Proverbs 15:7 – "*The lips of the wise disperse knowledge: but the heart of the foolish doeth not so.*"

11. Proverbs 12:23 – "*...heart of fools proclaimeth foolishness.*"

12. Proverbs 15:2, 14 – "*...the mouth of fools poureth out foolishness...the mouth of fools feedeth on foolishness.*"

13. Ecclesiastes 10:12-14 – "*...the lips of a fool will swallow up himself...*"

14. Ecclesiastes 5:1-3

15. Ephesians 5:4 – "*Neither filthiness, nor foolish talking...*"

16. Proverbs 30:32 – "*If thou hast done foolishly in lifting up thyself, or if thou hast thought evil, lay thine hand upon thy mouth.*"

G   Other Biblical traits of a fool

1. Psalms 14:1 (Psalms 53:1) – "*The fool hath said in his heart, There is no God. They are corrupt, they have done abominable works, there is none that doeth good.*"

2. Ecclesiastes 10:15 – *"The labour of the foolish wearieth every one of them, because he knoweth not how to go to the city."*
3. Psalms 92:5-6 – *"...A brutish man knoweth not; neither doth a fool understand this."*
4. Proverbs 26:11 – *"As a dog returneth to his vomit, so a fool returneth to his folly."*
5. Jeremiah 10:6-8
6. Proverbs 14:17 – *"He that is soon angry dealeth foolishly..."*
7. Proverbs 22:15 – *"Foolishness is bound in the heart of a child..."*
8. Proverbs 14:9 – *"Fools make a mock at sin..."*
9. Mark 7:18-23
10. Ecclesiastes 7:9 – *"...anger resteth in the bosom of fools."*
11. I Corinthians 2:14 – *"But the natural man receiveth not the things of the Spirit of God: for they are foolishness unto him..."*
12. Proverbs 27:3 – *"...a fool's wrath is heavier than them both."*
13. Proverbs 13:19 – *"...it is abomination to fools to depart from evil."*
14. Proverbs 14:33 – *"...that which is in the midst of fools is made known."*
15. Ephesians 5:15
16. Proverbs 10:23 – *"It is as sport to a fool to do mischief..."*
17. Proverbs 13:16 – *"...a fool layeth open his folly."*
18. Proverbs 17:12 – *"Let a bear robbed of her whelps meet a man, rather than a fool in his folly."*
19. Proverbs 17:24 (Ecclesiastes 2:14) – *"...the eyes of a fool are in the ends of the earth."*
20. Proverbs 19:10 – *"Delight is not seemly for a fool; much less for a servant to have rule over princes."*
21. Proverbs 20:3 – *"...every fool will be meddling."*
22. Ecclesiastes 4:5 – *"The fool foldeth his hands together, and eateth his own flesh."*
23. Ecclesiastes 7:6
24. Proverbs 15:21 – *"Folly is joy to him that is destitute of wisdom..."*
25. Jeremiah 4:22 – *"For my people is foolish, they have not known me..."*
26. Jeremiah 5:21-25
27. Romans 1:20-32
28. Ecclesiastes 7:4 – *"The heart of the wise is in the house of mourning; but the heart of fools is in the house of mirth."*
29. Matthew 23:15-19 (Luke 11:38-40)
30. I Corinthians 15:36 – *"Thou fool, that which thou sowest is not quickened, except it die."*
31. II Corinthians 12:11 – *"...a fool in glorying..."*
32. Psalms 73:3-12
33. Proverbs 9:13 – *"A foolish woman is clamourous..."* (full of noise)
34. Proverbs 14:1 – *"Every wise woman buildeth her house: but the foolish plucketh it down with her hands."*

H. Rewards of the foolish

1. Psalms 107:17 – *"Fools because of their transgression...are afflicted."*
2. Proverbs 7:22 – *"He goeth after her straightway, as an ox goeth to the slaughter, or as a fool to the correction of the stocks"* His life is sacrificed foolishly; corrected by beatings (Proverbs 26:3, 19:29, Luke 12:47)
3. Proverbs 10:8-10 – *"The wise in heart will receive commandments: but a prating fool shall fall."*
4. Proverbs 11:29 – *"...the fool shall be servant to the wise of heart."*
5. Proverbs 26:1 – *"...honour is not seemly for a fool."*

6. Job 5:1-5 – *"1Call now, if there be any that will answer thee; and to which of the saints wilt thou turn? 2For wrath killeth the foolish man, and envy slayeth the silly one. 3I have seen the foolish taking root: but suddenly I cursed his habitation. 4His children are far from safety, and they are*

crushed in the gate, neither is there any to deliver them. ⁵Whose harvest the hungry eateth up, and taketh it even out of the thorns, and the robber swalloweth up their substance."

   a.   Killed
   b.   No only he but his family is affected
   c.   No harvest
   d.   A life of thorns (Mark 4:18-19, Proverbs 24:30-34)
   e.   Robber (type of Satan) steals their substance (John 10:10)

7. I Timothy 6:9
8. II Chronicles 16:9 – *"...Herein thou hast done foolishly: therefore from henceforth thou shalt have wars."*
9. Proverbs 14:18
10. Psalms 38:5 – *"My wounds stink and are corrupt because of my foolishness."*
11. Proverbs 3:35 – *"The wise shall inherit glory: but shame shall be the promotion of fools."*
12. Proverbs 14:24
13. Proverbs 19:29 – *"Judgments are prepared for scorners and stripes for the back of fools."*
14. Isaiah 35:8
15. Proverbs 19:3 – *"The foolishness of man perverteth his way: and his heart fretteth against the LORD."*
16. Ecclesiastes 10:15 – *"The labour of the foolish wearieth every one of them, because he knoweth not how to go to the city."*
17. Ecclesiastes 10:1 – *"Dead flies cause the ointment of the apothecary to send forth a stinking savour: so doth a little folly him that is in reputation for wisdom and honour."* In sum, a little foolishness can destroy a lifetime of wisdom and honor
18. Proverbs 13:20 – *"He that walketh with wise men shall be wise: but a companion of fools shall be destroyed."* Even a fool's friend is destroyed

I. What is the end of a fool?

1. I Samuel 13:13-14 – *"...Thou hast done foolishly...But now thy kingdom shall not continue..."*
2. I Samuel 26:21 – *"...I have played the fool, and have erred exceedingly."* For Saul, this was a sad end to a great start.
3. Jeremiah 17:5-11 – *"...at his end shall be a fool"*
4. Luke 12:16-21 – *"...Thou fool, this night thy soul shall be required of thee..."*
5. Proverbs 10:21 – *"The lips of the righteous feed many: but fools die for want of wisdom."*
6. Matthew 7:24-27 – *"And every one that heareth these sayings of mine, and doeth them not, shall be likened unto a foolish man..."*
7. Ecclesiastes 7:17 – *"...neither be thou foolish: why shouldest thou die before thy time?"*
8. Job 5:1-4
9. Psalms 5:5 – *"The foolish shall not stand in thy sight: thou hatest all workers of iniquity."*
10. Proverbs 17:5 – *"Whoso mocketh the poor reproacheth his Maker: and he that is glad at calamities shall not be unpunished."*

J. What are we to do with fools?

1. Proverbs 26:4-5 – *"Answer not a fool according to his folly, lest thou also be like unto him. Answer a fool according to his folly, lest he be wise in his own conceit."*
2. Proverbs 26:8 – *"...so is he that giveth honour to a fool."*
3. Proverbs 30:21-22 – *"...a fool when he is filled with meat."*
4. Proverbs 14:17 – *"He that is soon angry dealeth foolishly..."*
5. Proverbs 29:9 – *"If a wise man contendeth with a foolish man, whether he rage or laugh, there is no rest."*

6. Proverbs 13:20 – *"...a companion of fools shall be destroyed."*
7. Ecclesiastes 7:5 – *"It is better to hear the rebuke of the wise, than for a man to hear the song of fools."*
8. Proverbs 9:6 – *"Forsake the foolish, and live; and go in the way of understanding."*
9. I Peter 2:15 – *"For so is the will of God, that with well doing ye may put to silence the ignorance of foolish men."*
10. II Timothy 2:23 – *"But foolish and unlearned questions avoid..."*
11. Titus 3:9 – *"But avoid foolish questions, and genealogies, and contentions, and strivings about the law; for they are unprofitable and vain."*
421

Lesson 115
FRIENDSHIP ACCORDING TO SCRIPTURE

I.   Are We Supposed To Have Friendships?

    A.   YES!

        1.   Psalms 75:2 – *"When I shall receive the congregation I will judge uprightly."* – Hebrew for receive – Lagach – to take, to accept. This scripture says to us that we cannot begin to judge correctly until we are flowing with the congregation.

        2.   John 13:35 – *"By this shall all men know that ye are my disciples, if ye have love one to another."*

        3.   Acts 2:41-47

        4.   John 15:12-14

        5.   Romans 15:7 – *"Wherefore receive ye one another, as Christ also received us to the glory of God."* – This does away with every spirit or attitude or isolation, be it cliquish, sectarian, or just plain fear of people.

II.   How Do We Get Friends?

    A.   YOU step out first

        1.   Proverbs 18:24 – You won't have friends by acting ugly or nonchalant. We must reach out of ourselves and be kind, sweet, and friendly to others. By doing this, we shall receive.

        2.   Luke 6:38 – Dictionary definition of friendly – kind, helpful, favorably disposed, inclined to approve, help, or support, amicable, not hostile.

    B.   Recognize your need for the rest of the body of Christ.

        1.   I Corinthians 12 – We are not islands unto ourselves. We are part of the <u>body</u>, one small member in the midst that should be relating and flowing with the rest of the body. We cannot say "I have no need of thee".

III. God's Warning to Those Who Don't Receive the Body

    A.   Beware of them!

        1.   John 13:20

        2.   III John 8-11

        3.   Hebrews 10:23 -26

IV.   What Are Friends For?

    A.   Scriptural Examples

        1.   Proverbs 27:9 – To be sweet to someone.

        2.   Exodus 33:11 – Face to face (close relationship, heart. That friend will say it to his face, not through some other avenue.)

            a.   Proverbs 27:5-6 – A friend will tell you the truth because he loves you. You always know where you stand. You can receive anything from them because you know they love you.

3. Luke 15:29 – Someone to make merry with. "Merry" in Greek – Euphraino: to put in a good frame of mind, to make glad, or to rejoice.

4. Luke 11:5-8 – One who is willing to share his provision with you or who is willing to be inconvenienced.

5. John 15:13 – One whose love is so deep, they will lay down their life for you. Jesus said there is no greater love than this.

6. Acts 27:3 – One who refreshes and encourages you.

7. Proverbs 17:17 – One who loves at all times (good and bad) and one who will stand with you in adversity.

    a.   Matthew 26:50 – Example of Jesus with Judas.

    b.   John 13:1 and I Corinthians 11:23 – Examples of Jesus with disciples.

8. Lamentations 1:8

Lesson 116
GIVING

I. There are two types of giving – disciplined/systematic (the tithe) or spontaneous (offerings).

   A. Systematic giving is tithing.

      1. Proverbs 3:9 – *"Honour the LORD with thy substance, and with the firstfruits of all thine increase:"* The substance spoken of here is tithe.
      2. Malachi 1:6-9
      3. Malachi 3:8-13
      4. Hebrews 7:2 – *"To whom also Abraham gave a tenth part of all; first being by interpretation King of righteousness, and after that also King of Salem, which is, King of peace;"* (Genesis 14:26)

   B. Tithing before the law

      1. Voluntary (Genesis 14:18-20), Abraham gives tithes.
      2. Genesis 28:20-22 Jacob promises the tithe.

   C. Tithing under the Law of Moses was compulsory.

      1. Leviticus 27:30-32
      2. Malachi 3:10 – *"Bring ye all the tithes into the storehouse, that there may be meat in mine house, and prove me now herewith, saith the LORD of hosts, if I will not open you the windows of heaven, and pour you out a blessing, that there shall not be room enough to receive it."*
      3. Nehemiah 10:37-38

   D. Tithing under grace is done willingly

      1. Hebrews 7:1-17
      2. II Corinthians 8:5, 11-12

Giving is a responsibility. God is a giver so we must be. Israel would take the best of their crop and give it to the Lord. We are called upon to do the same. The tithe belongs to God and obedience to the law of tithing brings blessing. We give ourselves to God first then he requires a tithe which he promises to protect us from our adversary.

II. Spontaneous Giving (Offerings)

   A. Offerings are special gifts we give to God, to our church, to people under the spontaneous direction of the Holy Spirit.

      1. Luke 3:8 – *"Bring forth therefore fruits worthy of repentance, and begin not to say within yourselves, We have Abraham to our father: for I say unto you, That God is able of these stones to raise up children unto Abraham."*
      2. Matthew 6:1-4
      3. Proverbs 3:9 – *"Honour the LORD with thy substance, and with the firstfruits of all thine increase:"* First fruits spoken of here are offerings. Offerings are our worship gifts to God.

III. Some Principles Concerning Giving.

   A. Scriptural Examples:

1. II Corinthians 8:5 – *"And this they did, not as we hoped, but first gave their own selves to the Lord, and unto us by the will of God."* We give ourselves to the Lord first.
2. II Corinthians 9:7 – *"Every man according as he purposeth in his heart, so let him give; not grudgingly, or of necessity: for God loveth a cheerful giver."* We give cheerfully (Greek – hilariously)
3. II Corinthians 8:3, 12 – We give willingly
4. II Corinthians 8:2 – *"How that in a great trial of affliction the abundance of their joy and their deep poverty abounded unto the riches of their liberality."* (II Corinthians 8:9-13), we are to give generously, liberally.
5. I Corinthians 16:1-2 – *"Now concerning the collection for the saints, as I have given order to the churches of Galatia, even so do ye. Upon the first day of the week let every one of you lay by him in store, as God hath prospered him, that there be no gatherings when I come."* We are to give regularly, systematically (1 Corinthians 9:7).
6. II Corinthians 9:12-13 – We are to give as a ministry to the Lord and His saints.
7. II Corinthians 9:11-12 – *"Being enriched in every thing to all bountifulness, which causeth through us thanksgiving to God. For the administration of this service not only supplieth the want of the saints, but is abundant also by many thanksgivings unto God;"* We are to give thankfully.
8. II Corinthians 8:24 – *"Wherefore shew ye to them, and before the churches, the proof of your love, and of our boasting on your behalf."* We are to give lovingly. Giving is a test of our love for Jesus. It is to be done with our heart and it really is a part of our worship and praise to the Lord.

IV. God's Promises Are Strongest to Us Concerning Giving.

   A. His Promises:

   1. Proverbs 3:9-10 – *"Honour the LORD with thy substance, and with the firstfruits of all thine increase: So shall thy barns be filled with plenty, and thy presses shall burst out with new wine."*
   2. Malachi 3:8-13
   3. Ecclesiastes 12:1 – *"Remember now thy Creator in the days of thy youth, while the evil days come not, nor the years draw nigh, when thou shalt say, I have no pleasure in them;"*
   4. Luke 6:38 – *"Give, and it shall be given unto you; good measure, pressed down, and shaken together, and running over, shall men give into your bosom. For with the same measure that ye mete withal it shall be measured to you again."*

   B. God simply wants us to be willing.

   1. II Corinthians 8:11-14
   2. II Corinthians 9:2 – *"For I know the forwardness of your mind, for which I boast of you to them of Macedonia, that Achaia was ready a year ago; and your zeal hath provoked very many."*
   3. I Peter 5:2 – *"Feed the flock of God which is among you, taking the oversight thereof, not by constraint, but willingly; not for filthy lucre, but of a ready mind;"*
   4. Proverbs 31:13 – *"She seeketh wool, and flax, and worketh willingly with her hands."*
   5. Psalms 110:3 – *"Thy people shall be willing in the day of thy power, in the beauties of holiness from the womb of the morning: thou hast the dew of thy youth."*

V. Common Sense Concerning Giving

   A. We are to give according to our ability.

   1. We give according to what we have.

a. II Corinthians 8:12 – *"For if there be first a willing mind, it is accepted according to that a man hath, and not according to that he hath not."*

b. II Corinthians 9:8 – *"And God is able to make all grace abound toward you; that ye, always having all sufficiency in all things, may abound to every good work:"*

c. Ezra 2:6, 9

d. Deuteronomy 16:17 – *"Every man shall give as he is able, according to the blessing of the LORD thy God which he hath given thee."*

e. Mark 14:8 – *"She hath done what she could: she is come aforehand to anoint my body to the burying."*

f. Acts 11:29 – *"Then the disciples, every man according to his ability, determined to send relief unto the brethren which dwelt in Judaea:"* – We are never to compare ourselves or our giving with others. Our giving is based on what we have to give.

Lesson 117
GOD DESIRES ABUNDANCE (FATNESS) FOR HIS PEOPLE

I.   Psalms 65 (verse 11) – *"Thou crownest the year with thy goodness; and thy paths drop fatness."* Other translations:

"...and they footsteps are dropping with riches."
"...your paths overflow with a rich harvest."
"...abundance flows wherever you pass."
"...where thy feet have passed, the stream of plenty flows."
"...life giving rain is dropping from your footsteps."

    A.   Hebrew word for "Fat, fatness" – Abundance; it comes from a root word – to anoint, to fatten, to remove ashes.

    B.   Scriptures concerning His desire for us to be made fat. This happens if we do the following.

        1.   Proverbs 28:25 – *"...he that putteth his trust in the LORD shall be made fat."* – He wants us to <u>trust in Him</u>. – Other translations:

            "...he who trusts in the Lord grows fat and prosperous."
            "...he who trusts in the eternal thrives."
            "...whoso trusteth in Jehovah shall be made prosperous."
            "...shall be made rich."

        2.   Proverbs 13:4 – *"...the soul of the diligent shall be made fat."* – He wants us to <u>be diligent</u> – Other translations:

            "...the diligent man is amply supplied."
            "...the diligent grow fat and prosperous."
            "...the desire of the diligent is richly supplied."

        3.   Proverbs 11:25 – *"The liberal soul shall be made fat: and he that watereth shall be watered also himself."* – He wants us to <u>be givers</u> – Other translations:

            "One gives away, and still he grows richer."
            "Yes the liberal man shall be rich."
            "One man gives freely, yet grows all the richer."
            "The generous man shall be enriched."

        4.   Psalms 92:13-14 – *"Those that be planted in the house of the LORD shall flourish in the courts of our God. They shall still bring forth fruit in old age; they shall be fat and flourishing"* – He wants us to be <u>planted in a local church</u>.

        5.   Isaiah 55:2 – *"Wherefore do ye spend money for that which is not bread? and your labour for that which satisfieth not? hearken diligently unto me, and eat ye that which is good, and let your soul delight itself in fatness."* – He wants us to <u>eat the Word of God</u>.

        6.   John 10:10 – *"...I am come that they might have life, and that they might have it more abundantly."* – He wants us to <u>believe His promise</u> – Other translations

            "...and have it to the full."
            "...and have it overflowing in them."

    a.   Greek word for "abundantly" – Super abundant, superior, excessive, beyond measure, exceedingly very high, exceedingly abundantly above.

C.   He wants us satisfied with His fatness (abundance)

    1.   Satisfied in Hebrew – to sate, to fill, to have enough, to the full, to have plenty of.

    2.   Jeremiah 31:14 – *"And I will satiate the soul of the priests with fatness, and my people shall be satisfied with my goodness, saith the LORD."*

        a.   Satiate in Hebrew – to bathe, to make drunk, to take the fill, to soak.
        b.   Other translations: *"...and my people will have a full measure of my good things, says the Lord"*, *"...blessings my people shall have the Lord says, till they ask no more."*

    3.   Psalms 63:5 – *"My soul shall be satisfied as with marrow and fatness..."* – Other translations:

        "I am satisfied with a rich and sumptuous feast..."
        "As with fatness and richness shall my soul be satisfied..."
        "As with the riches of a banquet shall my soul be satisfied..."

    4.   Psalms 36:8 – *"They shall be abundantly satisfied with the fatness of thy house; and thou shalt make them drink of the river of thy pleasures."* – Other translations:

        "They shall be fully satisfied with the abundance of thy house..."
        "They shall be satisfied abundantly from your vase reserves..."
        "...and from thine Eden river thou refreshest them."

    5.   Psalms 132:13-18

        a.   Other translations of verse 15:

        "I will enrich her food supplies..."
        "I will bless her with abundant provision..."
        "I will richly bless its produce..."

    6.   Psalms 65:4 – *"...we shall be satisfied with the goodness of thy house, even of thy holy temple."* – Other translations:

        "...we shall be satisfied with the blessings of thy house. The holiness of thy temple."
        "...we shall be satisfied with the riches of thy house, Thy holy temple."
        "...may we be satisfied with the goodness of thy house, the holy place of Thy temple."
        "...let us enjoy the blessing of thy house, thy holy temple."

    7.   Other compatible Scriptures

        a.   Psalms 145:16
        b.   Psalms 103:5
        c.   Psalms 107:9
        d.   Psalms 91:16
        e.   Isaiah 58:11
        f.   Psalms 105:40
        g.   Psalms 22:26
        h.   Joel 2:19

Lesson 118
GOD IS DOING SOMETHING NEW

I. Isaiah 43:18-21 – *"Remember ye not the former things, neither consider the things of old. Behold, I will do a new thing; now it shall spring forth; shall ye not know it? I will even make a way in the wilderness, and rivers in the desert. The beast of the field shall honour me, the dragons and the owls: because I give waters in the wilderness, and rivers in the desert, to give drink to my people, my chosen. This people have I formed for myself; they shall shew forth my praise."*

A. Verse 18 – Leaving the old

   1. Matthew 4:4 – *"...Man shall not live by bread alone, but by every word that proceedeth out of the mouth of God."*
   2. Deuteronomy 8:3 – They moved from camp to camp as He spoke. There is a time and season after God speaks, that His Word is fulfilled.
   3. Ecclesiastes 3:1, 17 – *"To every thing there is a season, and a time to every purpose under the heaven:"*
   4. Luke 1:20 – When the Word of the Lord is fulfilled we must go on and seek Him for a new word.
   5. Isaiah 42:9 – *"Behold, the former things are come to pass, and new things do I declare: before they spring forth I tell you of them."*

B. Verse 19 – Wilderness: it seems like we're always in a wilderness when we need that proceeding word.

   1. *"...make a way..."* – Seems like there is no way
   2. *"...rivers in the desert..."* – We need fresh oil
   3. *"...give drink..."* – They've been thirsty

   4. What happens when we wait too long?

      a. I Samuel 3:1-3 – Fire goes out
      b. Proverbs 29:18
      c. Psalms 55:19
      d. Jeremiah 48:11-12 – It does not have to be this way

C. Verse 19 – We should know beforehand. God will always speak and tell us to prepare ourselves.

   1. How can we know?

      a. Isaiah 28:20 – Uncomfortable
      b. I Samuel 2:18-19 – Just doesn't fit
      c. Genesis 26:17-22 – Seems like there's no room – strife
      d. Isaiah 41:17 – Poor and needy, thirsty – provision dries up
      e. Continued frustration

D. What makes us hold back?

   1. Job 29:18 – We like nests
   2. Psalms 30:6 – Our prosperity speaks too loudly
   3. Luke 5:36-69 – We think the old is better
   4. Luke 18:18-23 – Fear

E.   Verses 19-21 – But God wants to do a new thing

    1.   Isaiah 54:1-5
    2.   Matthew 4:4
    3.   Psalms 4:1

F.   What happens when we obey and receive this new thing?

    1.   Verse 20 – He pours out His glory
    2.   Psalms 18:36 – He enlarges our steps

G.   Let's be ready

    1.   Psalms 110:3 – *"Thy people shall be willing in the day of thy power..."*

Lesson 119

GOD'S EYE IS ON THE NATIONS

I. God's eye is on the nations; He cares about the nations of the earth

    A. The Condition In The World Right Now

        1. Ephesians 4:14-15 – *"That we henceforth be no more children, tossed to and fro, and carried about with every wind of doctrine, by the sleight of men, and cunning craftiness, whereby they lie in wait to deceive; But speaking the truth in love, may grow up into him in all things, which is the head, even Christ:"*

        2. Isaiah 54:11-13 – *"O thou afflicted, tossed with tempest, and not comforted, behold, I will lay thy stones with fair colours, and lay thy foundations with sapphires. And I will make thy windows of agates, and thy gates of carbuncles, and all thy borders of pleasant stones. And all thy children shall be taught of the LORD; and great shall be the peace of thy children."*

        3. Amos 8:11 – *"Behold, the days come, saith the Lord GOD, that I will send a famine in the land, not a famine of bread, nor a thirst for water, but of hearing the words of the LORD:"*

        4. I Timothy 4:1-2 – *"Now the Spirit speaketh expressly, that in the latter times some shall depart from the faith, giving heed to seducing spirits, and doctrines of devils; Speaking lies in hypocrisy; having their conscience seared with a hot iron"*

        5. II Timothy 3:1-7, 13-6

        6. II Timothy 4:2-5 – *"Preach the word; be instant in season, out of season; reprove, rebuke, exhort with all longsuffering and doctrine. For the time will come when they will not endure sound doctrine; but after their own lusts shall they heap to themselves teachers, having itching ears; And they shall turn away their ears from the truth, and shall be turned unto fables. But watch thou in all things, endure afflictions, do the work of an evangelist, make full proof of thy ministry."*

        7. Matthew 24:4-14

        8. Daniel 7:25 – *"And he shall speak great words against the most High, and shall wear out the saints of the most High, and think to change times and laws: and they shall be given into his hand until a time and times and the dividing of time."*

        9. Matthew 9:36 – *"But when he saw the multitudes, he was moved with compassion on them, because they fainted, and were scattered abroad, as sheep having no shepherd."*

     10. Ezekiel 34:1-16

     11. Jeremiah 3:12-18

     12. I Samuel 3:1-4

    B. Psalms 66:7 – *"He ruleth by his power for ever; <u>his eyes behold the nations</u>..."*

        1. Psalms 67 – *"God be merciful unto us, and bless us; and cause his face to shine upon us; Selah. at thy way may be known upon earth, thy saving health among all nations. Let the people praise thee, O God; let all the people praise thee. O let the nations be glad and sing for joy: for thou shalt judge the people righteously, and govern the nations upon earth. Selah. Let the people praise thee, O God; let all the people praise thee. Then shall the earth yield her increase; and God, even our own God, shall bless us. God shall bless us; and all the ends of the earth shall fear him."*

        2. Matthew 28:19 – *"Go ye therefore, and teach all nations, baptizing them in the name of the Father, and of the Son, and of the Holy Ghost."*

        3. II Peter 3:9 – *"...not willing that any should perish, but that all should come to repentance."*

        4. Matthew 24:14 – *"And this gospel of the kingdom shall be preached in all the world for a witness unto all nations; and then shall the end come."*

        5. John 4:35 – *"...behold, I say unto you, Lift up your eyes, and look on the fields; for they are white already to harvest."*

6. Isaiah 11:12 – "*And he shall set up an ensign for the nations, and shall assemble the outcasts of Israel, and gather together the dispersed of Judah from the four corners of the earth.*"
7. Isaiah 66:18-19 – "*...it shall come, that I will gather all nations and tongues; and they shall come, and see my glory. And I will set a sign among them, and I will send those that escape of them unto the nations...to the isles afar off, that have not heard my fame, neither have seen my glory; and they shall declare my glory among the Gentiles.*"
8. Jeremiah 50:2 – "*Declare ye among the nations, and publish, and set up a standard; publish, and conceal not...*"
9. Haggai 2:7 – "*And I will shake all nations, and the desire of all nations shall come: and I will fill this house with glory, saith the Lord of hosts.*"
10. Zechariah 2:8 – "*For thus saith the Lord of hosts; After the glory hath he sent me to the nations...*"
11. Zechariah 2:10-11 – "*Sing and rejoice, O daughter of Zion: for, lo, I come, and I will dwell in the midst of thee, saith the Lord. And many nations shall be joined to the Lord in that day, and shall be my people: and I will dwell in the midst of thee...*"

C. Who will go?

1. Isaiah 6:8 – "*Also I heard the voice of the Lord, saying, Whom shall I send, and who will go for us? Then said I, Here am I; send me.*"
2. Matthew 9:37-38 – "*...The harvest truly is plenteous, but the labourers are few; Pray ye therefore the Lord of the harvest, that he will send forth labourers into his harvest.*"

D. Many of us are comfortable

1. We don't want to go to the nations

   a. Ezekiel 2

   b. We no longer decide

      1) John 21:18 – "*Verily, verily, I say unto thee, When thou wast young, thou girdedst thyself, and walkedst whither thou wouldest: but when thou shalt be old, thou shalt stretch forth thy hands, and another shall gird thee, and carry thee whither thou wouldest not.*"
      2) Luke 22:42 – "*...not my will, but thine, be done.*"
      3) Philippians 2:5-9 – "*...took upon him the form of a servant...*"

   c. God will be taking people from jobs, etc.
   d. Some will be martyrs (Acts 1:8 – "witnesses" in the Greek means "martyrs")
   e. Matthew 26:26 – God first blesses us then breaks us, only to give us away.

E. The nations are ours if we want them

1. Joshua 1:3 – "*Every place that the sole of your foot shall tread upon, that have I given unto you, as I said unto Moses.*"
2. Psalms 2:8 – "*Ask of me, and I shall give thee the heathen for thine inheritance, and the uttermost parts of the earth for thy possession.*"
3. Psalms 47:2-3 – "*...He shall subdue the people under us, and the nations under our feet.*"

II. What God has Called Us to Do

A. Scriptures

1. Matthew 24:14 – *"And this gospel of the kingdom shall be preached in all the world for a witness unto all nations; and then shall the end come."*
2. Matthew 28:19 – *"Go ye therefore, and <u>teach</u>* (Greek for teach – disciple, make pupils or scholars) *all nations, baptizing them in the name of the Father, and of the Son, and of the Holy Ghost."*
3. Mark 13:10 – *"And the gospel must first be published among all nations."*
4. Psalms 2:8 – *"Ask of me, and I shall give thee the heathen for thine inheritance, and the uttermost parts of the earth for thy possession."*
5. Song of Solomon 8:8-9 – *"We have a little sister, and she hath no breasts: what shall we do for our sister in the day when she shall be spoken for? If she be a wall, we will build upon her a palace of silver: and if she be a door, we will inclose her with boards of cedar."*
6. Song of Solomon 7:11-12 – *"Come, my beloved, let us go forth into the field; let us lodge in the villages. Let us get up early to the vineyards; let us see if the vine flourish, whether the tender grape appear, and the pomegranates bud forth: there will I give thee my loves."*
7. Nehemiah 8:10 – *"...Go your way, eat the fat, and drink the sweet, and send portions unto them for whom nothing is prepared..."*
8. Job 29:18 – *"Then I said, I shall die in my nest..."*
9. Proverbs 3:27 – *"Withhold not good from them to whom it is due, when it is in the power of thine hand to do it."*

C. We Have Been Chosen For This Purpose

1. John 15:16-19 – *"Ye have not chosen me, but I have chosen you, and ordained you, that ye should go and bring forth fruit, and that your fruit should remain: that whatsoever ye shall ask of the Father in my name, he may give it you. These things I command you, that ye love one another. If the world hate you, ye know that it hated me before it hated you. If ye were of the world, the world would love his own: but because ye are not of the world, but I have chosen you out of the world, therefore the world hateth you."*
2. Psalms 132:13 – *"For the LORD hath chosen Zion; he hath desired it for his habitation."*
3. I Peter 2:9 – *"But ye are a chosen generation, a royal priesthood, an holy nation, a peculiar people; that ye should shew forth the praises of him who hath called you out of darkness into his marvellous light:"*
4. Revelation 17:14 – *"These shall make war with the Lamb, and the Lamb shall overcome them: for he is Lord of lords, and King of kings: and they that are with him are called, and chosen, and faithful."*
5. Matthew 20:16 – *"So the last shall be first, and the first last: for many be called, but few chosen."*

D. The Need For Teachers

1. Luke 10:2 – *"Therefore said he unto them, The harvest truly is great, but the labourers are few: pray ye therefore the Lord of the harvest, that he would send forth labourers into his harvest."*
2. II Chronicles 15:3-7 – *"³Now for a long season Israel hath been without the true God, and without a teaching priest, and without law. ⁴But when they in their trouble did turn unto the LORD God of Israel, and sought him, he was found of them. ⁵And in those times there was no peace to him that went out, nor to him that came in, but great vexations were upon all the inhabitants of the countries. ⁶And nation was destroyed of nation, and city of city: for God did vex them with all adversity. ⁷Be ye strong therefore, and let not your hands be weak: for your work shall be rewarded."*
3. Hebrews 5:12 – *"For when for the time ye ought to be teachers, ye have need that one teach you again which be the first principles of the oracles of God; and are become such as have need of milk, and not of strong meat."*

4. Ephesians 4:11 – *"And he gave some, apostles; and some, prophets; and some, evangelists; and some, pastors and teachers;"*
5. Deuteronomy 6:7 – *"And thou shalt teach them diligently unto thy children, and shalt talk of them when thou sittest in thine house, and when thou walkest by the way, and when thou liest down, and when thou risest up."*
6. Psalms 51:13 – *"Then will I teach transgressors thy ways; and sinners shall be converted unto thee."*
7. Isaiah 28:9 – *"Whom shall he teach knowledge? and whom shall he make to understand doctrine? them that are weaned from the milk, and drawn from the breasts."*
8. Ezekiel 44:23 – *"And they shall teach my people the difference between the holy and profane, and cause them to discern between the unclean and the clean."*
9. Matthew 5:19 – *"Whosoever therefore shall break one of these least commandments, and shall teach men so, he shall be called the least in the kingdom of heaven: but whosoever shall do and teach them, the same shall be called great in the kingdom of heaven."*
10. Acts 1:1 – *"The former treatise have I made, O Theophilus, of all that Jesus began both to do and teach,"*
11. Acts 2:42-46 – *"[42]And they continued stedfastly in the apostles' doctrine and fellowship, and in breaking of bread, and in prayers. [43]And fear came upon every soul: and many wonders and signs were done by the apostles. [44]And all that believed were together, and had all things common; [45]And sold their possessions and goods, and parted them to all men, as every man had need. [46]And they, continuing daily with one accord in the temple, and breaking bread from house to house, did eat their meat with gladness and singleness of heart,"*
12. II Timothy 2:24 – *"And the servant of the Lord must not strive; but be gentle unto all men, apt to teach, patient,"*
13. Psalms 119:99 – *"I have more understanding than all my teachers: for thy testimonies are my meditation."*
14. II Timothy 2:2 – *"And the things that thou hast heard of me among many witnesses, the same commit thou to faithful men, who shall be able to teach others also."*

E. It's Time To Arise And Be Going

1. Hosea 10:12 – *"Sow to yourselves in righteousness, reap in mercy; break up your fallow ground: for it is time to seek the LORD, till he come and rain righteousness upon you."*
2. Esther 4:14 – *"For if thou altogether holdest thy peace at this time, then shall there enlargement and deliverance arise to the Jews from another place; but thou and thy father's house shall be destroyed: and who knoweth whether thou art come to the kingdom for such a time as this?"*
3. Matthew 26:46 – *"Rise, let us be going..."*

Lesson 120
GOD'S HIDDEN ONES

This is an illuminating revelation in Scripture. God has what are called some "hidden ones". It is nice to know that our precious God will hide us when the wicked and the world are oppressing and tormenting us. To be kept hidden and protected by Him is a joy no one could ever have expected. As we look at these "hidden ones", let us allow the Bible to give us a true picture of what it means to be a hidden one.

I. What saith the Scriptures?

A. Psalms 83:3 – "*They have taken crafty counsel against thy people, and consulted against thy hidden ones.*"

   1. Other translations:

      "*...Your hidden and precious ones.*"
      "*...Your treasured ones.*"
      "*...those you cherish.*"
      "*...Your sheltered one.*"
      "*...those you treasure.*"
      "*...those you love.*"
      "*...thy protected ones.*"
      "*...those whom you keep in a secret place.*"
      "*...against thy saints.*"

   2. Definition of "hidden" in Hebrew, *tsphan* – to hide by covering over, to hoard or reserve, to protect, to esteem, to keep secret.

God has a people He is hiding, sheltering, protecting, and keeping. They are to Him precious, treasured, cherished, and loved by Him. A great day is coming when He shall be revealed in glory through these "hidden ones".

B. God wants us hidden in Him

   1. Colossians 3:3 – "*For ye are dead, and your life is hid with Christ in God.*" – God wants us hidden for a reason.
   2. Exodus 33:21 – "*And the LORD said, Behold, there is a place by me, and thou shalt stand upon a rock:*"
   3. Psalms 90:1 – "*LORD, thou hast been our dwelling place in all generations.*"

C. Where is it He hides us?

   1. Psalms 32:7 – "*Thou art my hiding place; thou shalt preserve me from trouble; thou shalt compass me about with songs of deliverance. Selah.*"

      a. Psalms 119:114 – "*Thou art my hiding place and my shield: I hope in thy word.*"

He is our hiding place, like a great eagle, He watches over us, nurtures us, protects us, and shields us from the world, flesh, and the devil.

   2. Psalms 17:8 – "*Keep me as the apple of the eye, hide me under the shadow of thy wings,*"

        a.   Luke 13:34 – *"...how often would I have gathered thy children together, as a hen doth gather her brood under her wings, and ye would not!"*

        b.   Psalms 57:1 – *"...in the shadow of thy wings will I make my refuge, until these calamities be overpast."*

        c.   Psalms 91:1, 4 – *"He that dwelleth in the secret place of the most High shall abide under the shadow of the Almighty...He shall cover thee with his feathers, and under his wings shalt thou trust: his truth shall be thy shield and buckler."*

3.   Psalms 27:5 – *"For in the time of trouble he shall <u>hide me in his pavilion</u>: in the <u>secret of his tabernacle</u> shall he hide me; he shall set me up upon a rock."*

        a.   Pavilion in Hebrew – tabernacle, covert, tent or booth; it is an enclosed place, a temporary, moveable habitation – it is a type of the house of God.

4.   Psalms 31:20 – *"Thou shalt hide them in the secret of thy presence from the pride of man: thou shalt keep them secretly in a pavilion from the strife of tongues."*

        a.   Psalms 18:11 – *"He made darkness his secret place; his pavilion round about him were dark waters and thick clouds of the skies."*

D.   What we receive there

1.   Isaiah 45:3 – *"And I will give thee the <u>treasures of darkness</u>, and hidden <u>riches of secret places</u>, that thou mayest know that I, the LORD, which call thee by thy name, am the God of Israel."* – We learn to receive from Him even in the darkest moments in life and find treasures there.

        a.   Judges 14:5-6, 8-9, 14

"[5]Then went Samson down, and his father and his mother, to Timnath, and came to the vineyards of Timnath: and, behold, a young lion roared against him. [6]And the Spirit of the LORD came mightily upon him, and he rent him as he would have rent a kid, and he had nothing in his hand: but he told not his father or his mother what he had done...[8]And after a time he returned to take her, and he turned aside to see the carcase of the lion: and, behold, there was a swarm of bees and honey in the carcase of the lion. [9]And he took thereof in his hands, and went on eating, and came to his father and mother, and he gave them, and they did eat: but he told not them that he had taken the honey out of the carcase of the lion...[14]And he said unto them, Out of the eater came forth meat, and out of the strong came forth sweetness. And they could not in three days expound the riddle."

2.   Isaiah 48:6 – *"Thou hast heard, see all this; and will not ye declare it? I have shewed thee <u>new things</u> from this time, even hidden things, and thou didst not know them."* – We learn as we are hidden in Him to know the Holy Spirit who shows us things to come.

3.   Revelation 2:17 – *"...To him that overcometh will I give to eat of the <u>hidden manna</u>, and will give him a <u>white stone</u>, and in the stone a <u>new name</u> written, which no man knoweth saving he that receiveth it."*

        a.   We learn to overcome, Revelation 12:11 – *"And they overcame him by the blood of the Lamb, and by the word of their testimony; and they loved not their lives unto the death."*

        b.   Hidden manna – we learn the deep things of God

        c.   White stone – pronounced not guilty

        d.   New name – a new character

These are just some of the wonderful things that we obtain as we stay and remain hidden in Him!

4. I Corinthians 2:7 – *"But we speak the <u>wisdom of God in a mystery</u>, even the <u>hidden wisdom</u>, which God ordained before the world unto our glory:"*

Revelation will dawn on us as we abide and are hidden in God. As we continue to give ourselves to Him in worship and sit at His feet hearing His Word (Luke 10:38-42), we can begin to understand the deep, hidden mysteries of God.

E. We are hidden until the time of the manifestations of the sons of God

1. Isaiah 32:1-3 – *"Behold, a king shall reign in righteousness, and princes shall rule in judgment. And <u>a man shall be as an hiding place</u> from the wind, and a <u>covert from</u> <u>the tempest</u>; as <u>rivers of</u> <u>water</u> in a <u>dry place</u>, as the <u>shadow of a great rock in a</u> <u>weary land</u>. And the eyes of them that see shall not be dim, and the ears of them that hear shall hearken."* – Yes, it's true. A man can become so much like His God, having His image, that he can do all these things simply because He now has God's nature.

2. Isaiah 49:2 – *"And he hath made my mouth like a sharp sword; in the shadow of his hand hath he hid me, and made me a polished shaft; in his quiver hath he hid me;"* – This means our mouths are full of His Word and we become arrows of truth

    a. Psalms 127:4-5 – *"As arrows are in the hand of a mighty man; so are children of the youth. Happy is the man that hath his quiver full of them: they shall not be ashamed, but they shall speak with the enemies in the gate."*
    b. Psalms 45:5 – *"Thine arrows are sharp in the heart of the king's enemies; whereby the people fall under thee."*

3. Bezaleel – We find a true type and example in Scriptures of these last day sons of God in this man who was commissioned by God of making the Tabernacle with all its luxurious and intricately designed furnishings.

    a. Exodus 31:1-5

"¹And the LORD spake unto Moses, saying, ²See, I have called by name Bezaleel the son of Uri, the son of Hur, of the tribe of Judah: ³And I have filled him with the spirit of God, in wisdom, and in understanding, and in knowledge, and in all manner of workmanship, ⁴To devise cunning works, to work in gold, and in silver, and in brass, ⁵And in cutting of stones, to set them, and in carving of timber, to work in all manner of workmanship."

1) Bezaleel in Hebrew means – in the shadow of God, under God's shadow – He is a type of the sons of God
2) He was the son of Uri; Uri in Hebrew – light of the Lord, enlightened.
3) Hur in Hebrew – cavern (cave), a hole, noble, splendor, white
4) He was of the tribe of Judah which means praise.

As we see what happened to this man who lived His life under the shadow of God, we find these precious things had been worked into him and he was called to build the house of God.

5) Verse 3

    a) Filled him with the Spirit of God
    b) He had wisdom and understanding (obviously in the Word)

       c)   Knowledge in all manner of workmanship (Ephesians 1:17, I Corinthians 3:10 – Paul a wise masterbuilder)

    6)   Verse 4 – He had wisdom to teach and to help build these things into the people of God

       a)   To devise cunning works (artistic and creative)
       b)   In gold (the nature of God)
       c)   In silver (redemption)
       d)   Brass (judgment)

    7)   Verse 5

       a)   Cutting of stones – laying the foundation (Isaiah 54:11 – "*...I will lay thy stones with fair colours, and lay thy foundations with sapphires.*")
       b)   Carving out timber (wood is a type of humanity or flesh)
       c)   To work in all manner of workmanship (to make a people prepared, throughly furnished, II Timothy 3:17 – "*That the man of God may be perfect, throughly furnished unto all good works.*")

b.   Exodus 35:30-35

"*30And Moses said unto the children of Israel, See, the LORD hath called by name Bezaleel the son of Uri, the son of Hur, of the tribe of Judah; 31And he hath filled him with the spirit of God, in wisdom, in understanding, and in knowledge, and in all manner of workmanship; 32And to devise curious works, to work in gold, and in silver, and in brass, 33And in the cutting of stones, to set them, and in carving of wood, to make any manner of cunning work. 34And he hath put in his heart that he may teach, both he, and Aholiab, the son of Ahisamach, of the tribe of Dan. 35Them hath he filled with wisdom of heart, to work all manner of work, of the engraver, and of the cunning workman, and of the embroiderer, in blue, and in purple, in scarlet, and in fine linen, and of the weaver, even of them that do any work, and of those that devise cunning work.*"

    1)   Verses 34-35

       a)   He hath put in his heart to teach
       b)   Filled with wisdom of heart
       c)   To work all manner of work of the engraver – to stamp God's image on other believers

       d)   Embroider – a feminine term showing He is a type of the bride.

          (1)   Blue – all things heavenly
          (2)   Purple – royalty
          (3)   Scarlet – suffering and sacrifice

c.   Exodus 36:1-3

"*1Then wrought Bezaleel and Aholiab, and every wise hearted man, in whom the LORD put wisdom and understanding to know how to work all manner of work for the service of the sanctuary, according to all that the LORD had commanded. 2And Moses called Bezaleel and Aholiab, and every wise hearted man, in whose heart the LORD had put wisdom, even every one whose heart stirred him up to come unto the work to do it: 3And they received of Moses all the offering, which the children of Israel had brought for the work of the service of the sanctuary, to make it withal. And they brought yet unto him free offerings every morning.*"

1) Verse 1 – How to work all manner of work for the sanctuary – these will be trained in every way
2) Verse 2 – Whose heart stirred him up to come unto the work to do it
3) Verse 3 – Received of Moses all the offering which the children of Israel had brought for the work of the service of the sanctuary. These were trusted to take the money received from the people of God.

4. Colossians 3:3-4 – *"For ye are dead, and your life is hid with Christ in God. When Christ, who is our life, shall appear, then shall ye also appear with him in glory."*

   a. Isaiah 60:1-3

"1Arise, shine; for thy light is come, and the glory of the LORD is risen upon thee. 2For, behold, the darkness shall cover the earth, and gross darkness the people: but the LORD shall arise upon thee, and his glory shall be seen upon thee. 3And the Gentiles shall come to thy light, and kings to the brightness of thy rising."

   b. II Thessalonians 1:7-10

"7And to you who are troubled rest with us, when the Lord Jesus shall be revealed from heaven with his mighty angels, 8In flaming fire taking vengeance on them that know not God, and that obey not the gospel of our Lord Jesus Christ: 9Who shall be punished with everlasting destruction from the presence of the Lord, and from the glory of his power; 10When he shall come to be glorified in his saints, and to be admired in all them that believe (because our testimony among you was believed) in that day."

Those who allow themselves, those who place themselves in Him, hidden under the shadow of the Almighty, protected, kept, taught, trained, filled with wisdom and a willingness to work, and also who have come to understand the mysteries of God and can be trusted to handle God's money will be the sons of God in the last days! So let us be His hidden ones!

Glory Publishing, Inc.
www.glorypublishinginc.com

SEARCHING THE SCRIPTURES
is the first volume in the
<u>FOUNDATIONAL SERIES – Hebrews 6:1-3:</u>

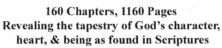
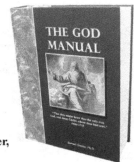
Jesus Is Precious!